Property of Joan Smith

ENCYCLOPEDIC DICTIONARY OF ENGLISH USAGE

ENCYCLOPEDIC DICTIONARY OF ENGLISH USAGE

by N. H. Mager and S. K. Mager

•

PRENTICE-HALL, INC.
Englewood Cliffs, N.J.

PRENTICE-HALL INTERNATIONAL, INC., *London*
PRENTICE-HALL OF AUSTRALIA, PTY. LTD., *Sydney*
PRENTICE-HALL OF CANADA, LTD., *Toronto*
PRENTICE-HALL OF INDIA PRIVATE LTD., *New Delhi*
PRENTICE-HALL OF JAPAN, INC., *Tokyo*

Library of Congress Cataloging in Publication Data

Mager, Nathan H
   Encyclopedic dictionary of English usage.

   1. English language--Usage--Dictionaries.
I. Mager, Sylvia K.,   joint author.
II. Title.
PE1628.M23   428'.003   78-37656

A WORD FROM THE AUTHORS

Encyclopedic Dictionary of English Usage was compiled from experience—the experience of answering thousands of questions through the years: "How do you say . . . ?" "How do you write . . ?" Basically, it is a selection from many reference books, from clippings, and from original inquiry. It has taken the gist of the Style Manual of the Government Printing Office, which is our first authority; *A Manual of Style,* the University of Chicago Press; the Style Book of the *New York Times;* some basic grammars and government writing manuals; various primers of thousands of words misspelled, misused, misunderstood or mispronounced; and some basic writings on filing, spelling, pronunciation and usage. It is more than a dictionary, more than a grammar, more than a manual of style—in many ways it serves the purposes of all three. To the numerous compilers before them, the editors express their sincere appreciation.

Included, too, are definitions and explanations of commonly used—or misused—expressions and abbreviations: terms such as B-52 bomber, the MiG 15, fore and aft, the ducat and the furlong. These are terms that most of us accept without a clear valuation, and often with a misconception as to significance.

This encyclopedic dictionary is a composite tool to help you speak and write more correctly and more specifically, to understand more completely the terms you commonly use or read, to resolve your doubts about what is incorrect and what is best usage, and to suggest a uniform style in matters where good usage permits a choice of several alternatives.

How is this book different from other manuals of style, usage and grammar? First, because it is an integrated work, combining a variety of the most common problems into a single, alphabetically arranged unit. Second, it explains by example rather than by exposition. The editors feel that this provides the answers more specifically, more expeditiously, and usually more simply. Third,

v

this manual provides the answers to more everyday problems because the answers are more concisely put, and because only common problems are presented. Frequency of use is the major criterion for inclusion.

In making selection of people and places, the importance of those selected was of minimum consideration. It was the difficulty involved in pronunciation, spelling or comprehension that finally determined the choice, and the fact that the name or word appeared in writings or conversation that nominated the item for inclusion. In a few instances, a family tree is recited to distinguish between generations and families of similar names. the Rockefeller, the Roosevelt.

In creating a pronunciation explanation system some of the subtleties have been eliminated to provide a universally understandable system with minimum reference to a code.

Vowels

Sound Expressed By		Webster Phonetic	
a			
ae	=	a̅	as in may, day, delay
a	=	a	as in map, bad, pass
ai	=	ai	as in hair
ah	=	á	as in bother, father
aw	=	ó	as in saw, all, prawn
e			
ee	=	e, é	as in meat, bleed, tree
eh	=	e, eú	as in bed, elk, operate
eu	=	ëü	as in few
i			
ie	=	ī	as in why, side, buy
ih	=	i, í, ú	as in tip, wish, iln
o			
oh	=	o̅	as in woe, snow, toad
oi	=	oi	as in coin, employ, coy
oo	=	u̅	as in rule, spittoon, truth
ou	=	oú	as in now, plow, denounce

u

u	=	u̇	as in stood, soot, could
uh	=		as in duchess, hurry

Consonants

wh	as in what, when, whale
sh	as in shock, shun, dish
th	as in either, then, dipthong
zh	as in division, azure

Cross references are indicated by:

SEE. Where little or no information is given in the original listing, and *Cf.* where additional information is given in another listing.

To use this encyclopedic dictionary effectively, you need take only two steps: 1) determine the word or subject that presents a problem, and 2) seek it out in alphabetical order. Explanations are purposely limited, but proper usage is indicated for each situation.

Most problems in the use of language can resolve themselves into single words. Some may involve spelling, capitalization, or pronunciation; others, meaning; still others may involve confusing grammatical usage. These words are integrated in alphabetical order and easily found.

Where two spellings are correct, the first spelling, alphabetically, is used in listing. Problems in grammar, punctuation, filing, and style are listed under a subject heading: CAPITALIZATION, COMMA, HYPHENIZATION, MEASUREMENT, NAMES, NUMBER, PREDICATE and so forth. Finding the listings is thus as easy as ABC.

Many shortenings have been utilized; the elimination of articles, the use of some non-standard, but understandable abbreviations, the designation of "adj." for unit modifier, and a general conciseness. In most instances, examples of correct usage are given without explanation or exposition, as the simplest answer to imaginary questions. In indicating proper endings, the last letter has been repeated rather than merely the addition of a suffix; the editors felt this was the way it was most explicable in ordinary situations.

Finally, in compiling and editing the selection contained in this work, the editors have attempted to create a tool with maximum

usefulness as determined by our own experience. We hope that readers in the business and professional worlds, students at high school and college levels, and indeed any individual who seeks to improve his ability to communicate in speaking and writing will find the book useful, enlightening, and entertaining.

N H and S K Mager

TYPICAL LANGUAGE PROBLEMS
THIS ENCYCLOPEDIC DICTIONARY SOLVES

How to pronounce

Bogota, N.J.   Sinn Fein
bona fide   Taliaferro County
Cairo, Ill.   Tyrol
Albert Camus   Uruguay
maniacal   vive voce
Schism   Worcester, Mass.

When to capitalize

a.d.   court
b.c.   DeGaulle
a.m.   state
the bible   tours
calliope   union

How to abbreviate

California   New Mexico
Canadian dollars   pence (penny)
Doctor of Literature   Quebec
Hawaii   Senate concurrent resolution
kilograms   subparagraph

Differentiate between

Algiers and Algeria   1 lb. avoirdupois and 1 lb. troy
amoral, immoral, unmoral   the Republic of the Congo and
catboat, cutter, sloop (SEE boat)   the Congo Republic
emerge and immerge   scherzo and scherzando
fervent and fervid   sensual and sensuous
hue, brilliance, color   technic and technique
insidious and invidious   valance and valence

Define or explain

caduceus	a palindrome
didactic	samurai
embrasure	Scandinavia
empiricism	subjunctive mood
Latin America	tendentious
monopsony	a usufruct

Which to write

caret, carat, or carrot	judgement or judgment
Cameroon or Cameroun	Michiganer or Michiganite
different from or different than	Scotsman or Scotchman
farther or further	10 or ten (SEE Numbers)
FCC or F.C.C.	X ray, Xray or X-ray

How much is

a dekaliter	a league
a fathom	an octavo
a hogshead	a septimillion
one horsepower	a talent
a knot	a tun

Which is the correct spelling

accommodate or accomodate	perseverence or perseverance
acoustics or accoustics	pronunciation or pronounciation
arbitrator or arbitrater	sacrilegious or sacreligious
encumbrance or encumberance	supercede or supersede
irrascible or irascible	wierd or weird
merringue or meringue	

. . . and many thousands more.

x

ENCYCLOPEDIC DICTIONARY OF ENGLISH USAGE

A

a. As an article, use *a* before all consonants except silent *h. a history, a humble man, a 4-H club.* ALSO before a consonant sound in a vowel. *a union, a UFC station, a one-time champion. Cf.* an.

a. (abbr.) ampere; are (metric system), area.

A. (abbr.) altitude, atomic weight, area, areage, absolute (temperature).

A-bomb. A-flat, A-frame, A-pole, A-sharp.

aa. author's alteration.

A.A. Alcoholics Anonymous; athletic association; *Boston A.A.*

AAC. *anno ante Christum* (Lat.) Year before Christ.

Aachen [AH-k'n]. (Fr.) Aix-la-Chapelle, [AEKS-la-sha-PEHL] city, W. Germany.

Aaron [AIR'n].

A.B. or *a.b.* (abbr.) able-bodied seaman.

A.B. or *B.A.* (abbr.) bachelor of arts.

abaca. Manila hemp; also the plant from which it comes.

abacus. Pl. abici, abacie, or abacuses. A calculating instrument.

abattoir [ab-a-TWAR]. Slaughterhouse.

abbe [a-BAE]. (Fr.) A secular ecclesiastic.

Abbot (Catholic). ADDRESS: His Excellency, The Right Reverend John Jones, Abbot of Briarcliff. SALUTATION: Your Excellency.

Abbot (Protestant). ADDRESS: The Lord Abbot of Briarcliff, or The Right Reverend Abbot Brown. SALUTATION: Dear Father Abbot; My Lord Abbot.

abbreviation. A shortening of a word or phrase. abbreviated abbr. —ated, —ating, —able.

ABRIDGMENT. Shortening by selection of most important portions.

ABBREVIATIONS. Some abbreviations have evolved into commonly used words. They are then treated as words with points omitted: *NATO, co-op, etc.*

Although styles differ, the tendency is for abbreviations to lose their points as they increase in use. Thus GPO style drops the points on almost all federal and international agencies, the *New York Times* on some, and some publishers on only a few. When an abbreviation is made up of letters from one word, it generally does not require a point, *TV*; but where two or more words are involved, *N. Y. Times* usually uses abbreviation points, *R.F.D.*

In most writings, abbreviations are to be avoided, but more extensive use is made of them in tabular material, headlines, indexes, and addresses. The chief factor in deciding when to use an abbreviation is reading facility—the readiness with which the reader can determine the meaning and the technical space limitations.

A large number of words, particularly new ones, are so distracting to the eye or so difficult to pronounce that abbreviation is necessary for good communication. Such abbreviations are proper both in writing and in speech: *DDT, DP, R.S.V.P., D.A.R., V.I.P., G.I., M.C., KLM.* (Imagine spelling out Koninkli jke Luchtuaart Maat-schaapi jvoor Nederland en Kolonien N.V.!)

The Abbreviation Point looks like a period and is used after many abbreviations. Although the abbreviation point is combined with a period into one dot at the end of a sentence, it remains before any other punctuation mark. Customary usage eliminates the point for abbreviations of governmental organizations. DO NOT use the abbreviation point after: (1) chemical symbols (H_2O); (2) formal signs of books (*8vo*); (3) initials used as titles of technical publications or organizations in technical matter (*PAIS, Public Affairs Information Service*); (4) linguistic epochs (*IE, Indo-European*); (5) per cent; (6) contractions (can't); (7) shortened forms of names (*Sam*); (8) Roman numerals (XIX); (9) letters not used as abbreviations (*A and B met and discussed the matter.*) BUT: If *A* and *B* are abbreviations for actual names, the abbreviation point is used.

ABC. (abbr.) atomic, biological, and chemical (war weapons).

ABC's. The alphabet.

Aberdeen [AB-ehr-DEEN]. City in Scotland; City in Maryland.

abettor. Preferred to *abetter*, especially in law.

abide. For p.p., abode is preferable to abided (in the sense of dwelt) BUT *He abided by his statements.*

abjure. Forswear; renounce on oath; disavow.
   ADJURE. Charge or command solemnly; entreat or appeal to earnestly.

—able. When added to a transitive verb, drop any final silent *e* or *ate* of polysyllabic words: *abominable, rebatable, accumulable. —ible* is an alternative established by custom for some forms. The general rule: (1) When there is a corresponding noun that ends in *—tion* preceded by *a*, the adjective ending is *—able: quotation, quotable; presentation, presentable.* (2) When there is a corresponding noun ending in *—tion* or *—sion* not preceded by a, the adjective ending is *—ible: expansible, extensible, admissible.* Words formed from them by adding the prefixes *in-, un-, non-*, also have the *—ible* ending.

able-bodied. (adj.), able-minded (adj.).

abolition. abolishing, abolishment, in order of preference.

aborigine. [AB-oh-RIHJ-ih-nee]. Pl. —ines; —inal (adj.).

about. Informal for approximately. BUT NEVER *about forty to fifty*. NOT: *He estimated about 15,000 were present.*

about-face.

above. (adv.) Generally, at a higher level. Also, foregoing.
   OVER. Indicates a higher level, sometimes with intimation of motion.
   ON. Indicates touching.
   UPON. Formal for *on*.
   UNDER, UNDERNEATH. SEE below.

above statement, above-listed, above-mentioned. Avoid as stilted. *The example above* is pref. to *the above example*. ALSO acceptable: *statement given above, this*.

abridgment. Preferred to *abridgement*; *—eable. abridged from, abridgment of. Cf.* abbreviation.

abrogate [AB-roh-gaet]. Annul; abolish; repeal. —gable.

ABRUPT MODIFICATION. A rhetorical device in which the modifier appears immediately after the subject at the beginning of a sentence. This places an emphasis on the subject. *The law, although unenforceable, was a major deterrent to fraud.*

abs. (abbr.) absolute; abstract.

abscess [AB-sess]. Infection; collection of pus.

absence. absentee; -teeism.

absent-minded.

ABSOLUTE CONSTRUCTION (nominative absolute). A literary construction in which the participial phrase is not connected with the main clause. *The facts being proved, he won his point.*

absolve [ab-SAHLV]. Free from a bond or obligation, or from condemnation for sin. *He was absolved from sin after confessing.*

absorb [ab-SAWRB]. Take into.
   ADSORB [ad-SAWRB]. To condense and hold by absorption, the adhesion of a thin layer of molecules to the surface of a solid body.

abstemious [ab-STEE-mee-uhs]. Displaying habitual moderation in food and liquor.
   ABSTINENT. Displaying forbearance from indulgence, (as in certain foods). Habitual restraint, especially from intoxicating beverages, is *total abstinence*.

ABSTRACT NOUN. A noun that names a quality, state or idea: *peace, freedom, whiteness.* Abstract is also used to mean the general class (*fruit*) as opposed to the particular (*apple*). Lower-case except where a proper name is involved. Overuse of abstract nouns makes a writing difficult to read. A concrete noun names a specific member of a group: *snake* rather than *reptile.*

abutting. Touching, sometimes with a protruding portion.

abysmal [a-BIHZ-m-1]. Deep; bottomless.

    ABYSSAL. (Unfathomable; tech., water depth over 300 fathoms.)

abyss. bottomless, unmeasurable.

    CHASM is deep, long, and narrow.

Abyssinia [ab-uh-SIHN-ih-uh]. SEE Ethiopia.

A.C. (abbr.) athletic club.

a.c. (abbr.) alternating current.

academician [uh-kad-uh-MISH-'n].

academic degrees and titles. John J. Smith, Ph.D; John J. Smith, Doctor of Philosophy; Prof. John J. Smith; Professor Smith; the professor. Degrees and titles are listed separately in this sequence; theological degrees, degrees earned in course, and honorary degrees in order of bestowal.

academic departments. Lower-case department of philosophy, department of French literature, etc.

Academy. Andover Academy, the academy; Merchant Marine Academy, the academy (BUT GPO uses Academy for a second reference). Most styles capitalize a second reference to National Academy of Science; the Academy of Sciences; French Academy; the United States Military, Naval, and Air Force Academies. BUT the service academies.

Acadia [uh-KAE-dih-uh]. Original name of Nova Scotia.

a cappella [ah-kah-PELL-ah]. Unaccompanied choral music.

Acapulco de Juarez [ah-kah-POOL-koh dthae-HWAH-raes]. South Mexico Pacific seaport-resort.

accede [ak-SEED]. (v.) Assume an office; assent to.

    EXCEED. Surpass.

ACCENT. When the same multisyllabic word is both noun and adjective, the adjective is usually accented on the last syllable; the noun on the first syllable: (n.) an *EX-pert*; (adj.) *ex-PERT player.* When the word is both a noun and a verb, the verb is usually accented on last syllable; progress (n.) [*PRAHG-rehs*;] (v.) [proh-GREHS]. Sometimes the consonantal sound at the end is hard in the noun, soft in the verb; use (n.) yoos; (v.) yooz; excuse (n.) ex-KYOOS; (v.) ex-KYOOZ. There are no general rules regarding accent in the English language, but new words tend to follow the accent of similar older words. The tendency is towards recessive accents, and towards accenting the first syllable.

accept. Receive willingly. *I accept your gift.*

    EXCEPT. Leave out, exclude. *He gave a gift to everyone except me.*

acceptance. In general, approval. Act of accepting.

    ACCEPTATION. The meaning of a word as it is generally understood.

accepter. Preferred to —*or.* In law, acceptor.

access. Opportunity of admission.

    EXCESS. Too much.

accession [ak-SESH-uhn]. Approach; adherence; something added; reaching an office or condition.

accessory [ak-SES-oh-ree]. (n. or adj.) Preferred to *accessary.* (adj.) Aiding or assisting; (n.) that which (or one who) assists or contributes.

accidentally. NOT *accidently.*

acclimate [uh-KLIE-miht; AK-luh-maet]. Also acclimatize [uh-KLIE-muh-tiez].

accolade [ak-oh-LAED]. A ritual embrace; award.

accompanied by, with. *By* is used to indicate an additional person. *With* is used to indicate supplementary activity. *He arrived, accompanied by his valet. She introduced her fiancee and accompanied her remarks with an affectionate hug.* —nying, —niment.

accommodate. -ted, -ting.

accompanist. Preferred to -*nyist*

accordion. NOT accordian.

accouchement [uh-KOOSH-mahn or mehnt]. Delivery in childbirth; confinement period of pregnancy.

account of ... *describe* is redundant. NOT: *An account of his adventures is described in* ... *Cf.* cause.

accouter [uh-KOOT-er]. Pref. to accoutre. Furnish with equipment or dress; *accouterment.*

acct. (abbr.) account. Also a/c.

accumulate [a-KYOO-myuh-laet]. —ting.

accurate [AK-yoo-riht] —racy.

accursed. Preferred to *accurst.*

ACCUSATIVE CASE is used for objects of a verb or a preposition; more commonly called the objective case: I hit *him.* It is on the *table. Cf.* Objective Case.

accuse of. Charge with: *I accuse him of theft.*

acetic [a-SEE-tihk]. Pertains to vinegar.
ASCETIC [a-SEHT-ihk]. Given to self-denial; austere.

Acheson, Dean Gooderham [AT-chehs-ihn]. (1893–1971) U.S. statesman; Sec. of State, 1949–1952.

achieve. Implies effort. AVOID: *achieving old age.*

ack-ack. Antiaircraft gun, or its fire.

acknowledgment. Preferred to *acknowledgement.* BUT acknowledgeable.

acoustics [uh-KOOS-tihks]. The science of sound; qualities that determine the clarity of sound in a room.

acquiesce [ak-wee-EHS]. Accept or comply passively.

acre. Unit of area measure. =,40469 hectare = 4,046.8726 sq. meters = 10 sq. surveyor's ch. = 160 sq. rods = 4840 sq. yd. = 43560 sq.ft. = approx. 2/3 city square block.

acreage.

acre-foot. Measure of water = 1 foot covering 1 acre = 325,900 gals. Also acre-inch.

acrid [AK-rid]. Irritating; corrosive.

acrostic. Verse in which initial letters of words or lines form a word or words.

Act. (federal, state, or foreign). Capitalize short or popular title: *Classification Act, Economy Act, Lend-Lease Act.* BUT: the act.
ACT. A simple deed.

act of God. Unpreventable accident.

Acting. Capitalize if part of complete capitalized title: *Acting Secretary of State.* BUT: *the acting secretary.*

activate. To make active, esp. through chemical treatment.
ACTUATE [AK-tyoo-aet]. Put into action; incite to activity; arouse. Implies communication of power.

acumen [a-KYOO-m'n]. Keenness of mind.

A.D. (abbr.) anno Domini (of the year of our Lord). The specific year should follow, NOT precede: *A.D. 1964.* NOT: *the tenth century A.D.* In type, often written with small caps : A.D.
B.C., before Christ; the year should precede: *70 B.C.* In type, often small caps : B.C.
B.C.E. Before the Christian Era. *70 B.C.E.*
C.E. The Christian Era.

ad. (abbr.) Shortening of "advertisement." No period.
ADD. Increase.

ADA. (abbr.) Americans for Democratic Action, liberal political organization.

Ada. Adah [ae-dah].

adagio [uh-DAH-joh]. A slow, graceful musical composition or dance. Pl. -gios.

adapt. -ed, -ing, -ter; -able (adj.), -ability (n.) ; -ive (adj.), -ation (n.). To make suitable; to fit or suit. *He adapts himself well to new situations.*

ADOPT. Take as one's own. *They adopted a new policy.*

addendum. Addition; supplement. Pl. -da.

add. Join to or unite with; append. addible.

addicted to. Must be followed by a noun.

Addis Ababa [AHD-ihs AH-buh-buh]. Capital of Ethiopia.

addict [AD-ihkt (n.) or -dihkt (v.)]. give oneself over to; (n.) one addicted to a habit, especially to taking drugs. -ed, -ing; -ed (adj.); -edness (n.), -tion (n.).

addle. Confuse; muddle.

addle. —brain, —head, —pate.

address [uh-DREHS]. (v.) Address, lecture, speech are in descending order of formality.

ADDRESS. In general, the address should stand out clearly from the body of a letter and should be specific and complete on the envelope. Principal words are capitalized. Mr., Miss, Mrs., Dr., Rev. or Hon. precede a name; Esq., Jr., Sr., 2d and academic degrees follow the name. BUT: When a degree or Esq. follows a name, there should be no preceding title. Write out North, South, West and East. In an address NW., SW., NE., SE., indicate divisions of a city. Do not abbreviate *street* or *building* as part of a name, *Court Street Building*, but street, avenue, place, road, square, boulevard building, terrace, or court may be abbreviated following a name or numbers. Write out names of U.S. states, territories or possessions when standing alone, but abbreviate after the name of a city (except Alaska, Hawaii, Idaho, Maine, Ohio, Utah, Canal Zone, Puerto Rico, Samoa, and Virgin Islands). Unofficial abbreviations widely used are: Alas., Ida., Me., O., Ut., C.Z., P.R., V.I. Where it is known, the zip code should appear on an envelope, following the names of city and state: New York, N.Y. 10020. Where the zip code is not known and the postal zone is known, the postal zone should appear between city and state, followed by a comma: New York 10, N.Y.

adduce. Offer as an argument; cite. -ced, -cing; -cible (adj.) Preferred to -*eable*.

adept [uh-DEHPT]. Skilled: *She is adept with a needle. Adept in* is preferred to *adept at.*

adequate. Sufficient.

adhere. Stick; cling. -ed, -ing; -ent (n. and adj.); -ence (n.).
ADHERENCE. Mental or moral attachment.

ad hoc [ad hahk]. (Lat.) For this (special purpose): *ad hoc committee.*

ad hominem [ad HAHM-in-ehm]. (Lat.) To the man; refers to an argument that appeals to one's prejudices rather than to reason.

adieu [uh-DYEU]. Farewell. Pl. —s or —x, leave-takings.

adj. (abbr.) adjective.

adjacent. . . . *to* . . . Not *of.*

ADJECTIVE. A word used to qualify a noun. It generally has no special forms to denote singular, plural, or gender, but most adjectives have comparative and superlative forms. *Cf.* Comparison. Nouns, pronouns, verbal forms of verbs, and some adverbs, may be used as adjectives: *sink washers, frightening crowds, frightened crowds.* Adjectives are classified as adherent when they are placed before a noun; apposite when they are placed after a noun; predicate when they follow a linking verb; objective complement or factitive when they follow the object of a verb. In a series of adjectives, the usual order is: (1) definitive adjectives (*a, the, this*); (2) ordinal numbers (*second, third,* BUT NOT *first, last,* and *others*); (3) cardinal numbers (*seven, two*); (4) fractions (*one-half*); (5) units (*tenths, dozens*); (6) adjective of degree (*more, least*); (7) judgment words (*true, happy, ugly*); (8) descriptive adjectives (*bright*); (9) adjective of size (*tall, slight*); (10) adjectives of color (*blue, green*). Phrases and clauses follow the noun. Exceptions have been established by popular usage in some forms and when *of* is needed: *half of the men, half the men.*
Compound adjective forms are hyphenated for clarity when they precede the noun: *The first-class passengers.* BUT: *The scholastic standing of the school is first class.*
Adjectives (and adverbs) are compared in three forms: positive, comparative (with -*er* added, or prefixed by *more*) and superlative (with -*est* added, or prefixed by *most*).

adjoining. Having a common boundary, contiguous.

ADJACENT. Near. Next to, but not necessarily connected; i.e., *a road may run between adjacent farms.*

ATTACHED. Fastened to, connected.

Adj. Gen. adjutant general. Pl. adjutants general,

adjoin [a-JOIN]. -ed, -ing; -ing (adj.). See adjoining.

ADJOURN [a-JEHRN, NOT ad—]. -ed, -ing; -ment (n.). *Cf.* prorogue.

adjudge [a-JUHJ]. Decide; determine; order or decree. -ed, -ging.

adjudicate [a-JOO-dih-kaet]. Decide judicially. -ting, -cable.

adjure [a-joor]. Command solemnly; entreat earnestly. *Cf.* abjure.

ad-lib. (Theatrical slang). To speak lines not in the script. -bbed, -bbing. (n.) ad lib, pl. ad libs; (adj.), ad-lib.

Adm. (abbr.) admiral. Used with a name.

administer. Manage; direct. -ed, -ing; trable (adj.), -trant (adj.), -trate (v.), -tration (n.)

administrate. -ed, -ting, -tive (adj.); -tion (n.), -tor (n.), -torship (n.), -tratrix (n.).

Administration. Capitalize with name when referring to specific agency appointed by the President and standing alone if referring to a federal unit: Farmers Home Administration, Food and Drug Administration, Maritime Administration, Veterans Administration, etc., the Administration. BUT: Roosevelt administration; administration bill, policy, etc.

administration. British use *government* or the *ministry.*

Administrator of Veterans Affairs; the administrator.

administrator. In law, a person who administers an estate.

administratrix. Female administrator. Pl. -tratrices [trae-TRIE-seez or TRAE-trih-seez].

admirable [AD-muh-ra-uh-b'l]. *Cf.* strong opinion words.

admiral. Charles F. Hughes, rear admiral, United States Navy; the rear admiral; Admiral Hughes.

Admiralty. Lord of the (British, etc.).

admire. -red, -ring; -ring (adj.); -rer (n.).

admission. More generally used than admittance (entrance) to suggest accompanying rights, obligations, and so on: admission to a church, a group.

admit. -tted, -tting; -ttance (n.).

admit of. *He will admit of no other solution.*

ad nauseam [ad-NAW-shee-am or NAW-see-am]. To the point of disgust.

adobe [uh-DOH-bee]. Sun-dried brick; a building made of such brick or clay.

adopted (adj.) Refers to the child.

ADOPTIVE (adj.). Refers to the parent.

adore. -red, -ring; ration (n.), -rer (n.).

adulate [AD-yoo-laet]. Praise or flatter obsequiously. -d, -ting; -tory [AD-yoo-luh-tawr-ee] (adj.); -tor (n.).

adult [uh-DUHLT; AD-uhlt].

adulterate. Corrupt or defile by adding a baser substance. -rable.

adv. (abbr.) adverb.

ad val. (abbr.) ad valorem.

ad valorem. (Lat.) according to value. A tax or duty of a percentage of the value of the taxed goods. *ad valorem duty.*

advance. (n.) Progress, improvement; rise in price, -ced, -cing; -d (adj.) *Advance warning, advance planning* are redundant.

advancement. (n.) Progression; often refers to promotion. DISTINGUISH from progress. *The student received an advancement in rating for the progress he had made in his studies.*

advantageous. Profitable; favorable.

ADVENTITIOUS. Accidental; fortuitous.

ADVERB. (adv.) A word, phrase or clause that modifies a verb, adjective, or other

6

adverb. It answers such questions as where, how, how much, when: *speedily, directly, only, very.*

An adjective or a noun may be used as an adverb; *light blue dress; He was there Tuesday.* Adverbs are classified as adverbs of time: *now, soon;* place: *here, everywhere;* manner: *softly, hurriedly;* and degree: *mostly, scarcely.* They are also classified as interrogative: *when, how.* (*She didn't know when he came*); relative (used to introduce a sentence); negative: *not, never, hardly;* directional: *back, up, down;* and descriptive: *slowly, beautifully, brightly.* Only descriptive adverbs are compared in three forms. *Cf.* Comparison.

With a compound verb, place an adverb between the auxiliary and the verb: *He has always slept well.* With a copulative verb, usually place the adverb between noun and complement: *He is ever ready to go.* With a transitive verb, the adverb does not intervene between verb and complement: *He selected the material wisely.* NOT: *He selected wisely the material.* Split an infinitive with an adverb only when necessary for greater clarity: *He hopes to at least see the prisoner. Cf.* adjective.

ADVERBIAL ADJ. Formed from an adverb and a participle, sometimes omitted: *the down (going) stairway.*

adverbial accusative. A noun not in the genitive used as an adverb in a prepositional phrase: *The miles we walked over road and field.*

ADVERBIAL GENITIVE. A noun used as an adverb, formed from the archaic genitive case, usually marked by its —*s* ending. *I work days.* Often such words as *since, needs, sometimes,* are adverb genitives.

ADVERBIAL CLAUSE may be placed (1) at the beginning of the sentence, either to emphasize the main clause or to avoid piling up adverbial clauses after the main clause; or (2) after the main clause, in its natural position. *If he loves me, he will come. He will come if he loves me.* Long or complex modifiers placed at the end of a sentence are anticlimactic and weaken the sentence.

adversary [AD-vuhr-sehr-ee]. Antagonist, enemy.

adverse [ad-VURS or AD-vurs]. Opposing. *There were many adverse conditions to be met.*

AVERSE [a-VURS]. Unwilling, reluctant. *I am averse to seeing bad movies.*

advert [ad-VURT]. Allude. -ed, -ing; -ent (adj.); -ence (n.), -ency (n.).

advertisement [ad-VUHR-tis-ment or AD-vihr-TIEZ-ment]., -sing, -tised; -tiser; (n.), -tise -ment (n.). Also -ize.

advice [ad-VIES]. (n.) A recommended opinion.

ADVISE [ad-VIEZ]. (v.) counsel, warn.

INFORM (v.) Communicate. AVOID use of *advise* for *inform.* NOT: *He advised me that it was raining.*

advise -vising, -vised; -visable (adj.), -vised (adj.), -viser, -visory (adj.) -visability (n.), -visableness (n.), -visedness (n.), -visement (n.).

advisedly. Deliberately; after consideration.

INTENTIONALLY. By plan.

adviser. Preferred to *advisor;* BUT advisory.

advocate. Support or plead for: *He advocated free speech.* NOT: *He advocated that liquor be served.* -ating, -d; -atory (adj.); -ator (n.), -tion (n.).,

adze [adz]. Ax, hatchet with cutting edge perpendicular to handle.

ae. oe. The *e* (or ae) alone is used for these ligatures in English: *aesthetic* or *esthetic: aesophagus* or *esophagus.*

A.E.C. (abbr.) Atomic Energy Commission. (GPO uses no periods.)

AEF. (abbr.) American Expeditionary Forces (World War I).

Aegean Sea [A-JEE-'n]. Between Greece and Turkey.

aegis [EE-jihs]. Also *egis.* The shield of Zeus; by extension, a protection.

Aeneid [ee-NEE-id]. Epic by Virgil.

Aeolian [ee-OH-lih-an]. Member of a Greek tribe that colonized Lesbos.

aeolian. Produced by wind, as rock sculpture.

aeolian harp. Stringed instrument on which the wind produces tones.

aeon. [EE-ahn]. *Eon* is preferred. Extremely long period of time.

aerate [AE-ehr-aet]. Preferred to aerify.

aerial [ae-EER-ee-uhl; AIR-ee'l]. Pertains to the air; insubstantial; radio antenna is preferred to *aerial*.

aerie [AE-ehr-rih]. A nest. Preferred to *aery, eyry, eyrie*.

aero. Combining form, meaning air or gas: *aerodrome, aerodynamic*.

Aerolineas Argentinas. Argentinian airline.

Aeronaves de Mexico. Mexican airline.

aeroplane [AE-ehr-oh-plaen or AIR-uh-plaen]. SEE airplane.

aerospace. The total expanse beyond the earth's surface.

Aeschylus [EHS-kih-luhs]. (525–456 B.C.) Greek playwright.

Aesop [EE-sahp]. (c.620–560 B.C.) Greek fabulist.

aesthete [EHS-theet]. One who emphasizes (or overemphasizes) appreciation of beauty. Preferred to Brit. *esthete*.

aesthetic [ehs-THEHT-ik]. Pertains to the beautiful. More generally used than esthetic.

AFB. (abbr.) Air Force Base. (with name).

Afghan hound.

A/c. (abbr.) airman, first class.

a few. a good many, a great many, a very few, many a man. BUT NOT: an extremely few, a good few.

affect. (v.) Influence, change, produce an effect upon. *The fire affected all the houses.* affectible.

    EFFECT (v.) Bring about, fulfill. *He has effected many improvements in management.*

    EFFECT (n.) Result, consequence. *The effect of the fire was bankruptcy to the business.*

affidavit [af-ih-DAE-viht]. Written statement made under oath.

affiliate. Correct; associate. -liable.

affix [AF-fihks]. (n.) Something added; e.g., a seal.

AFFIX (v.) [a-FIHKS]. Join to or add. SEE prefix.

afflict. He is afflicted with arthritis.

    INFLICT. Cause to suffer; impose. *He inflicts his presence on them.*

affluence. Abundance; connotes plenty.

    OPULENCE. Riches; connotes luxury.

A.F.L. (abbr.) American Federation of Labor. Preferred to *A.F. of L.*

Afghanistan [af-GAN-ih-stan]. Native, Afghan (s); adj. Afghan. Cap., Kabul [KAE-bul]; Currency, afghani (Afg), pul.

afore-. Combining form meaning before: *aforecited, aforementioned*.

aforesaid. AVOID as pedantic. Use *this*.

a fortiori [ae fawr-shih-OH-ree]. (Lat.) On yet firmer grounds; all the more. In logic, used to introduce a fact previously mentioned, from which it follows: *He was a millionaire; a fortiori, the expense of the trip was not a factor.*

afoul. In collision. From *run foul of.* (U.S.)

afraid. Any degree of apprehension. NEVER use directly after a noun. NOT: *An afraid child.*

afranchise. Free from bondage or obligation.

    ENFRANCHISE. Set free; endow with citizenship or its privileges, esp. the right of suffrage.

Africa. East, East Coast, North, South-West. West Coast.

African refers only to Negroes. *Cf.* South Africa. Negro refers only to native Negroes. Current usage prefers Black.

Afro. Combining form meaning Africa. *Afro-American*.

Afrikaner. SEE Union of South Africa.

after-[AFT-uhr]. Combining form meaning subsequent in time or place: · *afterbirth, afterthought, aftereffect*.

afterward. Subsequently. Preferred to -s. in U.S.; Brit. use—s. *Cf.* backward.

again [uh-GEHN, or uh-GAEN].

against [uh-GEHNST or uh-GAENST].

agar-agar [AH-gahr AH-gahr or AG-ahr AG-ahr]. A gelatinous substance obtained from seaweeds, used as a solidifying agent in culture media.

agate line [AG-iht or AG-at]. Unit used in computing newspaper advertising rates = $5\frac{1}{2}$ points = approx. 1/14th inch.

AGE. Use figures for the age of persons and animals. *Paul Jones, 37 years old; a 9-year old girl; open to 3-year olds. 22 years of age; aged 22 years; NOT aged 22 years old; 7 years old; 42 years 10 months 3 days.* BUT in a text, write out numbers greater than nine. *twenty-two years old.* Ages of inanimate objects are spelled out from one to nine but use figures for numbers greater than nine. *A six-year voyage; the doll is 16 inches tall.* BUT UCMS spells out references to the age of a person or object regardless of number. *At the age of 50* pref. to *age 60. Cf.* animals.

age. aged [aejd] (v.). aging; (adj.) aged [AE-jehd].

ageless. agelong; age-old (adj.), age-stricken (adj.), age-weary (adj.).

agency. Legal relationship between a principal who authorizes and an agent who acts for him.

Agency. Capitalize if part of name; cap. standing alone if referring to a federal unit. *Chippewa Agency; the agency.* Omit periods and spacing in abbreviations of agencies of government, unions, associations, and committees.

agency shop. Place of employment where employees need not join a union, but must pay fees equivalent to dues to the union.

agencywide.

agenda [uh-JEHN-duh]. Things to be done, or a list of such things. Singular is *agendum*, but plural form is usually used. *The agenda was amended.*

agent provocateur. Subversive agent who stimulates riot or revolt in order to expose opposition.

AGES, HISTORIC. Capitalize historic and geological eras that are generally recognized: *Age of Discovery, Dark Ages, Elizabethan Age. Christian Era, Renaissance, the Bronze Age, Golden Age* (of Pericles only), *Middle Ages, Dark Ages.* BUT use lower-case *age* or *era* when doing so would not be confusing to the reader. *Cambrian age, Colonial days, Victorian period.* DO NOT capitalize eras not generally recognized as such: *missile age, rocket age, space age, atomic age.* UCMS caps *Ice Age* and *Stone Age* and N.Y. Times capitalizes *Copper Age,* but GPO carries these in lower case. *Cf.* Numbers.

aggravate. Worsen. NOT annoy or irritate.

agreeable to. NOT *with.*

aggregate [AG-ruh-gaet]. (v.) Bring parts together into a whole; (n.) the total; also a mix of rocks for cement.

aghast [uh-GAST]. SEE afraid.

agile [AJ-ihl or AJ-iel].

ago. *He died a year ago.* NOT: *It is scarcely a year ago since he died.* Use: that he died.

AGREEMENT. A verb (except *may, can, might,* and a few others) agrees with its subject in number and person but changes form only in the present tense (except *to be*). A pronoun agrees with its antecedent in person, number and gender. *Cf.* Number, Pronouns.

agriculturist. Preferred to *argiculturalist.*

AGRONOMIST. Specialist in soils and field crops.

ague [AE-gyoo]. A shaking chill.

Agulyi-Ironsi, Johnson, Thomas [ag-WEE-yee i-RAHN-see]. (1914–   ) Congolese general.

Aida [ah-EE-da]. Opera by Verdi.

aid [aed]. (n., v.) Help. But *aide* [aed] is preferred for *assistant,* both civilian and military.

aide-de-camp [AED-dee-kamp]. Officer who is a general's personal assistant. Pl. aides-de-camp.

aide-memoire [AED-MAE-mwahr]. Notes to refresh memory.

aigrette [AE-gret]. Spray of feathers.

EGRET [EE-greht]. Heron.

aim at. *aim for* is colloquial; *aim to be* is obsolete in Britain.

ain't. Accepted by some authorities in the sense of am I not (ain't I), but still considered ungrammatical by most authorities. BUT NOT accepted for *is not, are not, have not, had not*. In Britain, *aren't I* is accepted by some, but it is usually considered ungrammatical.

airbase. -bill, -blast, -blown, -borne, -bound, -brained, -brake, -brush, -burst, -cargo, -coach, -craft, -crew, -crewman, -drome, -drop, -field, -flow, -foil, -frame, -freight, -freighter, -gap, -glow, -hammer, -head, -hole, -hose, -lane, -lift, -line (aviation), -liner, -link, -load, -mail, -man, -mark (v.), -marker, -mass, -minded, -park, -path, -photo, -plane, -port (all meanings), -power, -scoop, -ship, -show, -sick, -sickness, -sleeve, -space, -speed, -stream, -strike, -strip, -tight, -ward, -wave, -way, -wayman, -wise, -woman, -worthy (all one word); air-blasted (adj.), air-condition (v.), air-conditioned (adj.), air-conditioning (n. or adj.), air-cool (v.); air-cooled (adj.), air-dried (adj.), air-driven (adj.), air-dry (adj. & v.), air-floated (adj.), air-formed (adj.), air-slaked (adj.); air bends, air duct, air line (line for air), air navigation, air raid, air time (radio and TV), air train, air twist, air well.

Airedale terrier [AER-dael].

Air Force. Air Explorers, Air National Guard; Civil Air Patrol, Civil Patrol, the patrol; Command; Reserve; Reserve Officers' Training Corps; WAF, Women in the Air Force; Air Force Academy, the Academy.

Air France. French airline.

à la king. In a seasoned cream sauce.

à la Marengo [ah-lah mah-REHNG-goh]. With mushrooms or truffles.

Alamo [AL-uh-moh]. Scene in Texas of massacre during Texas War of Independence, 1836.

à la mode. Or alamode. In a special fashion; e.g., with ice cream.

Alaska [uh-LAS-kuh]. Alas. Native Alaskan; Cap., Juneau.

Albania [al-BAE-nih-uh]. Native, adj., Albanian. Cap., Tirana (Tirane); Currency, lek, quidar.

albeit [awl-BEE-iht]. Even though.

Alberta. (abbr. Alta.) Province in Canada. AVOID using the abbreviation. Cap., Edmonton.

albino [al-BIE-noh]. Person or animal lacking skin and hair pigment. Pl.—s.

albumen [al-BYOO-mihn]. Egg white.

ALBUMIN (chem). Protein found in the blood; also in eggs, milk, and meat.

Albuquerque [AL-buh-KUHR-kee]. City in New Mexico.

Aleutian Islands [al-OO-sh'n]. Chain of islands extending west from Alaska.

Alfaro Siqueros, David [al-FAH-reh see KEH-ee-rohs]. (1898–   ) Mexican muralist.

alfresco [al-FREHS-koh]. In the open air. *Cf.* fresco.

alga [AL-juh]. Low form of plant life. Pl., algae [AL-jee].

algebra [AL-jeh-bruh]. Branch of mathematics dealing with the relations and properties of numbers.

Algeria [al-JEER-ih-uh]. Fr., Algerie, Natives, Algerians. (Formerly Algiers; the Barbary State) Fr. Algier, Cap., Algiers. Currency, dinar (AD).

alias [AE-lih-uhs]. SEE nom de plume.

alibi [AL-ih-bie]. Plea of having been elsewhere; Colloq., any excuse. *What alibi have you for not getting your work done?*

alien [AEL-yehn]. Strange; different; belonging to another country. —ate; —able. *Cf.* corporation.

alien to. Preferred to *alien from*.

Alien Property. Office of.

alight. —ighted. Step down; dismount; descend.

align. aline.

alignment. Preferred to *alinement*.

alike. Similar.

aliquot part. A part of a number that divides the whole with no remainder.

Alitalia Airlines. Italian airlines.

alkali [AL-kuh-lie]. Soluble salts with acrid taste and ability to neutralize acids. Pl. —is or —ies.

all. With a singular noun, the whole; with a plural noun, the total or everyone. Never *all's.* all-American, all-clear (n. and adj.),

all-out (adj.), all-round (adj.), all-star (adj.); all fours, all hail, all in.

allege [uh-LEHJ]. (v.) alleged. State without positive proof. As a disclaimer of responsibility for a statement, e.g., in libel actions, the word has no legal value.

Allegany [AL-ee-gae-nee]. The name of counties in New York and Maryland.
> ALLEGHANY. A county in Virginia.
> ALLEGHANY CORPORATION.
> ALLEGHENY. The mountains, the river, the city, and the county in Pennsylvania.
> ALLEGHENY AIRLINES.
> ALLEGHENY MOUNTAINS. Pl. Alleghenies.

allegory. Illustrative story in which characters and things represent other things or ideas; a sustained metaphor.
> PARABLE. A short illustrative story about things that could actually happen, designed to make a single point, usually to teach a lesson.

allegretto [al-eh-GREHT-oh]. Not quite as quick as allegro. *Cf.* Slow Music.

allegro [al-LAE-groh]. Brisk, lively. Pl. -os.

Allende Gassens, Salvador [ah-YEHN-dae]. (1908–1973) President of Chile, 1970–1973.

alliances and coalitions. Allied Powers; the powers (World Wars); the Axis, Axis Powers; Benelux (Belgium, Netherlands, Luxembourg); Big Four (European); Big Three; Central Powers, the powers (World War I); SEATO, CENTO.

Allied (World Wars). armies, Governments, Nations, peoples; Allied Powers, the powers;

BUT European powers. N.Y. Times lower-cases references to post-W.W. II alliances and allies. NATO allies, CENTO allies, Western allies. BUT capitalize W.W. I and W.W. II alliances and similar alliances where the name includes Allies or Allied.

Allies. the (World Wars); BUT our allies.

alliteration. In rhetoric, repetition of the same sounds in sequence of words. *"The sad, sea-sounding wastes of Lyonesse."*

all of. Eliminate *of* unless followed by a pronoun: *All of us. All the books,* NOT *all of the books.*

allot. —tting; allottee.

allow of. Permit.
> ALLOW FOR. Leave a margin.

alloy [AL-oi]. Combination of two or more metals.

all ready. Prepared.
> ALREADY. Previous. *If they are all ready, we can proceed. They had already left.*

all right. Always two words. NOT *all-right* or *allright* or *alright.*

all-round. NOT *all around athlete.*

allspice [AWL-spiess]. Berry and aromatic spice from allspice tree; pimento. NOT allspices.

all-time. AVOID as applied to a sport or other record.

all together. The group in unison.
> ALTOGETHER. Entirely.

allude, allusion. An indirect reference. NOT: *He alluded to Mr. Olson by name.*
> REFER. Mention directly. *Although his statement alluded to a previous marriage, he never referred to a former wife.*
> ELUDE. Avoid or evade. (n.), elusion. *The criminal eluded the police for months.*
> ILLUSION. A fanciful but not harmful impression. *His stage sets were so clever we had the illusion of being in a foreign land.*
> DELUSION. A false belief. *He is under the delusion that someone is persecuting him.*

ally [a-LIE]. (n. v.) Pl. allies. An associate. *France was our ally in the war.*

ALLEY. Pl. alleys. A narrow passageway. *There is an alley between the two buildings.*

alma mater [al-muh MAE-ter; AHL-muh MAH-tehr]. (Lat.) Foster mother. One's school.

almanac. —ack is used only in old titles.

Almanach de Gotha [ahl-mah-NAHK deh GOH-tah]. German periodical of data on royalty and nobility, founded 1763.

almighty. Possessing all power.

almost is closer than *nearly. almost no, scarcely any, hardly any, practically no.* But *almost quite* is an impossible combination.

alone. SEE Placement of Words.

along. With one, in company. *He took a book along.* BUT NOT meaning *some way on* or *about.* NOT: *His job ended along October.*

along. Colloquial when used meaning approximately. *Along about breakfast time.*

along this line. Trite. Use *in this direction, like, similarly, and so on.*

aloof [uh-LOOF]. Removed; reserved.

Aloysius [al-oh-IHS-ih-uhs or -IHSH-uhs].

A.L.R. (abbr.) American Law Reports.

already. (adv.) Prior to a specified time. *The book has already been returned.* Cf. all ready. *Already existing* is redundant.

Alsatian wolfdog.

also. (adv.) As well (as). Avoid use as *and. He also brought cake.* NOT: *He quoted Shakespeare and Johnson; also Keats.*

also-ran. (n. and adj.) Pl. also-rans.

altar. A table for worship. *The minister stood at the altar.*
 ALTER. Change; modify. *She gained so much weight that her clothes had to be altered.*

alternately. Two things following each other.
 ALTERNATIVELY. Choosing one of two things.

alternating [AWL-tuhr-NAET-ihng]. Occurring by turns.

alternative. Offering a choice between two things or (loosely) among several. *They had no alternative. The alternatives are liberty and (NOT or) death. The only alternative is war or (NOT and) surrender. The alternative (NOT other) is to surrender. The only alternatives to surrender are arming and (NOT or) fighting. Cf.* Hobson's Choice.

alternatively. SEE alternately.

although. More formal, emphatic and more used in stating a fact than in making a hypothetical statement, than *though.* Only *though* may be used as an adverb and in the idiom *as though.*

altogether. Entirely. *This is altogether too weak to hold us.*
 ALL TOGETHER. All in one place. *We are all together for dinner.*

aluminum [a-lyoo-mih-nuhm]. British and some U.S. texts use aluminium [al-yoo-MIHN-ih-uhm].

alumnus [a-LUHM-nuhs]. Pl. alumni [-nie] (masc. or both m. and f.); (fem.) alumna [-nah], pl. alumnae [-nee].

always. (adv.) All the time.
 ALL WAYS. In all possible manners.

AM. (abbr.), amplitude modulation.

A.M. (abbr.) *anno mundi.* In the year of the world.

A.M. or M.A. (abbr.) master of arts.

a.m. (abbr.) Ante meridiem, NOT meridian. Period between midnight and noon. *9 a.m.* NOT 9 a.m. *in the morning* or *9 o'clock a.m.* In type, often A.M.

A.M.A. (abbr.) American Medical Association. American Marketing Association, American Management Association.

amanuensis [a-man-yoo'-EHN-sihs]. A secretary. Pl.—enses.

amateur [AM-uh-chehr or AM-uh-tuhr]. One who does something because he loves doing it; a non-professional.
 CONNOISSEUR. One who knows about aesthetic aspects, especially one capable of judging.

12

DILETTANTE. An amateur who is superficial and affected.

NOVICE. A beginner—amateur or professional.

amazing. *Somewhat amazing* is an impossible combination.

Ambassador, ambassadorial. Ambassador John J. Smith; John J. Smith, Ambassador to India, the Ambassador. BUT *a penchant for meeting ambassadors, an ambassador of goodwill.*

ambassador (American). ADDRESS: His Excellency the American Ambassador to France; The Honorable Benjamin Franklin, American Ambassador to France. SALUTATION: Sir, Your Excellency, My dear Mr. Ambassador.

ambassador (British, etc.). The Ambassador, the Senior Ambassador, His Excellency Extraordinary and Plenipotentiary; the Ambassador; Ambassador at Large. ADDRESS: His excellency the Ambassador of Great Britain, or His Excellency, the Rt. Hon, Sir Oliver Sherwell Franks, Ambassador of Great Britain. SALUTATION: Sir, Excellency, Your Excellency, Dear Mr. Ambassador.

ambassador at large. Pl. ambassadors —. Capitalize when referring to a specific person holding this official title.

ambidextrous. —ly. —ness. Able to use both hands with equal facility; ambidexterity.

A.M.C. (abbr.) American Maritime Cases.

Am. Dec. (abbr.) American Decisions.

ameliorate [uh-MEEL-yuh-raet]. Make better; improve. —rable.

amen [AE-MEN; BUT AH-MEN for singing].

amendent. Social Security Amendments of 1954, 1954 amendments, the social security amendments, the amendments; Tobey amendment to the Constitution (U.S.); first amendment, 14th amendment; etc. BUT N.Y. Times prefers capitals when referring to a specific amendment to the U.S. constitution: *First Amendment.* Spell out first to ninth, use figures for 10th and higher.

amenity [uh-MEHN-ih-tee, uh-MEE-nih-tee]. Civility; social niceties. Pl. —ties.

America, Americas. Includes both North and South America, but Americans usually refers to citizens of the U.S. If the context makes the meaning clear, *Americans* may be used to refer to natives of the two continents, but for Canadians, Mexicans, and the like, specific designations are better.

American. American Federation of Labor and Congress of Industrial Organizations (AFL-CIO); the federation; American Gold Star Mothers, Inc., Gold Star Mothers, a Mother; the American Legion; National Red Cross, the Red Cross; American Veterans of World War II (AMVETS); American War Mothers, a Mother.

Americana [uh-mehr-ih-KAE-nuh, uh-mehr-ih-KAH-nuh]. Collection of documents, facts, and so on, pertaining to U.S.

American Embassy, British Embassy.

American Geographical Society. *Cf.* National Geographic Society.

American plan. In hotels, a plan in which room and board are included in the charges. *Cf.* European plan.

American nations.

American Stock Exchange. In New York City.

American Telephone and Telegraph Company. (A.T. & T.).

America's Cup. Yachting trophy.

AMERICAS CUP. Golf trophy.

AMG. (abbr.) Allied Military Government.

Amherst [AM-uhrst]. Town and college in Massachusetts.

amiable [AE-mih-ab'l]. Good-natured; agreeable;or describes the disposition of a person.

AMICABLE [AM-ih-kuh-b'l]. Friendly; peaceful;describes a relationship.

amicus curiae. (Lat.) Friend of the court, by ext. a brief entered by one not a party to a lawsuit who may have an interest in the result.

amid. N.Y. Times prefers to amidst.

amidships. Toward the middle of a ship.

Amish [AHM-ish]. (adj.) Of an orthodox sect of the Mennonites, from Jacob Amen. Also (n.), the sect.

amoeba [a-MEE-ba]. Preferred to *ameba* except by GPO. Simple one-celled animal. Pl. —s or —bae [—bee].

among. Preferred to *amongst*. Division of things made among three or more. BUT *between two. He divided the money among the three of us. He divided the money between the two of us.*

amoral [ae-MAW-ral]. Not involving moral principles: *"The survival of the fittest," is a law of nature.*

IMMORAL. Contrary to moral principles: *Criminals are immoral.*

UNMORAL. Having no moral perception: *Animals are unmoral.*

amortization. Process of extinguishing the value of an asset or liability as carried in the books of a company.

amount. Use for bulk, mass.

NUMBER. Use for individuals, units.

amour [uh-MOOR]. Love affair.

Amoy [uh-MOI]. City in China.

ampere (abbr. a.).

ampersand (&). Use only in names and titles to follow form: *Baltimore & Ohio Railroad, B. & O.*

ampoule [am-POOL], **ampule** [AM-pyool], **ampul.** Hermetically sealed vessel containing material for injection.

Am. Repts. (abbr.) American Reports.

amuck [uh-MUHK]. Preferred to *amok* [uh-MAHK]. In a frenzied manner.

amusing. Preferred to *amusive*.

AMVETS (abbr.) American Veterans of World War II and Korea; (individual) Amvet(s).

an. As an article, use before vowel sounds: *an AEC report, an FCC rule, an 11 year-old, an VIII class, an herbseller, an NSC request, an RFC investigation. Cf.* a.

anachronistic [uh-nak-ron-nihs-tihk]. Preferred to *anachronic*. Out of its proper historical time; e.g. a horse and carriage at Cape Kennedy.

anacoluthon [an-uh-koh-LYOO-thahn]. In grammar especially, the abrupt shift from one uncompleted construction to another: *There's no reason to—all right, go ahead.* Also, construction that does not follow logically from another: *If he is bright and there are books for everyone why is he not well read?*

anadiplosis [an-uh-dih-PLOH-sihs]. In rhetoric, repetition at the beginning of one clause of the last word in the preceding clause: *He loved money—money he could hold on to.*

analogous [an-AL-oh-guhs]. Similar in some attributes. analogy. -gize (v.), -gist, -gic, -ical.

analogy. In rhetoric, reference to a likeness between same attributes of two things: *The kingdom of heaven is like a mustard seed.*

analyst. One who analyzes or studies in detail: *an investment analyst.*

ANNALIST. A chronicler: *A summary of the year was prepared by the annalist.*

analyze. Preferred to Brit. *analyse*. Break into fundamental elements; study in detail. analytic, analytical, —cally.

anapaest [AN-uh-pehst; Brit. -peest]. A metrical foot consisting of two unaccented syllables and one accented syllable (written uu-): *o-ver-come.*

anaphora [uh-NAF-oh-ruh]. In rhetoric, use of the same word or phrase to begin a series of sentences, clauses, etc.: *"I have seen war. I have seen war on land and sea. I have seen blood running from the wounded. I have seen men coughing out their gassed lungs."*

anastrophe [uh-NAS-troh-fee]. In rhetoric, the reversal of the usual order of words. *Came the dawn.*

anathema [uh-NATH-uh-muh]. Curse; cursed object.

ancestress. Use ancestor.

anchorite [ANG-koh-riet]. Preferred to *anchoret* (-eht) in U.S. A hermit.

anchovy [an-CHOH-vee, AN-choh-vee].

Ancient Free and Accepted Masons. a Mason, a Freemason.

and may be used to begin a sentence.

and joining parts of a subject signals a plural verb. *The pros and cons have been discussed.* BUT when the parts form a unit, use the singular verb. *Dollars and cents is the chief issue. Her adviser and confidante is here.*

and. In a series, must connect something common to all. NOT: *He often writes to his mother, talks to his wife and business associates. Talks to his wife and telephones his business associates* would be correct in this sentence; AVOID use of *and* as a substitute for *to.* NOT: *He'll try and do it. Cf.* also, *which.* The use of the comma before and in a series—*His mother, wife, and child*—is still a matter of disagreement.

and/or. Its use is decried by all, but is sometimes necessary in business and law. The number of the following verb is determined by the singular or plural concept. *Any check and/or cash paid* (considered as one unit) *is entered in the book. Any money and/or jewelry found* (considered as various items) *are his.*

and which, and who. Use only after *which* and *who: Women who work, and who also keep house, find themselves under great tension.* NOT: *Stout women of middle age and who do light work should watch their diets.*

Andalusia [AN-duh-LOO-zhuh]. Region in in S. Spain; city in Ala.

Andean [an-DEE-'n, AN-dee'h]. Pertains to the Andes.

Andes [AN-dees]. South American mountain system.

Andorra [an-DAWR-uh]. Coprincipality between France and Spain. 191 sq. miles. Currency, Fr. franc, Span. peseta. Natives, Andorran(s); (adj.) Andorran.

Andromeda [an-DRAHM-e-duh]. (Greek Mythology) Princess saved from a sea monster by Perseus. In astronomy, a northern constellation.

anemia [a-NEE-mee-ya]. Condition in which red blood corpuscles are deficient in hemoglobin or reduced in number —ic.

anemone [uh-NEHM-oh-nee]. Buttercup-like plant with white, star-shaped flowers.
    SEA ANEMONE. Invertebrate marine animal somewhat resembling a flower.

anesthetic [an-ehs-THET-ihk]. (n.) An agent that causes loss of feeling or sensation.

aneurysm [AN-yoo-rihs'm]. Also —ism. In medicine, a permanent, blood-filled sac in an artery.

angel [AEN-j'l]. Supernatural messenger.
    ANGLE [ANG-g'l]. Corner

angina pectoris [an-JIE-nuh PEHK-toe-rihs]. Disease characterized by pain and feeling of suffocation.

angl. Anglicized.

angle hook. anglemeter, anglesight, anglewing, anglewise, angleworm; angle iron.

anglicized. Changed to conform with English style.

Anglistics. (n.) Study of English language and literature. Anglicist.

Anglo-Indian. In India, a Eurasian. In England, an Englishman who has spent much time in India.

Angola [an-GOH-luh]. Portuguese African province on the Atlantic Ocean. Cap. Luanda. Currency, escudo.

angstrom. (abbr.) A. Unit of length—0.000 000 1 mm. = 0.0001 micron = 0.1 millimicron = 0.000 000 004 in.

Anheuser-Busch [AHN-hie-zuhr].

ANIMALS. Terms used for male, female, young, and groups of well-known species are listed in the table below.

Animal	Male	Female	Young
antelope	buck, bull	doe, cow	calf
bear	he-bear	she-bear	whelp, cub
beaver	—	–	kit
bison	bull	cow	calf
bovine	bull (steer, castrated)	cow	calf
cat	tom	tabby	kitten
chicken	rooster, cock (capon, castrated)	hen	chick
deer	hart, stag, doebuck, ram	doe, hind, roe	fawn
dog	dog	bitch	whelp, pup
duck	drake	duck	duckling
elephant	bull	cow	calf
falcon	tiercel	falcon	passager
fallow deer	buck	doe	fawn
fox	dog	vixen, bitch	whelp, cub
goose	gander	goose	gosling
giraffe	bull	cow	calf
goat	buck, ram, billy	nannygoat	kid
hare	buck, ram	doe	leveret
horse	stallion (gelding, castrated)	mare	colt, filly (f)
hippopotamus	bull	cow	calf
kangaroo	buck	doe	joey
lion	lion	lioness	whelp, cub
moose	bull	cow	calf
pig	hog	sow	farrow, piglet
rabbit	buck	doe	—
rat	buck	doe	—
red deer	hart	hind	calf
reindeer	buck	doe	fawn
rhinoceros	bull	cow	calf
seal	bull	cow	calf
shark	bull	cow	—
sheep	ram	ewe	lamb
swan	cob	pen	cygnet
tiger	tiger	tigress	whelp, cub
turkey	tom	hem	—
walrus	bull	cow	calf
weasel	boar	weasel	—
wolf	dog	bitch	whelp, cub
zebra	stallion	mare	colt

ANIMAL COLLECTIVES

ants	colony	chickens	peep
apes	shrewdness	colts	rag
asses	pace	crows	murder
badgers	cete	curs	cowardice
bass	shoal	dogs	pack
bears	sloth	doves	dule
bees	swarm or colony	ducks	paddling
birds	dissimulation	eggs	clutch
bison	troop or herd	elephants	herd or host
boars	singular	elk	gang
bovine	herd	falcons	cast
caterpillars	army	ferrets	business
cats	clowder	finches	charm
cattle	drove	fish	school
		foxes	skulk

geese	flock, gaggle or plum in flight, skein	plover	congregation
goats	trip	ponies	string
hares	down or husk	pups	litter
hawks	cast	quail	covey, bevy
hens	brood	rabbits	nest
herons	siege	ravens	unkindness
hogs	drift	reindeer	herd
horses	herd or harras	rhinoceroses	crash
jackals	troop or herd	roebucks	bevy
jellyfish	smack	rooks	building
kangaroos	troop	seals	pod, trip, herd, school
kittens	kindle	sheep	flock, drove
lapwings	deceit	snipe	walk, wisp
larks	ascension or exaltation	sparrows	host
leopards	leap	squirrels	dray
lions	pride	starlings	murmuration
locusts	host or plague	storks	mustering
mallards	sort	swine	sounder
magpies	tidings	teal	spring
martens	richness	toads	knot
moles	labor	trout	hover
monkeys	troop	turkeys	rafter
mules	barren	turtledoves	pitying, dule
nightingales	watch	turtles	bale, bevy
owls	parliament	whales	gam, herd, pod, shoal
partridges	covey	wolves	route, pack
peacocks	muster	woodcock	fall
pheasants	nye or bouquet	woodpeckers	descent
		zebras	herd

animals' ages. Write in figures. *Sale of 2-year olds.*

Ankara. Turkey. NOT Angora.

anklebone. anklejack; ankle-deep. (adj.)

Annapolis. [uh-NAP-uh-lihs]. Site of U.S. Naval Academy, Maryland.

annex. [uh-NEHKS]. (v.); [AN-ehks] (n.)

Annex. Cap. if part of name of building; the annex.

annihilate [uh-NIE-ih-laet; -hih-laet]. -lable.

anniversaries. biennial (2nd); triennial (3rd); quadrennial (4th); quintennial (5th); sexennial (6th); septennial (7th); octennial (8th); novennial (9th); decennial (10th); undecennial (11th); duodecennial (12th); quindecennial (15th); jubilee (25th); also (50th); centennial (100th); sesquicentennial (150th); bicentennial (200th); trentenary (300th); quadricentennial (400th); sexcentenary (600th); millennial (1000th). For the period of 100 years, the —ary form is pref. —centenary, bicentenary, tercentenary, quadricentenary, quincentenary, sexcentenary,

septingentenary, octocentenary or octingentenary, nongentenary, millenary.

DESIGNATIONS. 1st, paper, clocks; 2nd, cotton, china; 3rd, leather, crystal, glass; 4th, fruit, flowers, silk, electrical appliances; 5th, wood, silverware; 6th, sugar and candy, iron, wood; 7th, wool, copper, desk sets; 8th, bronze, pottery, linen, laces; 9th, willow, pottery, leather; 10th, tin, aluminum, diamond jewelry; 11th, steel accessories; 12th, silk, linen, pearls, gems; 13th, lace, textiles, furs; 14th, ivory, gold jewelry; 15th, crystal, watches; 16th, silver holloware; 17th, furniture; 18th, porcelain; 19th, bronze; 20th, china, platinum; 25th, silver; 30th, pearl, diamond; 35th, coral, jade; 40th, ruby; 45th, sapphire; 50th, golden; 55th, emerald; 60th and 75th, diamond.

annuity. Series of sums paid annually for a period of years, for life, or in perpetuity.

annul [uh-nuhl]. Cancel; make void. —lling, —lled; *annulment*.

anomalous [a-NAHM-a-luhs]. Abnormal; irregular; anomaly, —lism, —listic.

anonymous [a-NAHN-ih-muhs]. Abbr. anon.

another. Another person is coming. (NOT: *Another person is coming, too.*) *He will go to another school than* (NOT from) *hers. She prefers some kind or other.* (NOT *... some kind or another*).

ANTA. (abbr.) American National Theatre and Academy.

Antarctic [ant-AHRK-tihk]. Region near the south pole. Antarctica; Antarctic Circle, Antarctic Continent, Antarctic Ocean, Antarctic zone; BUT antarctic regions, antarctic ice, and so on.

ante-[AN-tee]. Prefix meaning before. Omit the hyphen except before proper nouns and words beginning with *e. antedate*; *ante-Christian*; *ante bellum, antemeridian, ante mortem*; *anteroom.*

ANTI-[AN-tih]. Prefix meaning against or opposite. GPO hyphenates before proper nouns, words beginning with a vowel, coined words, and words of temporary usage: *anti-discrimination*; but N.Y. Times prefers antiaircraft, antislavery, antisocial, antitrust. Hyphenate before a proper noun: *anti-Freud, anti-British.* BUT: *Antichrist.*

anteater, anthill.

ANTECEDENT. In grammar, the word or words that are represented by a pronoun. The pronoun must agree with the noun in person, number and gender. The antecedent must be identified (not merely implied) whenever practical. NOT: *Notwithstanding the stenographer's fatigue, it was typed perfectly.*

antedate [an-tee-DAET]. (v.) Fix a date earlier than the actual one; (n.) the date so used. Also, (v.) anticipate; precede.

antediluvian. Before the Deluge; by extension, very old; antiquated.

antenna [an-TEHN-uh]. Pl. -s [antennae, -ee in zoology].

anti-. SEE ante-.

antibiotic. (n. and adj.) Pl. -s.

anticipate. Do beforehand, expect. NOT *believe.*

Antietam [an-TEE-tam]. Site in Maryland of 1862 Civil War battle.

Antigua [ann-TEE-gua or ah]. Island in West Indies, Cap., St. John.

antilog (no period) antilogarithm.

antiphrasis [an-TIHF-rah-sihs]. The use of a word in a sense opposite to the usual meaning, as in irony. *A herculean task is this putting out the garbage. A little man only seven feet two inches tall.* Pl.-es.

antiphrastic. —tically.

antipode [AN-tih-pohd, an-TIHP-oh-dee]. Pl. -s. Two points on the earth's surface directly opposite each other. Hence, opposite; contrary.

antithesis. [an-TIHTH-uh-sihs]. In rhetoric, placing contrasting phrases in sequence or parallel. *They promised food and provided famine.* Pl. —ses.

antitype. Foreshadowed by a type or symbol; also, opposite type.

PROTOTYPE [PROH-toh-tiep]. ARCHETYPE [AHR-kee-tiep]. Original or model.

antonomasia [an-toh-noh-MAE-zhih-a]. In rhetoric, use of a person's name as a common noun or as a characteristic: *a Quisling, a Benedict Arnold.* Also, defining a person with a nickname: *the Profile.*

Antony and Cleopatra. 1623 play by William Shakespeare.

Anuradhapura. [uh-nyou-RAH-dah-poo-rah]. City in Ceylon; site of sacred Bo Tree grown from slip of tree of Buddha Gaya.

anxious. Full of anxiety. NOT eager. SEE afraid.

anybody. (pron.) anyhow, anyone, anyplace (adv.), anything, anyway(s) (in any event), anywhere, anywise; any more, anybody else, anybody else's, anyhow.

any, anyone, anybody, anything, each. All take a singular verb.

any more. Use only at the end of a thought to heighten a negative meaning, except in a question. NOT: *Any more, it's hard to find a good five cent cigar.*

anyone. Any person. BUT: *Any one of the three is good.*

anyway. (adv.) In any case: *Anyway, I will try.*
ANY WAY. Any one way. *Any way he does it is all right.*

anywhere. NOT anywheres.

anywise. (adv.) In any way; at all.

Anzac. (abbr.) Australian and New Zealand Army Corps.

Anzio [AHN-tsyoh; angle., AN-zih-oh]. Seacoast resort town, south east of Rome, scene of Allied landings in 1944.

Anzus. (abbr.) Australia, New Zealand, U.S. alliance.

Apache [uh-PATCH-ee]. Warlike Indian tribe. Pl. -s. [−cheez] ; Fr. [uh-PASH]. Paris underworld person.

Apalachin [ap-AL-ae-kihn]. Tioga County, N.Y. scene of 1961 U.S. underworld meeting.

appanage [AP-ah-nihj]. apinage. A perquisite or grant given to royal younger children.

apart from. Aside from.

apartheid [ah-PAHRT-hiet]. In South Africa; separation of races.

apartment. In Brit., a single room.

Apennines [AP-eh-nienz]. Mountain chain in Italy.

aperitif [uh-par-uh-TEEF]. Alcoholic appetizer.

aphelion [uh-FEE-lih-uhn, uh-FEEL-yuhn]. Point on an elliptical orbit around the sun that is farthest from the sun. (For the earth, about 94,500,000 miles.)

aphesis [AP-ee-sihs]. In grammar, loss of an unaccented initial vowel: *vanguard* from *avant-garde.*

aphid [AE-fihd]. Plant louse. Pl. -s. Pref. to aphis.
APHIS [AE-fihs]. Pl. aphides [AF-ih-deez].

API. (abbr.) American Petroleum Institute.

apiary [AE-pee-ehr-ee]. Place where bees are kept. Pl. -ies.

apiece. To each.
A PIECE. A fragment.

apish [AEP-ish]. Like an ape, silly or affected.

APO. (abbr.) Army post office.

apocope [a-PA'HK-oh-pee]. In grammar, loss of a final unaccented letter or syllable: *th'* '*for the*

apologia [ap-oh-LOH-jih-uh]. Pl. apologias. A formal apology, especially in defense of an idea. Apologize.

aporia [uh-poh-ree-uh]. In rhetoric, a passage presenting a difficulty or doubt.

a posteriori [ae-pahs-TEE-rih-OH-rih]. (Lat.) Reasoning by generalizing principles from observed facts. *Cf. a priori.*

apostle. One who hears and teaches principles.
APOSTATE. One who has abandoned principles.

Apostles' Creed. Augsburg Confession, the Twelve Apostles, the Apostle Thomas.

APOSTROPHE (*'*). used (1) to indicate the omission of letters or numbers in a contraction; *haven't. I've. '76;* BUT NOT in abbreviations, *Sgt., phone, Frisco;* (2) in the possessive use of nouns (*John's, boys'. America's*) BUT NOT personal pronouns; *hers, its, theirs;* (3) with a gerund; *The army's fighting;* (4) in the plural of figures and letters: *P's and Q's,* 2's and 3's.
The apostrophe should not be used after names of countries and other organized bodies ending in *s,* or after words more descriptive than possessive (not indicating personal possession), except when plural does not end in *s. United States control, Southern States industries, Bureau of Ships report.* BUT *children's hospital.* EXCEPTION: Veterans' Administration (so specified in the law).
There are exceptions to the above practice that have become established by usage: *a day's pay, the sun's rays, at death's door, the earth's orbit, ten dollars' worth, stone's throw, for goodness' sake, the world's problems, country's destiny. Cf.* Possessives.

apostrophe [uh-PAHS-troh-fee]. In rhetoric, a digression or aside addressed to an absent person, a thing, or an idea; "*O judgment, thou art fled to brutish beasts.*"

apothegm. Preferred to Brit. *apophthegm*. A maxim.

apotheosis. [uh-pahth-ee-OH-sihs, uh-poh-thee-of-SEHS]. A glorification; an ideal. Pl., —oses.

app. apps. (abbr.), appendix, appendixes, -ices.

appall. —ed, —ing.

Appalachia. Nine-state, poverty-stricken mountain area from northeast Pensylvania to Alabama.

apparatus [ap-uh-RAE-tuhs, ap-pa-RAT-uhs]. Pl. —tuses or —tus.

apparel. Clothes; dress. —ed, —ing.

apparent —ly. [uh-PAR-ehnt-lee, uh-PAIR-ehnt-lee]. Greater emphasis is given by commas before and after the word.

appearance. U.S. idiom substitutes appearances: *Keeping up appearances*, to all *appearances*.

appendix. Pl. —dices, —dixes; esp. med. —dices.

appendix. i, A, II, etc.; the appendix; BUT Appendix II, when part of title: *Appendix II: Education Directory*.

applicable [AP-lih-kuh-b'l]. Suitable; pertinent.

appliqué [ap-lih-KAE]. Ornamentation laid on in relief.

Appomattox [ap-oh-MAT-aks]. River town in Virginia; scene of Lee's surrender, April 9, 1865.

apposite [AP-oh-zeht]. Appropriate, relevant.

appositive. In grammar, a word or group of words used as a noun placed after another noun, denoting the same person or thing. When these words in apposition are not essential to the meaning, they are set off by commas, but when they limit the meaning, they are not set off. *Johnny, that little genius, loves school. Mary's book "Silas Marner" was found on his desk.*

appreciate [uh-PREE-shee-AE-shuhn]. Recognize the worthiness of; NOT a substitute for understand, as in *I appreciate your viewpoint*. In business, increase in value. -ciable, -ciation.

apprehend (v.) Perceive; anticipate fearfully.

COMPREHEND. (v.) Include; understand.

apprehensible. Capable of being understood.

apprise. (also apprize) Inform.

APPRIZE. (also apprise) Appraise.

appropriation bill. deficiency. Department of Agriculture bills, and so on.

approx. (abbr.) approximately.

Apr. (abbr.) April. Not usually abbreviated.

apricot [AE-pri-kaht, AP-ri-kaht].

April-fool (v.,adj.), BUT (n.) April fool.

a priori [AH-prih-OH-rie; AE-prie-OH-rie; AH-prie-OH-rie; AH-prih-OH-reel]. (Lat.) Reasoning from principles considered self-evident; denotes that which may be known through reason alone, without experiences. *Cf. a posteriori.*

apropos [ap-roh-POH]. Suitably; with respect to.

Aqaba [AH-kah-bah]. Ancient Elath; seaport in Israel on gulf of Red Sea.

aqua [AK-kwa]. Combining prefix meaning water; aquamarine, —meter, —plane, —puncture, —tint, —tone; aqua fortis, aqua green.

aquarium, Pl.,-iums; pref. to —ia.

aquatic [uh-KWAT-ihk, uh-KWAHT-ihk]. Pertains to water.

aquavit. NOT akavit. A caraway-flavored clear brandy.

aquiline [AK-kwin-lien or lihn]. curving, hooked.

Aquinas, St. Thomas [uh-KWIE-nas]. (1275-1335) Italian theologian.

Arab. (adj.) Of the Arabs; specif. *Arab horse*.

ARAB NAMES SEE Names.

Arabian. Of Arabia or Arabs: *Arabian desert*.

Arabic [AR-uh-bihk]. (adj.) Pert. to Arabic or Arabians; of the language of the Arabs. (n.) the *Ŀrab* language.

Arab League. Egypt, Iraq, Jordan, Saudi-Arabia, Syria, Lebanon, Yemen, Tunisia, Morocco, Sudan, Algeria, Kuwait, and Libya.

Arabic numerals. 1, 2, 3, 4, 5, 6, 7, 8, 9, 0. *Cf.* Numbers, Roman Numbers.

Arab States.

Arapahoe [uh-RAP-uh-hoe]. North American Indian tribe.

arbiter [AHR-bih-tehr]. One empowered to judge: *social arbiter.*

arbitrator. One selected to hear and decide a dispute.

arbor. U.S.; Brit., —our. Garden; orchards. Also a shaded retreat; bower.

arboretum [ahr-boh-REE-tuhm]. Place where trees and shrubs are grown for scientific or educational purposes. Pl. —tums; Brit., —ta.

arborway.

ARC. (abbr.) American Red Cross

arc. Arced, arcing. Brit., arcked, arcking.

arcanum [ahr-KAE-nuhm]. Pl. arcana. Secret; secret remedy; elixir.

arch. (abbr.) archaic.

arch [ahrch-]. except in archangel [AHRK—]. Combining form meaning chief, Archbishop, archduke.

    ARCHE—, ARCHI— [AHR-kih]. Prefix meaning chief (architect) or, original, primitive archetype.

archaic [ahr-KAE-ihk]. (Abbr. arch.) Applied to words, indicates an earlier usage that should be applied in modern context only with great caution. *Cf.* antique.

archangel [AHRK-aen-jhl]. A chief angel.

Archbishop (Anglican). ADDRESS: His Grace the Lord Archbishop of London. SALUTATION: My Lord Archbishop, Your Grace.

Archbishop (Catholic). ADDRESS: The Most Reverend Francis P. Keogh, Archbishop of Baltimore, Baltimore, Md. SALUTATION:

Your Excellency. *In England,* The Most Reverend Archbishop Keogh (followed by postal address). SALUTATION: Your Grace, My Lord, My Lord Archbishop.

Archdeacon. ADDRESS: The Venerable Sidney Smith, Archdeacon of San Francisco. SALUTATION: Venerable Sir; Dear Archdeacon Smith.

archae-, archaeo-, archeo-. Combining form meaning ancient: *archeology, archeozoic.*

archerfish.

Archimedes [ahr-kih-MEE-deeze]. (c. 237–212 B.C.). Greek mathematician, inventor.

Archipelago [ahrk-ih-PEHL-uh-goh]. Capitalize in singular when following a name: *Philippine Archipelago;* the archipelago.

architect [AHR-kih-tehkt]. Building designer.

Architect of the Capitol, the Architect.

archives [AHR-kievs]. The Archives (U.S.); in general, the archives.

Archivist of the United States [AHR-kih-vihst, or -kie-.]. the Archivist.

arcing [ark-ing]. arched. *Cf.* arch-.

arctic [AHRK-tihk]. Pertains to the region near the North Pole.

arctic clothing, conditions, fox, grass, night, seas; Arctic Circle, Current, Ocean, zone. BUT: subarctic, the arctics, arctics (overshoes).

area. (Abbr., n.) Extent of surface.

    ARIA. Melody.

Area. Capitalize if part of name. Cape Hatteras Recreational Area; the area; BUT area 2; free-trade area; Metropolitan Washington area.

areaway.

arena. Pl. arenas or arenae.

Arezzo [ah-REHT-soh]. Community southeast of Florence, Italy.

Argentina [ahr-jehn-TEEN-uh]. Argentine Republic, [AHR-jehn-teen, —tien]. Native, Argentine(s); adj. Argentine. Cap., Buenos

Aires; Currency, peso (M/N) or m/n for monedo nacional); O/S or o/s for gold coins; centavos. Written: M/N 297,360 or $297,360 (m/n).

Argonne [ahr-GAHN]. Wooded plateau in France, near Belgian border; scene of W.W.I. Meuse-Argonne offensive, September-November 1918.

argot [AHR-goh, gaht]. Slang of a lower element; e.g., of thieves. SEE Language.

arise. P., arose; p.p., arisen. SEE arouse.

aristocrat [uh-RIHS-toh-krat, AR-ihs-toh-krat]. One of a small privileged or ruling class.

aristocratic [uh-riss-toh-KRAT-ihk].

Aristotle [AR-ihs-taht'l]. (384–322 B.C.). Greek philosopher.

Arizona. (abbr. Ariz.). Native Arizonian (Webster prefers Arizonan). Cap., Phoenix.

Arkansas [AHR-kan-saw, sometimes ahr-KAN-zas]. (abbr. Ark.) Native Arkansan. Cap., Little Rock.

Arlington Memorial Amphitheater. the Memorial Amphitheater, the amphitheater; Arlington Memorial Bridge, Arlington National Cemetery.

Arm. (Military) The Cavalry Arm, the Infantry Arm, etc.; the arm.

arm. Pl. arms. Weapon is preferred in the sing.

armband.

armada [ahr-MAE-duh or ahr-MAH-duh]. Fleet of military ships or airplanes.

armadillo [ahr-mah-DIHL-oh]. South American armored mammal. Pl. -s.

Armed Forces. (as synonym for overall military establishment). Armed Forces Day.

armed services.

armful. Pl. -fuls.

armistice [AHRM-ihs-tihs]. Temporary suspension of hostilities.

Armistice Day. Now Veterans Day.

armorplate. armor-clad (adj.).

Armory. Springfield Armory, etc.; the armory.

arm's length. Applied to business dealings which personal relationships cannot or are not permitted to influence. (adj.) *arm's-length transaction.*

Armstrong-Jones, Antony. Married Princess Margaret Rose of England, 1960.

army. Lower-case. Lee's army; BUT Clark's Fifth Army, mobile, mule, shoe, etc.; of occupation, occupation army; Red.

Army. American or foreign, capitalize if part of name; capitalize standing alone only if referring to U.S. Army. Capitalize with Active, Adjutant General, the Band, all branches; Gordon Highlanders, Royal Guards, etc.; Brigade, 1st, etc.; the brigade; Robinson's brigade, Command, Command and General Staff College, Company A; A Company, BUT the company. Confederate (referring to Southern Confederacy); the Confederates, Continental; Continentals, Corps. District of Washington (military); the district, Division, 1st, etc.; the division; Engineers (the Corps of Engineers); the Engineers, BUT Army engineer; Establishment, Field Establishment; Field Forces; Finance Department; the Department, First, etc.; General of the Army, BUT the general; General Staff, the Staff; headquarters; 1st Regiment; Headquarters of the, the headquarters; Hospital Corps, Medical Museum; Organized Reserves; the Reserves.

army corps. Designate a U.S. Army corps by Roman numerals: *XI Corps.*

ARMY ORGANIZATION. In U.S., pentagonal organization provides an army with two or more corps, each of two or more divisions, each made up of five battle groups (larger than triangular battalions, but smaller than the regiment), each with five rifle companies plus one headquarters company plus combat support. Armored battalions are organized separately for combat support. Company formations remain as under the triangular system.

The triangular organization used prior to 1956 provided each corps with three divisions, each with three battalions, each with three regiments, each with three rifle companies and one weapons company, each rifle company with three rifle platoons and one weapon platoon, each rifle company with three rifle squads and one weapons squad. The squad consisted of twelve men until 1948, nine men after that date.

Army, Air Force, and Naval Officers.
ADDRESS letters to an officer in accordance with his exact rank. However, the salutation should ignore the "lieutenant" in "lieutenant colonel," or "lieutenant commander" and the prefixed titles to general, admiral, etc. A retired army officer is addressed by his title, followed by his name and "U.S.A., Ret." A member of the armed forces who is also a doctor, a dentist, or a clergyman may be addressed either by his professional rank or his army rank in a personal letter, but his military rank should be used in official correspondence. Army rank is always used for administrative officials. A Warrant Officer is always addressed as Mister. In writing to military or naval personnel, the serial number and tactical unit or ship should always be part of the address, followed by the post and state or an APO number, c/o Postmaster of N.Y., or San Francisco, etc. Brigadier General James Johnson, U.S.A., Commanding Officer, 3rd Corps Area (followed by postal address); Major General Robert Ryan, U.S.A., Commanding Officer, 2nd Tank Corps.
SALUTATION: Sir (formal), Dear General, Dear Colonel, Dear Sergeant, Dear Corporal, Dear Sir, Sir (formal), Dear Captain, My dear Captain Jones. In all written correspondence rank and rating precede the name and are written out. All generals, colonels, sergeants and privates are so called without prefix title. Dear General, NOT: *Dear Lieutenant General.* For officers below the rank of captain in the army or air force or below lieutenant commander in the navy use: Dear Mr.—. For official correspondence omit ceremonial salutations and closings. *Cf.* Officers.

armyman, armywoman.

around. Brit. use round. *Hall hung round with flags; spring comes round.*

arouse. Stimulate. Usually used with abstract words: *fear, suspicion, love, desire.*

ROUSE. Preferred form, particularly in the physical sense. *—from sleep.*

arrant. Particularly guilty.

Arsenal. Rock Island Arsenal, etc.; the arsenal.

art. (abbr.) article.

article. In English grammar, *a, an,* and *the* used as adjectives.

article 15. But Article 15, when part of title. *Cf.* Capitalization.

article, repetition of. SEE *the first and the second.*

Articles of Confederation (U.S.). Compact under which the American colonies were united, 1781–89.

artifact. Preferred to *artefact.* A product of simple, primitive workmanship.

artificer [ahr-TIHF-ih-suhr]. Skilled worker; (mil.) weapon maker.

artillery. The weapon takes a singular verb; the military unit takes a plural verb.

artilleryman.

artisan [AHR-tih-zan]. One skilled in a craft or trade.

artist [AHR-tihst]. Male or female practitioner in the fine arts.

ARTISTE [ahr-TEEST]. Male or female public performer.

artistically [ahr-TIHS-tihk-uh-lee].

as. Use only when referring back to *as, so, the same,* or *such. Such of you as have finished may leave the room. The hat she wears is the same as her mother's.* NOT: *Let those as love pigs keep them.*

as. When used to mean *in the capacity of,* avoid unattached-participle error. NOT: *The gift was presented as president of the society.* Correct: *As president . . . he presented the gift. The gift was given by him as president. . . .*

as, since, because. These have one meaning in common and all may be used to introduce clauses of reason, but to avoid confusion use *since* only for its distinctive meaning, for the introduction of clauses of time, duration. *Since the rule was passed there have been no more omissions.*
    as, may follow *express, regard, account, it, consider it,* but DO NOT use *as* as a substitute for *that* or *whether* after *say, believe,*

know, think. NOT: *I don't think as I believe you.*

as, is usually used in a positive statement. *As long as she has come, let her remain. He is equally good. He is as good as* ... NOT: *He is equally as good as* ... AVOID construction where unpaired *as as* occurs. NOT: *It is not so much as a Frenchman that he loves France as,* as a gourmet.

SO AS. Is usually used in a negative statement. *The technique is not so difficult as it appears.* Cf. because.

as. The case of the pronoun that follows will change the meaning. *He loves her as much as I* (love her.). *He loves her as much as* (he loves) *me.*

AS ARE, AS DID. AVOID. *The student—as did his fellows—made a practice of breaking curfew.* Use *like all students.* as follows. NOT *as follow. as for* pref. to *as to. As for me, I like spicy foods.* Cf. as to. as if, as though (subordinate conjunction). Follow *as* with a conditional form of verb *She acted as if she were not there.*

AS IS. Applied to merchandise sold "in present condition, subject to any present faults."

AS MANY AS. *As many as if not more than.* NOT: *As many if not more than.*

AS OF. is acceptable in commercial use only, *effective as of this date.*

AS PER. Is acceptable as a commercial shortening of *in accordance with* but should not be used in other correspondence. *The product was made as per your specifications.*

AS REGARDS. Is not acceptable as a substitute for concerning or regarding. SEE regards.

AS TO. Use only when necessary to bring a subject to prominence. *As to France, her attitude is predictable.* BUT NOT *As to whether France will vote for the measure or not, no one can say.*

ASCAP. American Society of Composers, Authors and Publishers.

ascendancy. Pref. to ascendency. Domination, supremacy, NOT rising trend. *The ascendancy of the party is acknowledged. The party is in the ascendant.*

ascent. (n.) Rise, ascending, ascension.

ASSENT (n.) Consent.

ACCENT (n.) Emphasis.

ascertain [as-er-TAEN]. Make certain. Implies study, investigation or experiment, beyond mere reference.

ascetic [as-SEHT-ihk]. Given to self-denial.

ash. Pl. ashes. But singular is collective.

Ash Wednesday. The first Wednesday of Lent among Western Christians.

Asian. Some natives consider *Asiatic* offensive.

askance [uh-SKANSS]. Obliquely; by extension, with mistrust.

aspect. In grammar, a function of the verb that indicates action or state as beginning, duration, completion, or repetition, with reference to tense; in some languages, also a set of inflectional forms: completive, imperfective, iterative, perfective. In English, aspect is indicated by the verb meaning (*find* is momentary, *seek* is continuing), by the progressive form (*I am speaking*), and by modifiers (*sit, sit down, while I was sitting*).

asphalt [ASS-fawlt, AS-falt].

aspirant [as-PIE-rant or ASS-pih-rant]. One who aspires.

ASPIRATE. The breathed sound of *h* as in *home*, distinguished from the inaspirate *h* in *hour* or the fused *h* in *phonograph.*

assay. Test, analyze, weigh or evaluate.

ESSAY. Try. (n.) A short, interpretive composition.

assemble. Congregate; fit together. *Assemble together* is a tautology.

assembly. A meeting, gathering.

ASSEMBLAGE. A formal assembly, a collection.

Assembly (United Nations). Capitalize General Assembly, the Assembly.

Assembly of New York. N.Y. Times, the Assembly; GPO, the assembly, an assembly, a state assembly, assemblies. First Assembly District. Capitalize specific references. Second Assembly District, 23rd Assembly District.

assemblyman; assembly line, assembly room.

assess. Fix value, usually for tax purposes.

asset. Pl. assets. Any item of value owned; e.g., property, accounts receivable, copyright.

INTANGIBLE ASSET. An item of value with no physical being; e.g., goodwill, patents.

LIQUID ASSET. Property owned which is readily convertible into cash; e.g., notes and accounts receivable.

NET ASSETS. Value of assets less liabilities.

WATERED ASSET. Property or rights carried on the books at overstated values.

assiduity [ass-sih-DYOO-ih-tee]. Diligence.

assiduously [uh-SIHJ-yoo-uhs-lee].

assign. Appoint, designate; apportion; (law) transfer to another. -nable, -nation, -nor, BUT -ner is acceptable in nonlegal sense; -ned, -ning.

assignee [AS-ih-NEE].

assignation [ASS-ihg-nae-shuhn]. Assignment; also, appointment for a love tryst.

assimilate [uh-SIM'l-aet]. Incorporate; absorb. -lable.

Assistant. Capitalize if part of capitalized title of a specific individual and before names. Lower-case especially for subordinate positions, and where there is more than one person with the title: *the assistant*; *assistant, Presidential*; *Assistant Secretary. The assistant district attorney spoke.*

assistant attorney. Pl. —attorneys, —commissioners, —corporation counsels, —directors, —general counsels, —secretaries.

assistant attorney general. Pl. —attorneys—.

assistant chief of staff. Pl. —chiefs—.

assistant comptroller general. Pl. —comptrollers—.

assistant surgeon general. Pl. —surgeons—.

associate [as-SOH-shih-aet] (v.). [as-SOH-shih-yht] (n. and adj.) [-sih-AE-shuhn] association.

Associate Justice (Supreme Court).

Association. Capitalize if part of name; capitalize standing alone if referring to federal unit:

American Association for the Advancement of Science, the association; Federal National Mortgage Association; the Association. Lower-case a second reference. BUT Association football (British).

assonance [AS-oh-nans]. Resemblance of vowel sounds, but not a rhyme: *Safe* and *take*.

CONSONANCE. Resemblance of consonant sounds, but not a rhyme: *move and moose.*

assume [uh-SYOOM, uh-SOOM]. In the sense of suppose, follow by that: *He assumes that you like him.*

PRESUME. Indicates greater belief. *I presume you are cousins.*

assure, assurance. In the sense of insure, use is limited largely to insurance trade terminology. In the sense of provide certainty, *assure* requires an indirect object: *James assured them that credit would be available.* OR Substitute gave assurance.

ENSURE. (v.) Make certain.

INSURE. (v.) Make secure or protected.

A.s.t. Atlantic standard time.

THE ASTERISK.* Used to indicate a footnote. A second footnote may be indicated by two asterisks, a third by three, etc. *Cf.* Footnotes.

Three asterisks are used to indicate an omission of paragraphs in a quotation or to denote passage of time.

asthma [AZ-muh]. Disease affecting breathing.

Astrophysical Observatory.

asyndeton [uh-SIHN-dee-tahn]. In rhetoric, omission of the conjunction ordinarily used: *The tide rises, the tide falls. I came, I saw, I conquered.*

Aswan Dam, Egypt [ahs-WAHN].

A.t. Atlantic time.

at. *Where are you staying?* NOT *Where are you staying at?*

at, in. Although these may often be used interchangeably, when they are used in phrases giving the place or locality of an action, these distinctions should be noted: (1) *In* is used to refer to the interior, when the site itself is stressed. (2) *In* is usually used before countries and sections. (3) *At* is used before business firms, office buildings, etc. (4) *In* is used before a city to leave an impression of permanence; *at* is used to suggest a temporary stay. (5) In addresses, *in* is used before the name of city; *at*, before the street number of the residence or office.

at about. Redundant. USE *at one o'clock* or *about one o'clock*.

atheism [AE-thee-ihz'm]. Belief that no God exists.

    AGNOSTICISM. Belief that neither existence nor nature of God can be known.

    DEISM. Belief that God exists, but outside the range of human experience as creator and judge alone.

    GNOSTICISM. Belief that knowledge brings emancipation from matter.

    PANTHEISM. Belief that the universe or the laws of the universe are God. Polytheism.

    POLYTHEISM. Belief in many gods.

    THEISM [THEE-ihz'm]. Belief in a deity, supernatural revelation, providence, personal relationship with God.

athenaeum or atheneum [ath-ee-NEE-uhm]. (Rom.) School for law, poetry, and oratory; library building; scientific or literary association.

athlete [ATH-leet].

Atkinson, Topeka & Santa Fe Railway. the Sante Fe.

Atlantic. Charter; coast; Coast States; Destroyer Flotilla; Fleet; Pact; seaboard; slope; time; standard time; BUT cisatlantic; transatlantic. North Atlantic, South Atlantic, mid-Atlantic. the destroyer, the flotilla.

Atlantic shoreline. The Atlantic coast; the region around the shoreline is the Atlantic Coast or the Atlantic Seaboard; the coast; the West Coast is known as *the Coast*.

at large. DO NOT hyphenate ambassador at large, representative at large. Capitalize in referring to a specific person in a government position: *John J. Smith, Councilman at Large*.

atlas. Pl. atlases.

at least. SEE Placement of Words.

atm., atmosphere. Air surrounding earth or any planet.

    TROPOSPHERE. Ground level to 10 miles up.

    STRATOSPHERE. Orig. ground to 10 miles up; now 10 to 16 miles (Webster 7 miles) from ground.

    MESOSPHERE. 16 to 300 miles from ground.

    EXOSPHERE. 300 to 1000 miles from ground.

    IONOSPHERE. Region of several layers of electrically charged air beginning 25 miles from ground, varying by season and time of day.

atoll [AT-awl]. Coral island formed by a reef enclosing a lagoon.

atom. One of the minute particles of which matter is composed.

    ELECTRON. Particle with elementary charge of negative electricity found in the atom.

    PROTON. Particle with elementary positive charge of electricity, believed present in all atomic nuclei.

    NEUTRON [NYOO-trahn]. Uncharged particle found in atomic nuclei.

    MOLECULE [MAHL-ee-kyool]. Smallest portion of a chemical substance that retains identity.

atomic bomb. But usage permits atom bomb, A-bomb.

atomic weight (at. wgt.). Measure of relative weight of an atom of an element, based on oxygen = 16.

atrocious [a-TROE-shuhs]. Violently and brutally savage; (colloquial) of poor quality or in bad taste.

attaché [at-ash-AE]. Diplomatic staff member. *Timothy S. Smith, naval attaché.*

attached hereto. *Hereto* is superfluous.

attacked [at-TAKT]. As a journalistic euphemism for raped, *sexually attacked*, is more precise.

attic. The usual term.

    GARRET. Suggests poverty.

at the present time. Now is pref.

attorney at law. Pl. attorneys at law; attorney at law's fee.

attorney, United States.

attorney general. Pl. attorneys general; attorney general's cases. But Webster *also* accepts attorney generals.

Attorney General (U.S.). BUT attorney general of Maine, etc. *Cf.* Cabinet member.

Attorney General (State). ADDRESS: The Honorable Louis J. Lefkowitz, Attorney General of New York, Albany, N.Y. SALUTATION: Sir; My dear Mr. Attorney General, Dear Mr. Lefkowitz.

attribute [uh-TRIHB-yoot] (v.). [AT-trih-byoot] (n.).

attributive adjective. Describes a quality of a person or thing. *good man, red apples.*

Aubusson [oh-beu-SAWN]. Carpet and tapestry center in France.

audacious [aw-DAE-shuhs].

audible [AW-dih-b'l]. Capable of being heard.

audience [AWD-ee-ehns]. Implies the act of listening, not merely witnessing. Thus, NOT of an accident, arrest, crime or fire.

audiofrequency, audiogram, audiometer, audiovisual.

auf Wiedersehen [ouf-VEE-der-zae-'n]. (Ger.) See you again.

Aug. (abbr.) August. May be used before a numeral.

auger [AW-ger]. Hole-boring tool.

auger box, auger drill.
AUGUR [AW-ger]. (v.) Foretell.

aught. A cipher or zero in mathematics. *Six times aught is aught.* But naught is pref.
OUGHT. Should. *You ought to be in pictures.*

au gratin [oh-gra-TANN]. With browned covering of bread crumbs, butter and cheese.

auld lang syne [ald-lang-ZIEN]. Literary, old long since; times long ago.

au revoir [OH rih-VWAHR]. (Fr.) Until we meet again.

Auriol, Vincent [ohr-YOHL, VEHN-sahnn]. (1884–1966) Stateman, president of France (1947–1954).

AUS. (abbr.) Army of the United States.

Aus. (abbr.) Australia.

Ausable Chasm [aw-SAE-bl KAS'm]. Scenic gorge in New York State.

Auschwitz [OU-schvihtz]. (Oswieciem) Site of Nazi concentration camp in Poland.

Australia. (abbr. Aus.) Native, Australian(s); (adj.) Australian. Cap., Canberra. Currency, pound (A), shilling(s), penny (p).

Austria. (abbr. Aust.) Native Austrian (s); (adj.) Austrian. Cap., Vienna. (Wien) [Veen]. Currency, schilling (S), groschen (sing. and pl.).

autarchy [OH-tahr-kee]. Autocratic rule; absolute sovereignty. SEE -archy.
AUTARKY [OH-tahr-kee]. Economic self-sufficiency.

author. Male or female. Use as a verb is not the best usage. AVOID *authoress* in the U.S.

authoritative [aw-THAH-rih-tae-tihv].

Authority. Capitalize standing alone if referring to government unit: National Shipping Authority; the Authority; Port of New York Authority; the port authority; the authority; St. Lawrence Seaway Authority of Canada, the authority; Tennessee Valley Authority, the Authority.

auto. *Car* is preferred.

autobahn [AW-toe-bahn]. Pl. —s. German throughway. Capitalize in German.

auto-da-fé [AW-toh-da-FAE]. Pl. autos-du-fe. Ceremony accompanying judgment of a heretic during the Inquisition; by extension, execution, especially burning.

automaton [aw-TOM-ih-tahn]. Pl. -s or -ta. Self-moving machine
AUTOMATION [aw-toh-MAE-shuhn]. Automatic operation of an apparatus, especially of machinery for manufacturing.

autopsy [AW-tahp-see]. Post-mortem examination, to determine cause of death, etc.

autumn. fall.

auxiliary [awg-ZIHL-yair-ee]. Helping, supporting.

AUXILIARY VERB. A verb that helps or supplements another verb. *Be, have, can, may, shall, will* combine with main verbs to form verbal phrases.

avail. (v.) Be of use; *availed oneself of*: make use of.

avant-garde [ah-VAHN-GARD]. Vanguard; unconventional experimentalists and innovators.

avdp. (abbr.) avoirdupois.

Ave. (abbr.) avenue. In an address, 505 Fifth Ave. Avenue is preferred.

avenge. (v.) Punish or exact satisfaction for a wrong, especially one done to another; thus, a justified act.

RETALIATE. (v.) To give like for like, sometimes in self-defense.

REVENGE. (v.) Punish or give pain because of a wrong done to revenger; thus, a selfish act.

avenue [AV-uh-nyoo]. Capitalize with name: Constitution Avenue, etc.; the avenue.

average [AV-uhr-ihj or AV-rihj]. Arithmetic mean; the sum of quantities divided by the number of quantities. $1 + 2 + 3 + 5 + 9$ divided by 5 equal the average of 4.

MEAN. The figure midway between two extremes. In the series $1, 2, 3, 5, 9$ the mean is 5 $(1 + 9 \div 2)$.

MEDIAN. Point in a series where half are on each side. In the series $1, 2, 3, 5, 9$, the median is 3.

GEOMETRIC MEAN. The root of the product of a number of quantities where the root is the number of quantities. $\sqrt[4]{2 \times 4 \times 6 \times 8}$ = the geometric mean of 2, 4, 6, and 8. The figure (4.75) is generally less than the arithmetic mean. *Cf.* harmonic mean, mode.

MOVING AVERAGE. A graph showing simple averages over a period of time; e.g., Dow Jones average of stock prices.

Avignon [ah-vee-NYAWN]. City near confluence of Rhone and Durance Rivers, France.

avocado [av-oh-KAH-doh]. Alligator pear. Pl. -s.

avoirdupois [av-uhr-du-POIZ]. (abbr. avdp.) System of weights in English-speaking countries. Based on a pound of 7000 grains or 16 ounces.

avow. Acknowledge openly. *He avowed his willingness to kill if necessary.*

awake. (v.) P., awoke; p.p., awaking; awaken, -ed. Awaked for past and awoke for p.p. are rarely used. They suggest coming to full consciousness.

WAKE. (v.) P., woke; p.p. waking; waked, waken, -ed. Waked for past and woke for p.p. are rarely used. Suggests the process of throwing off sleep or lethargy.

Award. Distinguished Service Award, Merit Award, Mother of the Year Award, the award.

aweigh. Clear of the ground: *anchors aweigh.* BUT: *The ship is under way.*

awful [AW-fuhl]. Filling or filled with awe. Colloquial, very bad; ugly; very great.

awhile. (adv.) For a short time: *We'll* stay awhile. Prefer: *We'll stay for a while.*

a.w.o.l. (abbr.) absent without official leave.

awry [uh-RIE]. Askew; amiss.

ax. Preferred to *axe.* Pl. axes.

axis. Pl. axes.

Axis, the. World War II Alliance between Germany, Italy and Japan.

azalea [uh-ZAEL-yuh]. Spring flowering shrubs.

Azores [a-ZAWRZ or AE-zawrz]. Islands in North Atlantic.

azure [AZH-ehr]. Blue.

B

B. (abbr.) brightness.

B. (abbr.) Baume. Hydrometer scale.

b. Usually silent before *t*. *subtle, debt* ; and after *m*. *bomb, crumb, dumb*. BUT the addition of a suffix will often cause the silent letter to be sounded.

b. (abbr.) breadth or width; boils at.

B.A. or A.B. (abbr.) Baccalaureus Artium, Bachelor of Arts.

baccalaureate [bak-uh-LAW-ree-eht]. Degree of bachelor; commencement ceremony.

bacchanal [BAK-uh-nal]. (n.) Devotee of Bacchus, reveler; an orgy. The male form is usually used for both sexes.

Bach, Johann Sebastian [bahk, YOH-hahn zae-BAHS-tee-ahn] (1685–1750) German composer.

back formation. In grammar, a word that appears to have been formed from another word: *enthuse* from enthusiasm.

backgammon [BAK-gam'n]. Board game.

back of, in back of. (colloquial, U.S.) Use behind.

back-order. (n. and v.) Portion of an order that cannot be filled immediately, held for future delivery.

backward(s). (adv.) Both forms are acceptable with euphony determining choice. The *s* form is preferred for manner. Only backward may be used as adjective to modify a noun immediately following.

bade (bad). P. of bid.

badinage [bad-ih-NAHZH, BAD-ih-nahzh, BAD-ih-nihj]. Banter.

badland(s). (geol.) Badlands. (S. Dak. and Nebr.).

badly. AVOID use meaning *very much*. NOT: *His venture is badly in need of capital.* Do not use for *ill: He feels badly* means his sense of touch is faulty.

baggage. (Brit.) luggage. baggage car, baggage man, baggage master; baggage rack, baggage room, baggage train.

Baghdad or Bagdad [BAG-dad]. Holy capital city of Iraq.

Bahai [bah-HAH-ee]. Religious system founded in 1863 emphasizing spiritual unity of man. Bahaism. (adj.) Bahai.

Bahama Islands [bah-HAH-mah; also -HAE-]. Chain of Atlantic islands. Cap., Nassau. Bahamas, Bahamian. Currency, pound (Bf), shilling (s), penny, pence (d).

Bahrein [buh-REIN]. Also Bahrain Island. Archipelago in Persian Gulf.

bail. To draw water (from Fr. *baille* bucket).
BAIL. Legal security for appearance in court.
BALE. Commercial bundle (cotton, paper, hay).

baker's dozen. Also long dozen, 13.

Baku [bah-KOO]. City in U.S.S.R., on Caspian Sea.

balance. Should be used only in reference to money or in bookkeeping; otherwise, *remainder*.

balance of payments. Difference in a statement of national trade, investment, tourist transactions, etc. showing the amount which must be settled in gold. A favorable balance of payment indicates that the nation is to receive gold.

balance of trade. Difference between a nation's exports and imports. A favorable balance indicates that exports exceed imports.

balding. Preferred to *baldening*. BUT *getting bald* is much more acceptable.

Balearic Islands [bal-ih-AR-ihk]. Spanish island group in Mediterranean.

baleful. SEE baneful.

Balkan States, the Balkans [BAWL-kanz]. On the Balkan Peninsula: Yugoslavia, Romania, Bulgaria, Greece, Albania, and Turkey in Europe.

ballot box.

baloney. SEE boloney.

Baltic States. Countries bordering east side of Baltic Sea—Latvia, Lithuania, Estonia (all absorbed by U.S.S.R., 1940), sometimes also Finland, Poland.

Baltimore & Ohio Railroad, the B. & O.

balustrade [bal-uhs-TRAED or BAL-uhs-traed]. Banister.

banal [BAE-nal or bae-NAL]. Trite; flat.

Band. Capitalize if part of name; the band: Army Band, Marine Band, Navy Band, Sousa's Eastern Band, etc. of Cherokee Indians; the band.

bandsman.

bandy-ball; bandy-legged. (adj.)

Bangladesh [BANG-lah-dehsh]. Sometimes Bangla Desh. Formerly E. Pakistan. Cap. Dacca [DAH-kuh]. Natives, Bengali, Pl. -s. Adj. Bengali. Independent 1971. Currency: rupee, anna.

banjo. Pl. -jos or -joes.

Bank. Capitalize if part of name; the bank. Capitalize when standing alone if referring to international bank: Export-Import Bank of Washington (Eximbank), Export-Import Bank, the Bank; Farm Loan Bank of Dallas; Dallas Farm·Loan Bank; First National Bank, etc.; International World Bank, the Bank; BUT blood bank, central reserve bank, soil bank.

bank. The left or right bank is determined as one looks downstream.

bankruptcy.

bantamweight. In boxing, weight class (not exceeding 118 pounds).

barkeeper. -maid, -man, -master, -post, -room, -tender, -way, -wise (all one word); bar-wound (adj.); bar bit.

baraka. Islamic concept of pulsating vitality, especially in the arts.

Barbados Islands [bahr-BAE-dohs]. Islands in Lesser Antilles. Native, Barbadian(s).

barbarian. (adj.) Used in the sense of being, belonging to, or usually with a barbarian. *barbarian tribes, huts, lust.*
   BARBARIC. Implies no condemnation; barbaric simplicity, splendor, ceremonies.
   BARBAROUS. Implies condemnation; barbarous torture, practices. Thus a barbarian ruler (of barbarians) may be neither barbaric (uncultured) nor barbarous (cruel).

barbed wire.

barbiturate [bahr-BIHT-tyoo-raet]. Drug used as sedative, hypnotic, etc. NOT barbituate.

barely. By a narrow margin.
   HARDLY. Implies physical strain: *We hardly had enough strength to get up. We barely arrived in time.*

bargainer. In law, bargainor.

bark. See boat.

barley field. barleymow, barley water.

bar mitzvah [bar-MIHTS-vah]. Sometimes bar mizvah, bar mitzvot. A Jewish boy who has reached his 13th birthday; also, the accompanying ceremony. Pl. -s.

barn. British use only for a place of grain storage; animals are kept in a stable.

barnman. -stormer, -yard, barn dance.

baron [BAR-uhn]. Peer of the realm, orig. holding directly from the king. In Britain member of the lowest grade of peerage. ADDRESS: The Right Honourable Lord Milford, or The Lord Milford. SALUTATION: My Lord.

baron. (colloq.) A powerful industrialist, etc.

baronage. All the barons.

Baroness. ADDRESS: The Right Honourable the Baroness Milford or The Lady Milford. SALUTATION: Madam.

baronet. Rank next below a baron but above a knight. ADDRESS: Sir Sidney Milford, Bt. (or Bart.) SALUTATION: Sir.

baronial. Pertaining to a baron or baronage.

barony. Rank of baron.

Barracks. Capitalize if part of name; the barracks; Carlisle Disciplinary Barracks (Leavenworth); BUT A barracks; barracks A; etc.

Barranquilla [bahr-rahn-KEE-yah]. City in Colombia.

barratry. Illegal or grossly negligent action of a master or crew of a ship which results in loss to the owner; also the practice of stirring up lawsuits or quarrels to annoy a competitor.

barrel. In U.S., 31–1/2 gallons or 105 dry quarts. (2) Unit of petroleum capacity = 42 U.S. gal. = 34.97 imperial gal. = 158.9 liters, (3) Unit of dry measure = 7056 cu. in. = 105 dry qt. = 3.281 bu. = 115.62 liters. (4) Unit of cranberry measure = 5826 cu. in. = 86-45/46 dry qt. = 2.709 bu. = 95.47 l. (5) Unit of liquid measure = 31.5 gal. = 119.237 l. (6) Measure of beef, pork, fish (U.S.) = 200 lbs. = 90.72 kilograms. (7) Measure of flour = 196 lbs. = 88.9 kilograms. (8) Measure of cement = 396 lbs. = 170.55 kilograms. (9) Measure of lime, U.S., small = 180 lbs. = 81.65 kilograms; large = 280 lbs. = 127.01 kilograms.

barrel. -ed, -ing.

barrister. SEE lawyer.

basal. Forming the base.
BASIC. Of the essence; fundamental.

Base. Andrews Air Force Base; Air Force base; the base; Naval base.

Basel [BAH-zehl or BAS'l]. Originally Basle (Bahl), Fr. Bale. City & Canton in northwest Switzerland.

Basenji [BAH-sehn-yee]. A breed of dog.

basis. Pl. bases.

bas-relief [BAH-]. Low relief; figures slightly raised from a bass-[baes].
BASS. [baes] Deep toned.
BASS DRUM. bass horn, bass viol; bass bar.

bassinet. Basket used as a cradle. NOT bassinette.

bastille. A fortress; the Bastille (Paris), Bastille Day (July 14).

Bastogne [bahs-TOHN-y]. Town in Belgium.

Bataan [bah-TAHN]. Peninsula in Manila Bay, Philippine Islands; scene of U.S. last stand, January-April 1942.

batblind. bat-man, bat-wing; bat-eyed (adj.).

bath [bath]. (n.); bathe [baethe] (v.), Brit. (v.) bathe = swim.

bathhouse. -mat, -robe, -room, -tub; bath towel.

bathroom. Avoid as a euphemism for toilet where no bathing facilities are available, e.g. a gas station.

bathysphere. Diving bell for studying deep-sea life. (From Greek *bathy*, deep.) Created by Dr. William Beebe.

batman. Officer's orderly (Brit.).

batman = 6.5 lbs. avdp. (Iran).

baton [bah-TAHN].

battallion. Capitalize if part of a name: Second Battallion. SEE Army Organization.

batter. cake; batterman.

battery [BAT-uhr-ee]. the Battery (N.Y.C.).

Battle. Capitalize if part of name; the Battle of Gettysburg, of the Bulge, and so on. BUT the battle of the sexes.

Batum [bah-TOOM]. City on Black Sea, U.S.S.R.

bavarian cream. A dessert.

bay-bolt, bayman; bay rum.

bayou. [BIE-oo]. A creek.

Bayreuth. [bie-ROIT, BIE-roit]. Bavarian music festival center, West Germany.

bay window. Projects from a room in any form.
BOW WINDOW. Projects from a room in curved form.

bazaar. A place where goods are sold: *The church held a bazaar to raise money.*
BIZARRE. Strage; odd. *Many bizarre animals roam the veldt.*

B.B.C. (abbr.) British Broadcasting Corporation.

bbl. (abbr.) barrel.

B.C. (abbr.) Before Christ. Written 610 B.C. *This is the seventh century B.C.* Usually printed in small capitals (B.C.). *Cf.* A.D.

B.C.E. Before the Christian era.

bd. -ft. (abbr.) board-foot.

be. P., was; p.p., been.

beakhead. -iron; beak-shaped (adj.)

bear. (v.) Carry, used formally, bore [BOHR], bearing, borne, BUT for birth, p. bore; p.p. borne; p.p. passive, born. *He was not born yesterday.*

beat. P. beat, p.p. beaten.

beater. beater-out, beater-up; beater press.

beau [boh]. Suitor; admirer, Pl. beaux, beaus [bohz].

beauty [BYOO-tee]. beautyproof; beauty-blind (adj.), beauty-clad (adj.) beauty shop.

beaver board. beaverpelt.

because. Literally, caused by. Assigns a reason immediately and explicitly. The reason was that NOT the reason was because.
SINCE. Assigns a reason more incidentally than because.
AS. Even more casual than since.
INASMUCH AS. Implies a concession or qualification.

FOR. Introduces a reason, evidence, or justification for what has preceded it.

become. Became, becoming, become.

Bedouin [BEHD-oo-ihn]. Arab nomad, singular, plural and adjective.

beechnut. -wood.

beef. Pl. beefs, pref. to beeves. To mean complaint. (Colloquial) beef, beefs.

beefeater. -steak, -tongue; beef-faced (adj.); beef extract.

been [bihn; Brit. bean].

beermaker. beer cellar, beer yeast.

bees wax.

beet. field; beet pulp, beet sugar.

Beethoven, Ludwig van [BAE-tohv'n, LOOT-vik fahn; angl., LUHD-wig]. (1770–1827) German composer.

before [bee-fawr]. beforehand; before-cited (adj.), before-mentioned (adj.), before-named (adj.).

beget. P., begot; p.p., begotten, begot.

beggarman. beggarwoman.

begin, began, beginning. Rarely passive: *The project was begun.*

behalf. Side; interest; defense; on behalf of. On his behalf implies representation.

behoof [be-HOOF]. Advantage, interest: *He conquered for his own behoof.*
BEHOOVE [be-HOOV]. Brit., behove [be-HOHV]. To be necessary for; *It behooves you to be careful.*

behold. P. & p.p., beheld.

Beirut [bae-ROOT]. Capital city of Lebanon.

Belgium [BEHL-juhm] [BEHL-gih-uhm]. Native Belgian(s); (adj.) Belgian. Cap. Brussels or Bruxelles or Brussel. Currency, franc (B. Fr.), centime (c.)

Belgrade [BEL-graed or -GRAED]. Capital city of Yugoslavia.

believable. Worthy of belief and confidence.

CREDIBLE. Stresses intellectual assent. A story is believable; his report is credible. A credible witness.

belittle. Depreciate; minimize. -ler, -ling.

Bellefonte [BELL-fahnt]. City in Pennsylvania.

belles-lettres [behl-LEHT'R]. Literature for art's sake, rather than for informational values: poetry, fiction, drama, essays.

below. Anywhere on a lower plane. Opposite of above.

UNDER. Lower than, usually in terms of vertical position; also, subject to: *Under the umbrella; under a superior officer. He swam under the trestle to a beach below* (lower on the river). Opposite of over.

BENEATH. Below or under, often suggests lower in special station (and place) or prestige. *He is beneath contempt.*

UNDERNEATH. Suggests underlying, hidden.

belowstairs.

belly. A good word too often avoided.

Belt, the belt. Capitalize if part of name: Corn Belt, Cotton Belt, Dairy Belt, Ice Belt, Wheat Belt. Bible Belt, goiter belt.

Bench. Capitalize only if used as a substitute for Supreme Court.

bend. P. & pp., bent.

bends. In U.S., an air-pressure disease.

beneath. SEE below.

benedict. Newly married man, especially one considered a confirmed bachelor.

BENEDICK. A bachelor in "Much Ado About Nothing."

beneficent.

beneficial trust. SEE trust.

benefit. -fited, -fiting.

Benelux countries. Belgium, the Netherlands, and Luxembourg.

Benet, Stephen Vincent [beh-NAE]. (1898–1943) American poet William Rose Benet (1886–1950). American poet and novelist.

Bengal [behn-GAWL]. Area in northeast Indian subcontinent. *Bengali* preferred to *Bengalese. Cf.* Bangladesh.

Bengasi or -zi or -shi [ban-GAH-zee]. Capital of Cyrenaica and Libya, scene of W. W. II battles.

benighted. Overtaken by darkness, esp. moral or social.

benign [bee-NIEN]. Of gentle disposition, especially as to effect.

BENIGNANT [bee-NIHG-nant]. Refers to disposition or intention, especially toward inferiors. The two are often used interchangeably.

benthoscope. Deep-sea observation sphere.

bentwing. (n. & adj.) bentwood.

benzo-. Combining form meaning benzoine: benzoate, benzoic.

Beowulf [BAE-oh-woolf]. (c. 700) Hero of Ancient Anglo-Saxon epic.

Berchtesgaden [behrk-tehs-GAH-dehn]. Town in Bavaria, (West Germany) scene of Hitler's mountain estate.

bereave. P., p.p. bereaved. Bereaved implies more emotion than bereft: *The bereaved wife. She was bereft of her senses.*

Berenice [behr-eh-NIE-see]. BUT Bernice [buhr-NEES]

Bering Sea [BEER-ihng or BEHR- or BAIR-]. North Pacific Ocean strait between Siberia and Alaska.

Berkeley. (California)

Bermudas, Bermuda. British colony of 360 islands 640 miles east-south-east of Cape Hatteras, North Carolina, Cap. Hamilton, Native Bermudian.

Bermuda shorts.

Bernice. SEE Berenice.

berth. A bunk or resting place. *She selected a lower berth on the train.*

BIRTH. Coming into life.

Bertillon System [behr-tee-YAHN; BUHR-tih-lahn]. Method of criminal identification based on body measurements.

beseech. Beg; entreat. P. & p.p., besought, although beseeched is sometimes used.

beside. (prep.) At the side of, next to.

besides. (adv.) In addition to.

besiege [bee-SEEJ]. Surround with armed forces; lay siege to.

bespeak. Arrange for in advance; foretell. P., bespoke; p.p. bespoken.

bestir. Always used reflexively. *He must bestir himself.* NOT: *The gold outflow bestirred the State Department to stimulate exports.*

best-seller. bestselling (adj.); best-clad, best-dressed, best-known; best man.

bet. P. & p.p., bet; betting.

bête noire [baet-NWAHR]. (Fr., bat—); object of dread or aversion.

betide. Happen to, NOT forecast. Used only in third person sing. present: *Woe betide them.*

betimes. Soon, early. (archaic).

better. Wagerer. Usually pref. to bettor. BUT N.Y. Times, bettor.

betterment. Improvement, particularly of property. Use carefully of people. *He is on a self-betterment campaign.* NOT: *he is working for the betterment of the underprivileged.*

better than. Avoid use for more than. NOT: *There went better than a million warriors.*

between. Refers to two alternatives. Differences between you and me. Between two players or the players BUT NOT between each of the players or every player. The usual form when two terms are specified is *between . . . and.* Avoid repeating *between*, even in long sentences.

between you and I. Not standard Eng., but widely used for *between you and me.*

between. betweendecks, betweenwhiles.

Bev. (abbr.) billion electron volts. Measure for atom-smashing machines.

betwixt and between. Correct although redundant. BUT avoid as a cliché.

Bevan, Rt. Hon. Aneurin [BEV-an, uh-NIE-rhin]. (1907–1960) British Labour Party leader.

bevy. A somewhat obsolete collective use for belles, beauties, maidens, ladies.

bevel. -eled, -ling-. (Brit. -elled, -elling.)

beware. There is no other tense.

bf. (abbr.) boldface. Heavy type; e.g., the type in which *bf.* appears.

B-flat.

b. hp. (abbr. bhp.) brake horsepower.

Bhumibol Adulyadej [poo-MEH-bawl ADOON-dehj]. (1927–   ) King of Thailand, 1964; married 1950, Princess Sirikit Kitiyakara, daughter of Prince Nakkhatra Mongkool, Krommun Chandaburl Suranat.

Bhutan [buh-TAHN or boo-TAN]. Bhutanese. Singular plural and adjective. Independent protectorate on China border in Himalayas. Cap. Thimphu. Currency, India rupee (Rs).

Bhutto, Zulfiqar Ali [ByOO-TOH]. (1928–   ). Prime Minister of Pakistan (1972–   ). Second reference, President Bhutto.

bi-. Prefix meaning two or twice. Bi-weekly, can mean twice a week or every other week. Avoid use in time context; to avoid ambiguity, use semiweekly, every other week, etc. bifocal, bifoliate, biennium.

Biarritz [byah-reets]. Resort community on Bay of Biscay, France.

bias. -ed, -ing; pl. biases.

Bible. Holy Scriptures, Scriptures; Koran; also Biblical; Scriptural, Koranic. BUT some authorities lower-case biblical, koranic, talmudic.

Bible. Abbreviate the books: OLD TESTAMENT: Gen., Exod.,Lev., Num., Deut., Josh., Judg., Ruth, I and II Sam., I and II Kings., I and II Chron., Ezra, Neh., Esther, Job, Ps. or Pss., Prov., Eccles., Song of Sol. or Cant., Isa., Jer., Lam., Ezek., Dan., Hos., Joel., Amos, Obad., Jonah, Mic., Nah., Hab., Zeph., Hag., Zech., Mal.

NEW TESTAMENT. Matt., Mark, Luke, John, Acts., Rom., I and II Cor., Gal., Eph., Phil., Col., I and II Thes. I and II Tim., Titus, Philemon, Heb., Jas., I and II Pet. I, II and III, John, Jude., Rev.

APOCRYPHA. (Apoc.) - I and II Esd., Tob., Jth., Rest of Esther, Wisd. of Sol., Eccles., Bar., Sus., Song of Three Children, Bel and Dragon. Pr. of Man., I and II Macc.

APOCALYPTIC - En., Sib. Or., Assmp. M., Apoc. Bar., Ps. Sol., XII P., Bk Jub., Asc. Isa.

BIBLIOGRAPHY. A list of books on a particular topic or by a particular author. In a book, place bibliography as part of reference matter following the appendix supplement and the glossary and preceding the index. Notation should include maximum information concisely.

PUBLISHED WORK. Shirer, William L. *The Rise and Fall of the Third Reich,* New York: Simon and Schuster, 1960.

EDITED WORK. Mager, N.H. and S.K. (ed.) *Index to English.* Englewood Cliffs, N.J.: Prentice Hall, 1964.

UNPUBLISHED WORK. Weiss, Raymond. *Accuracy of Reporting in New York Metropolitan Newspapers,* unpublished study. Education Library, New York University, 1957. pp. 427-432.

ANONYMOUS WORK. *Crimes of the Soviet Union.* New York: Freedom House, 1959.

BOOK IN A SERIES. *Statistical Abstract of the United States,* 1960. Superintendent of Documents. Washington: U.S. Government Printing Office.

MAGAZINE ARTICLES. Sempich, Frederick, Jr. *Honolulu, mid-Ocean Capital.* The National Geographic Magazine. (Washington) CV (May, 1954) 577-624.

PRIVATELY PRINTED WORK. Peters, Alison. *Political Almanac.* New York: Privately printed. 1938.

For second references to articles by the same author in the same publications, use *ibid, pp.* —.

When more than one work of an author appears on the list.

Mager, N.H. *Office Encyclopedia,* New York: Pocket Books, Inc. 1953.

Complete Letter Writer. Pocket Books, Inc. 1955.

Cf. Footnotes

Biblical. GPO and N.Y. Times, BUT UCMS lower-case.

bicentennial. Preferred to bicentenary in U.S.

biceps. Pl. -cepses; triceps. Pl. -cepses.

bicycle. tricycle [sihk'l].

bid. (At auction or contract bridge), bid, bidding, bid.

bid. Bade, bidding, p.p., bidden. AVOID in the sense of attempt. NOT *He bids to become the richest man in town.*

bid and asked prices. Bid price is the price at which someone is willing to buy; asked price, to sell.

bide. Wait. Bode, bided, biding, Also, to wait for, in *to bide one's time.*

bid in. Repossession by an owner at an auction by topping the last bid.

biennium. A period of two years. Pl. -s or biennia.

BIENNIAL. Every two years.

BIANNUAL. Avoid as ambiguous. USE semiannual to mean twice a year.

big. Most widely used for size, amount, quantity. Emphasizes bulk, weight, or volume: *big house, nose, animal.*

GREAT. Used for important meanings, a high degree of distinction, magnitude, amount, quantity or size. Also implies wonder or admiration: *great man, idea, composition.*

LARGE. Used for size, amount, quantity, indicates extension in many directions beyond the group average: *large area, country, collection.*

big board. N.Y. Stock Exchange.

Big Inch; Little Inch. (oil and gas pipelines).

bill. In Brit., refers to a pound note.

bill. Kiess Senate bill 217, House bill 31.

Billerica [bihl-RIK-ah]. Town in Massachusetts.

billet-doux [bih-lae-DOO]. (Fr.) Love letter. Pl. billets-doux [bihl-ae-doo].

billet. head, billetman.

billiards. Takes a singular verb.

Billingsgate [Brit., -giht]. London fish market noted for foul language.—: by extension, the language, billingsgate.

billion. In U.S., 1000 millions; in Brit. a million millions. Milliard refers to 1000 million. in Brit.

TRILLION. In U.S., 1000 billions; in Brit., a million billions *Cf.* Numbers, zillion.

bill of fare. Menu. Pl., bills of fare.

bill of lading. List of items in a shipment.

Bill of Rights. (historic document) BUT, GI bill of rights. N.Y. Times, G.I. bill of rights.

B/L. (abbr.) bill of lading.

bimetallism. Use of two metals as a currency base at the same time; e.g. *gold & silver.*

binary number system. System with 2 as radix (instead of 10 as in metric system); used for electronic computers. Binary 13 thus = 1101.

bind. P. & p.p., bound.

binoculars [BIE preferred to BUH]. Field glasses; opera glasses.

Birdie. (abbr.) battery integration and radar display equipment. Transistorized version of central system for Nike, Ajax & Hercules.

birds'-eye. bird's-nest (n., adj., v.); bird's nest (literal) (n.).

Birobidzhan or Biro-Bid jan [bih-roh-bih-JAHN]. Jewish Autonomous Republic, U.S.S.R.

biscuit. Bread baked in a roll shape. Brit., cracker or cookie.

Bishop (Catholic). ADDRESS: The Most Reverend Joseph A. Burke, Bishop of Buffalo; or, The Right Reverend Bishop SALUTATION: Your Excellency; Dear Bishop Burke.

Bishop (Episcopal). ADDRESS: The Right Reverend Timothy Brown, Bishop of St. Louis. SALUTATION: Right Reverend and dear Sir, My dear Bishop Brown, My dear Bishop, Right Reverent Sir.

Bishop (Methodist). ADDRESS: The Reverend Bishop Frederick Jones. SALUTATION: Dear Sir, My dear Bishop Jones, Dear Bishop Jones.

bishopric. Bishop's rank, see, diocese or office. Diocese is preferred for the province of a bishop.

SEE. Seal of bishop's authority.

DIOCESE. District (and population) under a bishop.

bison. Sing & pl.

bite. P., bit; p.p., bitten.

bivalve. Animal with two-valved shell; e.g., oyster, clam.

bivouac [BIHV-wak, (n.) BIHV-ou-ak]. (v.) Encamp. -uacked, -uacking. (n). Temporary encampment.

bizarre. See bazaar.

Bizerte. (or —erta) [bee-ZUHRT: angl., bih-ZUHRT or big-z-UHR-tee]. City in Tunisia.

black. (v.) Intentional coloring.

BLACKEN. Unintentional coloring or figurative use: *Blacken his reputation, city blackened by soot.*

blame. -mable, -med, -ming.

blameworthy.

blanc mange. [blahnk-MAHNZH] Molded dessert of gelatine or starch substance and milk.

blanket·maker. -making.

blasé [blah-ZAE]. Satiated and bored.

blaspheme [BLAS-feem]. Speak irreverently; revile. (n.) blasphemy [BLAS-fee-mih]. Pl. -mies. -mous, -mously; blasphemer [blas-FEEM-ehr].

blatant [BLAE-tant]. Noisy; obtrusive; bellowing.

bldg. (abbr.) building.

bleed. P. & p.p., bled.

bleeding. In textile industry, loss of color in wet cloth because of improper dyeing or the use of poor dyestuffs. Fabrics that bleed stain white or light shade fabrics in contact with them while wet.

In printing, extending type or illustration

beyond the edge of the type page, often leaving no margin.

blessed [BLEHS-ehd]. (adj.) Holy. Also blest (poetical adj.) (v.) bless, blessed (sometimes blest: *He is twice blest.*), blessing.

blithe [blieth]. Preferred to *blithesome*. Gay.

blithe-hearted. blithe-looking (adj.).

blitz-buggy. blitzkrieg.

blizzard. SEE Winds.

bloc. Group, especially of legislators: *the farm bloc.* In Europe, a group of political factions combined for a purpose; also a combination of political or racial units: *the Central European bloc.*

blond. Preferred to *blonde*, except when referring to a woman: *Her blond hair. She is a blonde.*

bloom. Refers to flowering; the height of a period.
　　BLOSSOM. Implies promise of fruit; the rise of a period: *Flowers bloom while the fruit trees blossom. The flower of youth; the bloom of maturity.*

blouse [blouz or blous].

blow. P., blew; p.p., blown.

blowup. Enlargement esp. art work for advertising; (v.) blow up.

BLS. (abbr.) Bureau of Labor Statistics.

blue. blued, bluing.

blue-chip. Security of a well-established, usually well-known company.

blue-collar worker. Factory, trade and technical workers. Contrast white-collar (office) worker.

Bluegrass Region. Bluegrass State (Kentucky).

blue-sky law. State law designed to regulate sales of securities.

blunderbuss. blunderhead.

Blvd. (abbr.) boulevard. May be abbreviated in an address or a news report.

b.m. (abbr.) board measure.

BMEWS. (abbr.) Ballistic Missile Early Warning System.

BMT. (abbr.) Brooklyn Manhattan Transit, N.Y.C. subway system.

B'Nai B'rith. Jewish fraternal organization.

b.o. (abbr.) buyer's option.

Board. Capitalize if part of name; capitalize standing alone only if referring to federal, interdepartmental, District of Columbia, or international board: Civil Aeronautics Board, the Board; Board of Education, the Board. Do not abbreviate.

board foot. Unit of measure for lumber equal to 144 cu. in.

boardmaker. -man, -walk (U.S. only); board foot, board measure.

boarding house. boarding school.

boast. AVOID use for have. NOT: *The company boasts more than $ 1 million in assets.*

boarskin. boarspear, boarstaff.

boardwalk. Atlantic City Boardwalk.

boat. Small open vessel usually moved by oars. General terms: vessel, any craft that travels on water; ship, any large seagoing vessel.
　　BARK, BARQUES. three-masted vessel with square fore and aft rigging.
　　BRIG. Two-masted vessel with square sails
　　CAIQUE. Light rowboat used on the Bosporus.
　　CARAVEL. Light 15th century mailing boat originally from Spain and Portugal, used by Columbus. *Cf.* Caravel.
　　CATBOAT. A sailboat with one forward mast, one sail, cat-rigged.
　　CUTTER. A ship's boat; also, a one-masted, fore and aft rigged vessel.
　　FRIGATE. Small mail vessel. Also an 18th century square-rigged warship, usually with 28 to 60 guns on two decks.
　　GALLEON. Large 15th-16th century 3 or 4 decker used by Spaniards and Venetians.
　　GIG. Long, narrow, light racing boat; small boat attached to a large ship; officers' boat.
　　KETCH. Two-masted boat with small mast (mizzen) aft.

SCHOONER. Vessel having two, three or more masts with fore and aft rigging.

SLOOP. One-masted vessel similar to a cutter, but with jib stay and bow sprit.

PINNACE [PIN-nihs]. Small vessel with two schooner-rigged masts and oars; a 6-8 oared boat on a man-of-war. Also, a ship's boat.

TRIREME. Galley with three rows of oars.

XEBEC [ZEE-behk]. 3-masted Mediterranean vessel with overhanging bow and stern.

YACHT. Pleasure vessel with a deck; a pirate's ship.

YAWL. Two-masted boat with mizzenmast far aft. Also a shipboat, usually 23 to 28 feet long.

boatswain [BOH-s'n]. Warrant officer.

bobcat. bobsled, bobstay, bobtail, bobwhite.

bobby pin. bobby-soxer.

Boeing 707 and 747. Turbine-powered jet engine transport planes.

Boer [BOOR]. South African of Dutch or Huguenot descent.

Boettiger [BAT-tihg-hr, (BAHT)].

Boeynants, Van [BWEE-nants]. (1919–   ) Belgian premier (1965–1968)

bogland. -man, -trot (v.) -trotter, bogway; bog-eyed (adj); bog iron.

Bogota [buh-GOHT-ah]. Boro in New Jersey, [Boh-goh-TAH] Capital city in Columbia.

bogy [BOH-gih]. Bugbear. Pl. bogies.

bogie [BOH-gih]. A low cart; weight-carrying wheel on a tank tread.

BOGEY [BOH-gih]. Golf score one stroke above par.

bohemian. Sometimes capitalized. An unconventional, especially artistic person.

Bohr, Niels Henrich David [bohr, neels]. (1885–1962) Danish physicist.

boilerplate. News material and art work provided on stereotyped plates or mats; by extension, stereotyped material.

boiler room. Office where sales are made by group of high-pressure telephone salesmen.

boiling house. boiling point.

Bois de Boulogne [BWAH deh boo-LOHN]. Fr., [BWARD-boo-lawn-(y)]. Park in Paris.

boldface type. (abbr., b.f.) Form of a typeface heavier than normal. The word boldface above is set in boldface type.

Bolivar, Simon [bohl-LEE-vahr see-MOHN]. (1783–1830) Liberator of South American nations.

Bolivia [bohl-LIHV-ih-ah]. Native, Bolivian(s); (adj.) Bolivian. Cap., Sucre; seat of govt., La Paz; Currency, boliveano (Bs.) centavo.

Bologna [buh-LOH-nya; angl., boh-LOHN-yah]. North Italy community. Bolognese.

BOLOGNA [buh-LOH-nee]. A sausage. Also bologna sausage.

boloney. Slang for a false statement, buncombe.

Bolshevik [BAWL-shih-vihk, Bol —]. (sometimes l.c.) Bolsheviki (collective plural), Bolshevist, bolshevism. The Communist Party from "majority of the party," as opposed to the Mensheviks, the minority group.

Bolshoi Theatre [bohl-SHOI]. Moscow theater.

bolsterwork.

bolt. Unit of (1) cloth length = 40 yd.; (2) wallpaper length = 16 yd.; (v.) break away from; gulp.

bolt·cutter. -head, -header, -heading, -hole, -maker, -smith, -strake, -work (all one word); bolt-shaped (adj.)

bombazine [bahm-bah-ZEEN, BAHM —]. Preferred to -sine. Twilled dress fabric of silk or cotton warp and worsted filling.

Bombers. U.S.: B-10 (By Martin) 1930, 250 mph; B-17G, Flying Fortress (by Boeing) 1937; B-18, (by Douglas) 1939; B-24, Liberator, 1940; B-25J, Mitchell (by North American) 1941; B-26, Invader (by Douglas) and Marauders (by Martin) 1942; B-29, Superfortress (by Boeing) 1943; B-36 (by Convair) for Strategic Air Command with 10,000 mi. range; B-45A, Tornado (by North American); B-47 B and E Stratojet (by

Boeing) 1957, 600 mph, 40,000 ft. ceiling, 3000 mi. range; B-50 (by Boeing) improved B-29; B-52, Stratofortress (by Boeing), 650 mph, 50,000 ft. ceiling, 6000 mi. range, missile platform (cost $8 million); B-57B (by Martin); B-58 Hustler (by Convair) speed, 1500 mph, 60,000 ft. ceiling, Mach 2, air refueled (cost $11 million); B-66B, Destroyer (by Douglas) 700 mph, ceiling 45,000 ft., range 1500 mil, air refueled; B-70 Valkyrie (by North American) Mach 3, 2000 mph, 70,000 ft. reconnaissance-strike ceiling.

SOVIET. I-28 (by Ilyushin) Beagle; Tu-16 (by Tupchev) Badger; Tu-14 Blowlamp; T-16, Badger; T-20, Bear; T-85, Barge; T-88, Badger; T-91, Boot, Tarzan; T-95, Bear.

BRITISH. B.1, B.2 Avro Vulcan; B.2, B.6, B(I).6, Electric Canberra; B.1, Handley Page Victor; B(K).1, Vickers Valiant. *Cf.* DC-, Fighter Planes.

bona fide [BOH-nuh-FIE-dee]. (Lat.) (adj.) in good faith.

bona fides. (Lat.) (n.) Evidence of good faith. *He produced his bona fides.*

Bonaparte, Napoleon [BOH-nuh-pahrt]. (1769–1821) Emperor of France. His brothers: Joseph (1768–1844), King of Naples & Spain; Lucien (1775–1840), Prince of Canino; Louis (1778–1846), King of Holland, father of Napoleon III; Jerome (1784–1860), King of Westphalia.

bond. A written agreement, under seal, to pay a certain sum at a certain time, usually at least one year later. Brit. debenture.

bondholder. bondman, bondslave, bond paper.

bonding. Process of pressing fibers into thin sheets or webs that are held together by adhesive, plastic, or cohesion (self-bonding).

bondsman. bondswoman.

bonhomie [bahn-oh-mee]. Cheerful disposition.

bon mot [bawn moh]. (Fr.) Witty remark. Pl., bon mots.

bon voyage [bahn vwa-AZH]. (Fr.) A good journey.

booby trap. booby hatch.

boogie-woogie. (piano) Rhythmic way of playing blues.

bookbinder.

bookmaker. Professional bet-taker. Not generally used for makers of printed books.

book titles. Place in quotation marks (GPO, N.Y. Times), or italicize (UCMS). Capitalize first letters of important words, except in extensive bibliographies, tables, books of the Bible, and ancient mass.

book. Books of the Bible, First Book of Samuel, etc.; Good Book (synonym for Bible); book I, II, etc.; BUT Book I, when part of title: Book I: The Golden Legend; book II. *Cf.* Bible.

book value. (1) Net assets of a company; (2) proportionate allocation of the net value of a business as shown on the company's books, applicable to each share of stock.

boondoggling.

boot. (British) for shoe.

border, United States-Mexican. SEE boundary.

born. Brought into life.

borne. Carried or endured. *The tribulations borne by the pioneers seemed unendurable.* *Cf.* bear.

borderland. borderline.

bore hole.

Borough [BUHR-oh]. Capitalize if part of name. *Borough of the Bronx; the borough.*

borscht. Beet or cabbage soup, Russian style.

bo's'n [BOHT-suhn]. Boatswain. Also bosun, bos'n.

Bosporus [BAHS-pawr-uhs]. The Bosporus. Straits in Turkey connecting Sea of Marmara and Black Sea.

Botanic Garden. (National) the garden.

botanical. Preferred to *botanic.*

both. (adj.) both men; (pronoun). Both have happy homes. (conj.) Both you and I will go. Both (adj.) *follows* a single pronoun. (*They both went*) but PRECEDES a single noun (*Both men went*) and FOLLOWS a double noun (*Tom and Jerry both went*). NOT: The men both went to town. However, after a linking verb, both FOLLOWS a single noun; *The men were both happy.*

Both involves two elements connected by *and*: *They are both strong and rich.* AVOID placement before a preposition. NOT: *They are both strong, rich, and intelligent. Oatmeal is pleasing in both flavor and consistency.* OR: *both in flavor and in consistency.* NOT: *both in flavor and consistency.* In the genitive, *both's homes. Both takes a plural verb. Both Tom and Jerry are here.*

both. AVOID redundant use with equal, alike, agree, together. NOT: Both are equal, both agree, and so on.

both of. Must be followed by a pronoun: *both of them.* BUT: *both girls*; NOT: *both of the girls.*

Botswana. (Formerly British Bechuanaland.) Surrounded by Union of South Africa. Cap., Gaberones. Independent since 1966. Natives, s. and pl. and adj. Botswana. Currency, South Africa rand (R).

Botticelli, Sandro [boht-tee-CHEHL-lee, angl. baht—, SAHN-droh]. (1444–1510) Italian painter.

bottom land. bottom plate.

bottom of the page. Preferred to *foot of the page.*

Bouganville Is. [BOO-gan-vihl]. Solomon Is. Site of W.W. II landing. Australian territory.

bouillon [bool-YAHN, buhl-yuhn, buhl-yahn]. Soup.

bullion [BUHL-yuhn]. Metal.

boulder. Large, rounded rock.

boulevard [BOOL-eh-vahrd, BUHL -]. (Abbr. blvd.)

bound. Obliged. Used as *determined*, it is colloq. NOT: He is bound to succeed.

boundary. A definite geographical limit: *The boundary between France and Germany.*

BORDER. Line or area extending along a boundary: *The Franco-German border.*

EDGE. A terminal line between any two areas; *The edge of a precipice.*

FRONTIER. Region approaching a foreign, new or different area: *France's German frontier; the New Frontier.*

bounden. Under obligation. Use only in bounden duty.

bountiful. Preferred to *bounteous* (Poet).

bouquet [boo-KAE, boh-kae]. Bunch of flowers; aroma.

Bourbon. The family [boor-BUHN]; the whisky [BUR-BUHN].

bourgeois [boor-ZHWAH; -ZHWAHZ]. (fr.)-oise. (n.) One of the middle class; (adj.) middle-class.

bourgeoisie [boor-zhwah-ZEE]. The middle class.

Bourguiba, Habib [boor-GHEE-bah, hah-BEEB]. (1903–   ). Prime Minister of Tunisia, 1956–   .

bourn or bourne [bohrn, buhrn]. (Arch. and poet.) boundary; goal.

boutonniere [boo-tuh-NYAIR]. Flower worn in a buttonhole.

bouw. 7,096.5 m² = 1.754 acres (Indonesia).

bovine [BOH-vien -vihn]. Pertains to the ox or the cow.

bowdlerize [Boud-lehr-ieze]. Expurgate prudishly. From Thomas Bowdler.

bowerbird [BOU-ehr-buhrd]. Any Australian birds that build playhouses to attract females.

bowie knife [BOH-ih, boo-ih]. Knife used for hunting and fighting.

Bowl·Dust. Bowl, Ice Bowl, Rose Bowl, the bowl.

bow window. See bay window.

Boxer Rebellion. Uprising in China, 1900.

Boxing Day. British holiday, first weekday after Christmas and traditional tipping day.

boycott. (v.) Withhold business or social intercourse. From Captain Boycott, Irish land agent. *Cf.* secondary strike.

Boy Scouts. (the organization) a Boy Scout, a Scout, the Scouts.

brace. Two, used in referring to game, dogs, pistols, or contemptuously, of people. He brought in 12 brace. But two braces equal one pair of suspenders.

THE BRACE. Used to show the relationship of an inclusive element to a group of subordinate elements. It is used instead of an outline or a table with headings. The point of the brace faces the more inclusive term.

$$\text{Verbs} \begin{cases} \text{Voices} \begin{cases} \text{Active} \\ \text{Passive} \end{cases} \\ \text{Tenses} \begin{cases} \text{Past} \\ \text{Present} \\ \text{Future} \end{cases} \end{cases}$$

brackets [ ]. Used to indicate (1) a correction, (2) a supplied omission, (3) an interpolation, (4) a comment, or (5) a warning, that an error is reproduced literally. *The general [Eisenhower] ordered the invasion. "The playing fields of Eton [an English public school] are credited with preparing many fine officers." The meeting will be a short one [laughter], and I propose to keep it orderly [applause]. The statute [sic] was the law of the land.* (6) In bills, contracts and other documents, used to indicate material to be omitted. (7) In mathematics, used to denote that enclosed matter is to be treated as a unit. When matter in brackets extends beyond one paragraph, start each paragraph with a bracket and place the closing bracket at the end of the last paragraph.

brag. Avoid use as a noun. NOT *his brag that the team would win was borne out.* BUT *His brag and bluster* (one characteristic) *was warranted* is correct.

braggadocio [brag-uh-DOH-shee-oh]. A braggart; empty boasting.

Braille, Louis [BRAH-y; angl. brael]. (1809–1852) French teacher of the blind, inventor of printing for the blind.

brains. May take a singular or plural verb when referring to more than one person.

brake. (v.) Retard or stop, (n.) an overgrown area: canebrake. Brit.—a shooting brake is a station wagon.

Branch. Capitalize if part of name; capitalize standing alone only if referring to a federal or District of Columbia unit. Accounts Branch. BUT: executive, judicial, or legislative branch.

brandnew. (adj.)(GPO). Webster, brand-new. *Cf.* bran-new.

brandyman, brandywine; brandy-burnt (adj.).

Brandywine, Pa. (BRAN-dih-wien). Creek in Pennsylvania; scene of 1776 battle.

bran-new. An acceptable variant of brand-new.

brass. Alloy of copper and zinc.

brasier, brazier [BRAE-zhehr]. A brass worker.

BRASSIER [BRASS-ee-ehr]. With more brass; bolder.

BRASSIERE [bruh-ZEER]. Woman's undergarment.

BRAZIER. Pan for holding coals or one for exposing food to fire.

bravado [bra-VAH-doh]. Swagger, simulated bravery.

brazen. From bronze, but frequently used in a figurative sense; brazen impudence.

brazenface. brazen-browed (adj.).

Brazil. (Estados Unidos de Brasil). Native, Brazilian(s); (adj.) Brazilian. Cap., Brasilia; formerly Rio de Janeiro. Currency, cruzeiro (Cr.) [croo-ZAE-roo], Brazil nut.

breach. (n.) Gap; (v.) make an opening in.

breach. Rear or lower part.

break. P., broke, p.p., broken.

breathtaking. breath-blown (adj.), breath-tainted (adj.).

breech [breech]. Part of a gun behind the bore; the buttocks.

breeches [BRIHCH-ehz, -ihz]. (Colloquial) Trousers.

breed. P. & p.p., bred, breeding.

breezeway. breeze-borne (adj.), breeze-lifted (adj.), breeze-swept (adj.).

Breton. Native of Brittany.

Bretton Woods [breht'n.]. Resort town in New Hampshire; Scene of U.N. conference, July, 1944.

breviary [BREE-vih-ary, BREHV-ih-ary]. Book of daily prayers.

brew·house. brewmaster.

Brezhnev, Leonid Ilyich [BRAEJ-nehf]. (1906–) First secretary, Soviet Communist Party (1964–   ).

briar. Preferred to *brier*. Tree used for making pipes.

bric-a-brac [BRIHK-uh-brak]. Knicknacks.

bridesmaid. -man.

Bridge. Capitalize if part of name. *The bridge. Arlington Memorial Bridge, Memorial Bridge, BUT a Pennsylvania Railroad bridge.*

bridle·man. -wise; bridle gate.

brief. Implies short in duration. May refer to time or distance; sometimes implies incompleteness or curtailment.

BRIEF. (Law) Statement of a client's case, or of the points of a legal argument.

briefcase.

brig. SEE boat.

brigand [BRIHG-uhnd]. Bandit.

Brig·Gen. (abbr.) brigadier general, brigadier generals.

brilliance. Brightness.

brilliancy. Used when noting degrees of brightness.

brilliant-cut. (adj.), brilliant-green (adj.).

brimstone. Sulphur.

bring. P. and p.p., brought; bringing; —er. Cause to come toward or with the writer or speaker. NOT *bring to the enemy.* Opposite of *take.*

briquette, briquet [brih-KEHT]. (n.) Block of pressed coal dust.

Brit. (abbr.) British, Britain.

Britain [BRIHT-ehn, -n]. The island of Great Britain.

British. Of Great Britain or the British Empire or State. Also of the Celtic language of Britons.

Briton. The Celt native to England at the time of the Romans. Poet., for native of Great Britain. *Cf.* England, Breton.

Britisher. An Americanism for native of Great Britain.

ENGLISHMAN, ENGLISHWOMAN, THE ENGLISH.

Britannia. Poetic for Great Britain; represented by a seated, helmeted female figure holding a trident.

British Columbia. (abbr. B.C.) Canadian province. Capital, Victoria.

British Commonwealth. Association of Britain's former colonies, established by Imperial Conference in 1926 and Statute of Westminster, Dec. 11, 1931.

British Honduras, C.A. Native, adj., Honduran. Brit. colony in Central America. Cap., Belize. Currency, dollar (BH$), cent.

British Guiana [gee-ANN-uh]. South American British crown colony in northeast South America; granted independence Aug. 21, 1961. Cap. Georgetown. Currency, dollar (BWl$).

Brittany [BRIHT-n-ih]. Fr., Bretagne [breh-TAHN-y]. Region in northwest France. Native, Breton.

broad. wide; extended from side to side; applies particularly to surfaces or areas: broad arrows, backs, blades, bosom, chests, fields, forehead, hands, mind, pen stroke, plains, shoulders; also broad daylight, hint, humor, outline.

WIDE. Extensive; over a great distance; to the greatest extent. Often suggests an aperture or opening. Generally: Wide distribution, eyes, mouths, range, sleeves, trousers, influence, world, eyes wide open.

Broad and wide are often used interchangeably, but occasionally with different meaning. *The wide plains were difficult to cross,* BUT *broad plains brought bountiful harvests. A wide generalization covers a large area,* BUT *a broad one neglects possible exceptions. A wide difference suggests a great difference,* BUT *a broad difference is apparent.*

broadcloth. A cotton material used for shirts or dresses. Brit., poplin. In Britain, broadcloth is a napped, calendered wool usually used for black coats.

Brobdingnag [BRAHB-dihng-nag]. Imaginary country on a gigantic scale. From Jonathan Swift's *Gulliver's Travels*. Brobdingnagian.

brochure [broh-SHOOR]. Pamphlet.

brogan [BROH-gan]. Heavy, coarse shoe.

bronchial [BRAHNK-ee-uhl].

bronchi [BRAAHNG-kie]. Subdivisions of the windpipe. Sing., bronchus; adj., bronchial, bronchia. Pl. The bronchial tubes.

broncobuster, bronchobuster. One who breaks (tames) broncos.

bronze [braahnz]. Alloy of copper and tin.

Bronze Age. Period following Stone Age.

brooch [brohch, brooch]. Ornamental clip or pin.

broom·maker. -stick, -tail; broom-leaved (adj.), broom-making (adj.); broom handle.

Brother(s). (adherent of religious order) ADDRESS: Brother Timothy Stone, F.S.C., Superior, 121 Peach Street, etc. SALUTATION: My dear Brother, Dear Brother, My dear Brother John.

brotherhood. brother-German, brother-in-law, Pl., brothers-in-law.

brown study. Serious absorbtion.

bruit [broot]. (v.) (Now usually passive). Rumor or noise about.
BRUT. Not sweet. Drier than extra sec.

brunet [broo-NEHT]. (adj. masc. or fem.)
BRUNET. (n. masc.); brunette (fem.).

brusque [bruhsk]. Rough, abrupt.

brussels carpet. lace, sprouts. (Webster: *Brussels carpet*, etc.)

brutal. Savage, cruel, animal-like. Implies moral condemnation: *brutal treatment*.

brute. Having animal powers and appetites. Usually implies no condemnation; *brute force*.

brutish. Irrational; stupid: *Neanderthal man was brutish*.

B.S. or B.Sc. (abbr.) Bachelor of Science.

B.t.u. or B.T.U. (abbr.) British thermal unit.

bu. (abbr.) bushel.

bubble gum.

buccaneer [buhk-uh-NEER]. Pirate.

buck. Male deer (except red deer), antelope, reindeer, hare, rabbit, rat, goat or (colloquial) reindeer, hare, rabbit, rat, goat or (colloquial) sheep. Male moose and elk are bulls. *Cf.* hart, animals.

bucket shop. Unlicensed dealer or broker, esp. in securities. Orders are placed on the basis of current prices, but there is no actual selling or buying.

Buddha. SEE Gautama Buddha.

Buddhism [BUHD-ihsm]. Religion of Gautama Buddha; holds that nirvana (escape from suffering and mortality) is goal, attainable by "Eightfold Path" of right belief, right resolve, right word, right act, right life, right effort, right thinking, and right meditation. Buddhist; Buddhistic.

budget. department, estimate, message; federal budget, performance-type, President's, etc.

Budget of the United States (publication). the Budget (Bureau implied); the budget.

budtime. budwood; bud rot.

buffalo. Pl. -oes.

buffaloback. (fish) buffalo dance.

Buffalo Bill. William Frederick Cody (1846–1917). American scout, showman.

buffet [bu-FAE or BUFF-iht]. Cupboard.
BUFFET [BUHF-eht, -iht]. A blow; slap.

build. P. & pp., built; building.

Building. Capitalize if part of name; the building: Capitol Building, Colorado Building, House (or Senate) Office Building, Investment Building; Chrysler Building; Empire State Building; Church of Christ Building

build-up. (n. & adj.)

built-in. (adj.) built-up (adj.).

bulb. As lily, onion, tulip.

TUBER. As dahlias.

CORN. As gladiolus.

Bulgaria [buhl-GAR-ih-a; BUL-]. Native, Bulgarian(s); adj., Bulgarian, Cap., Sofia. Currency, lev, leva; stolinka, -ki.

bullet. The bullet is discharged from the muzzle of a gun; the cartridge holds the explosive charge and the bullet before firing, and may be ejected in some weapons. *Cf.* caliber.

bullion. SEE bouillon.

bull's eye. (nonliteral), bull's-foot.

bumboat. Provision boat selling to vessels in port.

bumper. (Automobiles) Brit., fender. Brit., wing.

bunch. AVOID use meaning a lot, especially of people.

buncombe [BUHNG-kuhm]. Preferred to *bunkum* in U.S. Anything said for show; nonsense.

bunion.

bunkhouse. -load.

Bunsen burner. Gas burner producing a hot flame.

buntline. Rope attached to the foot of a square sail; used in furling the sail.

buoy [BOO-ih (n.) (U.S.); boi (Brit.)]. Moored float marking a channel, rock, etc.

buoy No. 1.

buoyant [BOO-yuhnt; BOI-uhnt]. Tending to float; having lightness of spirit.

burden [BUHR-d'n]. Preferred to *burthen* [BUHR-thehn]. Load; encumbrance; obligation.

bureau [BYOO-roh]. Chest of drawers; business office; government department, or one of its subdivisions.

Bureau. Capitalize if part of name; capitalize standing alone if referring to Federal, District of Columbia, or international unit: Bureau of Customs, Bureau of Engraving and Printing; the Bureau.

bureaucracy [byoo-RAHK-ruh-sih]. Government conducted by means of bureaus; hence, officialism characterized by elaborate routines, red tape, etc.

bureaucrat [BYOO-ruh-krat].

burgh [buhrg].

BOROUGH. [Scotch, BUHR-oh]

burgher [buhr-guhr]. Freeman of a burgh.

burglary. Burgle and burglarize are still considered colloq. Burglary involves breaking and entering. A robbery involves taking by force. Holdup is robbery with a weapon. Theft is any taking of another's property.

Burlingame [BUHR-lihn-gaem, or ling-gaem]. City on San Francisco Bay, California.

Burma [BUHR-muh]. Native Burman(s) (preferred); adj., Burmese. Cap., Rangoon. Currency, kyat (K), pya.

burn. -ed, -ing. Participial adjective is burnt: (burnt offering). British use burnt as past or p.p.

burned-over. (adj.)

burner-off.

burnt-out. (adj.) burnt-up (adj.).

burr. Preferred to *bur* except for the prickly seed.

burst. Preferred to *bust* except in bronco busting and other colloquial uses.

Burundi. Constitutional monarchy under king (mwani). Natives, Burundian(s). Capital, Bujumbura. Currency, franc (RBF).

bus. Pl. buses. Preferred to *busses*.

busboy. Busdriver, busfare, busline.

bushel. (abbr. bu.) Unit of dry measure (1) U.S.; 4 pecks = 32 dry qts. = 8 dry gal. = 2150.42 cu.in. (2) Brit.: 1.032 U.S. bu. = 33.026 U.S. dry qt. (3) heaped (U.S.) = 1.278 U.S. bu. struck measure = approx. $1\frac{1}{4}$ bu. struck measure = 2.747.715 cu. in.

bushelman., -women.

businessman. business woman, small businessman.

bust. (v.) Applies to broncos; otherwise burst.

bustling [BUHS-lihng].

busybody.

but. Used (1) for except (SEE below); (2) for only: *He had but one life to give.* (3) for that . . . not: *There was not a page but had an error on it.* (4) to introduce a parallel clause: *He studied hard, but he looked it.* (5) to introduce a negative clause: *He studied hard, but he did not learn.*
    But is considered a preposition when followed by a noun or pronoun: *Everyone was here but him.* However, some grammarians (including Fowler) consider *but* a conjunction: *Everyone was here but he (was not).*

butt. Unit of capacity measure equals 2 hogsheads equals 126 long gallons.

Butte [byoot]. City in Montana.

buy. (n.) (colloquial) purchase; bargain. AVOID: *He made a good buy.*

buyers' market. One in which supply exceeds demand.

buzz bomb. buzz saw, buzz wig.

buzzerphone.

Bvt. (abbr.) brevet.

by. (adv.) *He is standing by.*
  BY. (prep.) *He passed by the house.*

bygone. bylaw, byplay, byroad, bystander, byway, byword; by-line, by-the-way (n., adj.),

by-your-leave. (n., adj.) by-election, by-product; by and by, by the by, by the way.

by-product. One produced incidentally to the major process of manufacture.

bye. (n.) Something aside or secondary. Now obs. except in *by the bye.*

Byelorussia [Bie-loh-RUHSH-uh]. White Russia, region near Poland. Native, Byelorussian(s) adj., Byelorussian. Cap., Minsk.

by the hundred. dozen, score, etc. BUT by hundreds, dozens, scores.

Byzantine Empire [BIH-zan-teen or -tien or BIE-]. Outgrowth of Eastern Roman Empire, 474–1453. Cap., Constantinople.

C

c, ck. A word ending in *c* adds *k* before a native suffix *-ed, -er, -ing* or *-y*: *panicky, picnicking.* This does not apply when classical suffixes *-ian, -ism, -ist, -ity, -ize* are added: *criticism.*

C. (abbr.) Catholic, Celsius, Celtic.

C. or c. (abbr.) centigrade.

C-sharp. C-star, C-tube.

c. (abbr.) centi = one-hundredth (0.01); cycle (Kc. only); curie.

c., ct. (abbr.) cent, cents.

c., ca. (abbr.) circa.

c. and s.c. (abbr.) caps and small caps.

CAB (abbr.) Civil Aeronautics Board, N.Y. Times, C.A.B.

cabal [kuh-BAL]. A secret association of a few persons.

cabala [KAB-uh-luh]. Esoteric doctrine or science.

cabana [kuh-BAN-uh]. Bathhouse.

cabdriver.

Cabell, James Branch [KAB-ehl]. (1879–1950). American novelist.

cabinhouse. cabin car.

Cabinet, American or foreign. Capitalize if part of name or standing alone: *British Cabinet: the Cabinet; the President's Cabinet; the Cabinet: Cabinet officer, member.* Cf. Minister, Foreign Cabinets. Secretary of Defense, John J. Smith; Minister of War; the Minister.

cabinetmaker. —making, —work, —worker, —working (all one word).

cableholder. —man, —way; cable-laid (adj.); cable car, cable ship.

cacao [kuh-KAE-oh, kuh-KAH-oh]. Pl. -s. Cf. cocoa.

cache [kash]. hiding-place.

cachet [ka-sh-AE]. seal.

cacodemon [kak-oh-DEE-muhn]. Preferred to *cacodaemon.* An evil spirit.

cacophony [ka-KAHF-oh-nih]. Discord.

cactus. Pl. -ti or -uses.

cadaver [kuh-DAV-uhr or kuh-DAE-vuhr]. A dead body.

caddy. Tea box.

caduceus [kuh-DYOO-see-uhs]. Pl. -cei. Staff with separate twining snake about. Symbol of physicians and medical corps.

caecum [SEEK-uhm]. Blind end of a canal, especially of the intestinal canal.

Caedmon [KAD-muhn]. (c. 670). Anglo-Saxon poet.

C.A.F. (abbr.) Cost and freight.

café [ka-FAE]. Coffee house.

café au lait [—oh—LAE]. (Fr.) Half coffee, half hot milk.

café noir [—NWAHR]. (Fr.) Black coffee.

cafeteria.

caffeine [KAH-fee-ihn; KAF-een]. Stimulant alkaloid in coffee, tea, etc.

Cairo [KIE-roh]. City in Egypt.

Cairo [KAE-roh]. City in Illinois.

cakebaker. —box, —maker.

Calais [Kah-LAE, Kal-ae; angl., Kuh-LEH]. French seaport on the English Channel.

caldron [KAWL-dr'n]. Preferred to *cauldron* in U.S. Large kettle or pot.

calèche [kuh-LESH]. Two wheeled buggy with folding top.

Caledonian. Native of ancient Scotland.

Calendar. Capitalize if part of name; the calendar, Consent Calendar, etc., House Calendar, Calendar No. 99, Calendar of Bills and Resolutions, Private Calendar, Wednesday Calendar (legislative).

calendar. A list of dates. Also, a smooth paper finish.

COLANDER. A strainer. *She placed the spaghetti in a colander to remove the water.*

caliber. Preferred to *calibre* in U.S. 0.30 caliber = 0.3 inch diameter bore. *Cf.* bullet, gun.

calico. In U.S., printed cotton cloth; Brit., white muslin.

calicoback. (fish); calico bass.

Calif. (abbr.) California.

caliper. calliper [KAL-ih-pehr]. Pl. -s. Measuring instrument. Usually used in plural.

caliph [KAE-lif;, KAL-ihf]. Temporal and spiritual ruler.

calisthenics. Preferred to *callisthenics* in U.S.

calix [KAE-lihks, KAL-lhks]. Pl. calices. Chalice.

calk. *Caulk* is preferred in the U.S.

calligraphy [ka-LIHG-ra-fih]. Elegant penmanship.

Calliope [Kuh-LIE-oh-pee]. Muse of poetry and eloquence.

calliope [kuh-LIE-oh-pee]. Steam whistle musical instrument. Battlefield 3.5 = in. rocket.

callus [KAL-uhs]. (n.) Pl. -uses, (adj.) callous. Hard thickened skin area.

caloric [kuh-LAHR-ihk].

calorie (or calory). Unit of heat required to raise temperature of 1 liter of water 1 degree centigrade. Used in expressing energy value of food.

gram-calorie or small calorie. Unit of heat required to raise 1 gram of water 1 degree centigrade.

calumny [KAL-uhm-nee]. Slander.

Calvary. The place where Christ was crucified.

CAVALRY. Soldiers on horseback.

calyx [KAE-lihks; kal-ihks]. Leafy part of flower. Pl. —es or calyces [KAL-ih-seez, KAE-lih-seez].

cambist [KAM-bihst]. Dealer in foreign notes or money.

Cambodia. Native, Cambodian(s); adj., Cambodian. Cap., Phnom Penh. Webster prefers Pnom Peenh [P'NAHM-peen]. Currency, riel, centime.

Cambria [KAM-brih-uh]. (Lat.) Wales.

Camel. The Bactrian camel has two humps; the Arabian camel or dromedary has one hump.

camel's-hair. (adj.) camel's hair (n.).

camellia [kuh-MEHL-ih-uh or —MEEL-yuh].

camelopard [cuh-MEHL-oh-pahrd or KAMehl-oh-pahrd]. A giraffe. NOT *leopard.*

cameo [KAM-ee-oh]. Pl. -os. Relief-carved stone gem.

cameraman. camera lucida, camera obscura.

Cameroons [kam-ehr-OONZ]. British Cameroons. Former U.N. Trust Territory. After March, 1961, plebiscite, North portion joined Nigeria in June, 1961; South portion joined Cameroun Republic in October 1961.

CAMEROON [ka-m'-ROON] French and Webster prefer Cameroun. Former French Ind. mandate in West Africa. Became independent on January 1, 1960. Capital Yaounde [YUH-oon-DAE]. Currency, CFAF franc. "Reunified" October, 1961.

Camp Gary. etc.; the camp.

camshaft. cam switch, cam wheel.

Camus, Albert [kah-MUE, al-BEHR]. (1913-1960). French writer, social reformer.

can. P., could: *She could talk before she was a year old.* The subjunctive *could* does not require *if* preceding. *Could he have passed the test, he would have won.*

can and may. Can expresses mental or physical ability; may expresses permission: *What is possible can be done. You may have an apple.*

Canaan [KAEN-nan]. Canaanite [—iet -Brit., KAEN-yan-iet].

Canada. Native, Canadian(s). Adj., Canadian. Cap., Ottawa. Currency, dollar (Can.$), cent.
CANADA [can-YUH-duh]. (Sp.) A narrow valley.

canaille [KUH-nael; Fr. kan-IE]. The rabble.

Canal. Capitalize with name. Isthmian; Panama; the canal; Canal Zone (Isthmian), the zone.

canal. boat, —man, —side.

Canal Zone. (abbr., C.Z.) U.S. leasehold in Panama, 10 mi. wide.

Canandaigua [can-an-DAE-gwuh]. City in New York State.

canapé [kan-uh-PAE]. An appetizer.
CANOPY [KAN-oh-pih]. An overhanging covering.

Canaveral, Cape [can-AV-ehr-al]. U.S. Army rocket-launching site in Florida; renamed Cape Kennedy.

candelabrum [kan-deh-LAH-bruhm; -LAE-bruhm, -LAB-ruhm]. Branched candlestick. Pl. —bra is pref. to —brums; NOT —bras.

cancapper. —maker, —making; can buoy, can opener.

cancel. —led, —ing, pref. in U.S.; Brit. *ll.* cancellation, canceler.

candidate [KAN-dih-daet].
CANDIDACY. British prefer *candidature.*

candor [KAN-der]. (Brit., candour) Frankness.

candy. Pl. (same type) pieces of candy; (various types) candies. British use sweets; candy is rock candy.

canebrake.

cane sugar.

canine [KAE-nien].

canister.

canker.

Cannes [kann]. French town on the Riviera.

cannon. (Sing. and collective). Pl. -s. cannon-ball, —proof.

cannot. One word except in special meanings or for emphasis.

cannot help. cannot but, cannot help but, pref. in that order.

canon [KAN-yuhn; Sp., kah-NYOHN]. Variation of canyon.
CANON [KAN-uhn]. Law; rule.

cantabile [kahn-TAH-bee-lae]. Singable.

can't seem. AVOID. Use seem unable: *I seem unable to concentrate.* NOT: *I can't seem to concentrate.*

cantaloupe [KAN-tuh-lohp; Brit., -loop]. (Brit.) cantaloup muskmelon.

cantata [kan-TAH-tah]. Dramatic choral composition.

canto [KAN-toh]. Division of a long poem. Pl. —s.

canvas. (n. and v.) Hemp or flax material.
CANVASS. (n. and v.) Solicitation, (n.) detailed examination.

canyon [KAN-yuhn]. Deep, steep-walled valley; *Cf.* canon.

caoutchouc [KOO-chunk, KOU-chook]. Pure rubber.

capital; capitalize. (abbr. cap.) Cap. and small cap (or c. & s.c.). Instructions to printer to set type in CAPITAL and SMALL CAPITAL letters.

capable of. Able to.

Cape Girardeau [jih-RAH(r)-doh or duh]. City in Mississippi.

Cape of Good Hope. the cape.

Cape Kennedy. See Cape Canaveral.

Cape Verde Is. [kaep VUHRD]. Portuguese islands in Atlantic Ocean.

capital. City.

CAPITOL. The building.

Capital. Capital City, National Capital (Washington, D.C.); BUT the capital (state).

capital gain (or loss). Profit (or loss) from sale or exchange of a capital asset, i.e., an asset owned for the purpose of producing income.

CAPITALIZATION. Capitalize (1) the first word of a sentence, of an independent clause or phrase, of a direct quotation, of a line of poetry, of a formally introduced series of items: *The question is, Will they agree? He asked, "And where are you going?"*
Lives of great men all remind us
We can make our lives sublime.
(2) BUT NOT the first word of a fragmentary quotation: *He objected to "the phraseology," not to the ideas.* (3) Capitalize the first word following a colon, an exclamation point or an interrogation point unless the matter following is merely a supplementary remark: *Revolutions are not made: they come.*
The vote was as follows: In the affirmative, 16; in the negative, 11; not voting, 2.
(4) Capitalize proper names, *John Brown; New York; the Jones family,* and derivatives in English, Latin and Dutch texts. *Italian, Romanize,* (5) BUT capitalize only proper nouns (not adjectives) in French, Italian, Spanish, Norwegian, and Swedish texts. All nouns are capitalized in German. (6) Lower-case derivatives from proper nouns which have acquired independent common meaning: *roman type, plaster of paris, pasteurize.* (7) Capitalize adjectives or common nouns which are an essential part of a proper noun. *Statue of Liberty, Amsterdam Avenue, Union Station.* BUT NOT the common noun standing alone: *the statue, the avenue, the station;* AND NOT when a common noun intervenes: *Union passenger station.* (8) Capitalize the plural forms of proper nouns: *First and P Streets,* (9) and when the common noun is used as a short form of a well known name previously mentioned: *the Capitol, the Court (for the Supreme Court).*
(10) Capitalize a title preceding a name: *Professor Jones.* (11) Capitalize eminent distinctions, titles of heads of state or of members of the diplomatic corps following a name: *Nelson Rockefeller, Governor of the State of New York.* (12) BUT NOT military titles: *Charles F. Hughes, admiral,* (13) or scholastic titles: *Cloyd H. Marvin, president of George Washington University.* (14) Capitalize the titles of acts, articles, books, captions, chapters, editorials, essays, historical events, laws, lectures, parts of a book, poems, reports, short titles of acts, songs, television and radio programs, treaties, wars, and usually any noun followed by a numeral, especially a roman numeral, when used as a title. (15) BUT titles in a foreign language conform to the rules of that language. (16) Lower-case general titles of a bill not yet enacted into law: *minimum wage bill.*
(17) When an article is part of a name or title, it is capitalized: *The New York Times,* BUT NOT when the article is used adjectively; *the Hague Court, the Herald Tribune.* (18) In general, lower-case the articles in reference to newspapers, periodicals, vessels, airships, trains, and firm names: *the Netherlands, the News, the Queen Mary, the U-2.* (19) In foreign names, articles *d', da, della, du, van,* and *von* are capitalized when not preceded by a forename or title: *De Gaulle* BUT *Charles de Gaulle.* (UCMS capitalizes *Van* and *Von* in all cases.) *Cf. Filing.* (20) BUT in anglicized versions, the articles in names are capitalized unless personal usage is otherwise: *Thomas De Quincey; Irenee du Pont* (his usage).
(21) Capitalize the full name of organized bodies and shortened names, but substitutes are regarded as common nouns and are lower-cased except to indicate preeminence or distinction. *U.S. Congress, 82d Congress; U.S. Navy, the Navy, naval shipyard, naval station; Republican party.*
(22) Capitalize the names of administrative, judiciary, or legislative bodies of government: *Office of Civilian Defense, Budget Bureau:* BUT NOT general designations: *the national parliament, United States government bodies, federal courts.* (23) Capitalize the names of adherents of organized bodies: *a Republican, an Elk, a Communist:* BUT lower-case those with a common belief designated as a group: *liberals, democrats, conservatives, freethinkers.* (24) Capitalize official designations of countries, administrative divisions, regions, and geographic features as nouns or adjectives, including an area direction if part of the name: *British Commonwealth, the Commonwealth, the East, the Eastern States.* BUT *eastern section, east* (as a direction), *the valley of the Missouri River, the river Elbe, the Indian peninsula, western Europe.* (UCMS lower-cases county referring to Irish counties: *county Kildare.*)

(25) Capitalize epithets and fanciful appelations; *the Dust Bowl;* (26) vivid personifications; *When Nature wields her scepter mercilessly;* (27) religious terms denoting the Deity or a sacred book: *Heavenly Father, the Scriptures, Talmud, Exodus, Gospel of Mark;* BUT NOT derived adjectives: *scriptural, talmudic* (28) Capitalize calendar divisions and holidays: *Sunday, January, Thanksgiving Day*; BUT NOT the seasons: *fall, winter.* (29) Capitalize historic events and periods: *the Renaissance, the Iron Age, the Bronze Age. Cf.* Ages. (30) Capitalize trade names: *Band-Aid, Fiberglas;* (31) the scientific name of a phylum: *Arthopoda*; class: *Crustacea*; order: *Hypoparia*; family: *Agnostidae*; or genus: *Agnostics*; BUT NOT species. *Cf.* CLASSIFICATION OF PLANTS AND ANIMALS. (32) BUT lower-case coined terms derived from proper names: *menodontine.* (33) Capitalize soil names, *Bog*; (34) planets, *Venus*; (35) BUT lower-case sun, moon, and earth unless used in association with other planets.

(36) Capitalize Volume, Chapter, Book, etc. when followed by a number when part of a title, legend, or citation of a publication, report, case, etc.: *Book I: The Golden Legend: Chapter II of the Penal Code.* BUT do not capitalize a common noun merely because it is used with a date, number, or letter, for the purpose of reference or record: *article* 1. (UCMS capitalizes a noun followed by a number except minor subdivisions.) (37) Lower-case freshman, sophomore, junior, and senior. (UCMS capitalizes these.)

(38) Capitalize the first word following an enacting or resolving clause (usually *That*): *Resolved, That . . . and be it further . . . Provided, That . . .* But not the first word following *Whereas* in resolutions, contracts, etc.: *Whereas the law provides, etc.* (BUT UCMS always capitalizes the first word following *Whereas.*) (39) Capitalize the exclamatory *Oh*! or *O. Cf.* TITLES. the Capitol, (the building in Washington): BUT state capitol; Building (State), the capitol. Referring to the Capitol at Washington, D.C.: Architect of the Capitol, Capitol caucus room, Capitol Chamber, Capitol dome, Capitol Grounds, Capitol Hall of Fame, the Hall; Capitol Hill, the Hill; Capitol Police; Capitol Power Plant; Capitol Prayer Room.

Capote, Truman [kah-POH-tee]. (1924–   ). American author.

Capri [KA-prih]. Island in Bay of Naples, Italy.

capsule [KAP-sool, not suhl].

Capt. (abbr.) Captain [KAP-tihn].

caption. Title or explanation of an illustration. U.S. only.

captious. Unreasonable or unnecessary. Criticism. Peevishness.

    CAVILING. Petty criticism.

    CARPING. Ill-tempered criticism.

capuchin [KAP-yoo-chihn; kap-yoo-CHEEN]. A hooded cloak; also a South American monkey; also an order of monks.

captivate.

car. Preferred to auto.

carabao [kah-rah-BAH-oh]. Singular and plural. Water buffalo.

Caracas [kah-RAH-kahs]. Capital city of Venezuela.

carat. Measure of weight of precious stones = 3.0865 grains = 200 mgr.

    KARAT. Measure of gold purity in 24ths; 14 karat is 10 parts alloy. Also *carat.*

    CARET. A mark ($\wedge$) used to indicate an insertion.

    CARROT. The vegetable.

caravansary [kar-ah-VAN-suh-rih]. Also -serri [—seh-rie, —seh-rae]. Inn for caravan travelers.

Caravel (le). (By Sud Aviation) 2-engine turbojet transport plane. *Cf.* boat.

carbine [KAHR-bien]. Short-barreled rifle.

carburet [KAHR-byou-reht]. (v.) Combine chemically with carbon; charge with volatile carbon compounds. —ed, —ing.

carburetor [KAHR-byoo-reht-er]. (Brit., —rettor) Device in which air or gas is carbureted.

carcass [KAHR-kuhs]. Dead body. Preferred to *carcase.*

Carcassonne [kuhr-kuh-SAHN]. City in France.

carcinogen. Cancer-causing substance.

Cardinal. Terrence Cardinal Cooke, Cardinal Cooke, the Cardinal. ADDRESS: His

Eminence The Most Reverend Terrence Cardinal Cooke, Archbishop of New York. SALUTATION: Your Eminence; Most Reverend Sir; Dear Cardinal Cooke.

CARE. (abbr.) Cooperative for American Relief Everywhere.

Caribbean Sea [kar-eh-BEE-an; kuh-RIHB-ee-an].

carload.

Carnegie, Andrew [KAHR-nae-gih]. (1835–1919). American steel magnate and philanthropist.

caroled. -ing.

carping. SEE captious.

carrierborne.

carryall. (m. & adj.).

carte blanche [kahrt BLAHNSH]. (Fr.) Blank page with signature; by ext; blank check; unlimited authority.

cartilage [KAHR-tih-lihj]. Elastic tissue composing parts of the skeleton, as in the nose.

cartridge. SEE bullet.

Caruso, Enrico [kah-ROO-zoh; angle., —soh]. (1873–1921) Italian tenor.

Casablanca [kah-sah-BLAHN-ka]. Seaport in Morocco.

case. A particular instance, especially legal or medical: *In case of accident*; or a situation involving a problem: *a case of bad blood*; or an argument: *a case law case.* AVOID: *in any case* meaning *anyhow* or *from any point of view; in many cases* meaning *usually; in all cases* meaning *always; in the case of* meaning *in this connection; as was formerly the case* meaning *in the past; that is not the case* meaning *that is not correct; as is the case* meaning *as is true; such is the case* meaning *it is true; in each case* for *each time.*

CASE. In grammar, the property of a noun or pronoun indicated by change of form, inflection, or position, that shows the relation of the noun or pronoun to other parts of the sentence; *e.g.*, as subject (nominative); object (objective or accusative); or modifier (possessive or genitive). In old English, case was indicated by word endings.

All nouns and some pronouns retain the same form in the nominative and objective cases; the case or function is indicated by their position in the sentence. Some pronouns change form (or inflection) in all three cases.

The subject of a sentence or a clause is in the nominative case, as is a noun following a form of the verb *be* (called the predicate nominative). Also in the nominative case are (1) a noun in a phrase that consists of a noun or pronoun and a participle (nominative absolute, and (2) noun in direct address. The direct object, the indirect object (at one time called the dative case), the subject of an infinitive, the subject of a participle, and the word before *to be* are in the objective case. *We believed him to be honest.*

Pronouns change form to show case: (1) subjective or nominative: *I, we, she, who, they*; (2) objective or accusative: *her, him, them, whom*; (3) possessive or genitive; *your, our, his, their.*

In a compound, both members must be in the same case. A word or group of words standing in opposition remains in the same case as the antecedent. Expressions like *I believe, he thinks* between the subject and the verb do not change the case: *He is the man who I think was there.* A relative pronoun (*who, whoever, which, whichever*) used as the subject of a clause is in the nominative case. *Return the money to whoever loaned it to her.* In a subordinate clause, the case of the relative pronoun depends upon its use within the clause. *Cf.* Aspect.

casebearer. —book, —bound, —hammer, —harder, —load, —maker, —making, —mate, –mated, –wood, –worm (all one word); case binding, case work, case worker.

cashbook. —box, —boy, —girl, —keeper (all one word).

casket. A box. A corpse lies in a coffin.

Cassiopeia [kas-see-oh-PEE-uh]. Northern constellation.

cast [kast]. P. and pp., cast; casting. Throw; mold; select actors in a play. Also (n.) the actors.

caster. Stand for holding cruets; furniture wheels.

CASTOR. A type of beaver, bean, medicine, hat.

CASTOR OIL.

CASTER-OFF, CASTER-OUT.

Castiglione, Conte Baldassare [kahs-teel-YOH-nae. KOHN-tae bahl-dah-SAH-rae]. (1478–1529). Italian statesman-writer.

castlebuilder. Dreamer.

Castro, Ruz, Fidel [KAHS-troh, Rooz, fee-DEHL]. (1927–   ). Prime Minister of Cuba, 1959–   .

casual. Offhand, unforeseen, etc.

CAUSAL. Implying cause.

catalyst. Substance which speeds or slows chemical reactions, remaining unchanged itself.

catboat. SEE boat.

catalog. In wider use than the more proper -ogue used by N.Y. Times. -ed, -ing, -er.

catarrh [kuh-TAHR]. Inflammation of a mucous membrane.

catch. P. and p.p., caught.

catchall. (n. & adj.)

catchup. Preferred to *catsup*. British use ketchup.

categorical [kat-ee-GAWR-ih-kul]. Absolute, unqualified; of or in a category.

category [KAT-ee-goh-rih, ih-goh-rih]. Division formed for discussion or classification.

class. Group of persons or things with common characteristics.

cater-corner. —cornered. caterwauling.

Cather, Willa [KATH-uhr]. (1873–1947). American novelist.

Catherine de Médicis [kat-REEN duh mae-dee-SEE]. Queen of France, wife of Henry II. (1519–1589).

catholic. Universal; general.

CATHOLIC. Pertaining to the Western Christian Church. Use Roman Catholic for the religion and its adherents. catholicly, catholically; catholicism [ka-THAHL-ih-sihsm].

cat's-eye. (nonliteral) cat's-paw (nonliteral). Pref. to catspaw.

catsup. N.Y. Times, *catchup*; Brit., *ketchup*.

catty [katih]. 1⅓ lb. avdp. (China).

Caucasian. A misnomer for the white race, based on the supposition that the people of the Caucasus were typical of the white race.

causa mortis. (Lat.) In contemplation of death: *A gift causa mortis.*

cause. (n.) Produces an effect.

REASON. (n.) Explains the cause.

cause. (v.) may be followed by an infinitive: *You caused him to fail;* a noun: *You caused his failure;* or a gerund: *You caused his failing.*

cause. Avoid redundancy. *It is due to* or *The cause is,* NOT: *The cause is due to.*

cause célèbre [kohz-sae-LEHBR]. A widely-publicized case.

caused by. NOT caused from.

cause of . . . *is that,* NOT *is on account of* or *is due to: The cause of the delay is that he was late.* NOT . . . *is on account of his being late.* BUT as a preposition, CORRECT: *We were delayed on account of his lateness.*

causeway. causewayman.

cautious. SEE afraid.

cavalcade. (Procession) Literally, parade on horseback.

"Cavalleria Rusticana" [Kahv-ahl-lyeh-REE-ah roos-tih-KAH-nuh]. (Rustic Chivalry) Opera by Pietro Mascagni.

cavalryman.

caveat [KAE-vee-at]. Beware; a warning. *caveat emptor,* "let the buyer beware."

cavedweller.

caviar.

cavil. —led, —ling or —lling, —ler. SEE captious.

cayenne [kie-EHN; kae-EHN]. Hot red pepper.

Cayuse [kie-YOOS]. Oregonian Indians. Lower case when meaning small hardy horse.

c.b.d. (abbr.) cash before delivery.

C.B.S. (abbr.) Columbia Broadcasting System.

cc. or c.c. (abbr.) cubic centimeter. Also cm.

C.C.A. (abbr.) Circuit Court of Appeals.

CCC. (abbr.) Commodity Credit Corporation; Civilian Conservation Corps.

cd.-ft. (abbr.) cord-foot.

C.E. (abbr.) Common Era. *Cf.* A.D.

CEA. (abbr.) Council of Economic Advisers.

cease. *Stop* is preferred BUT: *cease-fire* (n. and adj.).

cedar·bird. —maker, —ware; cedar-colored (adj.); cedar leaf.

cedilla [see-DIHL-uh]. Mark placed under *c* to indicate soft pronunciation. (Common in French and Spanish. In English, often used in façade.) *Cf.* Diacritical Marks.

Celebes [SEHL-ee-beez or seh-LEE-beez]. Island of Indonesia, south of Philippines.

celebrant. One who conducts a Mass or other religious ceremony.

CELEBRATOR. One who celebrates.

CELEBRITY. A well-known person.

celerity [see-LEHR-ih-tih]. Speed, applied to living things.

VELOCITY. Speed, applied to objects.

celi-. Combining form meaning unmarried; *celibacy, celibate.*

cellar·man. —way, —woman.

cell·house. —mate; cell tester, cell wall.

cello [CHEH-loh]. Pl. -os. Shortened from violoncello. Modern use permits elimination of the apostrophe.

Celt [SEHLT or, esp. Brit., kehlt]. Of an ancient ethnic group now native in Ireland, Scotland, Wales, Brittany. Celtic. *Cf.* Cymric.

cement [see-MEHNT]. See concrete.

cement·maker. —making; cement-covered (adj.), cement-temper (v.).

Cemetery. Capitalize if part of name: *Arlington National Cemetery, the cemetery.*

censer [SEHN-suhr]. Vessel for burning incense; the person using it.

CENSOR [SEHN-suhr]. One who passes on acceptability of material for publication.

CENSURE [SEHN-shoor]. Condemn; criticize adversely.

Census. Seventeenth Decennial Census (title), Seventeenth Census (title), the census; 1950 Census of Agriculture, the census of agriculture, the census; the 14th decennial census (descriptive).

centare [SEHN-taer]. (abbr. ca.) Also centiare. Unit of area = 1.196 sq. yd. = 10.764 sq. ft. = 1 m.^{2} = 0.01 are.

centennial [sehn-TEN-ee-al]. 100th anniversary.

CENTENARY [SEHN-tee-nehr-ih, sehn-TEHN-ehr-ih; Brit., TEE-na-rih]. Pertaining to 100 years.

center. Preferred to *centre* in U.S. BUT (N.Y.C.) Centre St.; Brit., centring, centreless

center. The central point. Half is on each side, in time, space, or material. *The middle surrounds the center.*

Center. Agricultural Research, etc.; the center

center. board, —head (printing), —line, —most, —piece; center-second; center bit, center point.

centi-. Combining form meaning hundred or hundredth part; centipede, centigrade, centiloquy. *Cf.* hecto.

centigrade [SEHNT-ih-grade]. Temperature scale 0° (freezing)—100° (boiling). Compares with Fahrenheit, 32° (freezing)—212° (boiling). *Cf.* temperature.

centigram. (abbr., cg.) Unit of weight = 0.15432 grains = 0.01 gram.

centiliter. (abbr. cl.) Unit of capacity = 0.3381 fluid oz. = 0.011 liter = 0.6102 cu. in.

centimeter [SEHN-tih-mee-tahr]. (abbr., cm.) Unit of length = 0.3937 in. = 0.01 m. = 10 mm.

centistere [SEHN-tih-steer]. Unit of volume = 0.353 cu. ft. = 0.01 m.^{3}

centner. 110.23 lbs. avdp.

cento. Pl. -os. Literary work of selections.

Central African Republic. Formerly French: Ubangi-Shari [oo-BANG-ee SHA-REE]. Situated north of Congo (Leopoldville). Native, Centrafrican. Cap., Bangui. Independence, Aug., 1960. Currency, CFAF franc.

central Asia. central Europe, etc.; Central States; central time, central standard time.

century. The first includes years 1 to 100. The 20th, years 1901 through 2000. Year 1900 is in the 19th century. Lower-case and spell out the first through the ninth centuries, BUT *the 10th, 11th, etc. century.* Hyphenate the adjective form. *20th-century artist.*

cerebral [SEH-ree-bruhl]. (adj.) Pertains to the brain, physically or intellectually: *cerebral music.*

cerebrum [SEH-ree-bruhm]. (n.) The brain, figuratively and anatomically. Specifically, the forebrain; the seat of voluntary and conscious mental processes. Pl. -s, -bra.

Cervantes Saavedra, Miguel de [dae ther-VAHN-taes sah-ah-VAE-thrah, mee-GAHL]. (1547–1616). Spanish novelist. *Cf.* Don Quixote.

Cesarean. [see-ZAIR-ee-an]. Var. of Caesarean. *Cf.* Caesar.

cesium [see-zih-uhm]. Soft, silver metallic element.

cesspipe. —pit, —pool.

Ceylon. Native, Ceylonese. adj., Ceylonese, Cingalese, or Singhalese. Brit., Sinhalese, Cap., Colombo. Currency, rupee, (Cey Rs) anna. Name changed to Sri Lanka, 1972.

Cezanne, Paul [sae-ZAHN]. (1839–1906). painter.

Cf. (abbr.) confer, compare.

CFA. (abbr.) Colonies Francaises d'Afrique.

c-factor. In psychology, measurable zest, alertness, and energy computed by psychometric tests.

c.f.m. (abbr.) Cubic feet per minute.

c.f.s. (abbr.) cubic feet per second.

c.g. (abbr.) centigram.

c.-h. (abbr.) candle-hour.

ch. (abbr.) chapter.

Chad. Nation situated south of Libya. Formerly French. Officially Tchat. Native, Chadian(s), Tchadien(ne). Independent Nov. 28, 1958. Cap., Fort Lamy. Currency, CFAF franc.

chagrin [shuh-GRIHN; Brit., shuh-GREEN]. Mortification resulting from failure. —ined, —ining.

Chair, the. Capitalize if personified.

chairman. Used for either sex in U.S. Also chairwoman.

Chairman. of the Board of Directors; the Chairman (federal), BUT chairman of the board of directors; (non-Federal); Chairman of the Committee of the Whole House, the Chairman; Chairman of the Federal Trade Commission, the Chairman; Chairman of the Loyalty Board, the Chairman; BUT chairman of the Appropriations Committee, chairman of the committee, the chairman.

Chaldea [kal-DEE-ah]. Ancient nation on Euphrates River, Persian Gulf, now Iraq, Iran. Native, Chaldean [kal-DEE-an]. Cap., Bit Yaki. Prominent in history 811–681 B.C.

chalet [sha-LAE]. House built on style of Swiss herdsman's mountain cottage.

chambermaid. —woman.

chamber of commerce. the Chamber of Commerce of Boston; Boston Chamber of Commerce, the chamber; the Chamber of Commerce of the United States, U.S. Chamber of Commerce.

chameleon [kuh-MEE-lee-uhn, kuh-MEEL-yuhn]. Also cameleon. Lizard that can change color. Fig., *a fickle person.*

chamois [SHAM-mih]. (Sing. and pl.). Soft leather. The antelope [SHAM-mih or sham-WAH].

champion [CHAM-pih-uhn; NOT cham-PEEN].

Champs-Élysées [shah'n-zae-lee-ZAE]. Boulevard in Paris.

chance. —cy, —d, —cing.

chancellery [CHAN-seh-lehr-ih]. Position, court, or department of a chancellor.

chancery [CHAN-suhr-ih]. U.S., a court of equity; a court of record or office of public records.

Chanel [shah-NEHL]. French couturier.

change. —eable.

change·house. —over (n. and adj.).

changeling. Child left in place of another, especially by fairies. One who changes from animal to human or vice versa.

the Channel (English Channel). channel 3 (TV); the channel; channeled, —ing.

chantey, chanty [SHAN-tih]. From French *chantez*. Sailors' song.

chaos [KAE-ahss]. Complete disorder. *Complete chaos* is redundant.

chapbook. —fallen.

chaparral [shahp-uh-RAL]. Thicket of thorny shrubs.

Chapei [CHAH-bae or JAH/bee]. Suburb of Shanghai, China.

chapel·going. —man.

chaperon, —one [SHAP-uhr-ohn]. Person who accompanies unmarried women. chaperonage.

character . AVOID use as quality, kind or sort. NOT: *He carries antiques of the highest character.*

characters in books, plays, etc. Capitalize names. Do not place in quotation marks. She played the role of Cleopatra.

chapter. chapter III; BUT (title) *Chapter 5: Research and Development.*

charade [shuh-RAED]. Brit. [shuh-RAHD]. Guessing game in which words or syllables are acted out.

charcoal. charcoaled, charcoaling. charpit, charwoman.

charge. *The store is in his charge* implies responsibility. *He is in charge of the store* implies authority.

charge·man. —off (n. and adj.), —out (m. and adj.), charge book.

chargé d'affaires [SHAHR-ZHAY-duh-FAER]. Substitute for an ambassador. Pl., charges d'affaires; British, *Charge d'Affaires*, the Charge d'Affaires, the Charge.

charivari [shah-ree-VAH-ree; also U.S., sha-rihv-uh-REE, shohv-uh-ree]. Traditional mock serenade of a bridal couple.

charlatan [SHAHR-luh-tan]. Quack; pretentious imposter.

Charlemagne [SHAR-leh-maen]. (742–814). Also Charles I, Charles the Great. King of the Franks, Emperor of Europe.

Charles the First, Charles I.

charley horse.

Charlotte Amalie [uh-MAHL-yuh]. Capital of St. Thomas, Virgin Islands.

chart·house. —room.

chart 2, A, II. BUT Chart 2, when part of legend: *Chart 2, Army strength.*

Charter. Capitalize with name; Atlantic Charter, United Nations Charter; the charters.

chassis [SHASS-ee]. Body or framework of a vehicle (or instrument). Pl. chassis [SHASS-ihs].

chasten [CHAES'n]. Punish; discipline; purify.

chastise [CHAS-tiez]. Punish or discipline by whipping.

château [sha-TOH]. Large country house. Pl. -teaux or —s. Circumflex is omitted with —s plural and often in sing. in U.S.

chatter·box. —mark.

chauffeur [shoh-FEUR in U.S.; SHOH-fuhr in Brit.].

Chautauqua [shuh-TAW-kwah]. Summer educational center, N.Y. Hence (often lower-case), a type of educational assembly combining lectures, entertainment, and outdoor activities.

Chavez, Dennis [SHAH-vehs]. (1888–1962) Senator from New Mexico (1935–1962).

chauvinism [SHOH-vihn-ihzm]. —ist, —istically, —istic. Exaggerated patriotism.

JINGOISM [JIHNG-goh-ihzm]. Bellicose policy in foreign affairs.

cheapskate.

check (U.S.) Bank draft, Brit., cheque.

CHECK. Hold back. (U.S. and Brit.)

checkerboard. —breast (bird), —wise, —work; checker-in, checker-off, checker-out, checker-up.

Cheddar [CHEHD-ehr]. A smooth cheese.

cheekbone. —piece, —strap.

cheerful. Applies principally to feelings.

CHEERY. Applies to appearance. *He took his losses cheerfully. His wife looked cheery enough.*

cheerleader.

cheese. Camembert, Cheddar, Roquefort, etc.

Cheka. SEE MVD.

Chelsea [CHEHL-sih]. Town in Massachusetts. Borough of London. Section of N.Y.C.

CHEMICAL FORMULAS. Use full size figures before the symbols or group of symbols to which they relate and inferior figures after the symbols. *6 Ph S. (Ag. Cu)$_2$ S. AS$_2$ S$_2$.* Lower-case the names of elements and formulas. *strontium 90, oxygen.* Do not use a hyphen, even in a unit modifier. *uranium 235; freon 12;* BUT *U^{235}; Sr^{90}; $_{92}$U^{234}.*

Chennault, Claire Lee [sheh-NAWLT, klayr]. (1890–1958) American Air Force general; commander of the Flying Tigers in China and Burma.

Cheops (Gr.) **or Khufu** (Egypt) [KEE-ahps, KOO-foo]. (c, 2900) King of Egypt, pyramid-builder.

Cherbourg [SHAIR-boorg; Fr., -boor]. Port in Northwest France.

cherry-colored. (adj.) cherry pie, cherry pit, cherry stone (literal), cherry wine.

Cherokee [chehr-oh-KEE or CHEHR –]. Iroquoian Indian tribe in Oklahoma.

cherubic [chehr-OOB-ihk].

chess. Lower-case chess terms, unless the term includes a proper name, *queen's gambit, Philidor's defense.*

CHESS. board, —man.

chesterfield. The overcoat.

chestnut-colored. (adj.) chestnut-red (adj.).

Chevalier, Maurice [chuh-val-YAE, moh-REES]. (1888–1972). French actor, singer.

chevy [CHEV-ih]. A hunt.

Cheyenne [shie-EHN, or ANN]. City in Wyoming; also river in South Dakota.

Chiang Kai-shek [jee-AHNG kie-SHEK]. (1886–). Chinese statesman, general; president National China, 1943–1949, 1950– .

Chianti [kih-YAN-tih]. Italian dry red wine.

Chianti Mts [KYAHN-tee]. Mountains in Italy.

chiaroscuro [kih-ah-roh-SKYOO-roh]. Form of drawing or painting using only light and shade; arrangement of light and dark parts. – scurist.

chic [SHEEK]. Stylish.

Chicago [shih-KAH-goh]. City in Illinois.

Chicago Great Western Railway. the Great Western.

Chicano. SEE Mexico.

chicanery [shih-KAEN-uhr-ee]. Trickery.

chicken pox. A plural form which takes a singular verb.

chide. P., chided or chid; —iding.

Chief. Capitalize if referring to head of a federal agency, the Chief Forester, Chief Intelligence office, Chief Justice (U.S. Supreme Court); BUT chief justice (of a state), Chief Division of Publications, Chief of Staff, Chief of Naval Operations.

Chief Clerk. Capitalize if referring to head of federal unit.

chiefest. Used only ornamentally.

Chief Justice of the United States. NOT Chief Justice of the Supreme Court of the United States.

chief-justiceship. chief justice, chief mate.

chiffon [SHIHF-ahn, shih-FAHN]. A sheer fabric.

chiffonier [shihf-oh-NEER]. High chest of drawers.

Chihuahua, Mex. [chee-WAH-wah]. Largest cattle state.

childish. Like a child; disparagingly, unless of a child. Silly, immature: *Childish actions.*
CHILDLIKE. Implies good qualities. Innocent, sweet, confiding: *Childlike trust.*

Chile. Native, (adj.), Chilean. Cap., Santiago. Currency, peso ($); centavo.

chili [CHIHL-ih]. Pepper. Pl. -ies. (U.S.) from Spanish: *chile con carne,* peppers with meat.

chilli. (Brit.) From Mexico. Dried pod of red pepper.

chill-room. chill-cast (adj. and v.).

chimera. [kih-MEE-ruh or kie-MEE-ruh]. Foolish fancy; from mythological she-goat monster. chimerical [kiem-MEHR-ih-kal].

chimney [CHIHM-nih].

chimpanzee [chim-pan-ZEE].

China. Native, Chinese; adj. , Chinese. China-man is a demeaning term. Chinese may be used for singular or plural noun, is always used for large numbers, the whole nation, and the feminine.

MAINLAND CHINA. Peoples' Republic of China. Cap., Peking. Founded Sept. 21, 1949.

REPUBLIC OF CHINA. On Taiwan (Formosa). Cap., T'ai pei, angl. Taipei. China, (adj.) Chinese. Currency, New Taiwan Yuan. (NR$).

Chinatown. china-ware; china-blue (adj.); china bark, china shop.

chindit. Allied jungle fighters in Burma, 1943; from native word for mythological griffin-lion.

Chinese Names. SEE Names.

Chinese Red. The color.

chip-board. —munk; chip shot.

Chippewa [CHIHP-eh-wuh]. Indian tribe. River rising in Wisconsin.

chiropodist [kie-RAHP-oh-dihst]. Foot doctor.

chisel. -led, -ing. But Brit. *ll.* Slang, to bargain; to cheat in a small way.

chitchat. Small talk. N.Y. Times, chit-chat.

chitter-chatter.

Chiusi [KYOO-see]. Town in Italy.

chivalry [SHIHV-al-ree]. Dignity, spirit, or manner of knighthood.
CHIVALRIC [SHIHV-al-rihk]. Implies medieval; is emotionally neutral.
CHIVALROUS [- - ruhs]. Implies gallant, generous, etc.

chloride [KLOH-ried].

chlorine [KLOH-reen].

chlorophyll.

cho. 0.4506 acres. (Jap.)

Choate School [CHOHT].

chockablock. chock-full (adj.).

chocolate [CHAHK-oh-liht].

choirboy. —man. —wise; choir master, choir school.

Choiseul [shwah-zuhl]. Island in Solomon Islands.

chol, chole, cholo. Combining forms meaning bile; *cholecystectomy, choledology.*

cholera [KAHL-eh-ruh]. A disease.

   CHOLERIC [KAHL-ehr-ihk]. Quick tempered; enraged.

Cholmondeley [CHUHM-lee]. Village and parish in England.

choose. P., chose; p.p., chosen; choosing.

chophouse. —stick; chop-chop; chop suey.

Chopin, Frederic [shoh-PAN]. (1810–1849) Polish pianist-composer.

chops, chaps. Jaws. Lick one's chops is the preferred form.

chord. String of a musical instrument; hence an emotion: *touch the right chord* (of emotion). Also, straight line intersecting a curve; *chord of an arc.*

   CORD. Rope, string, ribbed cloth; measure of wood (128 cu. ft.), vocal cords, spinal cord.

chore [CHAWR]. Small or odd job. In Brit., chare [CHAHR].

Chou-En-lai [JOH-ehn-lie]. (1898–   ). Chinese Foreign minister, prime minister, (Mainland) Chinese Peoples Republic.

chorus [KAWR-uhs].

chowchow. chow mein. BUT N.Y. Times, chow-chow, the dog.

Christian. Christian name, etc.; Christendom; Christianity; Christianize; BUT christen (v).

Christian Era. Middle Ages; 20th century.

Christian name. Use first or given name (in baptism).

Christian Science. Church of Christ Scientist is the organization; the Mother Church, in Boston, is the principal church. Members are practitioners, lecturers, or readers, but are never referred to as *reverend.* Capitalize titles before a name: *Reader Sam Jones,* BUT *Sam Jones, reader.*

Christmas. Xmas is an old abbreviation, from χ (Chi), the Greek initial of Christ.

chronic, -ically. Of long standing; NOT bad or intense.

chronological. Preferred to —*ic.*

chrysalis. Pl. —ises.

chunkhead.

Church. Capitalize if part of name of organization or building: *the Catholic Church; Christ Church; the church.*

church and state. Lower-case.

church calendar. Capitalize Christmas, Easter, Lent, Whitsuntide (Pentecost).

Churchill, Winston Leonard Spencer [CHUHRCH-ihl]. (1874–1965) British prime minister 1940–1945, 1951–1955.

churnmilk. churn-butted (adj.).

CIA. (abbr.) Central Intelligence Agency. N.Y. Times, C.I.A.

ciao [chahoh]. Italian (colloquial) for hello, so long.

-ciation. Words which add *shuhn* should pronounce *ci* as *si: pronunciation, emaciation, denunciation.*

cicatrix. [SIK-uh-trihks]. Pl. -trices.

Cid [the sihd]. (1040–1099). Title given to Rodrigo Diaz de Bivar, Spanish hero.

cider-maker. —making.

c.i.f. (abbr.) cost, insurance, and freight. When added to a quotation, indicates that these items are included in price.

   C.I.F.C. cost, insurance, freight, and charges or commission.

   C.I.F.E. cost, insurance, freight and exchange.

   C.I.F.I. cost, insurance, freight and interest.

cigarette [sihg-uh-REHT, SIHG-uh-reht]. Preferred to *cigaret.*

cigarette-making. (adj.) cigarette case, cigarette holder, cigarette maker, cigarette paper.

cigars. belvedere (short corona); cheroot (blunt, long and narrow); cigarillo (cigarette sized); corona (long, blunt, round ended); Havana (of Cuban tobacco); panatela (thin, tapering, short); perfecto (long with narrow pointed ends); stogie (cheap, thin).

Cimabue, Giovanni [chee-mah-BOO-ae, joh-vahn-nee]. Real name Cenni di Pepo. Florentine painter (c. 1240—c. 1302).

Cincinnati [sihn-sih-NAT-eh; or -ih]. City in Ohio.

cinema [SIHN-ehmah]. British for motion pictures.

Cingalese. SEE Ceylon.

cinquecento [chihnk-wee CHEHN-toh]. 1500's. 16th century in Italian art. *Cf.* trecento.

cinquefoil [SIHNCK-voil]. Preferred to *cingfoil*. Five-leaved rose plant or similar design.

Cinzano [chéen-ZAHN-oh]. Italian apératif.

cion [SIE-uhn]. Scion is preferred in horticulture. Detached part of plant suitable for propagation.

cipher [SIE-fehr]. Preferred to *cypher*. Secret writings using disarranged letters. Also a number, a symbol for naught.

DIGIT. A number from 0 to 9.

code. Use of substituted words or groups of letters.

circa. (abbr. ca., c., circ.). With dates, about; *c. 1900; circ. 1622.* NOT *circa the 19th century.*

Circe [SUHR-sih]. In the Odyssey, Island sorceress who turned men into beasts.

Circle. Capitalize if part of name; *Arctic Circle, Logan Circle; the circle.* BUT *great circle.*

circuitman. circuit breaker, circuit rider.

circuitous [suhr-KYOO-ih-tuhs]. Roundabout.

Circular. Capitalize if part of a title; *Circular 420; the circular.*

circumcise.

circumference of a circle. $= \pi r^2$.

circumlocutional. —nary, —utory are awkward. *Periphrastic* is suggested.

circumstance [SEHR-kuhm-stanss]. An accompanying condition or event. Pl. circumstances; *Under the circumstances.*

cirrus. Pl. cirri., adj. cirrose (for the curl), cirrous (clouds).

citable. Preferred to *citeable.*

cite. (v.) Quote. (n.) citation.

SIGHT. (n.) Vision

SITE. (n.) Location.

Cities, Sections of. Capitalize official or popular names; East Side, Latin Quarter, the Loop, North End, Northwest Washington, etc. BUT northwest (directional).

Citroen [SIH-troh-EHN]. French automobile.

City. Capitalize if part of corporate or popular name; Kansas City; the two Kansas Cities, Mexico City, Twin Cities; Washington City, but city of Washington; Windy City BUT Reserve City, the city, the city government. Capitalize when used with an official title; the City Court, City Controller Abraham Beame. The City (London financial district), the City of New York.

city editor. U.S. editor who assigns reporters and controls editing of local news; Brit., financial editor.

Ciudad Trujillo [see-oo-DAHD troo-HEE-yoh]. Capital city of Dominican Republic. Until 1936, and after 1961, Santo Domingo.

Civil Air Patrol.

Civil Service. Capitalize only when word "Commission" follows or is implied; *the Civil Service has ruled,* BUT *civil service employee, examination, etc.*

Civil War.

C.J. (abbr.) corpus juris, body of law; Chief Justice.

cl. (abbr.) centiliter.

clambake. —cracker (fish), —shell, —worm.

clamor. Preferred to *clamour* in U.S. —ous.

clampdown. (n. and adj.).

Clan. Capitalize if part of tribal name; the clan.

clandestine [klan-DEHS-tihn].

clangor. Brit. clangour. Both, clangorous.

clansman. —woman.

clapboard. —net, —trap.

claque [klak]. Paid applauders.

clarify. Clear up, NOT answer, unless the question is obscure. NOT; *He addressed the group to clarify questions raised.*

clarinet. Preferred to *clarionet.*

class I, class 2, A, II. But Class 2 when part of title; *Class 2: Leather Products.*

class book. —man, —mate, —room, —work; class-conscious (adj.); class consciousness, class day.

classic. Preferred in ornate context and in conveying emotional admiration, especially meaning first rank art or literature, or the methods used by Greeks and Romans.

    CLASSICAL. Generally preferred and required in contrast with *romantic*, in reference to studies and teaching methods, and in reference to the school of composers.

CLASSIFICATION OF ANIMALS AND PLANTS. Kingdom, animal; phylum, pl. phyla; *chordata;* sub-phylum, *vertebrata;* class, *mammalia;* sub-class, *theri;* infra-class, *eutheria;* order, *Primates;* sub-order, *Simiae* or *Anthopoidea;* infra-order, *Hominoidea;* family, *Hominidae* (adj. *hominid*)*;* genus, pl. genera, *Homo;* species, pl. species, *sapiens,* Capitalize the Latin scientific names of orders, families, and genera BUT NOT English derivatives and NOT names of species. In printed matter, italicize the names of genus and species used either separately or together: *Homo sapiens.*

CLASSIFICATION OF GEOLOGICAL AND PALEONTOLOGICAL GROUPS. Capitalize Latin scientific names of divisions.

classified information. U.S. government information for restricted circulation.

clastic. Capable of being taken apart.

CLAUSE. A group of related words containing subject and predicate. An independent, principal, or main clause can stand alone as a complete sentence; a dependent clause cannot. A dependent or subordinate clause depends upon a word or words in the independent clause to complete its meaning.

Clausewitz, Karl von. [KLOU-zeh-vihts, kahrl fawn]. (1780–1831). Prussian military scientist and general.

claustrophobia [klaws-troh-FOH-bih-uh]. SEE —phobia.

clean, cleanness.

cleanly [KLEHN-lee]. (adj.) Habitually clean, not necessarily clean at the moment. Thus *cleanliness,* quality of being cleanly.

    CLEANLY [KLEEN-lee]. In a clean manner; *He cut out the picture cleanly.*

clearly [KLEER-lee].

cleave. Split. p., clove, cleft, or cleaved; pp., cloven, cleft, or cleaved. Split apart. *Cleft palate, cloven hoof, a cleft stick.* By extension, position where retreat or advance are both impossible.

    CLEAVE. Adhere. P. and p.p., cleaved. (Note opposite meanings.)

clematis [KLEHM-at-ihs]. Vine of the crowfoot family.

Clemenceau, Georges [klae-mahn-SOH, zhuwrzh]. (1841–1929) Fr. prime minister (1917–1919).

clench. Applies to parts of body, e.g., jaws, nails, etc.

    CLINCH. Applies to a sale, an argument. Fasten as with nails. *Clinch a bolt.*

Cleopatra [klee-oh-PAT (or PAET or PAHT)-ruh]. (69–30 B.C.) Egyptian queen.

Clergymen. The titles of clergymen vary among the faiths. Accepted forms are; Anglican, priest; Bahai, chairman of the assembly; Baptist, pastor and minister; Christian Science, reader; Congregationalist, minister; Eastern Orthodox, rector; Episcopalian, rector, if of the chief church of the parish; if not chief official, vicar [VIH-kuhr]; but all other clergymen are priests after serving six months as a deacon; Evangelical, pastor; Greek Orthodox, pastor; Jehovah's Witnesses, minister; Jewish, rabbi; Lutheran, pastor (applied to all clergymen); Methodist, minister; Muslim, mulla or mullah; Presbyterian, pastor (others are minister); Reformed, pastor; Roman Catholic, pastor, priest; Seventh Day Adventist, pastor; Unitarian, minister.

The title Father is used by Roman Catholics and most Episcopalians in addressing their clergymen. Roman Catholics ADDRESS; The Reverend Joseph B. Hunter, Dear Father Hunter or Dear Father; refer to Father Hunter. Episcopalians ADDRESS; The Reverend Father Johnson, O.H.C. (without a Christian name), and refer to Father Johnson. Some orders use the title Father and address Father John, The Reverend Father John, C.S.F. Lay brothers may be addressed Brother Thomas, O.H.C. For forms of address of other clergymen, Cf. minister and each of the titles. ADDRESS; The Reverend Samuel Brown or The Reverend and Mrs. Samuel Brown or (if a doctor of divinity) The Reverend Dr. Samuel Brown; The Reverend Dr. Brown. SALUTATION; Dear Sir; Reverend Sir, Dear Mr. Brown, Dear Dr. Brown. Never "Reverend" or address as "Reverend Brown". Cf. Minister, Rabbi. In conversation, address as mister or doctor.

clergyman. —woman.

clerk [klehrk, Brit., klahrk].

Clerk, the, of the House of Representatives. of the Supreme Court of the United States.

clew, clue. A ball of thread or cord. Nautical, lower corner of a sail. Hint, suggestion, piece of evidence. (v.) To make or provide these.

cliché [klee-shae].

clientele [klee-ahn-TEHL; klie-en-TEHL]. A body of customers or clients.

cliffsman.

climacteric [klie-MAK-tehr-ihk or TEHR]. A critical period of change, especially menopause.

CLIMACTIC. Refers to a climax.

CLIMATIC. Refers to climate.

CLIMACTIC ORDER. Arrangement of ideas in rising order of importance. *She distributed pennies, nickels, and dimes.*

CLIMAX. (v.) Arrange in ascending order.

climb down. This use is acceptable.

clime. Poetical version of climate, but applied only to a region.

clinchwork. clinch-built (adj.).

cling. P. and p.p., clung; clinging.

clink-stone. clink-clank.

clip-board.

clipper. Preferred to clippers for one pair.

clique [kleek]. -quy or -quey. Derogatory for a small, exclusive group.

cloak-maker. —making, —room.

cloak-and-dagger. (n. and adj.).

clockwise. counter-clockwise.

close-connected. (adj.) close-out (adj.), close-fertilize (v.).

close . Block an opening.

SHUT. Close so as to bar going in or out.

closed-circuit. (adj.) closed end, closed shop.

close to. AVOID use in the sense of ALMOST. NOT: Close to 5,000 attended the meeting.

close proximity is a tautology.

closure [KLOH-zhuhr]. Brit., provision for limiting debate in Parliament. In U.S. Senate, CLOTURE. N.Y. Times follows British style.

clothe [klothe]. p. and p.p., clothed, also clad; clothing.

CLOTHES [klohz]. May be singular or plural in meaning, but takes a plural verb.

clothes closet.

clothes tree.

cloud burst.

club foot.

clue. SEE clew.

cm. (abbr.) centimeter.

c.m. (abbr.) circular mil (wire measure).

cm.² (abbr.) square centimeter.

cm.³ (abbr.) cubic centimeter. cc. is preferred.

C.O. commanding officer.

Co. company. Pl. Cos.

co-. Combining form meaning with; *coacervate, coadventure.* Use hyphenated form (1) to distinguish from other words; *co-respondent, correspondent;* (2) to safeguard against mispronunciation; *co-worker;* (3) in made words; *co-partnership;* (4) Webster hyphenates *co-o* words and some dictionaries distinguish by use of diaeresis (..) *coordinate, coördinate.*

coagulate [coh-AG-yoo-laet]. Clot, congeal; solidify.

coal sizes. pea, barley, buckwheat, stove, etc.

coalesce. Grow together. —escing.

coarse. Not fine.
COURSE. Direction of movement; path.

coast. Atlantic, east, gulf, west, etc. West Coast, the region.

Coastal Plain. (Atlantic and Gulf).

Coast Guard, U.S. the Coast Guard, Coastguardsman Smith; BUT a coastguardsman; a guardsman.

coast land.

coat of arms. Pl. coats—.

coauthor. codefendant, coed, coeducational, cooperate, coordinate, co-owner, co-partner, copilot, co-star.

cobalt bomb. Atomic bomb containing cobalt, designed to produce large contaminated radioactive area.

cobblestone.

COBOL. Common Business Oriented Language, for computers.

cocaine [koh-KAEN]. Narcotic drug.

coccus [KAHK-uhs]. Spherical bacterium. Pl., cocci [KAHK-sie].

CoCCYX. End of the vertebral column.

Cochin [KOH-chihn]. Former state in southwest India.

Cochin China [KOH-chihn or KAHCH-ihn CHIE-nuh]. Region in South Vietnam.

cock. Male of a bird.
ROOSTER. In U.S., male of domestic chicken. *Cf.* animals.

cockleboat.

cockscomb. First comb of a rooster.
COCKSCOMB, COXCOMB. Colorful plant of amaranth family.
COXCOMB. Red cloth strips worn by a jester; by ext., a fop.

cocksure. Brit., cock-sure.

cocoa [KOH-KOH]. Drink, bean, or powder from which made.
COCONUT. Preferred to *cocoanut.*
COCO FIBRE.

c.o.d. (abbr.) cash on delivery.

Code. Capitalize in shortened title of a publication; the code: District Code, Federal Criminal Code, Internal Revenue Code, Penal Code, Criminal Code, etc. Pennsylvania State Code, Uniform Code of Military Justice, United States; BUT civil code; flag code; Morse code.

code. SEE cipher.

codebook.

codex. Manuscript book. Pl., codices.

codicil [KAHD-ih-sihl]. An addition to a will.

coelacanth [SEE-luh-canth]. 350 million-year-old fish believed extinct (*Latimeria Chaluminae*), found surviving in 1934 off African coast.

coerce, coercible.

coffee [KAHF-ee].

coffee cake.

coffer. Box for storage of valuables.

COFFIN. (NOT casket) The box containing the corpse.

coffin-maker. —making; coffin-headed (adj.); coffin bone.

cogitate. cogitable.

cognac [KOHN-yak]. Brandy from the white wine of Charente district of France.

cognate. Having common blood. In grammar, having the same origin; e.g., Spanish and French are cognate languages.

cognizance [kahg-nih-sans]. Apprehension; heed; notice. -zant, -zable. [kah- niez-abl, or KAHG-nihz-abl].

COGNOSCIBLE [kahg-NAHS-ih-bl]. Knowable; (n.) a knowable thing.

COGNIZE [KAHG-niez]. Know; recognize.

cognomen [kahg-NOH-m'n]. Family name (originally a third name). Sometimes a nickname, a first name.

cog-way. —wheel.

coiffeur, -feuse [kwah-feur; -fyoos]. Hair dresser.

COIFFURE [KWAH-fyoor]. Hairdo.

COIN. (abbr.) Air Force counter-insurgency (guerrilla) forces. *Cf.* Seal.

coin-box. —holder, —maker, —making; coin-operated (adj.); coin silver.

coincide [koh-ihn-SIED]. Occupy the same place or time; agree exactly.

co-insurance clause. Provision in an insurance policy limiting liability of the insurer to "no greater proportion of any loss than the amount insured bears to the percentage specified of the actual cash value of the property described at the time when such loss shall happen."

Col. (abbr.) colonel, used with name.

col. (abbr.) column.

colander [KUHL-ehn-dahr; KAHL —]. Bowl-shaped sieve. Preferred to *cullender.*

Coleridge, Samuel Taylor [KOHL-rihj]. (1772–1834) English poet.

cole-seed. —slaw.

coliseum [kahl-ih-SEE-uhm]. Any large structure for entertainments or sporting events. BUT the Colosseum, Rome.

collaborate together is a tautology.

collage [kahl-lazh]. Miscellaneous materials assembled into an artistic composition.

collation [kahl-LAE-shuhn, koh-]. Formal term for light repast or refreshments. Also, gathering together.

collected together is a tautology.

collectible. Preferred to —*able* in U.S.

collection. Brady collection, etc.; the collection.

collective bargaining talks.

COLLECTIVE NOUNS. By extension a group of people or things (mass nouns), usually expressed in a singular form, whose number is not clear, may be treated as singular or plural according to the sense intended. *The Committee approves the bill. The membership are active in many sports. My family are all sick.* Some collectives are always treated as singular: *apparatus, news, summons, whereabouts.* Some collectives are always treated as plural: *assets, earnings, means* (income), *odds, premises, proceeds, quarters, savings, wages, winnings.* Some are treated as either singular or plural, according to the meaning: *ethics, goods, gross, headquarters, mechanics, politics, series, species, statistics, tactics. Ethics is taught in high school. His ethics are above reproach. Misfortunes follow them in their travels.* Types of words treated as collectives include: (1) Certain pronouns: *all, any, many, more, most, none, some, who, which: All the books are here. All the glue is here.* (2) Units of measure: *Six months have passed. Six months is a short time to wait.* (3) Group nouns: *committee, people.* (4) Company names: The sound may determine whether a singular or plural verb is to be used: a name ending in *company* or *corporation* usually takes a singular verb (5) Abstract collectives: Use singular form for reference to qualities, emotions, feelings, or actions of a group: *Love is here to stay.* Use plural form when there is no generalization. *His loves are legion.* (6) Nouns that have the same form in singular and plural: *deer, sheep.* (7) Nouns which use singular forms to denote the plural: *fish, duck, cannon.* (8) Abstract singulars used for concrete plurals: *nobility*. (9) Nouns which derive from the material content: *straw, fur, linen, silver, glass, china*. (10) Nouns which may mean all or one of a thing: *timber, cheese;* (11) Nouns of indefinite quantity: *butter, wine;* (12) Nouns which have a plural but which are used in the singular as collectives: *shot*. (13) Nouns of quantity: *pair, fathom*. (14) Nouns of multitude: *cattle, shot*. (15) Animal collectives: *flock of sheep, pride of lions, skulk of foxes, gaggle of geese. Cf.* Animals.

College. Capitalize if part of name; the college: Armed Forces Staff, Command and General Staff, National War, of Bishops; BUT electoral college.

College Degrees. bachelor of arts, master of arts, etc.

collegian [KAHL-LEE-jih-an]. college student.

collision. Meeting of two moving bodies.

colloquial. (abbr. colloq.) Applied to words used in informal speech but not suitable for formal writing.

colloquy [KAHL-oh-kwih]. Mutual discourse.

Colo. (abbr.) Colorado.

Cologne [koh-LOHN]. Koln; Coln [kuhln]. City on Rhine River, West Germany.

Colombia. Native, Colombian(s); adj., Colombian. Cap., Bogota [boh-goh-TAH]. Currency, peso (Col$), centavo (Ctvo.).

Colombo. Capital of Ceylon.

COLON. Is used: (1) after a formal introduction; (2) before a quotation or example; (3) after the salutation of a letter: *Gentlemen:*; (4) to separate two main clauses in a sentence, especially when they are not joined by a conjunction or are in antithesis: *I sow: he reaps;* (5) before a final summary in a sentence: *Flying is not dangerous: it is merely untried;* (6) to introduce material that follows, in effect often replacing *as follows, that is,* or *for example: He mentioned the following passages: Section 317, p. 17; Section 819, p. 141; and Section 320, p. 6;* (7) in indicating time, between the hour and the minute: *2:30 P.M.;* (8) in citations of volume and page numbers, or chapter and verse numbers: *Exodus 6:9.*

DO NOT use a colon between a verb or preposition and its objects, NOT: *He gave books to: Tom, Dick and Harry;* or *His friends are: Mary, Jane, Alison, and Sally.*

Usually capitalize the letter following a colon but not an explanatory element following; *He has three attractive qualities: physique, intelligence, and money.*

Colonials. (American Colonial Army) BUT colonial times, etc.

Colonies, the. the Thirteen Colonies, Thirteen American Colonies, Thirteen Original Colonies. BUT: 13 separate Colonies.

colonists, the.

colonnade.

Colony. Crown Colony of Hong Kong; the colony, crown colony.

color. The quality of visible phenomena such as "red of blood", made up of three elements:

HUE. Quality which distinguishes one color from another, e.g. red, yellow, green.

BRILLIANCE. Value or measure of lightness or darkness of a color, on the scale O is black; as maroon to pink in reds.

SATURATION. Measure of vividness of a color, e.g. a greyish or watery red compared with a carmine.

color. -rable, -rist. Brit., colour, -ourable, -ourist.

COLORATION. Blueish green, blueish-green feathers; iron gray, iron-gray hair; etc.

color-bearer. -blind, (N.Y. Times, color-blind), -fast, -maker, -making, -man, -type (printing) (n.); color-free (adj.), color-washed (adj.); color blindness, color guard, color line.

Colorado. (Colo.) Coloradan. Cap., Denver.

colored. in U.S., Negro or other non-white. In South Africa, one of mixed blood; a colored. Current usage prefers "Black."

colossal [koh-lahs-'l].

COLOSSUS. Pl. —ssuses or —ssi.

colt [kohlt]. See foal.

column [KAHL-hum]. columnist, [KAHL-um-nihst] (v.), (a slight Y sound is usual).

column 2.

column inch. Unit of advertising, 1 column wide, 1 in. deep.

comatose [KAHM-uh-tohs, KOHM—]. (adj.); as in a coma.

comb holder. -maker, -making; comb-toothed (adj.); comb brush, comb case.

combat. -ed, -bating; combatant [KAHM-buh-tht].

combine [kahm-BIEN]. (v.), [KAHM-bien] (n.), *Combined together* in a tautology.

combustible.

Comdr. (abbr.) commander.

come. P., came; p.p., come; coming.

Comecon. Council for Mutual Economic Assistance. Composed of U.S.S.R., Poland, Czechoslovakia, Hungary, Rumania, Bulgaria, East Germany, Outer Mongolia, and nominally, Albania.

comely [KUHM-lih]. Of pleasing appearance.

comedian [kom-EE-diehn]. Fem., —ienne.

Comedie Francaise.

come-on. Pl. come-ons.

comestible. Food. Pl. -s.

comforter. U.S., a quilted bedcover; Brit., a woolen scarf.

comic. Pertains to comedy.

comical. Causing laughter.

comic book, comic opera.

Cominform. Comintern.

comings-in. (Pl.)

comity [KAHM-i-tih]. Courtesy. *Comity of nations.* Courtesy and respect for one another's laws and institutions among civilized states.

COMMA, THE. Is used: (1) To indicate that a word or phrase has been omitted; *To err is human, to forgive, divine.* (2) When two or more qualifying words modify the same word without a conjunction between them;

her small, red hat. But when the first adjective modifies the combination of second adjective plus noun, no comma is used. The rule-of-thumb test is; Could you comfortably put *and* between the adjectives? If you could, a comma belongs there; (3) After a subordinate clause at the beginning of a sentence, especially between introductory modifying phrase and subject modified: *The sun shone all day, drying all the puddles.* (4) Before the conjunction in a compound sentence if the second clause is complete with subject and predicate. (5) To separate an introductory phrase from a question. The test is: Will the sentence retain its sense if the introductory phrase is omitted? (6) To set off incidental or parenthetic words, phrases, or clauses: *Mr. Kennedy, then Senator from Massachusetts, repudiated the statement.* BUT a phrase or clause that restricts or limits the meaning of a word is not set off by commas: *The man standing beside her is her husband.* (7) To set off words in apposition or explanation when they are not restrictive: *Sam, the butler, opened the door.* But when the word in apposition restricts or limits the subject, do not use commas: *The renowned scientist Einstein developed the formula $e = mc^2$.* (There are other scientists.) BUT: *My wife, Sylvia, is here.* (I have only one wife.) (8) Following an introductory phrase before a direct quotation: *He said, "Now is the time."* BUT when the quotation is the subject or object of the sentence, so that the part of the sentence that is not quoted serves as more than a mere introduction, a comma is not used: *Don't say "Yes."* (9) To separate two words or figures that might otherwise be misunderstood; *September 17, 1945.* (10) Before Jr., Sr., Esq. Ph.D., M.D., etc.; *Tom Brown, Jr.* BUT: John Smith II (or 2nd), (11) After each member of a series of three or more words, phrases, letters, or figures when *and, or,* or *nor* precedes only the last. (Many authorities omit the last comma before the conjunction.) *The flag is red, white, and blue.* BUT usually; *She was four years one month and three days old.* (12) After a noun or noun phrase in direct address: *Gentlemen, please be seated.* (13) Between the name and number of an organization. (14) Inside closing quotation marks when there is no question mark, exclamation mark, or dash, and the sentence continues: *She answered "No," and perhaps meant no.* BUT: *"Will you?" he demanded.* (15) In numbers of four or more digits: *7,267.* BUT SEE exceptions under (19) below. (16) In addresses, between the city and the state: *Teaneck, N.J. 07666.* (17)

After the year in complete dates within a sentence: *The Declaration of Independence, first read July 2, 1976, was applauded.*

The comma is NOT used: (18) Between months and year in dates: *December 1960; 5th of May 1916. June and December 1910.* (19) In built-up fractions, decimals, and serial numbers: *3.4196, Beekman 3–6018, 1630 Fifth Avenue, Motor No. 1013, 2800 meters (no comma unless more than four figures).* (20) Between superior figures or letters in footnote references; *Numerous instances may be cited.*[123] (21) Before ampersand: (&) *John, Jeffreys & Jones.* (22) To set off an adverb. NOT: *Suddenly, the appeared.* (23) Before and after Jr., Sr., Esq., Ph.D., etc., within a sentence except where possession is indicated. *John Smith, Jr., Chairman; Motorola, Inc., factory.*

Command. Capitalize with name: Air Materiel Command, GHQ Far East Command, Joint Far Eastern Command, Zone of Interior Command, the command.

commandant [KAHM-uhn-DANT].

commander-in-chief. Pl. commanders-in-chief.

commandos, the. Commando raid; a commando; a commandoman.

commence. Formal for begin, commencement. Graduation ceremony; *The 1963 Yale commencement.*

comment [KAHM-ehnt].

commingle [KUH-mihng-gl]. Mingle.

commiserate [KAHM-mihs-uhr-aet]. (v.) Show compassion.

Commission. Capitalize if part of name; capitalize standing alone if referring to federal or international commission: *Alaska Road Commission, Atomic Energy Commission, Civil Service Commission.*

committee.

Committee. Capitalize if part of name; if referring to an international or noncongressional federal committee; the Committee of One Hundred, the Committee; the committee on Finance, the committee; Committee Print No. 32; the committee print.

committeeman, committeewoman.

committable.

commodity.

common law. That body of law developed by custom and precedent.

Common Market. (European Economic Community) Also Common Market Treaty. *Cf.* European Economic Community.

COMMON NOUNS OR ADJECTIVES. In grammar, those which apply to one of a class or group; *boy, sample, door. Cf.* proper noun. A common noun used with a date, number, or letter, merely to denote time or sequence, or for the purpose of reference, record, or temporary convenience, does not form a proper name and is therefore not cap.

Commonwealth of Australia. of Massachusetts, etc.; British Commonwealth; the commonwealth.

communal [KAHM-yoo-nal, kuh-MYoo-nal].

Commune. (of Paris).

communicate [kuhm-yoo-nik-KAET]. A communique [kuh-myoo-nih-KAE].

Communist Party. Capitalize when referring to the political party, otherwise, lower-case.

Communist. (member of the party); communism; communist philosophy (preferred to *communistic*).

Comp. Dec. (abbr.) Comptroller's Decisions & Treasury.

Comp. Gen. (abbr.) Comptroller General General Decisions.

compact. U.S. marine fisheries compact, etc.; the compact.

compactible. Capable of being made compact.

companion ship. —way.

companionship. SEE acquaintanceship.

company. As a synonym for guests, has been used since 1579, but is still considered colloquial.

Company. (abbr. Co.) Capitalize if part of name; lower-case standing alone. *Procter & Gamble Co.; the company.* If a government agency, *Panama Railroad Company, the Company.*

company union. Union sponsored by the employer.

companywide.

comparable [KAHM-puhr-uh-b'l].

comparatively few. NOT *a comparatively few.*

compare with. When the objects are side by side to show their relative value; *compare to* when one is said to be like the other. *She compared John with Bill. She compared John to a horse and Bill to a mule. He compared himself with Shakespeare. He compared himself to Shakespeare.* The last sentence implies near-equality, i.e., conceit in this case. The previous one does not imply equality.

comparison : other, else. In a comparison, two elements must appear, and the item compared must be separated from the group. NOT; *He is better than any man.* BUT; *He is better than anyone else* (or *any other man*).

COMPARISON: adj. and adv. An adjective or adverb changes its form to express greater or lesser degrees. The forms are positive; *big;* comparative; *bigger;* and superlative; *biggest.* Most adjectives of three or more syllables and most adverbs use *more* and *most* or *less* and *least* to denote the comparative and superlative forms. Adding *er* or *est* to a word emphasizes the quality; using *more* or *most* emphasizes the comparison. A few modifiers have irregular comparisons, notably: *good, well, bad, badly, far, late, little, many, much* (which SEE).
More and *most* are the required forms for adverbs ending in *-ly,* for words which can be used predicatively, for unusual or foreign words, and for *eager. More* and *most* forms are preferred for long modifiers, for words of more than one stressed syllable, and for words ending in *-s, -ish, -est, -ive, -or, -ile, -ed,* or *-ing.* Absolute words (*perfect, unique, extreme, complete, equal, square, chaste, pregnant*) should not be compared. For comparisons of these qualities, use *more nearly perfect,* etc.

comparison shopper. Retail store employee who checks merchandise and prices at competing stores.

compass. SEE shears.

Compass Directions. N., NE., E., SW., S., NNW., W., ESE., 10°N. 25°W., NW. by N.; north, northerly, northern, northward, northeast, north, northeast, east Pennsylvania, eastern region, southern France; BUT West Germany, the East (region), West Coast. In description of a tract of land, omit periods: *lot 4, NE ¼ sec. 2 T 6N, R 1W. Cf.* points of the compass, latitude and longitude.

compatible. Capable of living together in harmony.

compendious. (adj.) Abridged. (n.) —dium, pl., —diums or —dia. Compendium is a brief, not an exhaustive compilation.

compensate [KAHM-pehn-saet]. compensatory [kahm-PEHN-suh-toh-ree].

competence. Preferred to *-cy.*

Compiegne [kawm-PYEHN-y]. Town on Oise River, France.

complacent. Self-satisfied, pleased. -cency.
COMPLAISANT [KAHM-plae-zants]. Willing to please; obliging.

complement. (v.) Complete. In grammar, a word or words which follow the verb and complete the meaning of the sentence. A complement may be a direct object, an indirect object, a predicate adjective, or a predicate nominative.
COMPLIMENT. Praise.
SUPPLEMENT. Something additional.

complete. NEVER more or most complete. BUT *most nearly complete.*

complete. Having attained the limit of its development.
ENTIRE. Continuous or unbroken.
WHOLE [hohl]. Undivided, unbroken; with all parts present.

COMPLEX SENTENCE. A sentence composed of one independent clause and one or more dependent clauses.

COMPLIMENTARY CLOSE. Formal business letters should close *Yours truly,* or *Very truly yours.*; more informal letters may close, *Sincerely yours, Very sincerely yours, Cordially yours, Very cordially yours.*
For social letters, wording of a formal closing is rigidly set by custom. *Sincerely, Sincerely yours, Very sincerely yours,* and *Very sincerely* are correct for formal social

letters. Informal letters permit greater flexibility, but letters from men are more formal than letters from women. In decreasing formality, accepted closings may be: *Yours cordially, Faithfully yours, As ever, Fondly, Yours affectionately, Lovingly yours, Devotedly.*

complexioned. Used in combinations: dark-complexioned. NOT dark-complected (dial.).

comply with. NOT -to.

composition. (1) In printing, the setting of type; (2) in law, agreement between debtor and group of creditors for partial payments in settlement.

compost [KAHM-pohst in U.S.; -ahst in Brit.].

compound [KAHM-pound]. (n.) [kahm-POUND]. (v.)

COMPOUND SENTENCE. A sentence containing two or more independent clauses.

COMPOUND-COMPLEX SENTENCE. A sentence composed of two or more independent clauses and one or more dependent clauses.

comprehend. Know as well as can be known. -ed, -nding, -ensible.

comprehensive. Covering the entire field: *A comprehensive view of the subject.*

compressible.

comprise. Preferred to —*ize.* Consist of, include, contain. NOT compose. *New York City comprises five boroughs.*
  COMPOSE. Create by putting together. *Cement is composed of lime, clay, and water.*

compromise.

Comptroller [kuhn-TROHL-uhr]. Used in titles by most government agencies, esp. New York City, N.Y. and U.S., for controller of funds.

Comptroller. of the Currency, the Comptroller; Comptroller of the Post Office Department, the Comptroller; Comptroller General (U.S.); the Comptroller.

comradery [KAHM-rad-ree]. (-ie is Fr.)
  CAMARADERIE. The spirit of good will.

CONARC. (abbr.) Continental armv command.

conative future. In grammar, compulsative form: *I will do it.*

concave [kahn-KAEV]. Hollow.

convex. Rounded; protuberant.

conceive.

concentrate [KAHN-sehn-traet].

conception. Preferred to *concept,* except in philosophical use.

concertmaster.

concerto [kahn-CHAIR-toh]. Pl. -os. (Ital. -i).

concessionaire [kahn-sehsh-uhn-AER]. Preferred to *nn.*

conch [kahngk]. shell. Pl. -s.

conciseness.

concrete. Cement (burned clay—limestone) plus sand, mixed with gravel and/or crushed rock and set with water.

concupiscent [kahn-KYOO-pih-sehnt]. Lustful. -ence.

condescend [kahn-dee-SEHND]. Forego privileges or dignity of a superior position; usually implies a patronizing manner.

conditions met.

condolence [kahn-DOH-lehns]. Expression of sympathy.

conductible.

conduit [KON-doo-iht preferred to Webster's kahn-diht; Brit., kuhn-diht].

Conelrad. (abbr.) control of electromagnetic radiation (civil defense). Former emergency communications system at 640 and 1240 kc.

confectionery. Candies.

confederacy. confederation, federation. Strength of unity indicated increases in that order.

Confederacy (of the South). Confederate States of America; Confederate Army, government, soldier.

Confederation. Swiss; the Confederation.

Conference. Capitalize if referring to governmental (U.S.) or international conference: *Bretton Woods (Conference),the Conference.* Non-governmental: *Sixth Annual Conference of Southern Methodist Churches, the conference; conference of Governors; conference of mayors; Governors' conference.*

conference room.

conferrable [kahn-FUHR-ra-bl]. Capable of being given.

confessedly [kahn-FEHS-ehd-lee]. Admittedly.

Confession, Augsburg.

confidant(e) [kahn-fih-DANT]. m. and f. both. -ent is archaic.
　CONFIDENT [KAHN-fih-dehnt]. Fully assured.

confines [KAHN-fiens]. (n.) Boundaries.

confirmer. In law, confirmor.

confiscatory [kahn-FIHS-kuh-toh-ree].

conflux. Confluence. -luxible.

confrere [KAHN-fraer]. Colleague.

Congo, Republic of (Brazzaville). Native, Congolese. Independent Republic proclaimed August 15, 1960. Member of French Community. Cap., Brazzaville. Currency, CFAF franc.

Congo, Republic of (Leopoldville). Native, Congolese. Former Belgian Congo. Proclaimed June 30, 1960, Federal Republic of the Congo, name adopted May 1961. Changed to Zaire, Oct. 27, 1971. Cap., Leopoldville named changed to Kinshasa, Congo R. to Zaire R. Currency, Congolese franc.

congratulate. Expresses pleasure in another's good fortune.
　FELICITATE. Expresses a wish for continued happiness. A lucky bridegroom is congratulated; a bride is felicitated, NOT congratulated.

Congress (convention). Capitalize if part of name; cap. standing alone if referring to international congress; International Good Roads, Congress, Good Roads, Congress; the Congress of Parents and Teachers, National, the congress.

Congress (legislature). Capitalize if referring to national congress: Congress of Bolivia, etc., the Congress; Congress of the United States; First, Second, 11th, 82d, Congress; the Congress.

Congressional Directory. the directory; First Congressional District, 11th Congressional District, etc.; the First 11th District; the congressional district; the district; Congressional Library, the Library; Congressional Medal of Honor (SEE decorations) BUT congressional action, congressional committee, etc.

Congressional Medal of Honor. the Medal of Honor, the medal.

Congressman (U.S.). Congressman at Large; Member of Congress; Member; membership.

conjecture [kuhn-JEHK-chyoor].

CONJUGATION. In grammar, inflections of a verb, including forms for principal parts, and forms for its numbers, persons, tenses, moods, and voices.

CONJUNCTION. A word used to join words, phrases, or clauses; *and, but, nor. Cf.* Connectives.

CONJUNCTIVE ADVERB. An adverb which connects independent clauses and shows relationship between them. *A man has been selected; however, the choice is not final.*

conjure [kahn-JOOR]. Beseech. Conjurer.
　CONJURE [KUHN-jehr]. Do magic. Conjurer.

connecter. -or.

connectable. Preferred to -ible in U.S.

Connecticut [kahn-NEHT-ih-kuht]. (abbr. Conn.) Native, Connecticuter. Cap., Hartford.

CONNECTIVES. The most important connectives are conjunctions and prepositions. Coordinate conjunctions connect elements of equal grammatical importance: *and, but, or, not, for, yet.* Correlative conjunctions work in pairs to connect elements of equal rank: *either, or; neither, nor; not only, but also; both and.* Each member of this group must be followed by the same part of speech. Conjunctive adverbs connect independent clauses and show a relation between them: *therefore, however, consequently, accordingly, furthermore, moreover, nevertheless.* Several types of connectives may be used to join elements of unequal rank, subordinate conjunctions: *before, since, after, as, because, if, unless, until, although;* relative pronouns: *who, whom, that, which, whatever, whichever, whoever;* and relative adverbs: *how, when, where, while.* Subordinate conjunctions introduce dependent adverb clauses and join them to independent clauses. Relative pronouns introduce noun and adjective clauses and also act as pronouns within the clauses. Relative adverbs introduce subordinate clauses. The other connective, the preposition, is used to connect its object with the word in the main clause which is modified, showing the relationship between the word and the object of the preposition: *to, of, between, in, over, under, from, for.*

connection. Brit. —xion.

connoisseur [kahn-uh-SEUR]. An expert in a certain field.

connote. Suggest, imply. connotation.

DENOTE. Indicate, signify, express explicitly: *The dollar denotes 100 cents but connotes power, materialism, etc.*

conscious [KAHN-shush].

consecrator.

consensus. Agreement or unanimous agreement of opinion; *of opinion* is implied without being stated. Thus, NOT: *consensus of opinion.*

consequential. Following as a result. Also self-important. NOT meaning of consequence or having great consequences.

conservative. Tending to preserve existing conditions, thus cautious people or those of moderate views.

REACTIONARY. One who favors return to old philosophy or methods.

LIBERAL. One not bound by tradition in politics, etc.

PROGRESSIVE. One who favors social change.

conservatory. -ries. (Brit.); conservatoire (Fr.); conservatorium (Germ.); conservatorio (Ital.); Academy of Music (U.S.).

consider. *I consider her intelligent.* NOT: *to be intelligent* or *as intelligent.*

considerable. Used as *a great deal* (colloq.) in U.S. but is applied to immaterial things in Brit.

consist of. Applies to parts which make up the whole; *The omelet consists of vegetables and eggs.*

CONSIST IN. Applies especially to inherent qualities or introduces a definition: Truthfulness *consists* in not lying.

consolatory [kuhn-SAHL-uh-toh-rih]. Comforting.

consommé [kayn-soh-MAE]. Clear soup.

consonant [KAHN-soh-nant]. Consistent; having agreement.

CONSONANT ENDINGS. When adding a suffix which begins with a vowel to a one-syllable word ending in a single consonant or a multi-syllable word which is accented on the last syllable, double the final consonant: *sit, sitting.* BUT NOT when the final consonant is *c, h, j, q, w, x,* or *z.* EXCEPTIONS: *defer-ence, refer-ence, infer-ence, prefer-ence, prefer-able, transfer-able, chagrin-ed, gaseous.* Do not double the final consonant in words of more than one syllable where the accent is on any but the last syllable. BUT: *cancellation, questionnaire, crystallize.* NOTE: Do not double the consonant if (1) the word ends in more than one consonant: *resist, resistance;* (2) when the word ends in a single consonant preceded by more than one vowel; *detain, detainable;* (3) when the suffix begins with a consonant: *loyal, loyalty.* A word ending in a double consonant usually retains the double consonant: *skill, skillful.*

consort [KAHN-sawt]. (n.) Partner; companion. (v.) [kuhn-SAWRT]. Associate.

conspectus. Pl. -uses. Synopsis.

conspicuousness. Preferred to -cuity.

constable [KAHN-stuh-b'l].

constitution [kahn-stih-TYOO-shuhn].

Constitution. Capitalize with name of country; capitalize standing alone when referring to a specific national constitution; *the Constitution of the United States, the Constitution.* BUT New York constitution; the constitution, constitutional.

constitutional amendments. Capitalize when referred to by name or number. *First Amendment.*

constitutionalist. Preferred to constitutionist.

construct. SEE translate.

constructive trust. SEE trust.

construe [kuhn-STROO]. SEE translate.

consul. Commercial representative of a foreign state. consular. British consul; consul general, British consul general; British consulate, etc.

consul general. ADDRESS: John J. Smith, Esq. American Consul, London, England. SALUTATION: Sir, My dear Mr. Smith, Dear Mr. Smith.

consulter.

consummate [kahn-SUHM-iht]. (adj.) Perfect.

CONSUMMATE [KAHN-suh-maet]. (v.) Complete. Applied to marriage, it implies sexual intercourse.

consume entirely is a tautology.

cont. (abbr.) continued.

contact. There is some objection to the use as a verb meaning *get in touch with.*

contagious. Communicable by contact or by contact with breath, clothing, etc. Colloquial, catching.

INFECTIOUS. Communicable by micro-organisms through air, water, food, insects, etc.

contemn [kahn-TEHM]. Despise, treat with contempt. -emning, -emned; -mner or -nor.

contemplate [KAHN-tehm-plaet]. Think; meditate; intend. Contemplative [kahn-TEHM-pluh-tihv].

contemptible [kahn-TEHMPT-ih-bl]. Worthy of contempt.

CONTEMPTUOUS [kahn-TEMPT-tyoo-uhs]. Full of contempt.

content. Significant material in a work.

contents. Topics covered in a work.

content oneself with. NOT by.

contentment. Preferred to content except in poetical use.

contest [KAHN-tehst]. (n.) [kahn-TEHST] (v.)

Continent. Capitalize only if following name; American Continent, the continent; BUT the Continent, meaning continental Europe.

Continental Army. the Army; Continental Congress, the Congress; Continental Divide (see Divide); Outer Continental Shelf, the shelf.

continental. *Don't care a continental.* Lowercase before Europe, United States, etc.

Continentals (Revolutionary soldiers).

continual. Going on or recurring at short intervals.

CONTINUOUS. Uninterrupted; *a continual flow of trade, a continuous pavement.*

continuance. (n.) A continuing in a state or direction. In law, adjournment to a specified time.

CONTINUATION. (n.) Extension; prolongation; resumption; *continuation of a story, the cold war.*

CONTINUITY. Quality of being continuous.

contour [KAHN-toor]. Outline.

contra-. Prefix meaning against; *contraband, contraceptive.*

contract [KAHN-trakt]. (n.) U.S. (v.), meaning undertake [KAHN-]; in other senses [-TRAKT].

contractible.

contraction. SEE abbreviation.

contractual. NOT contractural

contralto. Pl. -os.

contrary [KAHN-trehr-ee]. Opposed; opposite, *All sheets are white;* contrary, *No sheets are white.* OR: *All sheets are colored.*

CONVERSE. *All white things are sheets.*
OPPOSITE. *No sheets are white.*

contrast [KAHN-]. (n.) [-TRAST] (v.)

contravene [KAHN-truh-veen]. Oppose; act contrary to.

control. -lled, -lling, -llable.

controvertible. Capable of being disputed.

contumacy. Preferred to -*aty*. Defiance of authority.

contumely. [KAHN-tyoo-mee-lih]. (n.) Insult.

Convair 880 and 990. 4-engine turbo-jet transport planes.

Convention. Capitalize governmental (U.S.), international, or national political; the convention; Constitutional Convention (United States, 1787), the Convention; Democratic National Convention; Genocide Convention; 19th Annual Convention of the American Legion, Universal Postal Union Convention, Postal Union Convention, International Postal Convention; Warsaw Convention; BUT convention of 1907 (not formal name).

conversant [KAHN-vuhr-sant]. Acquainted; familiar.

converter.

convertible.

conveyor.

convincible.

cook book. (Brit. cookery book).

Cook County. the county.

cooky.

cool, coolly. Preferred to *cooly*.

coolheaded. —house.

coolie.

coonskin.

cooped-in. (adj.) cooped-up (adj.)

cooper [KOOP-uhr]. Barrelmaker.

cooperate. Preferred to *co-operate* or coöperate.

co-ordinate. In grammar, of equal rank and importance. In an outline, of equal significance.

COORDINATE OR COORDINATING CONJUNCTION. A conjunction joining sentence elements of equal value.

Coordinator of Information. the Coordinator.

copperbottom. (v.), -head, -hose, -plate, -proof, -sidesman, -smith, -ware, -wing (butterfly), -worker, -works; copperbottomed (adj.), copper-colored (adj.), copper-headed (adj.), copper-plated (adj.); copper mine, copper miner.

copper age. BUT N.Y. Times, Copper Age. *Cf.* Capitalization, Ages, Time.

copula. In grammar, linking verb which ties subject and predicate.

copyright. Brit. copyrighted.

coquet [koh-KEHT]. (m.), coquette (f.), (n. and v.) -quetry [KOH-keht-rih].

Coquilaville [kah-keel-ah-VEEL]. City in the Congo.

coral [KAWR-uhl]. Marine skeletons forming underwater deposits.

CORRAL [kuh-RAL]. Enclosure for confining animals.

CHORAL [KOH-ruhl]. Sung by a chorus or choir.

coral bound. coral-beaded (adj.), coral red (adj.); coral reef, coral stitch.

cord. (abbr. cd.) Unit of volume is 127 cu. ft. or 3.625 m.^{3}; usually 8 ft. long $\times$ 4 ft. $\times$ 4 ft. *Cf.* chord.

cord foot. (abbr., cd. ft.). Unit of volume is $\frac{1}{8}$ cord is 16 cu. ft.

Cordier, Andrew Wellington [kawrd-YAE]. (1901–   ), U.N. official, 1946–1962, educator.

cordon [KAWR-dn]. Line or circle of people; *a police cordon.*

CORE. (abbr.) Congress of Racial Equality.

coremaker. —making; core drill, core print.

coriolis effect. Tendency of a projectile to be deflected right in the northern hemisphere, left in the southern hemisphere, by earth's rotation.

CORRELATIVE CONJUNCTION. Conjunctions used in pairs to connect sentence elements of equal value: *either-or, neither-nor, not only – but also, both—and.*

corespondent [KOH-rehs-PAHN-dehnt]. The third party in a divorce suit. *Correspondent* is acceptable, but fails to make the distinction.

CORRESPONDENT [kahr-eh-SPAHN-dehnt]. The writer of a letter.

corn. Seeds of cereal grass. U.S., Indian Corn, maize; Brit., wheat; Scotland and Ireland, oats.

Corneille, Pierre [kawr-NEH-y or -NAE]. (1606–1684) French playwright.

cornetist.

cornucopia. Pl. —as.

corollary [KAHR-uh-leh-ree; Brit., koh-RAHL-uh-rih]. Something that logically follows.

corona [kah-ROH-nuh]. Crownlike structure or radiation. Pl. —nas or —nae. coronal (n.) [KAH-roh-nal]. A crown or coronet (adj.) [kah-ROH-nal].

Corot, Jean Baptiste Camille [koh-ROH, zhahn bah-TEEST kah-MEEY]. (1796–1875) French impressionist painter.

Corp. (abbr.) Corporation.

corporal. Of the physical human body. *Cf.* Officers.

Corporal punishment.

corporeal. Of the nature of the human body; tangible: *Goblins are fears given corporeal form.*

Corporation. Capitalize if part of name; the Corporation, if referring to unit of Federal government: Commodity Credit Corporation; Federal Deposit Insurance Corporation. BUT: Rand Corp., the corporation; St. Lawrence Seaway Development Corpor-

ation, the corporation; Union Carbide Corp., the corporation.

Corps [cohr]. Capitalize if part of name; the corps (see also Reserve); Adjutant General's Corps, Army Hospital Corps, Artillery Corps, Chemical Corps, Counterintelligence Corps, Enlisted Reserve Corps; Corps of Engineers, Army Engineers; BUT corpsman, army engineer, diplomatic corps, hospital corpsman.

corps. Sing. and pl. Sing. [kohr]; pl. [KAWRZ]. An organized body. SEE Army Organization.

CORPSE [kawrps]. Dead body. Pl. -ses

corpulence. Preferred to *corpulency.* Fatness.

corpus. Pl. -pora. Body. Thus, corpus of knowledge, of writings, of capital.

corpuscle [KAWR-puhs-'l]. Free floating blood or lymph cell.

corral [kuh-RAL, koh-RAL, U.S. West., kaw-REHL]. (n.) Enclosure for animals. (v.) To pen animals. -lled, -lling.

correctitude. Propriety.

Correggio, Antonio [kohr-RAED-joh]. (1494–1534) Italian painter.

correlative [koh-REHL-uh-tihv]. (n. and adj.) Mutually related. In grammar, ordinarily used together: e.g., *either . . . or.*

correspondence.

corrigendum. Pl. -da. Error or (pl.) list of errors in a manuscript.

corrigible. Capable of being corrected.

corroborate. -rable. confirm.

corrodible or corrosible. Capable of being eaten away gradually, as by acid.

corrosion [kuh-ROH-zhun]. Eating away by chemical action; corrosion of copper, corrosible.

EROSION. Wearing away by action of water or wind: *erosion of soil.*

corruptible.

corsage [kawr-SAHJ].

corsair [KAWR-sair]. Privateer.

cortege [KAWR-tehzh or taezh]. A group of followers.

Cortes [KAWR-tehz]. National legislature of Portugal and Spain (before France).

corvette. Small, fast anti-submarine ship. *Cf.* boats.

cos. (abbr.) cosine.

Cosa Nostra. (Ital.) "Our Thing." Organization of U.S. crime syndicate, alleged name of Mafia.

cosh. (abbr.) hyperbolic cosine.

cosmetics [kahz-MEHT-ihks].

cosmopolite [kahz-MAHP-oh-liet]. A person at home in any country.

cosmos. The universe.

cost. P. and p.p., cost; costing.

cost and freight. (abbr., c.a.f.) Term of sale including these items. *Cf.* c.i.f.

Costa Rica. Native, Costa Rican(s); adj., Costa Rican. Cap., San Jose [san-hoh-SAE]. Currency, colon, pl. colones; centimo (Ctmo.)

costume [KAHST-tyoom].

cot. (abbr.) cotangent.

-cote [kaht]. Suffix meaning shed or coop; *sheepcote, dovecote.*

Côte d'Or [koht-dawr]. Department in East France. Cap.,Dijon.

coterie [KOH-tuh-ree]. Congenial group of people.

coth. (abbr.) hyperbolic cotangent.

cotterway. cotter pin

Cotton Belt. (see Belt).

couchant [KOUCH-ant]. Lying down.

coulee [KOO-lih]. Solidified lava stream. In U.S., a steep-walled valley.

coulomb [koo-LAHM]. Unit of measure of quantity of electricity which flows in a specified period of time: 1 ampere in 1 second.

Council. Capitalize if part of name; capitalize standing alone if referring to federal or international unit: Boston City Council, the council; Choctaw Council, etc., the council; Federal Personnel Council, the Council; His Majesty's Privy Council, the Privy Council, the Council; Philadelphia Common Council, the council. *Cf.* United Nations.

council. -cilor. A governing body, or a meeting of one: city council.

COUNSEL. -selor, -sellor. Advice, or the one who gives advice: They hired counsel to defend them. (v.) counsel, -seled or -selled; -seling or -selling.

councilman. -woman.

councilor. Member of a council.

COUNSELOR. One who gives counsel; also title of an embassy official.

countdown. (n. and adj.) count-down (v.); count wheel.

countenance. Face; implies expression.

FACE. Refers to a part of the body.

PHYSIOGNOMY. Implies character, as revealed by type of features.

VISAGE. Face (literary).

counter-. Combining prefix meaning opposite, retaliatory, or complementary; counterclaim, counterthrust.

counterpart. A similar or complementary thing. NOT opposite. *Cf.* contrary.

countess. In Britain, the wife of or female equivalent of an earl; in other countries, the wife of or female equivalent of a count. The title is often territorial: *the Countess of Derby, Lady Derby; Countess Attlee, Lady Attlee.*

Countess. ADDRESS: The Right Honourable the Countess of Haddington or the Countess Haddington. SALUTATION: Madam, Dear Lady Derby.

countryseat.

county. Capitalize in singular when part of a name; *Queens County, the county; County-Frederick, county of Frederick; County Kilkenny, etc.; the county, the county sheriff.*

countywide. county seat.

coup [koo, kooz]. Pl. coups. A successful blow.

COUP D'ETAT. [KOO deh-tat]. A sudden overthrow or subversion of government or state policy.

COUP DE GRACE [deh-GRAS]; putting one out of his misery.

coupé [koo-PAE]. Compartment – door, automobile

couple. Two related in some way; a pair.

coupon [KOO-pahn, NOT kyoo-; Brit. KOO-pahng].

Courbet, Gustave [koor-BEH, geus-TAHV]. (1819–1877) French painter.

Court (of law). Capitalize if part of name of a local, state, national, or international court, U.S. court, district court, or State court; lower-case if part of the name of city or county court; capitalize standing alone if referring to the Supreme Court of the U.S., to Court of Impeachment (U.S. Senate), or to an international court; Circuit Court of the United States for the Second Circuit, the circuit court, the court; Court of Appeals of the State of Wisconsin, etc., the court of appeals, the court; Court of Claims, the court; Court of Customs and Patent Appeals, the court; Court of Impeachment, the Senate, the Court; District Court of the United States for the Eastern District of Missouri, the district court, the court; Emergency Court of Appeals, United States, the court; International Court of Justice, the Court; Permanent Court of Arbitration, the Court; Supreme Court of Virginia, etc., the supreme court, the court; Tax Court, the court; U.S. Court of Appeals for the District of Columbia, the court. Appellate Division, Court of Appeals, Court of Claims, Court of Criminal Jurisdiction.

courtesan [KAWR-teh-zan]. Prostitute.

courtesy [KUHR-teh-sih]. [KOUR-teh-sih].

court-martial. Pl. courts-martial. Preferred to *court-martials.*

Court of St. James. St. James's Palace.

courthouse. BUT United States Court House.

courtier [KAWR-tih-ehr, KAWRT-yehr].

Courtlandt Ave. Bronx, N.Y.

COURTLANDT ST. N.Y. and Brooklyn.

cousin-hood.

couturier [koo-too-RYAE]. Designer of haute couture, man or woman. A male dressmaker.

COUTURIERE. A dressmaker (female).

Covenant. League of Nations Covenant, the covenant.

Coventry [KAHV-ehn-trih]. Ancient Warwickshire town. *To send one to Coventry* (Cap.) is to refuse to associate or speak with him.

coveralls.

covert [KUHV-uhrt]. Concealed.

covetous [KUHV-eh-tuhs]. Desirous of what belongs to others.

cowardice [KOU-uhr-dihs].

Cowles, John [KOHLZ]. (1899–   ) and Gardner (Mike) (1903–   ) Des Moines and Minneapolis publishers.

coxswain [KAHK-sn].

coyote [KIE-oht].

cozen [KUH-zihn]. cheat, defraud.

cozy. Brit. cosy. Comfortable; also, teapot warmer.

cp. (abbr.) candlepower; chemically pure.

CPA. (abbr.) certified public accountant. N.Y. Times, C. P. A.

CPI. (abbr.) Consumer Price Index.

Cpl. (abbr.) corporal.

c.p.m. (abbr.) cycles per minute.

c.p.s. (abbr.) cycles per second.

Cr. (abbr.) Cranch (U.S. Supreme Court Reports).

cr. (abbr.) credit; creditor.

crackleware.

cracksman.

craft or horizontal union. Union including workers with the same skills, e.g. carpenters. *Cf.* industrial union.

craft. Meaning boat, pl. craft. BUT other meanings, pl. crafts.

craftsman. —woman.

craft-work. craft union.

crane man. crane driver.

cranium. Pl. —niums,-nia. The skull.

crape fish. —hanger.

crash boat. —dive (v.), —land (v.).

C ration. Emergency military packet of 3500 calories including meat, biscuits, coffee and candy.

crawfish.

crawlup. (n. and adj.) crawl-a-bottom (fish).

crayon board. —stone.

creature [KREE-tchuhr].

crèche [kraesh, krehsh]. Christmas scene. Brit., day nursery [kraesh].

credence [KREE-dehnss]. Belief.

credible. Worthy of belief.
　　CREDITABLE. Worthy of praise.

credit man. credit union.

credulity [kruh-DYOO-luh-tih].

Creed, Apostles'. the Creed.

creek [kreek; NOT krihk].

creep. P. and p.p., crept.

creep hole. —mouse.

creme [krehm].

crenel [KREH-nehl]. crenelle [KREE-nehl]. Embrasure in a battlement. crenelated; Brit. use *ll*.

Creole. White person descended of French or Spanish settlers of the U.S. Gulf States; also the native French language, food, cattle, cooking style. Native of Negro or Creole and Negro blood. In Latin America, native of European ancestry, usually Spanish.

crêpe [kraep].

crêpe de chine. crêpe paper, crêpe rubber.

crêpe suzette. Pl. crêpes suzette.

crepuscule [KREE-puhs'l. kree-puhs-kyool, Brit., KREHP-uh-skyool]. Twilight.

crescendo [kreh-sh-EHN-doh].

crestfallen. —line.

cretin [KREE-tihn]. One congenital ailment due to thyroid insufficiency, resulting in deformity and idiocy.

Crichton, James [KRIE-tn]. (1560–1582) Scotch prodigy.

crime buster. —busting, —wave.

crimson. See red.

crinoline [KRIHN-oh-lihn, Brit., -leen]. Stiff cloth, lady's skirt.

crisis [KRIE-sihs]. Pl. -ses [seez].

crisscross. —crossed.

criterion [krie-TEER-ih-uhn]. Standard of judgment. Pl. criteria.

criticism. Judgment of a work, especially unfavorable.
　　CRITIQUE [krih-TEEK]. An estimate or discussion of a work, not necessarily unfavorable.

Croce, Benedetto [KROH-chae, bae-nae-DAE-toh]. (1886–1952). Italian philosopher-statesman.

crockeryware.

crocodile. Brit. tank flame thrower. Also LVT.

Croesus [KREE-suhs]. (–546 B.C.) King of Lydia renowned for his wealth.

Croix de Feu [krwah-da-FEU].

Croix de Guerre. *See decorations.*

crook [kruhk]. Hook: A crooked stick.

crooked. Dishonest. (This is not colloquial.)

crook. Combining form meaning bent; crook-backed.

croupier [KROO-pih-air; Fr. -pyae].

crow. -ed. BUT *The cock crew* is permissible.

Crown. Capitalize if referring to a ruler. BUT crown colony, lands, etc. *The Crown* for king or queen as constitutional monarch.

crow's-foot. (nonliteral) crow's-nest (nautical); BUT literally: crow's nest: *The crow's-nest is on the tree.* crowfoot, crowfeet.

CRP. (abbr.) C-reactive protein.

crucible [KROO-sih-b'l]. Pot for melting ores, etc.

cruel. —ler, —lest. Brit. *ll.*

cruise.

crux [kruhks]. Crucial point.

crybaby.

cryogenics. Science which deals with behavior of substances at temperatures close to absolute zero.

cryptic [krip-tihk]. Secret, hidden
CRYPTOGRAM, CRYPTODIROUS.

crystal. —lize, —line. [KRIHST-uh-lihn]

crystal-clear. (adj.)

csc. (abbr.) cosecant.

csch. (abbr.) hyperbolic cosecant.

Csepel [CHAE-pel or CHEH-pehl]. City in U.S.S.R.

CSS. (abbr.) Commodity Stabilization Service.

C.S.T. (abbr.) central standard time.

c.t. (abbr.) central time.

Ct. (abbr.) Court.

Cuba. Native, Cuban(s); adj., Cuban. Cap., Havana (La Habana). Currency, peso ($), centavo (ctvo.)

cubbyhole.

cubic. Three-dimensional; of third power; cubic content.

cubical. Cube-shaped.

cubic centimeter. (abbr., cc., cm³) Unit of volume is 0.061 cu. in.

cubic foot. (abbr., cu. ft.) Unit of volume = 1728 cu. in. = 0.037 cu. yd. = 0.028 m³.

cubic inch. (abbr., cu. in. or in.³) Unit of volume is 0.000579 cu. ft. = 16.3872 cm³.

cubic kilometer. (abbr., km³.) Unit of volume = 1 billion cm³.

cubic meter. (abbr., m³.) Unit (1) of volume is 1.3079428 cu. yd. = 35.31445 cu. ft. = 61,023.38 cu. in. = 1000 cu. decimeters; (2) of capacity is 264.1776 gal. = 1000 l.

cubic millimeter. (abbr., mm³) Unit of volume = .00006 cu. in. = .001 cm³.

cubic yard. (abbr., cu. yd.) Unit of volume = 27 cu. ft. = 46,656. cu. in. = 764559 m³.

cub master. cub shark.

cube. SEE -hedron.

cuckold [KUHK-uhld]. (n.) Man with an unfaithful wife.

cuddy. Pl. —dies. An ass.

cudgel. —led, —ling. Brit. —lled, —lling.

cue [kyoo]. A signal; also the stick in billiards.
QUEUE [kyoo]. Line of people waiting their turn. (Sometimes *cue.*)

Cuernavaca [kwehr-nah-VAH-kaha]. Resort capital of Moreles State, Mexico.

cui bono. (Lat.) *Who benefits from it?* NOT: *What is the use of it?*

cu. (abbr.) cubic.

cuisine [kwee-ZEEN]. Style of food preparation; the kitchen.

cul-de-sac. Blind alley.

culinary [KYOO-lih-nehr-ih]. Pertains to cooking.

cullboard. Stand for articles to be sorted.

cullender. *Colander* is preferred. [KUHL-anduhr]. Bowl-shaped strainer.

cullible. Capable of being chosen and gathered

culminate. (v.) Reach the highest point. —nation.

culottes. Woman's sport skirt divided into two legs.

cultivate. —vable.

cumulo [kyoo-myool-oh]. Combining form meaning a heap; *cumulative, cumulate.*

cuneiform [kyoo-NEE-ih-fawrm]. Wedge-shaped characters of ancient Babylonian, Asyrian, Persian, etc. writing.

cunning. Artful. —ness.

cupful. Pl. cupfuls. Preferred to *cupsful.*

cupola [KYOO-poh-lah]. Small structure over roof; a rounded ceiling.

Curacao [koo-rah-sou; angl. KYOO-rah-soh]. Island in Netherlands Antilles. Chief town, Willemstad. Also the liqueur, curaçao or curacoa.

curator [kyoo-RAE-tuhr]. Keeper, custodian.

curb. Preferred to kerb in U.S.; Brit. use kerb for foot path.

curbstone.

curé [kuh-RAE]. (Fr.) Parish priest.

cure-all. (n. and adj.).

Curie, Marie. (1867–1934) and Pierre (1859–1906) [keu-REE]. French chemists. Daughter, Eve, (1904–   ) Author.

curiosity.

curly head.

current. Passing from person to person; passing in time; *current fancy. currency.*

CURRANT. A small seedless raisin of Middle East; sour red berry.

Current. Capitalize if part of name; Arctic Current, Humboldt Current, Japan Current, North Equatorial Current; the current.

curriculum. Pl. —la. Pref. to —ums.

currycomb.

custom work. custom-tailored (adj.).

Customhouse. (a specific one) BUT a custom house; customs official, customs duty.

cut. P. and p.p., cut.

cut away. (n. and adj.)

cut-off (n. and adj.); cutoff or cut off (v.).

cute. (From acute). Colloquial. Shrewd; attractive.

cutlas. Pl. —es.

cuttlebone. —fish.

Cuyahoga Falls [kah-HOHG-a or HOHG-ah or kah-HAW-gah]. Town in Ohio. `

CWO. (abbr.) chief warrant officer.

cwt. (abbr.) hundredweight.

cybernetics [sie-ber-NEHT-ihks]. Study of electronic devices as brains.

cycle car. —smith.

cyclone. Low-pressure system. Also hurricane, typhoon, especially in Indian Ocean.

HURRICANE. Violent tropical cyclonic system.

cyclopedia. Brit. Prefer -paed-. Encyclopedia is preferred form., but shorter form is preferred for adjective; cyclopedic.

cyclops. Pl. -opes or —opses. Mythological one-eyed giants of Sicily.

Cymric or Kymric [SIHM-rihk or KIHM-rihk]. Of the Celts in Wales.

Cyn(e)wulf [KIHN-un-woolf]. (c. 750). Anglo-Saxon poet.

cynic(al). Faultfinding, captious. Distrustful of human nature. *Cf.* captiousness.

SARDONIC. Bitter, scornful, sneering, derisive.

cynosure [SIE-noh-shoor; Brit., SIHN-]. A center of attraction.

SINECURE [SIHN-ih-kyoor]. Valuable position with little responsibility.

Cyn Wyd [kihn-wihd]. Town near Philadelphia, Pennsylvania.

Cyprus. Native Cypriote (N.Y. Times). [-oht] or Cypriot, [-aht]. (Adj.) Cyprian. Cap., Nicosia. Currency, pound.

Cyrenaic (for Aristippus or Cyrene). One who believes that mental and moral pleasures are greater than physical pleasures.

Cyrenaica [sihr-ih-NAE-ih-kuh; Ital. chee-rae-NAH-ee-kah]. Region in northeast Libya.

C.Z. (abbr.), Canal Zone (Panama).

czar [zahr]. (pref. form), tzar (closer to the Russian) Capitalize when referring to a specific king; Russian monarch. —ist. Also, colloquial, one in complete charge: *baseball czar.*

Czechoslovakia. Native, Czechoslovak(s); (adj.) Czechoslovak, Czech [chehk]. Cap., Praha (Prague). Currency, koruna (Kcs); haler; pl., haleru (ha.).

D

D-day. D-handle, D-major, D-plus-4-day.

d. (abbr.) dyne; pence; deci.

d, dd. One-syllable words (or polysyllabic words with the accent on the last syllable) ending in d, preceded by a single vowel (but not a diphthong or double vowel or a vowel and r) double the d before suffixes beginning with a vowel: *reddish, bidden, baddish, bedridden.* BUT: *deaden, goodish, periodical, nomadic.*

Dachau [DAHK-hou]. Nazi concentration camp site, West Germany.

Daché, Lili [dah-SHAE]. French-American milliner.

dachshund [DAHKS-hoont]. Breed of dog.

dactyl. In poetry, metrical foot consisting of one stressed and two unstressed syllables (- · ·). -ic.

Dadaism [duh-DAE-iesm]. Movement in painting and literature characterized by shocking disregard of previous art materials, started by Tristan Tzara, Hugo Ball, etc. in Zurich, 1916.

dado [DAE-doh]. Pl. —oes. Lower part of room wall when specially decorated. Also, a carpenter's joint made by fitting one piece into a groove of the other; the portion of a column between the base and the surbase.

daemon [DEE-mahn]. Pl. —s. Greek mythological supernatural being. Also, variety of demon. —ic.

daguerreotype [duh-GAIR-oh-tiep]. Early photograph in negative form on glass. From L. J. M. Daguerre (1787–1851).

dahlia [DAHL-ya; Brit., DAE.].

Dahomey [duh-HOH-mih]. Situated on the Gulf of Guinea. Formerly French West Africa. Independent August 1960. Native Dahomean. Cap., Porto Novo. Currency franc (CFAF).

dais [DAE-ihs. Brit., daes]. Speaker's platform. Pl., daises.

Dakar [dah-KHAR]. African seaport in Senegal, closest to South America.

Dali, Salvador [DAH-lee]. (1904–   ) Spanish surrealist painter.

Dall Eireann [dawl-AIR-ehn; - doil—; or diel-]. Lower house of Ireland's legislature.

Dalles, The. BUT the Dalles region. Dalles City, Oregon.

Dalmatian [dal-MAE-shun]. Breed of dog.

dam. Lower-case with number or in conjunction with lock; capitalize with name; Boulder Dam, Boulder Dam site.

damage. -geable.

Damascus, Syria. Native, Damascene.

dame. A woman of station; wife or daughter of a lord; a lady. When used as a title: *Dame Margot Fonteyn, Dame Margot.* A dame who marries below her rank retains her title: *Dr. Robert Arias and Dame Margot Fonteyn de Arisa.* Cf. Lady.

damning [DAM-ing, DAM-ning]. Bringing damnation. Also, cursing.

DAMNED. (adj.) Condemned. (adv.) damnably.

dampen. (v.) Preferred to Brit. *damp.*

danger. Exposure to injury or evil.

RISK. Implies voluntarily accepting a chance of or exposure to loss, injury, etc.

DANGLING CONSTRUCTION. In grammar,

a modifier (usually an infinitive, participial, or prepositional-gerund phrase) which does not logically relate to the sentence element it modifies. NOT: *By submitting my application now, the Personnel Department has time to check my references.* CORRECT: *...I am allowing the Personnel Department time 'to check my references.*

Danish language capitalizes all nouns.

D'Annunzio, Gabriele [dahn-NOON-tsyoh, gab-bree-a-lah]. (1863–1938) Italian soldier, writer.

DAR. (abbr.) Daughters of the American Revolution.

dare. P., dared or durst; p.p. dared.

dardanelles, the Dardanelles [dahr-duh-NEHLS]. Narrow strait between Europe and Turkey. NOT Dardenelles Strait.

Darien [die-yrehn]. Port in China.

Darien [dar-ih-EHN]. Town in Connecticut.

darkly. Fig. dimly or gloomily. NOT pessimistically.

darky. Pl. -ies.

Darrieux, Danielle [dahr-YEH-, dan-YEHL]. (1917–) French actress.

DASH, THE. Printed in two widths, the em dash and the en dash. The em dash, a long dash (—), is used: (1) To mark a sudden break or abrupt change in thought or in construction: *If he goes—and it is not unlikely—she will come immediately.* (2) Instead of commas or parentheses, if the meaning is clarified: *She had bad things to remember—death and sickness—but she did not falter.* (3) To give emphasis to an element added to a sentence: *He spoke once—but it was enough.* (4) Before a final clause that itemizes a series of ideas: *Wealth, good health, a happy home—what more can a man desire?* (5) After an introductory phrase introducing a series set in separate lines (a colon is also correct for this purpose): *The proposal—that no further travel be permitted.*

(6) To indicate a faltering in speech or an interruption: *I—I don't know. "Will you —" he had begun when the alarm sounded.* (7) To precede the name of an author or a signature: *"Give me liberty or give me death."—Patrick Henry.* (8) To separate questions and answers in testimony. (9) After a sidehead of printing. BUT NOT at the beginning of a line (except 7) or after a comma, colon, or semi-colon. (10) To indicate a root omitted. dash, —ed, —ing, —board.

Use an en (short) dash (Not a hyphen), in combinations of figures and/or letters: Sec. *7–A*: or to denote a period of time: *1958-60.* BUT NOT when preceded by *from* or *between. Cf. HYPHEN*

dastard. (Mean.) coward, with an element of sneakiness. —ly.

DATA. (abbr.) Defense Air Transportation Administration.

data [DAE-ta, DAH-ta]. Pl., but commonly used with a singular verb. The singular is datum. *Data are available*: *Many data are...*

data processing. Handling masses of informations, especially by computers.

data-processing machine. Electronic magnetic, or punched-tape or punched-card device which multiplies, divides, subtracts, and stores information.

date. -table.

Dates. *May 1967; May 7, 1967;* (BUT NOT: *May, 1947) May, June, and July 1959; May and June 1959; May-September 1946; May 1, 1942-January 4, 1946; 4th of July;* (Fourth of July is the holiday); *the 1st (day); the last of April* (not a specific day), *In December, 1917; Christmas 1917. Cf.:* Time, Years, Ages, Days, Weeks, Months, Years, Decades, Centuries.

daub [dawb]. Smear with plaster, mud, etc.; paint in a coarse manner.

daughter [daw-tuhr]. daughter-in-law. Pl. daughters-in-law.

Daughters of the American Revolution. (Abbr.) (DAR). a Real Daughter, King's Daughters, a Daughter.

Davao [DAH-vou]. City in Philippine Islands.

davenport. U.S., a sofa. Brit., a writing table.

da Vinci, Leonardo. SEE Vinci.

dawnlight. —streak; dawn-gray (adj.).

Dayan, Moshe [DIE-an, moi-shuh] (1915–) Israeli general, politician.

daylight-saving time. System of time adjustment designed to provide longer summer days by pushing the clock ahead one hour in the spring (usually last Sunday in April), back one hour in the fall (usually in Oct.). *7 P.M. eastern daylight time* (or e.d.t.)

days of the week. U.S. *We will work Monday*; Brit. *on Monday.*

dazzling [DAZ-ling].

db. (abbr.) decibel.

d.b.a. (abbr.) doing business as.

d.c. (abbr.) direct current.

D.C. (abbr.) District of Columbia.

D.D. (abbr.) Doctor of Divinity.

D-Day. Date of Normandy landings, June 6, 1944. SEE holidays.

D.D.S. (abbr.) Doctor of Dental Surgery.

DDT. (abbr.) dichlorodiphenyltrichloroethane, an insecticide.

De-, de-. (Fr.) preceding a name. SEE Le-.

de-. Combining form meaning away from: *decentralize*; down: *depose*; intensification: *denude*; reversing a previous form: *denationalization.*

Deacon. Cleric or lay servant of the church who may preach and give communion. ADDRESS: The Reverend Deacon Smith. SALUTATION: Reverend Sir, deaconess, deaconate.

dead letter. Unclaimed mail; unenforced laws.

deaf [dehf]. deaf-dumb, deaf-dumbness.

deal. (v.) P., dealt; p.p., dealt.

deal. (n.) Colloquial for amount: *a great deal*; also for a transaction: *a business deal.*

Dean. ADDRESS: The Very Reverend the Dean Smith. SALUTATION: Very Reverend Sir, Sir.

Dean of a College or University. ADDRESS:

Dean Norman B. Gould, School of Fine Arts, Columbia College, or Norman B. Gould, Ph.D., Dean of the School of Fine Arts, Columbia College; or Dr. Norman B. Gould, Dean of the School of Fine Arts, Columbia College. SALUTATION: Dear Sir, Dear Dean Gould, Dear Dr. Gould, Dear Mr. Gould (if he does not hold a doctor's degree).

dean of the diplomatic corps.

dear. (adj. and adv.)
DEARLY (adv.).

dear. In a salutation, no affection is indicated by the term *dear. My dear* is more formal than *dear* in a formal letter, less formal than *dear* in an informal letter.

Deauville [doh-VEEL; angl., -vihl]. French resort, racecourse town on Bay of the Seine.

debacle [dee-BAH-kl, —bak'l]. A sudden breaking up; by ext., disruption, rout.

debar. Exclude, prevent.
DISBAR. (Law) Expel from the bar.

debonair, debonaire [dehb-oh-nair]. Gay and graceful.

Debré, Michel Jean Pierre [deh-BRAE]. (1912–) French Prime Minister, 1959–1962.

debris [deh-BREE or dae-BREE]. Rubbish; ruins.

debt [deht]. —or.

Debussy, Claude Achille [deh-beu-SIH, klohd-ah-SHEEL]. (1862–1918) French composer of modern music.

debut [DAE-byoo, dae-BOO; Brit., DAE-boo, DEHB-oo].

debutant [DEH-byoo-tahnt]. Fem., —ante.

Dec. (abbr.) December. Abbreviation is often permitted before numerals. *Dec.* 25.

deca-. Metric system prefix meaning multiplied by 10. *Cf.* deci—.

decade [DEHK-aed; Brit., deh-KAED].

decades. Spell out or write in figures; *the nine-*

teen-twenties; the 1950's. When the century is omitted, *the twenties*, the 20's. Capitalize special eras: *the Gay Nineties. Cf.* years, centuries.

decadent [dee-KAE-dehnt; DEHK-uh-dehnt]. Characterized by deterioration or decline. —dence pref. to Brit. —dense.

decagram. (abbr., dkg.) Unit of weight is 0.35274 ou. avdp. = 0.32151 ou. = 10 grams.

decalog. (Webster prefers *Decalogue*) The Ten Commandments.

decameter. (abbr., dkm.) Unit of length is 10.9361 yd. = 32.8083 ft. = 393.7 in. = 10 m.

decare. (no abbr.) Sing. and pl. Unit of area is 0.2471 acres = 10 ares.

decathlon [dih-KATH-lahn].

decease [deh-SEES]. Die, deceased (n.) The dead.

DISEASE [dih-SEEZ]. Illness, diseased. The sick.

decent. Proper, suitable; *decently dressed.*

decency.

DESCENT. Downward movement: *The descent to the ground floor.*

DISSENT. Disagreement: *The judge wrote a long dissent from the majority opinion.*

deci—. Prefix meaning divided by ten; one-tenth. *Cf.* deca.

decibel. Unit of sound measure. Threshold of hearing is o decibels; a whisper is 10–20; an automobile is 40–50; conversation is 60; a riveter is 90–100; threshold of pain is 120.

decided. Clear-cut.

DECISIVE. That which decides an issue: *Wellington's decided superiority made possible a decisive victory.*

decigram. (abbr., dg.) Unit of weight is 1.5432 grains = 0.1 gram.

deciliter. (abbr., dl.) Unit of (1) capacity = 0.1816 dry pt. = 0.211 liq. pt. = 0.8454 gill = 3.38147 fl. ou. = 0.1 liter; (2) volume = 6.1025 cu. in.

DECIMAL SYSTEM. (Numerical system based on radex of ten. 1 is unit; .1 is one-tenth; .01 is one-hundredth; .001 is one-thousandth; .017 is seventeen-thousandths; .117 is one hundred seventeen-thousandths; .0001 is one ten-thousandths; etc. Use figures for numbers which contain decimals. 2.5 Decimals without units should be preceded by 0:*0.72. Cf.* Fractions, Metric System.

decimate. (v.) Kill one in ten. By ext., kill a large number. But NOT: *Decimated the population by 50 per cent.*

decimeter. (abbr., dm.) Unit of length is approx. 0.328 ft. = 3.93 in. = 0.1 m. = 10 cm.

Declaration. Capitalize with name: Declaration of Independence; the Declaration; Declaration of Panama. BUT the declaration.

declare. Make a formal, explicit statement.

déclassé [dae-klass-AE]. Socially fallen; socially below standard.

declension. Inflection of n. and pron., including forms for gender, number and case.

decolleté [dae-kohl-TAE]. (adj.) Low-necked, of a gown. decolletage (n.).

DISHABILLE. Undressed. Loosely or carelessly dressed.

DISHEVELLED [dih-SHEH-vehld]. Mussed.

Decoration Day. Memorial Day. In May.

decorative [DEHK-oh-rae-tihv; ruh-tihv].

decorous [DEHK-oh-ruhs; Brit., dee-KOH-ruhs].

decrease [dee-KREES].

Decree. SEE Executive Decree; Royal Decree.

decrement. Opposite of increment.

decry. Belittle: *To decry talent is to stifle ambition.*

DESCRY. Discover by looking: *The astronaut descried the shape of continents below.*

Dedham [DEHD-am]. Town in Massachusetts.

dedicate. -cable.

deduce [dih-DYUHS]. deducible.

deductible clause. In an insurance policy,

provision that the first specified part of loss (e.g., $50.) is to be absorbed by the insured.

deduction. Drawing a conclusion from a general principle.

INDUCTION. Drawing a general conclusion from observation of similar situations.

deem it advisable. AVOID as trite.

de-emphasis.

Deep South. Georgia, Florida, Alabama, Mississippi, Louisiana, often also South Carolina, North Carolina, Arkansas, Tennessee, and Texas. BUT: Midsouth.

deer. Both singular and plural. SEE hart, animals.

defendant. The name is usually italicized in legal writings: *Jones v. Smith.*

defense. Brit. —ce. defense bond, defensible.

Defense Establishment. SEE Establishment.

deferrable.

deficit [DEHF-ih-siht]. Shortage in amount.

definite. Precisely defined, exact: *His meaning was definite.*

DEFINITIVE [deh-FIHN-ih-tihv]. Defining precisely; not alterable; final: *He wrote a definitive study.*

DEFINITIVE ADJECTIVE. Ordinarily the first adjective in a series which specifies which n. is modified: *a, the, his, whose, this, every, no.*

Degas, Hilaire Germain Edgar [deh-GAH, el-LAIR shehr-MANN ehd-GAHR]. (1834–1917) French impressionist painter.

de Gaulle, Charles Andre Joseph Marie [duh-GOHL, sharl ahn-DRAE zho-ZEHF ma-REE]. (1890–1970). French general, statesman, president. De Gaulle Free French, Free French, Fighting French; BUT de Gaullist.

degauss [dee-GOUS]. (v.) To neutralize magnetic field of ship's hull, for defense against mines.

degree-wise. degree-day (measure).

deign [daen]. To consider fit for oneself; condescend.

Deity. Capitalize nouns denoting deity and all but relative pronouns: *The word of the Lord; His word; God, who is good. Cf.* atheism.

dejeuner [dge-zhuh-naer; Fr., dae-zher-nae]. Breakfast.

delectus personae [duh-LEHK-tuhs puhr-SOHN-ae]. (Lat.) Choice of persons, as the right of a partner to reject other new partners.

dekaliter. (abbr., dkl.) Unit of (1) capacity = 2.6418 gal. = 10.5671 liq. qts. = 10.1; (2) volume = 0.284 bu. = 1.1351 pks. = 9.081 dry qts. = 610.25 cu. in.

Delaware. (abbr. Del.) Native, Delawarean. Cap., Dover.

delegate. (n.) (to a conference), the delegate, the delegation.

Delegate. (n.) (U.S. Congress).

delegate at large.

Delhi [Dehl-ih]. Indian province. New Delhi is the capital.

delineate. -neable.

delinquent [dehLIHN-kw'nt]. (adj.) Failing in duty; offending by neglect or law violation. (n.) One who thus fails or offends.

delirium. Pl. —s or deliria.

Delphi [dehl-fie]. Central city of Greece, noted for ancient oracles.

deliver. A mother *is delivered of* a child.

Delta. Mississippi River Delta, the delta.

Delta Dart. SEE Fighter Planes.

deltiology. Post card collecting as a hobby.

de luxe [de-LOOKS, dee-LUHKS]. Especially fine quality.

demagog [dehm-uh-gahg]. Also demagogue. Rabble rouser.

demagogy [dehm-uh-goh-jih]. Preferred to *demagoguery* [dehm-uh-GAHG-uhr-ih].

demarche [dae-MAHRSH]. A plan involving change in policy.

demimondaine. Woman of doubtful reputation.

de minimus. (Lat.) Of the least. An item of error too minor to be of concern.

demise. NOT -ize [dehm-iez]. Death. Used of royalty, or humorously of others.

democrat. Believer in democracy. —ic (adj.).
DEMOCRAT. Member of the political party.

Democratic National Convention. The national convention, the convention.

democratic party.

DEMONSTRATIVE ADJECTIVES. They tell which or what is meant. Definite: *the, this, that, other.* Indefinite: *a, any, another, certain.*

demote. (v.) Lower in rank.

demur [dee-MUHR]. —rred, —rring, demurs. Show scruples; object or delay.
DEMURE [dee-MYOOR]. Serious, modest; prim.

demurrage. A charge made for storage on merchandise not unloaded or picked up at the specified time.

demurrer. A legal plea admitting facts but denying that they create a legal cause of action.

dengué fever [DEHN-gae]. Painful, seldom fatal tropical viral disease carried by mosquito. Also called breakbone fever.

denier. Unit of fineness based on weight in grams of 10,000 m. (until recently 9,000 m.) of yarn. The lower the denier the finer the yarn.

denigrate [DEHN-ih-graet]. Defame, blacken. SEE deprecate.

Denmark. Native, Dane(s); adj., Danish. Cap., Copenhagen. [koh-pehn-HAE-gehn]. Currency, krone, pl. kroner. (Dkr); ore (s. and pl.).

dentifrice. Toothpaste. NOT dentrifice.

Department. Capitalize if part of name; capitalize standing alone if referring to federal or international unit: Highway Department, (District of Columbia) the Department;

Post Office Department; the Department; Yale University Department of Economics, the department of economics, the department.

department. Lower-case before clerk, legislative, executive, judicial departments.

departmentwide.

dependent. Brit. pref. -ant.

dependent clause. In grammar, a clause used as an adjective, adverb, or noun that cannot stand alone: *Because I love you* I say no.

depositary. Person or institution named to hold something of value. BUT: *A diary is a depositary of secrets.*
DEPOSITORY. A place where things may be left; e.g., for safekeeping or for sale.

depot [DEH-poh]. A reception, storage or classification center. BUT a railroad station is DEE-poh]. Capitalize if part of a name. (v.) —ed, —ing.

depressible.

Depression. Capitalize when referring to the 1930's: *the Great Depression, the Depression.*

deprivation [DEH-prih-VAE-shuhn]. Preferred to *deprival.*

depth charge.

Deputy. Capitalize if part of capitalized title; BUT the deputy.

deputy chief of staff. Pl. -chiefs —.

deputy judge. Pl. —judges, —sheriffs.

Derby [Brit., DAHR-bee]. But the Kentucky Derby [DUHR-bee].

de rigeur [deh-ree-GOOR]. With strict etiquette.

derisive [deh-RIE-sihv]. Mocking; scornful.

derisory [deh-RIES-uh-ree]. Implies not worth taking seriously. *A derisory recommendation.*

derivative.

derring-do. (n.) Archaic, daring-to-do.

Descartes, René [dae-KAHRT]. (1596–1650) French mathematician and philosopher.

desalting. Preferred to *desalinization*, which in turn is preferred to *desalinification*.

descendant. (n., adj.) Offspring.

DESCENDENT (adj.) Going down. Rarely used.

descendible. Or —able. That which can descend to an heir.

description.

desecrate. -crable, —crater.

Deseret. Name suggested by Joseph Smith for present Utah. A Deseret alphabet was created by Mormons with a symbol for each sound to simplify learning English speech.

desert [DEHZ-zuhrt]. (n.) Arid area.

DESERT [dih-ZUHRT]. (n.) Reward or punishment.

DESSERT [deh-ZUHRT]. (n.) Sweet course at end of a meal. Brit., fruit, nuts, raisins, etc. U.S. *dessert* is Brit. *sweets*.

DESERT [dih-ZUHRT]. (v.) Abandon.

deshabille [dehz-uh-BEEL]. *Dishabille* is preferred. Loosely or carelessly dressed; by ext., mentally disordered. *Cf.* decolleté.

designate. Chairman-designate, etc.

desist [dee-ZIHST]. —ance.

Des Moines [deh MOIN]. City in Iowa.

despair [dee-SPAIR].

despatch. Dispatch pref.

desperado [dehs-per-AE-doh; des-per-AH-doh]. Desperate criminal.

desperate. Without hope; reckless.

DISPARATE. Different; distinct.

despicable [Dehs-pih-kuh-b'l]. Contemptible.

despite. More formal than *in spite of*, but not as strong. *Notwithstanding* suggests a deterrent.

Dessau [DEHS-ou]. City in East Germany.

destructible.

desuetude [DEHS-wee-tood]. Not being used; *The regulation is nullified by desuetude.*

determinedly. With determination.

DETERMINATELY. In a fixed way, precisely.

detour [DEE-toor; Brit. deh-TOOR]. (v.)

detractor.

de trop [dee-TROH]. Out of place, too much.

deutsche mark [DOI-cheh MAHRK]. West German monetary unit since June, 1948.

Deutschland uber alles [doitsh-lahnt EE-bair AHL-less]. "Germany above everything." German national anthem.

develop. —ment. AVOID misuse of verb in the sense of arise, happen, occur, or take place. NOT: *Let's see what develops.*

developing nations. Underdeveloped nations.

device. Contrivance.

DEVISE. Convey; contrive.

Devil. Capitalize when meaning Satan. BUT devil, devils, (v.) devil, —led, —ling. Brit. *ll.*

devilry, deviltry. *Deviltry* is used esp. for pure mischief.

devise. Contrive, invent. —ser.

DEVISE. Distribute, especially in a will. —sor, —see.

deviser. One who invents.

DEVISOR. One who leaves property.

DIVISOR. Number which divides the dividend.

Devonian. SEE Time.

devotee [dehv-oh-TEE].

DEW (abbr.) distant early warning. DEW line.

Dewey Decimal Classification. System of arranging books by subject based on numbers for each subject. 000 is general works; 100 is philosophy; 200 is religion; 300 is social science; 330 is economics; 340 is law; 370 is education; 400 is language; 500 is pure science; 600 is technology; 610 is medicine; 620 is engineering; 630 is agriculture; 650 is business; 700 is the arts; 780 is music; 790 is sports; 800 is literature; 900 is history; 910 is travel; 920 is biography.

dexter. Right.

SINISTER. Left, of the shield bearer, in heraldry.

Dhahran [dah-RAHN]. Oil town in East Saudi Arabia.

Di-. (Ital.) preceding a name, SEE Le —.

di-. Prefix – meaning two; double; *diacid, dichromic.*

dia-, di-. Prefix meaning through or between, apart, across; *diaglyph, diagonal.*

DIACRITICAL MARKS. Appear on some letters in foreign words to indicate a deviation from normal pronunciation. Generally these are made by hand on typewritten material, since most English typewriters do not have them.

FRENCH use acute é [ae] *fiancé*; circumflex â/ah/ ê î ô û (*pâte*); (there is then no dot over the i); grave à è ù *première*; and dieresis on ë ï ü, *näivete* [nie-EEV-tae]. The two dots of the diaeresis take the place of the customary one on the *i*, and indicate that the vowel is to be pronounced separately. The cedilla under c, *reçu, façade* [RAE-soo, fuh-SAHD] is used before *a, o,* and *u* to indicate an *s* sound. Ordinarily the French a is pronounced *ah*; i is pronounced *ee*, j is pronounced y, and *u* is pronounced as the German *ü, Walküre.*

GERMAN language may use an umlaut on ä, ö, ü/ue/

SPANISH. The acute á é í ó ú is used to indicate stress or to distinguish two words otherwise alike in spelling but different in meaning. A tilde makes the ñ soft; thus, cañon is pronounced canyon. The ñ is a separate letter in the Spanish alphabet between *n* and *o*. The diaeresis is used in combination with ü on güe and güi, when the u is to be pronounced.

Typical foreign words commonly used which require diacritical marks; à l'américaine, attaché, bêton, blessé, calèche, cañada, cañon, chargé, congé, crédit foncier, crédit mobilier, curé, doña, entrepôt, exposé, longéron, mañana, maté, mère, nacré, outré, passé, pâte, père, piña, précis, raissoné, resumé, touché.

ENGLISH words sometimes carry the diaeresis to indicate the separate sound of two adjacent vowels. *Naïve, coöperate.*

diagnosis. Pl. —oses, pron. —sees.

diagonal expansion. Business extension by development of new products which can be made with similar raw materials and equipment.

DIAGONAL LINE. Is used: (1) To indicate word omitted in certain expressions. *B/L* (*bill of lading*); *L/C* (*letter of credit*). (2) To mean *or* between *and* and *or: He may pay in pounds and/or dollars.*

diagram. —ed, —ing. diagrammatic.

dialect. A local language. SEE Language. dialectal.

dialectic. Or dialectics. (n. and adj.) Branch of logic dealing with discussion and discrimination of truth from error. Pl. -s., adj. also -tical.

dialed. —ing.

dialog. Also dialogue.

dialysis. Pl. —ses. Separation.

diameter [die-AM-uh-tuhr]. Of a circle equals circumference × .3182 = 2 × radius

diamond [die-uh-muhnd].

diapason [die-uh-PAE-zn]. From music, the entire scope.

diaphragm [die-uh-fram].

diarchy. Government by two. SEE Government.

diaeresis. [die-er (or EER) -ruh-sihs]. Pref. to dieresis. Pl. ses. [-seez]. The mark (¨) over a letter indicating that two vowels should be pronounced separately. *aëration, coöperative.* Also, separation of one syllable into two. *Cf.* Diacritical Marks.

diarrhea.

diary [DIE-uh-rih]. A daily record book.

DAIRY [DAE-ree]. Milk establishment.

Diaspora [die-AS-puh-ruh]. Dispersion of Jews after the destruction of Jerusalem, 70 B.C.

diastole [die-AST-tohl-ee]. Rhythmic beat of the heart; correlative to systole. Diastolic [die-as-TAHL-ihk].

dichotomy [die-KAHT-oh-mih]. Pl. —ies. Division into two parts.

dictator [DIHK-tae-tawr].

diction. Style derived from choice of words; manner of speaking.

dictionary. Concerned with words.

    LEXICON. Concerned with words, but used often for ancient languages.

    ENCYCLOPEDIA. Concerned with things.

    HANDBOOK. Concerned with techniques.

dictograph. Interoffice telephone.

    DICTAPHONE. A dictation machine. Trademark (by Dictaphone Corp.)

dictum. Pl. -ta. Formal statement; a judge's opinion.

didactic [die-DAK-tihk]. In the manner of a teacher or moralizer. —ticism.

die. Pl. dice. gambling cubes.

Dieppe [dee-EHP]. Seaport in North France.

Dien-Bien-Phu [dee-EHN bee-ehn FOO]. City in North Vietnam. Scene of French military defeat, May 7, 1954.

dietary [DIE-uh-tehr-ee]. Dietitian preferred to —ician.

die with. Avoid. People die *of* a disease.

different [DIHF-ehr-ehnt]. Always followed by *from* NOT: *different than.*

differently.

differentia. pl. -iae. Fig., a distinguishing characteristic.

differentiation [dihf-ehr-ehn-shee-AE-shuhn].

diffuse. diffusible, diffuser.

dig. P. and p.p., dug or digged; digging.

digestible.

digit. Unit of length is 0.75 in.

dike or dyke. Lower-case. dike no. 1.

dilemma. Difficulty in choosing between a limited number of equally undesirable solutions. NOT difficulty in finding any solution: *Two horns of a dilemma.*

dilettante [dihl-uh-TAN-tee, —tahnt]. Pl. -ti [tee-ti]. Preferred to -s, -tism. SEE amateur.

dillydally. (v.) —dallied, —ies, —allying, —ier.

dim lit. dim-lighted (adj.).

dimensions. Write in figures. *1 by 2; 6 feet 2 inches by 2 feet 4 inches; 6 feet 3 inches tall; 14 years 2 months 7 days; 3 parts gin 1 part vermouth; 7 to 5; 10-to-1 shot, $2\frac{1}{2} \times 8$; 20-foot boat.*

Dimensions of Water. Weight of water is important because it is the basis for many calculations involving capacity and pressures. 1 cu. in. is 0.03617 lbs.; 1 cu. ft. is 62.5 lbs.; 1 cu. ft. is 7.48052 gals.; 1.8 cu. ft. is 112.5 lbs.; 35.84 cu. ft. is 2240.0 lbs. *Cf.* Numbers, Measurements.

dimeter [DIHM-ee-tehr]. In poetry, verse of two metrical feet or of two dipodies.

diminuendo. Pl. —os. Of sounds, diminishing in volume.

diminution [dihm-in-NYOO-shuhn]. Preferred to *diminishment.*

diner-out.

dinghy [DIHNG-gee]. Pref. to dingy. Small rowboat.

dinosaur [DIE-nuh-sohr].

diocese [die-oh-sees or sihs]. diocesan [die-AHS-eh-s'n].

Dionne Quintuplets [dee-UHN].

Dionysius [die-oh-NIHSH-ih-uhs; -NIHSH-uhs; -NIHS-ih-uhs; -NIE-sih-uhs]. Two tyrants of Syracuse. The Elder, c. 430–367 B.C.; the Younger, 367–344 B.C.

Dionysus [die-oh-NIE-suhs]. Greek wine god; Bacchus.

Dior, Christian [dee-OHR, Krehst-YAHN]. (1905–1957). French fashion designer.

dip. P. and pp., dipped or dipt.

diphtheria [dihf-THEER-ih-uh].

diphthong [DIF-thawng]. Sound changing continuously from one vowel to another: *out, yoo* in *beauty*. Loosely in the ligature; *ae*. Consonantal diphthongs: t + sh = ch; d + sh = j.

diplomat. Preferred to —*tist* in U.S.

diplomatic corps. *Cf.* corps; service.

dipody [DIHP-oh-dih]. Pl., —dies [-dihz]. A verse having two feet.

diptych [diph-tihk]. Series of pictures painted on two hinged tablets, from similar writing tablet. *Cf.* tryptich.

direct [dih-REHKT, die—]. (adv.) In some contexts the —ly may be omitted. *She came direct from school.*

direct address. A noun or pronoun used in direct address is in the nominative case and set off by commas. *I tell you, father, I will not be stopped.*

direct object. In grammar, the person or thing directly affected by the action of the verb: *I took the book.*

director. Fem. —tress or —trix.

Director. Capitalize if referring to head of federal or international unit; the Director: *District Director of Internal Revenue*, the Director; *Director of Fish and Wildlife Service*, the Director; *Director of the Mint*, the Director; BUT director, board of directors (non governmental).

dirigible [DIHR-ih-jih-b'l]. Steerable, engine-driven lighter-than-air craft.

disadvantageous [dihs-ad-van-TAE-juhs].

disappointed. In a person, place, etc., with a result, product, etc.

disbar. SEE debar.

disbeliever. One who refuses to believe.
UNBELIEVER. One who does not believe.

disc. Preferred for the anatomical part, records.
DISK. Preferred for other uses.

discern [dih-ZERN] [-SEHRN]. See, discriminate, discernible [dih-ZERN-ih-b'l]; dih-SEHRN-ih-b'l].

discharge [dihs-CHAHRJ]. (v.) [dihs-CHAHRJ pref. to DIHS-charj]. (n.)

discomfit. Frustrate, overwhelm. —ure.
DISCOMFORT. Make uneasy; (n.) uneasiness.

disconnection. Brit. -xion.

discordant [dihs-KAWRD-'nt].

discotheque [DIHS-koh-tehk]. discothequeries. From French record library. Dance club depending principally on recorded music, usually with a disc jockey.

discourse [dihs-KAWRS. DIHS-kawrs].

discreet [dihs-CREET]. Prudent, judicious.
DISCRETE. Separate, disconnected, distinct: *Light is not a continuous flow, but is made up of discrete particles.*

discriminate. —nable.

discussible.

disfranchise. Also disenfranchise. Deprive of the rights of a citizen.

disenthrall. —allment. Brit. -alment. From thrall, slave; enthrall, to hold spellbound.

disgraceful. SEE strong opinion words.

disguise.

dishabille [dihs-ah-beel]. Also deshabille. *Cf.* decolleté.

disheveled. -ing [deh-SHEH-vild].

disinterested [dihs-IHN-tehr-ehs-tehd]. Unbiased.
UNINTERESTED. Not taking any interest.
INDIFFERENT. Lacking in feeling.

disk. SEE disc.

dismissible.

disparage [dihs-PAR-ihj].

dispel. Must be followed by an object which can be dispersed in different directions: e.g., suspicion, cloud, darkness. NOT: *He dispelled the report that......*

dispense with. Do without. Also special legal and ecclesiastical meanings.

dispersible.

displacement ton. SEE ton.

disposition. *Disposition of* funds, possessions, etc., implies distribution or utilization.
DISPOSAL. *Disposal of* funds, possessions, etc., implies getting rid of.

disproved. Preferred to *disproven.*

disputable [DIHS-pyoo-tuh-bl, dihs-PYOO—].

disputant [DIES-pyoo-tant].

disregardless. Incorrect. Use regardless.

dissociate. Preferred to *disassociate.* Disunite.

dissociation [dihs-soh-sih-ae-shuhn]. *Disassociation* is preferred. BUT dissociate [dihs-soh-shih-aet].

dissoluble or dissoluable.

dissonance [DIHS-oh-nans]. Discord.

disyllable.

Dist. Ct. (abbr.) District Court.

distaff. Woman's domain; by ext., the female part of a group.

distensible. Preferred to *-tendable* or *-dible.*

distension. Preferred to *—tion* in U.S. Stretching.

distich [DIHS-tihk]. P. —s. A strophic couplet; usually a sense unit.

distill. -ed, -ing, -ment. Preferred to *distil.*

distinct. Marked out.

distingué [dihs-tang-GAE]. Elegant in appearance.

distrait [dihs-TRAE]. Absent-minded, owing to pain or anxiety.
DISTRAUGHT. Confused mentally: *After the death of her child, she was distraught.*

distributable.

DISTRIBUTIVE ADJECTIVE. Indicates the noun is to be taken singly: *each, either, every, neither.*

distributor.

District. Capitalize if part of name: *District of Columbia, the District; Alexandria School District No. 4, the school district; Chicago Sanitary District, the sanitary district; Congressional District; 1st Naval District, naval district;* BUT customs district No. 2; first assembly district; school district No. 4.

district attorney. Pl. —attorneys. ADDRESS: The Honorable Frank S. Hogan, District Attorney, New York County, Criminal Courts Building, New York, N.Y. 10013. SALUTATION: Dear Sir, Dear Mr. Hogan.

districtwide.

ditto mark.

diurnal. (1) Taking place during the day. Opposite, nocturnal; (2) recurring every day. *Cf.* annual
DAILY. Occurring every day.

diva [DEE-vuh]. Prima donna.

dive. P. Dived preferred to dove (colloquial); diving.

divers [DIE-vuhrs]. Various, several: *The catalog listed divers models.*
DIVERSE [die-VUHRS, DIE-vuhrs, dih-vuhrs]. Several, different, unlike: *They learned the same facts but reached diverse conclusions.*

diverter, divertible.

divestible.

Divide. Continental Rocky Mountain; the divide.
DIVIDE. Split according to a plan. Separate, disjoin.

divide up. *Up* is superfluous.

divine.

Divine Father. BUT divine guidance, divine providence, divine service.

divisible.

Division. Capitalize if referring to federal governmental unit; Electro-Motive Division; the division; division of General Motors.

Division, Army. Capitalize if part of name: *21st Division* (BUT spell out numbers from first to ninth), *the division. Cf.* Army Organization.

divorced from. NOT by. Strictly, the party sued is divorced.

divorcee [dih-vawhr-SEE]. A divorced person (m. or f.). BUT: divorcé [-SAE]. (m.), divorcée (f.) [-SAE]. Address a divorced woman by her maiden name plus her married name. *Mrs. Johnson Smith.* BUT prefixed by Mrs., unless she prefers Miss. This is formal etiquette but not necessarily practiced in normal everyday living.

Dixie, Dixiecrat.

Djakarta. SEE Jakarta.

Djiboutior Jibuti [ji-BOOT-tih]. Capital city of French Somaliland.

Djilas, Milovan [JEE-las]. (1911–　) Yugoslav statesman-writer.

dk. (abbr.) deka = ten (10)

D. Lit. (t). D. (abbr.) doctor of literature.

Dnieper R. [NEE-puhr]. Russ., Dneper., [d'NYEH-pr]. Russian river flowing into Black Sea.

Dnepropetrovak [NEHP-roh-peh-trawfsk]. (N.Y. Times, Dnie—) City in the Ukraine, U.S.S.R., on the Dnieper River.

do. P., did; p.p. done.

do. (abbr.) ditto, the same.

do [doh]. (musical note) Pl. dos.

do-all. (n. and. adj.), do-gooder, do-little (n. and adj.). do-nothing (n. and adj.), do-nought (n. and adj.).

Doberman pinscher. The dog.

docible. Teachable.

docile [DAH-sihl; Brit., DOH-siel, DAH-siel]. Tractable.

dock. (n.) The water between piers or wharves. But commonly used for *piers*.

dock no. 1. Lower-case.

docket No. 66. Lower-case.

doctoral.

doctrinal [DAHK-trih-nam]. Pertaining to teachings which are to be believed.

DOCTRINAIRE [dahk-trih-NAIR]. One who would apply theories regardless of practical considerations.

Doctrine, Monroe. the doctrine; BUT Truman doctrine.

Document. Capitalize if part of name; *Document No. 2, Document numbered One Hundred and Thirty; the document.*

dodo. Pl. —oes. An extinct bird.

doe. Female of antelope, deer, rabbit, hare, rat, etc. *Cf.* buck, hart, animals.

doesn't.

dog days. Refers to the belief in the pernicious influence of dog stars Sirius and Procyon, visible for six weeks between July and September.

doggerel. Preferred to *doggrel*.

dogma. Pl. —mas.

do have. *Do you have coffee or tea?* Despite objections on the ground of formality, the double auxiliary is permissible except where the meaning of *have* is *to possess* or refers to a single occasion. Avoid substitution of *do* for a previously used verb. NOT: *They cried profusely, as they had to do, to arouse sympathy.*

dollarbird. –fish; dollar mark.

Dollars and Cents. Write in figures: *2 cents, 10 cents, $4.00, $6.35, $1,000,000.* Round numbers and approximations may be spelled out: *a dollar, a million, the million-dollar robbery, forty billion, about a million.* Spell out cents when less than $1.00 except in tables: *7 cents, 98 cents. one red cent.* In tables: *7¢, 98¢.*

dolorous [DAHL-uhr-uhs, DOHL –]. Sorrowful.

Domesday Book. [DOOMz-dae, DOHMZ –]. Record of land survey by William the Conqueror, 1085–1086.

domicile. [DAHM-ih-sihl]. —ed. [DAHM-ih-sihld]. also -cil.

dominee. Pastor of Reformed Dutch Church; 18th century schoolmaster.

Dominican [duh-MIHN-ihk'n].

Dominican Republic. Native, Dominican(s); (adj.) Dominican. Cap., Santo Domingo (formerly Ciudad Trujillo). Currency peso (RD$), centavo (Ctvo.) Sit. on E. $^2/_3$ of Island of Hispaniola.

Dominion of Canada. of New Zealand, etc.; the Dominion; BUT British dominions, a dominion, dominion status.

domino. —oes. The game, although in the plural, takes a singular verb: *Dominoes requires both skill and intelligence.*

Dona [DOH-nyah]. (Sp.) Lady; dona. A lady.

dormitory.

Donbas [DAHN-bas; Russ., duhn-bas]. also Donets Basin [doh-nehts]. Region in Ukraine, U.S.S.R.

Don Juan [dahn-JOO-an; Sp., dawn-WAHN]. Traditional Sp. profligate-nobleman-lover.

Don Quixote [dawn-kee-HOH-tee; angl., KWIHK-oht]. Character in 16th century novel by Miguel de Cervantes.

doodlebug. One who does not stand up for his convictions; a divining rod.

doomsday. The day of judgment.

Doppler effect. Apparent change in wave length of light, sound, etc. caused by change in relative position; e.g., change in pitch of train sound as it moves away.

do's and don'ts.

dos-a-dos [doh-za-DOH; square dancing; doh-see-DOH]. Back to back.

dosimeter. Instrument for measuring absorbed radiation. *Cf.* ratemeter.

Dos Passos, John Roderigo [duhs-PAS-uhs]. (1896–1970). American writer.

dossier [DAHS-ee-ae, -uhr; Fr., daw-syae]. A record about a person or subject.

Dostoevski or Dostoyevsky, Fedor Mikailovich [DAHS-tuh-YEHV-skih, FYAW-dehr, myeh-KIE-luh-vyihch]. (1821-1881) Russian writer.

dotage [DOHT-ihj]. Excessive fondness; also senility

Douay Version of the Bible. *Cf.* Bible.

double-crostic. Trademark of word-definition puzzle in which letters properly entered form a sentence.

double-entendre [DOOBL-ahn-TAHN-dre]. Expression with two meanings of which the less obvious is indicated.

DOUBLE NEGATIVE. Use of two negatives in a sentence may serve to add emphasis to the negative: *No. I'll never do it!* In many instances, the construction is incorrect: *No one said nothing.* This construction, therefore, generally serves to confuse the reader or to indicate a lack of care in the sentence formation. Difficulties arise particularly with the use of negative pronouns, *no, none, nothing*; negative adverbs, *hardly, scarcely*; negative conjunctions, *but, neither, nor*; and negative verbs, *doubt, deny, refrain.* Although it is generally assumed that two negatives make a positive, the reader is often left to puzzle out the attitude: *I could hardly approve. It is scarcely possible that no one will either deny or confirm the possibility of the cabinet's fall.*

doubt. The word should always be followed by *whether* in the affirmative and by *that* in the negative and interrogative: *I doubt whether she knows. I do not doubt that he knows.*

doubtless. Without doubt.

UNDOUBTEDLY. Beyond doubt (the stronger word).

doughty [DOW-tee]. Valiant.

Douglas fir tree.

Doukhobors [DOO-koh-bohrs]. Var. of Dukhobors. Russian religious sect.

dour [door. Dow-r]. Sour, sullen.

dove. (v.) See dive.

dowager. A widow who has inherited from her husband; an elderly lady. In Britain, the earliest surviving widow of the holder of a title: *the Dowager Marchioness of Bute. Lady Bute, the Marchioness, Alice. Marchioness of Bute, Lady Bute.*

dower. Widow's share of property.

dowry. Portion brought by a bride.

Down East. Coastal area of northeastern U.S. and southeastern Canada.

downward. Preferred to *downwards*. SEE backward.

dozen. (abbr., doz.) 12. Pl. —s. *Dozens of cousins, two dozen eggs. Cf.* baker's dozen.

DP. (abbr.) displaced person.

dr. (abbr.) debit; debtor; dram.

Dr. (abbr.) doctor.

draft [draft]. Preferred to *draught* except for drinking, fishing and air currents. But Brit. distinguish draftsman (one who draws banking drafts) and draughtsman (one who draws). U.S., draftsman.

dragoon [druh-GOON]. (n.). Compel or try to compel.

dram [dram]. A small quantity.

DRACHM [dram]. Drachma.

DRACHMA [drak-muh]. 1. Pl. —s or —mae. Greek coin. —6 obols.

DRAM. apothecaries (dram. ap.) Unit of weight is 2.1943 dr. avdp. = 0.125 ap. cz. = 2.5 dwt. = 3 scruples = 3.888 grams = 60 grains.

dram, avoirdupois. (dram avdp.) Unit of weight is 0.4558 dr. ap. is 0.0625 av. oz =1.1393 divt. = 1.3672 scruples = 1.7713 grams = 27.344 grains.

dram, liquid. (1) U.S. = 0.125 U.S. fl. oz. = 60 U.S. minims = 2256 cu. in. = 0.03125 gill = 3.6966 milliliters; (2) Brit. unit of capacity = 0.125 fl. oz. Brit. or 0.9607 U.S. liquid drams = 60 Brit. minims = 0.2167 cu. in. = 3.5514 milliliters.

drama [DRAH-muh; DRAM-muh].

dramatis personae [DRAM-uh-tihs puh-SOH-nee]. The cast.

drapery. Pl. —ies.

drapes.

draw. P., drew; p.p., drawn.

drawing II, A, 3, etc.. BUT Drawing 2 when part of title: Drawing 2.—Hydroelectric Power Development.

dreadful. Preferred to *direful*.

dreadnought. -naught. Twentieth – century ship with large guns.

dream. P. and p.p., dreamed [dreamed or dremt, drehmt; Brit. drehmpt].

dressing room.

Dreyfus, Alfred [DRAE-fuhs, DRIE-fuhs; Fr. drae-FUES]. (1859–1935) French army officer, victim of anti-semitism.

drink. P., drank; p.p., drunk, drunken.

Drive. Do not abbreviate in an address or a news report.

DRIVE. P., drove; p.p., driven.

dropout. (n.)

drought [drout]. drouth [drouth]. Lack of rain.

drowned. Preferred to *was drowned*.

dry. drier, driest, dryly. (Brit. drily). dryness, dryish, dryer (v.); (n.) drier, one who dries; dryer, the machine.

drydock no. 1. Lower-case.

dry measure. System for measuring volume of dry commodities based on pint of 33.60 cu. in., one bushel is 4 pecks is 32 quarts is 64 pints.

Du. (Fr.) preceding a name. SEE *Le*.

dual. Double: *It was a dual solution: finding workers and housing them.*

DUEL. A fight with weapons between two persons.

Dubcek, Alexander [DOOB-chehk]. (1921–) Prime Minister of Czechoslovakia, 1969.

Dubois, Paul [doo-BWAH]. (1829–1924) French sculptor.

ducat [DUHK-uht]. Coin first used c.1150, worth approx. $2.25.

duce, il [eel-DOO-cheh]. Dictator. BUT il Duce, the Leader, title of Benito Mussolini.

Duchess. Female sovereign of a duchy, or the wife or widow of a duke; the Duchess of Argyle, the Duchess. ADDRESS: Her Grace, the Duchess of Atholl. Her Grace, the Most Noble Duchess of Atholl. SALUTATION: Your Grace, Madam. ADDRESS: Her Royal Highness, the Duchess of Kent. SALUTATION: Madam.

duck. (f.), drake (m.). Pl. ducks. As food, collective: *Too much duck for 100 people.* *Cf.* animals.

duel. (v.) dueled, dueling, duelist. Brit. *ll. Cf.* dual.

dues. For club dues, Brit. use *subscription.*

due to. Avoid use of *due to* as a preposition. Use *since* or *because* where appropriate.

dufflebag.

Dufy, Raoul Ernest Joseph [deu-FEE, rah-OOL]. (1877–1953) French progressive, painter.

dugout. (n.) (Brit. dug out)

duke. ADDRESS: His Grace, the Duke of Windsor. SALUTATION: My Lord Duke; Sir; Your Grace (for servants or retainers).

Dukhobors [doo-koh-bohrs]. Russian religious sect.

du Maurier, Daphne [deu-MAW-ryae]. (1907–). English novelist.

Dumas, Alexandre [doo-MAH; angl. DOO-mah]. (Dumas pere) (1802–1870) French novelist, author of *The Count of Monte Cristo.* (Dumas fils) (1824–1895) French realistic dramatist.

dumbfound. Preferred to *dumfound.* Amaze.

dumdum. A soft-nosed bullet which expands on impact.

dunderhead. —headed.

duodecimo. (12 mo). Pl. —os. Book size, approx. $4\frac{3}{4}'' \times 8\frac{1}{4}''$.

duodenum [dyoo-oh-DEE-nuhm, dyoo-AHD-n-uhm].

duologue [dyoo-oh-lahg]. Dramatic piece for two actors.

du Pont de Nemours [deu-PAHN; angl., doo-PAHNT, de neh-moor]. Pierre Samuel (1739–1817); son, Irenee, [ee-rae-NAE]. (1771–1834) American industrialists.

durance. Being in confinement.
DURESS. Being under constraint.

during the time that. *While* is better.

durst. SEE dare.

Dusseldorf or Duesseldorf [DEUSS-ehl-dawrf; angl., DOO-sl-dawrf]. City on Rhine River, West Germany.

Dust Bowl.

dusterman.

dutiful. Preferred to *duteous.*

Duvalier, Dr. Francois (1907–1970). President of Haiti, 1957–1970.

Dvorak, Anton [DVAWR-zhahk, AN-tawn]. (1841–1904) composer.

dwell. P., dwelt or dwelled; p.p. dwelt.

dwelling house.

d.w.t. (abbr.) deadweight tons.

dwt. (abbr.) pennyweight.

dyarchy. Rule by two. Applies to government of Indian provinces. 1919–37. Others, diarchy. *Cf.* government.

dye, dyed, dyeing.
DIE, DIED, DYING.

dynamo. Pl. —os.

dynasty [DIE-nast-ee].

dysphemism. *Cf.* euphemism.

Dzhugashvilli [JOO-gah-SHVEE-lee]. SEE Stalin.

E

e. (abbr.) erg. Unit of energy = 1 dyne acting through distance of 1 cm.

E. (abbr.) east.

each. (1) As subject, always followed by singular verb; *Each has her own hat. Each of the men has two hats.*
NOT: *Each has our own hat,* or *Each has their own hat.*
BUT: *The men have two hats each.*
(2) In apposition, with a plural noun, *each* takes a plural verb: *The boys have two hats each.* (3) When *each* is emphasized, it precedes the verb or part of the verbal phrase or its complement, and takes a plural pronoun. *We each have our own hats.* (4) When the verb is emphasized, *each* follows, and a singular pronoun is used: *Masqueraders are judged, each on his own costume.* Cf. between each. *Each or every* when used to modify a compound subject (joined by *and*) is treated as a singular subject: *Each governor and every senator has approved the measure.* When *each* is inserted parenthetically or in explanation between a plural or compound subject and its plural verb, the plural verb is not affected. *A, B, and C each are entitled to rebates. The Governors each want the plans enlarged.* Each other—one another is the preferred form for more than two: *The two spoke to each other. Three of us spoke to one another.* Possessive: each other's.

Earhart, Amelia [AIR-hahrt]. (1898–1937) American aviatrix.

earl. *Address*: The Right Honorable the Earl of Athlone, or the Earl of Athlone. SALUTATION: My Lord: Sir. *Cf.* Nobility

earl's wife. SEE countess, Nobility, Lady.

Early Spring. SEE Saint.

earnest. Serious: *He studied earnestly.*
EARNEST. Guarantee of serious intention: *He provided a substantial sum as earnest money.*

earth. Lower case unless used with names of other planets.
EARTHEN. Made of earth.
EARTHLY. Belonging to this planet.
EARTH SATELLITES: *Discoverer IV: Explorer II: Sputnik I.* BUT do not capitalize *sputnik, sputniks.*
EARTHY. Containing soil; materialistic; lusty.

earthenhearted. —ware.

easement. Right granted for the use of land owned by another, e.g. to traverse.

East. Capitalize East Coast (Africa), East Europe (political entity), East Germany (political entity), Middle East, Mideast (Asia), Near East (Balkans), East South Central States, the East (section of United States), East End (London). Also the East (Communist political entity); the East Side (section of a city).

east. east coast (U.S.) N.Y. Times, East Coast (U.S.); east Pennsylvania.

east. eastern, more eastern, easternmost.

east bound. east-central (adj.), east-northwest, east-sider, east-southeast; east end, east side.

Easter. Falls on the first Sunday following the Paschal full moon on or after March 21, and must therefore fall before April 25. If Paschal full moon falls on Sunday, Easter Day is the next Sunday. *Easter*-tide.

easterly. westerly, and so on. Towards the east. When used in connection with direction, implying present motion or position attained because of prior motion: *a westerly course; the most northerly outpost of our expansion.* BUT *east end of the city; west view; south position.* eastern France; eastern seaboard; eastern time; easterner; eastward; eastern standard time. SEE time.

Eastern. Eastern Europe (political entity); Far

Eastern (Orient) (*see* Far East); Eastern Germany (political entity); Eastern Gulf States; Eastern Hemisphere (see Hemisphere); Middle Eastern, Mideastern (Asia); Eastern North Central States; Eastern States BUT: eastern farming states; eastern United States.

easy. May be used as an adv., *take it easy,* but easily is generally pref.

eat. [eht] (in Brit.) P., ate. p.p., eaten.

EATABLE. Can be eaten.

EDIBLE. Can be eaten, but indicates that a question of healthfulness has been raised; *edible mushrooms.*

eavesdrop. —dropper, —dropping; eaves molding.

E-bond.

ebullience [eh-BUHL-y'ns]. Preferred to —cy. High spirits.

écarté [ae-kahr-TAE]. Card game for two.

ecce homo [EHK-see-HOH-moh]. (Lat.) Behold the man. BUT *Ecce Homo* when referring to Christ.

Ecclesiasticus [uh-klee-zee-ASS-tihk-kuhs].

echo. Pl. echoes.

eclair [AE-klair]. Filled pastry.

eclat [AE-KLAH]. Notoriety; acclaim.

eclectic [ehk-LEHK-tihk]. Selected from many sources.

ecology. The interrelationship of organisms and environment. NOT environment itself.

economics [EEK-pref. to EHK-oh-nahm-ihks].

ecru [ehk-roo, AE-kroo]. Beige color.

Ecuador [EHK-wah-dawr]. Native, Ecuadoran-(s); adj., Ecuadoran. Cap., Quito. Currency, sucre (/$/), centavo (Ctvo).

eczema [EHK-seh-muh]. Pl. —mas or —mata.

ed., eds. (abbr.) edition, editions.

edema [uh-DEE-muh]. Preferred to oedema. Pl. —mas, edemata. Body swelling, usually due to excess fluid.

edgeways. Or —wise.

Edinburgh [EHD-'n-Buhr-oh; Brit. —buh-ruh, bruh]. Capital city of Scotland.

e.d.t. (abbr.) eastern daylight time.

educate. —cable, —cative.

educe. —cible. Bring out something latent.

EEC. (abbr.) European Economic Community; the Inner Six. Originally Belgium, Luxembourg, the Netherlands, France, Germany, Italy.

EEE. (abbr.) eastern equine encephalitis.

eerie. Preferred to eery.

effect [eh-FEHKT]. (v.) Cause, bring about: *She has effected many improvements since she became principal.* Effectible.

AFFECT. (v.) Influence: *The announcement affected prices immediately.*

EFFECT. (n.) Result, consequence: *The effect of the price change was an immediate demand.*

effective. Applies to people, deeds, or measures producing or able to produce a substantial result: an *effective* speaker.

EFFECT OF ... IS PRODUCTIVE. Is redundant. NOT: *The effect of the new tax is to produce a new middle class.*

EFFECTUAL. Applies to means and actions and implies the achievement of the desired effect: *an effectual action.*

EFFICACIOUS. Applies to medicines, etc.; implies possession of a quality that makes it effective; *an efficacious drug.*

EFFICIENT. Applies to persons, machines or organizations and implies energy and competence.

effectuate. To carry into effect.

effervescible. Able to effervesce.

effluvium [eh-FLOO-vee-uhm]. Pl. effluvia or —ums. Something that flows out.

e.g. (abbr.) *Exempli gratia.* (Lat.) For instance. Always precede with a comma or a semicolon.

egoism. Excessive love of self; egocentricity. Opposite. *altruism.*

EGOTISM. Excessive reference to self; conceit

egregious [ee-GREE-juhs, —jih-uhs]. Outstanding (from the flock), usually for bad quality; used as a term of contempt: *That egregious liar. . .*

Egypt. SEE United Arab Republic. Cap., Cairo, [KIE-roh]. Currency, pound (Ef), piaster (Pi., Pias.).

EHF. (abbr.) extemely high frequency.

Ehrenburg, Ilya Grigorievich [AIR-ehn-buhrg, EEL-yah, gryih-gawr-yeh-vyihch]. (1891–1971) Russian journalist.

Eiffel Tower [ei-fehl].

8. 8 vo. (abbr.) octavo. Book of pages 6″ × 9″.

Eire [AE-reh]. (Gaelic) Ireland. Formerly Irish Free State.

Saorstat Eireann [SAIR-staht AIR-ihn]. (1922–1927). See Ireland for geographic and political references. Republic of Ireland is official name.

Eisenhower, Dwight David [IES-ehn-our]. (1890–1969) 34th President of U.S. (1953–1961).

either or [EE-thuhr; EI-thuhr]. Use to distinguish two choices, NOT more than two; *either of the NATO nations.*
 Although the meaning of *either* as *both* persists in U.S., it is not acceptable in Britain: *Curtains at either end of the room.*

either . . . or, neither . . . nor. A complete alternative should follow each of the words, and the alternatives should be in structural balance: *The men wanted either more days off or higher wages.* NOT: *The men wanted either to have more days off or higher wages.* Usually takes a sing. v., but where a subject contains a pl., a pl. v. is acceptable especially where pl. applies to both. *Neither of the men are coming. Are either coming?*

eke out. Stretch out the usefulness of something by adding to it: *He was able to eke out a living by taking an additional part-time job.* NOT: *He was able to eke out a living from his menial job.*

El Al Israel Airlines. Israeli airline.

élan [ae-LAHNN]. assumed enthusiasm.

Elbe [EAL-buh; angl., ehlb]. River that flows through Czechoslovakia, Germany, to the North Sea.

elder, eldest. Used in preference to *older, oldest* when speaking of age of members of a family, except when used in the comparative sense. *An elder son* is the oldest of two in the family; *an older son* is older than the one previously mentioned.

-elect. Elected, but not yet installed in office; president-elect. Capitalize titles preceding names, and when standing alone in specific references to government office: *Senator-elect John J. Smith. Cf.* suffix.

elective course. Optional course.

electoral college. the electors.

electric. Pertains to electricity; *electric bulbs, motors, house wiring, shock, —eel, —dynamo.*
 ELECTRICAL. Concerning electricity. *Electrical course, book, training.*
 ELECTRO-. Combining form meaning electric: electro-optics, electro-osmosis, electro-ultrafiltration.

electrolysis. Process of chemical decomposition by electricity in which negative ions move toward an anode while positive ions move toward a cathode.

electromagnetic radiation. SEE rays.

electromotive force. (abbr. e.m.f.) Pressure under which electricity flows, measured in volts.

electron. Negatively charged physical particle (−1/1840 of mass of hydrogen atom) which orbits around nucleus of an atom. *Cf.* atom.

electronics. (n.) electronic (adj.). Branch of physics which deals with electrons, especially with their action in gases and vacuum tubes. The field covers radio, TV, modern computers, the flow of electrons, etc.

elegiac, —al [ehl-ee-GIE-ak or GEE-ak]. Suitable for elegies; having the tone of an elegy.

elegy. A poem of mourning.
 EULOGY. Commentary on or praise of the deceased.

elemental. Refers to the elements; primal: *elemental spirit; drive.*
 ELEMENTARY. Pertains to basic components, great principles, simple, or a single element: *elementary school.*

elevator. British use lift.

elf. elves, elfish or elvish.

elicit. Draw out: *They tried to elicit more information.*

 ILLICIT. Unlawful or prohibited: *An illicit love affair.*

Elisha [ee-LIE-shuh]. Hebrew prophet.

Elizabeth II. (1926–) Queen of England (1950–) The Queen, the Crown, Her Most Gracious Majesty, Her Majesty.

Elizabethan Age [eh-lisz-uh-BEE-thuhn; eh-LIHZ-uh-behth'n]. 1533–1560. *Cf.* Ages.

elk. U.S. —Brit. red deer, wapiti. *Cf.* animals. an elk.

ell. British unit of cloth length = 45 in. = 1/32 bolt.

ellipse [eh-LIHPS]. A plane curve, roughly egg-shaped.

ELLIPSIS. Pl. —ses. Omission of word or words, in quotation, indicated by three dots in the middle of a sentence or four dots at the end of a sentence. When a complete paragraph or more is omitted, three asterisks (***) may be inserted as a separate line, or a complete line of dots may be made.
 "When in the course of human events it becomes necessary ... to assume, among the powers ..."
   ***
 "... it becomes necessary for one people ..."

elliptic. Usually refers to ellipse.

 ELLIPTICAL. Usually refers to ellipsis.

ELLIPTICAL CLAUSES. When parts of a dependent clause are omitted, the reader is presumed to understand the missing elements. However, the writer should be certain that the modifiers in the incomplete clauses identify, both logically and grammatically, the subject of the main clause. *If he is rich and I (am) poor, why tax me?*
 In a parallel writing, corresponding portions of expressions may be omitted, esp. (1) the parts of the verb *be: He is there and I here;* (2) compound verbs: *She cannot love him or leave him;* (3) subject after than: *No greater love is possible than* (the love) *she gives.* But NOT if the tense, voice, or number changes.

El Paso [ehl-PASS-oh]. City in Texas, on Mexican border.

else [ehls]. other; additional to. everyone else's preferred to everyone's else.

em. Measure of type = width equal to the height of the line. An em of 12 pt. type = 12 points = 1/6 in.

Emancipation Proclamation.

embargo. Pl., —oes. Prohibition of commerce or freight.

embarrass. embarrassment.

Embassy. British, etc.; the Embassy; BUT embassy when standing alone; consulate.

embed. —dded. Preferred to imbed.

emblematic. Preferred to —cal.

embrasure [ehm-BRAE-zhyehr]. Recess for a door or window.

emend. —ation. Correct, especially in a literary work.

Emerald Isle. Ireland.

emerge [ee-merj]. To rise out of: *The submarine emerged from the water; ... emerge from poverty.* Adj., emerged.

 IMMERGE, IMMERSE. To disappear, to plunge into: *The figure immerged into the shadows. He immersed himself in work.* (adj.) immersed.

emergence. Coming into notice.

 EMERGENCY. Situation requiring immediate help.

emeritus [ee-MEHR-iht-uhs]. Retired, with title; Dr. John J. Smith, professor emeritus or emeritus professor of English literature; NOT professor of English literature emeritus.

e.m.f. (abbr.) electromotive force.

emigrant. Person who leaves a country.

 EMIGRÉ [ae-mee-GRAE]. Political emigrant, especially Royalist refugee.

 REFUGEE. Political emigrant who has suffered great hardships or losses.

 IMMIGRANT. Person who comes into a country.

eminent domain. Power of a state, subject to

payment, to acquire private property for public use.

emir, emeer [eh-MEER]. (Arab.) Military commander or leader; (Turk.) title of dignity.

emollient [ee-MAHL-ih-ehnt, -yehnt]. A soothing medication. *emollient for a burn.*

EMOLUMENT [ee-MAHL-yoo-mehnt]. Remuneration: *She received a salary and other emoluments, including room and board.*

emotive. Expressing emotions.

emotional. Arousing emotions; prone to emotion.

empanel. Use impanel.

Emperor. Capitalize when part of a title or referring to a specific person; Emperor Haile Selassie; the Emperor.

Empire. Ethiopian, etc.; the Empire; BUT an empire.

Empire State. New York.

empirical [ehm-PIHR-ih-kal]. Preferred to empiric. Depending on experience or observation. —cally, —piricism.

employ. AVOID in the sense of use in informal writing.

employee, employe. Brit. employe [ehm-PLOI-ee]. Pl., —yees.

employ. Stresses the use of a person's services.

HIRE. Stresses the act of engaging a person's services.

emptor. (Lat.) Buyer. *Caveat emptor.* Buyer beware.

empyrean [ehm-pih-REE-an]. The highest heaven.

emu [EE-myoo]. Large Australian bird.

en. Measure of type. ½ em.

en-. Prefix meaning *in.*

enamor. Brit. —our.

encase. Use incase. Brit. en—.

encephal-. Prefix meaning *of the brain.*

Encino [ehn-SEE-noh]. Town in California.

enclasp.

enclave. Territory enclosed in a foreign territory.

enclose. Inclose is pref. only as legal term. enclosure.

ENCLOSED HEREWITH. Herewith is superfluous.

ENCLOSED PLEASE FIND. AVOID as trite and archaic commercialese.

encumber. encumbrance.

encyclopedia. SEE dictionary.

end. There is no comparative form. Superlative: endmost.

endeavor. Brit. —our.

ended. For references to the past: *The period ended (last) Dec. 31.*

ENDING. For references to the future: *Period ending (next) Dec. 31.*

endemic. Habitually prevalent; native.

EPIDEMIC. Temporarily widespread.

PANDEMIC. Affecting all people.

-e endings in adj. Drop the final *e* when adding *y; wave, wavy*; except: (1) To avoid confusion with another word: *hole, holey.* (2) Nouns ending in *-ue: glue, gluey.* Nouns ending in *y* take *ey* to avoid *yy* ending: *clay, clayey.*

endive [EHN-dieve, AHN-deev]. Variety of chicory.

endocrine [EHN-doh-krien; -krihn, -kreen]. (adj.) Secreting internally.

endorse. (v.) NOT *indorse.* Method of transferring title by signing on the back of a negotiable instrument, *e.g.* a check or note. Also, express approval: *They endorsed the product.* —ment. In insurance, addition to a policy.

end result. Unless there are intermediate results, *end* is superfluous.

endue. Preferred to indue. Endow.

endurable [ehn-DYOOR-uh-b'l].

endways. Pref. to —wise.

energumen [ehn-uhr-GYOO-mehn]. A raving devotee; one possessed by a devil or by frenzy.

enforce. (v.) Give force to execute: *Enforce the law.* Do not confuse with force. enforceable, —ment.

enfranchise. NOT —ize. Set free; admit to citizenship or its privileges.

engine. Used for steam-driven (except turbines), rocket-driven, some gasoline-driven and reciprocal electrical devices.

 MOTOR. Used for gasoline or electrically driven devices.

Engine Company. Bethesda; engine company No. 6; No. 6 engine company; the company.

Engineer officer. of Engineer Corps.

engineer's chain. (abbr. ch.) Unit in length = 100 ft. = 30.48 m.

engineer's link. (abbr. li.) (SEE *engineer's chain*) Unit of length 1/100 chain = 12 in. = 0.3048 m.

Engineers, Chief of. SEE Chief; Corps. of Engineers, SEE Corps.

England [IHNG-l'nd]. Refers to that part of the British Isles, but by ext. to the whole of Great Britain, in spite of qualms of Scots and Welshmen. For most situations, *British* may be substituted. BUT: *English language, history, fair play, gentleman; the word of an Englishman. Cf.* British, United Kingdom.

ENGLISH LANGUAGE. Derived principally from the Roman and the Germanic tribes (the Angles, Saxons, and Jutes) who came to Britain in 449 A.D. to help Romans control the native Celts, who spoke Gaelic. Word origins today can be traced to Greek and Latin (56%); German (33%); Oriental, African, and Amer. Indian (6%); and Celtic (2%).

engross. Copy or write. Also corner a market for a commodity (take all of).

 ENGROSSED. Absorbed; fully occupied.

enhance. Intensify; advance; make greater.

Enid [EE-nihd]. Wife of Geraint in *Idylls of the King. Cf.* Aeneid.

enjoin. Command, forbid.

en masse [ehn mass]. All together.

enmesh. Not inmesh.

ennui [ahn-WEE]. Boredom.

enough. Preferred as a noun and as an adjective of amount only, regardless of kind or quality.

 SUFFICIENT. Preferred as an adjective. As an adverb, the choice depends on the formality required.

enroll. —ed, —ing, —ment. Brit. *l.*

Ens. (abbr.) ensign [EHN-sihn]. SEE officers.

ensanguine [ehn-SANG-gwihn]. (v.) make bloody.

ensure. (v.) Preferred for most uses. To make sure.

 INSURE. (v.) To assure against loss by a contingent event, as in life insurance.

 ASSURE. (v.) Convince, make confident.

entente [ahn-TAHNT]. Friendly agreement; also those who join in an entente.

enterprise. Pl. —s; —sing.

enthrall. Preferred to —*l.* BUT —lled, —lling.

entire. —ty [ehn-TIER; en-TIER-tih]. Entirely completed is a tautology.

entity. An existing thing.

 NONENTITY. A thing or person of no consequence. In philosophy, a thing that does not exist.

entomology [ehn-toh-MAHL-oh-jih]. Study of insects.

 ETYMOLOGY [eht-ih-MAHL-oh-jih]. Study of the history of words; the derivation of a word.

 ETIOLOGY [ee-tee-AHL-oh-jih]. Science of causes, especially of diseases.

entr'acte [ahn-TRAKT]. an interval between acts; a short number between acts.

entree, entrée [both, AHN-trae]. Entrance; also, main course of a meal.

entrench. Preferred to in-.

entrepôt [AHN-treh-poh]. Warehouse.

entrepreneur. Person who assumes ownership, management, and risk of a business.

entrust. Preferred to intrust. Give into the charge of, or place in charge of something. NOT merely trust, or place trust in.

entry, entrant. Either may be used for one who enters a contest.

entwine.

ENUMERATION. Place numbers in an enumeration in parenthesis. *He wanted (1) cash payment, (2) a large house, and (3) a guaranteed income.* When the enumeration is formally introduced, capitalize the first word in each section of some length. *He listed three assets: (1) Cash in the bank; (2) A large house on Duane Street; and (3) A guaranteed income of $10,000 a year.* BUT do not capitalize brief items.
   Capitalize the first word in each element of an enumeration if it is presented in a sentence style, but do not capitalize brief items. Enumerations within a sentence take normal punctuation, using commas between simple elements and semicolons between long elements. If enumerated items are not complete sentences, omit the closing periods. Avoid ending a line with a division mark.
   Use a dash to set off added defining or enumerating elements: *These Indians—Apache, Shawnee, and Mohawk—had depended on treaties signed before 1900.* Use a dash to set off a phrase on a separate line.
   I say—*(1) That they are poor workers.*
        (2) That they should be retired.
   Complicated enumerations should be reduced to two or more sentences.

enunciate [ee-NUHN-shih-aet. -sih-aet. —ciation. -sih-ae-shun. -shih-].

enure. Variation of inure.

envelop [ehn-VEHL-uhp]. (v.) Surround. *The fog enveloped the house.*
   ENVELOPE [EHN-veh-lohp; AHN-veh-lohp]. (n.) A wrapper. *Place the letter in a No. 10 envelope.*

Envelope Sizes. Commercial, No. 5, $3\frac{1}{2} \times 5\frac{1}{2}$; $6\frac{1}{2}$, $3\frac{1}{2} \times 6$; $6\frac{1}{4}$, $3\frac{3}{8} \times 6\frac{1}{4}$. Official No. 7, $3\frac{1}{4} \times 6\frac{3}{4}$; No. $7\frac{3}{4}$, $3\frac{7}{8} \times 7\frac{1}{2}$; No. $8\frac{5}{8}$, $3\frac{5}{8} \times 8\frac{5}{8}$; No. 9, $3\frac{7}{8} \times 8\frac{7}{8}$; No. 10, $4\frac{1}{8} \times 9\frac{1}{2}$; No. 11, $4\frac{1}{2} \times 10\frac{3}{8}$. etc.

environs [ehn-VIE-ruhnz]. Suburbs; surroundings. There is no singular.
   ENVIRON (v.) Surround.

envoy [EHN-voi]. Postscript to a poem, essay, or book; also a messenger; diplomat ranking between ambassador and minister; Envoy Extraordinary and Minister Plenipotentiary.

the envoy.

enwrap.

Eocene. cf. Ages, Historic.

Eolian. SEE Aeolian.

e.o.m. (abbr.) end of month. A term of payment.

eon. Variation of Aeon. Division of geological time.

-eous, -ious. When preceded by *c*, sound *c* as *sh*. *precious.*

épée [ae-PAE]. Pointed sword with no cutting edges.

Ephesus [EHF-eh-suhs]. Ancient Ionian city in West Asia Minor.

EPIC. (abbr.) End Poverty In California, plan of Upton Sinclair, 1934.

Epictetus [ehp-ihk-TEE-tuhs]. (c.100 A.D.) Greek Stoic philosopher.

epicurean [ehp-ih-kyoor-EE-uhn]. SEE hedonist.

epidemic. SEE endemic.

epigram. -mmatic.

epilogue. Preferred to —log. epilogist. (v.) epilogue, —ed, —ing.

Epiphany [eh-PIHF-uh-nih]. Feast celebrating the coming of the Magi, Jan. 6.

Epirus, Epeirus [eh-PIE-ruhs]. Ancient Greek city-state on Ionian Sea.

episcopal. (adj.) Pertaining to bishops.

Episcopal. Pertaining to the Episcopal Church, an Episcopalian.

epitome [eh-PIHT-oh-mee]. A short statement of the contents of a work; part that typefies the whole. NOT: the high point.

epoch [EHP-ahk]. Period of event marking a distinct development.

epode [EHP-ohd]. Poem style in which short verse follows long verse.

equal. -ed, equaling. Brit. use *ll*.

EQUALLY AS. Redundant. Use: *He is as good as you. He is equally good.*

equerry [EHK-wehr-ee]. Personal attendant of a noble.

equilibrium. Pl. -iums (equilibria, scientific).

equivalence. Preferred to -cy.

equivocal [ee-KWIHV-oh-kuhl]. Questionable, ambiguous.

eradicate. -cable.

erasable [ee-RAES-uh-bl]. Able to be erased.

IRASCIBLE [ih-RAS-ih-bl]. Quick-tempered.

ere long, ere now.

ergo [uhr-goh]. (Lat.) Therefore; often used facetiously.

Ericson, Leif [EHR-ihk-s'n, Laev]. (c.1000) Norwegian discoverer of Vinland, North America, somewhere between Labrador and New Jersey.

Erie [EE-rih]. City in Pennsylvania.

Erie-Lackawanna Railway.

Erin. Ireland. (Poetic.) *Cf.* Ireland

ERIN GO BRAH. Ireland forever. Ancient battle cry.

Eritrea [ehr-ree-TRAE-uh]. Country in northeast Africa, federated with Ethiopia since 1950.

erodible. Preferred to —able. Capable of being worn away.

ERP. (abbr.), European recovery program.

errant. Wandering: A knight errant. Also, erring.

ARRANT. Confirmed: *An arrant fool.*

errata [air-AH-tuh]. Sing. erratum. The plural refers to a list of errors and may take a singular verb.

errorproof.

erstwhile. Archaic for formerly.

erudite [AIR-oo-diet, AIR-yoo-diet]. Learned.

eruption. A bursting out of something confined: *a volcanic eruption, a skin eruption.*

IRRUPTION. A bursting in or invasion: *An irruption of children into the study made work impossible.*

erysipelas [ehr-ih-SIHP-eh-luhs]. A skin disease.

Esau [EE-saw].

escapable.

eschew [ehs-CHOO]. Shun.

escrow [ehs-KROH, EHS-kroh]. An agreement to place property in the hands of a third party to be held until certain acts are performed.

escudo. (abbr. Esc.) Pl. —os. Monetary unit of Portugal and several former Spanish countries.

Eskimo. Pl. —s.

esoteric. Private; understood only by the initiated.

EXOTERIC. Understood by the many.

EXOTIC. Of foreign origin.

esophagus [ee-SAH-fuh-guhs]. Pl. —i [jie].

especially. Separates the pre-eminent. SEE special.

SPECIALLY. Separates the peculiar or individual.

espionage [EHS-pih-oh-nihj, EHS-pih-oh-nahzh]. Spying.

esplanade [ehs-pluh-NAED, NAHD]. Walkway.

espresso, expresso. Strong, black, steam-brewed coffee (Ital.).

Esquire [ehs-KWIER; BUT EHs-quier magazine].

ESQ. (abbr.) esquire. Used in Brit. after surname, only where there is no title (Sir, Dr., Prof. etc.) to denote a gentleman: John Jones, Esq. NOT Mr. John Jones, Esq. In U.S., an affectation.

essay. (v.) attempt.
ASSAY. Test.

essence. Preferred in use for spirit and quality.
SUBSTANCE. Preferred in use for materials and quantities.

essential. Being such in essence; absolute, needful: *Light is essential for plant growth.*
INDISPENSABLE. Cannot be spared, even though only an adjunct: *No man is indispensable to a well run organization.*
NECESSARY. Required for an end or condition; compulsory: *It is necessary to be at work early.*
REQUISITE. Required if the purpose is to be accomplished: *The first requisite is paper and ink.*
However, the four words are often used interchangeably.

essential modifier. SEE restrictive modifier.

E.S.T. (abbr.) Eastern Standard Time.

establishment. Capitalize if part of name; BUT the establishment, civil establishment; legislative establishment.

esthete. Variation of aesthete. British pref. e—

estimate. -matable, -mation.

estivate. Brit. aestivate. Spend the summer. Opposite, hibernate. Spend the winter.

Estonia. Native Estonian(s). Adj. Estonian. Cap., Tallinn. Since 1940, part of U.S.S.R.

estimate. An approximation of value or cost.
ESTIMATION. The process of arriving at an estimate; also, esteem.

estuary [EHS-tyoo-ehr-ih]. Where the tide meets a river current.

e.s.u. (abbr.) electrostatic unit.

e.t. (abbr.) eastern time.

et al. (*et alia*) (Lat.) And others.

et al., et alibi. (Lat.) And elsewhere.

et alii, et aliae. (Lat.) And others; (masc. and fem. pl.).

etc. etcetera, and so forth. NOT suitable for literary works. Always preceded by a comma or a semicolon. In printing a speaker's language, the words *and so forth* or *et cetera* are used—not the abbreviation *etc.*

ethics. The science, especially of honor.
MORALS. The practice, especially of sexual acts.

Ethiopia [EE-thih-OH-pih-ah]. East African republic on the Red Sea. Formerly Abyssinia. Adj., Ethiopian. Cap., Addis Ababa. Currency, Ethiopian dollar, (Eth. $); cent.

etiology. *Cf.* entomology.

Etna, Aetna [EHT-nah]. Volcano in N.E. Sicily.

étude [AE-tyood]. Study; especially musical practice piece.

etymology. *Cf.* entomology.

Euclid [YOO-klihd]. (c. 300 B.C.) Greek mathematician. euclidean.

eugenic [yoo-JEHN-ihk]. Pertains to the production of good offspring.

euphemism. -mistic, -mize. A mild or vague acceptable term substituted for a disagreeable one: *disadvantaged* or *underprivileged* for *poor; passing away* for *dying.* Opp. dysphemism.
EUPHUISM. Affectation in literary style, usually with excessive figures of speech, especially characteristic of the Elizabethan Age.
EUPHONY. Harmony of sound.

Euphrates [yoo-FRAE-teez]. River flowing from East Turkey to Persian Gulf; site of Babylonian civilization.

Eurasian. One of mixed European and Asiatic descent.

European. A native of Europe. In Union of South Africa, a white person; a Negro European is called a European (or French, German, etc.).

European Economic Community. (EEC) The Common Market. France, West Germany, Italy, Belgium, Netherlands, Luxembourg, Britain, Denmark, and additional members.

European Free Trade Association. (abbr.

EFTA). The Outer Seven. Austria, Denmark, Great Britain, Norway, Portugal, Sweden, Switzerland, and associates.

Euratom. European Atomic Energy Community.

European plan. In a hotel, plan under which charges cover rooms only, not meals.

AMERICAN PLAN. Charges include meals.

CONTINENTAL PLAN. Charges include continental breakfast of roll, coffee, sometimes orange juice.

MODIFIED AMERICAN PLAN. Charges include two meals daily.

European theater of operations. the European theater; the theater.

Eustacian tube [yoo-STAE-kih-an]. Tube connecting the middle ear and the nose.

evacuate. —cuable; —ee (either sex).

evaluate. —uable.

evanescent [ehv-uh-NEHS-ehnt]. Fleeting.

evasion. An illegitimate avoidance. Evasiveness, evasible.

AVOIDANCE. Keeping clear of.

eve. The evening, or day before: *Christmas eve.*

even. SEE placement of words.

evenness.

ever. Always; at any time; in any case.

evert. Turn inside out. eversible.

everybody, everybody else. Both take singular verb and pronoun.

every one. Each individual.

every which way. A U.S. colloquialism. In every direction, in every manner.

everywhere. (adj.) Every place.

evidence. Part of proof.

evidently [EAV-ih-dehnt-lee]. Obviously as is clear from the evidence. NOT seemingly.

APPARENTLY. Clear, manifest, visibly.

evince [ee-VIHNS]. Display, exhibit; give some evidence of. evincible.

evolution [ev-oh-LYOO-shuhn]. Brit., ee—.

-ex, -ix. Plural form in Latin is —*ices*, in English, —*exes*: index, indexes, indices. Scientific and technical words tend toward the Latin; popular words usually use the English form. Words of questionable status may take either form, the immediate use determining.

exacerbate [ehg-ZASS-ehr-baet]. Irritate.

exactly. Precisely, accurately.

JUST. Closely; nearly; almost; precisely; particularly as to time: *It is just six o'clock.*

exaggerate.

ex cathedra [ehks-kuh-THEE-druh]. (Lat.) From the seat of authority.

exceeding. -ly. More than the average; extraordinary. (v.) Going beyond.

EXCESSIVE. —ly. More than enough: *In spite of excessive spending, he was not exceeding his ability to pay.*

excellence. High quality or virtue.

EXCELLENCY. Title of high station.

excellency. His; Their excellencies.

excellent. AVOID use with more or most. SEE strong opinion words.

except. To introduce an exclusion, *except* is stronger than *but.*

excepting. Properly used only with *not: Everyone makes occasional errors in language, not excepting the teacher.*

exercises. Meaning a ceremony, is used only for religious exercises in Britain.

excerpt [EHK-suhrpt]. (n.) Extract.

Exchange. New York Stock Exchange, the stock exchange; the exchange.

EXCLAMATION POINT. Designates surprise, admiration or emotion. It should be used sparingly. Excessive use is equivalent to overexcited speech. *And mark this well!* place inside parentheses and quotation marks where sentence ends within. In Spanish, an inverted exclamation point also precedes the appropriate sentence.

exclosure. Area separated from outside elements.

excommunicate. —cable.

Ex. Doc. (abbr.) (with letter) executive document.

execrate. (v.) Curse.
EXECRABLE [EHKS-ih-kruh-b'l]. Detestable.

Executive (President of the United States); Executive Decree No. 100; Executive Decree 100; but Executive decree, Document No. 91; Executive Mansion; the mansion; the White House; Executive Office; the Office; Executive Order No. 31; but Executive order power.

executive agreement. branch, communication, department, document, paper.

executor [ehk-SEHK-yoo-tawr]. Pl. -s. Agent of an estate; one who executes something. Fem. -trix, pl. -trices.

exegesis [ehk-see-JEE-sihs]. Pl. exegeses. Exposition, especially of Scriptures.

exemplary [ekg-ZEHM-pla-ree; EGG-zehm-plehr-ih]. Serving as a pattern, warning or example.

exhale [ehks-HAEL, ehg-ZAEL]. Breathe out.

exhalation [ehks-ha-LAE-shuhn].

exhaustible.

exhibit 2, A, II, etc. BUT Exhibit 2, when part of title: *Exhibit 2: Capital Expenditures 1935–49.*

exhilarate [ehgs-ZIHL-uh-raet]. Gladden.

exigency [EHK-sih-jehn-sih]. Preferred to -ce. Urgent requirement.

exigible [EHKS-eh-jih-b'l]. Chargeable.

exiguous [ihg-ZIHG-yoo-uhs]. Scanty, diminutive.

existence.

existentialism. A pessimistic system of philosophy based on belief that all sensations have

"existence" as states of mind; therefore, there is no difference between external and internal worlds. Assuming an individual is contingent and free, he is responsible for what he is. The individual must oppose his hostile environment by exercise of free will. There is no God and therefore no system of values.

ex officio [ehks-uh-FISH-ih-oh]. (n.) ex-officio (adj.) By virtue of an office.

exorbitant.

exordium [ehg-ZAWR-dih-uhm]. Pl. -ms or -ia. Introductory portion of speech.

exotic. From a foreign source. *Cf.* esoteric.

expansible or expandable.

ex parte [ehks PAHRT-ee]. (n.) and (adj.) (Lat.) In the interest of one side only: *An ex parte legal action.*

expatriate. NOT expatriot.

expect. May be used idiomatically for *expect to find that: I expect he will make the grade.*

expediency. Preferred to —ce.

expedite. Speed up. expeditious.

Expedition. Byrd; Lewis and Clark Expedition; the expedition.

expert [EHKS-puhrt]. (n.) [ehks-PUHRT]. (adj.)

expiate [EHK-spih-aet]. Atone for. —iable, -iation.

expletive [EHKS-plih-tihv]. In grammar, filler word used to introduce an intransitive verb: *There* are two people here. *It* is time to go.

explicit. Emphasizes detail; plainly stated. NOT full, absolute.
EXPRESS. Emphasizes *great* force.
EXPRESSED. Emphasizes intention.
All mean definite and specific terms set forth in words.

explosible. Capable of being exploded.
EXPLOSIVE. Suitable for causing an explosion; tending to explosion.

exponent [ehks-POH-nehnt]. One who expounds, interprets or represents.

Export-Import Bank. U.S. government corporation to finance or guarantee credit on exports; the bank.

exposé [ehks-poh-ZAE]. (n.) Exposure of something discreditable.
EXPOSE [ehks-POHZ]. (v.) Lay open.

Exposition. California-Pacific International Exposition; the exposition.

ex post facto [ehks-pohst-FAK-toh]. After the fact; retroactive: *In the U.S. an ex post facto law is not enforcible.*

Express. Capitalize if part of name: *The Federal Express.*

expressible.

express man. —way; express train.

exquisite [EHKS-kwih-siht].

extend. —ible ; increase, reach out. The use as *give* is questionable. NOT: *extend an invitation.* Also extensible.

extent. Range. Avoid qualifying with a descriptive adjective. NOT: *the exotic extent of men's fashions...*
EXTANT [EHKS-tant]. In existence.

external. That which is outside and apart. *External appearances, conditions, parts.* Opposite internal.

exterminate. -nable.

extol or **extoll** [ehks-TOHL] —ed, —ing. Elevate by praise.

extortionate [ehk-STAWR-sh'n-aet]. Excessive.

extract [EHKS-trakt]. (n.) [ehks-TRAKT]. (v.)

extraneous [ehks-TRAE-nee-uhs]. Coming from the outside; not pertinent; external; foreign.

extrasensory perception. (abbr. ESP). Unexplainable perception beyond the five senses; e.g., telepathy. *Cf.* parapsychology.
EXTRATEMPORAL PERCEPTION. Unexplainable ability to foresee the future.

extraterritorial. Preferred to exterritorial. Outside the limits of.

extravaganza [ehk-strav-uh-GAN-zah]. Spectacular dramatic or musical composition.

extricate [EHKS-trih-kaet]. (v.) Free from difficulties. -cable.

extrinsic. (n.) unessential. Opposite intrinsic. *Cf.* extraneous.

Eyck, Hubert or **Huybrecht von** [vahn-IEK, HEU-behrt or HOI-brehkt]. (1366–1428) brother Jan [yahn] (1370–1440) Flemish painters.

eye. (v.) eyed; eying, or eyeing.
EYEGLASSES. British prefer spectacles.
EYRIE, AERIE. A nest.

Ezekiel [ee-ZEEK-yehl]. (600–549 B.C.) Biblical prophet.

F

F. (abbr.), Fahrenheit [FAR-uhn-hiet, FEHR-]. Scale of heat measurement named for G.D. Fahrenheit. To convert centigrade to Fahrenheit, multiply centigrade degrees by 9, divide by 5, add 32. To convert Fahrenheit to centigrade, subtract 32 and multiply by $\frac{5}{9}$. $32°F = 0°C$ (freezing); $70°F = 21.1°C$ (ordinary room); $110°F = 43.3°C$ (bath); $212°F = 100°C$ (boiling). *Cf.* Kelvin, Reaumur, Temperature.

f. (abbr.), farad.

f. (abbr.), feminine.

f., ff. (abbr.), and following page (pages).

F-flat. F-horn, F-sharp.

F. (for focal) number. In photography, focal length of lens divided by effective diameter. The brighter the light, the higher F number required.

fabricate. Stresses skill; construct; put together: *The model was fabricated here.*

MANUFACTURE. Stresses labor. *The product was manufactured there.*

fabulous [FAB-yuh-luhs]. Like a fable; incredible.

façade [fa-SAHD]. The cedilla is used in the best form.

facetious [fuh-SEE-shuhs]. Given to jesting, sometimes crudely.

factbook. -finding (adj.) (GPO, one word).

factitious. [fak-TIHSH-uhs]. Sham; artificial.

faculty. In U.S., the teaching staff, in Brit., one of the university departments: *Faculty of Law.* Pl., faculties (more than one school). Unless singular is indicated, *a* or *the faculty*, singular or plural verb may be used.

Fair Deal. Policies of Pres. Harry S. Truman.

Fair. World's Fair; the fair.

fait accompli. (Fr.) [feht uh-KAHN-plee]. A deed presumably irrevocable, accomplished.

faker [FAEK-ehr]. Swindler; fraud.

FAKIR [fuh-KEER, FAEK-ehr]. Religious, beggar and wonder-worker.

Falangist. Member of Spanish fascist organization.

falcon [FAWL-kuhn, Brit., faw-kn]. Type of hawk.

falderal, folderol [FAL-deh-ral, -RAL; -reh-l, -AHL]. Old song refrain; a bit of nonsense.

fall. P., fell; p.p., fallen; falling.

fallible [FAL-ih-b'l]. Subject to error.

fallow land.

Falls, Niagara. the falls.

Falmouth [FAL-muhth]. Town in Massachusetts.

falsetto [fawl-SEHT-oh]. Pl. -os. Artifical voice.

fancies. Both singular and plural form.

Fanciful Appellations. Capitalize when used with or for a proper name. Bay State (Massachusetts), Big Four (powers, railroads, etc.), City of Churches (Brooklyn), New Deal, Fair Deal, Administration Policies, Great Father the President, Keystone State (Pennsylvania), the Hub (Boston).

Faneuil, Peter [FAN-l, FAN-y'l]. (1700–1743). American merchant. Faneuil Hall, Boston.

fangle. With new, a fashion: *a new-fangled automobile.*

Fannie Mae. N.Y. Times, Fanny May. Federal National Mortgage Association, which buys mortgages from banks at a small discount. Fanny Mays are the bonds.

fantasia [fan-tah-ZEE-ah, fan-TAH-zih-uh, fan-TAE-zih-uh]. Composition unrestricted by a set form.

FANTASY. Fanciful invention, caprice.

PHANTASY. Visionary notion.

FAO. (abbr.) Food and Agriculture Organization. N.Y. Times, F.A.O.

faraway. (n. and adj.) (Brit. hyphenate), —fetched, —flung (adj.), —going, —gone, —seeing, —sighted; —flung, —off (adj.) —reaching (adj.) (all one word); far cry.

Far East. China, Formosa, Japan, South Korea, North Korea, the Philippines, the Pacific littoral of the Soviet Union, and some Pacific Islands. Far Eastern (the Orient).
Far West (U.S.). but far western.

far from the madding crowd. (NOT maddening)

Farm. Capitalize if part of name; Johnson Farm; but Johnson's farm; San Diego farm; the farm.

Farouk I. also Faruk I [fuh-ROOK] (1920–1965). King of Egypt, 1936–52.

farther. Use only as comparative of far, esp. for distance.

FURTHER. Preferred in most cases, especially as a verb and for continuation, time, quantity, or degree: *They moved farther into the jungle. Let's carry the discussion one stage further.*

f.a.s. (abbr.) free alongside. Includes all risks and costs to delivery alongside ship. *Cf.* c.i.f.

FAS. (abbr.) Foreign Agricultural Service.

fasces [FASS-eez]. Bundle of sticks, originally carried before Roman magistrates; the symbol of fascism.

fascinate. Allure; captivate.

Fascist [FA-shihst]. Fascisti [fah-SHEES-tee]. fascism.

fastidious. Over-nice.

fathom. (abbr. fath.) Unit of depth 6 ft. or 8 spans, 1.829 m. Orig. an arm's length: *a seven-fathom line.*

fatherland. father-in-law, father-confessor.

Father. (clerical title) Use in direct address and in a second written reference to a Roman Catholic priest, or to a Protestant Episcopal clergymen: *The Rev.* John J. Smith, *Father* Smith.

Father of his Country. (Washington).

Father's Day. Third Sunday in June.

Fatima [FAT-ihmuh].

faucet. British use tap.

faultfinder. —finding, —line.

fauna [FAW-nuh]. May take singular or plural verb. Pl. —s or —ae. The realm of animals. faunal, -lly.

FLORA. Pl. —s or —ae. The realm of plants. Both from Latin goddess' names.

Faure, Francois Felix [fohr, frahn-SWAH fae-leeks]. (1841–1899). French statesman, president (1895–99).

Faust, Dr. Johann [FOUST, yo-HAHN]. (1480–1540). German astrologer-magician.

faux pas [foh-pah]. Singular and plural. False step especially an offense against good taste or propriety.

favor. Brit. -our.

faze. (v.) Disconcert.

PHASE. (n.) A transitory state.

FCA or F.C.A. (abbr.) Farm Credit Administration.

FCC or F.C.C. (abbr.) Federal Communications Commission.

FDA or F.D.A. (abbr.) Food and Drug Administration.

FDIC or F.D.I.C. (abbr.) Federal Deposit Insurance Corporation.

F.D.R. Franklin Delano Roosevelt.

feasible. Capable of being accomplished.

Feast of the Passover, the Passover. Pesach. Eight day Jewish festival of deliverance from Egyptian bondage, occurring in March or April.

Feb. (abbr.) February [FEB-roo-ehr-ih].

febrile [FEE-brihl; FEB-rihl]. Feverish.

feces [FEE-sees]. Excrement. fecal.

fecund [FEE-kuhnd]. Fruitful in offspring.
FERTILE. Capable of reproducing.

Fed. (abbr.), Federal Reporter; *F.* (*2nd*) (abbr.), Federal Reporter, second series.

Federal. Capitalize when used in titles as synonym for United States or other sovereign power, Federal District (Mexico), Federal government (of any national government), Federal grand jury, the grand jury; Federal land bank (SEE Bank); Federal Personnel Council (see Council); Federal Register (publication), the Register; Federal Reserve Bank (SEE Bank); Federal Reserve Board, the Board, Federal Reserve; Federal System, the System; Federal Reserve Board Regulation W, BUT regulation W.

federal courts. SEE courts.

federally.

federation. SEE confederation.

Federation of Rhodesia and Nyasaland [roh-DEE-zhuh, nih-AS-uh-land]. Situated north of Union of South Africa. Cap., Salisbury. Currency, Rhodesian dollar.

fedora [feh-DOH-ruh]. Wide-brimmed felt hat created for an 1882 play *Fédora* , starring Sarah Bernhardt.

fed-up. (adj.).

feed. P. and p.p., fed; feeding.

feel. P. and p.p., felt. Meaning *I am ill, I feel bad* (NOT *badly*) is correct. (*I feel badly* means *My sense of touch is impaired.*)

felicitate. Extend wishes for happiness. *Cf.* congratulate.

feline [FEE-lien]. Pertains to the cat family.

fellah [FEHL-uh]. Arabian peasant. Pl. fellahin, fellaheen.

fellow, fellowship. (academic) lower-case with name: *a fellow at Harvard.* BUT N.Y. Times, *a Woodrow Wilson Fellow, Woodrow Wilson Fellowship in History.*

fellow. bedfellow, schoolfellow, playfellow. *fellow American* (no hyphen).

fellowship. SEE acquaintanceship.

felo-de-se [FEE-oh-dee-SEE]. (Lat.) One who has committed suicide.

female. (n.) Applies to plants, animals, girls. etc. (Adj.) Of the female sex.
WOMAN. (n.) Applies to a grown human female.
LADY. (n.) Applies to a woman of social distinction.
LADY. (adj.) Title of the nobility. *Cf.* Lord and Lady.
GENTLEWOMAN. (n.) A woman of good family; also one attending a lady of rank.
FEMININE. (adj.) Having the distinctive attributes of a woman.
WOMANLY. (adj.) Having the attributes of a good or developed woman; suggests the family, dignity, homemaking.

Feminine Designation. Avoid authoress, paintress, songstress and manufactured designations. BUT: abbess, actress, administratrix, adultress, adventuress. ambassadress, duchess, enchantress, executrix, grantess, goddess, governess, hostess, Jewess, princess, procuress, stewardess, waitress, etc.

fer-de-lance [fehr-duh-LAHNSS]. Snake of South and Central America.

ferret. (v.) Search out. —eted, —eting.

ferule. Teacher's stick, used to discipline children.
FERRULE. A ring or cap to strengthen a stick, cane, or the like.

fervid. Intense, implying feverish or vehement.
FERVENT. Intense, implying spiritual, warm, earnest.

fervor. Brit. —our.

festal. In connection with a festival: *festal day, costume, ceremonies.*
FESTIVE. Like a festival: *festive mood, meal, manner.*

fete [faet]. Festival.

fetid [FEHT-ihd, FEE-tihd]. Stinking.

fetish [Brit., FEHT-ihsh; FEET-ihsh]. That which is irrationally held sacred.

Feuchtwanger, Leon [FOIKT-vahng-air, LEE--awn]. (1884–1958) Pseudonym of J.L. Wetcheek, German writer and dramatist.

feudal [FYOO-d'l].

few. Takes a plural verb. Not many. *A few, comparatively few.* NOT *a comparatively few*; *very few, a very few.*

few in number is redundant.

    SOME. Considerable; but followed by a number, approximately.

    FEWER. Refers to numbers: *He has fewer cases of failure.*

    LESS. Refers to quantity or degree: *He earns less on his new job.*

    SMALLER. Refers to size.

fez. Pl. —zzes; (adj.) fezzed.

FHA. (abbr.) Federal Housing Administration; Farmers Home Administration. N.Y. Times, F.H.A.

FHLBB or F.H.L.B.B. (abbr.) Federal Home Loan Bank Board.

fiancé [fee-ahn-SAE; fee-AHN-sae]. The man to whom a girl is engaged.

    FIANCÉE [-SAE]. The girl to whom a man is engaged.

fiasco [fee-ASS-koh]. Pl. —oes or —os. Dramatic and ridiculous failure.

fiber glass. BUT *Fiberglas* is a trademark.

FICA. (abbr.) Federal Insurance Contributions Act.

fictitious. Imaginary.

    FICTIONAL. Of fiction.

    FACTIONAL. Of a faction or clique. SEE factious.

fidget. —eted, —eting.

fiducial [fih-DYOO-shal]. Founded on trust, especially religious beliefs.

FIDUCIARY [-shih-ehr-ih]. Of the nature of a trust; pertains esp. to financial matters.

-fied. Nouns ending in *y*, change *y* to *i* or add *i* in forming an adjective, except when noun provides a convenient connecting syllable: *countrified, bountiful.*

Field. Byrd Field, Stewart Field, etc.; the field.

fiend [feend]. A demon.

fiery [FIER-ih].

FIFO. Inventory system in which merchandise first in is counted first out. Assumes that all stock has been acquired recently, and thus is valued at current market prices.

fifth. —ly. Pron. *f.* and *th.*

fifty-fifty.

fig. (abbr.) figure.

fight. P. and p.p., fought; fighting.

fight with. To avoid ambiguity, use *fight against*, or *on the side of.*

Fighter Planes. U.S. planes are numbered: F-4, F-80, F-84, F-86, F-89, F-100, F-101B, F-102A, F-104, F-105 (Thunderchief), F-106 (Delta Dart), F-111.

    Soviet planes are designated M.6-15, M.6-17, M.6-19, M.6-21. Popularly MiG-23 (N.Y. Times, MIG-23).

figurehead. figure of eight (adj.); figure work (printing).

Figueres, Jose (Dr.) [fee-GAE-rehs, hoh-SAE]. Costa Rican politician, president.

figure 2, A, etc. (illustration); BUT Figure 2, when part of a legend: *Figure 2.—Market scenes.*

Figures. SEE Numbers

Fiji Islands [FEE-jee]. British colony of 250 Pacific Islands, 80 inhabited. Native, Fijuan(s).

filet mignon [fee-LEH meen-YAWN]. (Fr.) Steak from the ends of the fillet of beef.

    CHATEAUBRIAND [shaht-OH-bree-AHN]. Steak from the center of the fillet, two to four inches thick served with butter and lemon sauce.

filibuster. (n. and v.) Delaying speech in a parliamentary body. Brit., buccaneering.

filigree [FIHL-ih-gree]. Wire ornamental work.

FILING. Two systems of alphabetical order are recognized: dictionary order and directory order. Dictionary order recognizes all existing letters, ignoring spaces or word divisions; directory order considers each word as a unit, listing identical words in order of the second word. Thus dictionary would list: *American, Americanization, American states.* Directory system would alphabetize: *American, American states, Americanization.* In all cases, punctuation is disregarded. Numbers and abbreviations are alphabetized as if they were spelled out. (But some directories place all initials at the beginning of a letter: *aaa, AZC Co., Abraham & Co.*

In similar spellings, the shorter word precedes the longer: *John, Johns, Johnson.* Company names, corporations, and organizations are listed by the first word (initials are placed at the end): James Worth, Inc. under J. *Worth, J. J. Co.* But individuals are listed by their last or family names. *Born, James; Brown, T. M. Co.; Brown Water Works.* Identical names are listed in alphabetical order of state, city, name streets, numbered streets. In directories, government departments are listed under the government having jurisdiction: *New York State, Department of Conservation.*

Geographical-alphabetical listings (used for mailing lists) file alphabetically by state, then city, then postal zone if the list is properly marked, then name. But zip code order lists are filed under state then numerically by zip number. Compound names and names with a prefix present special problems. Webster ignores prefixes in alphabetizing, as does this text, but the American Library Association follows a set style: (1) The prefix is considered part of the name in *A, Ap, Fitz, M', Mac, Mc, O', Saint, San.* (2) BUT names beginning with a preposition, or article or a contraction or both vary with the country where the person is a resident. In general, follow the name style indicated by the person: *De La Rue, De Morgan, Du Maurier, Le Gallienne, Van Buren.* (3) Alphabetize with the prefix all names beginning with *Le, De, De La, Du, and Van* and all French names where the prefix consists of an article or a contraction of an article and a preposition: *Des Esse, Du Souleur, Le Sage.* (4) Also all Italian names where the prefix consists of an article: *La Farra, Li Gotti.* (5) Also Scandinavian names of romance language origin when the prefix consists of an article (but cross-reference). (6) In cases not specified, enter under the name following the prefix and refer from the name beginning with a prefix. Thus: French names which begin with a prefix which consists of a preposition, *de*; German names; Scandinavian names when the prefix consists of a preposition, *av or af* (the equivalent of the German *von*): *Hallstrom, Gunman Johannes af; Linne, Carl von.* Also Spanish and Portuguese names, with rare exceptions: *Rio, Antonio del; Ripo, Domingo le.*

A married woman's name is filed under her latest name unless she is prominently known by an earlier name, and it is then cross-referenced: *Eddy, Mary (Baker).* Compound names made up of surnames of husband and wife are treated as two words and filed under the first word. Spanish women customarily add to their own surnames the name of their husbands, connecting the two by the preposition *de*, but dropping the part which refers to the mother's surname. File these as compound words: *Molina y Vedia de Bastianini, Delfina* (her father's name was Octavia T. Molina, her mother's name was Manuella Vedia de Molina, her own maiden name was Delfina Molina y Vedia, and her husband's name was Rene Bastianini). Cross-refer to *Bastianini* and *Vedia.* In Portugal and Brazil, the style is similar to the Spanish but less consistent. File under the last (husband's) surname rather than the compound. In Dutch, the wife's name is a hyphenated compound of husband's name followed by wife's maiden name: *Ammers-Kullen, Jo van.* Cross refer to *Kullen.* In Italian, the wife's name is a compound of husband's and wife's maiden name, either one of which may precede. File as used and cross-refer.

Arabic, Persian, and Turkish names prior to 1900 are a compound of given name, the word *ibn* (son) or *aku* (brother), and patronymic name. *Abu al Ala Mohammad-ibn-Zakarya.* Hebrew names prior to 1800 are compounds of given name, *ben* (son) and patronymic name. *Itzhak-ben-Zvi.* File under *Ben-Zvi.* Hebrew articles *ha* and *he* are never capitalized. *Judah ha-Levi.*

Japanese names are filed under the family name followed by the given name: *Noguchi, Hideyo,* except in cases of well-known pseudonymns: *Jippensh Ikku.* Chinese names are listed under the family name (given first) separated from the given name by a comma: *Sun, Yat-sen* but are usually written without the comma: *Sun Yat-sen.* In modern works, the order of the names may follow western style. Annanese names are filed in full, *Tran-van-Trai,* but cross-refer from the third name (or from the second when the first name consists of two words). Burmese names are filed under the full name without inversion. *U Shan Maung Maung.* Refer from *Maung, Maung U Shan* and *Maung, U Shan Maung.*

Saints are generally alphabetized under their forename in the long Latin form: *Benedictus, Saint;* except Biblical saints, who are alphabetized by their forenames in English: *James, Saint, Apostle.* Modern saints are filed by vernacular name: *Luigi Gonzaga, Saint* with cross reference from *Ignatius Loyola, Saint* and *Ignacio de Loyola, Saint.* Popes and kings who have achieved sainthood are filed according to the rules for popes and kings.

Popes are filed under Latin pontifical name followed by title: *Pius XI, Pope,* with cross reference from *Pio* and *Ratti, Achille.* A patriarch is listed under the name under which he was known in his own country: *Cyrillus, Saint, Patriarch of Alexandria.* A cardinal is listed according to the custom at the time and place of elevation: *Richelieu, Armand Jean du Plessis, duc de, Cardinal.* An ecclesiastical prince is listed under his forename in the vernacular: *Neithard, Prince-Bishop of Bamberg.* A bishop or an archbishop is listed under his surname: *Waitz, Siegmund, Prince-Archbishop of Salzburg.* Where there are several bishops, etc. of the same name in one see, include a number. File names of sovereigns and rulers under their forenames: *James I, Napoleon III, Harun al-Rashid.* Consorts follow the same style: *Albert, consort of Victoria; Marie Antoinette* (under M).

Except Ming and Ching dynasties, Chinese emporers are filed under the name of the dynasty followed by the temple name given posthumously: *T'ang Hsuan-tsung, Emperor of China.* Ming and Ch'ing emperors who are known by reign titles are so filed: *Hang-wu, Emperor of China,* with cross references from personal name, name of dynasty, and temple names. Edicts, proclamations, and laws issued under a ruler's name are filed under the name of the country.

Princes and members of a royal family are filed under their forename (but Russian families include family names). Noblemen are listed under their latest title unless they are better known under a family name or an earlier title: *Wellington, Arthur Wellesly, 1st*

duke of; Scott, Sir Walter, bart.; Landseer, Sir Edwin Henry; Campbell Dame Jane Mary; Gordon, Lord George; Russell, Hon. Harriet.

fillet [FIH-leht, but commonly fih-LAE]. A ribbon; a strip of lean meat. BUT; *filet mignon; filet de sole.*

Fillmore, Millard [FIHL-mohr, MIHL-uhrd]. (1800–1874) 13th U.S. President, 1850–53.

filly. SEE foal.

film [FIHLM, one syllable].

finable.

finagle [fih-NAE-gl]. (v.) finagler. Also **fainaigue** [fa-NAEG]. Revoke at cards; by extension, cheat, use devious methods, to shirk work.

finale [feh-NAH-lae]. The concluding piece.

finalize. Conclude or complete are preferable.

finance [fih-NANS, fie-NANS, FIE-nans].

financier [fihn-un-SEER, fie-nan-SEER, fih-NAN-sih-ehr].

find. P. and p.p., found.

fin de siècle [FAN duh see-EHK-'l]. (Fr.) End of the century. (adj.) Characteristic of the end of the 19th century; by extension, decadent.

finesse [fih-NESS]. Delicate skill. In bridge, a play designed to by-pass a winning card.

finger. Unit of length = 0.125 yd. = 4.5 ins.; sometimes 3/4 inch to 1 inch.

Finland. Native, Finn(s). adj., Finnish. Cap., Helsinki (Helsingfors). Currency, markka (Fm), penni, pl. pennia (Pia.).

fiord. [fyawrd]. Preferred to fyord.

fire. (v.) Use for *dismiss* is colloq.

firearms. Brit. fire-arms. Pl.; singular ⸳ rarely used.

firm price. A binding price quotation.

first. Adverb, adjective or noun.

first and foremost. Use first.

first floor. The ground floor. British ground floor is first storey; two flights up is third storey.

First Lady. (wife of President).

firstly. Adverb only: *firstly, secondly, finally*.

1st Lt. (abbr.) first lieutenant.

1st Sgt. (abbr.) first sergeant.

First World War (W.W.I) SEE War.

fiscal year. Arbitrary year for accounting purposes. For the U.S. government, July 1 to June 30. *Cf.* year.

fix. (v.) —ed, —edly, —ety, —edness. Use meaning *in a predicament*, is colloq. NOT: *He's in some fix.*

fizz. Preferred to fiz. fizzed, fizzing.

Fla. (abbr.) Florida.

flaccid [FLAK-sihd]. Flabby.

flag, U.S.. Capitalize Old Flag, Old Glory, Stars and Stripes, Star-Spangled Banner.

flagitious [fla-JIHSH-uhs]. Wicked; villainous.

flags, foreign. Tricolor (French), Union Jack (British).

flail. A threshing instrument made of a short stick attached to a long handle, similar to a whip. flail-like.

flair. Instinctive taste and aptitude: *She has a flair for dressing.*

flambeau [flam-BOH]. Pl. —s or —x. Flaming torch.

flameproof, flamethrower.

flamingo. Pl. —os. Species of long-legged, aquatic bird.

flammable.

flaneur [flah-NEHR]. A lounger.

flatulence. Preferred to —cy. Intestinal gas.

Flaubert, Gustave [floh-BAIR, gues-TAV]. (1821–80) French writer.

flaunt. Display brazenly or ostentatiously: *She flaunted her wealth before all the neighbors who had snubbed her when she was poor.*

FLOUT. Insult, scorn, mock. *She flouted all standards of morality.*

flautist [FLAWT-ihst]. Flute player. Also flutist [FLOOT-ihst].

flaxen. (adj.) Preferred to flax.

flection. A fold.

fledge. Acquire feathers necessary for flight.

flee. P. and p.p., fled, fleeing.

FLY, FLEW, FLOWN, FLYING. Both mean run away from danger. *fled, fly* and *flying* are most commonly used.

FLEECE. —eable, —cy.

Fleet. Capitalize if part of name; the fleet: Atlantic Fleet, Channel Fleet, Grand Fleet, High Seas Fleet, Marine Force Fleet, Naval Reserve Fleet, Pacific Fleet, etc. (naval), 6th Fleet, United States Fleet.

fleshly. Worldly, unspiritual; bodily; sensual. Sometimes, plump.

FLESHY. Containing flesh; plump; corpulent.

fleur-de-lis [fleur-duh-LEE]. Pl. fleur-de-lis. Conventionalized lily, symbol of French monarchy. N.Y. Times, no hyphens.

flex. (abbr.) flexible.

flier. Preferred to flyer.

flimflam, flimflammer.

fling. P. and p.p., flung; flinging, —er.

flock. Pl. —s, flock. Applied to traveling birds, domestic sheep, goats, and to a Christian congregation.

floor. (House or Senate).

floorwalker. U.S.; Brit., shopwalker.

flophouse.

flora. Pl. —s or —ae. Plants or plant life. *Cf.* fauna.

Florence [FLAHR-ehns]. Ital. Firenze, [fee-REHN-tsae]. Tuscan city on Arno River, Italy, noted for Renaissance art.

Florida. (abbr. Fla.). Floridian. Cap., Tallahassee.

flotage [FLOH-tihj]. State of floating; also, that which floats.

FLOTATION [floh-TAE-shuhn]. Process of floating.

flotsam [FLAHT-suhm]. Objects found afloat; wreckage.

JETSAM [JEHT-suhm]. Objects thrown overboard to lighten a distressed ship; especially such objects washed ashore (from jettisoned.)

flow chart. Diagram of production sequence in a plant showing transformation of materials to finished product.

flush tank.

Flushing Meadow. Site of N.Y. World's Fairs, 1939, 1964.

flute. SEE flautist.

flux. Fluid discharge; copious flow. fluxible.

fly. SEE flee. P., flew; p.p., flown; flying.

fly-leaf. Blank page at beginning or end of book.

FM. (abbr.) frequency modulation.

FMB or F.M.B. (abbr.) Federal Maritime Board.

FMCS or F.M.C.S. (abbr.) Federal Mediation and Conciliation Service.

FNMA or F.N.M.A. (abbr.) Federal National Mortgage Association. SEE Fannie Mae.

foal. (m. and f.); colt (m.); filly (f.). All young horses.

f.o.b. (abbr.) free on board. Term of sale including all costs and risks to point mentioned.

Foch, Ferdinand [FAWSH, FEHR-dee-nahnn]. (1851–1929) French W.W. I marshall.

focus. Pl. focuses or —ci; focused, -cusing.

foil. (n.). That which is used to set off another thing advantageously.

foist. (v.) Pass off something spurious as worthy; insert surreptitiously.

Fokine, Michel [FAW-kihn, mee-SHEHL]. (1880–1942) Russian-American choreographer.

—fold. Combining form meaning times as many: tenfold.

foldup. (n. and adj.) fold-in.

f°. (abbr.) folio. Pl. —os. Sheet folded once.

folium. Pl. —s, folia. Thin layer of rock. In geom., a leaf-shaped arc.

folk. Singular and plural. Folks is colloquial.

follow-up.

following. For use meaning after, use after.

font. Brit. fount. An assortment of type of one size and style.

Fontainebleau [FAHN-tn-bloh]. Community near Paris, residence of former French kings.

foolscap. Sheets of paper, approx. 13 × 16 or 17 in.; from an old watermark.

foot. (abbr., ft.) Pl., feet. Unit of length. 12 in. = 1/3 yd. 1.515 links = 0.3048006 m. A 17-foot boat; a 6-footer; about 7 feet; 12 foot-pounds; a ten-foot wall.

footing. Total at the end of a column of figures.

FOOTNOTES. Indicated by superior figures or symbols in the text placed after the punctuation mark (BUT in German, before the punctuation marks). Numbers are used consecutively and written as superior figures. Symbols are used in order * (asterisk), † (dagger), ‡ (double dagger), § (section mark), ‖ (parallels), # (number sign). Footnotes may be placed at the bottom of the page or at the end of the work segregated by chapters. All footnotes take a paragraph indentation.

The first mention of a work is given with full detail except where the author or title is mentioned immediately before the footnote in the text. In the second mention of the same work, eliminate the author's initials.

UCMS is most widely accepted in listing references. In a footnote or bibliography, the form is highly standardized.

For books: 1. AUTHOR, FIRST NAME OR INITIALS FIRST, FOLLOWED BY A COMMA. Omit listing degrees unless especially relevant to the work. A pseudonym is followed by a true name in brackets; if the pseudonym is acknowledged, this is noted by (*pseudonym*) following the name. If there are three authors, all are cited; if more than three, the first is cited followed by *et al.* Editors of compilations are treated as authors.

2. TITLE, UNDERLINED AND FOLLOWED BY A COMMA. If part of a whole published work, the facts of publication are included, with the numbers of volumes noted, followed by a semicolon. The title should follow exactly the style of the book title page except that punctuation must be added to clarify the elements shown on different lines and in different type sizes. The titles of holy books are neither underlined nor quoted.

Capitalize the first and last words of titles, and all verbs, nouns, adjectives and adverbs; or capitalize only the first word and all proper nouns and adjectives. Titles in French, Italian, and Spanish require capitalization for the first word and for all proper nouns. Titles in German require capitalization for all nouns and words used as nouns and adjectives derived from personal names. A part of a work followed by a number should be abbreviated. Capitalize *Bk.*, *Fig.*, *MS*, *Vol.*

3. FACTS OF PUBLICATION. (all in parenthesis) including edition, if more than one, followed by a semicolon; place of publication, followed by a semicolon; publisher, followed by a comma; date of publication, followed by a comma; volume number in cap. Roman numerals, followed by a comma; page number, followed by a period. When a serial publication has no identifiable volume number, give the year number, but place this outside the parenthesis. If some element differs from the rest of the items, place the reference to this edition after the volume number, not after the title.

The words and abbreviations *infra*, *supra*, *passim*, *et al* and *ca.* should be underlined to indicate that they would be printed in italics.

FOR PERIODICAL REFERENCES—
1. author (first name or initials first) followed by a comma;
2. title of article in quotation marks;
3. name of periodical underlined followed by a comma;
4. date of the periodical followed by a comma;
5. volume number of the periodical in capitals. Roman numerals followed by a comma;

6. month and year of publication followed by a comma;
7. page numbers. Where only both volume and page numbers are given, they need not be identified, but if one is given or other designations are made, all must be identified.

legal publications use a special style: volume, journal, page, and date in parenthesis. *6 Yale L. Rev. 1321 (1927)*

When references to the same work follow consecutively, use *ibid.* (the same) for as much of the reference as can be carried forward. When the reference is to material cited previously, but not immediately prior, use *loc. cit.* (in the place or passage cited) or *op. cit.* (in the work cited.)

For volume, book, part, or division of a modern work, use capital Roman numerals. For introductory material, page numbers, use lower-case Roman numerals. For periodical numbers and page numbers, use Arabic numerals.

EXAMPLES:
1. W.L. Shirer, *The Rise and Fall of the Third Reich* (New York; Simon & Schuster, 1960), p. 37.
2. Shirer, *op. cit.* p. 47.
3. A Manual of Style, 11th ed. (Chicago; University of Chicago Press, 1940), p. 140.
4. J.F. Wharton, "The Plight of the Promising Play, "*Saturday Review*, XLIV, No. 17 (1961), 9.
5. *The New York Times*, CXXI, June 28, 1973. p. 8, col. 2.
6. Wharton, *loc. cit.*, *supra* note 4.

Abbreviate a designation followed by a number: *Vol. III, sec. 2*, except parts of a play: *Act I, scene 2, line 7.*

for. SEE because.

for-. Combining prefix meaning out, away completely, refusal to do: *forbear.*

FORE-. Combining form meaning before: *foreordain.*

forbear. Refrain, avoid, shun: *Forbear from asking futher questions.*

FOREBEAR. Ancestor: *One of his forebears fought in the Revolution.* Brit. forbears.

forbid. P., forbade or forbad; p.p., forbidden; forbidding, forbidder.

force de frappé. (Fr.) Striking force.

force de dissuasion. (Pref.) Armed forces independent of NATO created by De Gaulle; the French own deterrent force.

force of circumstances. Avoid as trite.

Force(s). Capitalize if part of name; the force(s); Active Forces, Air Force (*Cf.* Air Force), Armed Forces (synonym for overall Military Establishment); Army Field Forces; the Field Forces; Fleet Marine Force, Navy Battle Force (SEE Navy), Navy Scouting Force (SEE Navy); 7th Task Force, the task force BUT task force report (Hoover Commission); United Nations Emergency Force, the Emergency Force, The Force; BUT United Nations police force.

force majeure. (Fr.) An irresistible force; e.g., an act of God or government agency, which excuses fulfilling a contract.

forceful. Of great force: *forceful personality.* Preferred for abstract use.

FORCIBLE. Effected by force: *forcible invasion.* BUT British usage is the reverse.

forceps. Pl. usually the same, or —ses or —cipes.

fore and aft. Lengthwise on a vessel; contrasted with *athwart.* Also, near both bow and the stern.

FORE. Toward the bow or forward end.

AFT. Toward the stern or rear end.

fore. (adj.) Comparative, former; superlative, foremost.

fore-age, fore-and-aft. (n. and adj.) (which SEE), for-and-after (n.), fore-edge, fore-end, fore-exercise.

fore-. SEE for-.

forearm.

forecast. Preferred to -ed. for past and p.p.

forecastle [FOHK-s'l]. Upper deck forward of the foremast, site of crews' quarters.

foregone. What has gone before. Avoid *a foregone conclusion* as trite.

FORGONE. Gone without, renounced: *His rights forgone, the Duke fled to America.*

forehead [FAWR-ehd].

foreign cabinets. Foreign Office, the Office;

Minister of Foreign Affairs, the Minister; Ministry of Foreign Affairs, the Ministry; Premier; Prime Minister.

Foreign Legion. (French) the legion.

Foreign Service. Capitalize the Service, and preceding officer; Officer Corps; BUT the corps; Reserve officer, Reserve Officer Corps; and the Reserve Corps; BUT the corps; Staff officer, the Staff officer; Staff Officer Corps, the Staff Corps; BUT the corps.

forenoon.

forensic. Of the law: *forensic medicine.*

foresee.

Forest. Capitalize if part of name; the national forest, the forest: Angeles National Forest, Black Forest, Coconino and Prescott National Forests: BUT state and national forests.

forestall [fawr-STAWL].

Forester. Chief of Forest Service, the Chief, Chief Forester.

forever. Brit., for ever.

foreword. For material at the front of a book, preface is more popular today.

forfeit [FAWR-fiht].

forget. P., forgot; p.p., forgotten; forgettable.

forget-me-not. Pl. -nots.

forgo. Relinquish, refrain from.

FOREGO. Precede.

form 2, A, II, etc.. But Form 2, when part of title: *Form 1040: Individual Income Tax Return* BUT *withholding tax form.*

former. Refers to the first of two things. Not to be used when three or more things are involved. *Cf.* latter. Preferred to *ex-* in most cases.

FORMERLY. In time past: *He was formerly a general.*

FORMALLY. In accordance with form: *She was formally introduced to the Queen.*

formidable [FAWR-mih-duh-b'l, except for Brit. ships, -MIHD-].

Formosa (Taiwan) [fawr-MOH-suh]. N.Y. Times, Taiwan. Native and adj., Formosan. Island in southeast China Sea. Japanese 1895–1945; now headquarters of Free China. Cap., Taipei.

formula [FAWR-myuh-luh]. Pl. -s, or -lae.

fornication. —tor. Implies that participants are not married.

ADULTERY. Indicates that one or both of the parties are married.

forsake. P., forsook; p.p., forsaken; forsaking.

forswear. To renounce under oath; also, to swear falsely.

forsythia [fawr-SIHTH-ee-uh]. Ornamental shrub with yellow spring flowers, for William Forsyth, 1737–1804.

Fort. Capitalize and spell out when part of a name: *Fort McHenry*, etc.; the fort. BUT abbreviate in lists, tabular matter, etc.

forte [fawrt for a strong point; FAWR-tae for musical term].

fortissimo [faw-TEESS-uh-moh]. In music, very loud.

fortitude. Strength in adversity.

Fort Lauderdale [LAU-dehr-dael]. City in Florida.

fortnight [FAWRT-niet; Brit., —niht]. Two weeks.

fortuitous. Undesigned, accidental. (Not necessarily fortunate)

fortune [FAWR-tyoon].

forty. four, forties, (no apostrophe); forty-niner. *Cf.* four.

forum. A public meeting for open discussion.

DISCUSSION. Consideration of a question for sake of arriving at truth or common ground.

SYMPOSIUM. Presentation of various viewpoints on a single subject.

DEBATE. Formal public argument between opposing points of view.

forward. (1) Near the front; advanced in position; (2) of a person, overready; (3) of the future; (4) the direction, towards.

FORWARDS. A direction in contrast with backwards, sideways.

fossil [FAH-sihl]. Preserved remains, impressions, footprints of an animal or plant of past ages, found in the earth.

foul. foully.

foulard [FOO-lahrd]. Necktie material.

Foundation. Capitalize if part of name; capitalize standing alone if referring to federal unit; Chemical Foundation, the foundation; Infantile Paralysis Foundation, the foundation; National Science Foundation; Russell Sage Foundation, the foundation.

Founding Fathers (Colonial).

fountain [FOUN-tihn].

fountainhead. The source of anything.

4°, quarto. Book page $9\frac{1}{2} \times 12\frac{1}{2}$ in.

four. 4, Roman IV; fourth, 4th; fourteen, Roman XIL or XIIII, fourteenth; forty, 40, XL or XXXX, fortieth, 40th; forty-one, XLI; forty-first; four hundred.

Fourth Estate. The Press. The other three: Lords Spiritual, Lords Temporal, and the Commons.

Fourth of July. the Fourth.

fourscore. Eighty.

fowl. SEE Collectives.

foyer [FOI-yehr.]. Lobby.

fox. Fem. vixen, bitch-fox, or she-fox. *Cf.* animals.

FPC. N.Y. Times, F.P.C. (abbr.) Federal Power Commission.

f.p.m. (abbr) feet per minute.

FPO. (abbr.) fleet pos office.

f.p.s. (abbr.) feet per second, frames per second.

FPV (abbr.) free piston vessel.

Fr. (abbr.) France, French.

F.R. (abbr.) Federal Register.

fracas [FRAE-kuhs; Brit., FRAK-ahz]. Brawl. pl. —ases.

FRACTIONS. In general, follow the style of numerals spelling out one to nine. (Some styles include *ten.*) Spell out a fraction when it appears by itself in a text; *one-half gallon, ten-hundredths* (NOT ten one-hundredths). BUT use numbers when fractions apply with a full number and in ages. dimensions, measures, sizes, etc.: $3\frac{1}{2} \times 6$ *inches*, $6\frac{1}{2}$-*pound bird*, $\frac{1}{4}$, $\frac{2}{3}$, $\frac{7}{8}$. Do not use comma in fractions of four or more digits: $\frac{3}{1787}$. Use only one hyphen in spelling out: *one-seventh; one thirty-seventh.* Fractions which modify a noun of distance drop final s: *three-tenth feet.*

fragile. Applies only in the physical sense, likely to be fragmented or broken.

France. (abbr. Fr.) Native, Frenchman (—men), Frenchwoman; adj., French. Cap., Paris. Currency, new franc, (N.F.), centime. French-minded (adj.); French Army.

Frances. (f.), -cis (m.).

Francesca, Piero della [dee-lah frahn-CHAES-kah, PYEH-roh]. (1420–92) Italian painter.

franchise tax. Tax on the right to conduct business, esp. corporate franchise tax.

Franco, Francisco. [FRAHNG-koh, frahn-thehs-koh]. (1892–) Spanish general, dictator. Called Caudillo (leader) 1939–1973

Francois [fran-SWAH].

francs and centimes. Spell out when written with figures. *8 francs; 1,000,000 francs; 25 centimes.*

frangible [FRAN-jih-b'l]. Breakable.

Franjié, Soliman [fran-JEE, soo-lae-MAN]. (1910–) Pres. of Lebanon (1970–).

Frankenstein [FRANK-'n-stein]. One who builds something which will destroy him. (NOT the monster itself, although often used erroneously in this sense.) From the character in Mary W. Shelley's 1818 romance.

Frankfort [FRANGK-fehrt]. Capital of Kentucky.

FRANKFURT [FRANK-fehrt; Ger., FRAHNGK-foort]. District in Germany.

FRANKFURT AM MAIN [FRANGH-foort ahm MIEN]. German city.

frappé (frap-PAE). Iced. *Cf.* force de frappé.

fraternal organizations. Capitalize names: *Odd Fellow;* capitalize titles of officers: *Sachem, Grand Regent.*

fraternize with the enemy. Associate in a friendly way with occupying troops, or (by troops) with population of occupied areas.

Frau [frou]. (Ger.) Mrs.

Fraulein [FROI-lien]. (Ger.) Miss; young lady.

Fraunces Tavern [frownchehs]. In New York. Scene of Washington's Farewell Address.

freedman. One freed from slavery.

FREE MAN. One not subject to any arbitrary external power.

FREEMAN. One not a slave in a State which permits slavery.

free list. BUT: Title I: Free List.

freely. Without stint.

FREE. Without charge.

free trade area.

free will. (n.), free-will (adj.).

free world.

freeze. P., froze; p.p., frozen; freezing.

freight [fraet.].

freight-mile. freight house, freight room.

Frelinghuysen, Frederick Theodore [FREE-lihn-hie-zn]. (1817–1885) American statesman.

French bulldog. French cuff, French door, French-fried potatoes.

French leave. Leave taken without notice or permission.

Frenchman. SEE France.

Freneau, Philip Morin [free-NOH, maw-RANN]. (1752–1832) American poet.

frenetic. Preferred to phrenetic. Frantic.

frenzied. SEE frantic.

frequency. Preferred to frequence.

frequency modulation. (FM) Improved noise-reduction radio reception process through varying radio-frequency wave without varying amplitude. *Cf.* amplitude modulation.

frère.

fresco. Pl. —oes. Painting on freshly spread plaster.

ALFRESCO. In the open air.

freshman. But UCMS caps. for name of a class or a member of the class in a college.

Freud, Sigmund [froit; angl., froid, ZEEK-muhnt, angl. SIG-muhnd]. (1856–1939) Austrian neurologist, founder of psychoanalysis.

F.R.G. (abbr.) Federal Republic of Germany (West Germany).

friable [FRIE-uh-b'l]. Capable of being crumbled. *Cf.* fryable.

friar. Mendicant monk who lives outside a monastery.

MONK. Male member of a religious order, usually segregated in a monastery.

Fri. (abbr.) Friday [FRIE-dih].

Fribourg [FREE-bahr; Fr., FREE-boor]. Ger., Freiburg [FRIE-buhrg]. Town and canton in Switzerland.

fricassee [frihk-uh-SEE].

friendly. (adj.) friendly (adv.).

friendship. SEE acquaintanceship.

Frisco. (abbr.) San Francisco. Natives dislike the term.

frogman. Skindiver equipped to stay underwater for long periods, esp. for military operations.

from [FRAHM].

frontier. SEE boundary; frontiersman.

frontispiece [FRUHN-tihs-pees]. Illustration facing the first or title page of a book.

FRS. (abbr.) Federal Reserve System. N.Y. Times, F.R.S.

F.R.S. (abbr.) Fellow of the Royal Society.

fruition [froo-IHSH-uhn]. Attainment of thing desired; coming to fruit; realization.

fryable [FRIE-uh-b'l]. Able to be fried, e.g. potatoes.

FRIABLE [FRIE-uh-b'l]. Able to be crumbled, e.g. soil.

fryer. For a chicken, NOT frier.

frying pan.

F. Supp. (abbr.) Federal Supplement.

ft. (abbr.) foot.

ft. b.m. (abbr.) feet board measure.

ft.-c. (abbr.) foot-candle.

FTC (abbr.) Federal Trade Commission. N.Y. Times F.T.C.

Ft.-l. (abbr.) foot-lambert.

ft.-lb. (abbr.) foot-pound.

Fuad I [foo-AHD]. (1868–1936) Sultan and king of Egypt (1917–1936).

fuchsia [FYOO-shuh]. A decorative shrub named for Leonhard Fuchs. More commonly, the pink color of its flowers.

fuel. -led, -ling; Brit. *ll.* fueler.

fuelwood. fuel line, fuel oil.

Führer [fe-rehr]. (Ger.) Leader. For Adolf Hitler.

-ful. Pl. spoonfuls NOT spoonsful.

fulcrum [FUHL-kr'm]. Pl. -s or -cra. Support about which a lever turns.

fulfill. —ed, —ing, —ment.

full-fashioned. Shaped on a flat knitting frame; applies to construction of hose, sweaters, and underwear shaped to form-fit.

fullness.

fulsome. Offensively excessive or insincere.

Fund. Capitalize if part of name; capitalize standing alone if referring to international or United Nations fund: Common Market Fund, the Fund; Development Loan Fund, the Fund (U.S. government corporation); International Monetary Fund, the Fund; Rockefeller Endowment Fund, the fund; Special Projects Fund; BUT civil service retirement fund; mutual security fund, national service life fund, insurance fund, revolving fund.

funeral. (n.) Observance for the dead. (adj.) funereal, funebrial, funerary.

fungi [FUHN-jie]. Plural of fungus.

fungus. Pl. fungi or -guses. fungoid, attributive adjective.

funnel. funneled, —ling. Brit. *ll.*

funny. Humorous. Do not use meaning *strange.* NOT: *That was a funny accident.*

furbelow [FUHR-bee-loh]. Ruffle; frill.

furlong. (abbr. fur.) Unit of length = 0.125 statute mi. = 10 chains = 40 rods = 220 yd. = 201.168 m.

furor [FYOO-rohr]. Rage, anger, maniacal fit. Contagious excitement, general commotion.

further. SEE farther.

fuse. All meanings. Fusible.
FUZE. Sometimes in Army printing.

fuselage [fyoo-zehl-LAHZH, FYOO-z'l-ihj].

fusible [FYOO-zih-bl]. Easily melted.

fusillade [FYOOS-zih-LAED]. A rapidly repeated or simultaneous discharge, especially of firearms.

fustian [FUHS-chuhn]. Corduroy, velveteen, or bombast; formerly cotton or linen cloth.

futures. In commodity trading, contract for delivery of specified commodities at specified future dates.

FWD corporation. From four-wheel drive auto.

G

g. Usually silent before *m* or *n*: *gnat, phlegm, sign.* BUT the addition of a suffix will often cause the letter to be sounded. *Phlegmatic.*

g. (abbr.) gram, gravity. 3 g. = three times the force of gravity.

-g. Words ending in single vowel and *g*, double the *g* before a suffix beginning with a vowel: *bigger, begging, zigzagging.*

G-1. Personnel; G-2, Intelligence; G-3, Operations and Training; G-4, Supply and Evacuation. (Sections of U.S.A. armed forces.)

G-major. G-man, G-minor, G-sharp.

Ga. (abbr.) Georgia.

gabfest.

Gabon [gah-BAWN]. Formerly French; Independent since August, 1960. Situated on the Atlantic Ocean. Native, Gabonese; Adj. Gabonese. Cap., Libreville. Currency, CFAF franc.

Gadsden Purchase.

Gael. One of Celtic inhabitants of Ireland, Scotland, and Isle of Man.

Gaelic [GAEL-ihk]. Native language of Celts of Ireland and Scotland.

gaff-topsail.

Gagarin, Maj. Yuri [gah-GAH-rihn]. Soviet astronaut, 1961.

gage. A challenge.
    GAUGE. Measure. BUT *gage* for technical use.

gala [GAE-luh, GAH-luh]. Festival; celebration.

Galapagos [guh-LAE-pah-gus; -LAP-ah-]. Sometimes Colon Archipelago. Island group 600 miles from Pacific coast of Ecuador, known for primitive animals.

galaxy [GAL-ak-sih].

Galen [GAE-lehn]. (c.130–200) Greek physician.

Galilean [gal-ih-LEE-un]. Pertains to (1) Galilee, the region in which Jesus lived; or (2) Galileo Galilei, Italian scientist (1564–1642).

gallant [GAL-lant]. Stately; noble; [often gal-LANT] courteously attentive to women.

galley. Pl. -eys.

Gallic [GAL-ihk]. Relating to Gaul or France; characteristically French.

Gaulish [GAWL-ihsh]. language, etc. Gallican [GAL-ih-kan].

Gallicism or gallecism. Anglicized French words or expressions, usually those used improperly.
    GALLICANISM. Policy favoring autonomy of French Church from papacy.

Gallipoli [gah-LIHP-oh-lih]. Seaport on Dardanelles, Turkey.

gallon. (abbr. gal.). Unit of capacity. (1) U.S. = 0.82368 Brit. gal. = 4 U.S. qts. = 8 U.S. pt. = 32 U.S. gills = 128 fl. oz. = 231 cu. in. = 3.78531. (2) Brit. or Imperial = 1.20094 U.S. gal. = 4 qt. Brit. = 8 pt. Brit. = 160 fl. oz. = 277.42 cu. in. = 4.5460.

gallop. -oped, -oping. Leaping gait of a horse.
    GALOP. -oped, -oping. A 19th century dance in double measure.

gallows. Pl. -ses.

galosh. Preferred to golosh. Overshoe.

Galsworthy, John [GAWLZ-wuhrthee, NOT GALS-]. (1867–1933) British writer.

galvanize. Plate with zinc.

Gambia, The [GAM-bih-uh]. British commonwealth in West Africa. Situated on the Atlantic Ocean. Natives, Gambian(s). Cap., Bathurst. Currency, pound (WA £), shilling, penny, pence.

gambit. From the chess term meaning an opening move in which a pawn, or other piece, is sacrificed. NOT merely a play or series of plays.

gambol [GAM-buhl]. (v.) Frolic; frisk. -ed, -ing.

GAMBLE [GAM-b'l]. Wager.

game. Use for plucky is acceptable. Of animals, in U.S. any animal hunted, BUT Brit. use for birds and hares only.

gamut [GAM-uht]. The entire range of notes, prices, or choices.

gamy [GAEM-ih].

Gandhi, Mohandas Karamachand [GAHN-dee, MOH-huhn-dahs KUHR-uhm-chuhns]. (1869–1948) Mahatma [muh-HAHT-muh, angl.-HAT-]. Ascetic Hindu nationalist.

Gandhi, Shrimati Indira [GAHN-dee, shrih-mah-tih in-dee-rah]. (1917–   ). Indian politician, prime minister, social worker. Daughter of S.J. Nehru, wife of Feroze Gandhi; no relative of Mohandas Gandhi.

GAO. (abbr.) General Accounting Office.

gaol. Obsolete in U.S. Use jail. -or.

G.A.R. (abbr.) Grand Army of the Republic.

garage [guh-RAHZH, Brit. GAR-ihj]. garageman.

Garand rifle.

garble. Sift or mutilate facts to present only one side of a question, mislead. NOT: mix up.

garçon [gahr-SAWNN]. Pl. -s. (Fr.) Boy, waiter.

Garibaldi, Giuseppe [GAR-ih-BAL-dih; Ital., gah-ree-BAHL-dee, joo-SEHP-pae]. (1807–1882) Italian revolutionary patriot.

garnishment. Warning or legal proceeding attaching money or goods against payment to a debtor.

garrote [guh- ROHT, -RAHT]. Brit. -tte. Strangulation; Spanish method of execution.

garrulity [guh-ROOL-uh-tih]. garrulousness [GAR-yoo-luhs-nehs]. Talkativeness.

gas. Gasoline in U.S.; Brit. use *petrol.*

gaseous [GAS-ee-uhs].

gasoline. Brit. -ene.

Gasperi, Alcide de [deh-GAHS-peh-ree, ahl-CHEE-deh]. (1881–1954) Italian statesman.

Gaspé Peninsula [GAS-pae or -PAE]. Southeast Canada, south of St. Lawrence River. Native, Gaspesian [gas-PEE-zhan].

GATT. (abbr.) General Agreement on Tariffs and Trade.

Gatun [gah-TOON]. Town, locks on Panama Canal.

gauche [gohsh]. Awkward, especially in social intercourse.

Gaucho [GOU-choh]. Pl. -os. (Span.) Cowboy.

gauge. -geable. Preferred to gage.

Gaughin, Eugene Henri Paul [goh-GAN, UH-zhehn AHN-ree]. (1848–1903). French painter.

Gaul. Ancient name of area now South France, Belgium, parts of Holland, Germany, and Switzerland, 600 B.C.-A.D. 486. *Cf.* Gallic.

Gautama Buddha [GAH-uh-tah-mah, BUHD-dah; angl., GOU-tah-mah BUHD-ah]. (c. 563–483 B.C.) Indian philosopher, founder of Buddhism.

Gautier, Theophile [GOH-tyae, TAE-aw-feel]. (1811–1872) French writer.

G.A.W. (abbr.) guaranteed annual wage.

gay. -er, -est, -ly, gaiety. Also gaily, gayety.

gay nineties. British use naughty nineties.

Gaza [GAH-zuh]. Arab, Ghazze [gaz-zih]. Arab strip, seaport now occupied by Israel on Mediterranean; in ancient times, land of the Philistines.

gazetteer. A geographical dictionary. N.Y. Times accepts *Columbia Lippincott Gazetteer of the World* as authority.

GCA. (abbr.) ground control approach.

g.c.d. (abbr.) greatest common divisor.

G.c.t. (abbr.) Greenwich civil time.

Gdynia [guh-DEEN-yah]. Baltic seaport, Poland.

Geiger counter.

geisha [GAE-shuh]. Pl. geisha or -s. Japanese girl trained to entertain men. *Geisha girl* is redundant.

gelatine. But British nonscientific use, -tin.

gemination. In rhetoric, a doubling or immediate repetition. *The Yanks! the Yanks!*

gendarme [ZHAN-dahrm]. (Fr.) Police organized and drilled as soldiers.

gender. In English grammer, the property of nouns and pronouns relating to the sex of the object named; e.g., *masculine, feminine, or neuter.*

genealogy [jeen-ee-AL-oh-gee]. History of ancestry of a family or person; also, the study of family pedigrees.

General Agreement. SEE Agreement.

General Assembly. (United Nations) the Assembly.

General Counsel. the Counsel (federal).

General Order No. 14. General Orders, No. 14; a general order.

generalissimo. Pl. -os. Commander of combined armed forces.

general rule. AVOID as redundant.

Genghis Khan, Jenghiz Khahn [JEHNG-gihs KAHN]. (1162–1227) Mongol conqueror.

Gent [kehnt]. Also *Ghent* [gehnt], *Gand* (Fr.) [gahnn]. City on Schelde and Lys Rivers, Belgium.

genie [JEEN-ee]. Pl. genies or genii [JEE-nee-ie]. Also jinni. Nature spirit.

genitive case. Possessive case in grammar used for noun modifiers: *Tom's book, a dog's life.*

genius. Pl. geniuses, or genii. Great inborn mental or creative power.

TALENT. A natural capacity.

genoa. (the sail) genoese jib.

genre painting [ZHAHN-'r]. Style of painting depicting life realistically.

genteel. -lly. Polite; well bred. Used only in mockery.

gentile [JEHN-tiel]. An outsider. Used by Jews to distinguish a non-Jew; by natives of India, a non-Moslem; by Mormons, a non-Mormon.

gentlewoman. SEE female.

genuine [JEHN-yoo-ihn]. Not spurious or adulterated; of the reputed origin; *genuine diamond, genuine Stradivarius.* Also sincere, free of hypocrisy.

AUTHENTIC. Authoritative; trustworthy; true; not fictional: *authentic document, letter, writing.*

genus [jehn-uhs]. Pl. genera. Scientific division of living things after family, and itself divided into species. Names are written in italics, with the first letter capitalized, except medical terms. In a list or second reference of species of the same genus, abbreviate the genus. *Lepomis gibosus, L. megolatis.* Cf. Classification of Animals and Plants.

geogenous [gee-AHJ-eh-nuhs]. Growing in the ground.

geographical terms. Capitalize if part of name; lower-case in general sense. *rivers of Virginia and Maryland, Erie Basin.* For place names, *Cf.* gazetteer, Arabic place names.

geographical. Preferred to geographic. But geographic latitude, environment.

geometric. Preferred to —cal in U.S.

Georgia. (abbr. Ga.). Native and adj., Georgian. Cap., Atlanta.

German. (Ger.) Language spoken in S. (mountainous) Germany including Thuringian, Franconian, Swabian, Alsatian, Swiss and Bavarian dialects, and known as High

German. Low German, spoken in the northern regions, refers to the group of languages including Flemish, Dutch, Frisian, and English. In German language, capitalize all nouns, and all adjectives derived from names of persons.

German measles. Rubella.

germane. Appropriate or relevant.

Germany. Native, German(s); adj., German. Pl., Germanys.

WEST GERMANY. Federal Republic of Germany; Cap., Bonn. Currency, Deutsch Mark (DM); pfennig.

EAST GERMANY. German Democratic Republic; Cap., East Berlin. Currency, Ost (East) mark, pfennig, pfennige.

gerund. -ial. In grammar, a verbal noun in the form of the present participle, thus ending in -ing. There are two tense forms, present: *Hating him gave her courage.* and perfect: *She can't help John's having cared for her.*

Gestapo [geh-STAH-poh]. Gerheime Staatspolizei. Nazi German state police force.

get, got or gotten, getting. *get the better hand,* NOT to be confused with *get the upper hand.*

Gethsemane [gehth-SEHM-uh-nee]. Scene of arrest and agony of Jesus.

geyser [GIE-sehr]. Hot spring that erupts jets of water and steam.

Ghana [GAH-nah]. West African republic named for ancient empire; independent since March, 1957. Formerly British Gold Coast. Native, Ghanaian(s) [GAH-nah-yan; gahn-yon]. Cap., Accra. Currency, New Cedi (N¢), New Peservas (NP).

Ghent [gehnt]. SEE Gent.

gherkin [GUHR-kihn]. Small cucumber used for pickling.

ghetto. Pl. -os.

ghoul [gool]. Evil being that feeds on the dead; grave robber.

GI. N.Y. Times, G.I.; Pl. G.I.'s (abbr.), general issue; Government issue; by extension, U.S.

soldier. GI bill of rights. N.Y. Times, G.I. bill of rights.

Giap, Vo Nguyen. SEE Vo Giap, Nguyen.

gibberish [JIHB-; Brit., GIHB-]. Foolish chatter.

gibbet [JIH-beht]. Gallows where executed were hung in chains.

gibe [JIEB]. Taunt.

JIBE [JIEB]. Match.

Gide, André [zheed, ahn-DRAE]. (1869–1951) French novelist.

gigolo [JIHG-uh-loh]. Paid male escort.

Gijon [hee-HAWN]. Seaport on Bay of Biscay, Spain.

gild. paint in gold.

GUILD. Association of men with similar interests, especially trade or vocation.

gill [jihl]. Pl. -s. Unit of capacity. (1) U.S. = $\frac{1}{8}$ qt. = $\frac{1}{4}$ pt. = 4 fl. oz. = 7.2188 cu. in. = 0.1183 1. (2) Brit. gill = 1.20094 U.S. = $\frac{1}{8}$ qt. Brit. = $\frac{1}{4}$ pt. Brit. = 8.6694 cu. in. = 0.1421.

Giotto. Giotto di Bondone [JAWT-toh de bohn-DOH-nae]. (c. 1276–1337) Florentine painter, architect.

Giraudoux, Jean [zhee-roh-DOO]. (1882–1944) French writer.

gird. -ing, -ed or girt.

Girl Scouts. (organization) a Girl Scout; a Scout.

Giscard d'Estaing, Mr. Giscard d'Estaing. Valery [zhee-SKAHR dehs-TAN, va-lae-REE]. (1926-   ) President of France, 1974-   ).

gist [jihst]. Main point; pith.

Gitmo. SEE Guantanamo Day.

give. P., gave; p.p.,given; giving.

giveaway. (n. and adj.) N.Y. Times, give-away (n.); give-and-take (n. and adj.); give consideration to. (Consider is preferred.)

given name. Not used in Britain.

Gizenga, Antoine [ghee-ZEHN-gah, ehn-TWAHN]. Congo politician (Stanleyville).

glacé [glas-SAE]. -éed, éing. Candied. Usually italicized. (French "iced") Also, a glistening lustrous effect imparted to fabrics in finishing.

glacial [GLAE-shal; Brit., GLA-sihal].

glacier [GLAE-shehr; Brit., GLAS-yehr].

gladiolus. (s. & pl.), or pl. -luses [glad-ee-OH-luhs or glad-IE-oh-luhz]. Also gladiola.

glamour. pref. to glamor [GLAM-ehr]. From Scotish glam-oor, magic. —ous, BUT glamorize.

glassful. Pl., glassfuls.

glaucoma [glaw-KOH-muh]. Condition of the eye causing impairment of vision or blindness.

glazework. glaze wheel.

glazier [GLAE-zhehr]. Glass worker.

glidepath.

glimpse. What is seen at a glance.

glissade [glih-SAHD]. Gliding descent in the snow; a ballet glide.

glossary. Explanation of unfamiliar words appended to a work.

  VOCABULARY. Stock of words known or available for use.

Gloucester [GLAW-stehr]. Town in Massachusetts. Gloucestershire [GLAW-stuh-shihr]. Town in England.

gluey.

G-man. Government man, especially representative of Federal Bureau of Investigation.

G.m.a.t. (abbr.) Greenwich mean astronomical time.

G.m.t. (abbr.) Greenwich mean time.

gnaw. -ed, -ing. Arc. gnawn.

gneiss [nies]. —ic, —oid. Metamorphic rock similar to granite.

gnomic [NOH-mihk, NOHM-ihk]. Containing maxims.

Gnossus. SEE Knossos.

Gnostic [NAHS-tihk]. Cf. atheism.

GNP. (abbr.) Gross National Product; N.Y. Times, G.N.P.

gnu [noo, or nyoo]. African antelope.

go. P., went; p.p., gone; going.

Goa [GOHah]. Former Portuguese territory on Indian subcontinent; liberated by India, 1962.

goat's-hair. goat's-horn.

gobbledegook. Slang for officialese; i.e., use of long words and circumlocution.

Gobelin [GAHB-eh-lihn]. Type of tapestry made at the Gobelin works in France.

go-between. Pl. go-betweens.

Gobi [GOH-bee]. Central Asian desert, mostly in Mongolia.

God. Capitalize. Most authorities capitalize personal pronouns, *He, Him. His,* BUT lower case relative pronouns *who, whom, whose.*

goddess.

God's acre. A churchyard.

Godunov, Boris Fedorovich. Sometimes Godounov [guh-duh-NAWF; angl. GOH-d'n-of FYOH-duh-raw-vyehch]. (1552–1605) Czar of Russia, 1598-1605.

Goebbels, Joseph Paul [GUEH-bels]. (1897–1945) German Nazi propagandist.

—goer. concertgoer, playgoer, theatregoer, etc.

Goering or Göring, Hermann Wilhelm. sometimes Goring [GEHR-ihng]. (1893–1946) German Nazi polit.

Goethe, von, Johann Wolfgang [fawn GEU-teh, YOU-hahn VAWLF-gahng]. (1749–1832) German poet, dramatist.

Goethals, George Washington [GOH-thalz]. (1858–1928) American general and engineer.

go-getter. go ahead.

Gogh, Vincent Van [vahn KAWK, vihn-SEHNT]. (1853–1890) Dutch painter.

Gogol, Nikolai Vasilievich [GAW-guhl; angl., GAW-gawl, nyih-kuh-LIE vuh-SYEEL-yeh-vyihch]. (1809–1852) Russian writer.

goings-on. (Pl.)

gold. For literal use.
    GOLDEN. Especially for figurative use.

Golden Age. SEE Ages; Golden Rule.

Gold Star Mothers. SEE American.

golf course. Preferred to golf links.

golf tees.

Golgotha [GAWL-guh-thuh]. Calvary.
    GOLGOTHA. A burial place.

Goliath [guh-LIE-uhth].

golosh. Use galosh.

-gon. Combining form meaning closed geometric plane figure: polygon (many sides and angles); trigon, triangle (3 sides and angles); tetragon, quadrangle, quadrilateral (4); pentagon (5); hexagon (6); heptagon (7); octogon or octangle (8); nonagon (9); decagon (10); undecagon (11); dodecagon (12); quindecagon (15); (adj.) -gonal.

gonad [GAHN-ad]. An essential sexual gland.

gondola [GAHN-duh-luh].

gondolier [gahn-duh-LEER].

good-by. Preferred to -bye in U.S.

Good Friday. Christian holy day commemorating the Crucifixion.

good will. BUT goodwill of a business enterprise, good-will for the attributive adjective; *A good-will gesture.*

googol. Figure 1 followed by 100 zeros = 10^{100}.

Gorgonzola [gawr-gahn-ZOH-luh]. An Italian cheese.

gorilla [goh-RIHL-luh].

Goring, Herman Wilhelm. SEE Goering.

Gospel. Capitalize if referring to the first four books of the New Testament; BUT *gospel truth.*

gossamer [GAHSS-uh-mehr].

gossip. -ed, -ing, -y.

Gotham. New York City.

Gothic.

gotten. See get.

"Gotterdammerung." (Ger.) "Twilight of the gods;" fourth and last opera of Wagner's *Ring of the Nibelung.*

Gouda [GOU-dah]. Dutch town in South Holland; also hard eyeless cheese from the area.

Gounod, Charles Francois [goo-NOH, angl. GOO-noh]. (1818–93) French composer.

gourd [gohrd or goord]. Family of vine-growing plants (cucumber, melon, squash, pumpkin), especially inedible varieties. gourdhead.

gourmand [GOOR-mand]. A lover of eating; a greedy eater.
    GOURMET [GOOR-mae]. A connoisseur of food and drink.

Gov. (abbr.) governor.

government [GUHV-uhr-mehnt]. (abbr. govt.)

government. Churchill government, Communist government, European governments, Federal government, State government, municipal government; insular, island; military government; seat of government; Provincial government; Territorial government.

Government. Cap. British Government, Soviet Government, the Government; Canal Zone Government, the government; Government (U.S.) department, officials, publications, (U.S. Government); National and State Governments; Government Printing Office (SEE Office); U.S., National, Federal, Central, General Governments.

governmental. Lower-case unless part of a name.

Governor of Puerto Rico. the Governor; Governor of the Federal Reserve Board, the Governor; Governor of the Panama Canal, the Governor; Governor of Wisconsin, the Governor; State Governor(s); Governors' conference; a Governor.

Governor of a State. ADDRESS: His Excellency Nelson Rockfeller, The Governor of New York, Albany, N.Y. 10024 or The Honorable the Governor of New York, Albany, N.Y. SALUTATION: Sir, Dear Sir, or His Excellency, The Governor of New York, Your Excellency, Dear Governor Rockefeller:

governor general. Pl. governors general. Governor General of Canada, the Governor General.

governorship.

g.p.m. (abbr.) gallons per minute.

g.p.s. (abbr.) gallons per second.

GPU. SEE MVD.

gr. (abbr.) grain, gross, gram.

gr. wt. (abbr.) gross weight.

Grace, your. Title of address to a duke or duchess.

gradation [grae-DAE-shuhn].

grade, market. SEE market grades.

grades. British for all school marks.

gradual [GRAD-joo-uhl].

graduate. (n.) one who has completed a school course. As a verb, the active form is preferred to the passive. *She graduated from* preferred to *—was graduated from.*

grain. Unit of weight $= \frac{1}{5760}$ troy lb. $= \frac{1}{7000}$ avoirdupois lb. $= 0.05$ scruple $= 64.799$ milligrams.

gram. (g.) Preferred to Brit. gramme. Unit of weight in the metric system $= 0.03215$ oz. sp. $= \frac{1}{1000}$ kilogram $= 15.432$ grains $= 0.03527$ ou. Based on weight of 1 cc. of pure water at 4° centigrade.

Grand Army of the Republic. (abbr. G.A.R.) The Grand Army, the Army; Grand Army

Post No. 63; Post No. 63; Grand Army Post; the post.

grand jury. SEE Federal.

Grange, the (National).

grangerize. Of a book, extra-illustrate with material from other sources. From techniques used by James Granger in 1769, who left blank pages for additional illustrations.

grant-in-aid Pl. grants-in-aid. Sum given, especially by government, to contribute to cost of a project such as roads, schools, housing.

graph 2, A, II, etc. But capitalize Graph 2, when part of title: *Graph 2.—Production Levels.*

gratis [GRAE-tihs or GRAT-ihs]. Without recompense. Free. *The service was gratis.*

gratuitous [gruh-TOO-ih-tuhs]. Freely given. Gratuitous advice, coinage.

grave. P.p., graved or graven.

grave accent (`) [GRAHV]. In French, an open quality of *è*, a falling inflection, pronounced "eh." In English, used occasionally on any vowel to indicate stress on syllable or to distinguish two words otherwise alike in spelling but different in meaning. *armed vs. armèd.*

gray. Preferred to grey in U.S.

gray market. Unofficial but legal market on which prices of scarce goods are higher than standard prices.

Greece. Native, Greek(s); adj., Grecian, Greek, Grecize, [GREE-siez]. (Greco—. combining form). Cap., Athens (Atheinai). Currency, drachma (DR), lepton, lepta. SEE Hellenes.

GRECIAN. Used to refer to facial or architectural features.

GREEK. For ordinary usage: *Greek people, islands, church, history.*

Greenwich mean time [GRIHN-ihj or GREHN- or -ihch]. (abbr. G.m.t.) The hour in London, based on the zero meridian which runs through Greenwich. New York time is 5 hours earlier, Tokyo time is 9 hours later.

Greenwich Village [GREHN-ihch or GRIHNihch]. Area in New York City bounded roughly by 14th St., Canal St., 4th Avenue, and the Hudson River, noted for unconventionality.

grey. Gray is preferred, BUT greyhound.

great. SEE big.

Great Basin. Great Beyond, Great Divide, Great Father (SEE fanciful appellations), Great Lakes, the lakes, lake(s) traffic; Great Plains, BUT southern Great Plains; Great Rebellion (SEE Rebellion), Great War (SEE War), Great White Way (New York City).

Great Britain. (England, Scotland, and Wales.) Native, Briton(s), British (collective, pl.); adj., British. Cap., London. Currency, pound, (£), shilling (s.), penny (d.), pence changed to decimal system in 1968, £1 = 100 pence. *Cf.* United Kingdom, Britain.

UNITED KINGDOM. Great Britain and Northern Ireland. (Prior to 1922 also Eire.)

COMMONWEALTH OF BRITISH NATIONS. Canada and other autonomous communities.

great circle (navigation). Shortest distance between two points on earth, allowing for earth's curvature.

Greater Los Angeles. Greater New York.

grid. Metal grating or plate.

GRIDDLE. Flat pan for cooking cakes.

GRIDIRON. Metal plate or grid used for broiling food. Colloq., football field.

GRILL. (v.) Broil; (n.) broiler.

GRILLE. Lattice: *An iron grille stretched across the porch.*

griddlecake.

griffin. Preferred to —fon. (1) A type of vulture; (2) a French dog's name; (3) a mythological monster, half lion, half eagle. *Cf.* hippogriff.

grimace [grih-MAES]. (n., v.) —cer, —ced, —cing.

grimy [GRIE-mee].

grind. P. and p.p., ground; grinding.

grindstone.

gringo. Pl. -os. Among Spanish Americans,

contemptuous term for a foreigner, especially an Englishman or American.

grippe, grip [GRIHP]. Influenza.

grisly. (adj.) Inspiring horror.

GRIZZLY. Gray: *Grizzly bear.*

Gris-Nez, Cape [GREE-nae]. Cape in France; Point on European mainland nearest Britain.

gristmill.

Gromyko, Andrei A. [groh-MEE-koh; Russ., gruh-MIH-kuh, UHN-drya]. (1909–   ) Russian economist, diplomat.

groom. British use bridegroom, to distinguish from one who cares for horses.

grosbeak [GROHS-beek]. Species of finch.

gross. 12 doz. = 144.

GREAT GROSS. 12 gross = 1728.

Gross National Product. (abbr. GNP) Value of all goods and services produced in a nation each year. *Cf.* National Income.

gross-minded. (adj.) gross weight.

Grosvenor, Gilbert Hovey [GROHV-nehr]. (1875–1966) American geographer.

growth rate. For a nation, annual percentage increase in GNP.

grottowork.

Group. Military Advisory Group, the group; Standing Group. SEE Army Organization.

group 2, II, A, etc. But capitalize Group 2, when part of title: *Group II: List of Countries by States.*

group-connect. (v.) group insurance.

group nouns. (flock, family, crowd) take a singular verb except where the sense is individualized or plural: *The football team were given letters. Cf.* animals.

groups. triad (3); tetrad (4); pentad (5); hexad (6); heptad (7); ogdoad (8).

grouse. Singular and plural. A bird. In slang, complain.

grovel [GRUHV'l]. —ling, —led. Brit. *ll.*

grow. P., grew; p.p., grown.

grown-up. (n. and adj.) grownupness.

gruel [GROO-uhl]. (n.) A thin porridge.
GRUEL. (v.) -ling. Brit. —*ll*—. Punish; try beyond one's endurance.

Gruenther, Alfred M. [GRUHN-thehr]. (1899–) U.S. General and NATO commander.

gruesome. Repulsive; grisly.

Gruyere [groo-YEHR]. Cheese made chiefly in Switzerland.

GSA or G.S.A. (abbr.) General Services Administration.

G.T.C. order. Good till cancelled order, especially to a stockbroker, or for advertising.

GTS. (abbr.) gas turbine ship.

Guadeloupe Is [gwahd-LOOP]. Islands in French West Indies.
GUADELUPE, TEX., North Mexico mountains and river.

Guam [GWAHM]. (no abbrev.) U.S. territory largest and southernmost island in Mariana group; U.S. naval base. Native, Guamanian.

guano [GWAH-noh]. Dung of seafowl used as fertilizer.

Guantanamo Bay [gwahn-TAH-nah-moh]. Site of former U.S. naval base on southeast coast of Cuba. In slang, shortened to Gitmo.

guarantee, guaranty. Guarantee is more common as a verb and as a noun in reference to the security or pledge offered, or the one who offers security. BUT guarantor in the last mentioned sense is simpler. Guaranty is more usual as a noun in reference to the act of guaranteeing or offering security: *The agency guaranteed his mortgage to the bank. The bank holds a guarantee from the government agency on his mortgage. The agency acts as guarantee (guarantor) of our mortgage. The certificate of guaranty is good until the mortgage is completely repaid. The agency has always honored its guaranty.*

guaranteed annual wage. (abbr. GAW)

guardsman. SEE Coast Guard; National Guard.

Guatemala. Native, Guatemalan(s); adj., Guatemalan. Cap., Guatamala City. Currency, quetzel, quetzales (Q), centavo (Ctvo.).

gubernatorial [goo-behr-nuh-TAWR-ee-uhl]. Of the state governor or government.

Guernica [gehr-NEE-kah]. Town in northeast Spain, site of former Basque parliament.

guerrilla [guhr-IHL-uh]. (n. and adj.) One who engages in irregular warfare in connection with a regular war, especially as a member of a predatory band. *Cf.* Seals.
GORILLA. Ape.

guffaw [guhf-FAW]. Loud burst of laughter.

Guervara, Ernesto "Che" Dr. (Major) [goo-aw-VAH-rah "CHAE"]. (1932–1967) Cuban Revolutionary.

Guiana [gee-AH-nah or -AN-ah]. Sections of South America including parts of Brazil, Venezuela, Surinan (Dutch), British and French Guiana.

guide. -dable.

guided-missile. (adj.)

guider-in.

guidon [GIE-dun]. Small flag, as a military company banner. *Cf.* pendant.

Guienne, Guyenne [gew-ee-YEHN or gee—]. From Aquitaine, historical region of southwest France on Atlantic Ocean.

guild. Organized trade group. SEE gild.

Guillaune, Charles Edouard [gee-yohn, SHAHRlz ae-DWAHR]. (1861–1938) French physicist.

guillotine [GIHL-oh-teen]. Beheading machine created by French physician J. I. Guillotin in 1789.

guilty. SEE hold guilty.

Guinea [GIHN-ih]. West Africa nation and region from Gambia to the Cameroons. Natives, Guinean(s). Formerly French.

Independent since October 1958. Cap., Conakry, Currency, Guinea franc = 100 centimes.

guinea fowl. guinea hen, guinea pig.

Guise, de, 1st Duc [de-GEEZ, sometimes GWEEZ; Fr., GEEZ]. (1519–1563) French soldier, politician.

guitar [gih-TAHR].

Guitry, Sacha [gee-TREE, sah-CHAH]. (1885–1957) French actor-playwright.

gulden [GOOL-dehn]. Dutch and early German coin.

Gulf Coast States. gulf coast; Gulf of Mexico, the gulf; Gulf States; Gulf Stream, the stream.

gullible.

guns. Use figures for caliber: .22 rifle; .45 caliber revolver; .410-gauge shotgun; 12-gauge shotgun; 7.3-inch gun; 125-mm. gun. *Cf.* bullet, caliber.

Gunter's chain. SEE surveyor's chain.

gunwale [guhn-el]. Sometimes gunnel. Part of vessel where topsides and deck meet.

Gustaf VI, Adolf (1882–   ) King of Sweden, 1950–   . Married (1) Princess Margaret, daughter of Duke of Connaught, died 1920;

(2) Lady Louise Mountbatten, daughter of Marquess of Milford Haven in 1923.

Gustavus [guhs-TAE-vuhs, -TAH-vuhs]. Name of five kings of Sweden.

Gutenberg, Johann [GOO-tehn-behrk, YOH-hahn]. (1400–1468) Inventor of movable-type printing, 1440. The town is sometimes written Guttenberg, due to ancient error.

Guyana. Nation in northern South America, formerly British Guiana. Independent since May 1966. Adj., natives (s. and pl.) Guyanese. Capital, Georgetown. Currency, Guinea franc (G. Fr.) = 100 centimes.

guy. In U.S. slang, a fellow. Originally from Guy Fawkes; also one of grotesque appearance.

gybe. British form of jibe. See gibe.

GYMNASIUM. Pl. —s or —ia.

gymp. Use gimp.

gynecology [jihn-nec-KAHL-uh-jee, gie-, or jie-].

gypsy. Preferred to gipsy in U.S.

gyrate [JIE-raet].

gyroscope [JIE-roh-skohp]. Spinning disk which rotates on perpendicular axis, used to control torque.

gyves [jievs]. Shackles.

H

h. Silent in nihilism, philharmonic, and other multisyllable words where the syllable is not accented; *h* is usually aspirate (made with an impulse in breath) as in *hate, home, behave,* and is sounded only before vowels and *w.*

h. (abbr.) hecto = (100) in the metric system.

H-bar. H-beam, H-bomb, H-hour, H-piece.

ha. (abbr.) hectare.

Haakon VLI [HAW-kohn]. (1872–1957) King of Norway; 1905–57.

habitué [huh-biht-yoo-AE]. Frequent visitor or resident.

had better. *He had better be here. He had better have been here. NOT: He had better been here.*

Hadrian [HAE-drih-an]. (76–138) Pope, Emperor of Rome.

The Hague. BUT: the Hague Court, the Second Hague Conference.

Haifa [HIE-fah]. Mediterranean seaport, Israel.

Haile Selassie [HIE-lee sih-LAH-syeh; angl., HIE-lee seh-LAS-ih or -LAH-sih]. (1891–) Emperor of Ethiopia, 1930– , 225th descendant of Solomon.

hailstone. hailstorm; hail fellow.

hairdresser. hairline, hairsplitting, hair ribbon, hair trigger.

hairdo. Pl. – dos.

hairbreadth or hairsbreadth. Unit of width = $\frac{1}{48}$ in. = $\frac{1}{4}$ line.

Haiti. Native, Haitian(s); adj., Haitian. Cap., Port-au-Prince. Currency, gourde (G), centime.

halcyon days. From ancient fable, 14 days about December 21.

hale. Shout.
> HALE. Force to go along. *He haled a cab and haled the drunk home.*

half. (1) *cut in half* is preferred to more correct *cut in halves;* (2) (v.) halve; (3) A yard and a half is pref. to one and a half yards, even when written $1\frac{1}{2}$ yards. The verb of a mixed number is singular: *Seven and a half tons is here.* (4) Half again as much is 150 per cent. Avoid as subject to ambiguity: *He got a 10 cent price increase in June, and half again as much in September.* (The total of the two increases is 25 cents, but might be misunderstood as 15 cents.)

half past four. 4: 30.

half title. A short title of a book or a subdivision, printed on a separate page before the section it introduces.

halfback (football). half-breed, half-caste, half-hearted, halfpenny, halfpennyworth, half title, half-tone (printing), half-track, halfway; half-and-half (n. and adj.), half-afraid, half-alive, half-baked (adj.), half-bred (adj.), half-clear, half-hourly (adj.), half-mast, half-miler, half-ripe, half-strength (adj.), half-true, half-truth, half-witted (adj.).

half binding. half cent, half hour, half load, half measure, half mile, half moon, half nelson, half past, half speed.

Hall. (U.S. Senate or House).

hallboy. hallmark, hallway.

hallelujah [hal-luh-LOO-yuh. NOT loolya].

halliard. Use halyard. A hoist for flags.

Halloween. Brit., e'en.

Halls of Congress.

halo. Pl. -os. Brit. -oes.

Hammarskjöld, Dag Hjalmar Agne Carl [HAHM-ahr-shuld, dahg YAHL-mahr AHNG-neh]. (1905–1961) Swedish U.N. secretary-general, 1953–61.

Hammurabi [hahm-uh-RAH-bee]. (c. 1955–1913 B.C.). King of Babylon.

hamstring, hamstrung. -ed is correct but rarely used.

hand. Unit of length = 4 in. = 10.16 centimeters.

hand and glove. Preferred to *hand in glove.*

hand-tailored. (adj.) hand-tooled (adj.).

handful. Pl. —fuls.

handicap. -pped, -pping.

handkerchief [HANG-kuh-chihf].

hand-me-down. Pl. -downs.

handyman. One who does odd jobs.
HANDY MAN. One who is handy.

hang. -ed (of persons so killed); otherwise, hung.

hanger-back. hanger-up.

hanger-on. Pl. hangers-on. Colloquial for dependent.

hanker. (for). Have a craving (for).

Hanukkah, Hanukka, Chanukah, [HAH-nuh-kah]. Transliteration of Hebrew word for Jewish festival of lights, (in December).

haply. Perhaps; by chance (archaic).

happen into. Avoid: *I happened into the shop.*

happen to. Avoid: *I happen to know (or think).*

happy-go-lucky.

hara-kiri [HAR (or hohr) -uh-KIHR-ih]. Japanese ritual suicide.

harass [HAR-uhs; huh-RASS].

harbor master. -side.

hard. (adj. and adv., except in sense of scarce) *I worked very hard. I had hardly enough for myself.*

hard-and-fast rule.

hard-pressed. (adj.) hard-set (adj.), hard-won (adj.); hard rubber, hard shell, hard up, hard wheat, hard work.

hardly. Is followed by when. *He had hardly been seated when the curtain rose,* NOT *... than the curtain rose.* AVOID double negatives. NOT: *He saved hardly nothing.*

harebrain. -brained.

harem [HAE-rehm, HAIR-ehm].

harken.

Harlequin [HAHR-lee-kwihn, -kihn].

harmless. *More* or *most harmless* should not be used.

harmony. In music, a group of notes forming a pleasing chord.
MELODY. A series of notes in an expressive succession.

harnessmaker. harness-making (adj.); harness race.

Harpers Ferry, W. Va. Scene of John Brown's raid. NOT: *Harper's.*

hart. Male deer, especially red deer; especially after its 5th year. *Cf.* animals.
STAG. A male deer, especially after its 5th year.
BUCK. Male of fallow deer, reindeer, chamois, hare, rabbit, and similar animals.
HIND. Female deer, especially red deer; especially after its 3rd year.
DOE. Female fallow deer and similar animals. *Cf.* reindeer, hare, rabbit, rat, etc.

harum-scarum.

Harun-al-Rashid [hah-ROON al-ra-SHEED; angl. har-roon al-RASH-ihd]. (764–809) Caliph of Bagdad.

has-been. (n.)

hasenpfeffer [HAH-zehn-fehf-ehr]. Rabbit stew.

has got. meaning possesses, is redundant.

hashish. Preferred to -sheesh.

hateful [HAET-fuhl].

haulageway.

hauteur [haw-tuer]. Haughtiness of manner.

have-not. (n. and adj.)

haversack.

havoc. -cked, -king.

Hawaii [hah-WIE-ee or -WAW-yee]. (no abbr.) Native, Hawaiian. Chain of islands in North Central Pacific. 50th U.S. state. Formerly Sandwich Islands. Capital, Honolulu.

Hawker. SEE Fighter Planes.

hay fever.

hazelnut. hazel-eyed (adj.).

H.B. (with number) (abbr.). House bill.

H.C. (abbr.) House of Commons.

h.c.f. (abbr.) highest common factor.

H. Con. Res. (with number) (abbr.) House concurrent resolution.

H. Doc. (with number) (abbr.) House document.

HE (abbr.) high explosive.

Head of a state department. ADDRESS: The Secretary State, or The Secretary of State, Commonwealth of Pennsylvania, or The Honorable John J. Jones, Secretary of State. SALUTATION: Sir, Dear Sir, Dear Mr. Jones, Dear Mr. Secretary.

headache. headband, head-on (adj.); head tax.

header-up.

headquarters. Alaska Command Headquarters, the command headquarters; 4th Regiment Headquarters, regimental headquarters; 32nd Division Headquarters; the division headquarters.

heal-all. (n. and adj.).

healthcraft.

healthful. Conducive to health: *healthful foods.*

HEALTHY. Generally, containing health, in good health. BUT a healthy *climate, place, influence.*

heaps. Use a singular verb except when followed by of: *There is heaps more work to do.*

hear. P. and p.p., heard.

hearken. Preferred to harken.

heartache. heartbeat, heartbreak. halfhearted. lionhearted, softhearted; heart-leaved (adj.), heart-throbbing (adj.), heart-weary (adj.).

heart condition. AVOID as indefinite. Use heart ailment, disease, injury, etc., as appropriate.

hearthman. -rug, -stone.

heathland.

heave. P.p., heaved is preferred to hove. heaved-to, hove-to, heaving-to.

Heaven. (Deity) heaven (place): *I thank Heaven.*

heaven, heavens. The words are interchangeable, but heavens is preferred for the sky.

heavenly bodies. Names are not capitalized unless used in connection with the names of planets or stars that are always capitalized: *sun, earth, moon, stars, polestar, lodestar.* BUT: *studying Mercury, Arcturus, the Sun, Mars, the Earth.* Fanciful names in English are always capitalized. *the Milky Way, the Great Bear, the Dog Star.*

Heavenly Father. the Almighty, Thee, Thou, He, Him; BUT himself; (God's) fatherhood.

heaven's sake. NOT heavens' sake.

heavenward. heaven-inspired (adj.), heaven-sent (adj.).

heaver-off. heaver-out, heaver-over.

Hebrew. Used for the people in past or patriarchal, literary contexts. Hebraic, -aism, -aist, -aize. Cf. Jew.

hecatomb [HEHK-uh-tahm]. A great slaughter; from public sacrifice of 100 oxen.

hectare. (abbr. ha.) Unit of area = 2.471 acres = 1 hm.^{2} = 100 acres = 10,000 m^2.

hectic. At a high pitch of excitement.

hecto-, hect-. Combining prefix meaning hundred. *Cf.* centi-.

hectogram. (abbr. hg.) Unit of weight = 100 g. = 3.5274 oz. = 0.1 kg.

hectoliter. (abbr. hl.) Unit of (1) capacity = 100 liters. = 2.838 bu. = 2 bu. 3.35 pk. = 26.418 gal.; (2) volume = 6102.5 cu. in. = 0.1 m.^{3}

hectometer. (abbr. hm.) Unit of length = 100 m. = 109.361 yd. = 328.083 ft.

hectostere. Unit of volume = 100 m.^{3} = 130.794 cu. yd. = 100 steres.

-hedron. Combining form meaning sides of a solid. polyhedron (many); trihedron (3); tetrahedron (4); pentahedron (5); hexahedron (6); cube (6 equal); cuboid (approx. cube); heptahedron (7); octahedron (8); decahedron (10); dodecahedron (12); icosahedron (20); tetrahexahedron (24 equal triangular); trisoctahedron (24 equal); (adj.) trihedral, etc.; prismatic.

Hegel, George Wilhelm Friedrich [HAE-gehl, GAE-awrk VIHL-helm FREE-drihk]. (1770–1831) German philosopher.

hegemony [hee-JEHM-oh-nih, HEHJ-ee-moh-nih, HEE-jih-meh-nih]. Leadership, especially of a government or state.

hegira [hee-JIE-ruh, HEHJ-ih-ruh]. Also hejira. Flight of Mohammed from Mecca, A.D. 622, Moslem yr. 1. By extension, any flight.

height [hiet]. Preferred to highth. But NOT heighth or hight.

heinous [HAE-nuhs]. Infamous; odious.

heir. (m. & f.) One who inherits anything (including characteristics, etc.)
HEIRESS. (f.) Used usually in connection with wealth.

heir apparent. Heir regardless of any possible births (usually the oldest son).

heir at law. Pl., heirs at law.

heir presumptive. Heir subject to birth of a more legitimate heir; e.g., the oldest daughter where a son might be born and would inherit.

Hejaz [heh-JAZ]. Since 1932, region of Saudi Arabia on Red Sea. Cap., Mecca.

Helena [HEHL-uh-nuh]. City in Montana.

helicopter [HEHL-ih-kahp-tihr]. Wingless aircraft, supported and driven solely by overhead propellers revolving on a horizontal plane. *Cf.* STOL, VTOL.

helio-, heli-. Combining form, meaning the sun: heliocentric, heliograph.

heliotrope [HEE-lih-oh-trohp].

heliotropism. Movement toward sun.
APHELIOTROPISM. Movement away from sun.

helium [HEE-lee-uhm]. (abbr. He) Gaseous element first found in the sun's atmosphere.

helix [HEE-lihks]. Pl., helices [HEHL-ih-seez]. Anything having a spiral form.

hell. BUT Hades.

Hellas [HEHL-as]. Greece.

Hellenic [hehl-ehn-ihk]. Hellene, Hellenist, Hellenize, -zation. Classical Greek. In modern times, used to signify pro-Greek feeling, pan-Hellenism. *Cf.* Greece.

hellbender. -bent, -born, -bound, -box, (printing), -bred, -cat, -diver, -dog, -fire, -hole, -hound, -ship (all one word); hell-dark (adj.), hell-red (adj.).

Hells Canyon. NO apostrophe. Canyon.

Heloise [ae-law-EEZ or HEHL]. (1101–1164) French abbess, wife of Abelard.

help. Avoid use for *must.* NOT: *Don't miss more dates than you can help.*

helter-skelter.

Helvetia. Switzerland (poetic).

Helvetius, Claude Andrien [ehl-vae-SYUES, klohd]. (1715–1771) French philosopher.

hem-, hema-, hemato-, hemo- or haem- [HEEM]. Combining prefixes meaning blood. U.S. uses *hem-* except in scientific terms. British use *haem-: hemastatic, hematoblast, hemoglobin.*

he-man.

hematoma [hem-uh-TOH-muh]. Bloody tumor.

hemi-. Prefix meaning half: *hemisphere, hemiatrophy.*

Hemisphere. Eastern; Western Hemisphere, etc.; the hemisphere.

hemoglobin, haemoglobin [HEE-moh-gloh-bihn]. Pigment in the red blood corpuscles.

hemorrhage. Preferred to haemorrhage. Blood discharge caused by injury. -ic.

hempen. (adj.) Preferred to hemp.

hence. From this place, time, or source.

THENCE. From that place, time, or source.

WHENCE. From what place or source.

WHITHER. To what place.

In these forms, the preposition (from or to) is understood and should not be repeated: *Go hence immediately; whence you have come concerns me not.* NOT: *Go from hence..*

henceforth, henceforward.

Henie, Sonia [HEHN-ee, SOHN-yah]. (1913–1967). Norwegian-American skater, actress.

her, hers. *This book of hers. Your and our and her courses. Her* (NOT hers) *and his towels. His house and hers. The law applied to you and yours, her and hers, me and mine. Cf.* him.

her, she as personification. Avoid except when commonly used or in poetic context. NOT: *The nation deserves the best we can give her.* BUT *she* and *her* may be used for a ship, the Queen, and other nouns of traditional gender.

herb [uhrb; Brit. huhrb]. Seed plant used for medicines or cooking. An herb; a herbal [HUHR-bal].

herbacious [huhr-BAE-shuhs]. Of an herb or a leaf.

Herculaneum [huhr-kyoo-LAE-nee-uhm]. Ancient city northwest of Vesuvius in Italy.

Herculean [huh-KYOO-lih-an]. Pertains to Hercules; requiring great strength; difficult. N.Y. Times, *herculean.*

hereabout. —after, —at, —by, —from, —in, —inabove, —inafter, —inbefore, —into, —of, —on, —to, —tofore, —under, —unto, —upon, —with (all one word).

heredity. Used in the biological sense.

DESCENT. Used in the social sense. BUT Darwin's "Descent of Man."

Hereford [EHR-uh-fuhrd]. Capital of Herefordshire, England.

herein. Here is preferred.

herewith. AVOID *enclosed herewith* and similar commercialese.

heroicomic. High burlesque: *a heroicomic poem.*

Herr. Pl., Herren. (Ger.) Mister.

herringbone.

Herriot, Edouard [eh-RYOH, ae-DWAHR]. (1872–1957) French prime minister, 1924–1925, 1926, 1932.

hesitation. More usual than *hesitancy* or *hesitance.* Hesitancy is used to indicate the tendency to hesitate: *After a moment of hesitation, he drove ahead. There was a hesitancy in all his decisions after he learned of this disability.*

Hesperia. The Western Land. Of Italy to the Greeks, of Spain to the Romans.

HESPERIDES. Mythological garden of the golden apples; also the nymphs who, with the aid of a dragon, guarded it.

heterography. Spelling in which the same letters sound differently; spelling different from current usage. *sow* [sou; soh].

Heuss, Theodor [hoiss]. (1884–   ) President, Federal Republic of Germany, 1949–1959.

hew. P. and p.p., hewed in U.S.; Brit., hewn.

HEW. (abbr.) Department of Health, Education, and Welfare.

hexagon. Regular six-sided polygon. Area = diameter of inscribed circle × 0.860.

hexameter [hehks-AM-ee-tehr]. In poetry, verse of six metrical feet.

HF. (abbr.) high frequency.

hg. (abbr.) hectogram.

hiatus [hie-AE-tuhs]. Pl. —es or hiatus. A gap. In grammar, slight pause between two vowels, each distinctly sounded: *egoism. Cf.* diaresis.

Hiawatha [hie-uh-WAHTH-uh].

Hibernia. Ancient Ireland. Hibernian.

hiccup [HIHK-uhp]. -uping, uped. Or hiccough [HIHK-uhp].

hide. P., hid; p.p., hidden.

hideaway. (n. & adj.) hide-and-seek (n. & adj.).

hie. Hasten; hied, hieing.

hierarch [HIE-uhr-ahrk]. Leader of a sacred order. hierarchy.

Hierosolymitan. Native of Jerusalem.

high. Both an adjective and an adverb.

highly. Often carries a note of condescension in a compliment: *A highly amusing project.*

High Church.

High Commissioner.

High Court. SEE Supreme Court.

higher-up. (n.) Pl., higher-ups.

highfalutin.

High Holy Days (Jewish).

highlight. (n. & v.)

Highness. Title of address to member of a royal family. *Your Highness* is followed by you and your: *Your Royal Highness is correct in your decision regarding your voyage. NOT her decision, etc.*

High School. Capitalize if part of name: Western High School. BUT the high school.

Highways. U.S. 40, U.S. No. 40, U.S. Highway No. 40; Route 40; State Route 9; the highway. Fifth Avenue; Belt Parkway; East River Drive.

hijack. -ed, -ing; -er.

hi-fi. High fidelity.

hilarious [hih-LAIR-ih-uhs, HIE -].

hillbilly.

him. Informally, but not in formal writings, *him* may be used after *is* or *than: It's him or me, but rather me than him.* FORMALLY: *It is he or I, but rather I than he. Cf.* Predicate Nominative.

Himalayas [hih-MAH-luh-yuh or hih-MAHL-yuhz; angl. hihm-ah-LAE-az]. Mountain range between India and Tibet.

hindermost. Use hindmost.

hindrance [HIHN-druhnss].

Hinds' Precedents.

Hindu. One of the native races of India. Language is Hindi; religion is Hinduism; (adj.) Hindustani [hihn-doo-STAH-nae]. *Cf.* India.

hinge. hinging.

Hippocratic oath [hihp-uh-KRAT-ihk]. Code of medical ethics by Hippocrates, (c. 460–357 B.C.)

hippogriff or -gryph. Fabulous medieval monster, part horse, part griffin.

GRIFFON. Part lion, part eagle. Also horse entered in race for the first time.

hippopotamus. Pl. -muses is preferred to -mi.

hire. Applied to labor, automobiles, halls.

RENT. Applied to buildings, equipment, halls.

CHARTER. Applied to vessels, buses, planes.

hiring hall. Official employment agency especially in maritime, music and printing trades.

Hirohito [hee-roh-HEE-toh]. (1901–   ) Reigning house of Yamato (since 500 B.C.). Emperor of Japan, 1926–   . Married Princess Nagako, 1924.

Hiroshima [hee-RAWSH-mah; angl. HEE-roh-SHEE-mah]. Site of first A-bomb destruction, Japan.

His Excellency. The Duke of Athol, etc.; His Excellency; Their Excellencies. Similarly, His Majesty, His Royal Highness.

Hispanola, -niola [hihs-pahn-YOH-lah]. Caribbean Island containing Dominican Republic and Haiti.

historic [hihs-TAHR-ihk]. Worthy of a place in history, memorable. Also in grammar, historic present tense. *A historic event is momentous.*

> HISTORICAL. Part of history. *A historical event* took place in the distant past.
>
> HISTORICITY. Historical existence.

Historic Events and Epochs. Reformation, the; Renaissance, the; Restoration, the (English); Revolution of July (French); Revolution, the (American, 1775; French,1789; English, 1688). *Cf.* Ages.

history [HIHS-toh-ree, -trih].

hit. P. and p.p., hit; hitting; hitter.

hit-and-miss. (adj.) hit-and-run (adj.), hit-or-miss (adj.).

hitchhiker. —hiking.

hither, thither. Here and there, for poetical use only.

hitherto. Until now.

H.J. Res. (with number) (abbr.) House joint resolution.

H.L. (abbr.) House of Lords.

hl (abbr.) hectoliter.

hm. (abbr.) hectometer.

hm.² (abbr.) square hectometer.

hoarfrost.

hoary-headed. hoary-haired (adj.).

hobbyhorse.

hobgoblin.

Ho-Chi-Minh [hoh-chee-MEEN]. (1890–1970) President of Democratic (Communist) Republic of Vietnam (North), 1955–1970.

hockshop.

hocus-pocus.

hodgepodge. A mixture, in a derogatory sense.

hodman. hod carrier.

hoe. hoeable, hoeing.

Hoess [hehss]. (The family name.)

Hogarth, William [HOH-gahrth]. (1697–1764). Engineer, engraver, painter.

hogback. (geol.)

hogshead. (abbr. hhd.) Unit of capacity. (1) U.S. = ½ butt = 63 U.S. gal. = 2 liquid bbl. = 238.476 1.; (2) Brit. = 52.4 imperial gal.

Ho-Ho-Kus, N.J.

hoi polloi [hoi-puh-LOI]. The many. Ordinary people; the rabble.

hoist. -ed, -ing, -er. *Hoist with his own petard:* killed with his own weapon. *Cf.* petard.

hoistaway. (n.)

Holbein, Hans [HAWL-bien; angl. HOHL-bien]. Father (1465–1524), son (1497–1543). German painters.

hold. P. & p.p., held; holding. *The judge held him guilty.* NOT *to be guilty.*

holder-forth. holder-on, holder-up.

hold in abeyance. *Suspend action* is preferred.

hold steady is idiomatically correct for *hold steadily.*

hold up. (v.) holdup (n. & adj.): A holdup man holds up the victim of a holdup.

hole-in-one. (n. & adj.)

holidays. Individual days or mid-season week.

> VACATION. Annual or summer vacation. British summer holiday(s).

holidays and special days. Admission Day, All Fools' Day (also April Fools Day), Arbor Day, Armed Forces Day, Christmas Day, Christmas Eve, Columbus Day, D-Day; D-plus-4 day, Father's Day, Flag Day, Founders' Day, Fourth of July, Halloween, Inauguration Day, Independence Day, Labor Day, Lincoln's Birthday, M-day, Memorial Day (also Decoration Day), Mother's Day, New Year's Day, New Year's Eve, Thanksgiving Day, V-E Day, V-J Day, Veterans (no apostrophe) Day, Washington's Birthday; BUT election day; primary day.

Holland. A medieval country on the North Sea, presently the Netherlands.

Holland-America Line.

holy. Sacred.

HOLEY. Full of holes.

HOLLY [HAH-lee]. A plant commonly used for Christmas decoration.

WHOLLY. Completely.

Holy Scriptures. Holy Writ (Bible). SEE Bible.

Home, Earl of [YOOM]. (1903–   ) Name changed in 1963 to Sir Alec Douglas-Home. British Secretary of State for Foreign Affairs, 1960–1963; Prime Minister, 1963.

home. A place where a person or family lives.

HOUSE. A structure suitable for a home.

Home. Naval Home, Soldiers' Home; the home.

homely. Plain, simple. By extension, in U.S., ugly.

homeo-. Combining form meaning like: *homeopathy* [hoh-mee-AHP-uh-thee] (medical system which uses medicines that produce like symptoms); *homeomorphism* (like crystalline forms in unlike chemicals). *Cf.* homo-.

homeward.

homicide [HAHM-ih-sied]. Killing of a human being.

MANSLAUGHTER. Unlawful homicide without malice.

MURDER. Unlawful homicide with malice and premeditation.

homo-, hom-. Combining form meaning same or equal: *homonyms, homochromatic, homocentric.*

homogeneity [hoh-moh-jehn-EE-uh-tee]. Homogeneous character.

homogeneous [OH-moh-GEE-nee-uhs]. Of the same kind or nature.

homogenized milk.

homologue, —log. (n.) Thing whose similarity to something else is attributed to a common origin.

homonyms. Words having the same sound but different meanings: *bark* (of a tree), *bark* (of a dog); *hole, whole*; *rite, right, wright.*

heteronymns. Words spelled alike but with different sound and sense: *sow* (pig) [sou]; *sow* (seed).

SYNONYMS. Words with identical meaning (quite rare). By extension, words with similar meanings.

ANTONYMS. Words with opposite meanings. *Cf.* heterography.

homo sapiens [HOH-moh SAE-pee-uhnz]. (Lat.) Man.

Hon. (abbr.) Honorable. Title preceding the Christian name or initials of a public official, especially a judge: *Hon. John Collins* or *Hon. J.T. Collins.* NOT *Hon. Mr. Collins,* or *Hon. Collins,* or *the Hon. Mr. Collins.*

Honan [HOH-NAHN]. Province in China.

Honduras. Native, Honduran(s); (adj.) Honduran. Cap., Tegucigalpa. Currency, lempira (L), centavo (Ctvo.).

honeycomb.

Hong Kong [HAHNG-kahng]. British crown colony island and adjacent mainland, southeast China, 391 sq. mi. Currency, dollar (HK$), cent.

honor. Brit. -our.

honorbound.

hood (auto). British use bonnet; a hood is the top of a convertible.

hoodcap.

hoof. Pl., -s is pref. to hooves.

Hoover Dam. the dam.

hope chest.

Hopei, Hopeh [HOH-pae]. Province in China.

Hoppe, William Frederick [HAHP-ih]. (1887–1959) American billiard champion.

horde.

horehound. Preferred to hoar-.

horror-struck.

hors de combat [AWR-duh-kohm-BAH]. Out of action.

hors-d'oeuvre [awr-deuvr]. Appetizer.

horse. For cavalry, plural is horse. horsy.

horsepower. Measure of power = 33,000 ft. lbs. per sec. = 0.746 kilowats = 4241 B.t.u.

horse races. Capitalize names: *Kentucky Derby.*

Hosea [hoh-ZEE-ah]. Old Testament prophet.

hose. Pl., hose, except tubing, which may be *hoses.*

hosiery [HOH-zhuhr-ee].
   HOSE. (stockings) Pl. hose.
   HOSE. (rubber tube) Pl., hose or hoses.

hospitable [HAHS-piht-abl].

Hospital. Capitalize if part of name; the hospital. BUT naval (marine or Army) hospital.

host. (m. & f.); hostess (f.)

hostile [HAHS-tihl; Brit., -tiel].

hostler [HAHS-luhr or AHS-luh]. One who takes care of horses.

hotbed.

hotelkeeper.

Houphouet-Boigny, Félix [HOOF-weht BOIYN-yee] (1906–) Physician-President of Ivory Coast, 1961–

houri [HOOR-ih or HOUR-ih]. Mohammedan nymph.

house. SEE home. In Britain, an impressive building or residence.

houseful. Pl, -fuls.

House. Capitalize if part of name; Johnson house (private residence); Lee House (hotel); House of Representatives; the House (U.S.); House of the Woods (palace), the house; House Office Building (SEE Building); Ohio (State) House, the house; BUT both Houses, lower (or upper) House (Congress).

House of Commons. the Commons.

House of Lords. the Lords.

Houston [HYOOS-tuhn]. City in Texas.

hover [HUHV-ehr, HAHV-ehr].

How. (abbr.) Howard (U.S. Supreme Court Reports).

howbeit. Nevertheless: albeit, although (archaic).

however. Stress is usually placed on the word that precedes *however* in the sentence.

however. *But . . . however* is redundant.

how ever. *How ever can you manage?* is colloq.

however. howsoever; how-do-you-do (n.).

how-to-be-beautiful course.

Hoxho, Enver, Col. -Gen. [HAHDZ-hah]. (1906–) First Secretary, Albanian Communist Party.

hp. (abbr.) horsepower.

hp. -hr. (abbr.) horsepower-hour.

hr. (abbr.) hour.

H. Rept. (with number) (abbr.) House report.

H. Res. (with number) (abbr.) House resolution.

Hruska, Roman Lee [RUHS-kah]. (1904–) U.S. Sen. from Nebraska.

Hrvatska [huhr-VAHT-kah]. City in Yugoslavia.

Hudson's Bay Co. NOT: Hudson Bay Company.

hue. SEE color.

Hué [HWAE, Hyoo-AE], Seaport, former Capital of Annam, Provincial capital in S. Vietnam.

hull-less.

human. Pertaining to people: *the human race.* Do not use noun as a substitute for *human being.* —ism, —istic, —itarian, —ity, —ize, —kind, —ly.
   HUMANE. Having tenderness, compassion; *humane character, actions.*

humankind.

humbly [HUHM-blee].

humdrum.

humpty-dumpty.

humus [HYOO-muhs]. Organic part of soil, brown or black, formed by decomposition.

hundred. = 100 = C. Several or many hundred; hundreds of books. One hundred, one hundred and one, one hundredth, one hundred and first, two hundred, two hundredth. *Cf.* million.

hundredfold. —weight; hundred-legged (adj.), hundred-percenter, hundred-pounder.

hundredweight. (abbr., cwt.) Unit of weight = $\frac{1}{20}$ ton; gross or long = 112 lbs. = 50.802 kgs: (2) net or short = 100 lbs. = 45.359 kg. *20 hundredweights,* BUT *a few hundredweight.*

hung. P.p. of hang; but persons are *hanged.*

Hungary. Native, Hungarian(s); adj., Hungarian. Cap., Budapest. Currency, forent (Ft.), fillér (sing. & pl.).

hunger-mad. (adj.) hunger-worn (adj.).

hung-up. (adj.) hung jury.

huntsman.

Hurricane Carol. etc.

hurt. P., p.p., hurt.

husbandman.

hush up. (n., adj.) hush-hush; hush money.

hussar [huh-ZAHR]. European cavalryman.
HUZZA [huh-ZAH]. Hurrah!

Hussein, Ibn Talal [hoo-SAEYN]. (1935–   )
King of Hashemite Jordan, 1952–   .

hussy [HUHZ-ee]. Disreputable woman.

hybrid. Cross-breed.

hydrangea [hie-DRAN-jee-uh].

hydrometer. Instrument for measuring specific gravity.

HYGROMETER. Instrument for measuring moisture content.

Hydrographer, the. (Navy Department).

hydropathy [hie-DRAHP-uh-thee]. Treatment of diseases by copious use of water, internally and externally.

hyena [hie-EE-nuh]. Preferred to -aena.

hygiene [HIE-jeen].
HYGIENIC [hie-jih-EHN-ihk].

hymns. Capitalize principal words in titles and place titles in quotation marks.

hyper-. Combining form meaning above, over, super-, extra-: *hyper-Dorian, hyperacidity, hypermeter.*
HYPO-. Combining form meaning under, less than normal: *hypoplasia, hypotention.*

hyphen. hyphenate preferred to hyphenize.

HYPHENATED COMPOUNDS. In general, compound two or more words to express a literal or figurative unit that would not be clearly expressed in unconnected succession. Hyphenate: (1) to avoid doubling a vowel or tripling a consonant: *anti-inflation, brass-smith.* BUT GPO does not hyphenate after a short prefix: *co-, de-, pre-, pro-, re-;* (2) when the vowel end of the prefix and the vowel beginning of the base word create a diphthong: *co-author;* (3) when the un-hyphenated prefix may lead to confusion in pronunciation or meaning: *co-op, co-worker, re-formation, re-cover;* (4) when the prefix is duplicated: *re-redirect examination;* (5) to join a prefix to a capitalized word: *pre-Victorian, un-American;* (6) where the terms are repetitive or conflicting: *walkie-talkie, pitter-patter, young-old;* (7) to join a capital letter to a noun or participle: *U-turn, I-beam;* (8) in chemical formulas: *Cr-Ni-Mo;* (9) in technical compounds: *candle-hour;* (10) in improvised compounds: *to blue-pencil;* (11) unit modifiers (in this volume, termed adjective) formed of an adjective or a noun plus a present or past participle, a *slow-rising elevator;* (12) unit modifiers formed of a present or past participle or a preposition not governing a following noun: *double-twisted cord, self-winding watch, lying-in hospital, hard-of-hearing class;* BUT NOT when the meaning is clear without the hyphen: *child welfare program, flood control project;* (13) unit modifiers made up of a verb plus a noun or pronoun: *make-believe, has-been, be-all*; (14) any adjective phrases made up of words not normally considered a unit which might be ambiguous: *high-school building, matter-of-fact manner, second-class citizen, Spanish-speaking community*; BUT NOT when the phrase is made up of two words normally considered a single unit, especially chemical, geographical or political ideas: *North American customs* (BUT UCMS hyphenates Latin-American), *New York traffic, Old English cheese, civil service jobs, family welfare studies, public school enrollment, social security payments, social service studies*; and foreign expressions: *laissez faire policies*; (15) a compound of which the base word is derived from a transitive verb: *wage-earner, fun-loving Office-holder*; BUT expressions formed of a transitive or intransitive verb as the first word are written as two words: *frying pan.* (16) Although GPO usually makes one word of agency compounds, UCMS hyphenates such compounds ending in *collector, dealer, driver, hunter, maker, etc.: toy-maker, book-critic, gun-dealer*. BUT commonly used words in this category are always treated as one word; *bookkeeper, bookdealer, bookmaker, copyholder, dressmaker, proofreader, serviceman, shopgirl, taxpayer, washerwoman*; (17) Usually, hyphenate compounds beginning with *mother, father, brother, sister, daughter, parent, fellow, foster: sister-city, fellow-members*; BUT compounds with a distinct unit meaning are written as one word; *fatherland, fellowship, motherland*; (18) hyphenate compounds beginning with *cross; cross-purpose*; with *great: great-grandfather*; with *life: life-line*; BUT NOT: *lifeblood, lifelong, lifetime*, and similar unit ideas; with *self; self-respect*; BUT NOT *selfless, selfsame*, and other unit ideas; with *half* and *quarter: half-mile, quarter-final*, BUT NOT *halfpenny, halftone, quarterback, quartermaster*; with *master: master-plumber*, BUT NOT *mastermind, masterpiece*; with *vice: vice-president*; BUT NOT *viceroy, vicerregent, vicereine*; with *ultra; ultra-elegant*, BUT NOT *ultra microscopic, ultra montane, ultraviolet*; with *quasi: quasi-judicial*; (19) hyphenate compounds of *god: sun-god; like* (if the base word has more than one syllable): *Spanish-like*; (20) titles in which the last element is *elect* or *designate: governor-elect*; (21) spelled-out fractions: *three-fifths, five-sevenths*; (22) Also hyphenate the following compounds: *after-years, bas-relief, blood-feud, blood-relation, court-martial, loan-word, object-lesson, sea-level, sense-perception, thought-process, title-page,*

trade-mark, trade-union, well-being, well-nigh. (23) A compound containing another compound is separated with an en (short) dash between the parts: *New Orleans-Nashville* run; (24) When multiple compounds have a common unit, the common unit may be omitted: *6- and 7- year olds, third- and fourth-year students.*

Make a single word of compounds containing: (1) two nouns making a third: *fishmonger*; (2) a short verb and an adverb; *blowout, showdown*; (3) a one-syllable noun prefix, especially most compounds of *book, eve, horse, house, mill, play, room, school, shop, snow, way, wood, and work*; BUT when the two components constitute a commonly accepted special meaning, write as two words: *tailor shop, bond house, book work, case work, field work*; (4) words beginning with *non*, BUT *non-civil service, non-European, non-pressed, non-tumor bearing, non sequitur*; (5) words ending in store or fold, if preceded by a one syllable word: *drugstore, twofold*; BUT these compounds are written as two words if preceded by words of more than one syllable; *tailor store, grocery store, twenty fold*; (6) compounds ending in *berry, blossom, boat, book, borne, bound, brained, bush, collector, dealer, driver, fish, flower, grower, hearted, holder, house, helper, keeping, light, like, maker, man, master, mate, mill, mistress, monger, piece, power, proof, room, shop, skin* (when preceded by a one-syllable word), *smith, stone, store, tail, tight, time, word, weed, wide, wise, woman, wood, work, worker, working, worm, writer, writing, yard*; BUT NOT if preceded by a long or unwieldy word and where no confusion would result from writing as two words: *encyclopedia maker*; (7) compounds ending with *one*, beginning with *any, every, no, and some*, BUT NOT when meaning a single or particular person or thing: *any one of these three*; also, write *no one* to avoid confusion; (8) all personal pronouns: *himself*; (9) compass directions of two points: *northeast*; BUT hyphenate when three points are combined: *north-northeast*; (10) technical terms in anthropology: *shortheaded.*

Write as separate words; (1) a predicate adjective or predicate noun when the second element is a participle: *The problem was price fixing; the cost was price fixed*; compounds in the predicate modifier where the first element is in the comparative or superlative: *The merchandise was of the better class*; BUT *lighter-than-air craft, higher-than-market price, bestseller (n.)* are exceptions; (3) compounds which are combinations of an adverb and an adjective or an adverb and a participle: *a never ending flow*; (4) compounds where the first element is an adverb ending in —ly: *eagerly awaited arrival*; (5) compounds where the first two words in a three-element modifier are adverbs; (6) compounds where a unit modifier contains a number or a letter as a second element: *Class II railroads*; (7) compounds which have an element in quotation marks; *"blue sky" laws*; (8) compounds where colors are separate words: *bluish green*; BUT hyphenate compound colors when used as unit modifiers: *bluish-green paper*; (9) independent adjective preceding a noun; *big gray houses*; (10) civil or military titles denoting a single office: *sergeant at arms, attorney general*; BUT not if two offices are involved: *secre-tary-treasurer*; and not *vice president*, (BUT Webster: *vice-president*); (11) a modifier with one element in the possessive case: *a week's pay*; except when used in a figurative sense; *cat's-paw*; (12) technical and chemical terms: *carbon monoxide poisoning*; (13) many elements usually hyphenated or written as one word, when preceded by words of two or more syllables: *grocery store, seventeen fold*; (14) two-word compounds containing an apostrophe: *science teacher's text*.

hypotenuse [hie-PAHT-eh-nuhs; Brit., hihp-].

hypoxia. Insufficiency of oxygen at high altitudes, resulting in excess water vapor in lungs.

I

-i. Plurals made by *-i* are usually pronounced *ee*, except for Latin and Greek words with singular ending in *-us* or *-os*, which are pronounced *ie: bacilli.* But the plurals of some Latin words have irregular endings: *hiatus, corpus, octopus, virus, callus.* When in doubt, use the *-uses* form for plural.

I. Nominative case: *I am. It is I.* BUT: *Between you and me.*

I-bar. I-beam, I-iron, I-nail.

IADB. (abbr.) Inter-American Defense Board, or I.A.D.B.

IAEA (abbr.) International Atomic Energy Agency, or I.A.E.A.

iamb [EI-am]. Poetic foot consisting of an unaccented and accented syllable (u-): *upset.* Pl. —s in U.S. Brit. iambus, Pl. —es or —bi. SEE Scansion.

IANF. (abbr.) Interallied nuclear force.

Iberia [ie-BEER-ih-ah]. Iberian peninsula containing Spain and Portugal; also ancient region now Georgia, U.S.S.R.

ibex [IE-behks]. Old World goat. Pl., ibexes, ibices or ibex.

ibidem. (abbr. ibid.) (Lat.) In the same place. Used in citations to avoid repetition of a source. *Cf.* footnotes.

ibis [IE-bihs]. Wading bird. Pl., ibises.

IBM. International Business Machine Corporation.

ibn-Saud, Abdul-Aziz [ihb'n-sah-OOD, uhb-dul a-ZEEZ]. (1880–1953) King of Saudi Arabia. 1932–53.

ICA. (abbr.) International Cooperation Administration. N.Y. Times, I.C.A.

Icarus [IK-uh-ruhs].

ICBM. (abbr.) intercontinental ballistic missile, range exceeding 5000 mi.

ICC. (abbr.) Interstate Commerce Commission. N.Y. Times, I.C.C. Also International Control Commission (in Laos, Canada, India, Poland).

ice age. SEE Ages. UCMS, Ice Age.

iced tea [EIS TEE].

Iceland. Native, Icelander(s); adj., Icelandic. Cap., Reykjavik. Currency, krona, kronur, (IKr); ore, aurar.

iconoclast [ie-KAHN-oh-klast]. Image (idol) smasher.

-ics, -ic. Most branches of study have -ics endings: *classics, dynamics, physics, tactics.* But a few take -ic endings: *logic, music, rhetoric.* Words ending in -ic and those which are used strictly for a branch of study take a singular verb: *Magic* (or *mathematics* or *metaphysics*) *is an interesting subject.* But in a general sense, a plural verb is required: *Her ethics are strong but her mathematics is weak.* This form is often indicated by a preceding pronoun.

IDA or I.D.A. (abbr.) International Development Association (of the World Bank).

Idaho. (no abbr.) BUT Webster abbr. Id. Native Idahoan. Capital, Boise.

idea [ei-DEE-uh].

idée fixe [EE-dae feeks]. One dominating idea.

idem. (abbr. id.) (Lat.) The same. In a citation, the same source.

identical (with). Preferred to identic.

ideology [ihd-ee-AHL-uh-jee, ie-dee-].

id est. (abbr. i.e.) That is. Always precede by a comma or a sem-colon.

idiom. In grammar, an accepted form of expression not necessarily in accord with other grammatical rules or with the ordinary meaning of the words used: *She made friends with them.*

idiot. SEE Mental Retardation.

idiosyncracy.

idleheaded.

Idlewild Airport. Officially, John F. Kennedy International Airport.

Idris I, Sayyid Mohammad Idris Al-Senussi [ih-DREES]. (1890–   ) King of Libya (1951–1969). Married Emira Fatima, his cousin, 1951.

idyl [IE-dihl]. Preferred to Brit. *ll*. Description of rustic life.

idyllic. Full of natural charm.

i.e. SEE id est.

-ie, -ei. Use *i* before *e* except after *c* or when sounded as *a*. BUT: *either, seize, seizure, neither, either, height, sleight, weird.*

IF. (abbr.) intermediate frequency.

if. Use to introduce a subjunctive clause of condition or supposition. Use *whether* where an alternat ve is indicated, expressed or understood. *Tell us whether you sent the package (or not). If* must be followed by a verb in the present or past tense. *If* may be omitted and understood. *Were I to go, he would object. Cf.* Subjunctive, was, were.

IFC. (abbr. I.F.C.) International Finance Corporation.

IFF. (abbr.) identification, friend or foe.

Ifni [EEF-nee]. Territory southwest of Morocco, administered by Spain.

ignitible or ignitable.

ignominy [IHG-noh-mih-nih]. Disgrace.

ignominious [ihg-noh-MIHN-ih-uhs].

ignoramus [ihg-noh-RAE-muhs]. Pl. -uses.

i. hp. (abbr.) indicated horsepower.

ikon. Use icon.

I.L.A. (abbr.) International Longshoreman's Association.

Ile-de-France, or **Isle-de-France** [eel-deh-FRAHNNS]. Region around Paris.

I.L.G.W.U. (abbr.) International Ladies' Garment Workers Union.

ill. Comparative, worse; superlative, worst.

ill-advised. (adj.) ill-born (adj.), ill-bred(adj.), ill-fated (adj.), ill-treat (v.), ill breeding (n.), ill fame, ill health, ill usage, ill will.

Illinois. (abbr. Ill.) Native, Illinoisan. Cap., Springfield.

illusive [ih-LYOO-sihv]. Illusory; unreal.

illustrate [IHL-uhs-traet, ih-LUHS-traet]. illustrative [IHL-uhs-trae-tihv].

ILO. (abbr.) International Labor Organization. N.Y. Times I.L.O.

Il Trovatore [eel-troh-vuh-TOH-reh]. Opera by Guiseppe Verdi.

imagery [IHM-ihj-rih].

imbed. Use embed.

imbibe. -bable.

imbroglio [ihm-BROH-lyoh]. Complicated confusion.

imbue with. Saturate, inspire:
INFUSE INTO. Pour into.
INSTILL INTO. Infuse gradually.
INCULCATE WITH. Impress by repetition.

IMCO. (abbr.) International Maritime Consultative Organization.

imitate. -table, -tator.

immanent. Intrinsic, indwelling: *God is immanent in nature.* immanence [IHM-uh-nehnss].
IMMINENT. Threatening to occur immediately: *Rain was imminent, so we sought shelter.*
EMINENT. Prominent, lofty.

immaterial. Not material, unimportant.

immediately. Avoid using for *as soon as*. NOT: *He will call you immediately he comes in.*

immersible. Capable of being plunged into liquid. *Cf.* emerge.

immiscible. Not capable of being mixed.

immobile [ihm-MOH-bihl].

immoral. SEE amoral.

immovable. Cannot be moved.
IRREMOVABLE. May not be removed.

impale. [ihm-PAEL]. Preferred to em-.

impanel. -led, -ling. Brit. *ll.*

impartible.

impassable. Cannot be passed (from passable): *The road was impassable.*
IMPASSIBLE. Incapable of feeling pain or emotion: *The torturer was impassible.*
IMPASSIVE. Not feeling or, especially, showing emotion: *His face was impassive.*

impasse [ihm-PAS, IHM-pas]. A blind alley; predicament from which escape is impossible; direction without a future.

impawn. (v.) Preferred to empledge.

impecunious [im-peh-KYOO-nee-uhs]. Without money. -ly, -ity.

impel. -lled, —llable.

impenitence. Pref. to -cy.

imperceptible.

imperil. NOT em-. -led, -lling. Brit. *ll.*

impermeable [ihm-PUHR-mee-uh-b'l].

impermissible.

imperscriptible. Unrecorded.

impersonate. -nable, -tor.

impersuasible.

imperturbable [im-puh-TUHRB-uh-b'l]. Incapable of being disturbed.

impetus. Pl. -tuses.

impinge. -ging. Encroach.

impious [IHM-pih-uhs]. Irreverent.

implausible.

implicate. -cable.

implicit. Implied. Opposite explicit.

imply. Suggest.
INFER. Conclude: *When she asked "Can you afford it?" She implied that he did not have enough money. He inferred that she was offering to pay the check.*

impolitic. -icly. Not good policy.

import. Meaning, significance.
PURPORT. Intention, purpose (less importance is implied).

important essentials is a tautology.

importune [ihm-pawr-TYOON]. Pester; urge.

importunate [ihm-PAWR-tchoo-niht]. Pressing in solicitation.

impossible.

imposter.

impotent [IHM-poh-tehnt].

impracticable. Not capable of being accomplished: infeasible.
IMPRACTICAL. Not adapted to actual conditions; theoretical.

impresario [ihm-prae-SAR-ih-oh]. (not -ss-) Pl., -os.

impress [IHM-prehs]. (n.). Mark, stamp.

impressible.

impromptu. Pl. -us.

impugn [ihm-PYOON]. Oppose as false with words. -er.

impugnation [ihm-puhg-NAE-shuhn]. Opposition. (v.) impugn, -able.

impuissant [ihm-PYOO-ihs-sahnt]. Weak; powerless.

in-. Prefix meaning in, into, on, within: *innate, incise, inside;* or not (un-): *incest, intangible, inept, inadmissible.* Usually employed for Latin words.

    UN-. A form of *not* usually employed for English words: *unmasked, untouched, unspeakable.*

    IL-. A form of in- meaning not: *illegitimate;* or in-: *illuminate.*

    IM-. A form of in- meaning not: *immaterial;* or in-: *imbue.*

    IR-. A form of in- meaning not: *irresponsible.*

inasmuch. inasmuch as, insofar, in-and-in (adj.), in-and-out (adj.), in-and-outer, in-being (adv. and adj.), in-flight (adj.), in-law (n.); in re, in rem, in situ, etc.

inability.

inacceptable. Un- is preferred.

inaccessible.

inadequate. Not equal to the need.

inadmissible.

inadvertence. Preferred to -cy.

inadvisable. Preferred to un- in U.S.

inalienable [ihn-AEL-yehn-uh-bl, Preferred to -AEL-ih- –]. Now preferred to un-, used in Declaration of Independence. Incapable of being surrendered.

inamorato. (m.) Lover. Pl. —tos. (f.) inamorata; pl., —as.

inane [ihn-AEN]. Empty; pointless.

inanimate.

inapprehensible.

inartistic. Without artistic taste.

    UNARTISTIC. Not a work of art.

inasmuch as. SEE because.

inaudible.

inaugurate [ihn-AW-gyoo-raet]. Install; initiate.

incarnadine [ihn-KAHR-nuh-dihn]. Flesh-colored; by extension, blood red.

incarnation. Embodiment of a spirit, ideal, character in human flesh: *The incarnation of murder.* NOT: *The incarnation of a murderer.*

incase. Brit. en-.

incessant.

inch. (abbr., in.) Unit of length = 1,000 mils = 2.54 centimeters = $\frac{1}{12}$ foot = $\frac{1}{36}$ yard.

inch worm. inch-deep (adj.), inch-long (adj.), inch-pound, inch-ton.

inchoate [ihn-KOH-iht; Brit., IN-koh-aet]. (adj.) Just begun; incomplete, elementary. NOT related to chaos.

Inchon [in-CHAHN]. Seaport in South Korea.

in. -lb. (abbr.) inch-pound.

Inc. (abbr.) incorporated.

incident. -al. Incident implies a closer and more certain relationship than incidental: *Old age and its incident illnesses. . . . The incidental expenses of old age.*

incidentally. Preferred to incidently.

inclose. Use *en-* except for legal purposes.

include. Refers to a part of the content.

    COMPOSE, COMPRISE. Refers to the whole content.

includible.

incombustible.

incommensurable. Having no common measure. Of a ratio not expressed in whole numbers. 7.42 : 11.6

incommiscible. Cannot be mixed.

incommunicative. Refusing or not inclined to talk; reserved. Also uncommunicative.

incomparable [ihn-KAHM-puh-ruh-bl]. Peerless.

incompatible. Not harmonious.

incompetence. In legal use, often -cy.

incomplete. But uncompleted.

incomprehensible.

inconceivable.

inconcussible. Cannot be shaken.

inconsolable. Preferred to un-.

incontrollable. *Un-* is preferred.

incontrovertible.

inconvincible.

incorporate. -rable.

incorrigible.

incorrodible.

incorruptible.

incredible. Beyond belief. SEE strong opinion words.

> INCREDULOUS. Skeptical: *The reporter was incredulous: he would not believe the incredible story.*

incredulity [ihn-crehd-DYOOL-ih-tih].

incriminate [ihn-KRIHM-uh-naet].

incrust. -station. Brit. encrust, incrustation.

incubus. Pl. -bi or buses. Evil spirit which lies upon a sleeper; nightmare; a burden. SEE obsession.

inculcate [ihn-KUHL-kaet; Brit., IN-]. Teach by repetition.

> IMPRESS. Leave an impression on the mind.

incunabula [ihn-kyoo-NAHB-yoo-luh]. Infancy, beginnings; also, books printed before 1500 A.D.

incur. -rred, -rring.

Ind. (abbr.) Indiana, India, Indo-.

IND. (abbr.) Independent Subway System, N.Y.C.

ind. (abbr.) Independent.

indecorous [ihn-DEHK-oh-ruhs; Brit., ihn-deh-KOHR-uhs].

indefatigable [ihn-dee-FAT-ih-guh-b'l].

indefensible.

INDEFINITE PRONOUNS. Pronouns which do not specify a person: *anyone, each, either, everyone, none, someone.* When used to modify a noun they are indefinite adjectives. All except *neither* and *none* take a singular verb when followed by *of* plus a plural noun. A plural verb is also acceptable, but a plural pronoun then must follow: *Each of the women were in favor, and they so voted.*

indelible. *Cf.* delible.

indenture. Deed between two or more persons in which each assumes specific obiligations.

independence. *In the year of our independence the one hundred and seventy-sixth.*

indeprehensible. Cannot be found out.

indescribable.

indestructible.

index. Pl., indexes. Scientific, indices.

index-digest.

India. Native, Indian(s); adj., Indian. Cap., New Delhi. Currency, rupee (Rs), anna. SEE Hindu.

India ink. india paper, india rubber.

Indian. In U.S.; Brit. use American Indian.

Indians. Shawnee Indians; Eastern (or Lower) Band of Cherokee, the band; Five Civilized Tribes, the tribes; Shawnee Tribe, the tribe; Six Nations (Iroquois Confederacy).

Indian summer. Period of mild weather in October or November. In Britain, also St. Luke's summer (Oct.), St. Martin's summer (November).

Indiana. (abbr. Ind.). Native, Indianian. Nickname: Hoosier. Cap., Indianapolis.

indicate. When followed by an explanatory clause, use *that: He indicated that he would go.*

indict [ihn-DIET]. (v.) -able, -ment. Accuse: *After the grand jury indicted him for larceny, he engaged an attorney.*

> CONVICT. (v.) Find guilty of an accusation.

> INDITE. (v.) Compose or put into writing: *He was told to indite the resolution.*

indifferent to. Not interested in.

indigestible.

indigo. Pl., -os. indigo-blue (adj.), indigo-carmine (adj.).

indirect object. Verbs like *give, pay, send,* and *write* take an indirect object not essential to the meaning of the verb but indicating the person or thing affected by the verb. *Pay* her *the money. Read* him *the letter.*

indirect question. In grammar a question placed in another form: *Tell me where he went. I asked where he went.*

indiscernible [IHN-dih-ZUHR-nih-bl]. Imperceptible.

indiscreet. Lacking discretion.
INDISCRETE. Not divided into distinct parts. *Cf.* discrete.

indiscriminate. Not discriminating (in choices). *Cf.* undiscriminating.

indispensable.

indisposed. Unfit.
UNDISPOSED. Not disposed of.

indisputable [ihn-DIHS-pyoo-tuh-bl].

indissoluble. Not capable of being dissolved, annulled, or disintegrated. indissolubly. *Cf.* soluble.

indistinguishable.

indivertible.

individual. Use only for contrast with a group: *The only individual who opposed the measure was....* NOT: *Any individual* (person) *can win. Cf.* special.

indivisible.

Indochina. Former French Indochina is now the independent Cambodia, Laos, North Vietnam, and South Vietnam.

indocible. Not teachable. Opposite. docible.

Indonesia. Native, Indonesian(s); adj., Indonesian. Cap., Djakarta [juh-KAHRT-uh]. Currency, rupiah (sing. and pl.) (Rp.); cent.

indubitable [ihn-DYOO-bih-tuh-b'l]. -bly. Too evident to doubt.

induce. -cible.

induction. Drawing a generalization from known cases.
DEDUCTION. Drawing a conclusion from a general principle.

indue. (Brit. en-) Endow; invest with a quality.

indurate [IHN-dyoo-riht]. Hardened.

industrywide.

ineffaceable. Preferred to un-.

ineffective. —fectual, —ficacious. *Cf.* effective.

ineffervescible. effervesce, effervescence, effervescent.

ineligible.

ineludible.

inept. Not fit; inappropriate; absurd.
UNAPT. Not likely.
INAPT. Unskilled; not suitable.

inequity. Unfairness.
INIQUITY. Sin.

inescapable. Use un—.

inessential. Use un—.

inestimable. NOT un—, except in British use.

inevasible.

inexhaustible.

inexpansible

inexplicable [ihn-EHKS-plih-kuh-b'l].

inexpressible.

inexpressive. Un—is preferred.

infallible.

infamous [IHN-fuh-muhs]. Notoriously evil.

infant. In general usage, under 1 year; in common law, under 21; in some areas.

BABY. Generally under 6.

CHILD. Generally under 12; in law, any legitimate offspring.

infanta [een-FAHN-tah]. Daughter or daughter-in-law of king of Spain or Portugal.

infantile. SEE childish.

infeasible.

infer. Deduce. —rred, —erable, —erence. *Cf.* imply.

inferrible. Used in logic.

inferno. Pl. -os.

infidel. An unbeliever, especially by Christians of Mohammedans; by Mohammedans of Christians and Jews. In modern usage, one who believes in no God. *Cf.* gentile.

HEATHEN. Especially one ignorant of Christianity. Suggests adherence to idolatry.

PAGAN. Especially one who ignores Biblical ethics. Now one who is not Christian, Mohammedan, nor Jew.

infinite (ly).

infinitive. Form of a verbal noun which performs a verbal function, takes an object and verb modifiers. It has two tense forms, present and perfect, and has no subject when standing alone as an infinitive. *To see, To have seen.* Cap. *To* when used in an infinitive form. *Cf.* split infinitive.

inflection. Brit., -exion. Grammatical changes in the form of a word to make it conform in person, number, tense.

inflexible.

inflict. *He inflicted himself upon them...*

AFFLICT. *He afflicted them with his constant company. They were afflicted with a contagious disease.*

infold. Brit. en—. Envelope, embrace.

inform. —er, —ant. An informer gives information against another; an informant merely provides information. *Cf.* advise.

infrangible. Not capable of being separated into parts.

infrared. Wave lengths longer than visible light but shorter than radio waves.

infringe. -able, -ging. Damage, weaken, violate. AVOID *infringe on, upon. Cf.* frangible.

IMPINGE. impingement, impinger. Strike sharply, encroach: *impinge upon, on.*

-ing. Both the gerund (noun form of a verb) and the participle are usually formed by adding —*ing: Racing* (gerund) *was his hobby. The racing* (participle) *group* ... AVOID using a modifying pronoun unless necessary: *He was certain of being elected* (NOT: *of his being elected*).

ingenious [ihn-JEEN-yuhs]. Resourceful, showing ingenuity: *an ingenious invention.*

INGENUE [ahn-zhae-NYOO]. A naive girl, or the actress playing such a part. Pl. ues.

INGENUOUS [ihn-JEHN-yoo-uhs]. Artless, free from dissimulation: *an ingenuous young lady.*

ingrained.

ingratiate [ihn-GRAE-shih-aet]. Bring oneself into the favor of another. Always used in the reflexive with *with: I tried to ingratiate myself with my superiors.*

inherent [ihn-HEER-'nt]. Firmly fixed by nature. (v.) inhere; inherence, —cy, pl. —cies (especially for an inherent attribute).

inherit. —tor, (f.) —tress or trix.

inhibition [ihn-hih-BIHSH-'n].

inimitable.

initiate. —iable, —iator.

initiative. (n.) The first step, or the ability to take it: *He took the initiative in denouncing the program.*

injustice.

in lieu of. *In place of* or *instead of* are pref.

inmesh. Use enmesh.

innavigable. Use un—.

innocuous [ih-NAHK-yoo-uhs]. Harmless. —ly, —ness.

innuendo. Pl. -oes.

Innsbruck [IHNZ-bruhk]. Resort city in Tirol, Austria.

—ino. Combining form, from Spanish, used to form noun of adjective: *albino, bambino.*

inoculate.

in order that. Follow with *may* or *might, shall* or *should: In order that he might be able to rest comfortably. . .*

inquietude. Uneasiness.

inquire. -ry. Preferred to en-.

inquiry [ihn-KWIER-ee, IHN-kwih-rih].

Inquisition, Spanish. the Inquisition.

in re. (Lat.) In the matter of; concerning.

in rem. (Lat.) A thing. In law, an action *in rem* is against a property rather than against a person.

insanitary. SEE unsanitary.

insatiable [ihn-SAE-shih-uh-b'l, -shuh-b'l]. Incapable of being satisfied.

insidious. Full of plots; intended to entrap; sly.
  INVIDIOUS. Tending to create envy, ill will.

inscriptible. Capable of being inscribed.

insect-borne. (adj.).

insensible.

insigne. Pl., insignia.

insofar as.

insoluble. (1) Cannot be dissolved or (2) cannot be solved.
  INSOLVABLE, UNSOLVABLE. Preferred for (2).

insomuch. (adv.) AVOID.

insouciance [ihn-SOO-see-anss]. Indifference.

Insp. Gen. (abbr.) Inspector General.

inspector general. Pl., inspectors general.

inspire. *inspire ambition in; inspire a person with ambition.*

install. —ed, —ing, —ment. installation. Brit. pref. instalment.

installment plan. British, hire purchase plan.

instill. —lled, —lling. *Into* should follow; *He inspires hope. He instills hope into every man.* Cf. *imbue.*

Institute. Capitalize if part of name; capitalize standing alone if referring to government or international organization: National Cancer Institute, the Cancer Institute, the Institute: National Institute of Health; the Institute of International Law, the Institute; Woman's Institute, the institute.

Institution. Capitalize if part of name; capitalize standing alone if referring to federal unit: Carnegie Institution, the institution; Smithsonian Institution, the Institution.

instructible.

instructor.

Instructor in a College or University. ADDRESS: Robert B. Cadugan, Ph.D., Department of Physics, Rutgers University, New Brunswick, N.J., or Dr. Robert B. Cadugan, Department of Physics, Rutgers University; or (if the instructor does not hold a doctor's degree) Mr. Robert B. Cadugan, Department of Physics, Rutgers University. SALUTATION: Dear Sir, Dear Dr. Cadugan, Dear Mr. Cadugen.

instrumentman.

insubmergible.

insubstantial. Un- is preferred.

insufficient. (adj.) Should qualify a quality, quantity, or amount. NOT: *There were insufficient people present. There were an insufficient number of people.*

insular [IHN-suh-luhr]. Of or like an island: insular government.

insulin [IHN-suh-lihn].

insupportable. Preferred to un-.

insuppressible.

insure. Against a loss.
  ENSURE. Make certain.
  ASSURE. Convince; give confidence to.

insusceptible. NOT un—.

intactable. —ible. Not perceptible to touch.

integer. A whole number. 3, 66, 421.

    INTEGRAL [IHN-teh-gruhl]. Of an integer; also, whole, complete; essential.

integrate. -grable, -tor, -tion.

integrity [ihn-TEHG-rih-tee]. Quality of being complete; soundness; honesty.

intelligent. Having a high mental capacity.

    INTELLECTUAL [ihn-t'l-EHK-choo-uhl]. Relating to a high degree of knowledge and understanding.

intelligentsia [ihn-tehl-uh-JEHNT-see-uh, —tziha (Ital.)]. The intellectual class. In U.S.S.R., —siya, [ihn-tehl-ih-GENT-tsih-uh]. The professional and highly educated classes.

intelligible. Capable of being understood.

intense. In an extreme degree: *Intense sunlight.*

intensive. Concentrated effort for a limited objective: *Intensive farming utilizes large quantities of fertilizer on a small area.*

intensives. Adverb and auxiliary verb used to emphasize a verb: *do, too, very, terribly. I do know him.*

intensive pronouns. *himself, herself, myself, yourself, itself,* are used to emphasize another noun or pronoun: *I, myself, will call the teacher. Cf.* reflexive pronouns.

intention of doing. – to do.

intentionally. *Cf.* advisedly

inter alia. (Lat.) Among others (things).

    INTER ALIOS. Among others (persons).

intercalary [ihn-TUHR-kal-luh-ih]. Interpolated into the calendar, as February 29.

interceptor.

intercoastal waterway. SEE waterway.

interdepartmental.

interest [IHN-tuhr-ehst].

interjection. In grammar, an ejaculatory word. *O, Oh, lo, say, ah.* Set off with commas or follow with an exclamation point.

Interlaken [IN-tuh-LAH-kehn]. Resort town on Aare River, Switzerland.

interment. Burial.

    INTERNMENT. Detention.

intermit. —tted, —tting, —ssible, —ttent. Stop for a time.

intern. British, interne. Graduate medical student in a hospital; also, detained alien.

internal revenue. British, inland revenue.

international banks. (SEE Bank); international date line, international law, international Morse code (SEE code).

International Court of Justice. SEE court.

International Geophysical Year. SEE year.

International Ladies' Garment Workers' Union.

International Postal Convention. SEE convention.

internecine [ihn-tehr-NEE-sihn, -sien]. Mutually destructive; deadly. NOT intramural, intertribal, internal.

interpellate, -ation, [ihn-tuhr-PEHL-aet, ihn-TUHR-peh-laet]. Interrupt to ask a formal question, as to a minister in parliamentary procedure.

interpolate [ihn-TUHR-pohl-aet]. Change a text by adding new material; insert between other things. -ation.

interpretative. Preferred to interpretive by Fowler, but not in common usage.

interprovincial.

interruptible.

interstate. Between states.

    INTRASTATE. Within a state.

Interstate Commerce Commission. (abbr. ICC or I.C.C.); the Commission.

interstice [ihn-TUHR-stihs]. Pl. —ces. [stih-seez]. Space between close things; a crevice.

intervener. In law, intervenor.

intervisible.

intervivos trust. SEE trust.

intestate [ihn-TEHS-taet]. Without a will: *He died intestate.*

in the amount of. *For* is preferred.

in the course of. Use *during* or *when.*

in the event that. *If* is preferred.

intimacy. See acquaintanceship.

intimidate. —dable, —dation, —dator.

in to. Indicates joining; *She came in to the club, group, family, play. The suspect turned himself in to the police.*
 INTO. Indicate motion, coming from outside. *She came into the room, theater, house.*

in toto. Entirely. NOT *on the whole.* Usually used in a negative sense; *She rejected the plan in toto.*

Intracoastal Waterway. the waterway. *Cf.* waterway.

intractable. Not easily governed.

intransigent. (n. and adj.) Refusing compromise. *Cf.* recalcitrant.

intrastate. SEE interstate.

intrench. En—is preferred.

intrigue [ihn-TREEG]. Cheat; entangle; puzzle; plot.

introduction. SEE preface.

intrude. Thrust in, or force in or upon.
 OBTRUDE. Thrust out; expel.

intrust. En— is preferred.

intwine. En— is preferred.

intwist. En— is preferred.

inure [ihn-YOOR]. Preferred to enure.

invaluable. Priceless; of value beyond counting. AVOID use for *valuable.*
 UNVALUABLE. Of no value.

UNVALUED. Not greatly wanted or not appraised; by ext., disregarded.

inveigh (against.) (v.) Dispute (with words); rail bitterly.
 INVECTIVE. (n.) The result of vigorous inveighing; violent denunciation.

inveigle [ihn-VEE-gl or in-VAE-gl]. (v.) Lead astray by deceit.

inventible.

inversion. In grammar, changing the usual order of subject and predicate object: *Never the twain shall meet. How wonderful is nature.*

invertible.

invincible.

invisible.

invited guest. Redundant except in contrast to paying guest.

invoice. Original bill giving quantity, prices, and charge for a shipment.

inward. *Cf.* backward.

inwrap. En— is preferred.

ion [EI-uhn]. Electrically charged atom. *Cf.* electrolysis.

Ione [ie-OHN, ie-OH-nee].

Ionic [ie-AHN-ihk]. In architecture, pertains to an order of architecture distinguished especially by the spiral volutes of its capital.

ion propulsion. Use of recoil from ejection of high-velocity charged particles as a propellant, especially in space.

IOU. (spaces, no periods) (abbr.) I owe you. N.Y. Times, i.o.u.

Iowa. (abbr. Ia.) Native, Iowan. Cap., Des Moines.

ipse dixit. (Lat.) So he says. An individual's unsupported testimony.

I.Q. (abbr.) intelligent quotient. A measure of aptitude (usually verbal and numerical) based on a comparison with normal mental age (= 100), but always quoted plus or minus 10. A boy of 120 months with a mental age (M.A.) of 144 months has an I.Q. of 120. plus or minus 10.

Iran [ie-RAN]. Formerly Persia. Native, Iranian(s); adj., Iranian. Cap., Teheran (Tehran). Currency, rial, dinars.

Iraq [ie-RAK]. Natives, Iraqui(s). Capital, Baghdad. Currency, Iraqui dinar (ID), fil(s), riyals.

irascible [ei-RAS-ihbl, ih-]. Prone to anger.

IRBM. (abbr.) intermediate range ballistic missile.

IRE. (abbr.) Institute of Radio Engineers.

Ireland. Native, Irishman (men); adj., Irish; collective, plural, Irish. Cap., Dublin. Currency, pound (£), shilling, penny, pl. pence. *Cf.* Eire.

Irgun Zvai Leumi [IHR-goon TSVIE lee-OO'M-ee]. Israeli radical underground under British rule.

iridescent. From iris, (Lat.) rainbow. Having a rainbowlike play of colors.

Irishwoman. Irish-American, Irish-born (adj.); Irish potato.

Irkutsk [ihr-KOOTSK]. City in Southern Asia on Angara River, Siberia, U.S.S.R.

irnoratio elenchi. (Lat.) Fallacy of the irrelevant conclusion.

IRO. (abbr.) International Refugee Organization. N.Y. Times, I.R.O.

iron [IE-urn].

Iron Curtain. the curtain.

ironer-up.

Iron Guard. Rumanian fascist organization, especially pre-W.W. II.

Iroquois [IHR-uh-kwoi]. Originally Five Nations of Indians, comprising Mohawk, Oneida, Onondaga, Cayuga, and Seneca (1722). Later expanded.

irreconcilable [ihr-EHK-ahn-SIEL-un-b'l].

irredeemable.

irreducible.

irrefragable [ihr-REHF-ruh-guh-b'l]. Indisputable.

irrefrangible [ihr-ree-FRAN-gih-b'l]. Cannot be refracted.

irrefutable [ihr-REHF-yoo-tuh-b'l, ihr-ree-FYOOT-uh-b'l]. Cannot be proven false.

irregardless. Incorrect. Do not use. *Regardless* is correct.

IRREGULAR VERBS. There are 227 irregular verbs in English, most of them noted in this text. Regular verbs form the past tense and past participle by adding *-ed*, the present participle by adding *-ing*.

irrelevance. (n.) Preferred to -cy.

irremediable [ihr-ruh-MEED-ee-uh-b'l]. Incurable.

irremissible. Unpardonable, inescapable.

irreparable [ihr-REHP-uhr-a-b'l].

irreprehensible. Free from blame.

irrepressible.

irresistible.

irrespective of. Without regard to.

irrespective. Having no regard for persons or things (rare).

irresponsible.

irresponsive. Un- is preferred.

irreversible.

irrigation district. SEE District; irrigation. project no. 1.

irruption. SEE eruption.

IRS or I.R.S. (abbr.) Internal Revenue Service.

IRT. (abbr.) Interborough Rapid Transit, New York City.

is, are. *Two times three is (or are) six. What is wanted are two horses. (Two horses is the subject.) One and one are two. His goods, his money, and his reputation are at stake.* SEE Number.

is. (abbr.) island.

Isbrandtsen Company, Inc.. Isbrandtsen freighter.

-ise, ize. SEE -ize.

-ism. Suffix meaning a disposition to be; an act, state, process or doctrine. *realism. spiritualism.*

-ITY. Suffix meaning the quality of being: *reality, spirituality.*

Ishmael [IHSH-mae-uhl]. Son of Abraham and Hagar; a social outcast.

Islam. SEE Mohammedan.

Isle of Man. Island northwest of England. Native, Manxman (men), Manx (collective); adj., Manx.

Ismailia [ihz-mae-ih-LEE-ah]. Half-way station on Suez Canal, Egypt.

Ismalian Mohammedans. SEE Aga Khan.

is of the opinion that. *Believes* is preferred.

isolate [EI-soh-laet; in U.S., also IHS-oh-laet].

isosceles [ie-SAHS-eh-leez]. Of a triangle, having two equal sides.

isotope. Form of an element distinguished by atomic weight and different radioactive transformations.

ISOTROPE. (adj.) Having the same properties in all directions.

ISOTYPE. In statistics, graphic presentation in which a figure represents a unit quantity, other quantities being represented by additional figures or fractions of figures.

Israel [IHZ-rae-ehl, IHZ-rih-ehl]. Medinat Israel. Native, Israeli(s); (adj.) Israel. Established May 14, 1948. Cap. (de facto), Jerusalem. Currency, pound (£), prutah, prutot. Native born Jewish Israeli, Sabra. *Cf.* Jew. Also ancient kingdom before and after division, 979-719 B.C.

issued. issuing, issueless.

Istanbul [ihs-tam-BOOL]. City on Bosporus and Sea of Marmara, Turkey. Formerly Constantinople, Byzantium.

isthmus. Pl. -uses [IHS- or IHSTH-muhs].

it. (pronoun) Used to refer to things without gender and as an indefinite pronoun.

it . . . it. Avoid use of both expletive and personal pronoun in the same sentence. NOT: *It is their idea that it should be done.*

ITALICS. The form of a type face approximating handwriting, used in printing for differentiation of material, emphasis, foreign words, formulas, scientific names, vessels, the title of a book (if not in quotation marks), publication, or law case, the name of a fictitious character. Also the words *Resolved, Resolved further, Provided, ordered,* etc., and letters used as symbols, except chemical elements.

Italy. Native, Italian(s); (adj.) Italian. Cap., Rome. Currency, lira, pl. lire (Lit); centisimo, pl. centesimi (Ctmo.).

I-T-E Circuit Breaker. From inverse time element.

itinerary [ei-TIHN-uhr-ehr-ee]. Outline of a route. —ant, —ancy, —ate.

its. Possessive of it.

it's. it is, preferred in formal writing.

itself. SEE intensives, reflexive pronouns.

ITU. (abbr.) International Telecommunication Union; International Typographical Union. Sometimes I.T.U.

Iturbi, José [ee-TUHR-bee, hoh-ZAE: Span., ee-TOOR-vee]. (1895-1969) Spanish-American pianist-conductor.

Ivory Coast. French, Cote d'Ivoire. Natives, Ivoriens. Formerly French possession; situated on the Atlantic Ocean. Independent since August, 1960. Cap., Abidjan. Currency, CFA franc.

Ivy League. Sports association of Harvard, Princeton, Yale, Dartmouth, Columbia, Cornell, Brown, and University of Pennsylvania.

Iwo Jima [EE-woh- JEE-mah]. Island 660 nautical miles south of Tokyo. Scene of U.S. landing in W.W. II, February-March, 1945.

-ize. American practice where British 1 is followed by yze if the word expresses an idea of separating (analyze). Other words, except those ending in mise, end ize. *circumcise, chemise, surmise.*

J

j (abbr.) joule.

J-. U.S.S.R. prefix for short-range missiles. J-1, surface-to-surface radio controlled missile with 370-mi. range; J-2, anti-submarine missile with 525-mi. range; J-3, anti-sub missile with 450-mi. range.

J-bolt.

jabot [zhah-BOH].

jackanapes [JAK-uh-naeps].

jack-in-the-box. jack-of-all-trades, jack-o'-lantern, jack-plane (v.); jack towel.

jack-in-the-pulpit. Pl. -pulpits.

Jacobean [jak-uh-BEE-uhn]. Of James I of England.

Jacques [zhahk]. In *As You Like It*, [JAE-kweez].

jaguar [JAG-wahr].

jai alai [HIE (ah)-LIE]. Court game resembling squash played by two teams of two.

jail. -er. Brit., gaol.

Jakarta [juh-KAHR-tah]. Also Djakarta, Djokjakarta, Jogjakarta, Jogjakarta [johk-yah-KAHR-tah]. Capital city of Indonesia on Java Island, formerly Batavia.

jalopy.

jamb. (v.) Preferred to jambe. Upright piece forming the side of a door, etc.

Jamaica. Island in West Indies. Former British colony. Territory in West Indies Federation, 1958–61. Independent, 1961. Native, (adj.) Jamaican.

James. St. James's, Court of St. James's; St. James's Palace; King James Version of the Bible.

Jan. (abbr.) January.

Japan. Native, Japanese (sing. and pl.); (adj.) Japanese. Cap., Tokyo [TOHK-yoh]. Currency, yen (sing. and pl.) (y), sen (sing. and pl.). *Cf.* Nippon. AVOID Jap as derogatory.

jardiniere [jahr-dihn-NEER]. Ornamental flower stand.

Jaroszewicz, Piotr [yah-roh-SHAE-vitch]. (1909–   ) Chairman of the Council of Ministers, Poland (1970–   ).

Jarring, Gunnar Valfid [YAH-rihng]. (1907–   ) Swedish diplomat, conciliator.

jasmine [JAZ-mihn].

jato. (abbr.) jet-assisted takeoff.

jaywalker.

jealous of. about.

Jeanne d' Arc [zhahn DAHRK]. (1412–1431) French saint and heroine. Joan of Arc, the Maid of Orleans.

Jehovah [jeh-HOH-vuh].

Jehovah's Witnesses.

jejune [jee-JOON]. Meagre, uninteresting.

jellybean.

jeopardy. —dize.

jerry-built. Constructed only for temporary use.

Jersey cattle.

Jerusalem. Native, Hierosolymitan.

jestbook.

Jesuit [JEHZ-yoo-iht].

jetsam. SEE flotsam.

157

Jetty. Barnegat Jetty, etc.; the jetty; jetty no. 1.

Jew. Jewess. -ish. Descendant of the tribe of Judah, or one whose religion is Judaism. Hebrew, Hebraic is usually used of the ancient people and their language. *Cf.* Hebrew.

    ISRAELI. Citizen of Israel; Sabra, native-born Israeli; Israelite, inhabitant of ancient Israel. Semite, one of the Semitic races. *Cf.* Israel.

jewel [JOO-ehl, JYOO-ehl]. -led, -ling, -ler, -ry. Brit. -ll.

jew's-harp.

jg. (abbr.) junior grade.

jibe. Preferred to *gibe* in U.S. (jieb). Agree; nautical, shift.

Jim Crow. Pertains to discrimination against Negroes, from a stereotype of a Negro in an 1860 play by Thomas D. Rice. *Jim Crow law, car, etc.*

Jiminez, Perez, Col. Marcos [HEE-mehn-ehz]. (1914–   ) President of Venezuela, 1953–58.

jingles. In writing, unintentional repetition of similar sounds; *His dizziness contributed to a business failure.*

jingoist. Chauvinist, blatant patriot.

jinn. Pl. of jinni, -ee. SEE genie.

job lot. Mixed assortment of merchandise, usually offered at a price concession.

jiujitsu. SEE ju-jitsu.

Joffre, Joseph Jacques Cesaire [zhawfr, zhoh-ZEF zhahk sae-ZAER]. (1852–1931) French W.W. I marshall.

John XXIII, Angelo Giuseppe Roncalli. (1881–1963) 263rd Pope, 1958–1963.

Johns Hopkins University [jahnz HAHP-kihns]. In Baltimore.

joiner. British for carpenter.

joint account. (abbr. J/A) Account in the name of more than one person, any of whom may claim benefit.

Joint Chiefs of Staff. Chiefs of Staff, the Joint Chiefs.

Joint Committee on Atomic Energy. SEE Committee.

jokebook.

Joliet [JOH-lih-eht]. City and state prison in Illinois.

Jolliet or Joliet, Louis [zhoh-LYEH; angl., jahl-ih-EHT or joh-lih-ET]. (1645–1700) French-Canadian explorer.

Jolo. SEE Sulu.

Jordan. Native, Jordan(s), Jordanian(s); (adj.) Jordan or Jordanian. Cap., Amman. Currency, dinar (JD), fil.

José [hoh-ZAE].

joule. (abbr. J-) (joul). Energy unit in the MKS system=the energy needed to exert a force of 1 newton over a distance of 1 meter=approx. ¾ ft. lb.=10^7 ergs.

Journal. (House or Senate) Journal clerk, the clerk.

journalese. Typical of bad, hastily formulated newspaper writing.

journey. Pl. -eys. Prolonged travel. *Cf.* voyage.

journeyman. -work.

Jr. (abbr.) junior. James Smith, Jr. is distinguished from his father James Smith, Sr. Do not use without a first name or initial. A young lady may be referred to as the younger Helen Smith, but no feminine equivalent to Jr. exists.

Juanita [wah-NEE-tah].

Juarez, Benito Pablo [HRAH-raes, bae-NEE-toh PAH-vloh]. (1806–72) President of Mexico, 1857–1872.

jubilate [JOO-bih-laet]. Rejoice.

Judaism [JOO-dae-ihz-m]. SEE Jew, Hebrew.

Judea, Judaea [joo-DEE-uh]. Ancient region of South Israel under Persian, Greek, and Roman rule. Judaean. 979 B.C.–70 A.D.

Judge. Title of a member of the judiciary.

    JUSTICE. Used in place of Judge for Justice of the United States (Supreme Court); in New York State, for Justice of the Supreme Court, Justice of the Appellate

Division, Justice of the Peace, and Police Justice.

The distinction is based on an ancient concept of the difference between courts of law and courts of equity.

judge advocate. Pl. advocates.

Judge Adv. Gen. (abbr.) Judge Advocate General.

judge advocate general. Pl. - - generals.

Judge of a Federal District Court. ADDRESS; The Honorable John Clark Knox, United States District Judge, Southern District of New York. SALUTATION; Sir, Dear Sir, Dear Judge Knox.

judgment. Preferred to Brit., judgement.

judicial. Of a judge or court.

judicious. Exhibiting good judgment.

judiciary [joo-DIHSH-ih-ehr-ih]. The body of Judges.

ju-jitsu [joo-JIHT-soo; Jap., JOO-jiht-soo]. Japanese art of self-defense.

jukebox.

Juliana, Louise Emma Marie Wilhelmina [yoo-lee-AHN-ah]. (1909–   ) Queen of the Netherlands, 1948–   . In 1948 married Prince Bernhard Leopold Frederik Everhard Julius Coert Karel Godfried Pieter of Lippe-Biesterfeld. (1911–   ).

July. Do not abbreviate.

jumbo. Pl. -os.

June. Do not abbreviate.

junior. (abbr. jr.; Brit. jun.). SEE freshman.

junk mail. Unsolicited 3rd class mail, especially

when addressed without specific names; e.g., to *Occupant*.

Junker [YOON-kuhr]. A young German of the old aristocracy.

Juno. Pl. -os.

junto [JUHN-to]. Pl. -os. Group combined especially for political purpose.

JUNTA [HUHN-tuh]. Council or committee, especially for administration or legislation.

Jupiter. (adj.) Jovian or Jupiterian.

juror. Member of a jury. -man, -woman.

jury-fixing. (adj.) jury-rigged (adj.); jury box, jury fixer.

just. Avoid repetition in a sentence. AVOID; *just exactly. Cf.* exactly.

just as. Precisely as, in the same way as; NOT *just the same as: He was graduated just as his classmates were.*

Justice. (Associate) of the United States (the Supreme Court). ADDRESS; The Honorable William O. Douglas, Associate Justice of the Supreme Court, Washington, D.C.; or, Mr. William O. Douglas, United States Supreme Court, Washington, D.C. SALUTATION; Sir, Mr. Justice, My dear Mr. Justice, Your Honor, My dear Justice Douglas, Dear Justice Douglas.

Justice. (Chief) of the United States (NOT of the Supreme Court). ADDRESS; The Chief Justice, The Supreme Court, Washington, D.C.; or, The Honorable Earl Warren, United States Supreme Court, Washington, D.C. SALUTATION; Sir, Mr. Chief Justice, My dear Mr. Chief Justice, Dear Mr. Chief Justice.

juvenile [JYOO-vehn-ihl; Brit., JYOO-vehn-iel].

juxta-. Combining form meaning situated near; *juxta-ampullar, juxta-articular, juxtaposition.*

K

K. (abbr.) Kelvin. *Cf.* Temperature.

k. (abbr.) kilo = one thousand; knot.

K-ration. K-term.

Kadar, Janos [kuh-DAHR, YAHN-aws]. (1912–) First Secretary, Hungarian Communist Party 1956–57; Prime Minister, 1956–58.

Kahane, Melanie [kuh-HAEN]. (1910–)

kaleidoscope [kuh-LIE-doh-skohp]. Instrument of loose colored glass and mirrors which creates variety of patterns; by extension, a changing scene.

Kalif. Use Caliph.

Kalinin, Mikhail [kah-LEE-neen, mee-KIEL]. (1875–1946) Soviet Russian statesman. City, Kalinin, in West Central U.S.S.R. on Volga River; formerly Tver.

Kemal Ataturk, Mustafa [ke-MAHL ah-tah-TUERK]. (1881–1938) President of Turkey (1923–1938).

kamikaze [kahm-ih-KAH-zee]. Japanese suicide planes used in W.W. II.

kangaroo court. An unauthorized court, usually created to circumvent normal justice.

Kansas. (abbr. Kans.; N.Y. Times Kan.) Native and adj. Kansan. Cap., Topeka.

Kansas City, Mo. also Kans. Pl. Kansas Citys.

Kant, Immanuel [kahnt, ih-MAH-noo-el; angl., kant, ih-MAN-yeu-ehl]. (1724–1804) German philosopher. Kantian, -ianism.

kapok [KAE-pahk].

karat. SEE carat.

Karelia [kah-REE-lih-ah or -REEL-yah].

Region in northwest Russia between Gulf of Finland and White Sea. Karelo-Finnish Soviet Socialist Republic.

Kasavubu, Joseph [kah-sah-VOO-boo]. (1910–1969) President of Congo (Leopoldville), 1960–1961.

Katyn Forest [KA-tihn]. Scene in U.S.S.R. of massacre of Polish soldiers, 1939.

Kazakh [kah-ZAHK]. Kazakhstan or Kazakstan. Russian Republic in Central Asia, bordering on China.

Kazan, Elia [kah-ZAHN, EEL-ee-ah]. (1909–) Greek-American theatrical director.

kc. (abbr.) kilocycle.

K.C.B. (abbr.) Knight Commander of the Bath.

keen. keenness, keenly, keener.

keep. P. and p.p., kept; keepsake, keepworthy.

keg, nail. Unit of weight = 100 lbs. = 45.359 kg.

Kekkonen, D. Urho, Kaleva [KEHK-oh-nehn, AWR-hah KAH-lae-vah]. (1900–) President of Finland, 1956– .

kelpie, or -y. Water sprite, usually in shape of horse.

kempt. P.P. of kemp (comb.) Opposite. unkempt.

kennel. -led. Brit. -lled.

Kentucky. (abbr. Ky.) Native, adj. Kentuckian. Capital, Frankfort.

Kenya [KEHN-yuh; Brit. locally, KEEN-yuh]. Former British crown colony in East Africa on Indian Ocean. Native, Kenyan. Cap., Nairobi [nie-ROH-bee]. Currency, East African shilling, cent.

Kenyatta, Joma [JOH-moh]. (1891–   ) Premier of Kenya, 1963–   .

kerb. U.S. form is curb.

kerneled. -ing.

kerosene. British is paraffin.
   GASOLINE. Brit. petrol, or petroleum spirit.

ketch. SEE boats.

ketchup. Brit. In U.S., catchup is preferred.

kettledrum. -drummer, -stitch.

Kev. (abbr.) kilo-electron volts.

key. -eyd, -ing.

the Keystone State. Pennsylvania.

kg. (abbr.) kilogram.

KGB. SEE MVD.

khaki [KAK-ee; KAH-kee].

Khan, Agha Mohammed Yahya. (1917–   ) Pakistani General, Prime Minister, 1969–   . General Yahya Khan or General Yahya.

Khartoum [kahr-TOOM]. Preferred to Khartum. Cap., Republic of Sudan.

Khmer [KEH-mehr]. Pl. Khmers. Aboriginal people of Cambodia and their 13th Century civilization.

Khrushchev, Nikita Sergeyevitch [KROOSH-chawf, nuh-KEET-uh sehr-GAE-yehv-vihtch]. (1894–1971) Soviet premier, Communist leader 1954–1963.

Khyber Pass [KIE-buhr]. Between Afghanistan and Pakistan.

kibbutz. Israeli communal agricultural settlement.

kidnap. -ped, -ping, -per. Brit. *pp.*

Kiev [kee-EHF]. On the Dnieper River, U.S.S.R.

kill. In the graphic arts, destroy the type for the matter indicated.

kilo- [KEEL-oh]. Metric system prefix meaning multiplied by 1000. *Cf.* milli-, divided by 1000. kilogram-meter, kilovolt-ampere,

kilowatt-hour. Also shortened form of kilogram, or kiloliter (colloquial).

kilocycle [KIHL-oh-SIE-kl]. (abbr. kc.) 1000 cycles, especially in radio.

kilogram [KIHL-oh-gram]. (abbr. kg.) (colloq. kilo) Unit of weight = 2.2046 avoirdupois lb. = 2.6792 apothecaries lb. = 1000 grams.

kiloliter [KIHL-oh-lee-tehr]. (abbr. kl.) (colloq. kilo) Unit of (1) capacity = 28.378 bu. = 264.18 gal. = 1000 l.; (2) volume = 1.308 cu. yd. = 35.315 cu. ft.

kilometer [KIHL-oh-mee-tehr, kih-LOHM-ee-tehr]. (abbr. km.) Unit of length = 0.621370 miles = approx. $\frac{5}{8}$ mi. = 1093.611 yds. = 3280 ft., 10 in. = 1000 m.

kilostere. Unit of volume = 1308 cu. yds. = 1000 m^3. = 1000 steres.

kiloton. Measure of explosive power = 1000 tons of TNT.

kilowatt-hour. Unit of measure = 1000 watts used for one hour.

Kim Sung Chu [kihm suhng choo]. (1912–   ) Known as Kimil-Sung after early 20th century hero. Premier North Korea, 1948–1967.

kimono [kuh-MOH-nuh]. Pl. -os. -ed.

kin. Relatives, collectively.
   KITH. Friends, neighbors, or relatives, collectively (archaic).

kindheart. -hearted.

kind. *Of what kind are these oranges? This kind of apple. These kinds of apples.*

kind of. Class or variety of. AVOID use as somewhat: *kind of frightened.* And NOT *kind of a . . . .*

kindergarten.

kindly. Avoid use for please. NOT: *Kindly give me some peaches.*

kindred [KIHN-drihd]. Relationship; relations.

King. (or any member of the Royal Family) ADDRESS; To His Royal Highness George, or The King's Most Excellent Majesty, or His Most Gracious Majesty, King George. SALUTATION; Your Royal Highness, Sir.

King of England. etc.; the King.

kingly. Of or worthy of a king.
REGAL. Of the office, dignity, or majesty of a king; *regal bearing*.
ROYAL. Of the person of a king or crown.
SOVEREIGN. Of highest power.

kinsfolk. (preferred to kinfolk) -man, -people, -woman.

Kinshasa [kihn-SHAH-suh]. Formerly Leopoldville, Capital of Congo.

kiosk [KEE-ahsk]. Outdoor newsstand, etc.

Kirov, Sergei Mironovich [KEE-ruhf, sych-GAE-ih myih-RAW-nuh-vyihch]. (1888–1934) Murdered Russian revolutionist.

kiss-off. (n. and adj.)

kitchenmaid. -man, -ware, -wife, -work.

kiteflier. -flying.

kittenhearted.

kl. (abbr.) kiloliter.

klang association. Carryover of meaning because of similarity of sounds; e.g., fakir (religious beggar) suggests faker.

Klansman. -woman.

Klee, Paul [klae]. (1879–1940) Swiss modern painter.

km. (abbr.) kilometer.

km.^{2} (abbr.) square kilometer.

km.^{3} (abbr.) cubic kilometer.

knapsack. -sacked, -sacking.

kneel. P. and p.p., knelt, kneeled.

knickknack.

knife. Pl., knives; -fed, -fing.

knifeboard. knife edge, knife grinder.

knight-errant. Pl., knights-errant.

knighthead. -hood.

Knight Templar. Pl., Knights Templar.

knit. P. p., knit or -tted. The long form is used for individual needle works. BUT *factory knit goods*.

knock-kneed. (adj.) knock-on (n. and adj.).

knoll [nohl].

Knossos, Chossus, or Gnossus [NOH-suhs]. City in ancient Crete.

knot. (abbr. k.) Unit of speed = 1 nautical mile (6080.2 ft.) per hour. *Speed of 30 knots*, NOT *30 knots per hour*. Brit., 6080 ft. per hour.

knothole.

knout [nout].

know. P., knew; p.p., known.

know-all. (n. and adj.) know-how (n. and adj.), know-it-all (n. and adj.), know-little (n. and adj.), know-nothing (n. and adj.).

knowledgeable.

Knudsen, William S. [NOOD-s'n]. (1879–1958) American industrialist.

Kobe [KOH-beh]. City in Japan.

Kobenhavn. (Copenhagen) Capital city of Denmark.

Koestler, Arthur [KEHST-lehr]. (1905–   ) Hungarian-English writer.

kohlrabi [KOHL-rah-bee]. A large-stemmed cabbage.

Konoye, Prince Fuimimaro [koh-NOH-yeh, fuh-mee-MAH-roh]. (1891–1945) Japanese statesman.

kopek [KOH-pehk]. 1/100th ruble. *Cf.* U.S.S.R.

Koran, the [koh-RAHN, KAW-rahn]. Koranic. BUT UCMS, koranic.

Korea [kaw-REE-uh]. Also Chosen; Choson. Native, Korean(s). Divided roughly by 38th parallel.
NORTH KOREA. Capital, Pyongyang. [pyahng-yahng]. Currency, won, chong.
SOUTH KOREA. Cap., Seoul (sool). Currency kwan, singular and plural; chon.

Kosciusko Mt. [kahz-ih-UHS-koh]. Mountain in New South Wales, Australia.

Kosciusko, Thaddeus [kahs-ih-UHS-koh]. (1746–1817) Polish patriot.

Kosygin, Aleksei Nikolaevich [kuh-SIH-gin, uh-LYEHK-syae-ih nyih-kuh-LAH-yeh-vyihch]. (1905–) Premier, U.S.S.R., 1963– .

Koussevitsky, Serge. Russ., Sergei. [koo-sae-VEETS-kee, sehrj-e; sehr-GAE]. (1874–1951) Russian-American conductor.

kowtow [Properly koh-TOU, but popularly kou-TOU]. Preferred to kotow.

K-ration. Highly concentrated three-box food packet of meat, biscuits, malted milk tablets, coffee, chewing gum, sugar, bouillon paste, and lemonade powder. *Cf.* C-ration.

Krishna Menon, V.K. [KRIHSH-nuh MEHN-uhn]. (1897–) Indian barrister; Defense Minister, 1957–1963.

Kroiger [KROO-guh].

KRUEGER [KROO-guh].

krona. Pl., kroner. Swedish currency.

krone. Pl., kroner. Danish, Norwegian currency.

kt. (abbr.) carat, kiloton.

ktenology. Science of putting people to death.

Kublai Khan [kyoo-blie KAHN]. (1216–94) Mongol conqueror, Emperor of China.

Kuibyshev [KOO-ih-bih-shehf; angl., KWEE-bih-shehf]. City on Volga River, U.S.S.R. Formerly Samara.

Ku Klux Klan [KOO kluhks klan]. the Klan.

Kultur [kool-TOO'R]. (Ger.) Culture regarded as a force moving toward higher levels of development.

Kuomintang [kwoh-mihn-TAHNG]. Not Kuomintang party; *tang* means party.

Kuril Is. or Kurile Is. [KOO-reel]. Russian island chain between Japan and Asian mainland, formerly Japanese (1875–1945).

Kurland, Courland [KUR-land]. Region of Latvia on Baltic Sea.

kurtosis. Analysis of cases concentrated around the mode of a frequency curve.

Kuwait or Kuweit [koo-WIHT, —WAET]. Native Kuwaiti(s); (adj.) Kuwait or Kuwaiti. Oil-rich British former protectorate, northwest corner Persian Gulf; area 1930 sq. mi. Cap. Al Kuwait. Currency, Kuwait dinar (KD) of 1000 fils.

kv. (abbr.) kilovolt.

kv.-a. (abbr.) kilovolt-ampere.

kw. (abbr.) kilowatt.

kw.-hr. (abbr.) kilowatt-hour.

Ky. (abbr.) Kentucky.

L

l. (abbr.) liter, line.

L-bar. L-beam, L-block, L-square.

La. (Fr.) Preceding a name, see *Le*.

La. (abbr.) Louisiana.

Laban [LAE-ban]. A given name, masculine, from Hebrew.

label. -led, -ing. Brit., *lled*, *lling*.

"La Boheme" [lah boh-EHM]. 1897 opera by Giacomo Puccini.

labor. Brit. -our. Labor Day. Brit., Labour Party.

laboratory. [LAB-oh-ruh-toh-ree; Brit., lab-AH-ruh-toh-rih].

Laboratory. Capitalize if party of name; Forest Products Laboratory, the Laboratory; BUT the laboratory (non-federal).

laborious [luh-BAWR-ee-uhs].

labor-saving. labor union.

labyrinthine [lab-uhr-IHN-thihn]. Preferred to -thian. From labyrinthe [LAB-ih-rihnth]. Maze-like.

lacerate [LASS-uhr-aet]. Tear; mangle.

lachrymal. Also lacrimal, lacrymal. Of tears. -matory, -mose.

lackadaisical.

Lackawanna [lahk-uh-WAHN-ah]. City in New York on Lake Erie, south of Buffalo.

lackey. Pl. -eys.

lacquer [LAK-uhr].

lacuna [la-KYOO-nuh]. Pl., -nae [—nee]. Missing portion in a writing.

Ladakh [lah-DAHK]. East Kashmir district on Tibet border, India.

lade. Load. -ded, -den, -ding.

Lady. The title *Lady* is held by all peeresses under the rank of duchess, and by daughters of dukes, marquises, and earls, by the wives of knights, baronets, barons, viscounts, marquesses, knights, and lords of session. REFER TO: (1) A peeress in her own right, or a peer's daughter; *the Countess of Cromartie, Lady Pamela Berry*. Her title does not apply to her husband. If she outranks him, refer to *the Countess of Cromartie and her husband, Col. Edward Walter Blunt-Mackenzie*. (2) A widowed or divorced lady as *Nancy Viscountess Astor* or *Anne, Lady Orr Lewis*. For a second reference use *Lady Astor, NEVER Lady Nancy Astor*. (3) A daughter of an earl, marquess, or duke is *Lady Mary Grosvenor, Lady Mary*, but NOT *Lady Grosvenor*. ADDRESS; *Lady Martha Sperling*, or *Lady Sperling*, or *The Honorable Lady Sperling*. SALUTATION; *Madam, My Lady, Your Ladyship. Cf.* Nobility, Lord.

lady. Means woman in U.S., but use should be avoided except where a matter of etiquette is involved; *Gentlemen stand behind the ladies' chairs*. There is a tendency to associate lady with a person of higher social status. NOT; *I'm the lady next door*. BUT: *I'm your next door neighbor*. And, of course: *Ladies and gentlemen*; and to a waiter: *The lady will have a martini*.

ladybug. British use ladybird.

La Fontaine, de, Jean [de lah fawn-TEHN] (1621–1695) French fable writer.

lager [LAH-guh].

La Guardia Airport. Flushing, New York City.

LaGuardia, Fiorello Henry [lah-GWAHR-dih-ah, fee-aw-REHL-oh]. (1882–1947) New York City Mayor, 1934–1945.

laid. SEE lay.

laissez aller [leh-SAE AHL-lae]. Let's go, in the spirit of abandon.

laissez faire [LEH-sae-FEHR]. N.Y. Times. laissez-faire. Let (them) do as they please. In economics, freedom from government interference.

La Jolla [lah-HOI-ah]. Section of San Diego, California.

Lake Erie. Lake of the Woods, Salt Lake; the lake.

Lakes, Great. see Great Lakes.

lamé [lam-AE]. Fabric with gold or silver threads.

lameduck. (nonliteral) (n. and adj.) (Webster, *lame duck.*) An elected official who is serving an unexpired term after a successor has been chosen.

lamentable [LAM-ehn-tuh-bl]. -tably.

laminated. Composed of layers of material (cloth, wood).
lamppost.
lamprey. Pl. -eys.

Lancaster [LANG-kas-tuh]. The city.

Lancelot [LAHN-seh-laht]. Knight of the Round Table.

landau [LAND-aw]. Covered four-wheel carriage with rear portion which can be opened.

landaulet [land-dau-LEHT]. Preferred to —ette. Automobile with open front and convertible rear section.

landing craft. (abbr. LCC, LCI, LCK, LCM, LCP, LCR, LCS, LCT, LCM, LSD, LSM, LST, LVT, etc.) Special-purpose amphibious landing vehicles for communications, infantry, kitchen equipment, mechanical equipment, personnel, rubber, fire support, tanks, etc., used in W.W. II.

Lane. Capitalize if part of name; Maiden Lane, the lane.

language. Means of communicating thought.
ARGOT. Language of thieves and hobos, designed to hide meanings.
CANT. Phraseology of a class or occupation; also, pious or insincere speech.

COMMERCIALESE. Typical business writing.

DIALECT. Local language.

GIBBERISH. Unintelligible language.

GOBBLEDYGOOK. Extensive use of government terminology and circumlocution.

IDIOM. Characteristic expressions of native speakers.

JARGON. Barbarous language or mixture of languages; hybrid or technical language, difficult to understand.

JOURNALESE. Semi-colloquial, reportorial style.

LINGO. Foreign language, often in a contemptuous sense.

OFFICIALESE. Typical government wording. SEE gobbledygook.

PARLANCE. Manner of speaking. Must be associated with a modifier; *Nautical parlance.*

PATOIS [PAT-wah]. Dialect; often combination of two languages.

SLANG. Popular, but unauthorized, words or expressions.

VERNACULAR. Local or native language.

languor [LAN-gger; —gwehr]. Lassitude; dullness. languorous [LAN-geh-ruhs].

languid [LAN-gwihd].

languish [LAN-gwihsh].

lanolin [LAN-uh-lihn]. Wool grease used in ointments.

lanternman. lantern-jawed (adj.); lantern slide.

Laocoon [lae-AHK-oh-ahn]. Mythological Trojan priest who distrusted the wooden horse and, with his two sons, was destroyed by sea serpents sent by Athena.

Laos [LAH-ohs, lous]. Native Lao (s); (adj.) Lao or Laotian. Cap., Vientiane. Currency, kip (K), centime.

lapis lazuli [LAP-ihs LAZ-yuh-lih, or LAE-pihs—]. Azure blue stone of silicate and sulphur; its color.

larder [LAHRD-uhr].

Laredo [lah-RAE-doh]. City in Texas.

large. Denotes extension in several directions and beyond the average for the class. It is not so emphatic as, but more dignified than, *big.*

large. -gish. *Large size, large-sized. large scale, loom large, bulk large* NOT -*ly*. *Cf*. big.

largess, largesse [LAHR-jehs]. Liberal giving.

Larissa [la-RIHS-sa]. Ancient city, department in Greece.

larkspur. lark-colored (adj.).

larva. Pl. -vae.

larynx. Pl., larynxes.

lascivious [luh-SIHV-ee-uhs]. Lewd.

laser. Device which amplifies light. *Cf*. maser.

lasso [LASS-oh]. Pl., -os.

last. *The last three* pref. to *the three last*. In an enumeration, *firstly, secondly, lastly*. Indicates that none follow; not to be confused with *latest*. NOT: *This was the last burglary in the area*. SEE late.

last-born. (adj.) last-cited (adj.)

Las Vegas [lahs VAE-guhs]. City in Nevada.

lat. (abbr.) latitude.

late. When attached to a name or title, means that the bearer is dead. Comparative; *later, latter*; superlative; latest or last. The comparative form means *nearer the end*, but *latter* is also used in contrast with former. *The latter part of the 19th century. He preferred the former to the latter.* The superlative form of *latter* is *lattermost*. Many writers limit the use of *last* to the meaning of *final* rather than *immediately preceding* or *latest*.

latecomer. —coming; late-born (adj.)

latent [LAE-tehnt]. Hidden; not necessarily dormant.

latex [LAE-tehks]. Rubber (natural or synthetic) particles suspended in water. Pl. latexes or latices.

lath [lath]. Wood or metal strip base for plaster, tiles, etc.

lathe [laethe]. Machine for turning and shaping material.

Latin America. Spanish America, Brazil, and Haiti.
North American and South American

nations governed by people of Latin ancestry. Native, Latin American. Latin American States. SEE States.

latitude. (abbr. lat.) Figured in equal degrees of 68.703 statute miles north and south of the equator, written; *latitude 49 26'14" N.* N.Y. Times, Lat. 48 degrees N. Long. 28 degrees W.

latter. Refers to the second of two things. Opposite: former. Avoid when more or less than two are mentioned.
LATER. Coming afterward.

Latvia. Native, Latvian, Lett; (adj.), Lettic; Lettish, of the original people. Latvian Soviet Socialist Republic. Cap., Riga [REE-guh]. Incorporated into U.S.S.R., 1940.

laugh [LAHF is pref. to LAFF].

Launcelot [LAWN-seh-laht].
LANCELOT [LAN-suh-laht].

launch [lawnch].

laundrymaid. laundry room.

laureate [LAWR-ee-eht]. Crowned with laurel, a mark of honor; hence, distinguished; *poet laureate*.

laureled.

lavabo [luh-VAE-hoh]. Washing ceremony in the Mass; by extension, the basin, any wash basin. Pl. -os.

lavaliere [lav-uh-LEER]. or —ier, lliere. Pendent of jewels on a chain.

law. Walsh-Healey law; law 176; law No. 176; copyright law; Ohm's law.

lawn mower.

lawyer. A member of the legal profession.
ATTORNEY. pl. -eys, one (usually a lawyer) empowered to do business for another.
ATTORNEY IN FACT. One authorized to act for another.
BARRISTER. One who pleads in court.
COUNSEL. A legal representative engaged especially for a particular case.
SOLICITOR. In Britain, a lawyer permitted to conduct litigation but to plead only in lower courts.

lay, laid, laying. A transitive verb which requires a direct object; *Lay the book on the table. I must have laid it somewhere.*

LIE, LAY, LAIN. An intransitive verb which cannot take a direct object. *Lie down on the bed. I lay down on the bed. He has lain there for an hour.*

layaway plan. Method of selling by accepting payments in installments before delivery.

layman. Not a professional. Pertaining to the laity, compared with the clergy, and by extension to those not doctors, lawyers, engineers, teachers, or the like.

lb. (abbr.) pound. Pl., lbs. For weight only.

lb. ap. (abbr.) pound, apothecary's.

lb. av. (abbr.) pound, avoirdupois.

lc. or l.c. (abbr.) lower case; lower-case.

l.c.l. (abbr.) less-than-carload lot.

l.c.m. (abbr.) least common multiple.

Le, le. (Fr.) Capitalize preceding a name only when not preceded by a first name; *Le Fevre says . . . ; Jean le Fevre. Cf.* filing.

lead. P. and p.p., led.

leadenhearted. leaden-eyed (adj.).

leaderwork. leader line.

leading question. In law, one which leads a person on. NOT the most important question.

league. (1) Unit of length = 3 statute miles = 4.82805 km.; (2) marine league = 3 nautical mi. = 3.45 statute mi. = 5.56 km. At various times league has measured 2.4 to 4.6 miles. Square league = 4439 acres = 1796 hectares.

lean-faced. (adj.) lean-looking (adj.), lean-to (n. and adj.).

Leander [lee-AN-dehr]. (Greek mythology) Lover of Hero, who swam the Hellespont nightly to visit her.

leap. P. and p.p., leaped is preferred to leapt.

leapfrog.

leap year. 366 days. Occurs each 4th year, excluding century years (but not 2000). The additional day is February 29th.

learn. P. and p.p., learned is preferred to learnt. But do not confuse with learned (adj.).

leasehold.

leave. P. and p.p. left; leaving.

leave. Avoid the use meaning *let. Leave me alone* means depart and allow me to be in solitude. *Let me alone* means do not disturb me.

leaved. Preferred to -leafed in *broad-leaved plant.*

leavetaking.

Lebanon. Native, Lebanese; (adj.) Lebanese. Cap., Beirut. Currency, pound (L), piaster.

Lebensraum [LAE-b'nz-roum]. (Ger.) Living space.

leeward [LYOO-ahrd]. Opposite of *windward* or *weather.* The side farthest from the point from which the wind blows.

Leeward Island. Southeast of Puerto Rico. Antigua, Virgin Islands, St. Kitts, Nevis, and Montserrat.

Lefevre, Theodore Joseph Alberic Marie [l'FAE-vr]. (1914–   ) Lawyer, Premier of Belgium, 1961–   .

left. leftist, left wing.

leftmost.

left bank. When facing downstream.

Left Bank. The intellectual section of Paris.

left-hand. *Left-hand drawer, left-handed person.*

left-handed compliment. A roundabout, ambiguous, clumsy, or possibly insincere compliment.

Legal Adviser of the Department of State. the Legal Adviser.

legate [LEHG-iht]. A commissioned deputy; e.g., ambassador.

LEGATEE [lehg-a-TEE]. One to whom a bequest is made.

Legation. Finnish Legation, etc.; the Legation.

Legion. American Legion, the Legion, a Legionnaire; French Foreign Legion, the legion.

Legislative Assembly. Capitalize if part of name; Legislative Assembly of New York, the legislative assembly; the assembly of Puerto Rico; the legislative assembly; the assembly.

legislative branch. clerk, session, etc.

Legislator. ADDRESS; The Honorable Peter D. Smith, The State Legislature; or The Honorable Peter D. Smith, Member of Legislature, The State Capitol. SALUTATION; Sir; Dear Sir; Dear Mr. Smith.

Legislature. National Legislature (U.S. Congress), the Legislature; Ohio Legislature, Legislature of Ohio, the legislature. BUT N.Y. Times, Legislature, when referring to a specific state body.

Le Havre [luh-AHVR]. Seaport in France.

Leicester [LEHS-tehr]. City and county in England.

Leicestershire [—shihr]. County in central England.

leisure [LEE-zhoor; Brit., LEZH—].

leitmotiv [LIET-moh-teef]. Melodic phrase associated with an idea, person, or situation.

Lemass, Sean [le-MAHSS, shawn]. (1899–1971) Prime Minister of Ireland, 1959–1966.

lemma. Pl. -s or -ata. An accepted preliminary proposition used to demonstrate another proposition.

Le Monde [l'MAWND]. (Fr.) noted newspaper. The World.

lend. P. and p.p., lent; (n.) loan. NOT; *Loan me some books.*

lend-lease. (all meanings).

lengthwise. Preferred to -ways.

lengthy. Long, especially of speeches, writings, etc.

leniency. Preferred to -ce.

lenient [LEE-nih-ehnt; LEEN-yehnt].

Lenin, Vladimir Ilyich [LYAE-nyihn]. (1870–1924). Born Ulyanov. Sometimes listed Nikolai from pen name N. Lenin taken from wife's name Natalya.

lens. Pl. lenses.

Lent. 40-day spring fasting and penitence period preceding Easter.

lentissimo. lentando, lentanente, lento. SEE Slow Music.

Leonidas [lee-AHN-ih-das].

lesè-majesté [leez MAJ-ehs-tih]. (Fr.) Crime against sovereign power.

Lesotho, Kingdom of. (Formerly British Basutoland) Independent since 1966, member British Commonwealth. Native, Basatho (s. & pl.). Cap., Maseru.

less. Lesser, least; much less, much more, STILL LESS, STILL MORE.
A LITTLE. Less, least.
LITTLE. Smaller, smallest.

-less. Suffix added to nouns meaning without; *careless, headless,* or to verbs, meaning not able to or not subject to; *tireless, restless.*

let. P. and p.p., let.

letdown. (n. and adj.)

let-George-do-it attitude.

lethargy [LEHTH-ehr-gih].
LETHARGIC [lehth-ahr-jihk].

letters, plural. a's, b's.

letters illustrating shape and form: U-*shape* (d), A-*frame,* T-*bone,* T-*rail,* etc., are set in Gothic (sans serif) type.

Letters Patent No. 378,964. BUT patent No. 378,964; letters patent.

lettuce [LEHT-ihs].

letup. (n.) Abatement.

leukemia.

Levant [leh-VANT]. The eastern shores of the Mediterranean, West Greece to West Egypt. Levantine.

levee [LEHV-ee]. Embankment. levee no. 1.

levelheaded. level-line.

lever [LEE-vuhr, LEHV-ehr].

Leyte Is. [LAE-tae]. Site of U.S. sea battle W.W. II, Philippine Islands.

L.F. (abbr.) low frequency.

lf, or l.f. (abbr.) lightface. Cf. b.f.

L.I. Long Island.

liable. Responsible, obliged; also exposed to risk; *He was liable for his partner's debts.*

   APT. Have a tendency to. *It is likely that he will be elected, and he is apt to vote for a liberal program. In such a case, he is liable to lose a great many followers.*

   LIKELY. Probable.

liaison [lee-ae-ZAWN; Brit., lee-AE-zn]. Connecting link; bond.

Liberal Party. (Brit.) Successor to Whig Party, with program directed toward greater freedom. Comparable to U.S. New Deal Democrats. Cf. Conservative.

liberal-minded. (adj.) liberal arts.

Liberia [lie-BEER-ih-uh]. Native, Liberian (s); (adj.) Liberian. Ind. republic on Atl. Ocean, since 1847. Cap., Monrovia. Currency, U.S. dollar ($), native cent.

Liberty Bell. Liberty ship.

Liberty Island, N.Y. Formerly Bedloes Island, site of the Statue of Liberty.

Librarian of Congress. the Librarian.

Library. Army Library, the library; Franklin D. Roosevelt Library, the Library of Congress, the Library; Public Library, the library.

libretto [lih-BREHT-oh]. Pl. -etti, or -os [lih-BREHT-tee, -ohs].

Libya [LIHB-ih-uh]. Native, Libyan(s); (adj.) Libyan. Caps., Tripoli and Benghazi. Currency, Libyan pound (L) = Brit.

license. Brit. n. -ce.

lichen [LIE-kehn, - -kihn]. Plant of fungus and alga.

licorice [LIHK-uhr-ihs; LIHK-uhr-ihsh]. Brit., liquorice.

Lidice [LIHD-ih-see]. City in Czechoslovakia, destroyed by Nazis in 1942, following assassination of Heydrich.

lie. P., lay; p.p., lain; lying. Cf. lay.

   LIE. (tell a falsehood) P., lied; p.p., lying.

Lie, Trygve, Halvdan [lee, TREUG- veh; angl., TRIHG-vee]. (1896–1967). Norwegian United Nations Secretary-General 1946–1953.

Liechtenstein [LIHK-tehn-shtien]. Native, Lichtensteiner(s); (adj.) Liechtenstein. Independent principality between Switzerland and Austria on the Rhine River. Area 62 sq. mi. Cap., Vaduz. Currency, Swiss franc.

lief [leef]. Willingly, freely, gladly. Used only in *I would as lief, had as lief.* The word is not related to leave.

Liege [lih-AEZH]. City in Belgium.

lien [lee-ehn, leen]. In law, a claim against property. Cf. lean.

lieu [loo]. Stead. *Ir lieu of.*

lieutenant [loo-TEHN-ant; Brit. lehft-; nautical LEHT-eh-ꞁant].

lieutenant colonel. Pl. -colonels. lieutenant-colonelꞁy.

Lieutenant Governor of Idaho. etc.; the Lieutenant Governor; lieutenant governorship.

Lieutenant Governor of a State. ADDRESS; The Lieutenant Governor, State of New York, or The Honorable Malcolm Wilson, Lieutenant Governor of New York. SALUTATION; Sir, Dear Sir, Dear Mr. Wilson.

life-belt. lifesaving, lifetime, life-size (adj.), life-sized (adj.); life buoy, life everlasting, life mask, life net, life rate.

lift. British for elevator.

lift-off. (n. and adj.)

ligature [LIHG-uh-tchehr]. A binding; two or more letters printed together: æ, fl.

light. Capitalize if part of name; Buffalo South Pier Light 2, light No. 2, light 2; Massachusetts Bay Lights.

light. P. and p.p., lighted or lit.

lightborne. —face (printing), —house, —weight (n. and adj.), —wood (all one word); light-armed (adj.), light-clad (adj.), light-colored (adj.), light-drab (adj.), light-draft (adj.), light-footed (adj.), light-producing (adj.), light-struck (adj.) light-year; light buoy, light housekeeping (domestic).

lighterman. lighter-than-air (adj.).

lighter-than-air-craft.

Lightship. Capitalize if part of name; Grays Reef Lightship, North Manitou Shoal Lightship; the lightship.

Light Station. Capitalize if part of name; Watch Hill Light Station, the light station, the station.

light year. Unit of measure = distance light travels in 1 yr. = 6 trillion miles.

ligne. Unit of measure for the diameter of a watch movement = 2.2559 millimeters = approx. $\frac{1}{11}$ inch.

likable.

likewise. like-looking (adj.), like-minded (adj.).

-like. childlike, lamblike, lifelike, tigerlike, etc.; bill-like. Hyphenate suffix when joined to one-syllable words. BUT ladylike, businesslike.

like. (n.) *I never saw his like.* BUT *the likes of her* is colloquial.

like. (v.) Enjoy, be attracted towards; *I like him, I like to study. I like studying. I like it that you came.* BUT NOT *I like that you came. I would* (Brit., *should*) *like you to sing.* NOT *for you to sing.*

like. Meaning likely is archaic. *She is like to die of it.*

like. (adj., adv., prep.) Similar; *A man like him.* BUT NOT a mitigator: She was *pretty-like.*

like. (conj.) Meaning *as* (colloquial); *The paint won't peel like the wallpaper does. Winston*

tastes good like a cigarette should. BUT meaning also, *as if* (colloq.); *He acts like he knows everything.* Webster III accepts this form.

likely. Highly probable; *It is likely that he will arrive soon.*

LIABLE. Bound by law or legally answerable for an action. NOT; *He is liable to arrive soon.* SEE liable.

-lily. The sound is best avoided by using adjective form for lovelily, heavenlily, timelily. NOT; *He spoke timelily to us* BUT *at a timely occasion.* But some forms are widely used; *sillily sentimental.*

Lilliputian [lihl-ih-PYOO-shuhn].

lilyhanded. lily-shaped (adj.), lily-white (adj.).

Lima [LIE-mah]. City in Ohio.
LIMA [LEE-muh]. City in Peru.

limbo. Pl. -os.

limehouse. -juice, -light, -lighter, -pit, -stone, -water (all one word).

limit. Point which marks the end of the area specified.
LIMITATION. Point which marks the end of conditions or circumstances.

limn [lihm]. -ed, -ing. Draw, paint.

Limoges [lee-MOHZH]. City in France; type of porcelain.

limousine [lihm-u-ZEEN].

linage, lineage [LIE-nihj]. Number of lines, as in a newspaper advertisement.
LINEAGE [LIHN-ee-ehj]. Descent; race; family.

Line(s). Capitalize if part of name; Burlington Lines (railroad), Greyhound Line (bus), Holland-American Line (steamship); the line(s).

line. DEW line, Mason-Dixon line or Mason and Dixon's line, Pinetree line, State line.

lineament [LIHN-ee-uh-ment]. An outline or contour of the body or, especially, the face.

Lingayen Gulf [lihng-gah-YEHN]. Inlet of South China Sea, Luzon, Philippine Islands.

lingerie [LAN-jeh-ree; lahn-jeh-RAE].

lingo. Pl. -ōes. SEE language.

link. SEE surveyor's link, engineer's link.

LINKING VERB. (copulative verb) A verb which connects a subject with a predicate by telling what the subject is. It is followed by a predicate nominative; *I am a man*—or by a predicate adjective; *She looks beautiful. He is big. The flower smells sweet.* In addition to the verb *to be,* common linking verbs are *remain, grew, seem, keep,* and the verbs referring to the senses—*see, taste, smell, feel.* AVOID the use of an adverb for the predicate adjective NOT; *He feels badly.* Although the predicate nominative is properly in the nominative case, *It is I,* popular usage of the objective case is often permissable; *It is me,* especially in complicated sentences. Always use the objective case after *to be; He expected the caller to be me.* A noun or pronoun not in the genitive case after *being* is also in the objective case; *Would you like to try being me?*

links. Singular and plural. A golf course.

Linnaeus, Linnaean. System of plant classification and nomenclature including genus and species. For Karl von Linne, Swedish naturalist.

lionheart. -hearted, -like, -proof; lion-headed (adj.), lion-maned (adj).

lipread.

lipstick.

liquefy. -faction.

liqueur [lih-KEUR, -KOOR]. A sweet, flavored dessert brandy.

lira [LEE-rah]. Pl. lire. Monetary unit of Italy. *Cf.* Italy.

lissome, lissom [LISS-uhm]. Limber; agile.

listener-in. Pl. listeners-in.

litany. Prayer form of supplication and responses.

liturgy. Body of rites for public worship.

liter. (abbr. l.) Unit of capacity = 1.0567 liquid qt. = 0.9081 dry qt. = 61.025 cu. in. = approx. 1 dm^3.

literature [LIHT-ehr-uh-tchoor].

lithe [liethe]. Flexible, limber.

Lithuania. Native, Lithuanian (s); (adj.) Lithuanian. Cap., Kaunas. Incorporated into U.S.S.R., 1940.

litotes [LIE-toh-tees, LIHT-]. In rhetoric, use of a negative or understatement to make an affirmative statement; *This is not the best way of explaining the problem. He has no small talent.*

Litt. D. or D. Litt. (abbr.) Doctor of Literature.

little. Comparative, littler, less, lesser; superlative, littlest, least. SEE small.

Little Inch. Big Inch. Pipelines.

Littleneck. (clam); little-known (adj.), little-used (adj.).

littoral. Pertains to a shore, especially of the sea; used in describing marine life in shallow coastal water.

livable.

livelong [LIEV lawng]. -stock, -wire (nonliteral); live load, live weight, live wire.

livelily. The correct adverb form before an adjective. *The dance, livelily executed* ... NOT; *lively.*

livid. Pale, bluish. NOT flushed.

PALLID. Pale, wan.

living room.

llama. South American animal.

LAMA. Buddhist priest.

LL.B. (abbr.) bachelor of laws.

LL.D. (abbr.) Doctor of Laws.

Lleras Restrepo Carlos [YEH-rohss rae-STRAE-poh]. (1908–   ) Pres. of Colombia (1966–1970). Dr. Llera Restrepo.

Lloyd's. NOT -ds or ds'. London insurance company.

loan. (n.) Use lend for verb; *He would not lend me the money. He lent me the money. I borrowed the money from him. He gave me a loan.*

loath, loth [LOHTH]. Reluctant; averse.
 LOATHE [LOHTHE]. Detest. -thsome.

lobsterproof. lobster-tailed (adj.); lobster pot.

Local. Capitalize Teamsters Local Union No. 15; BUT local No. 15.

locale [loh-KALL]. Neighborhood.
 LOCAL. (adj.) In or from the neighborhood.
 LOCUS [LOH-kuhs]. Place. Pl. -ci.

Locarno [loh-KAHR-noh]. Town in Switzerland. Scene of pact in 1925.

loch. [lahk]. (Scot.) Lake.

loc. cit. (abbr.) loco citato (Lat.) *In the place cited.*

lock no. 1. Lower-case.

lockerman. locker room.

locus. Place. Pl., loci or locuses.

lodestar. Preferred to loadstar. Guiding star, especially polestar.

loadstone. Preferred to lodestone. That which attracts; from magnetite.

lodgment or lodgement. Lodging place.

Lodz [looj; Russ., LAWTS-y]. City in Poland.

log. (abbr.) logarithm.

logbook. logroll.

loggerhead.

loggia [LOHJ-uh]. Open-roofed gallery. Pl., -s.
 LOGIA [LAH-jih-uh]. Christ's words not in the Bible. Pl. of *logion,* pointed sayings of a religious teacher.

logo-. Combining form meaning word; *logogram, logometric.*

loll [lahl]. Droop.

long. (adj.) *long journey*; (adv.) *we will long remember*; (v.) *I long to see you.*

Longchamp [lohn-SHAHN]. Race track in Bois de Boulogne, near Paris.
 LONGCHAMPS. N.Y.C. restaurant chain.

long distance call. Brit., trunk call.

longeron [lawnzh-RAWN]. Part of airplane frame.

Longueil [lawnn-GAEL; Fr., lawnn-GEU-y]. City opposite Montreal on St. Lawrence River, Canada.

longways or -wise. Lengthwise.

looker-on. Pl. lookers-on.

lookout. (n.) look out (v.).

looseleaf. (adj.) loose-mouthed; loose-tongued (adj.).

lopsided. lop-eared (adj.).

loquacity [loh-KWAS-ih-tih].

loran. (abbr.) long-range navigation.

Lord and Lady. The titles of address, Lord and Lady, are applied to all members of the English peerage except dukes and duchesses. The wife of a peer takes the title corresponding to that of her husband—duchess, marchioness, countess, viscountess, baroness. The wife of a baronet or a knight receives the title of Lady. The placement of this title depends on its source. The daughter of a duke is *Lady Mary (Pierrepont) Wortley Montague,* the wife of a peer is *Lucie (Custin), Lady Duff-Gordon.* The daughter of a viscount or baron married to a baronet or knight keeps her own title and keeps the title of Lady; *Hon. Anna Emily, Lady Acland.* The wife of a younger son of an earl or the son of a viscount or baron without title in her own right is *Margaret (Wilson) Montague, Hon. Mrs. Charles Montague.* A maid of honor retains her title after her marriage, unless it is merged with a higher title. The eldest son of a duke is called by his father's second title (marquis or earl); the younger son of a duke or a marquis is called Lord his first name, and his wife is Lady her husband's first name; *Lady George.* Daughters are *Lady Jane,* etc. *Bertrand Lord Russell, Lady Russell. Sir Tom,* NOT *Sir Brown. Lady Cynthia Brown, Dame Cynthia.* When in doubt use *Sir. Cf.* Nobility and the various titles.

Lorelei [LAWR-uh-lie]. Legendary German siren on the Rhine.

lose. P. and p.p., lost; losing.

loth [lohth]. SEE loath.

Lothario. Libertine. From Rowe's "The Fair Penitent." Pl., -os.

lotus. Pl. -uses.

loud. May be used as adv. after *talk* and *laugh*; *Laugh loud.*

loudmouthed. loud-speaker (radio); loud-voiced (adj.).

Louis [LOO-ih]. French kings; XIII, Louis Treize [traez]; XIV, Quatorze [kat-AWRZ]; XV, Quinze [kanz]; XVI, Seize [sehz].

Louis, St. Louis.

Louisiana. (abbr. La.) Native, Louisianian. Cap., Baton Rouge.

Louisiana Purchase.

louse. Pl., lice.

louver. Slatted panel.

Louvre [LOOV'r]. Art Museum in Paris.

love-making. -seat, -sick; love-inspired (adj.); love knot.

low. Comparative, lower; superlative, lowest, lowermost.

lowborn. low-built (adj.); low-lying (adj.); low-power (adj.); low-pressure (adj.); low frequency, low tide, low water.

Low Church. Group in Anglican Church which holds evangelical views. Low-Churchman.

Lower. Capitalize if part of name, Lower California (Mexico); Lower Colorado River Basin; Lower Egypt; Lower Peninsula (of Michigan); Lower House (U.S. House of Representatives); BUT lower (or upper) House of Congress, lower Mississippi.

lowerclassman, lower class.

lower case. (abbr. lc or l.c.) Printers term for small letters. Opposite, upper case-capitals. (v.) lower-case.

lox. (abbr.) liquid oxygen.

lozenge [LAHZ-ehnj]. SEE shapes.

LSD. (abbr.) lysergic acid diethylamide. Hallucinogen synthesized by Dr. Albert Hofmann in 1943.

l.s.t. (abbr.) local standard time.

l.t. (abbr.) local time.

Lt. (abbr.) lieutenant.

Lt. Col. (abbr.) lieutenant colonel.

Lt. Comdr. (abbr.) lieutenant commander.

Lt. Gen. (abbr.) lieutenant general.

Lt. Gov. (abbr.) lieutenant governor.

Lt. (jg.) (abbr.) lieutenant (junior grade).

Ltd. (abbr.) limited. Brit. for U.S.,Inc. Limited-liability company—a corporation.

Lualaba [loo-ah-LAH-bah]. Region in former Belgian Congo.

lucent. Bright, clear, translucent.

lucite. SEE acrylic.

Lufthansa [LOOFT-hahn-seh]. German airline.

Luftwaffe [LOOFT-vah-fuh]. German airforce.

lukewarm.

Luluabourg [lool-wah-boor]. Town in Congo.

lumberjack.

lumen-hour. Foot-candle hour.

Lumumba, Patrice [luh-MUHM-buh]. (1926-1961) Prime Minister of Republic of. the Congo (Leopoldville), 1960.

lunatic. loony.

lunch. A casual midday meal.
LUNCHEON. A formal midday meal.
BRUNCH. A late breakfast-lunch.

lunchroom.

lunging.

luster. Preferred to -tre. Gloss, lustrous.

lusty. Full of vitality. lustily.

LUSTFUL. Full of lust. lustfully.

Luthuli, Albert John. (1900–1968) Zulu chief, winner of 1960 Nobel Peace Prize.

Luxembourg [LUK-sehn-buhrg]. Pref. to Luxemburg. Native, Luxembourger(s); (adj.) Luxembourg. Grand Duchy of –. Cap., Luxembourg. Currency, franc (lux Fr.), centime.

Luxor [LUHK-sohr]. Town on the Nile River, Egypt; site of Ancient Thebes.

luxuriant. Fertile, profuse, florid.

LUXURIOUS. Pert. to indulgence in costly dress, food, or material abundance.

luxury [LUHK-zhyoo-ree].

Luzon [loo-ZAHN]. Chief island of Philippines.

Lyautey, Louis Hubert Gonzalve [lyoh-TAE, eu-BAIR gawn-ZUHLV]. (1854–1934) French marshal.

lyceum [lie-SEE-um]. Pl. -ms or —cea. Aristotle's garden school; by extension, his philosophy and followers; also a lecture hall, literary institution, a group which sponsors lectures.

Lydia. Ancient country in area now Turkey, prominent 685–546 B.C. Cap., Sardis. Native and adj., Lydian.

lying. P.p. of lie in either sense.

lying-in. (n. and adj.)

lyonnaise [lie-uh-NAEZ]. Cooked with fried onions.

lyrebird. -man, -tail; lyre-tailed (adj.).

lyrics. Poems.

lyricist. Lyrics writer. Brit., also poet.

lyrist. Lyre player.

Lysenko, Trofim Denisovich [lih-SYEHN-koh, troh-FEEM]. (1898–1943) Russian geneticist.

M

M. (abbr.) thousand. (From the Roman numeral.)

m. (abbr.) (1) milli = one-thousandth (0.001); (2) meter; (3) merides (noon), as 12 m., BUT use 12 A.M. to avoid confusion with 12 midnight. 12 p.m.—midnight; (4) masculine.

M. (abbr.) monsieur; *MM.*, messieurs.

-m.. Words of one syllable ending in *m* when preceded by a single vowel (but not a diphthong or a vowel and verb) become *mm* before suffix beginning with a vowel: *hummer, drummer,* BUT *dreamer, roomy.*

m.² (abbr.) square meter.

m.³ (abbr.) cubic meter.

ma. (abbr.) milliampere

MA. (abbr.) Maritime Administration.

Ma'am. Madam contracted. Colloquial British form of address by servant to employer. *Cf.* ladies.

Mac or Mc. File under Mac or before M.

macabre [muh-KAHBR]. Gruesome. From the dance of death.

macaroni. Pl., -nis (food); -nies. Archaic, Dandies.

Macao Is. [muh-KOU]. Portuguese colony southeast of China. 6 sq. mi. Cap., Macao. Currency, pataca (P), avo.

mace bearer. mace oil.

Mach number. Velocity compared to speed of sound. *Mach-2* is twice the speed of sound.

machete [mah-CHAE-tae or -CHEHT-teh; also mah-SHEHT]. Heavy knife used for cutting cane or brush.

Machiavelli, Niccolo di Bernardo [mah-kya-VEHL-ih, NEE-koh-loh de behr-NAHR-do; angl., mak-ih-uh-VEHL-ih]. (1469–1527) Florentine practical statesman who held that any means were justified to maintain a strong central government. Machiavellian [mak-ee-uh-VEHL-ee-uhn]. -ism.

machinate [MAK-ih-naet]. Contrive. machination [mak-ih-NAE-shuhn].

machine-gun. machine-finished, machine-hour, machine-made; machine shop, machine stitch, machine work.

machinist [muh-SHEEN-ihst].

mackerel [MAK-uhr-ehl].

Mackinac Is. [MAK-ih-nak]. Island in Straits of Mackinac, between lakes Michigan and Huron.

MACKINAW [MAK-ih-naw]. Pertaining to Mackinac; with lower case, a short, heavy plaid coat.

mackintosh. Waterproof outer coat or cloth, from Charles Mackintosh, 1766–1843, inventor.

Macleish, Archibald [mak-LEESH]. (1892–) American poet, professor librarian.

macron. Bar shown over a letter indicating a long sound, as in āce, ēat, īce, ōh, ūnit.

mad. Insane. Not synonymous with angry. *Cf.* frantic.

Madagascar. Native, Madagascan or Malagasy. *Cf.* Malagasy Republic.

madam [MAD-am]. (n.) Form of address to a lady. *Cf.* ma'am.

MADAME. (Me.) [MAD-am, ma-DAM], pl., mesdames (Mes.) [Mae-DAM]. Title given to a married woman in France. In English, foreign married woman. In U.S., also, the woman in charge of a brothel.

made-over. (adj.) made-up (adj.).

Madeira [muh-DEER-uh]. Portuguese Atlantic Ocean Islands, north of Canary Islands. Also, wine made on the island or similar wines.

mademoiselle [mad-mwa-ZEHL, mad'm-muh-ZEHL]. (Mlle., Mmle) (Fr.) Miss. Pl., mesdemoiselles, (Mlles., Mmles.) [maed-mwa-ZEHL].

Madison, Dolley. (Dorothea) née Payne. (1768–1849) Wife of 4th U.S. President.

Madras [muh-DRAS]. City in South India.

maelstrom. [MAEL-strahm]. Whirlpool.

maestro. [mah-EH-stroh, almost MIES-troh]. Pl., -stros. Master in an art, especially music.

Maeterlinck, Count Maurice (Dutch) [MAH-tehr-lingk; Fr., meh-tehr-LAN; angl., MAE-tehr-lihngk]. (1862–1949) Belgian writer.

Mafia [MAHF-fee-ah]. Ital. -ff-. Italian (Sicilian) organization devoted to crime. In Sicily, lower case *m*, hostility to law. *Cf.* Cosa Nostra.

MAG. (abbr.) Military Advisory Group.

magazine [MAG-a-zeen (publication) or mag-a-ZEEN (storehouse)]. Italicize names of publications, but place titles of articles in quotation marks.

Magdalen College [MAWD-lihn]. Oxford; -e at Cambridge.

magdalene [MAG-duh-lehn]. A reformed prostitute.

Magdalene, Mary [mag-duh-LEE-nee]. Repentant prostitute, forgiven and accepted by Christ.

maggoty.

the Magi [MAE-jih]. Singular and plural. Priestly caste of Persia and Media.

Maginot, Andre [MAH-zhee-noh; angl., MAZH-ih-noh, ahn-DRAE]. (1877–1932) French minister of war. The Maginot Line, "impregnable" fortifications on the Franco-German border to 1940.

Magna Charta (M.C.) [MAG-nuh KAHR-tuh]. The Great Charter of rights to which the English barons forced King John to affix his seal, 1215. *He referred to Magna Charta,* NOT *the Magna Charta.*

magna cum laude. (Lat.) With high honors.

Magnani, Anna [mahn-YAH-nee]. (1908–   ). Italian actress.

magnetite-spinellite.

magneto [mag-NEE-toh]. Magnetoelectric machine.

magnolia [mag-NOH-lih-uh, NOT —NOHL-yuh], although slight *y* sound is accepted.

magnum. Wine bottle of two champagne quarts, usually = 52 oz.

magnum opus. (Lat.) Great work.

Magyar [MAG-yahr]. Hungarian people and their language.

maharaja(h) [mah-HAH-RAH-juh]. Indian state sovereign. His wife is a maharani, or -nee [muh-hah-RAH-nee].

Mahendra Bir Kikram Shah Deua, Maharjadhiraja [mah-HAHR-jah-heer-AH-jah, mah-HEHN-drah]. (1920–1972) King of Nepal, 1955–1972.

mahjong [mah-jengg, mah-JAHNG]. Chinese game.

maid of honor. Unmarried attendant of the bride.

   MATRON OF HONOR. Married attendant of a bride.

   MAID OF HONOUR. (Brit.) attendant of the Queen in public appearance.

maidservant.

Mainbocher. (Bocher, Main Rousseau) [MA'N-bawsh-ae]. French couturier (1891–   ).

Maine. (abbr. Me.). Native, Mainer. Cap., Augusta.

maitre d'hotel [MEH-truh-doh-TEHL].

maize. Corn; Indian corn. *Cf.* corn.

   MAZE. Labyrinth.

Majesty, Your, His, Her, Their. SEE His Exellency. Title of address for a reigning sovereign. *Cf.* Nobility.

Maj. (abbr.) major.

Maj. Gen. (abbr.) major general.

Majorca [muh-JAWR-kuh]. Span., Mallorca [mah-YAWR-kah]. Largest of Balearic Islands in Mediteranean. Cap., Palma.

major-domo(s). major-leaguer, major key, major league.

major general. Pl., major generals.

Majority Leader Mansfield. the majority leader. (U.S. Congress).

majuscule [mah-JUHS-kyool]. A large letter; capital. *Cf.* minuscule.

make. P. and p.p., made.

makefast. (n.) —ready (printing), —shift, —up (n. and adj.), —weight (all one word); make-believe (n. and adj.).

makers-up. (pl.)

make inquiry concerning. *Ask about* is preferred.

making up.

mal-. Combining form meaning bad: *malediction, maladjustment.*

Malacca [mahl-LAHK-kah]. City in Malaya.

Malachi [MAL-eh-KIE]. Hebrew prophet.

Malaga [MAH-lah-gah]. City and province in Spain. Also, a white wine of that district.

Malagasy Republic [MAL-uh-GAS-ih]. Native, Malagasy. Independent, March, 1960. Cap., Tananarive. Formerly French Madagascar. Currency, Malagasy franc (FMG).

malaise [muh-LAEZ]. Indefinite body illness or discomfort.

malapropism [MAL-uh-prop-ihz'm]. Using the wrong word of approximately the right sound, from Mrs. Malaprop in Sheridan's "The Rivals."

Malawi [muh-LAH-wee]. Formerly Nyasaland. Independent since 1964. Natives, Malawian(s). Capital, Zomba. Currency, pound (M£), shilling, penny.

Malaya. Native, Malayan (s); (adj.) Malayan. Cap., Kuala Lumpur. Now part of Malaysia.

Malaysia. Federation of states established August 31, 1963, comprised of former Malaya, Singapore, Sarawak, and Sabah (North Borneo). Singapore seceded in 1965. Cap., Kuala Lumpur. Currency, dollar, cent.

Maldive Islands [maul-DEEV]. Sultanate cluster of 13 islands in the Indian Ocean. Natives, Maldivean(s). Capital, Male. Currency, Rupee (M Rs), lari.

malefactor [MAL-uh-fak-tawr]. Evildoer.

malevolent [muh-LEHV-uh-l'nt]. Wishing evil.

malfeasance. Performing an improper act.

MISFEASANCE. Performing a proper act improperly.

NONFEASANCE. Failure to perform a necessary act.

Mali [MAH-lee]. Native, Malian (s). Formerly French Senegal and the Sudanese Republic. Independent June, 1960. Situated west of Senegal. Cap., Bamako. Currency, Mali franc.

malinger [muh-LIHNG-ehr]. Pretend illness, generally to escape work or punishment. -er.

mall [mawl]. A shaded walk. BUT Pall Mall [pehl-mehl]. *Cf.* Pall Mall.

Malraux, André [mahl-ROH]. (1901–   ) Fr. propagandist, writer, politician.

Malta Is. Parliamentary state in the Mediterranean Sea. Native, Maltese. Cap., Volletta. Currency, Maltese pound (M£).

Malthus, Thomas Robert. (1766–1834) English economist.

Malthusian Theory [mal-THOO-zhan]. Population expands faster than food supply, tending to keep standard of living at subsistence level.

mameluke [MAM-eh-lyook]. In Mohammedan countries, a white or yellow slave.

mammon. Wealth, evil influence.

Man, Isle of. SEE Isle of Man.

manageable.

-man. Noun endings in combining forms or compound words usually use —men for pl. forms.

manana.

-mancy. Combining suffix meaning ability to foretell, divination, especially by means of a specified thing: *aeromancy* (from the air); *alectryomancy* (grains eaten by a cock); *astromancy* (stars); *austromancy* (south wind); *axinomancy* (ax on a post); *belomancy* (arrows); *bibliomancy* (books); *botanomancy* (plants); *capnomancy* (smoke of a burnt sacrifice); *cephalomancy* (head signs); *ceromancy* (wax droppings); *chiromancy* (palms); *chronomancy* (time); *cleromancy* (lots); *coscinomancy* (balanced sieve); *crithomancy* (crums at a sacrifice); *crystallomancy* (crystal ball); *dactyliomancy* (finger rings); *gastromancy* (ventriloquism); *geomancy* (lines or figures); *gyromancy* (walking in a circle); *halomancy* (salt); *hieromancy* (objects used in sacrifice); *hydromancy* (tides); *ichnomancy* (footprints); *ichthyomancy* (fish); *lithomancy* (stones); *molybdomancy* (lead); *myomancy* (mice); *necromancy* (word from the dead); *nomancy* (letters of the alphabet); *oenomancy* (wine); *oneinomancy* (dreams); *onomancy* (letters of a name); *onychomancy* (claws, nails); *ophiomancy* (serpents); *ornithomancy* (birds); *chiromancy*, *palmistry* (palms); *pedomancy* (soles); *pegomancy* (fountains); *psephomancy* (pebbles); *pyromancy* (fire); *rhabdomancy* (wands); *scapulimancy* (shoulder blade); *sideromancy* (burning straws); *stichomancy* (passages of a book); *theomancy* (divine oracles); *theriomancy* (wild animals).

man cook. Pl. men cooks.

mandamus [man-DAE-muhs]. Writ to enforce performance of a duty. Pl., -uses.

MANDATE. An authoratative command, especially to perform some act.

MANDATARY. (n.) The one to whom a mandate is given.

MANDATORY (n.) A mandatary. (adj.), obligatory.

mandible. Jaw, especially lower jaw.

man employee. Pl. men employees.

maneuver [ma-NOO-vuhr]. Adroit proceeding.

mango. Pl., -oes.

mangy [MAEN-jih]. Infected with mange; shabby.

Manhattan. Island and borough of New York City.

-mania. Excessive enthusiasm, craze, especially of psychotic proportions: *He has a mania for chocolate. andromania* (sex); *dipsomania* (alcoholism); *kleptomania* (morbid thievery); *megalomania* (grandiose delusions); *monomania* (in one area); *nymphomania* (sex); *pyromania* (setting fires); *schizomania* (and *schizophrenia*) (loss of sense of reality). *Cf.* obsession.

maniacal [ma-NIE-uh-kal]. Affected with madness.

manifesto. Pl., -oes; Brit., -os. A public declaration of policy and motives: *the Communist Manifesto.*

manikin. Anatomical model; a little man or dwarf.

MANNEQUIN. Dummy or female model for costumes.

manipulate. -lable.

Manitoba. (abbr. Man.) Province in Canada. Cap., Winnepeg.

man of war. Pl., men of war. (Webster, man-of-war, men-of-war.).

manly. Refers to admirable qualities in a man.

MALE. Refers to sex. Contrast with female.

MANNISH. Refers to qualities normal in a man, especially appearance, especially applied to a woman. *Cf.* masculine.

MASCULINE. Refers to male qualities.

man power. Preferred to manpower.

manslaughter. Unlawful but not willful killing. *Cf.* homicide.

mantel. Shelf.

MANTLE. Cloak.

mantelpiece. -shelf, -tree.

manuscript. (abbr., MS. or ms.; pl., MSS. or mss.).

many. Takes a plural verb; *many a* takes a singular verb. *Many are chosen. Many a man prefers his own home. Many men prefer to stay.*

manywise. (adv.)

Maori [MAH-oh-rih, MOU-rih, MAH-rih]. Polynesian aborigines of New Zealand. Pl., -ris.

Mao Tze-tung [MAH-oh dzuh-DOONG]. (1893–   ) Leader of Communist China, 1938–   .

map 3, A, II, etc. BUT cap. Map 2, when part of title: *Map 2. – Railroads of Middle Atlantic States.*

maquis [mah-KEE]. French underground in W.W.II. From Corsican outlaws.

Mar. (abbr.) March.

Maracaibo [mar-ah-KIE-boh]. Lake and channel in northwest Venezuela.

maraschino [mahr-a-SKEE-noh]. Pl. -os. Liqueur distilled from a bitter wild cherry.

Marat, Jean Paul [mah-RAH]. (1743–93) Swiss-French revolutionist.

marbleize.

marcescent. Withering without falling off. *marcescence.*

marchioness. Wife or widow of a marquis, or one of equal rank. ADDRESS: The Most Honourable, the Marchioness. SALUTATION: Madam. *Cf.* Nobility, Lord and Lady.

mare's-nest. Hoax; something which appears wonderful but which results in ridicule for the proposers.

mare's-tail. Cirrus cloud with a flowing tail.

margarine [MAHR-juhr-reen]. Butter substitute.

MARGARIN [MAHR-juh-rihn]. Chemical substance from lard and vegetable oils.

marginalia [mahr-jih-NAE-lih-uh]. (n. pl.) Marginal notes.

marijuana, marihuana [mah-rih-HWAH-nah]. Hemp; its dried leaves and flowers which are smoked in cigarettes.

Marine Corps. the corps; Marines (the corps); but marines (individuals); Marine Corps Organized Reserve, the Reserve; also a marine, a woman marine, the women marines (individuals).

Marine Officers. ADDRESS: U.S.M.C. (United States Marine Corps) should follow the branch of the service in which the person addressed is engaged. *Captain Howard T. Smith, Signal Corps, U.S.M.C.* SALUTATION: SEE Army Organization.

Mariner. NASA spacecraft designed to approach Venus.

marital. Pertains to marriage.

MARTIAL. Pertains to war.

Maritime Provinces (Canada). SEE Province.

markdown. (n. and adj.)

Market Grades and Classes. U.S. grade A; Western, Mixed, Malting Two-rowed (barley); Red Kidney, U.S. No. 2 Pea (beans); Prime, Choice, Good (meat); Yellow, White, Mixed, Dent (corn); Middling, Strict Good Ordinary, Strict Low Middling, Good Ordinary; (cotton); Timothy Light Clover Mixed, Upland Prairie (hay); White, Red, Mixed (oats); Yellow, Black, Mixed (soybeans), Flue-cured, Fire-cured, Cigar-wrapper (tobacco); Hard Red Spring, Red Durum, Durum, Hard Red Winter, White, Mixed, etc. (wheat); Grade 60's, or one-half blood (wool).

marketplace. (Webster, *market place*).

market quotations. Form: Pennsylvania Railroad, 29; gold is 107; wheat at 45; sugar, .03.

Marquand, John Phillips [mahr-KWAHND]. (1893–1960) American writer.

marquee. Tent or canopy leading to an entrance; a tent.

MARQUIS, MARQUESS [MAHR-kwihs; mahr-KEE]. Nobleman ranking above earl or count and below duke.

MARQUISE [mahr-KEEZ]. Wife of a marquis; marchioness.

Marquette [mahr-KEHT]. County in Michigan, Wisconsin.

Marquis. ADDRESS: The Most Honourable the Marquis of Donlan, or The Marquis of Donlan. SALUTATION: My Lord or Sir. *Cf.* Nobility, Lord and Lady.

marriageable.

marrowbone.

Marseillaise, La [mahr-s' – YAEZ]. French national anthem by Claude Joseph Rouget de Lisle in Marseilles.
MARSEILLES OR MARSEILLE [mahr-SAELZ or mahr-SAE; Fr., mahr-SAE-'y]. French port on Mediterranean Sea.
MARSEILLES [mahr-SAELZ]. Cotton fabric similar to pique.

marshal. An officer.
MARTIAL. Military.

Marshall plan. SEE plan.

Martin 202 and 404. Four-engine piston-propeller transport plane.

martini. Cocktail made of gin and vermouth.

marvel. -led, -ling, -lous. Brit., lled, -lling, -llous.

Mary. Capitalize any member of the Christian Trinity. *Savior, Logos.* BUT NOT derivatives. *messianic hope.*

Maryland. (abbr., Md.) Native, Marylander. Cap., Annapolis.

masculine. For appearance, qualities, companionship, nature, gender.
MALE. (adj.) Consisting of males. For choir, fertilization, sex, servant, voice. *Cf.* female, manly.

Mason-Dixon line. Surveyed by Charles Mason and Jeremiah Dixon in 1760, approximately south of Pennsylvania, through Southern New Jersey, to settle Maryland boundary dispute; later marked the division between free and slave states. *Cf.* line.

masonwork.

masque. Used for ball or entertainment. Otherwise, *mask.*

Mass. Is celebrated, said, or read; High Mass is sung; the Rosary is recited.

mass. Measure of inertia in a body.

Massachusetts. (abbr. Mass.) Native, Massachusettan. Cap., Boston.

massacre. -cring.

massage [muh-SAHZH].

masseur [muh-SEUR]. Male practitioner of massage. Female, masseuse [muh-SEUZ].

mass-minded. (adj.) mass-produce (v.).

mass nouns. SEE Collectives.

master. British for boss.

Mastroianni, Marcello [mass-troh-YAHN-ee]. Italian film producer, actor.

master at arms. Pl. masters – –. (Webster, *master-at-arms, masters-at-arms.*)

Masters, Mates & Pilots' Association.

Matawan [MAT-uh-wan]. Town in New Jersey.

maté [MAH-tae]. Paraguay tea.

material [muh-TEE-ree-ehl]. (n.) The substance of which something is made.
MATERIEL [muh-tee-ree-EHL]. (n.) Provisions and equipment: *An army requires both personnel and materiel.*

matin. Pl., matins. Morning prayers. Usually used in plural form with plural verb.

matinee [mat-ih-NAE]. An afternoon performance. *Matinee performance* is redundant.

matrimonial. Pertaining to marriage; the general theme.
NUPTIAL. Emphasis is on the marriage ceremony.
CONJUGAL. Connotes the persons joined together for life.
CONNUBIAL. Refers to the married state.
SPOUSAL. Emphasis is on the pledge and acceptance at the altar.
MATRONLY. Emphasis is on motherhood, homemaking.
MARITAL. Suggest that which pertains to the married state, especially to the husband.

matrix. Pl., matrices, matrixes.

MATS. (abbr.) Military Air Transport Service.

mature [ma-TYOOR].

maturity. Full development; also date fixed for payment of an obligation.

matutinal [muh-TYOO-tih-nal]. Of the morning. *Cf.* nocturnal.

matzo [MAHT-auh]. Pl., matzoth [MAHT-tzuhz]. Unleavened bread eaten by Jews during Passover.

maudlin [MAWD-lihn]. Over-sentimental.

Maugham, William Somerset [MAWM]. (1874–1966) English novelist and dramatist.

Maui Island. [MAH-oo-ee, MOU-ee]. Hawaiian island.

Mauna Loa [MOU-nah LOH-ah]. Volcano in Hawaiian Islands.

de Maupassant, Henri Renne Albert Guy [de MOH-puh-SAHNN, ahn-REE re-NAE ahl-BAIR-gee]. (1850–93) French short-story writer.

Mauritania [maw-reh-TAE-nih-uh]. Native, Mauritanian (s). Formerly French. Independent, November, 1960. Situated on the Atlantic Ocean. Cap., Nouakchott. Currency, CFAF franc.

Mauritius Is. [maw-RIHSH-ih-uhs]. British island colony in Indian Ocean.

Mauser, Peter Paul [MOU-zzuhr, PAE-tuhr PAWL]. (1834–82) German inventor of repeating rifle.

mausoleum [maw-soh-LEE-ehm]. Pl., -s or -lea.

mauve decade. 1891–1900.

maximum. Pl., -ma; occasionally, -s.

may. *May* is the accepted form; *can* refers to ability; SEE can. P., might. In asking permission, *may* is bolder than *might*. *Can* and *could* may also be used in asking permission, especially where ability is not in question. *Can I have that letter?*

Maya [MAH-yuh]. Mayan Indian of Central America.

Maypole. –tide, –time; Mayday (n.); May Day, May fly.

mayonnaise [mae-oh-NAES].

Mayor of a City. ADDRESS: The Honorable John V. Lindsay, Mayor of the City of New York, City Hall, New York, N.Y.; or The Mayor of the City of New York, City Hall, New York, N.Y. SALUTATION: Sir, My dear Sir, Dear Sir, My dear Mr. Mayor, My dear Mayor Lindsay, Dear Mayor Lindsay.

mayoralty [MAE-ehr-al-tih, MAIR-al-tih]. Office of a mayor.

mb. (abbr.) millibar.

M.b.m. (abbr.) thousand (feet) board measure.

M'Ba, Leon [m'BAH]. (1902–1967) Gabonaise politician, Prime Minister, 1958–1963; President, 1963–1967.

Mboya, Tom (Thomas Joseph) [em-BOI-uh]. (1930–1969). Kenya nationalist leader.

mc. (abbr.) megacycle.

M', Mc. Alphabetize as if spelled Mac.

M c f. (abbr.) thousand cubic feet.

Md. (abbr.) Maryland.

M.D. (abbr.) doctor of medicine.

MDAP. (abbr.) mutual defense assistance program.

M-day.

me. *Between you and me, him and me, her and me. He met my friends and me. She gave me the book.*

meager. Preferred to Brit. -re.

mealman. -time.

mealybug.

mealy-mouthed. Over cautious in voicing sentiments.

mean [meen]. (n.) The middle point: *The golden mean lies between two extremes.* SEE average.

MIEN [meen]. (n.) Demeanor, bearing: *His dejected mien suggested he had come upon misfortune.*

mean. P. and p.p., meant; meanness.

means. As income, takes a plural verb: *His means were very limited.*

meantime. Use as noun: *In the meantime.*
MEANWHILE. Use as noun or adverb: *Meanwhile they lived on her income.*

measles. Singular and plural: usually takes a singular verb.

measuredly [MEHZH-urd-lee].

MEASUREMENT. GPO style specifies that units of measurement, time and quantity are expressed in Arabic numbers, especially in reference to age, clock time, dates, decimals, degrees of latitude and longitude, distances, market quotations, mathematical expressions, money, percentages and proportions. N.Y. Times uses numbers for sports points, scores and time, as well as for all numbers of 10 and above. UCMS requires figures for numbers of more than three digits but excepts science writings or other writings where many numbers are used. GPO specifies; *3 feet by 1 foot 4 inches by 2 feet 2 inches; about 12 yards;* $1\frac{1}{4}$ *miles; 3 ems.* BUT *ten-penny nail, fourfold, sixfold; three-ply; six bales; two-story house; five votes; midthirties; between two and three hours* and indefinite expressions. *Cf.* Numbers, Dimensions. Without a numeral, a unit of measure is used in the possessive and takes an apostrophe: *It was a mile's hike.* But with a numeral, the compound form is used: *A ten-mile hike, a two-foot deep creek*, and the singular form of the unit is used. BUT when the measure does not modify a noun, the plural form is used: *It is two feet deep. Two feet are dug.*

measurement ton. SEE ton.

meatless.

medaled. -ing, ist.

medicate. -cable.

medicine [MEHD-ih-sihn; Brit., MEHD-sin].

Medici, Marie de' [MAE-dee-sees, MAH-ree de]. (1573–1642) Wife of Henry IV of France.

medieval. Preferred to mediaeval. [mee-dih-EE-val; Brit., mehd-ih-]. Pertains to the Middle Ages.

Medina [meh-DEE-nah]. City in Arabia.

mediocre [MEE-dih-oh-kehr, mee-dih-OH-kehr]. Ordinary.

Mediterranean.

medium. Pl., media, except spiritualists, -ums.

meet. P. and p.p., met.

meetinghouse.

mega-, meg-. Combining prefix meaning great; also, million: *megacephalic, megalith.*

megadeath. one million deaths.

megalo-, megal-. Combining form meaning large: *megalocardia, megalomaniac.*

megaton. Measure of explosion. Effect of one million tons of TNT.

megrim [MEE-grihm]. British for migraine. Also, especially plural, the blues.

mein Herr. German for *Sir.*

meiosis [mie-OH-sihs]. Pl. -oses. In rhetoric, use of understatement: *Some corn is grown in Iowa. The H-bomb—that's dynamite. Cf.* litotes. In biology, nuclear changes in cells with half the usual chromosomes present. *Cf.* mitosis.

Meir, Golda [mie-ehr]. (1898–   ) Russian-American Israeli politician, prime minister.

melange [mae-LANZH]. Mixture.

Melchior, Lauritz Lebrrecht Hommel [MEHL-kyohr, LAW-rihtz LIHB-rehkt HAHM-ehl]. (1890–1961) Danish-American opera singer.

melee [mae-LAE, MAE-lae, mehl-AE]. Confused battle.

mellifluous [mehl-LIHF-hoo-uhs]. Flowing sweetly as with honey.

melodic [mee-LAHD-ik]. Having melody: *A melodic tune. Cf.* hormonic.
MELODIOUS [mee-LOH-dih-uhs]. Agreeable in sound: *A melodious voice.*

melody. Agreeable series of notes.
HARMONY. Pleasing combination of notes in a chord.

Member. Capitalize if referring to Senator, Representative, Delegate, or Resident Commissioner of U.S. Congress; also Member at Large; Member of Parliament; BUT membership.

memento. NOT momento. Pl., -os.

memo. (abbr.) memorandum (colloq.).

memorabilia. (n. pl.) Souvenirs, old records worthy of remembrance.

memorandum. Pl. -dums, or -da for informal records.

menage [mae-NAZH]. A household; household management.

menagerie [mehn-azh-ehr-ee, mee-NAJ-ehr-ih, meh-NAZH-ehr-ih]. Collection of wild animals.

mendacity. Act of a liar.
MENDICITY. Act of a beggar.

Menderes, Adnan [MEHN-dae-rehs, AHD-nahn]. (1899–1961) Prime Minister of Turkey, 1950–1960.

menial. AVOID use for unskilled because of contemptuous connotation.

Menon, V.K. Krishna. SEE Krishna Menon.

mensuration [mehn-shehr-AE-sh'n]. Art of measuring.

-ment. Suffix meaning condition, action, state or quality, usually added to verbs to form nouns. From Lat. *-mentum*.

mental retardation. Classified in three steps: *idiot* (severely retarded) incapable of useful speech, with mental age index of 3; *imbecile* (middle grade) incapable of earning a living, with mental age 4 to 11; *moron* (high grade) incapable of learning beyond elementary school, mental age 12 to 14.

menu [MEHN-yoo]. Pl., -s.

Menuhin, Yehudi [mehn-OO-ihn, yeh-HOO-dee]. (1916–   ) American violinist.

Menzies, Robert Gordon. (1894–   ) Australian statesman, prime minister.

Mephistopheles [mehf-ih-TAHF-eh-leez]. Also Mephisto [mee-FIHS-toh]. Chief devil.

Mephistophelean [meh-fihs-toh-FEE-lee-an].

meq. (abbr.) milliequivalent.

mercantile [MEHR-kihn-tihl; Brit., -tiel]. Pertains to merchants and trade, or to mercan-.ilism.

mercantile agency. Credit information organization.

merchandise.

Merchant Marine Reserve. the Reserve. BUT U.S. merchant marine; the merchant marine.

Mercury. The smallest planet. Mercurian.

-mere. Combining form meaning part: *blastomere.*

meringue [meh-RANG]. Browned, stiffened, sweetened egg white used for pie covering.

merino. A fine-wooled sheep. Pl. -os.

meritorious. Deserving of honor.
MERETRICIOUS. Having the traits of a prostitute; deceitfully ornamental.

merit system. Employee relations program based on employment and advancement by competition, merit, or seniority, especially civil service.

Merrimack. NOT Merrimac. The 1863 ironclad warship.

mesa [MAE-sah]. Small, high plateau.

Mesabi Range [meh-SAH-bih]. Iron ore reserves in NE. Minn.

mesalliance [mae-zal-YANS, mae-ZAL-ih-ahns]. Misalliance; marriage with a social inferior. Cf. misalliance.

Mesdames [mae-DAM]. Plural of Mrs., madame. Cf. madam.

mesdemoiselles [maed-dehm-mwah-ZEHL]. Cf. mademoiselle, Miss, madame.

meso-. Combining form meaning intermediate, in the middle: *mesoderm, mesonasal.*

meson. also mesaton, mesotron. Sub-atomic particle with + or − electronic charge, short life, and mass between electron and proton, approx. 200 to 1000 times mass of an electron.

messieurs [MEHS-uhrz]. (abbr. Messrs.) Plural of mister, and of French monsieur.

Messina [meh-SEE-nah]. Seaport; Strait between Sicily and Italy.

mestizo. Pl. -os. Person of mixed blood, especially in Philippine Islands and Spanish America. *Cf.* Mexico.

metal. One of a class of substances (steel, gold, lead): *A metal bar.*
METTLE. Quality of disposition respecting honor and courage: *It tried his mettle.*

metaled. -ing, -ize.

metamorphosis [meht-uh-MAWR-foh-sihs]. Pl., -oses [-sees]. Change in form, structure, or substance.

mete. To apportion. meted, meting.

meteor. Celestial matter, heated by friction with the earth's atmosphere.

meteoroid. Matter which becomes a meteor when it enters the earth's atmosphere.

meteorite. Meteor which reaches the earth.

meteorology. Study of weather.
METROLOGY. Study of weights and measures.

meter. In rhetoric, systematic rhythm in verse divided into syllabic groups or feet. *Cf.* iambic pentameter.

meter. (abbr. m.) Unit of length = 1.093611 yd. = 3.280833 ft. = 39.37 in. Since January 1, 1963, "a length equal to 1,656,763.83 wavelengths in a vacuum of the radiation corresponding to the transition between the level 2 P 10 and 5 D 5 of the atom krypton 86," the wave-length of an orange light.

methodical. Preferred to methodic.

meticulous. Painstakingly careful of small details.

metonymy [mee-TAHN-ih-mih]. In rhetoric, substitution of a suggestive thing as substitute for the thing: *The Crown, the Book, the Carriage Trade. The pen is mightier than*

the sword. Those blue eyes walked into the office.

Metric Units. meter (m.) for length; gram (gm.) for weight or mass; liter (l.) for capacity.

Metric System Prefixes.
milli = 1/1000 = one thousandth
centi = 1/100 = one hundredth
deci = 1/10 = one tenth
deka = 10 = ten
hecto = 100 = one hundred
kilo = 1000 = one thousand

metric ton or millier. (abbr. t.) Unit of weight = 0.98421 long tons = 1.1023 short tons = 2204.622 lb. avoirdupois = 2,679.23 lb. troy = 1000 kms. *Cf.* ton.

metropolis. Pl. -lises or metropoles.

mettle. Figurative for courage, spirit. *The sad events tried his mettle. Cf.* metal.

Mev. (abbr.) million electron volts.

mews. Royal stables. Plural, but takes a singular verb.

Mexico. Native, Mexican(s); (adj.) Mexican. Cap., Mexico City (Ciudad de Mexico). Currency, peso (Mex. $), centavo. Written Mex. $257. In Mexico, citizens of mixed European and Indian ancestry are called mestizos [mehs-TEE-zohs]. In the U.S. Southwest, Mexicans are referred to as *Spanish, of Spanish extraction,* or *Spanish-speaking,* and *Mexican* has a derogatory connotation. Of U.S. resident Mexicans, *Mexican-American* is a more acceptable term. The term *Chicano* is accepted by some but others consider it degrading.

Meyner, Robert Baumle [MIE-nawr]. 1908-) Governor of New Jersey, 1957-1961.

mezzo-[MEHD-zoh]. Fem. mezza – -[MEHD-zah]. Combining form meaning middle, half, not extreme. *mezzosoprano, mezzotint.*

mf. (abbr.) millifarad.

MF. (abbr.) medium frequency.

mG. (abbr.) milligauss.

mg. (abbr.) milligram.

mho. (not an abbr.) Unit of conductance, reciprocal of ohm.

Miami [mie-AM-ih]. Resort city in Florida.

Michelangelo (Michelangniolo Buonarroti) [mie-kehl-AN-jehl-loh]. (1475–1564) Italian artist.

Michigan. (abbr. Mich.) Native, Michiganite. Nickname: *Wolverine.* Cap., Lansing.

Michiko Shoda (MEE-chee-koh]. (1935–   ) Wife of Crown Prince of Japan.

micro-. Combining form meaning small or millionth. *microscope, microvolt.* Opp., macro-, mega-.

μa. (abbr.) microampere.

microbe [MIE-krohb]. Minute organism.

μg. (abbr.) microgram.

μuf. (abbr.) micromicrofarad (one-millionth of a millionth part).

μu. (abbr.) micromicron (one-millionth of a micron).

μ micron symbol.   Unit of length=0.00003937 in. = 0.03937 mil = 0.001 mm.

μ². (abbr.) square micron.

μ³. (abbr.) cubic micron.

μsec. (abbr.) microsecond.

μv. (abbr.) microvolt.

μw. (abbr.) microwatt.

mid. Amid. (Webster, *'mid.*)

mid-. Combining form meaning middle; *mid-American, mid-April, mid-dish, mid-ice, mid-1958, mid-Pacific, mid-Victorian.*

midcontinent region.

Middle Atlantic States. New York, New Jersey, Pennsylvania, Maryland, Delaware (sometimes Washington, D.C.).

the Middle Ages. (c. 400–1400).

Middle East. Mideast; Mideastern; Middle Eastern (Asia); middle Europe; Middle West, Midsouth, Midwest (sections of United States); Middle Western States; Midwestern States; Midwesterner; BUT midwestern farmers, etc.

Middle West. U.S. area between Allegheny and Rocky Mountains, Illinois, Indiana, Michigan, Minnesota, Ohio, Wisconsin.

midnight. 12 p.m.

mien. SEE mean.

MiG. Soviet jet fighter plane. N.Y. Times, MIG. SEE Fighter Planes. MiG-23 or MIG-23.

mignon [mee-NYAWNN]. (Fr.) Delicate; graceful; petite.

migraine [MIE-graen]. British use megrim.

Mikoyan, Anastas Ivonovich [MEE-kaw-YAHN, or MEE-koh-yan, uh-nuh-STUHS ih-VAH-nuh-vyihch]. (1895–1969). Onetime Deputy Premier, U.S.S.R.

mil. (abbr.) military.

milage. Mileage is preferred.

mile(s). Not abbreviated. Statute mile. Unit of   length = 5280 ft. = 1760 yds. = 1.6093 km. = 0.868 U.S. nautical mile.

mile, nautical. Unit of length. (1) U.S. = 1.007 international nautical mile = 1.1515 statute mi. = 6080.20 ft. = 1.853248 km.; (2) Brit. = 6080 ft. = 1,8532 km.; (3) International Hydrographic Bureau mile = 0.999 U.S. nautical mile = 6076.10 ft. = 1.852 km.

mileage. Preferred to milage.

mil-foot.

miliary tuberculoses. TB caused by infection from another focus.

MILLIARY. Pertaining to 1000 or to the ancient Roman mile.

milieu [mee-LYUH]. Social environment.

Militia. Capitalize if part of name; 1st Regiment Ohio Militia, Indiana Militia, Naval Militia, Militia of Ohio, Organized Militia; the militia.

militiaman.

milkshed. Ohio, etc. (region).

mill. In U.S. currency, 0.1 cents or $0.001.

millenary. Pertains to a thousand.

MILLIARY. Pertaining to 1000 or to the ancient Roman mile.

MILLINERY. Hats.

millenium. Pl. —s or millennia. 1000 years, especially during Christ's reign. By extension, ultimate period of great happiness.

millimeter. (abbr. mm.) One thousandth meter. = 0.3937 inches.

mμ. (abbr.) millimicron.

Millet, Jean Francois [mee-LEH, angl., mih-LAE, FRAHN-swah]. (1814–75) French painter.

milliard. 1000 millions (Fr. and U.S.); in U.S., usually a *billion*.

millier. SEE metric ton.

milligauss. (abbr. mG).

milligram. (abbr. mg.) Unit of weight = 0.01543 grains = 0.001 gram.

milligram-. Combining form meaning a thousandth of a gram; *milligram-hour*.

milliliter. (abbr. ml.) Unit of (1) capacity = 0.27052 fluid dram = 16.231 minims = 0.001 1.; (2) volume = 0.06102 cu. in. = approx. 1 cm³.

millimeter. (abbr. m m.) Unit of length = 0.03937 in. = 0.001 meter.

millimicron. (abbr. mμ.) Unit of length = 0.001 micron. = 0.000 000 03937 in.

million. 1000 thousand. *Two million and a half* is preferred to *two and a half million. Ten million, a dozen million, a thousand million* BUT *a few millions, many millions, millions of dollars, he had millions* (of dollars).

millionaire.

milord [mih-LAWRD, mehl-AWR]. (from *my lord*). An English lord or important person (used on the Continent). ALSO *milady. Cf.* Lord and Lady.

Miltiades [mihl-TIE-ah-deez]. (540?–489 B.C.). Athenian general.

mime [miem].

mimeograph. Originally trade name (by A.B. Dick Co.) of stencil duplicating machine; now a generic term.

min. (abbr.) minute.

Mindanao [mihn-dah-NAH-oh]. Island in Philippines.

minatory. Preferred to minacious. Menacing.

mince. -ceable.

Mindzenty, H.E. Cardinal Jozef [meend-ZHEN-tee]. (1892–　) Primate of Hungary.

minestrone [mihn-ehs-TROH-nee]. Italian vegetable soup.

minesweeper.

miniature [MIHN-ee-uh-chuhr]. (n.) A small painting; a small copy; (adj.) on a small scale.

minim. A half note; anything very small.

minim. (U.S. min.). Unit of capacity (1) in U.S. = 1/60 fluid dram = 0.06161 ml. = 1/480 fluid oz. = 0.00376 cu. in. = 0.06161 m.; (2) Brit. = 0.96073 U.S. minim = 0.05919 ml. = approx. 1 drop.

minimize. Make the least (not less) of.

minimum. Pl. -s, -ma.

minion. A favorite or servile attendant. In printing, 7-point type.

minister. SEE clergyman.

Minister. (diplomatic), foreign. ADDRESS: His Excellency, the Rumanian Minister, the Rumanian Legation, Washington, D.C., or The Honorable George Macovescu, Minister of Rumania, The Rumanian Legation. SALUTATION: Your Excellency, Sir, Dear Mr. Minister, Dear Sir.

minister-designate. Pl., ministers designate.

Minister Plenipotentiary. Capitalize, the Minister; Minister Without Portfolio. *Cf.* foreign cabinets.

Minister (Protestant). ADDRESS; The Reverend J.J. Jones, D.D. or Rev. J.J. Jones. SALUTATION; Reverend Sir, My dear Dr. Jones, My dear Sir, Dear Dr. Jones, Dear Sir.

Minister (U.S.). ADDRESS; The Honorable John J. Adams, American Minister, Ottowa, Can. SALUTATION; Sir, My dear Mr. Minister, Dear Sir.

the Ministry. SEE foreign cabinets.

Minneapolis, Minn. SEE Saint Paul.

Minnesota. (abbr. Minn.) Native, Minnesotan. Cap., St. Paul. Nickname, *Gophers.*

minor-leaguer. minor key, minor league.

Minorca, Span., Menorca [mih-NAWR-kah]. Spanish islands of Balearic group in Mediterranean.

minority. Less than half the group.

Minority Leader Mansfield. BUT the minority leader (U.S. Congress).

minority of one. One person.

Mint. Philadelphia Mint; the mint.

Minuteman. U.S. ICBM, land-based strategic missile fired from hardened silos.

minuteman. minute book, minute band, minute mark.

minutemen (colonial).

minutia [mih-NYOO-shih-uh]. Trivial, precise detail. Pl. -iae.

Mirabeau, de, Comte Honore Victor Riqueti [duh MEE-rah-boh; angl., MIHR-ah-boh, kawnnt AWN-aw-rae gah-bree-EHL veek-TAWR REEK-tee]. (1749–91) French revolutionist orator.

mirabile dictu [mihr-RAB-ih-lee DIHK-too]. (Lat.) Wonderful to relate.

miracle play. Dramatization of a Bible portion.

Miro, Jan [mee-ROH]. (1893–   ) Spanish artist.

mirage [mih-RAHZH].

mirthmaking.

MIRV. (abbr.) Multiple intercontinental re-entry vehicle. A MIRVed warhead.

misalliance. [mihs-uhl-LIE-ans]. Pref. to mesalliance. Marriage to a social inferior.

miscegenation [miss-seh-jeh-NAE-shuhn]. Interbreeding of races.

miscellaneous.

miscellany [MIHS-sehl-ae-nee].

mischiefmaker. -making.

mischievous [MIHS-chihv-uhs].

miscible. Capable of being mixed. -ibility.

miscreant [MIHS-kree-ehnt]. Rascal.

misogynist [mih-SAHJ-ih-nihst]. Woman hater. MISOGYNY [mih-SAHJ-ihn-ih].

miss. Not an abbreviation. Pl., misses. *The Miss Browns.* BUT *The Misses Brown* (formal). *The Misses Brown and Smith. Miss Brown and Miss Smith. Miss Joan and Miss Cynthia Smith.* Do not use *Miss* as a form of address if the name is followed by an academic title. NOT *Miss Joan Smith, Ph.D.* British do not use *Miss* as a form of address. The word there has implications of youth and of a mild rebuke. AVOID use of *Miss* to call for someone's attention or to address a stranger. (*Madam* is preferred, except for addressing a very young person.) *Cf.* Mr., Ms.

missilemaker. -man, -work.

Mission. Capitalize if part of name; Gospel Mission, Mission 66, the mission; BUT diplomatic mission; military mission; Jones' mission.

Mississippi. (abbr. Miss.) Native, Mississippian. Cap., Jackson.

missive. (n.) A letter.

missile. Projectile.

Missouri (abbr. Mo.) Native, Missourian. Cap., Jefferson City.

Missouri-Kansas-Texas Railroad. the Katy.

misspell.

misstate.

mistake. P., mistook; p.p., mistaken. -nness.

mister. SEE Mr.

mistletoe [MIHS-l-tow]. Green shrub, emblem of Oklahoma, traditional for Christmas.

mistreat. Abuse. British prefer maltreat. BUT in U.S., maltreat is malpractice.

miter. Preferred to -re.

miter-lock. (v.) miter box.

mitigate. Moderate; meliorate. -gable, -tor.

mixblood. mixup (n.).

mizzenmast. mizzentopman.

ml. (abbr.) milliliter.

Mlle. (abbr.) mademoiselle.

mm. (abbr.) millimeter.

mm.[2] (abbr.) square millimeter. mm.[3] (abbr.) cubic millimeter.

Mme. (abbr.) madame.

Mmes. (abbr.) mesdames; plural of madame.

m.m.f. (abbr.) magnetomotive force.

mmfd. (abbr.) micromicrofarad.

mnemonic [nee-MAHN-ihk]. (adj.) Aiding memory.

Mo. (abbr.) Missouri.

mo. (abbr.) month.

Mobile [moh-BEEL]. City in Alabama.

mobile [MOH-bl, -beel]. Movable. Also, sculpture with movable parts capable of easy movement.

mobilization [moh-bihl-ihz-ae-shuhn].

moccasin.

Mocha [MOH-kuh]. Red Sea port in Yemen formerly noted for coffee shipments.

mocker-up.

model. -led, -ling. Brit. -lled, -lling. modeler.

modelmaker.

modern. -nness.

modicum [MAHD-ih-kuhm, NOT MOHD-]. A small quantity.
IOTA. Greek letter i; the smallest quantity.
MORSEL. A bite; mouthful.

Modigliani, Amedeo [moh-deel-YAHN-ee, ahm-ae-DAE-oh]. (1884–1920) Modern painter.

modiste [moh-DEEST]. (fem.) Dressmaker.

modus vivendi [MOH-duhs, vih-VEHN-dee]. (Lat.) A way of living. A temporary arrangement or accomodation.

Mogul [moh-GUHL, MOH-gul]. Of Mongolian race, especially of conquerors of India and their descendants.

mogul. A great personage.

Mohammedan. Pertaining to Mohammed or religion he founded. Moslems object to this term. SEE Moslem.

Mohave Indians [moh-HAHV-eh]. Mohave or Mojave Desert.

moiety [MOI-eh-tih]. One of two equal parts; a half.

moiré [mwohr, mohr]. (n.) Silk material with frosted or watered appearance.
MOIRE [MAW-rae; MOH-rae]. (adj.) Having a watered appearance.

MOL. (abbr.) Manned Orbiting Laboratory.

molasses. Takes a singular verb, except in some Western States.

mold. Preferred to mould.

molecule. SEE atom.

Moliere [mawl-YAIR]. (1622–73) Pseudonym of Jean Baptiste [BAH-teest] Poquelin [paw-KLANN]. French dramatist.

Mollet, Guy [MOH-lae, gee]. (1905–   ) French statesman; Prime Minister, 1956–57.

mollusk. (Brit. mollusc.)

molt. (Brit. moult.)

molten.

mol. wt. (abbr.) molecular weight.

moment. A short but indefinite period of time.
INSTANT. A point in time: *The instant the switch was turned the bomb exploded.*

momentarily. In or for a moment.
MOMENTLY. From moment to moment.
MOMENTARY. Lasting for a moment.
MOMENTOUS. Of great importance.

Mon. (abbr.) Monday.

Monaco [MAHN-ah-koh]. Native, Monegasque(s) or Monacan(s). Principality between France and Italy on the Mediterranean. 368 acres. Cap., Monaco. Currency, Fr. franc.

monad [MAH-nad, MOH-nad]. An indivisible unit, especially in philosophy.

monarchic [muh-NAHR-kihk]. Of a monarchy.

Monday [MUHN-dih]. (abbr. Mon.)

Mondrian, Pieter Cornelis [MAWN-dree-ahn, PEE-tuhr, kawr-NAE-lihs]. (1872–1944) Dutch modern painter.

Monet, Claude [maw-NEH, klohd]. (1840–1926) French painter.

money. *$2.75; $0.27; 14 cents; $2 per 100 pounds; 2¢ to 6¢* (no spaces); *£2 4s 6d; 2.5 francs; fr. 2.5;* Rs. 5,278,411 (Indian rupees); 85 yen; ¥190; T£127; $17 million; $1.7 million or $1,7000,000. BUT $750,000; $½ billion to $1½ billion. SEE individual countries for native currencies.

money market. The organization or machinery which deals in loans.

money rate. Interest rate for short-term loans.

money. monied (adj).
MONIES. Sums of money.

monger [MUHNG-guhr]. Trader; now often implies petty or discreditable dealing.

mongoose. Pl. -ooses.

monitory [MAHN-ih-tawr-ee]. Admonishing.

monogamy [muh-NAHG-uh-mee]. Marriage with one person at a time. -gamous; -gamist.

monogrammed. -ing.

monologue. Preferred to monolog. One person speaking or monopolizing a conversation. monologist [MAHN-ahl-oh-gihst].
SOLILOQUY. Speaking to oneself.

monopsony. Market condition with only one buyer. Similarly, duopsony, oligopsony.

monotonous. Implies sameness and boredom.
MONOTONIC. In one tone.

monseigneur. [MAWN-sae-yoor, -z]. Pl., -s. My lord. French title for church and court dignitaries. *Monseigneur the Archbishop.*

monsieur. (abbr. M.) pl., -s (abbr. mm or Messrs.) [meh-SYUH, -z]. French for Mr. or sir.

monsignor. [mawn-SEEN-ayawr]. Pl. -s or -ori. [mawn-see-NYOH-ree]. Pl., -i. Title of honor held by some prelates. ADDRESS: The Right (or Very Reverend) Monsignor Thomas Delaney. SALUTATION: Monsignor, Right Reverend and Dear Monsignor Delaney.
MONSIGNORE. Pl., -ori. Italian form.

montage [mahn-TAHJ]. Picture created by blending several others, or other materials.

Montana. (abbr. Mont.) Native, Montanan. Cap., Helena.

Monterrey. angl. *Monterey.* City in Mexico.

monthlong. (adj.) month-end (adj.).

Months. Abbreviate Jan., Feb., Aug., Sept., Oct., Nov., and Dec. in reports when followed by a numeral. Do not abbreviate March, April, May, June or July. (BUT Webster: *Mar.; Apr.; Je.* (June); *Jy.* (July).

Montserrat [mahnt-seh-RAHT]. British West Indies island.

Monument. Bunker Hill Monument, the monument; National Monument (SEE National); Washington Monument, the monument (District of Columbia).

mood. (or mode) In grammar, verb form which denotes style or manner: imperative, *Go.*; indicative, *I am going;* subjunctive, *If I go . . . Cf.* subjunctive.

moon. Lower case unless used with names of other celestial bodies.

Moonachie [moon-AHK-ee]. Town in New Jersey.

Moore-McCormack Lines.

moose. Pl. moose. U.S., British, elk or European elk.

moot. (adj.) Debatable. BUT a *moot court* is a mock court.

moonlight. Work at an extra job. moonlighter, moonlighting.

mopper-up. mopping-up (adj.).

moral. Pertaining to conduct of men as social beings, or a lesson to teach this.
MORALE. Mental condition.

Morales, Dr. Ramon Villeda [maw-RAE-lees, rih-YEH-dah]. (1908–   ) President of Honduras, 1957–1963.

morality play. Dramatized allegory; e.g., *Everyman.*

morals. SEE ethics.

morass [moh-RASS]. Marsh.

moratorium. Pl. -ia or -ums. Period of delay for payment.

more and more. Never follow by *than.* NOT: *The council required more and more taxes for school building than the community would pay.* BUT . . . *required more than they could pay.*

moreover.

mores [MOH-reez]. (n.) Social customs and manners.

more than one. Though plural in meaning, takes a singular verb: *More than one person is here.*

morgen. 2.1165 acres (U.S.A.).

Mormon. A member of the Church of Jesus Christ of Latter-day Saints, founded in 1830 by Joseph Smith. From *Book of Mormon,* believed to contain divine revelations.

Morocco. Native, Moroccan (s); (adj.) Moroccan. Cap., Rabat. Currency, dirham (DH).

Morpheus [MAWR-fee-uhs; more properly, MAWR-fyuhs]. Greek Mythology god of dreams.

morphology. In grammar, study of inflectional forms, their origin, development, and func-

tions; (biology) science of structural organic types.

Morris, Gouverneur [MAHR-rihs, guhv-uhr-neer]. (1752–1816) American statesman.

mortgagee. The lender.
MORTGAGER. [MAWR-gihj-uhr]. In law, -or. The person who pledges property.

mortgageholder. mortgage bond.

mortician [mawr-TIHSH-ehn]. Undertaker.
MORTUARY [MAWR-choo-air-ee]. Pertains to burial of the dead; place where dead bodies are kept.

mortise [MAWR-tihs]. Or mortice (n.). A cavity, or (v.) to cut a cavity: *fasten with tenon and mortise.*

MOS. (abbr.) military occupational specialty.

Moshoeshoe II [moh-schwae-shwae]. (1939–   ) King of Lesotho (1968–   ).

Moslem. Preferred to British, Muslim. Variations; Muslem, Muslim. Believer in the faith established by Mohammed.
MUSSELMAN. Orthodox believer in Islam.
ISLAM. The religion of the Moslems; lit., submission to the will of God. Also the whole body of Moslems. Moslems object to the term Mohammedan.
MOHAMMED, MUHAMMAD. (most nearly correct) Mohamet. SEE Mohammedan.

mosquito. Pl. -os, pref. to -oes.

most-favored-nation. (adj.)

motherhood. —land; mother-of-pearl; mother lode, mother ship.

mother-in-law. Pl. mothers-in-law.

Mother Superior of a Sisterhood. ADDRESS: Reverend Mother Superior, or Reverend Mother Sophie (followed by initials designating the order), or Reverend Mother Superior Louise (without the initials designating the order), or Mother Louise, Superior Convent of the Immaculate Conception. SALUTATION: Reverend Mother Louise, Dear Reverend Mother.

motif [moh-TEEF]. Theme or salient feature of a work.

motion pictures. Preferred to moving pictures. Movie(s) is colloquial. As a cultural influence, in U.S. use cinema. British, cinema for all uses.

Moulin Rouge [MOO-la'n ROO-ZH].

mountain [MOUN-tihn, —tehn].

mountainside. —top; mountain-high (adj.),

Mountain States. Colorado, Wyoming, North Dakota, South Dakota.

mountain time. mountain standard time. SEE time.

mousse [mooss]. A flavored frozen cream or gelatin dessert.

movable.

moviegoer. -land, -maker, -maker (All one word).

mow. P., mowed; p.p., mowed or mown; mowing.

Mozambique [moh-zam-BEEK]. Portuguese African overseas province on Indian Ocean. Native, Mozambique (seldom used). Cap., Lourenco Marques. Currency, escudo (Esc.).

Mozart, Wolfgang Amadeus [MOH-tsahrt, angl., MOH-zahrt, VOLF-gahng ah-mah-DAE-uhs]. (1756–91) Austrian composer.

m.p. (abbr.) melting point.

M.P. (abbr.) Member of Parliament.

MP. (abbr.) military police. N.Y. Times, M.P.

m.p.h. (abbr.) miles per hour.

Mr. (abbr.) mister. Pl. Messrs. (abbr.) messieurs. Title of address for a man. Use Mr., Mrs., and Miss for citizens of all countries which do not have titles which replace these terms: *Mr. Brown; Mr. John Brown; Messrs. Jones, Brown, and Smith.* Never use Mr. with a title, or with honorable, reverend, or esquire, or when an academic degree follows the name: *Rev. John Law or John Law, D.D.; Dr. Joseph Brown or Joseph Brown, M.D.; The Reverend Dr. John Smith, but John Smith, D.D.; Mr. Chairman; Mr. Secretary.*
    MESSRS. (abbr.) pl. of Mr.; *Messrs. Smith, Brown and Jones.* BUT NOT *Messrs. Smith, Brown and Jones Co.*

MRBM. (abbr.) Medium-range ballistic missile (100-to 5000-mile range).

Mrs. (abbr.) mistress. Pl. Mrs. (abbr.) *mesdames. Mrs. Smith and Mrs. Jones; Mesdames Smith and Jones. Referring to two women, Mesdames B. O. and A. R. Jones, or informal, the Mrs. Jones.* As a title of address for a married woman, *Mrs.* is always abbreviated. *Mrs.* may be used with reverend, honorable, or doctor: *The Reverend Mrs. Smith, the Honorable Mrs. Brown, or the Doctor Mrs. Jones.* (The last two are considered archaic.) In speaking to a married woman, *madam* may be used, but NOT as a substitute for *you.* NOT: *Has madam anything further to say. Cf.* madam, Ms.

MS. (abbr) motorship.

MS., ms. (abbr.) manuscript; MSS., mss., manuscripts.

M.S. (abbr.) master of science.

Ms. Feminist title representing non-committal designation for Miss or Mrs. Not widely accepted at present. AVOID use with married name, *Ms. John Smith* or *Mr. & Ms. John Smith.*

msec. (abbr.) millisecond. 1/1000 second.

Msgr. (abbr.) monsignor.

M. Sgt. (abbr.) master sergeant.

m.s.l. (abbr.) mean sea level.

m.s.t. (abbr.) mountain standard time.

MSTS. (abbr.) Military Sea Transportation Service.

mt. (abbr.) megaton; mountain.

m.t. (abbr.) mountain time.

muchly. Although correct, it is obsolete. Use *much.*

mucilage [MYOO-sihl-ihj].

muckrake (v.) -raker.

mucus. (n.) mucous (adj.).

muddlehead. -headed.

muezzin [myoo-EHZ-ihn]. Moslem prayer crier.

Mujibur Rahman, Sheik [SHAEK MOO-jihb-uhr rah-MAHN]. (Sheik is a title of affection.) (1921–   ) Second reference may be *Mujib* (N.Y. Times) or *Mr. Rahman*. Prime Minister of Bangladesh, 1972.

muleback. -man, -skinner; mule deer.

muleteer [myoo-leh-TEER]. Mule driver.

multiple-purpose. (adj.).

multiplication. double, triple, quadruple, quintuple, sextuple, septuple, octuple, nonuple, decuple.

Munchhausen, von, Baron Karl Friedrich Hieronymus [fawn MEUNK-hou-zehn, FREE-drihk, hee-ae-ROH-neu-muhs]. (1720–97) German soldier, hunter, hero of burlesque stories by Rudolf Erich Raspe, 1785.

Munich, W. Ger. [MYOO-nihk]. Munchen [mewn-kehn]. City in West Germany; capital of Bavaria.

Munoz Marin, Luis [MUHN-yohth mae-REEN]. (1898–   ) Governor of Puerto Rico, 1949–   . Mr. Munoz Marin, or Mr. Munoz.

Murat, Joachim [meu-RAH, zhoh-ah-KEEM]. (1767?–1815) French general.

mus. (abbr.) music.

Muscat [or Masqat] **and Oman** [MUHS-kat and OH-man]. Native, Omani(s) or Muscati(s). (adj.) Oman or Omani. Cap., Muscat (Masqat). Sultanate (1741–1970) and port on east cape of Arabian peninsular. Now independent. Currency, Gulf rupee (G Rs), naija paisa.

museum [myoo-ZEE-'m].

Museum. Capitalize with name; the museum; Army Medical Museum, the Medical Museum; Field Museum, National Museum; National Air Museum, the Air Museum.

Muses. Nine Greek goddesses of the arts and sciences: Calliope, Clio, Erato, Euterpe, Melpomene, Polymnia, Terpsichore, Thalia, Urania.

music Capitalize the title of an opera and place in quotation marks: "*Aida*." Capitalize characters, the titles of symphonies (but place nicknames in quotation marks), the

name of a movement: *the Scherzo,* BUT lower-case instrumentation which is added for explanation: *Sonata in F Major for piano.*

musicmaker. —making (GPO only), —room (GPO only); music-mad (adj.).

musical [MYOO-sih-kuhl]. (adj.) Of music.
MUSICALE [myoo-sih-KAL]. (n.) Program of music.

Muslim. SEE Mohammedan.

Muslims. Negro racist group seeking autonomous U.S. status.

muslin. A cotton cloth; in U.S., a coarse one; in India, a fine, thin one. Brit., calico.

Mussolini, Benito [moos-oh-LEE-nih, bae-NEE-toh]. (1883–1945) Il Duce [eel-DOO-chae]. Italian Fascist dictator, 1921–1945.

mustache [muhs-TASH, MUHS-tash]. Brit., moustache [moos-TASH].

mutual [MYOO-choo-uhl]. Shared equally and jointly by two or more for benefit of all.
RECIPROCAL. Returned in due measure by each of two sides.

mutual defense assistance program.

MV. (abbr.) motor vessel.

MVD. (abbr.) In U.S.S.R. the uniformed police of the Ministry of Public Law and Order, but from 1946 to 1953, the secret police of the Commissariat of Internal Affairs, replaced in 1953 by KGB. The secret police have been known as Cheka, for Chresvychainaya Kommissiya, 1917-1922; GPU, 1922–1934; OGPU, 1934; NKVD, 1934–1939; NKGB, 1940–1941; NKVD 1941-1946.

mya. (abbr.) myriare.

Mycenae [mie-SEE-nee]. Ancient city in southern Greece.

myopia [mie-OH-pee-uh]. Nearsightedness.

myriameter. Unit of length = 6.2137 miles = 10 km.

myrhh [muhr]. Fragrant, bitter-tasting resin of middle-Eastern shrub.

myth. Story concerning supernatural beings designed to explain a natural phenomena. mythology.

N

n. Usually silent after *m* in the same syllable: *autumn, solemn.* BUT the addition of a suffix will often cause the silent letter to be sounded. *autumnal, solemnity.*

-n. Words of one syllable ending in *n* preceded by a single vowel (but not a diphthong or vowel and *v*) double the *n* before a suffix beginning with a vowel: *Running, sinning,* BUT *darning, coining.*

Words of more than one syllable follow the same rule if the last syllable is accented: *beginning, unplanned,* BUT *womanish.*

N. (abbr.) normal: n., noun.

NAC. National Agency Check.

nacre, nacré. Mother of pearl and shellfish that yield it.

Nagasaki [nah-gah-SAH-kee]. Seaport in Japan.

Nagoya [nah-GOH-yah]. City in Japan.

Nagy, Imre [nawj, IHM-ruh]. (1896–1956) Hungarian premier, 1956.

naiad [NAE-ad, Brit., NIE-]. A water nymph.

nail. Unit of cloth length = $\frac{1}{16}$ yd. = 2.25 in. = $\frac{1}{4}$ span = 5.715 cm.

Nairobi [nie-ROH-bee]. Capital city of Kenya.

naïve or naive [nah-EEV]. Unsophisticated. naïvete [nah-eev-TAE].

name. namable.

Namibia. Governed by and called South West Africa by South Africa. Cap., Windhoek [vihnt-HOOK].

name plate. —sake; name-calling (adj.), name-dropping (adj.).

named for. Preferred to *named after.*

NAMES. In common usage, given names are written first, followed by a family name: *John Brown.* The first reference to a person should include the first name and initials, commonly used. BUT AVOID a single initial: *J. Doe.* Additional references should be to *Mr. Doe.*

Women in England and United States adopt the given and family names of husband, disregarding maiden name: *Mrs. John B. Doe* But in Scotland, women retain surname using husband's name for an alias. British Peers sign only given name with peerage designations; peeresses sign given names or initials with peerage designations *Cf.* Lady, Lord. Bishops sign initials followed by the name of the See.

ARAB NAMES are usually made up of Arab words and follow grammatical rules. Many incorporate *the* as *al.* The vowel may appear as *a, e,* or *u,* or not at all, and *l* may appear as *d, dh, n, r, s, sh, t, th,* or *z.* The article may be joined to any or both names, but *al* is usually hyphenated with the word following. Common names are: *Abdullah (Worshipper of God), Abdel (Worshipper of the Victorious One), Abdur (Worshipper of the Merciful One), Haj (Pilgrim).*

Most names have at least three or four parts, in this order; the given name, the father's and the grandfather's names, and sometimes a family name. Anglicized versions prefix Mr. to the last name for a second reference.

BURMESE NAMES are usually single words prefixed by a title such as U (something between *sir* and *uncle*) or Thaikin (*master*). In anglicized versions, the title is used in the first reference: *U Thant.* In second references, it is *Mr. Thant* or *Secretary-General Thant.* Where more than one name is given, all references include both names: *U Tin Maung, Mr. Tin Maung.* Women's names do not change at marriage.

CHINESE NAMES. Local family names appear first, but many Chinese adopt western style, at least for foreign use, putting their given names or initials first; K.C. Wu. Transliteration of Chinese words is based on the Wade-Giles system, but apostrophes are omitted. *Chiang Kai-shek, General Chiang; Sun Yat-sen, Mr. Sun.*

INDONESIAN NAMES often have only one name: *Sukarno, President Sukarno.* When there is no title, the name is written *Mr. Sukarno.*
For Western contacts, a first name may be adopted; e.g., *Achmed Sukarno.* In Bali, children are numbered.

KOREAN NAMES. Family names are written first in most Korean names. Use *Kim* in a second reference to *Kim Il Sung.* Unlike Chinese practice, the given names are not hyphenated. Some Koreans, like *Syngman Rhee,* use western style: *Rhee* is the family name.

SPANISH NAMES are usually made up of two surnames, father's family name and the mother's family name, often joined by a *y* (and). These are sometimes hyphenated. A second reference to *Jose Molina Valente* is usually Molina, NOT *Valente.* Some individuals prefer both the mother's and father's family names for a second reference.
A married woman usually adds to her own surname the name of her husband, connecting the two by the preposition *de,* but omitting the portion which refers to his mother's surname. *Cf.* Filing.

VIETNAMESE NAMES. Although family names appear first, use full names in second as well as in first references: *Ngo Dinh Diem,* NOT *Ngo or Diem. Cf.* Filing, Nobility.

Nansen, Fridtjof [NAHN-sehn, friht-yaw]. (1861–1930) Norwegian arctic explorer-statesman.

nape [NAEP].

napery [NAE-puhr-el].

naphtha [NAF-thah. NOT NAP-tha].

napkin. British use serviettes; napkins are diapers.

Napoleon Bonaparte. But Code Napoleon.

napoleon. The pastry.

naptime.

Narasimhan, Chakravarthi V. [na-RAHSH-ih-mah, chak-ruh-VAHR-thee]. (1915–   )

First assistant to Secretary-General. U.N., 1961–   . Under Secretary for General Assembly Affairs and chief of Cabinet.

narcissus. Pl., narci, ssuses or -cissi.

narcissism. [nahr-SIHS-ihzm]. -cissist or narcism, -cist.

narcosis [nahr-KOH-sihs]. Pl., -oses [-seez].

narrator [nar-RAE-tehr].

narrative [NAR-uh-tihv].

Narvik [NAHR-vihk]. Northern port in Norway.

NASA [NA-suh]. (abbr.) National Aeronautics and Space Administration.

nascent [NASS-ehnt; NAE-sehnt (or s'nt)]. Being born; coming into being.

Nashua [NASH-oo-uh]. Town in New Hampshire.

Nasser, Col. Gamal Abdel [NAH-saer, angl., NAS-SEHR, guh-MAHL-AHB-dihl]. (1918–1971) President of United Arab Republic, 1958–1971.

nasturtium [nuhss-TUHR-shuhm]. Herb with red and yellow flowers.

nation. In general lower-case when standing alone: *the nation.*

Nation. Capitalize when synonymn for United States; BUT nationwide; French nation, Balkan nations.

Nation (Indian). Greek Nation. Osage Nation; the nation.

National. Capitalize in conjunction with name; National Academy of Sciences (SEE Academy), and with State institutions; National Archives; National Capital (Washington), the Capital (Washington), the Capital; National Forest (SEE Forest); National Gallery of Art, the National Gallery, the gallery; National Grange, the Grange; National Guard, Ohio, Air National Guard, the National Guard, the guard, a guardsman, BUT a National Guardsman; National Institute (SEE Institute); National Legislature (SEE Legislature); National Monument, Muir, the national monument, the monument; National Museum (SEE Museum);

National Naval Medical Center (Bethesda, Md.); National Park, Yellowstone, Yellowstone Park, the national park, the park; National Treasury, the Treasury; National War College; National Woman's Party, the party; National Zoological Park (SEE Zoological).

national. Lower-case with agency, anthem, customs, spirit; British, Mexican; defense agencies; stockpile; water policy (SEE policy).

nationwide.

native. Born in a particular place. *Cf.* Union of South Africa.

native-born. (adj.)

nativity. [nae-TIHV-ih-tih]. Birth or the circumstances of birth.

Nativity. The birth of Christ.

NATO [NAE-toh]. (abbr.) North Atlantic Treaty Organization. N.Y. Times, nato.

naught, nought. A cipher, zero, nothing. Nought is customary in the mathematical sense, naught in other contexts: *Nought from six is six. He cares naught for money.* SEE aught.

nausea [NAW-shee-a, NAW-see-uh, NAWshuh]. Stomach sickness, e.g. seasickness: by extension, extreme disgust. Nauseated, of a person: *He was nauseated and nauseating.*
NAUSEOUS. Disgusting.

nautch [nawtch]. East Indian dance. *nautch girl.*

nautical mile. 1 minute of longitude at the equator = 6080 feet = 1.15 miles. *Cf.* mile.

Navaho, Navajo [NAV-uh-hoh]. Indian nation now in Arizona, Utah, New Mexico. Also a mountain in Utah.

Naval. Capitalize if part of name. Naval Academy (SEE Academy); Naval Base, Guam Naval Base, the naval base; Naval District; Naval Establishment (SEE Establishment); Naval Gun Factory, the gun factory, the factory; Naval Home (Philadelphia), the home; Naval Militia, the militia; Naval Observatory (SEE Observatory); Potomac River Naval Command (SEE Command); Naval Reserve, the Reserve, a reservist; Naval Reserve Force, the force; Naval Reserve Officer, a Reserve officer;

Naval Shipyard (if preceding or following name): Brooklyn Naval Shipyard; Naval Shipyard, Brooklyn. BUT the naval shipyard. Naval Station capitalize if preceding or following name): Key West Naval Station, Naval Station, Key West, the station; Volunteer Naval Reserve; Naval War College, the War College, the college.

Naval Officers. ADDRESS: Captain Horatio Blue. SALUTATION: SEE Officers.

navel orange.

Navy, American or foreign. Capitalize if part of name; capitalize standing alone only if referring to U.S. Navy. Admiral of the Navy, the admiral; Navy Battle Force, the Battle force, the force; Navy Establishment, the establishment; Navy Hospital Corps, hospital corpsman, the corps; Regular Navy; Navy regulation 56; Navy Scouting Force, the scouting force, the force; Navy Seabees (construction battalion), a Seabee; Navy 7th Task Force (SEE Forces).

Nazarene [naz-uh-REEN]. Christ.

Nazi [NAHT-see; NAT-see]. Member of National Socialist German Workers Party (Nationalsozialistische Deutsche Arbeiterpartei) led by Adolf Hitler 1921–1945; also adherents in other countries. Nazism.

N.B. (abbr.) New Brunswick, Canada.

n.b. (abbr.) nota bene. (Lat.) Note well.

NBS. (abbr.) National Bureau of Standards.

N.C. (abbr.) North Carolina.

N. Dak. (abbr.) North Dakota.

Ndola ['n-DOH-lah]. Site of conference in north Rhodesia resulting in death of Dag Hammarskjold.

NE. (abbr.) northeast. Also N.E.

nearby. Nearsighted, near-miss.

Near East. Until W.W. II, the Balkan States. Thereafter, countries bordering East Mediterranean Sea, the Middle East. *Cf.* Levant.

nearly. SEE almost.

neatline.

neat's-foot. (adj.)

Nebraska. (abbr. Neb.) Native Nebraskan. Nickname, *Huskers.* Cap., Lincoln.

Nebuchadnezzar [nehb-yuh-kuhd-NEHZ-uhr]. (605–502 B.C.) Chaldean king of Babylon.

nebula [NEHB-yoo-luh]. Pl. -lae. One of large class of cloudlike celestial structures. nebular [-lehr].

n.e.c. (abbr.) not elsewhere classified.

necessary [NEHS-eh-sehr-ih]. necessarily [Accent NEHS- or -SEHR-].

necessity for doing. NOT *to do.*

nectar. -ed, -rine, -ous.

nee, née. (fem.) né [nae]. (masc.) Born. *Mrs. Cynthia White, née Brown.* NOT *née Cynthia Brown.* (The given name is given after birth, not at birth.)

ne'er-do-well.

Nefertiti [NEH-fuhr-tee-tee]. Sometimes Nofretete. (N.Y. Metropolitan Museum of Art, *Nefretity.*) Queen of Egypt, 1379–1365 B.C., wife of Ak-henaton; noted for her beauty.

Nefos. New emerging forces. Opp. Oedfos (Old established forces).

NEGATIVES. Sometimes incorrectly assembled to say the opposite of what is meant, particularly in parallel clauses where the negative may or may not apply to the second clause. Incorrect usage: *None shall come but shall see that I am right. No person may enter unless he is a member, and (each member* omitted) *must pay his dues.* Cf. double negatives.

neglect, negligence. Both mean failure to attend to, but negligence generally connotes habitual neglect: *Neglect of duty is an offense punishable by court martial. The owner's negligence caused the building to deteriorate.*

negligee [nehg-lih-ZHAE, NEHG-].

negligible.

Negro. Pl. -oes. Negress. Negroid. Negrophile, -phobia. *Cf.* African. *Black* is preferred for American Negroes.

NEGRITO, NEGRILLO.

COLORED. Of a race other than white.

Nehru, Jawaharlal [NAE-roo, juh-WAH-hahr-lahl]. (1889–1964) 1st Prime Minister of India, 1947–1964.

neighbor. Brit. -our.

IN THE NEIGHBORHOOD OF ... Use *nearly* where appropriate.

Neiman-Marcus [NEEM-'n-MAHR-kuhs]. Dallas department store.

neither [NEE-thuhr, NIE-thur]. Usually refers to two, but may refer to more. Usually takes singular verb, but when plural is indicated in one part, verb agrees with closest subject: *Neither John nor Mary knows. Neither she nor they know. Neither* must be followed by *nor* (except when meaning *not yet*). Seldom: *neither, or.* Place neither before the word modified, excluding words from the parallel which apply to both subjects. NOT: *Who neither serves him nor his master. Cf.* either/or.

nelson. Wrestling hold, full nelson, three-quarters nelson, half nelson.

neo-classicism. Imitation of Greek and Roman arts.

neologism. In grammar, a new expression or new meaning of an old one.

Nepal [neh-PAWL]. Native Nepalese. Himalaya kingdom on northeast border of India. 5400 sq. mi. Cap., Katmandu. Currency rupee (Rs), pie, (pl., pice). *Cf.* Mahendra.

nephew [NEHF-yoo; Brit. NEHV-].

nepotism [NEHP-uht-ihsm]. Favoritism shown to relatives, especially in employment.

Nereid [NEE-reh-ihd]. Sea nymph, daughter of Nereus.

Nerva. Nuclear rocket engine.

nerve-racking. Preferred to nerve-wracking.

n.e.s. (abbr.) not elsewhere specified.

nescience [NEHSH-ih-ehns, NEHSH-ehns]. Ignorance.

nether. Lower, under: *Nether garments.*

Netherlands. Native, Netherlander(s), Dutchman, Hollander, (adj.), Netherland, Netherlandish. Cap., Amsterdam; seat of government, The Hague. Currency, guilder, florin (f), cent.

network. A chain of radio stations.

neurosis. Mental disorder. Pl. -oses [-seez].

Nevada [neh-VAD-ah or -VAH-duh]. (abbr., Nev.) Native, Nevadan. Cap., Carson City.

nevermore. —theless; never-ending (adj.).

New. Capitalize if part of name: New Willard.

New Brunswick. (abbr., N.B.) Province in Canada. Cap., Fredericton.

Newburgh, N.Y.

New Caledonia Is. [nyoo kal-eh-DOH-nyah]. French island near Australia. Cap., Noumea. Currency, C.F.A. franc.

the New Deal. Political-economic philosophy under Pres. F. D. Roosevelt. anti-New Deal.

New England States. Maine, New Hampshire, Vermont, Rhode Island, Connecticut, Massachusetts.

newfangled. This is an old, established word.

Newfoundland [noo-fuhnd-LAND]. (abbr. N. F. or N.Y. Times, Nfld.) Island and province in Canada. Native Newfoundlander(s); (adj.) Newfoundland. Cap., St. John's.

Newfoundland [nyoo-FOUND-land]. Breed of dog.

New Hampshire. (abbr. N.H.) Native, New Hampshirite. Cap., Concord.

New Jersey. (abbr. N.J.) Native, New Jerseyite. Cap., Trenton.

newly. (adj.) BUT new-baked bread, newmown hay. newlywed.

New Mexico (abbr. N.M. or N. Mex.) Native, New Mexican. Cap., Santa Fe.

New Orleans [noo-AWR-lee-anz]. City in Louisiana.

news. Singular and plural. Takes a singular verb.

newsboat. -boy, -caster, -dealer, -letter, -making, -man, -paper, -paperboy, -paperman, -paperwoman, -print, -reader, -reel, -room, -sheet, -stand, -teller, -worthy, -writer, -writing (all one word); news-greedy (adj.); news editor.

newspaper titles. Some include the name of the city in the title, but others do not. Follow the style set by the newspaper. *The New York Times, the Sun (Baltimore), The Times of London.*

newspaper work. newspaper worker.

New World.

New Year's Day.

New York. (abbr. N.Y.) Native, New Yorker. Cap., Albany. Residents of New York City, nicknamed *Knickerbockers.*

New Zealand. Native, New Zealander(s); (adj.) New Zealand. Cap., Wellington. Currency, pound (NZ£), shilling, penny, pence.

nexible. Can be knit together.

next of kin.

nexus. Pl.-es. Connection.

Ngo Dinh Diem [noh dihn zee-EHM]. (1901–1963) Vietnamese politician; Prime Minister, 1954–1955. President, 1956–1963. The Ngo family. Brothers: Ngo Dinh Can, once in control of central province; Archbishop Ngo Dinh Thuo of Hue [HWAE]: Ngo Dinh Luyen, Ambassador to Great Britain; Ngo Dinh Nhu, in charge of internal security. Acting first lady was Mrs. Nhu. The Diem regime.

N.H. (abbr.) New Hampshire.

niacin [NIE-a-sihn]. A B-vitamin; pellagra preventative.

Niagara [nie-AG-ruh]. Niagara Frontier.

"Nibelungenlied" [NEE-buh-luhng-uhn-leed]. 12th century epic of Attila and Burgundians. The Nibelungs are children of the mist in German mythology.

Nicaragua [nihk-uh-RAH-gwuh]. Native, Nicaraguan (s); (adj.) Nicaraguan. Cap., Managua. Currency, cardoba (C), centavo.

Nice [NEES]. Italian, Nizza. Resort seaport on the Mediterranean Riviera, France.

nice. Displaying close discrimination; subtle; fine. Also, pleasing; agreeable; well-mannered.

nicety [NIES-eh-tee]. A dainty feature, delicacy: *niceties of life.*

niche [nihtch].

nickelplate. (v.) nickel-plated (adj.), nickelplating (adj.).

Nicosia [nihk-oh-SEE-uh]. Capital city of Cyprus.

Niebuhr, Barthold Georg [NEE-boor, BAHR-tawlt gae-AWRK]. (1776–1831) German philologist-historian, statesman.

Niebuhr, Reinhold [NEE-boo'r, RIEN-hohlt]. (1892–1971) American (New York City) theologian, writer.

Niemoller, Martin, Rev. [NEE-muhl-uhr, MAHR-teen; angl., MAHR-tihn]. (1892–) German anti-Nazi Protestant minister.

Nietzsche, Friedrich Wilhelm [NEE-cheh, FREE-drihk VIHL-hehlm]. (1844–1900) German philosopher. Nietzscheism.

Niger [NIE-juh]. Formerly French. Independent, August, 1960. Situated north of Nigeria. Native, Nigerois s. & pl.). Cap., Niamey. Currency, CFAF, franc.

Nigeria [nie-JEER-ih-uh]. Native Nigerian(s). Formerly British. Independent, October, 1960. Cap., Lagos. Currency, Nigerian pound, shilling.

nigh, near. Comparative, nigher; superlative, nighest.

nihilism [NIE-uhl-ihzm]. Philosophical doctrine which denies any real ground of truth or moral principle.

Nijinsky, Waslaw [nih-ZHIHN-skee; Russ., nyih-ZHEEN-skih, VUHTS-lahf]. (1890–1950) Russian ballet dancer.

nimblebrained. -footed; nimble-fingered (adj.).

nimbus. Pl. -bi. Halo.

nimrod. Hunter.

nine. ninety, ninth, the nineties, ninefold, 9, IX, nineteen, ninetieth, ninety-one.

nine days' wonder.

ninepin. Pl., ninepins. The game ninepins, singular and plural, takes a singular verb. Cf. tenpins.

Nine Power Treaty. the treaty.

ninon. Sheer woven fabric of nylon, silk or rayon.

Nippon. -ese. Preferred by Japanese for Japan, -ese.

Nisei [nee-SAE]. American-born Japanese.

nite. Avoid this spelling.

niter. Preferred to Brit. -re. Native soda.

Nitze, Paul Henry [NIHT-see]. (1907–) U.S. Assistant Secretary of Defense for Internal Secrity, 1960–1963.

N.J. (abbr.) New Jersey.

Nkrumah, Kwame [n'KROO-mah, KWAH-mee]. (1909–1972) Prime Minister of Ghana, 1956–1966. Locally known as Osagyefo [oh-SAH-jee-foh] (Redeemer).

NKGB, NKVD. SEE MVD.

NLRB or N.L.R.B. (abbr.) National Labor Relations Board.

N. Mex. (abbr.) New Mexico.

No., Nos. (abbr.) number, numbers.

nobody. -how, -way (adj.), -where, -whit, -wise (all one word); no-account (n. and adj.), no-good (n. and adj.), no-hitter (n.), no-par (adj.), no-par-value (adj.), no-show (n. and adj.), no-thoroughfare (n.); no man's land.

Nobel prize [noh-BEHL]. Annual awards in literature, science, peacemaking, created by Alfred Bernhard Nobel, 1833–1896.

Nobility. In order of rank. Reigning sovereign (king and queen); member of the royal family (prince and princess); duke and duchess; marquis and marchioness; earl and countess; viscount and viscountess; baron and baroness; baronet; knight. Cf. Lord and Lady. Also: archbishops, bishops, abbots, priors.

noble. DO NOT use as an adv. NOT: *You did noble.*

noblesse oblige [noh-BLEHS oh-bleezh]. (Fr.) *Nobility constrains.* Rights entail responsibility.

nohow. Although some grammarians accept the term meaning *not in any way*, Webster calls it dialect. It is always incorrect in a double negative: *I wouldn't do .it nohow.*

noibn. (abbr.) Not otherwise indexed by name. Used in freight classification. Sometimes n.o.i.b.n.

noisemaker.

noisome. Poisonous; foul-smelling. NOT noisy.

nolle prosequi, nolle prosse [NAHL-ih PRAHS-ee-kwih]. (n. and v.) (Lat.) Being unwilling to prosecute further, as when prosecution of a criminal case is abandoned by a district attorney. nol-pros (v.), nol-prossed (adj.), nol-prossing (adj.).

nolo contendere. (Lat.) *I will not contest it.* A plea, in a criminal case which submits the defendant to conviction without admitting formal criminal guilt.

nomad [NOH-mad]. One of a tribe which wanders from place to place, especially for pasturing.

nom de plume [nahm-duh-PLOOM]. Pen name.
NOM DE GUERRE [nahm-duh-GAIR]. Name for a short period or single purpose.
PSEUDONYM. Assumed name; pen name.
ALIAS. Assumed name, esp. for concealment for questionable purpose.

nomenclature [NOH-mehn clae-choor]. System of naming.

nominative absolute or absolute. A clause resembling a participial phrase which modifies a whole sentence rather than any part. It is independent and does not dangle: *All things considered, he is a great man.*

nominative case. Used for subject of verbs. *Cf.* Case.

Nomura, Kichisaburo [noh-moo-rah, kee-chee-sah-buh-roh]. (1877–1967) Japanese admiral, diplomat.

non-. Prefix meaning not, un-, in-. non-civil-service. (adj.) non-European, non-pros (v.), non-tumor-bearing (adj.); non sequitur.

nonce. Time being; for one occasion.

nonce words. Coined words for temporary use: *Castrocize, cigargoyle.*

nonchalant [NAHN-shal-ahnt]. Unconcerned. —ance.

non compos mentis. (Lat.) *Not of sound mind.*

none. Meaning not one, takes a singular verb: *None of the candidates is qualified.*
NONE. Meaning *not any* may be treated as a plural: *None of the guests have arrived.*

nonentity [nahn-EHN-tuh-tee]. Person or thing of no account.
NON-ENTITY. Thing that does not exist. (Webster, *nonentity.*)

nonesuch. (Brit. nonsuch) Something unique; especially a paragon.

nonetheless. From the phrase *none the less.* (adv.) Nevertheless.

nonfeasance. SEE malfeasance.

nonfinite verb. A verb form that can only suggest action but cannot make a statement, e.g. gerunds, infinitives, and participles.

nongovernmental.

nonpareil [nahn-pah-REHL]. Unequalled. Also a printer's measure = 6 points or $\frac{1}{12}$th inch.

noplace. Of questionable use in U.S., but never used in Britain.

nonplus. (n.) State of quandary; (v.) -plussed, -plus (s) ing.

nonrestrictive modifier. A modifier not essential to the identification of the person or thing modified: *Lincoln, who loved all people, was a great president.* NOTE commas.

non sequitur [nahn-SEHK-wih-tuhr]. Inference which does not logically follow from the premise.

nonstatement. Declaration which says nothing but appears meaningful: *Life is just a bowl of cherries.*

noon. (abbr. 12 M.)

noonday. -light, -tide, -time.

no one. Preferred to nobody.

n.o.p. (abbr.) not otherwise provided (for).

no par value stock. Common stock which has no face value.

nor. And not. *Cf.* or; either, or; neither, nor.

Norodom, Sihanouk [nawr-ruh-duhm, SIH HAH-nook]. (1922–) Successor to throne, king 1940–41, and head of State in Cambodia, 1960–1970. (Family name is Norodom.)

north, northern. Comparative, more northern; superlative; northmost, northernmost. *Cf.* east.

North. North Atlantic, North Atlantic Pact (SEE Pact), North Atlantic States, North Atlantic Treaty (SEE Treaty), North Atlantic Treaty Organization (SEE Organization), North Equatorial Current (SEE Current), North Korea, North Pole, North Star (Polaris), the North (section of United States). BUT north Delaware; North Jersey, South Jersey are exceptions to the general rule.

North Carolina. (abbr. N.C.) Native North Carolinian. Nickname, *Tarheel.* Cap., Raleigh.

north-central region. etc.

North Dakota. (abbr. N.D.) Native North Dakotan. Cap., Bismarck.

northeast, northwest. British hyphenate. northeast-bound.

northerly. A direction; *northerly wind, most northerly city.* BUT *north side. Cf. easterly.*

northerner. BUT N.Y. Times, capitalize when used to designate a native or inhabitant of the northern part of the United States.

northern Ohio.

Northern States.

northward.

Northwest. (abbr. NW.) Section of United States.

Northwest Pacific. Northwest Territory.

Northwestern States. Idaho, Montana, Oregon, Washington.

Norway. (abbr. Norw.) Native, Norwegian(s); (adj.) Norwegian. Cap., Oslo. Currency, krone, pl. kroner (N Kr), ore (sing. and pl.).

n.o.s. (abbr.) not otherwise specified.

no sooner. Is followed by *than,* not *when: No sooner had he received a check than the creditors appeared.*

Nostradamus [nahs-trah-DAE-muhs]. (1503–66) French physician, astrologer.

nostrum [NAHS-truhm]. A quack cure.

not all, not everything. Preferred to *all is not, everything is not.*

noticeable.

not only ... but, but also. The first is always followed by one of the second. The portions of the sentence they introduce should be in structural balance: *She not only loved to read, but also loved to watch television.*

notorious. Ill-famed.

not un—. May be used to express a double negative situation, but is usually best avoided: *It is not unusual to find ...*

notwithstanding.

nougat [NOO-guht]. Candy made of nuts in sugar paste.

NOUNS. (common variety) These are just the names of places, persons, things, qualities. A proper noun is the name of a particular thing and is capitalized. Collective nouns refer to groups of things; concrete nouns, to specific things; abstract nouns, to general things. A verb must agree with the noun in number. A noun preceding a gerund should be in the possessive case; *in the event of Mary's leaving; the ship's hovering nearby.*

nouveau riche [noo-voh-REESH]. Newly rich (disparagingly). Pl. -veaux riches.

Nov. (abbr.) November.

Nova. NASA project for eight-stage rocket.

Nova Scotia. (abbr. N.S.) Province of Canada (with Cape Breton Island). Cap., Halifax.

Novgorod [NAHV-goh-rahd]. City in Russia on the Volkhov River.

novice. SEE amateur.

novitiate [NOH-vihsh-ih-aet]. Brit., noviciate.

now. In a special sense, may be used as an adjective: *The now generation.*

nowhere. NOT nowheres.

noxious [NAHK-shuhs]. Harmful.

nr. (abbr.) near.

NS. (abbr.) nuclear ship.

N.S. (abbr.) Nova Scotia.

NSC or N.S.C. (abbr.) National Security Council.

NSF or N.S.F. (abbr.) National Science Foundation.

n.s.p.f. (abbr.) not specifically provided for.

nth [EHNTH]. Mathematical symbol for an unspecified number: *the nth degree,* to an extreme. Italicize *n.*

nuance [NOO-anss]. Subtle difference in meaning.

nucleus [NOO-klee-uhs]. Pl. -lei [-klee-ie].

nugatory [NYOO-guh-toh-rih]. Worthless.

nuisance [NYOO-sans].

NUMBER. In grammar, the distinction between singular and plural. *Cf.* verbs.
(1) Sing. subjects take singular verbs; plural subjects, plural verbs; *I am here. They are here. I am many things. America is 50 states. The 50 sovereign states are America. He or she is coming. One or two are sick. She and he are coming. Everybody* (no one, each) *is here. All are here. The first ten of American parentage are here. Britain is one of those nations which are members.* BUT *Britain is only one of those nations which is a member. The flock of sheep is nearby. What men do is their own affair. What is there for children to do? There is heaps to do.*
(2) *Number* is itself singular BUT *A num-*

ber of people were sitting at the table. The number of books on the table is six.
(3) Subjects joined by *and* take a plural verb. Subjects joined by *or* or *nor* take a singular verb. Where a singular and a plural subject are joined by *or* or *nor,* the subject closest to the verb determines its number. It is best to place the plural subject closest to the verb. But where the subject is also the antecedent of a pronoun, reconstruct the sentence to avoid awkwardness: *He says that either the library or the three classrooms have cushioned seats.*
(4) Two indefinite pronouns joined by *and* remain singular in meaning: *anyone and everyone is here.*
(5) When a word is accepted as singular or plural in a sentence, the same number should be retained throughout the sentence and all verbs and pronouns must agree in number. NOT: *Because the nation bases its decisions on logic, we must express our voice in civic matters if a correct solution is to be found. Cf.* is, are; COLLECTIVES.

Numbers: *cardinals:* one, three, twenty; *ordinals: first, second, tenth; multiplicatives:* single, double; *arabic:* 1, 7, 100; Roman: I, V, X, C, L, D.

NUMBERS. The GPO and the N.Y. Times rule is, generally, that numbers *one* through *nine* are spelled out, numbers ten or above are written in figures. UCMS requires that numbers of less than three digits be written out in ordinary text but that figures be used in scientific and statisticals works with many numbers. Exceptions are made for percentages, decimals, dates, streets, telephone numbers, exact sums of money, numbers written with abbreviations, pages (except preliminary pages which are written in small Roman numerals). Additional exceptions specified by GPO and N.Y. Times are; age, clock time, degrees of latitude and longitude, distance, market quotations, mathematical expressions, and proportions. *Cf.* Measurement.
Use figures for numbers: (1) in groups of two or more numbers if any of the numbers is 10 or more; *I invited six boys and nine girls. She had 7 boys, 10 girls and 4 parents;* (2) For isolated numbers of 10 or more; (3) With units of measurement, *7 bushels;* (4) For serial numbers, *Book 2, Exhibit 7.* Colon preceding does not affect the use.
Spell out numbers; (5) At the beginning of a sentence: *Six dollars was the price;* BUT *Nine (9) dollars* NOT *($9) dollars;* (6) For serious and dignified texts: *the Thirteen*

Original States, the Eightieth Congress;
(7) For isolated units of time, money or measurement, if under 10: *seven years.* (8) For numbers less than 100 preceding a compound modifier containing a figure: *two ½-inch boards* BUT *200 1-inch boards;* (9) For indefinite expressions: *the seventies;* (10) For the words million and billion in large numbers, not tabulated: *$6 billion;* (11) For round numbers; *a thousand men.* (12) For fractions standing alone; *one-half.* UCMS also spells out numbers describing centuries, dynasties, chapters, decades, military bodies, political divisions and sessions of Congress. Numbers larger than 1000 are written: *one thousand nine hundred and seventy.*

Use Arabic numbers with abbreviations and for pages, chemical formulas, dates, decimals, degrees, dimensions, distances, fractions, market quotations, measurements, money, paces, temperature, time of day and years, weights, unit modifiers, except in formal invitations. Used as modifiers, numbers and units are hyphenated: *a 7-hour day.*

HIGHER NUMERATION. Follows two systems, one adopted by the U.S. and France, the other by Britain and Germany. In U.S., a billion is 1000 million, in Britain a million million. (Brit., 1000 million = 1 milliard). In U.S. a trillion is 1000 billion, in Britain a million billion. Thus, where the U.S. adds three zeros, Britain adds six for each unit. The number of zeros under U.S. and British systems respectively are indicated: million 6, 6; milliard, 9, 9; billion 9, 12; trillion 12, 18; quadrillion, 15, 24; quintillion 18, 30; sextillion 21, 36; septillion 24, 42; octillion 27, 48; nonilian 30, 54; decillion 33, 60; undecillion, 36, 66; duodecillion 39, 72; tredecillion 42, 78; quattuordecillion 45, 84; quindecillion 48, 90; sexdecillion 51, 96; septdecillion 54, 102; octdecillion 57, 108; novemdecillion 60, 114; vigintillion 63, 120. Place a comma after each group of three numbers in a text. BUT in Spanish and German a period is used; *1.423.612.* In India, a comma appears after each two zeros.

Capitalize numbers if spelled out as part of a name: *Charles the First, Committee of One Hundred, Fourteenth Census* (SEE Census). PLURALS: *twos, threes, sevens.* 2's, 7's, 42's. AGES: six years and three months; men between thirty and forty; a forty-one year old bridge. SEE also Ages, Time.

FRACTIONS. $\frac{1}{1000}$th, one-thousandth; $\frac{2}{3}$, two-

thirds; $\frac{2}{1000}$, two one-thousandths; $\frac{23}{30}$, twenty-three thirtieths; $\frac{21}{32}$, twenty-one thirty-seconds; $\frac{3}{4}$ inch, three-fourths of an inch. 0.9 ton. POSSESSIVES: 1 month's layoff, 1 week's pay, 2 hours' work, 3 weeks' vacation. ROMAN: SEE Roman Numbers.

SERIAL NUMBERS: Bulletin Number 72; document 27; pages 127–129; lines 2, 3, and 4; Genesis 39:20; 290 U.S. 325; the year 1925.

TIME: In general, use numerals. 3:00 p.m. or 3 a.m.; at 2:30 in the morning; at 2 o'clock; at half past three; 12 a.m. (noon); 12 p.m. (midnight); o'clock is not used with a.m. or p.m. Without a number, write a unit of time in the possessive, a day's journey. BUT with a unit, use the compound form; *a three-minute egg.* If the numeral is one or less than one, the possessive form may be used: *one-minute's wait, a half-hour's* wait. If the numeral is more than one, the form may be *ten-minutes wait, ten-minute's wait, or ten-minutes' wait.* With an intervening adjective, the singular form of the unit is preferred: *a two-year-old horse.* BUT a plural unit: *seven-days journey, a two-years old* may be used.

QUANTITY: Units usually take an *of* form; *a quart of wine.* In a compound, the singular form is used; *a twenty-gallon tank.* BUT in other constructions, the plural may be used, *four quarts of milk.* In weight measurements, the singular form is sometimes used, especially in Britain; *six ton of hay;* but the plural is preferred.

TITLES. Usually capitalized. Book 5; Book Five; BUT abstract B pages, article 3 provisions, class II railroad, grade A milk, point 4 program, ward D beds.

UNIT MODIFIERS: twenty-one, twenty-first, 6-footer, 24-inch ruler, 3-week vacation, 8-hour day, 10-minute delay, 20th-century progress, 3-to-1 ratio, 5-to-4 vote, .22 caliber cartridge, 2-cent-per-pound tax, four-in-hand tie, three-and-twenty, two-sided question, multimillion-dollar fund; BUT one hundred and twenty-one; 100-odd, foursome, threescore, foursquare, $20 million airfield, 2-inch diameter; 10-word telegram, 5-percent increase, 3-phase, 60-cycle, 115-volt, 2-glass jars; 5-gallon, 2-gallon, 1-quart cap; 2-inch, 1½-inch, ½-inch, ¼-inch. 2- or 3-em quads, NOT or 2 or 3-em quads; 2- to 3- and 4-ton trucks; 2- by 4-inch boards, but 2 to 6 inches wide; 2-, 10- and 16-foot boards; twofold or threefold, not two or threefold. eighties. NOT 'eighties. Use apostrophe only to avoid ambiguity. BUT '20's.

READ: 1500 as fifteen hundred, NOT one thousand five hundred.

SEE also figures, foot, one, three, four, eight, nine, ten, hundred, million, billion, trillion.

a number of –. Takes plural verb.

number. A term used in counting; the amount of units.

numeral. A word or figure, expressing a number.

FIGURE. A symbol expressing a number.

numskull. Webster, also *numbskull.*

Nun. ADDRESS: SEE Sister of a Religious Order.

nuncio [nuhn-shih-oh]. Pl. -os. Permanent, official representative of the pope.

nuptial [NUHP-shal]. SEE matrimony.

Nuri as-Said [noo-ree ah-sah-EED]. (1888–1958) Irani statesman, premier.

nutmeg. Tropical spice, a nut-like center is pear-sized mace. The pulp is also dried and used as spice.

N.Y. (abbr.) New York.

Nyasaland. SEE Federation of Rhodesia and Nyasaland.

Nyerere, Julius K.[nie-YEHR-ruh]. (1923–   ) Prime Minister of Tanzania, 1960–   .

O

-o ending. Becomes -oes in pl.: (1) usually when the word is most commonly used in the plural: *dominoes*; (2) for monosyllables: *noes*; (3) BUT not for rarely used plurals: *dos, dittos*; (4) nor for words where a vowel precedes -o, *intaglios*; (5) nor for foreign and strange words: *albinos*; (6) nor for curtailed words: *photos*; (7) nor for multi-syllable words: *archipelogos*; (8) nor for proper names; *Romeos*.

oaf. Pl. -s.

Oahu Is. [oh-AH-hoo]. Chief island of Hawaiian group.

oaken. Use oak.

O.A.S. (abbr.) Organization of American States, Formerly Pan American Union. Also, Organization de L'Armee Secrete, French Secret Army Organization.

OASI. (abbr.) old-age and survivors insurance (Social Security).

oasis. Pl. oases or oasises.

oath. Pl. -s. [ohthz as in clothes].

Obadiah [oh-bah-DIE-ah].

obbligato. pref. to obligato. A required accompaniment.

obdurate [AHB-deur-aet]. Hardened.

obeisance [oh-BAE-sehnts; —BEE-]. Homage, deference. Also, bow, curtsy.

obese [oh-BEES]. Fat. -sity.

obfuscate [AHB-fuhs-kaet]. (v.) Obscure.

obiter dictum [OHB-ih-tuhr DIHK-tuhm]. (Lat.) Pl. -dicta. Incidental opinion by a judge; by extension, an incidental observation.

object. *He objects to having to go.*

objective (accusative) case. In grammar, the case used to denote the receiver of the action of a verb as either the direct object: *I hit* the ball; the indirect object: *I gave* him the ball; as the object of a preposition: *I gave the ball to* him; as the subject of an infinitive: *I want him to have the* ball; as the subject of a participle; *Can you imagine* him *playing the piano*?

objet d'art [ahb-JAE dahr]. Pl., -objets. *Cf.* virtu.

obligated. refers to a legal obligation.

OBLIGED. Refers to a social favor: *He is obliged to you for your courtesy and obligated for the amount of the damage.*

obligatory [ahb-LIHG-uh-toh-ree].

oblique [oh-BLEEK]. Slanting, diagonal; (v.) bend aside.

obliterate [ahb-LIHT-ehr-aet]. Destroy, erase. —rable.

obloquy [AHB-loh-kwih]. Pl. —ies. Censorous speech: *described with obloquy.* Also, bad repute.

oboe [OH-boh]. Pl. —s. oboist.

obsequious [ahb-SEE-kwee-uhs]. Fawning. Opposite, officious.

obsequy. Pl., -quies [ahb-see-kwihz]. Used only in plural funeral rites.

observance. Carrying out a custom.

OBSERVATION. Noticing.

Observatory. Capitalize with name. Astrophysical Observatory, Naval Observatory, the Observatory.

obsession. Persistent mental concept, usually a delusion.

COMPLEX. System of desires and memories which exerts a strong influence on a person.

INCUBUS. A nightmare.

MANIA. Strong misconceptions and delusions which result in insanity. *Cf.* psychopathic.

obsolete. (abbr. obs.) No longer in use. *Cf.* antique.

OBSOLESCENT. Becoming obsolete.

obstacle to.

obstreperous [ahb-STREHP-uhr-uhs]. Aggressively noisy, disorderly.

obverse. Facing side. On a coin, *heads.* Opposite, reverse.

obviate. (v.) Anticipate and dispose of or prevent.

O'Casey, Sean [oh-KAE-sih, shawn]. (1884–1964) Irish dramatist.

occasion [oh-KAE-zhuhn]. occasionally.

the Occident [AHK-sih-d'nt]. The West. *Cf.* Orient, occidental.

occiput [AHK-sih-puht]. Back of the head.

occult [ahk-KUHLT]. Of magic, alchemy, etc.

occur. -rred, -rring, -rrence.

Ocean. Capitalize if part of name. Antarctic Ocean, Arctic Ocean, Atlantic Ocean, North Atlantic Ocean, Pacific Ocean, South Pacific Ocean, Southwest Pacific Ocean, etc. BUT; the ocean.

Oceania [oh-shee-AN-ih-ah]. Central and southern Pacific Islands, including Melanesia, Micronesia, Polynesia, Australia.

ocher. (Brit., -re.) Impure yellow iron ore; its color.

ochlocracy [ahk-LAHK-kruh-sih]. Mob rule. -crat. *Cf.* government, form.

Oct. (abbr.) October.

octagon. Regular eight-sided polygon. Area = (diameter of inscribed circle)^2 × .828.

octave [AHK-taev, also AHK-tihv]. Any group of eight.

octavo [ahk-TAE-voh]. (abbr. 8vo) Pl. -os. Book size $6\frac{1}{4}$ × 9 inches, 8 pages to a sheet.

octet (te). A group of eight. *Cf.* solo, duet, quartet.

octodecimo. (abbr. 18 mo.) Pl. -os. Book size 4 × $6\frac{1}{2}$ inches, from 18 leaves folded from sheet size.

octopus. Pl., octopuses is preferred to -podes.

oculist. An opthalmologist.

OCULARIST. Maker of artifical eyes.

OPTHALMOLOGIST. Physician who treats eye defects and diseases.

OPTOMETRIST. One who measures the range of vision and may prescribe eye glasses.

OPTICIAN. One who prepares eye glasses from a prescription.

OD. (abbr.) officer of the day.

o.d. (abbr.) olive drab.

odd. In the meaning of additional, write 1000-odd, 1000 and odd people. *1000-odd people are strange indeed.* twenty-odd, thirty-odd, etc. *Cf.* suffix.

odd-lot. Less than standard round lot. In securities round lot is usually 100 shares of stock or 10 bonds.

oddment. Part of a broken set. In printing, any portion of a book except the main portion.

Oder R. [OH-dawr]. River in Poland.

Odessa [oh-DEHS-ah]. Seaport on Black Sea, U.S.S.R. Also city in West Texas.

Odysseus [oh-DIHS-yuoos]. Ulysses. Greek hero of Trojan War.

"Odyssey" [AHD-ih-sih]. Homeric epic; not capitalized when meaning wanderings.

OECD. N.Y. Times, O.E.C.D. (abbr.) Organization for Economic Cooperation and Development.

Oedipus [EHD-ih-puhs]. Greek tragic hero who killed his father and married his mother.

OEDIPUS COMPLEX.

off. NOT *off of.*

-off. cut-off, play-off, take-off, etc.

offal [AW-fuhl]. Rubbish; garbage.

Off Broadway. *an Off Broadway play. Off Broadway produces some excellent works.*

offense. (Brit. -ce.)

offering. In business, a product, commodity, or security offered for public sale.

office [AW-fihs].

Office. Capitalize if referring to unit of government. Chicago Operations Office, the Operations Office; Executive Office, Foreign Office (SEE foreign cabinets); General Accounting Office, the Accounting Office; Government Printing Office, the Printing Office; New York regional office (including a branch, division, or section); the regional office; the Office of Alien Property; Office of Chief of Naval Operations; Office of Education, Office of Experiment Stations, Office of the Secretary (Defense).

officeholder. —seeker, —worker; office-seeking (adj.); office boy.

officer. Army officer, Marine officer, BUT naval and marine officers; Army, Navy, and Marine officers; Regular Army officer, Regular officer, a Regular Reserve officer; WAC officer, WAVE officer.

officer in charge.

OFFICERS. In the U.S. armed forces, in order of rank (and their insignia).

ARMY. general of the armies (5 stars); general (4 stars); lieutenant general (3 stars); major general (2 stars); brigadier general (1 star); colonel (eagle); lieutenant colonel (silver leaf); major (gold leaf); captain (2 silver bars); 1st lieutenant (silver bar); 2nd lieutenant (gold bar).
 Non-commissioned officers—platoon sergeant or sergeant first class (3 chevrons, 2 rockers); staff sergeant (3 chevrons, 1 rocker); sergeant (3 chevrons); corporal (2 chevrons); private 1st class (1 chevron); private; recruit.

NAVY. admiral of the fleet (5 stars); admiral (4 stars); vice-admiral (3 stars); rear-admiral (2 stars); in wartime only, commodore (1 star); captain (eagle); commander (silver leaf); lieutenant commander (gold leaf); lieutenant (2 silver

bars); lieutenant (jr. grade) (silver bar); ensign (gold bar); commissioned warrant officer (silver cord device).
 Non-commissioned warrant officer (gold cord device); master chief petty officer (3 chevrons, 2 rockers, 2 stars); senior chief petty officer (3 chevrons, 1 rocker, 2 stars); chief petty officer (3 chevrons, 1 rocker, 1 star); petty officer, 1st class (3 chevrons); petty officer 2nd class (2 chevrons); petty officer 3rd class (1 chevron); seaman, seaman apprentice, seaman recruit.

AIR FORCE. Commissioned officers follow style of the army.
 Non-commissioned officers—warrant officer (gold stripe with blue stops); chief master sergeant (6 chevrons, 2 rockers); master sergeant (6 chevrons); technical sergeant (5 chevrons); staff sergeant (4 chevrons); airman 1st class (3 chevrons); airman 2nd class (2 chevrons); airman 3rd class (1 chevron); airman, basic. *Cf.* Army.

offspring. Progeny. Although commonly used in the singular, offspring is usually plural.

often [AW-fn or AH-fn].

ofttime. Often.

ogive [OH-jiev]. A Gothic arch.

OGPU. (U.S.S.R.) SEE MVD.

ogre [OH-guhr]. A fairy-tale monster. (adj.) ogreish.

Oh! Capitalize an expression of surprise, grief.

oh-oh. Means "oops."

O. Henry. Pen name of William Sydney Porter (1862–1910). American short story writer.

Ohio. (abbr. O.) Native, Ohioan. Nickname, *Buckeye.* Cap., Columbus. AVOID abbreviation.

ohm. (Not an abbr.) Unit of electrical resistance = volts/amperes

Oise R. [WUHZ]. River in France; flows into Seine.

OIT or O.I.T. (abbr.) Office of International Trade.

OK. OK'd, OK'ing, OK's. Or O.K., etc. All right.

Okeechobee Lake [oh-ka-CHOH-bee]. Lake in south central Florida.

Okefinokee Swamp [ok-keh-fihn-NOH-kee]. Swamp in southeast Georgia, northeast Florida, area 660 square miles.

Okinawa Is. [oh-kih-NAH-wah]. Island in Ryukyu group south of Japan, site of W.W. II landing.

Oklahoma. (abbr. Okla.) Native Oklahoman. Cap., Oklahoma City.

Olav V. (1903–   ) King of Norway (1957–   ). Married Princess Martha of Sweden, 1929 (1901–1954).

old. -er, -est. But among members of a family, elder, eldest. Write; *A six-year-old girl. Cf.* Age.

Old Dominion. Virginia.

old-fashioned. old-fogyish.

Old Glory. The flag of the United States.

Old Guard. Members of the Old Guard. NOT: Old Guards.

Old Lady of Threadneedle Street. The Bank of England.

Old South.

Old World.

oleaginous [oh-lee-AJ-ih-nuhs]. Oily.

oleomargarine [oh-lee-oh-MAHR-jeh-reen]. Margarine, sometimes with additional butter substitutes.

olfactory. Connected with sense of smell.

oligarchy [AHL-ih-gahr-kee]. Government by a few.

oligopoly. Control of a market by a few.

olive-drab. (adj.) olive-skinned (adj.); olive oil.

Olympic games. Olympiad. Held every four years since 1896.

Olympus. -pia, -pic, -pian.

Oman. SEE Muscat and Oman.

Omar Khayyam [OH-mahr or OH-mehr kie-YAHM]. (c. 1123) Persian poet, astronomer, mathematician.

omega [oh-MEE-gah; Brit., -AH]. *O*, the last letter of the Greek alphabet.

omelet.

omit. -tting, omissible.

omni-. Combining form meaning all: *omnivorous, omnifarious.*

omnibus. Pl. -uses. Formerly used for bus; now a collection of works from a single source. (adj.) pertains to many things at once.

omniscient [ahm-NIHSH-'nt]. All knowing.

omnivore. Pl. -a. Animal which is both carnivorous and herbiverous.

Omsk [awmsk]. City in central Asian Russia.

on. In contact with the surface, especially upper surface; time when: *on March 15;* continued motion: *sail on, work on.*

onto. Preferred to *on to* (prep.). To a position on; upon. SEE above.

on-and-off. (n. and adj.), on-go (n.)

on the other hand. Indicates a reconciliation of fact: *It is not black now. On the other hand, it could be black tomorrow.*

> ON THE CONTRARY. Emphasizes the difference: *It is not black; on the contrary, it is white.*

once. twice, thrice.

once-over. (n.) once-run (adj.).

one. (pronoun) Used in three senses: (1) numerical: *One of us talks.* (2) as an average person: *One has to make the best of things.* (3) as an impersonal substitute for I: *He asked me for help; one knew better than to lend him money.* The last form of use should be avoided.

> ANYONE. any one, everyone, someone, no one, all take singular verbs.

one of. Follow by a plural noun and a plural verb. But the antecedent of a following pronoun is the plural noun: *One of the men who were here yesterday is sick.*

ONE OF MANY. May take a plural verb, if referring to persons in a plural concept: *One of every six doctors are specialists.*

Oneida [oh-NIE-duh]. Lake in New York State, from the Iroquois Indian tribe.

onerous [AHN-er-uhs].

oneself. Also one's self.

onetime. Means former: *A onetime governor.*

one-time. Means single occasion: *It was a one-time opportunity.*

on hand. Present, available.

TO HAND. Within reach. AVOID use as *received.* NOT: *Your letter to hand today.* . . .

onionpeel. -skin. (one word)

only. Placement in the sentence is an essential element in the meaning. COMPARE: *Only the lady came at noon yesterday: The only lady came. The lady came only at noon. The lady came at noon only yesterday.* When meaning can be misunderstood, place *only* before the word modified.

only one. Takes a singular verb: *Only one of the seven books was returned.*

onomatopoeia [ahn-ahm-aht-ah-PEE-ah]. -poetic. Formation of words from sounds, or use in imitation of sounds: *giggle, gobble, gabble; tintinnabulation of the bells; babble; cuckoo. "There come up the dull hum of the city, the tramp of countless people marching out of time, the rattle of carriages and the continuous keen jingle of tramway bells." And drowsy tinklings lull the distant folds.*

Onondaga [ahn-ahn-DAW-guh]. City in New York. From the Indian tribe.

Ontario. (abbr. Ont.) Province in Canada. Cap., Toronto.

on the occasion of. *When* is preferred.

on the street. British: *He lives in Regent Street.*

on to. She came on to the ship.

ONTO. She stumbled onto a solution. *Cf.* into, on.

onus [OH-nuhs]. Responsibility; burden; obligation.

onward. Preferred to -s. SEE backward.

oo-. Brit., oo- [oh-oh]. Combining form meaning egg: *oology, oosphere.*

opacity, opaqueness. Imperviousness to light; hence, figurative, obtuseness. Only the first form is suitable for figurative use.

Op. Atty. Gen. (abbr.) Opinions of the Attorney General.

op. cit. (abbr.) *opere citato* (Lat.) In the work cited.

open end. open house, open pit, open shop. BUT N.Y. Times, open-end, open-end fund, open-end mortgage.

opera bouffe [boof]. (Fr.) Light comic opera. Also opera bouffa [boo-fuh]. (Ital.)

OPERA-BOUFFE. (adj.) A parody of: *An opera-bouffe government.*

opera comique [kah-MEEK]. Distinguished from grand opera by spoken (usually farcical) lines between arias.

operagoer. -going; opera house.

operas. Capitalize principal words in title and place title in quotation marks.

Ophelia [oh-FEEL-yah]. Daughter of Polonius in Shakespeare's *Hamlet.*

opinion [oh-PIHN-yuhn].

ophthalmologist. SEE oculist.

opponent [oh-POH-nehnt].

opposite from. NOT *opposite than. Cf.* contrary, on the other hand.

Opposition. Capitalize when referring formally to a specific group opposing the party in power in a foreign country: *the Opposition proposal.*

oppress. -ssible, -ssor.

oppugn [oh-PYOON]. (v.) Controvert.

optative [AHP-tuh-tuhv]. In grammar, expressive of desire. *The optative mood.*

optimism. -ist, -istic.

opus [OH-puhs; Brit., AH-puhs]. Pl. opera. Work especially of music or literature.

opuscule. Pl.—s. A small or petty work.
OPUSCULUN. Pl. -ula. Minor work of music or literature.

or. (1) *He cannot walk or ride. He can neither walk nor ride.* BUT WRONG: *No person can trust them or* (use *nor*) *allow them credence.* (2) Where there are two negative alternatives, *or* is used to introduce the second if the negative (usually in the verb as part of the auxiliary) clearly applies to both alternatives. If, however, the first negative does not clearly carry over to the second alternative, either because the negative does not apply to both, or because the auxiliary is repeated without the negative, *nor* is used. *She never played or sang again* (the negative adverb *never* applies to both alternatives). *She cannot write or remember without pain* (the negative auxiliary *cannot* applies to both alternatives). *I will ask no more, nor will I go* (*no more* is the object of say, has no connection with the second alternative). *I will not write it myself, nor will I help him* (the auxiliary *will* is repeated without the negative). (3) Avoid unnecessary repetition after *or.* COMPARE: *He came without money or tickets* (he had neither). *He came without money or without tickets* (one was missing). (4) In a series: *I think he is either short or tall or in between. He never saw a man who was bigger or taller or fatter* (two *ors*). (5) In a series of alternatives, the verb is *always singular*: *A, B, C, or D is coming. Cf.* neither, nor.

-or. SEE -our.

oral [OH-rahl]. Spoken. *Cf.* verbal.
AURAL [AW-ral]. Heard.

orangeade. —peel, —wood; orange-colored (adj.), orange-red (adj.);

orange pekoe.

orangutan [oh-RANG-oo-tan]. Preferred to orang-outang [-tang].

orate. -ation, -ator, -atorical, -atory.

oratorio [awr-uh-TAWR-ee-oh]. In music, dramatic text, often from the Scriptures, set to music.

orchestra [AWR-kehs-truh]. orchestral [awr-KEHS-tral].

orchid [AWR-kihd].

order. *Called to order* is the expression used to open a meeting in U.S.; British use it as a rebuke for a violation of rules.

orderly room. Room for military personnel attending an officer.

Orderly Sgt. (abbr.) orderly sergeant.

ordinal numbers. *First, fifth.*
CARDINAL NUMBERS. *One, five. Cf.* Numbers

ordinance. A local law.
ORDNANCE. Military equipment.
ORDONNANCE. Arrangement in a work of art or literature.

ordinarily [AWR-dihn-ar-ih-lee].

Ord. Sgt. (abbr.) ordnance sergeant.

oread [AWR-ih-ad]. Mountain nymph.

Oregon [AWR-eh-guhn, NOT AHR-a-GAHN or OHR-]. (abbr. Oreg.; N.Y. Times Ore.). Native, Oregonian. Cap., Salem.

organdy. organdie. Stiff-finished muslin.

Organization. Capitalize if part of name; capitalize standing alone if referring to international unit; United Nations Educational, Scientific, and Cultural Organization (UNESCO); International Labor Organization; North Atlantic Treaty Organization; United Nations Organization.

Organized. Capitalize Marine Corps Organized Reserve, Marine Reserve, the Reserve; Organized Militia, Organized Naval Militia, the Naval Militia, BUT the militia; Organized Reserve Corps, the reserve.

orgy [AWR-jee]. Pl. orgies. Carousal; excessive indulgence.

the Orient [OH-ree-ehnt]. Preferred to *the East* to avoid confusion with U.S. eastern states. oriental.

orient. Preferred to *orientate* when used in the figurative sense of adjusting to new surroundings.

orientation [oh-ree-ehn-TAE-shuhn]. Adjustment to new circumstances; from "facing East."

Oriente Province [ohr-YEHN-tae]. In E. Cuba.

Oriental Province. Congo.

Orientale. Federal Republic of the Cameroon (southern half).

Orinoco R. [oh-rih-NOH-koh]. River in Venezuela, 1700 mi. long, flowing into Atlantic Ocean.

oriole [OH-rih-ohl]. Bright-colored bird.

Orion [oh-RIE-uhn]. Northern constellation; the hunter.

orison [AWR-ih-zuhn]. A prayer.

ormolu. Gold colored alloy of copper and zinc used for decoration in furniture and jewelry.

oro-. Combining form meaning mountain; also mouth: *orogeny* (process of mountain-making); *orotund* (sound made with round mouth).

Orphean [awr-FEE-an]. Pertains to Orpheus, Thracian poet and musician, whose music wrought an irresistible charm (Greek Mythology).

Orozco, Jose Clemente [oh-ROHS-koh, HOH-sae klae-MAEN-tae]. (1883–1931) Mexican painter, muralist.

ortho-. Combining form meaning straight, right: *orthography, orthogon.*

orthodontia [or-thuh-DAHN-shuh]. -tics. Branch of dentistry dealing with correction of irregularities. -dontist.

orthoepy [AWR-thoh-ehp-ih, awr-THOH-eh-pih]. The science of pronouncing words correctly.

orthography [awr-THAHG-ra-fih]. The science of writing and spelling words correctly.

orthopedia, orthopedic [awr-thoh-PEE-dihk]. Branch of medicine dealing with correction of deformities.

oscillate. -llable, -tor.

oscillograph [AH-sih-loh-graf]. Apparatus for recording electrical waves.

Osler, Sir William [OHS-luhr]. (1849–1919) Canadian physician.

ostensible. Avowed.

osteopath, -thist. Medical practitioner who applies theory that illness is due to mechanical defects, utilizing medicines, surgery, diet, psychotheraphy, etc. -thy [AHSS-tee-OP-uh-thee].

CHIROPRACTOR. Practitioner who uses system of curing disease by manipulating joints, especially of the spine.

ostracize. -zable. Banish from fellowship.

Oswiecim [awsh-VYEHN-tsehm]. Polish for Auschwitz [OUSH-vihts]. Town in Poland, site of German concentration camp, 1940–1945.

OTC. (abbr.) Organization for Trade Cooperation. N.Y. Times, O.T.C.

"Otello." Title of operas by Rossini (1815) and Verdi (1887).

"Othello, the Moor of Venice." Title of Shakespeare's play (1604).

other, others. *The spice here, as in the other* (or in others) *of her recipes, is essential. Others* takes a plural verb. *One horse and five others.* NOT: *One horse and the other five. Cf.* Comparison.

otherwise. —worldliness, —worldly; other world.

otiose [OH-shih-ohs]. Without purpose; indolent.

Ouagadougou, Upper Volta. [WAHG-uh-DOO-goo]. Capital city.

ought. (n.) Anything. Incorrect for *naught.*

ought. *Can and ought;* NOT *ought and can.* This verb has no infinitive or participle and may be used only as an auxiliary verb.

Ouija [WEE-juh]. Trademark of spiritualist reading board. (Fr. oui + Ger. ya.)

ounce. (abbr. oz.) (1) Unit of weight. In avoirdupois system = 437.5 grains = $\frac{1}{16}$ lb. = 28.35 grams = 0.91146 ounces troy weight.

(2) In troy and apothecaries' measure = 480 grains = $\frac{1}{12}$ lb. = 31.10 grams = 1.097143 ounces avoirdupois. (3) Unit of dry measure = 2.10002 cu. in. = $\frac{1}{16}$ dry pint. (4) In textile measurement, weight in ounces avoirdupois of 1 yard of 36 in. fabric. (5) In leather measurement, = $\frac{1}{64}$ in. thickness.

ounce, fluid. (abbr. fl. oz.) Unit of capacity; (1) U.S. = 1.041 Brit. fl. oz. = $\frac{1}{32}$ liquid qt. = $\frac{1}{16}$ liquid pt. = $\frac{1}{4}$ gill = 8 fl. drams = 480 minims = 29.5737 cm³. = 29.5729 ml.; (2) Brit. = 0.96073 U.S. fl. oz. = 1.734 cu. in. = 28.413 cm³. = 28.4122 ml. = app. volume of 1 oz. avp. water.

-our, -or. *our* is British usage for most U.S. *-or* spellings: *honor, honour.*

ours.

outcast. outlaw, etc.; out-and-out (adj.), out-loud (adj.), out-Machiavelli, etc., out-of-date (adj.), out-of-door(s) (adj.), out-of-state (adj.), out-of-the-way (adj.), out-to-out (adj.).

outermost. —wear; outer man.

out loud. Not to oneself. Use *aloud* for loudly, not in a whisper.

outré [OO-trae]. Bizarre: *An outré hat.*

outside. NOT *outside of.*

outstanding. Unpaid: *An outstanding note.* Also, stock in the hands of stockholders.

outward-bound. (adj.) outward-bounder. *Cf.* backward.

ovenbaked. —ware.

over. SEE below.

over-. Combining form meaning above, beyond, inverted; *overlook, overleap, overturn.*

overage. (surplus), overage (older) (n. and adj.), overall (all meanings); overalls (garment); over-the-counter (adj.).

-over. carryover, hangover, runover, turnover.

override. Trample down; also annul: *to override a veto.* A commission paid usually to supervisory sales personnel, above that paid to salesmen under them.

overly. Limited to few uses, especially speaking of virtues: *overly cautious, frank, deliberate, economical.*

overseas. (adv.) overseas (adj.). *He worked overseas. He had an overseas job.*

Ovid [AH-vihd]. (43 B.C.—17 A.D.) Roman poet.

ovum. Pl., ova. Egg or egg cell.

owing to. Preferred to *due to* when meaning *as a result of.*

owlhead. (bird) owl-eyed (adj.); owl car.

Owosso [oh-WAHSS-oh]. Town in Michigan.

ox. Pl., oxen.

oxblood. (color) oxcart, oxlike, ox team.

Oxonian. Native of Oxford, England. Of Oxford University.

oxymoron [ahk-see-MOH-rahn]. Pl., —s or —ra. In rhetoric, the use of two apparently contradictory terms in a single structure, from "wise foolishness." *An honorable thief.*

oyez [OH-yehz; also OH-yae, -yehs]. Hear ye!

oyster bed. —house, —man, -shell, -woman (all one word); oyster-white (adj.); oyster catcher (bird), oyster crab.

oz. (abbr.) ounce.

P

p. (abbr.) page; pp. (abbr.) pages.

p. (abbr.) past tense, especially in this text.

Pa. (abbr.) Pennsylvania.

PA. (abbr.) public-address system.

Paasikivi, Juho K. [PAE-sih-kih-vih, YUH-hun]. (1870–1956) Finnish businessman, President.

Paassen, Pierre van. [vahn-PAH-sehn, pyehr]. (1895–   ) Dutch-American writer.

Pac. (abbr.) Pacific Reporter; P. (2d), (abbr.), Pacific Reporter, second series.

pace [paes]. Unit of length: (1) common pace = 2.5, 3, or 3.3 ft.; (2) military double time = 3 ft.; (3) military quick time = 2.5 ft.

pacemaker. -making; pace-setting (adj.); pace setter.

Pacific. (Cf. Atlantic): Pacific Coast (or Slope) States; Pacific Northwest; Northwest Pacific; Pacific seaboard; Pacific slope; South Pacific; Pacific States; Pacific time, Pacific standard time (SEE time). BUT cispacific; transpacific.

pack horse. packsaddle; pack-laden (adj.); pack ice.

packinghouse. packing box.

packing list. Statement of contents inserted in a package. Cf. manifest.

Pact. Capitalize with name; lower-case standing alone: Atlantic Pact, Atlantic Defense Pact, Baghdad Pact, Four Power Pact, Kellogg Pact, North Atlantic Pact, North Atlantic Defense Pact; the pact.

padcloth. –lock, –stone, –tree; pad saw.

paddle wheel.

Paderewski, Ignace Jan [pah-de-REHF-skee; (angl., pad-eh-) ee-NJAHS yahn]. (1860–1941) Polish pianist, statesman.

padre [PAH-drih or drae]. Pl. —dres. Monk or priest, esp. in Italy, Spain or Portugal.

padrone [pad-ROH-nae]. Pl. -ni [nee]. Patron; master. In Italy, innkeeper; in U.S., Italian employment agent.

paean [PEE-an]. Hymn of praise or thanks.

page 2. Lower-case.

PAGINATION. Books are made up in the following order: (1) Frontispiece, facing title page; (2) False title (frontispiece, if any, on back); (3) Title page; (4) Back of title (listing publisher, copyright information, and frequently such useful bibliographic information as list of sponsors, note of editions and printings, etc); (5) Letter of transmittal (new odd page); (6) Foreword (an introductory note written as an endorsement by a person other than the author, on a new odd page; (7) Preface, by author, on a new odd page; (8) Contents, on a new odd page, immediately followed by list of illustrations and list of tables, as part of contents; (9) Text, which begins with page 1 (if half title is used, text begins with page 3); (10) Bibliography, on a new odd page ; (11) Appendix, on a new odd page; (12) Index, on a new odd page.

page-for-page. (adj.) page proof (printing).

PAGE NUMBERS. Always write in Arabic, except introductory material which is written in small roman numbers.

"Pagliacci" [pahl-YAT-chee]. Opera by Ruggiero Leoncavallo, 1892.

Pago Pago, Samoa. N.Y. Times, Pagopago. [PAN goh PAN goh, PON goh PON goh]. Capital city.

Pahlavi, Mohammed-Riza Shah. SEE Riza Shah Pahlavi.

Pahlavi, Pahlevi. Chief Persian language from third to ninth century.

pailful. Pl. -s.

painkiller.

painstaker. -taking, -worthy.

paintbox. -brush, -maker, -making, -mixer, -pot, -room, -work (all one word); paint-stained (adj.); paint filler.

paintings. Capitalize principle words in titles, and place titles in quotation marks.

pair. Two. Pl. *pairs* is preferred to pair: *Three pairs of socks.*
PARE. Cut off.
PEAR. The fruit.

pajamas [puh-JAH-mahs]. British. pyjamas [pih-JAH-mahs, pie-]. Even one set takes a plural verb: *My pajamas are green.*

Pakistan [pa-kih-STAN; pahk-ih-STAHN]. Native, Pakistani(s); (adj.) Pakistan or Pakistani. Cap., Karachi. Currency, rupee (PRs), anna, pice.

palanquin [pal-an-KEEN]. Enclosed litter on poles, used in India and China.

palaver [pa-LAV-uh or —LAHV—]. In Africa, a conference.

pale. palely, palish. Also, (n.) an enclosure: *beyond the pale.*

paleface. (n.); pale-blue (adj.), pale-cheeked (adj.), pale-faced (adj.), pale-looking (adj.), pale-reddish (adj.).

Palestine. Native, Palestinian(s); (adj.) Palestinian. Area of ancient Israel and Judah under British mandate 1923–48, since divided between Israel and Jordan. *Cf.* Israel.

palindrome. Word, phrase, etc. which is identical when read forwards or backwards: *madam, noon, Hannah;* (Lat.) *Ablat et alba* (secluded but poor); Or the first words ever heard, *"Madam, I'm Adam."*

palladium. Pl., -ia. A safeguard. From statue of Pallas Athena. Also, a soft metallic element similar to platinum, used as a gold alloy.

pallbearer.

pall-mall [pehl-mehl]. A game. Capitalize a street in London famous for its clubs. *Cf.* mall.

pallid. SEE livid.

palm. Unit of measure: either the length of a hand (7 to 10 in.) or its width (3 to 4 in.).

palmetto. Pl. -os. Variety of fan palm.

Palmetto State. South Carolina.

palpable. Easily apparent to the senses, particularly touch.

palsied [PAWL-zeed]. Paralyzed.

plausible. Reasonable at first view.

pan-. Combining form meaning every: *pan-Hellenic,* etc. *panacea.*

pan-broil. pan-ice.

Panagra. Pan American-Grace Airways.

Panama [PAN-uh-mah]. Native, Panamanian(s); (adj.) Panamanian. Cap., Panama City. Currency, balboa (B), centesimo.

Panama Canal. the canal.

pan-American. Pan American Union.

pander. (n. and v.) From Pandarus, who procured Cressida for Troilus.

panegyric [pan-nuh-JEER-ihk]. Formal eulogy.

panel. -led, -ling. Brit., -lled, -lling.

panelboard. panelwork; panel-lined (adj.).

Panel. Atomic Energy Labor-Management Relations Panel (federal), etc.; the Panel.

panful. Pl., fuls.

Panhandle of Texas. Texas Panhandle, the panhandle. A narrow strip of land.

panic. -icky, -icked.

panicproof. panic-stricken (adj.).

panoply [PAN-uh-plee]. Full suit of armor. Pl. —plies.

pantheism. SEE atheism.

Papeete [PAH-pae-AE-tae; angl., puh-PEE-tee]. Capital of Tahiti.

pantryman.

pants. In U.S., trousers; British colloquial for drawers or panties. Use plural verb.

paperback. (n.) board(s), —bound, —boy, —cutter, —hanger, —hanging, —maker, —mill, -shell (n. and adj.), -weight, -work (all one word); paper-shelled (adj.), paper-thin (adj.), paper-white (adj.); paper pulp.

papers. Woodrow Wilson papers, etc.; the papers. BUT white paper.

papier-maché [pap-PYAE-mahshAE; angl., PAE-per muh-SHAE].

papilla. Nipple. Pl.—ae.

paprika [pap-PREE-kuh]. From Hungarian *"Turkish papper."*

papyrus [pap-PIE-ruhs]. Pl. -ri.

par. Established or nominal value; common level.

par. (abbr.) paragraph.

paradigm [PAR-uh-dihm; PAR-uh-diem]. Model. In grammar, an example of complete conjugation or declension.

paradisiacal [par-uh-dihs-SIE-uh-kal]. Preferred to paradisiac. Heavenly.

paradox. In rhetoric, a statement seemingly absurd, which upon consideration makes sense. paradoxical, paradoxer, paradoxology.

paraffin [PAR-uh-fin]. Petroleum wax, used for sealing jars. In Britain, kerosene is called *paraffin oil.*

paragraph 4. Lower-case.

PARAGRAPHS. Used to break up a text into digestible thoughts. The appropriate length depends on the level of the reader, the type of material and formality. Technical material permits longer paragraphs.

Paraguay [PAR-ah-guie or -guae]. Native, Paraguayan(s); (adj.) Paraguayan. Cap.,

Asuncion. Currency, guarani, pl., guaranies (G), centavo.

parakeet.

parallel. -ed, -ing, -llelism.

parallelism. In rhetoric, a technique of placing ideas of equal importance in the same type of construction so as to emphasize their similarity... *"we cannot dedicate—we cannot consecrate—we cannot hallow this ground."*

parallelepiped, parallelepipedon [par-uh-lehl-ee-PIE-pehd, -PIHP-ee-dahn]. Geometric solid made up of six parallelograms, the opposite ones of which are equal, parallel and similar.

PARALLEL POSSESSIVE. A word standing parallel with a possessive should be in the possessive form: *His book, like his friend's, is lost.*

paralyze. (v.) Brit., -yse. (n.) paralysis. Pl. —ses.

paramount. Supreme. NEVER *most paramount.*

paranoia [par-uh-NOI-yuh]. Preferred to -noea. Severe mental illness, usually with delusions of persecution.

paraphernalia [par-uh-fehr-NAE-lih-uh, -NAEL-yuh]. Personal belongings.

paraplegia [par-uh-PLEE-jih-uh]. Paralysis of lower half of body. paraplegic.

parcel. -led, -ling; Brit., -lled, -lling.

parcel-plate. (v.) parcel carrier, parcel post.

parchment-covered. (adj.) parchment-making (adj.); parchment maker, parchment paper.

PARENTHESES. Used in pairs: (1) to enclose words not intended to be part of the sentence where confusion might arise from the use of other punctuation: *New York (population about 7,800,000) is the second largest city in the world. Jones (reading from his notes): Q (referring to the exhibit).* (2) To enclose a clause that takes a tangent thought: *They spoke in a language (if you could call it a language) that only their friends understood.* (3) To enclose an explanation not part of the statement: *The Springfield (Mass.) census showed a population increase.* (4) To enclose numbers or symbols designating items in a series: (*I*), (*B*), *etc.* (5) To enclose figures confirming numbers given in words, when the double form is used: *Delivery to be made in sixty (60) days from this date.*

A parenthetical statement within a sentence takes neither an initial capital nor a final period, even though it is a complete statement. Question marks and exclamation points, however, may be used if the statement calls for them: *His home (he lived there for about ten years) is next to the store. His store (did you know he had one?) is ... His store (he has a wonderful location!) is at ...* When the parenthetical statement is at the end of the sentence, the same rule applies. The closing period of the main sentence goes outside the parenthesis: *His home is next to the bank (he uses another bank, though) ... to the bank (isn't he foresighted?) ... to the bank (he has a wonderful location!).* A period goes inside the parenthesis only when the parenthetical statement is an independent sentence not standing with another. Then it also takes an initial capital.

Parenthetical expressions within parenthetical expressions are placed in brackets. [ ].

Parenthetical material exceeding one paragraph is written with an opening parenthesis at the beginning of each paragraph and a closing parenthesis at the end of the last paragraph.

parenthesis [pah-REHN-thee-sihs]. Pl. -ses [-seez]. British call them brackets. SEE PARENTHESES.

parenthetic expression. Parenthetical style of writing, parenthetically speaking.

paresis [pae-REE-sihs]. Partial paralysis.

par excellence [pahr EHK-suh-lahnss]. (Fr.) Pre-eminent.

parfait [pahr-FAE]. A frozen whipped cream dessert.

pariah [pah-RIE-uh; Brit., PAH-rih-uh]. An outcast; from India's lowest caste.

pari-passu. (Lat.) By equal steps. Progressing together with equal standing: *creditors pari-passu.*

parish. Area served and field of activities of a local church. British, a subdivision of a county. In Louisiana, a county. Caddo Parish; BUT parish of Caddo (Louisiana civil division); the parish.

parity. Equality of price between two markets.

Park. Fairmount Park; the park. *Cf.* National.

park. British use also for a private animal preserve or pasture.

parkway. park forest.

Parkway. George Washington Memorial Parkway, the memorial parkway; the parkway.

Parliament, Houses of. the Parliament.

parliament [PAHR-lih-m'nt].

Parliamentarian. (U.S. Senate or House).

parlor. Brit., -our.

parlormaid. parlor car.

Parmesan cheese [PAHR-mehz-an]. A hard, sweet, pressed Italian cheese.

parse. (v.) In grammar, analyze a sentence into its elements.

part. Less than the whole.
PORTION. A specific part.
SHARE. A receiver's portion.
PROPORTION. The ratio to the whole.
PERCENTAGE. The fraction of the whole in terms of hundredths.

partial. Affecting a part only: *A partial eclipse.* Opposite, complete or total.
PARTLY. In some measure. Opposite, wholly.

part-finished. (adj.) part-Japanese, part-time (adj.), part-timer; part owner, part way.

part 2, A, II. BUT capitalize Part 2, when part of title: *Part 2: Iron and Steel Industry.*

parti-. Combining form meaning divided: *particolored, partitive.*

partially. Has two meanings, in part and showing partiality. Avoid use which may be ambiguous. NOT: *The debate was partially documented.*

partible.

PARTICIPLE. Verbal adjective, also used to form verbal phrases. In English, the present or active participle is formed by adding -ing to the simple form of the verb: *write, writing;* the past participle is usually formed by adding -ed or -en to the simple form of the verb: *written.* Both participles are used to create compound verbs. The perfect form has the auxiliary *have: having written.*

The present participle refers to an action in progress. *Cf.* Tenses. The past participle is used with the auxiliary *have* in making completed tenses past, present or future. *Cf.* Verbals.

Participles may be used as adjectives: *shouting runners.* Participial phrases contain a participle and are used as adjectives. *The cakes, baked on Tuesday, were still fresh.*

PARTICIPLE MODIFIERS of a single word are often used in newspaper writing but should otherwise be avoided: *Divorced, she is the mother of three children.*

participating preferred stock. SEE stock.

particular. SEE special.

partisan [PAHR-tih-san]. A strong supporter of a faction; a guerilla fighter.

PARTS OF SPEECH. Words are classified by their function in a sentence as noun, pronoun, verb, adjective, adverb, preposition, conjunction, or interjection. SEE each part of speech individually.

party. Avoid use for *person,* except in legal forms.

partymaking. party line, party wall.

parvenu [PAHR-vee-nyoo]. Newly rich or powerful; often used disparagingly; an upstart.

pasquinade [pas-kwih-NAED]. A lampoon. Item anonymously written on a public place; graffitti; e.g., *Kilroy was here.*

pass. P. and p.p., -ed. But adj., past; passable.

Pass. Brenner Pass, Capitalize if part of name: the pass.

passageway.

Passaic [pa-SAE-ihk]. City in New Jersey

passback. (n.) -book, -key, -man, -out (n. and adj.), -over, -port, -way, -word (all one word).

passé [pa-SAE, PAS-ae]. Antiquated; past prime.

passenger-mile. Measure of railroad traffic—1 passenger carried 1 mile. Pl. passenger miles. Sum of distance traveled by each passenger on a carrier.

passe partout [pahs-pahr-TOO]. (Fr.) Picture frame or mat held together by gummed paper. In French, a pass everywhere; hence, a master key.

passer-by. Pl. passers-by.

passible. Learned, especially in theology; susceptible to feeling or suffering; sensitive.
PASSABLE. Able to pass.

passim [PAS-ihm]. (Lat.) (adj.) Here and there. Usually italicized.

Passion. (cap.) Refers to the suffering of Christ.

passion-driven. (adj.) passion-filled (adj.); Passion play.

past. Time gone by.
PASSED. Moved along.

pasteboard. -pot, -up (n. and adj.) (all one word).

pastel [pas-TEHL, Brit., PASS-tehl]. Pale color.

Pasternak, Boris Leonidovich [PAHS-tyirh-nahk]. (1890–1960) Russian writer, Nobel prize winner.

Pasteur, Louis [pahs-TEUR]. (1822–95) French chemist, immunologist.

pasteurize [PAS-tuhr-iez]. -ization.

past history is a tautology.

pastiche [pas-TEESH]. Literary or musical medley.

pastime [PAS-tiem]. Diversion.

past master.

pastor. Clergyman in charge of a church. British, only the Protestant churches. Refers especially to care of the personal problems of the congregation (pastoral duties); e.g., visiting the sick, comforting the bereaved.

pastoral [PAS-toh-ral].Relating to the care of souls. -ist, -ism. Also, rural. Music, pastorale.

pastryman. pastry cook.

pastureland.

patchwork. patch test.

paté [pah-TAE]. Pie; meat paste; *paté de foie gras,* paste of goose liver and truffles.

patent [PAT-ehnt. Brit. pae-]. Evident. SEE Letters.

patent-in-fee.

paterfamilias [PAE-tuh-fam-IHL-ih-as]. (Lat.) Head of a family. Pl. paterfamilias.

Paterson, N.J.
PATTERSON, N.Y.

pathbreaker. —finder, —finding, —way (all one word).

Pathet Lao [PATH-eht lou]. Communist force in Laos.

pathos [PAE-thahss]. Quality that elicits pity or sympathy.

patio [PAT-ih-oh; PAH-tee-oh]. Paved area adjoining building.

patois [PATwah]. Singular and plural. SEE language.

patriot [PAE-tree-aht]. -ic.

patrol. -led, -ling. patrol wagon.

patrolman. patrolwork.

patron [PAE-trun]. -ess, -ize; patronage [PAT-rahn-ihj].

patternmaker.

pattycake. patty shell.

Pau [poh]. University city in southern France.

Pavlov, Ivan Petrovich [PAHV-luhf, ee-VAHN pyih-TRAW-vyihch]. (1849–1936) Russian psychologist.

Pavlova, Anna [PAHV-luh-vah]. (1885–1931) Russian ballerina.

pawnbroker. pawnshop.

pay. P. and p.p., paid.

paycheck. —day, —dirt, —load, —master, —off (n. and adj.), —out (n. and adj.), —roll, —sheet (all one word); pay envelope.

PBS or P.B.S. (abbr.) Public Buildings Service.

pct. (abbr.) percent.

pea. Pl., -s.

peagreen. (adj.) pea-sized (adj.); pea coal, pea soup.

peacebreaker. —making, —monger, —mongering, —time (all one word); peace-blessed (adj.), peace-loving (adj.); peace pipe.

peaceable. Not inclined toward war.
PEACEFUL. Not at war.

peach Melba. An ice cream dessert.

peacock. (m).peafowl (f.).

peaked [peekt]. Pointed.
PEAKED [PEEK-ehd]. Wasted; thin.

peakload.

peanut. (Brit.), Monkey nut or ground nut.

pear-shaped. (adj.) pear gage.

pecan [pee-KAN].

peccadillo [pehk-uh-DIHL-oh]. Pl.-oes; Brit., -os. A small sin.

peck. (abbr. pk.) Unit of capacity; (1) U.S. = 1/4 bu. = 8 dry qt. = 16 dry pt. = 8.8096 l. = 537.605 cu. in. = 8.8096 l.; (2) Brit. = 1,0320 U.S. pk. = 554.84 cu. in. = 9.0919 l.

Pecos River [PAE-kuhs]. River in East New Mexico, West Texas.

peculiar.

pecuniary [pee-KYOO-nih-ehr-ih]. Consisting of money.

pedagogy [PEHD-uh-goh-jee]. The art of teaching.

peddler. Brit., -lar. Also pedlar.

pediatric [pee-dee-AT-rihk]. Of the health or illnesses of children.

peepeye. peephole, peepshow.

peer. Equal. NOT superior. Also a nobleman.

peerless. Without equal.

pegboard. pegleg.

pejorative [PEE-joh-rae-tihv, PEHJ-oh-rae-tihv, pee-JOHR-uh-tiv]. Depreciatory.

Peking [pee-KIHNG]. Pref. to Peiping [bae-JIHNG]. Capital of China, People's Republic of (mainland).

Pekingese or Pekinese. Breed of dog.

pekoe [PEEK-oh; Brit., PEK-]. A black tea leaf of India or Ceylon.

pellmell. (Webster, also *pell-mell*) In furious haste; mingled confusion. *Cf.* pall mall.

pellucid [peh-LYOO-sihd]. Easy to understand. Also translucent.

penal [PEE-nal]. penalize [PEEN-uh-liez].

penates [pee-NAE-teez]. Roman household gods.

pence. (abbr. *p.*) Before decimal system, p.

penchant [PEHN-chant or pahn-SHANN]. Strong inclination.
    Penholder, penknife, penmanship, penpoint, penpusher, pen-cancel (v.), pen-shaped (adj.); pen name, pen sketch.

pencilholder. pencil-mark (v.); pencil box.

penciled. -ing.

pendant. (n.) A hanging thing.
    PENDENT. (adj.) Handing; pending.
    PENNANT. (n.) Flags or nautical rigging.
    PENNON. (n.) Streamer or banner for military or heraldic use.
    GUIDON. Small flag for identification.

pendente lite [pen-DEHN-tih LIE-tih]. (Lat.) "Pending the suit."

pendulum. Pl.-ms.

penicillin [pehn-ih-SIHL-ihn].

peninsula. (n.) peninsular (adj.). BUT the Peninsula War.

Peninsula, Upper. (Lower) (Michigan); the peninsula.

penitentiary [pen-ih-TEHN-shar-rih].

Penitentiary. Albany Penitentiary, the penitentiary.

penman. Writer; also, one proficient in penmanship.

pen name. SEE nom de plume.

Pennsylvania. (abbr. Pa. or Penna.) Native, Pennsylvanian. Cap., Harrisburg.

Pennsylvania Dutch. People and habits of German and Swiss colonists now living in Pennsylvania.

penny. (abbr. p.) U.S. 1¢, pl., pennies. Brit., 1/12 shilling, pl., pence.

penny. (d.) Unit of nail measurement, originally price per hundred; now indicates length; $4d = 1\frac{1}{2}$ in.; $6d = 2$ in.; $10d = 3$ in.; $20d = 4$ in.; $40d = 5$ in.; $60d = 6$ in.

pennywise. pennyworth, penny-a-liner.

pennyweight. (abbr. dwt.) Unit of weight = 0.05 oz. troy; or ap. = 1.2 scruples = 24 grains = 1.5552 grams.

Penobscot [peh-NAHB-skaht or -skuht]. Inlet, river, and an Indian tribe in Maine.

pentameter. In poetry, a verse of five feet of a classical couplet.

Pentateuch [PEHN-tuh-tuook]. SEE Bible.

penthouse. pent-up (adj.); pent roof.

penult [PEE-nult]. Next to last, or penultimate [PEHN-uhlt-ih-mat].
    ANTEPENULT. Last but two, or the third from the end.

penurious. Stingy.

people. Singular and plural. BUT for people of several nations use peoples: *Aramaic speaking peoples.*

peptalk.

Pepys, Samuel [peeps; Preferred to pehps or PEHP-ihs]. (1633–1703) English diarist. (The modern family, [PEHP-ihs]).

per. (Lat.) Acceptable only in business writing; by; by means of; on account of.

per capita. By the head; from each person; average per person: *average per capita* is a tautology.

per annum. Yearly is preferred.

per cent. (abbr. pct.) Preferred to percent BUT GPO, percent. Never % in a text: *75 per cent, one-half of 1 per cent*, BUT *seven percentage points*.

percentage. percentile; per annum, per centum.

per curiam. (Lat.) By the court.

per diem. (Lat.) By the day.

per se. (Lat.) By itself.

père [pair]. (Fr.) Father or senior; *Dumas père; Dumas fils*.

peremptory. Absolutely final, destructive.
PREEMPTORY. Preferential.

perennial. Active throughout the year, or for a long time.
PERPETUAL. Of plants, having a life of more than two years.

perfect. Complete; flawless. NOT *more or most perfect*; use *more nearly perfect*.

perfectible.

pergola [PUHR-goh-luh]. Arbor.

Perigueux [pae-reeg-UH]. Community in southwest central France.

perihelion. The point in an elliptical orbit around the sun which is nearest to the sun. (For the earth, 91,500,000 miles.)

peril. -led, -ling. Brit. -lled, -lling. Both, -ilous.

periodic sentence. A sentence which cannot be concluded before its end: *If John loves Mary, they should be married.*

permanence. The fact of continued existence.

PERMANENCY. The quality of permanence.

Permanent Court of Arbitration. the Court; the Tribunal (only in the proceedings of a specific arbitration tribunal).

permeate. Pass through the pores. -meable, -tor.

permissible.

pernicious [puhr-NIHSH-uhs]. Highly injurious.

perorate. (v.) Harangue; also, conclude and summarize a speech.

perpendicular [puhr-pehn-DIHK-yoo-luh].

perpetrate. Commit: *He planned to perpetrate a crime.*
PERPETUATE. Make enduring: *He provided a scholarship fund to perpetuate his memory.*

persecute. Harass with unjust attacks: *Minority groups have been persecuted in the course of history.*
PROSECUTE. Follow through to an end: *The district attorney prosecuted the investigation and the legal action to conviction.*

Persepolis [puhr-SEHP-oh-LIHS]. Ancient Persian capital city.

Persia. SEE Iran.

person. An individual. Pl. persons.
PEOPLE. A body of persons. Usually both singular and plural. BUT different *peoples* when speaking of groups: *English-speaking peoples*. peoples. Cf. people.

persona [puhr-SOHN-uh]. Pl. -ae. Person. *Dramatis personae; persona non grata.*

personal [PUHR-suhn-n'l]. Private: *personal letters.*
PERSONNEL [puhr-suhn-NEHL]. Persons employed: *Government personnel are selected through civil service.*

personification. In rhetoric, attribution of a personal form: *The fog came in on little cat feet. The soft underbelly of Europe.* A vivid personification is capitalized: *The Chair recognizes the gentleman from New York.*

perspective. (n.) View.

PROSPECTIVE. (adj.) Expected.

perspicacity. Insight. -cious.

PERSPECUITY. Clarity of an idea; lucidity. -cuous.

persuade. -dable or -suasible.

Peru. Native, Peruvian(s); (adj.) Peruvian. Cap., Lima. Currency, sol, pl. soles (S/), centavo.

Perugia [pae-ROO-jah; angl., peh-ROO-jah or -jih-ah]. City in Italy.

peruse. Read carefully.

pervertible.

pesthole. pesthouse; pest-ridden (adj.).

pestle [PEHS-s'l, -t'l]. Tool used to crumble material in a mortar.

Petain, Henri Philippe [pae-TA'N, awn-REE fee-LEEP]. (1856–1951) French marshall 1918.

petaled. -ing.

petard [peh-TAHRD]. An explosive or fire-cracker. *Hoist with his own petard* (*blown up by his own bomb.*) *Cf.* hoist.

petcock. pet lamb.

petit [PEHT-ih; Fr., peh-TEE]. SEE petty.

petite [peh-TEET]. Small; dainty. petitgrain; petit jury, petit larceny, petit point.

petrel [PEHT-rehl]. Sea bird related to the gull: *Stormy petrel.*

PETROL [PEHT-rohl]. British, gasoline.

petty [PEHT-ih]. Small; mean; subordinate.

petty jury. Petit jury is preferred. Contrasted with a grand jury.

Peugeot [PUH-joh]. French automobile.

pewholder.

pewit [PEE-wiht]. A black-headed gull.

pF. (abbr.) water energy (p, logarithm; F, frequency).

Pfc. (abbr.) private, first class.

ph. (abbr.) phase.

pH. (abbr.) Hydrogen-ion concentration, used in expressing acidity and alkalinity in a range of 0-14, 0-highest acidity, 7-neutrality, 14-highest alkalinity. *pH-concentration of 10.5—* or a moderate acidity.

Ph. (abbr.) phenyl.

PHA or P.H.A. (abbr.) Public Housing Administration.

phalanx [fae-LANKS]. Pl., -xes. Ancient military formation of interlocked shields; by extension, a united group of persons.

phallus [FAL-uhs]. Pl., -li. The penis or clitoris; an image of one.

phantom. Delusion; apparition, principally visual; also, something only seemingly real.

PHANTASM. Illusive apparition; fantasy; also, mental image.

phantasmagoria. (sing.) Changing succession of imaginary things.

Pharaoh [FAE-roh].

Phar. D. (abbr.) doctor of pharmacy.

Pharisee. Ancient orthodox Jewish sect. -saic, -saism.

pharmaceutical.

pharmacopoeia.

phase [faez]. *Cf.* faze.

phasemeter. phase out (n. and adj.).

phenomenal. Of the kind apprehended by the senses. AVOID use for *extraordinary.* phenomenon. Pl. -ena.

Phi Beta Kappa [Commonly, FIE BAE-ta KAP-puh, although theoretically fee BEE-ta is more correct].

philately [fihl-AT-ehl-ih]. Postage stamp collecting. -ist, -telic.

-phile [fiel]. Suffix meaning *lover of: Anglophile, bibliophile.*

philharmonic [FIHL-ahr-mon-ihk (*h* is usually slighted or silent)]. Love of harmony; musical concert or organization.

Philippine Islands. The Republic of the Philippines. Native, Filipino(s) (adj.) Philippine. Old cap., Manila. New cap., Quezon City. Currency, peso (P), centavo.

Philistine [FIHL-ihs-teen]. An uncultured materialist.

philo-. Combining form meaning fond of, or loving: *philosophy, philharmonic.*

philoprogenitive [f ihl-oh-proh-GEHN-ih-tihv]. Loving offspring; also, prolific.

philter. Brit., —re. A love potion.

phlegm [FLEHM]. Mucous secretion.

phlegmatic [f lehg-MAT-ihk]. Sluggish.

Phoebe [FEE-bee]. (Greek Mythology) Artemis; poetical, the moon.

Phoenicia, Phenicia [fuh-NIHSH-ih-ah, -NIHSH-ah]. Ancient city-state in area of present Lebanon and Syria (c. 1200–1100 B.C.). Native, Phoenician(s). Cap., Tyre.

phoenix, phenix. (Egyptian myth.) Bird which rises from its own ashes.

Phoenix [FEE-nihks]. City in Arizona. Native, Phoenician(s).

phone. NOT 'phone.

phonology, phonetics. The science of word sounds.

phony. NOT phoney.

phosphorus. (n.) phosphorous (adj.).

photo. Pl. -os. Colloquial for photograph.

photoprint.

Phouma, Souvanna. SEE Souvanna.

phrase. In grammar, a group of related words without subject or predicate which may be used as a noun, adjective, adverb or verb. Phrases are classified as prepositional, participial, gerund, or infinitive.

phrasebook. phrasemaker.

phraseology [frae-zee-OL-uh-jee]. Way of speaking or writing.

Phrygia [FRIH-ih-ah]. Ancient country in area of West Turkey. Native, Phrygian. Cap., Gordium. Prominent c. 1400 B.C. to 300 A.D.

PHS or P.H.S. (abbr.) Public Health Service.

phthisis [THIE-sihs]. A wasting of tissue.

Phumiphon, Adulyadej or Adundet [POOM-ce-pohm, ah-DOON-deht or ah-DOOL-et]. (1927–) King of Thailand, 1950– .

Phyfe, Duncan [FIEF]. (1768–1854) Scottish-American cabinetmaker.

phylum. Pl., phyla. A primary biological division.

physic [fihs-ihk]. A cathartic. -cked, -cking, -cky; also natural science. SEE physics.
PHYSIQUE [f ih-ZEEK]. Body structure.
PSYCHIC [SIE-kihk]. Of the mind.

physician. One of the medical profession. *Cf.* medical specialties.

DOCTOR. Physician or other who has qualified by obtaining a doctorate degree in any field.

SURGEON. Physician who performs operations.

HOMEOPATHIC PHYSICIAN. Medical practitioner who applies theory of curing by remedies which produce effects in a healthy person similar to symptoms of the patient.

OSTEOPATHIC PHYSICIAN. One who practices medicine on the theory that disease is due chiefly to derangement of tissue.

physics. Science dealing with inorganic matter and energy.

physiognomy [f ihz-ih-AHG-noh-mih]. Face; external aspect.

physiology. Science dealing with the normal functions of living things. -logical.

pi. Greek letter π. In mathematics, the ratio of the circumference of a circle to its diameter = to a constant = 3.141592653589732846 or approximately $3\frac{1}{7}$.

pi [pie]. (Brit.) pie. (n.) In printing, an unorganized mass of type. (v.) to jumble. pied, pieing.

pianist [pih-AN-ihst; Brit., PEE-an-ihst].

piano [pih-AN-oh]. Musical instrument. Pl. -os.

PIANO [pih-AH-noh]. Musical direction: Softly.

pianoforte. pianoplayer.

piazza [pih-AZ-zuh, Ital. peh-AH-tza]. Veranda, public square.

pica [PIE-kah]. Printers measure of 12 points or ⅙ inch. SEE type size.

picaresque. Pertaining to, or characteristic of, rogues: *A picaresque novel about Henry Morgan.*

PICTURESQUE. Forming a pleasing picture: *picturesque scenery.*

Picasso, Pablo [pee-KAH-soh, PAHV-loh]. (1881-1973) Spanish modern artist.

picayune [pihk-uh-YOON]. Trifling.

Piccard, Auguste [PEE-kahr, oh-GUEST]. (1884–   ) Swiss physicist, baloonist.

piccolo. Pl., -os.

pickaback. —ax (Brit. -axe), -lock, —off (n. and adj.), —over (n. and adj.), —pocket, —pole, —up (n. and adj.) (all one word).

pick-me-up. Pl., -ups.

picker-up.

picket. (v.) -eted, -eting, picket line.

picnic. -icking, -icked.

picture [PIHK-tyoor].

picture maker. picture book, picture writing.

piebald. Black and white.

SKEWBALD. Color and white, especially of a horse.

piecrust. piemaker, piepan. pie-eater, pie-eyed (adj.), pie plate, pie tin.

piece. A standard length of a woven cloth, as 40, 60, or 80 yards.

piecemeal. pieceworker; piece goods, piece rate.

pièce de résistance [PYEHS-dee rae-sees-TAHNZ]. The most substanial dish of a meal.

pier no. 1. Lower-case. pier head; pier dam, pier table.

pierce. -ceable; pierced; piercing, -ly; piercer.

pieta [PYAE-tah]. Picture of Mary mourning over Christ's body.

piety [PIE-eh-tee].

pig-back. (v.), pig-backed (adj.), pig-faced (adj.).

pig iron. pig lead, pig tin.

pigeon hearted. —hole, —holed; pigeon-livered (adj.), pigeon-toed (adj.); pigeon blood, pigeon breast.

piggyback.

pigmy. Pygmy is preferred.

pilaster [pih-LAS-tuhr]. A rectangular column.

pile driver. –hammer, —up (n. and adj.); pile-driving (adj.).

pilfer. -ered, -ering.

Pilgrim Fathers. (1620) the Pilgrims, a Pilgrim.

pillbox. (military) pillmaker; pill-rolling (adj.), pill-taking (adj.).

pillowcase. pillowslip.

pilot. (v.) -ed, -ing.

pilothouse. —man; pilot boat, pilot burner, pilot light.

pilot plant. Plant designed to test a process or production method on a small scale.

Pilsudski, Jozef [peel-SOOT-skee, YOO-zehf]. (1867–1935) Polish general, statesman.

pilule [pihl-yool]. A small pill.

piña [PEE-nyah]. In South America, pineapple.

pince-nez [PANSS-nae]. Eyeglass clipped to nose by a spring.

pincers. (Brit.) pinchers. (pl.). Gripping device.
PINCHER. One who pinches.

pinchpenny. pinch-hit(v.), pinch-hitter.

Pinchot, Gifford [PIHN-shoh, GIHF-fuhrd].
(1865–1946) Pennsylvania governor, forester.

pinochle [PEE-nuhkl].

pint. Unit of (1) liquid measure = $\frac{1}{2}$ liq. qt. = 16 liq. ou. = 28.875 cu. in. = 128 fl. drams; (2) dry measure = 33.61 cu. in. = 0.5506 l. = 16 ou. = $\frac{1}{2}$ dry quart. (3) British imperial pint = 34.68 cu. in. = 20 fl. oz. = 1.032 U.S. dry pt. = 1.2009 U.S. liq. pt. = 34.6775 cu. in. = 0.5682 l.

pipe. Unit of capacity = $\frac{1}{2}$ tun = 126 gal = 476.952 l.

pipette, pipet. Tube for transfer of liquids.

piquant [PEE-kahnt]. Arch, provocative: *piquant face*. Also, pleasantly tart or pungent: *a piquant taste*. piquancy [PEE-kahn-see].

pique [peek]. Nettle, offend.
PIQUE [pee-KAE]. Cotton fabric with raised ribbing.
PIQUET [pee-KAE or -KEHT]. A card game.

Piraeus [pie-REE-uhs]. Greek seaport city for Athens.

Pisa [PEE-zah]. Commune on Arno River, Italy. *Leaning Tower of Pisa*.

pis aller [pee za-LAE]. (Fr.) "To go worst." The only course possible.

Pisces [PIH-seez]. Zodiacal constellation of the fish.

Pissarro, Camille [pee-SAH-roh, kah-MEEY]. (1830–1903) French painter.

pistachio [pihs-TAH-shee-oh; pihs-TASH-ih-oh]. Pl., -os. A nut; yellow-green color.

pistonhead. piston pin, piston rod.

pitchblende.

piteous [PIHT-ee-uhs]. Exciting pity or sympathy.
PITIABLE. Exciting pity or contempt.

PITIFUL. Feeling and deserving pity or contempt.

pitter-patter.

Pittsburg, Kans.
PITTSBURGH, PA.
PITTSBURGH LANDING, TENN.

Piute [PIE-yoot]. Pl., Piute or -s. American Indian tribe.

pizzicato [pihts-sih-KAH-toh]. Pl. -os. (Music) Plucked.

pk. (abbr.) peck.

pl. (abbr.) plate; plural.

placard [PLAK-ahrd].

placate [PLAE-kaet]. Appease; pacify. -cable.
IMPLACABLE [ihm-PLAK-uh-bl].

place. (v.) -ceable.

Place. Capitalize and spell out if part of name: Jefferson Place, the place.

placebo [pla-SEE-boh]. Harmless medical prescription given to placate a patient; figuratively, a soothing remark.

placecard.

PLACEMENT OF WORDS. To avoid confusion, modifiers should be placed as close as possible to the words they modify. Incorrect placement of a word may radically alter the meaning of a sentence. Words most commonly misplaced are *alone, at least, even, only: I alone can do it.* (Nobody else can.) *I can do it alone.* (I don't need any help.) *Only he can read a book a day.* (No one else can.) *He can only read a book a day.* (He can't do anything else.) *He can read only a book a day.* (He can't read any more.)

PLACE NAMES. (1) N.Y. Times uses as accepted authority the *Columbia Lippincott Gazetteer of the World.* However, The Times replaces the Egyptian *j* with *g*; the French *dj* with *j* and *ou* with *w.* (2) Avoid the repetition of geological formations in names where the foreign name includes the geological designation: *Rio Grande,* NOT *Rio Grande River; Sierra Nevada,* NOT *Sierra Nevada Mountains.*

placer [PLASS-uhr]. System of mining.

plague [plaeg]. -guable, -guing, -guy.

plagueproof. plague-infested (adj.).

plaice. A fish.

plaid [plad]. Scot. [plaed].

plain. -nness.

plainback. (fabric) -clothes (adj.), -clothesman, -hearted, -tail, -ward, -work, -woven (adj.) (all one word); plain-clothed (adj.), plain-headed (adj.), plain-looking (adj.), plain-spoken (adj.).

Plains. (Great Plains), the. Usually Kansas, Nebraska, Missouri, Iowa.

plain sailing.

plaintiff. In law, one bringing suit. The plaintiff makes a *declaration*, the defendant, a *plea;* the plaintiff's reply is a *replication*, to which the defendant makes a *rejoinder*. The plaintiff then files a *surrejoinder*, the defendant a *rebutter*, and the plaintiff, a *surrebutter*. Usually printed in italics in legal writings. *Brown vs. Smith.*

plait [plaet or pleet]. Brit. [plat]. A braid.

pleat [PLEET]. A fold.

plan. Lower-case Colombo plan, controlled materials plan, 5-year plan, Marshall plan (European recovery program); BUT Reorganization Plan No. 6 (Hoover Commission); plan no. 1.

Planck, Max Karl Ernst Ludwig [plahngk mahks, LOOT-vihk]. (1858–1947) German physicist.

planeload.

Planetarium. Fels; Hayden Planetarium; the planetarium.

planets. Mercury, Venus, Earth, Mars, Jupiter, Saturn, Uranus, Neptune, Pluto. *Cf.* heavenly bodies.

plangent. With deep reverberation, as the sound of breaking waves.

plantain [PLAN-tihn]. A weed.

planthouse. —life (Web., two words), —wide; plant food.

Plant. Rockford Arsenal Plant; the plant. BUT Savannah River (AEC) plant; United States Steel plant.

plaque [plak].

plasma physics. Study of electrically charged gases (as in space).

plaster board. —work.

plaster of paris.

plastic. (adj.).

plastics (n.).

plate 2, A, II. BUT Cap. Plate 2, when part of title: *Plate 2.—Rural Structures.*

plateau. Pl.-s.

plateful. Pl.—fuls.

plate glass.

plateholder. —maker, —making.

plate-incased. (adj.) plate glass.

platitude. -dinous.

Plattsburgh, N.Y.

plausible.

plaza [PLAH-zuh].

Plaza. Union Station (Washington, D.C.); the plaza.

plead. P. and p.p., pleaded, NOT pled. -ing.

pleasant.

pleasurebound. pleasure-bent (adj.), pleasure-seeking (adj.), pleasure-tired (adj.), pleasure-weary (adj.); pleasure boat.

plebeian [pleh-BEE-yan]. Pertains to common people; vulgar. -nness.

plebiscite [PLEHB-ih-siht]. Vote of the people.

plectrum [PLEHK-truhm].   Pl. -tra. Pluck used for playing a stringed instrument.

pledger. In law, pledgor.

Pleiad [PLEE-ad; Brit., PLIE]. Pl. -s or -es. A group of seven poets of the French renaissance.

PLEIADES. Seven daughters of Atlas; a contellation in Taurus of six visible stars.

plenary [PLEHN-uh-rih, although more properly PLEE-nuh-rih]. Entire, complete: *A plenary Congress.*

plenitude. Abundance.

pleonasm. (n.) More than enough. In grammar, redundancy.

plethora [PLEHTH-awr-uh]. —ic. Overmuch. From the medical, excess of red corpuscles.

pleurisy. Inflamation of the lining of the chest cavity.

plexus. Pl. -uses.

pliable. Flexible.

pliant. Bending; easily influenced.

plover [PLUHV-uhr]. A shore bird.

plow. Preferred to plough.

plumb [PLUHM]. Lead on a string used to determine the height or the depth. -er, -ing, -ery; -line.

plume. -my.

plumemaker. —making; plume-crowned (adj.).

PLURALS. (1) Usually form plural of nouns by adding *s*. Nouns ending in *o* preceded by a vowel add *s*; if preceded by a consonant, they generally add *es*; but there are many exceptions. *Cf.* *o* endings, *i* endings. (2) Nouns ending in *y* (except most names) change *y* to *ies*: babies, Alleghenies, Rockies, Sicilies. (3) In compound nouns, the significant word takes the plural; where only one word is a noun, the noun is pluralized; where no word is a noun, the last word takes an *s*. (4) Nouns ending in *-full* change to *fuls*: *3 cupfuls of flour* (1 cup filled 3 times). BUT: *3 cups full of coffee* (separate cups). (5) Some words invariably or occasionally take Latin plurals, changing the final *-a* to *-ae*, *-is* to *-es*, *-um* to *-a*, and *-us* usually but not always to *-i*. EXCEPTIONS: hiatus (pl., *hiatus or hiatuses*), dogma (pl., *dogmata*),

Saturnale (rare) (pl., *Saturnalia*). Sometimes the English form has a different meaning: *genii and geniuses.* (6) Letter abbreviations and symbols form plurals by adding the apostrophe and *s: 2's, T's, Y's, etc.* BUT contractions sometimes are treated as words. *co-ops,* AMVETS, vets (for veterinarians). (7) Some plurals have the force of singular: *pains, means, news, measles, gallows, gymnastics. A harvest of good fruit, fruits of Florida. Boatload of fish. Cf.* Collectives.

p.m. (abbr.) post meridiem; afternoon.

pneumatic [noo-MAT-ihk].

PO. (abbr.) petty officer.

Pocatello [poh-kah-TEHL-oh, or -uh]. City in Idaho.

pocket knife. —piece; pocket-sized (adj.), pocket-veto (v.); pocket battleship, pocket book (book), pocket lighter.

pocketbook. (Brit.) A book or wallet; NOT a lady's handbag.

pocketful. Pl., -s.

pockhouse. -mark; pock-marked (adj.), pock-pit (v.).

p.o.d. (abbr.) pay on delivery.

podium [POH-dee-uhm]. Pl., -ia. Dais. LECTERN. Raised speaker's table.

poet-artist. poet-painter; poet laureate.

poetess. Poet is preferred.

pogrom [POH-gruhm, Brit., pahg-GROM]. Organized massacre of helpless people.

poignant [POIN-yuhnt]. Brit. [POI-nant]. Keen, affecting, touching.

poilu [PWAH-loo]. (Slang) French soldier.

Poincare, Raymond [pwahn-kah-RAE, rae-MAWNN]. (1860–1934) President of France, 1913–1920.

poinsettia [poin-SEHT-ee-uh]. A tropical American plant popular at Christmas-time.

Point. Capitalize and spell out when part of a name: *Outlook Point.*

point. Unit of measure = $\frac{1}{100}$ carat. In printing, $\frac{1}{72}$ inch. *Cf.* type size.

pointblank. (N.Y. Times, point-blank).

point 4. point 4 program.

points of the compass. Spell out in ordinary text; abbreviate without periods in special material such as ship news. Otherwise N., NE., NNE. *Cf.* compass, latitude.

poisonmaker. poison-dipped (adj.); poison gas.

Poitier, Sidney [pwoi-TYAE]. (1924–) American actor.

Poiters [pwuh-TYAE]. City in west central France, scene of battles in 732 and 1356. Formerly Poictiers.

poke. -kable, -ky. pokehole. poke check.

Poland. Native, Pole(s); (adj.) Polish. Cap., Warsaw (Warszawa). Currency, zloty (ZL), grosz, pl. grosze, groszy.

Polaris. U.S. intermediate range (1200 miles) two-stage missile designed to be fired with nuclear warheads from a submerged submarine, adaptable for firing from ship or land.

Pole. North Pole, South Pole, the pole; subpolar.

polemic. (n.) Controversy. Pl. -s.
POLEMICAL. (adj.) Controversial.

Pole Star. (Polaris) polar star.

police. (v.) -ceable.

policeman. police dog.

Police. Capitalize if part of name. the police; Capitol Police, White House Police.

policyholder. —maker, —making; policy racket.

policy. national plan or principle.

Polish language. Capitalize all nouns.

polite. More polite, most polite are pref. to -er, -est forms.

politic. Expedient, discreet: *He did not think it would be politic to tell his boss about the errors.* -ly.

POLITICS. The science and art of government: *He selected politics as a career because he wanted to serve the public.*

political. -cally.

political parties and adherents. Party. Capitalize if part of name; BUT N.Y. Times and wire services lower-case party: Republican party, the party: Communist Party, a Communist; Conservative Party, a Conservative; Democratic Party, a Democrat; Free Soil Party, a Free Soiler; Independent Party, an Independent; Progressive Party, Progressive; Republican Party, Grand Old Party; BUT grand old Republican Party, a Republican; Socialist Party, a Socialist; States' Rights Party, States' Righter, a Dixiecrat; BUT States rights (in general sense). The unorganized groups are *conservatives, liberals, democrats.*

polity. Form of government or a government.
POLICY. A line of action.

pollbook. poll tax.

polo coat. polo shirt.

pollination.

poltergeist [PAWL-tuhr-geist]. Noisemaking ghost.

polyandry [PAHL-ih-an-drih]. Having more than one husband.

polygamy [puh-LIHG-uh-mee]. Having more than one wife or husband.
POLYGYNY [poh-LIHJ-ih-nih]. Having more than one wife or concubine.

polyglot. Of many languages. -ttal, -ttic, -thism.

Polynesia [pahl-ih-NEE-zhah or -zhi-ah or shi-ah]. Group of Pacific islands. Native, Polynesian. SEE Oceania.

polynomial [pol-ih-NOH-mee-al]. In algebra, an expression of two or more terms.

polyphony [puh-LIHF-uh-nee]. Multiplicity of sounds, as in an echo.

polysyllabic [pahl-ee-sih-LAB-ihk]. Having many syllables.

polytheism. Belief in many gods. SEE atheism.

pomelo. Pl., -os. Grapefruit.

pommel or **pummel** [puhm-mehl]. (n.) Rounded knob, as on a sword handle or a saddle. (v.) To beat, as with the pummel of a sword. -meled, -meling; Brit., -melled, -melling.

Pompel, Italy [pahm-PAE-ee or -PAE or -PEE (y) -ih]. Ancient city southeast of Naples.

Pompey [PAHM-pih]. (106–48 B.C.) Roman general, statesman.

Pompidou, Georges Jean Raymond [POHM-pee-doo, JAWR-juhs]. (1911–   ) Premier of France (1960-1968), President (1969-1974).

poniard [PAHN-yuhrd]. Dagger.

Ponte Vecchio [POHN-teh vehk-YOH]. Old Bridge, Florence.

pontificate. (v.) Speak as with the infallibility of a pontiff.

pontoon [pahn-TOON]. Mil., ponton. Portable float or boat.

pood. 36.1128 lb. avdp. (U.S.S.R.).

Pool. Northwest Power Pool; the pool.

poolroom. pool table.

Pope. ADDRESS: His Holiness the Pope, Vatican City, Rome, Italy. His Holiness, Pope Paul IV. SALUTATION: Your Holiness, Most Holy Father.

Popocatepetl [poh-poh-kah-TAE-peht-l; angl., poh-poh-kat-eh-PEHT-l]. Volcano in southeast central Mexico.

populate. -table.

p.o.r. (abbr.) pay on return.

porous [PAWR-uhs]. With many pores.

porphyry [POR-fuh-ree]. Feldspar base rock with feldspar crystals.

port [pohrt]. Formerly larboard. Left side when looking towards the bow of a ship.
  STARBOARD. Right side.

port. Town or city of a harbor.
  HARBOR. Place where ships may be accommodated.

HAVEN. Place of shelter from a storm.

Port. Capitalize if part of name. the port; Port of New York Authority (SEE Authority); BUT Baltimore port; port of Baltimore.

portal-to-portal. System (of wage payments) under which travel and other time spent (including time for wash-up, dressing, etc.) on company property is included in the work day.

Port-au-Prince [pohrt-oh-PRIHNSS]. Seaport capital of Haiti. Some publications use Port au Prince.

porte-cochère [pohrt-koh-SHAIR]. (Fr.) Large gate for vehicles.

portentous. NOT -tious. Ominous.

porterhouse steak. Choice cut from thick end of beef.

portfolio. Pl. —os. Portable case for keeping loose papers.

portico. Pl. -os.

portiere. Curtain area over a doorway.

portland cement.

portmanteau [pohrt-MAN-toh]. Pl.-s. Traveling bag, especially in Britain.
  PORTMANTEAU WORDS. Expressions coined by combining two or more words: *cigargoyle, persona non grata, brunch, cinemajestic.*

Portobelo [PAWR-toh-VAE-loh]. Also Porto Bello [PWEHR-toh BEHL-loh]. Seaport in Panama, on the Caribbean.
  PORTOBELLO [PAWR-toh-BEH-loh]. Seaport in Scotland.

Port of Spain. (Sometimes Port-of-Spain) Seaport capital of Trinidad, British West Indies.

Porto Rico. SEE Puerto Rico.

Port Said [sied or saed]. Seaport at Mediterranean end of Suez Canal, Egypt.

Portugal. Native, Portuguese(s); (adj.) Portuguese. Cap., Lisbon (Lisboa). Currency, escudo (Esc.), centavo.

portulaca [pawr-tyoo-LAK-uh]. Tropical low-growing succulent herb grown for its flowers.

pose. (v.) -sable.

poseur [poh-ZUHR]. Poser is preferred.

posse [PAHS-ee]. (Lat.) from *posse comitatus.* A legal armed band.

POSSESSIVE CASE. (1) The possessive of a singular or plural noun not ending in *s* is formed by adding '*s: man's, men's.* (2) Where the noun ends in *s,* or on an *s* sound, the possessive is formed by adding an apostrophe only: *Co.'s, Cos.'; hostess', hostesses'; prince's, princes'; princess', princesses';* For euphony, nouns ending in *-s* or *-ce* and followed by a word beginning with *s* form the possessive by adding an apostrophe only. *prince' shoe, for goodness' sake, Mr. Jones' service, for old times' sake.* Names of one syllable ending with *s* or other a *s* sound form a possessive by adding '*s Burns' poetry.* Names of more than one syllable with a silent sibilant add '*s. Syracuse's traffic.* (2) Compound nouns add the '*s,* to the element nearest the object possessed, thus the last word in the compound: *Mr. Smith of Chicago's book; attorney general's brief; John D. Brown, Sr.'s money.* (3) To show joint possession, place the apostrophe on the last element of the series. Individual possession requires an apostrophe with each element of the series: *Brown and Smith's store* (the store owned by Brown and Smith); *Brown's and Smith's stores* (the store of Brown and the store of Smith); *soldiers and sailors' home, John and Mary's home* (one home); *men's, women's,* and children's clothing; *Roosevelt's and Truman's administrations; Mrs. Smith's and Mrs. Allen's children; master's and doctor's degrees.* (4) In general, possession is attributed only to animate things. After names of countries or other organized bodies, use no apostrophe: *United States people, United Nations committee, Teamsters Union, teachers college, editors guide.* (5) Use an *of* phrase instead of an apostrophe or an apostrophe and *s* to form the possessive of inanimate things: *The sale of pictures is going on now.* (6) For geographic, trade, organization, or institution names or book titles, use the form established: *Harpers Ferry; Court of St. James's; Hells Canyon; Hinds' Precedents; International Ladies' Garment Workers' Union.* (7) Use the *of* phrase in forming the possessive to avoid "piling up" of possessives: NOT: *John's mother's sister's coat.* Also to form the possessive of names

consisting of several words: *The meeting of the chapter of the Daughters of The American Revolution.* (8) Sometimes both phrase and possessive are needed to express meaning accurately. NOT: *This is the Mayor's picture;* BUT: *This is a picture of the Mayor* (his portrait); OR: *This is a picture of the Mayor's* (his property). (9) Use the *of* phrase to avoid adding a possessive to a pronoun that is already possessive: *The covers of everyone's books are dirty.* (10) The possessive case is not used in expressions in which one noun modifies another: *day labor* (labor by the day), *quartermaster stores, State prison, city employee.* (11) Possessive personal pronouns take no apostrophe: *its, theirs.* (12) BUT possessive indefinite or impersonal pronouns require an apostrophe: *each other's books, someone's pen, somebody else's proposal, anyone's boat, anyone else's boat. Your, our, and my books.* NOT *Yours, ours, and my books.* BETTER: *Your books and ours are here.* (13) Singular possessive case is used in general terms such as the following· *author's alterations, cow's milk, fuller's earth, printer's ink.* (14) The possessive is often used in lieu of an objective phrase although ownership is not involved: *one day's labor* (labor for 1 day), *two hours' travel time, a stone's throw, two week's pay, for charity's sake.* (15) A possessive noun used in an adjective sense requires the addition of '*s: He is a friend of John's. The charity sale's merchandise ...* (16) If a possessive is followed by an appositive or an explanatory phrase, form the possessive on the explanatory word: *This was Mr. Keating, the Senator's proposal.* If the appositive is set off by commas, the possessive may be formed on both the main word and the explanatory word: *Here is John's, my teacher's, wallet.* OR, *Here is John, my teacher's, wallet.* (17) Possessives with participle take possessive: *The American Society's representative's joining the conference is a major step forward.* (18) Abbreviations follow rules for other words, with the apostrophe and *s* following the period: *The M.D.'s case, Smith Bros.' product.* (19) A noun or pronoun immediately preceding a gerund is in the possessive case. A participle, which may have the same form as a gerund, functions as an adjective; its subject is in the objective case: *His being early upset the schedule. Tom's coming here made her nostalgic.* (20) DO NOT use the possessive case for the subject of a gerund unless the subject immediately precedes the gerund. If subject and gerund are separated by other words, the subject must be in the objective case. *I could see no reason for him, with all his money, returning the merchandise. I can see no reason for a man with his background failing to pass the test. She could see no reason for the lady's returning the merchandise.* (21) There are no possessive forms for the demonstrative pronouns *that, this, these,* and *those.* When these words are used as subjects of a gerund, they do not change their form: *He could not be certain of that* (NOT that's) *being received.*

possible, possibly.

post. British for *mail.*

post restante [pohst rehs-TAHNT]. (Fr.) General Delivery.

post date. (v.) Date a document later than the current date. (Webster, *postdate).*

post diem. (Lat.) After the day.

postal card. The official variety. Brit. pref.
POST CARD. Especially a picture card.

postal savings account.

postern [POHST-uhrn]. (adj.) At the back or side.

posthaste. —mortem (nonliteral), —graduate.

post-Christian. post-free (adj.).

posthumous [PAHS-choo-muhs]. After death.

postilion. Preferred to *ll.* Guide who rides one of carriage horses.

postmaster general. Pl., postmasters general.

Postmaster General.

Post Office. (Department implied).

Post Office Box. (not abbreviated) Capitalize as part of address; otherwise lower-case.

postpone [pohs-POHN; Webster, pohst-POHN]. Defer; delay.

postprandial. After dinner.

postscript [pohst-skrihpt]. (abbr. p.s.)

postulate. Prerequisite or assumption in an argument.

Potemkin, Grigori Aleksandrovich [puh-TYAWM-kihn, grihch-GAW-ryih uh-lyihk-

SAHN-druh-vyihch]. (1739–1791) Russian marshal, statesman.

Potemkin Village. A facade city created for Catherine the Great to impress her falsely with how well Russian peasants lived.

potency. Power.
POTENTIAL. Possibilities.

potful. Pl. -s.

pot-pourri [poh-poo-REE]. (Webster and N.Y. Times, *potpourri*) Mixture; medley.

Poughkeepsie [poh-KIHP-sih]. City in New York.

poultry. (Sing. or Pl.) Domestic fowl. Never precede with a numeral.

pound. Pl. pounds: *ten pounds.* BUT: *a ten-pound turkey.*

pound, avoirdupois. (abbr. lb. avdp.) Unit of weight = 16 oz. = 1.215 lb. troy or apothecaries = 256 drams advp. = 350 scruples = 7000 grains = 543.592 grams.

pound, troy or apothecaries. (abbr. lb. t. or lb. ap.) Unit of weight = 12 oz. t. or ap. = 0.822286 lb. advp. = 96 drams t. or ap. = 240 dwt = 288 scruples = 5760 grains = 373.242 grams.

pound keeper. pound-foolish (adj.), pound-foot.

pound. (£) (orig. 1 lb. of silver.) Write; £ 12 16s. 8p. NOT 12/16/8. One pound was 20 shillings = 240 pence = 2.48828 grams of gold (1963). Indefinite sums and round numbers are usually spelled out. Spell out shillings and pence when used alone: *7 shillings, two pence; ten thousand pounds.* British decimal system now £1 = 100 pence.

pour. Cause to flow.
PORE. (v.) Gaze intently. Pore over a book.

pousse-café [poos-kuh-FAE]. Liqueurs of different specific gravities which form layers of different colors in a glass.

poverty. Poorness, when referring to money or property. BUT *the poorness of his singing.*

POW. (abbr.) prisoner of war.

Powers. Capitalize if part of name. the powers (SEE also alliances); Allied Powers (World Wars I and II); Axis Powers (World War), Big Four Powers. BUT European powers.

Poznan [PAWZ-nahn-y]. Polish city. Ger., Posen.

p.p. (abbr.) past participle.

PP (abbr.) pellagra preventive (factor).

p.p.i. (abbr.) policy proof of interest.

p.p.m. (abbr.) parts per million.

p.q. (abbr.) previous question.

PR. (abbr.) Proportional representation.

P.R. (abbr.) Puerto Rico.

practicable. Feasible, capable of being put into practice.

PRACTICAL. Useful, capable of being used profitably: *Television was practicable for many years before production techniques made it commercially practical.*

practically.

practice. (n. and v.) Brit. v. -se. (n.) A lawyer's practice. (v.) Practicing the piano.

Prado y Ugarteche Manuel [PRAH-doh, man-wehl]. (1899–1967) President of Peru, 1960–1962.

pragmatic. Skilled in legal, business or political affairs; practical.

PRAGMATICAL. Practical; officious, dogmatic, conceited.

Prague [prahg, praeg]. Capital of Czechoslovakia. Czech., Praha; Ger., Prag.

prairie chicken. prairie dog, prairie schooner.

Prairie States.

praiseworthiness. —worthy.

Prajadhipoh [pruh-chah-tih-pahk]. (1893–1941) King of Siam, 1925–35.

prandial. Pertaining to a meal, esp. dinner. Usually humorously.

pre-. Prefix meaning before. When placed before *e* (in Brit., also *i*), or a proper noun, or a possible misconception, hyphenate: *pre-eminent, pre-arranged, pre-Columbian, pre-position* NOT *preposition, prepared.* Usually not hyphenated: preplanning.

precede. Go before: *Ladies precede gentlemen into a room.*

PROCEED. Go ahead: *Where cars cannot travel, proceed on foot.*

precarious [preh-KAIR-ee-uhs]. Hazardous; insecure.

precedence [preh-SEED-ehns]. Priority: *Matters of health must take precedence over matters of money.*

PRECEDENTS [PREHS-ih-dehnts]. Instances that serve as authority or justification for future similar actions: *Legal precedents influence judicial decisions.*

PRESIDENTS [PREHS-ih-dehnts]. Presiding officers.

precinct. first; 11th precinct.

preciosity [prehsh-ee-OSS-ih-tee]. Excessive fastidiousness in diction.

PRECOCITY. Early development.

precipitate [PREE-sihp-ih-taet]. Brit. [-iht]. (adj. and v.) -itable.

precipitous. Steep.

précis [prae -SEE]. (Sing. and pl.) A statement of the gist. *Cf.* abbreviation.

predacious. Living by preying on other animals.

PREDATORY. Plundering.

predate. (v.) Date a document prior to current date.

predecessor [preh-dehs-SEHS-uhr; Brit., PREE-].

predicate [PREHD-ih-kaet]. (v.) -ted, -ting. Proclaim; predict. -cable, -cation.

predicate [PREH-dih-kiht]. (n.) In grammar, the part of a clause containing the verb, its complements and its modifiers.

predicate [PREH-dih-kate]. (v.) Proclaim publicly; base; imply.

predicate complement, predicate noun or predicate adj. A noun, pronoun, or adjective used after a linking verb to complete its meaning: *Tom is* a good boy.

predicate nominative. A word following a form of the verb *be* (except the infinitive if it has its own subject) must be in the same case as the word before the verb -i.e., the nominative: *Did you call John Brown? I am he. Is that he?* The verb *be* has the same weight as the (=) in mathematics. NOT: *Is that him?* A noun or pronoun following the infinitive *to be* is in the nominative case if the infinitive has no subject. *His sister was thought to be I.* In cases of double pronouns, decide which case would be appropriate if one pronoun were the simple subject or predicate nominative, and then use the same case for both: *The tellers selected are he and I.* Reverse positions: *He and I are the tellers selected.*

Preface. (v.) -ceable. (n.) Statement preceding a text, usually by the author.

FOREWORD. Usually by another.

INTRODUCTION. An introduction differs from a foreword or a preface in that it is the initial part of the text. If the book is divided into chapters, it should be the first chapter.

prefect [PREE-fehkt]. -orial.

prefer. -ring, -rred, -ence.

prefer, than. *He preferred to study rather than assume the problems of his father's business.* AVOID: *He preferred studying. . . .*

preferable [PREHF-ehr-uh-b'l]. NEVER *more* or *most* preferable.

preferential [prehf-uhr-ehn-sh'l].

prefix. Letters or syllables attached to the beginning of a word. (v.) *Prefix to*, NEVER *with*, or *by*.

AFFIX. A prefix or suffix.

SUFFIX. Letters or syllables attached to the end of a word.

COMBINING FORM. Word elements used with other word elements to form a compound or a new word. *phono graph; trade mark.*

PREFIXES AND SUFFIXES. Those that ordinarily combine into solid words are instead hyphenated under special circumstances; (1) Words ending in -like and -smith are written solid except when the *l* or *s* would be tripled, or when the first element is a proper name: *lifelike, bill-like, tinsmith, girllike, Florida-like, brass-smith.* (2) Use a hyphen when the prefix ends in the same vowel with which the root begins: *semi-invalid, semi-intellectual.* (3) Use a hyphen to join duplicated prefixes: *re-redirect, sub-subcommittee, super-superlative.* (4) Use a hyphen to avoid ambiguity: *re-sort* (to sort again), *re-treat* (to treat again), *re-creation* (second creation), *un-ionized* (without ions). (5) Unless usage demands otherwise, use a hyphen to join a prefix or combining form to a capitalized word: *pro-British, un-American*, BUT: *overanglicize, transatlantic.* SEE Hyphenated Compounds.

prehensible. Capable of being laid hold of.

PREHENSILE. Adapted for grasping.

prejudgment. A judgment made before hearing evidence.

prejudice. Preconceived attitude, usually unfavorable; bias. *prejudice: against, in favor of,* NOT *to* or *towards.*

prelate [PREHL-iht]. A church dignitary.

prelude [PREH-lood]. An introductory event. In music, capitalize in a title: *Gershwin's Prelude in B flat; the Prelude to the Second Act of "Pelleas-et Melisande."*

premature [pree-muh-TOOR, Brit., PREHM-uh-toor]. Occuring before the usual time.

premier [PREE-mih-uhr, PREHM-yehr]. Chief or principal; hence first minister of state, prime minister.

PREMIERE [preh-MYAIR]. First performance of a show.

Premier. SEE foreign cabinets.

premise [PREHM-ihs]. (n.) Proposition assumed before argument. (v.) [preh-MIEZ]. Explain before discussion.

PREMISES [PREHM-ihs-ihz]. Property conveyed in a deed.

premium. Pl. -s.

premonition [pree-moh-NIHSH-uhn]. Forewarning; foreboding.

preparation [prehp-uh-RAE-shuhn]. preparatory [pree-PAR-ih-toh-rih].

prepare [pree-PAER]. preparable [pree-PAER-uh-b'l].

preposition. A word used to relate a noun or pronoun to another word in the sentence: *at, on, by, from, toward.*

A preposition is permissible at the end of a sentence. To an aide who attempted to remove a preposition from the end of one of his sentences, Winston Churchill is said to have commented: "That is an impertinence up with which I will not put."

PREPOSITION, OMISSION OF. Repeat preposition before the second of two connected elements: *He seemed interested in us and in our problems.*

prepositional phrase. The number of the noun in the phrase controls the number of the verb. BUT a preceding verb indicates the number in the following prepositional phrase: *Some of the paper has been written. Some of the books have been read. Has some of the material been used?*

presage [PREH-sij; (v.) preh-SAEJ]. (n.) Portent (n.). Portend.

prescience [PREE-shih-ehnss]. Foreknowledge of events. prescient [PREE-shih-ehnt]. -ce.

prescribe. Lay down a plan of action: *The physician prescribes medicines for his patients' ailments.* prescriptible.

PROSCRIBE. Denounce, condemn or prohibit: *Under the Eighteenth Amendment, the sale of liquors was proscribed.*

presentation [prehs-en-TAE-shuhn]. A showing or a giving: *Presentation of a gift to the departing president is customary.*

presentiment [prih-ZEN-tih-mehnt]. Premonition: *They had a presentiment of danger ahead.*

PRESENTMENT [prehz-EHNT-mehnt]. Presentation: *The grand jury handed down a presentment of findings to the court.*

PRESENTIENT [pree-SEHN-shehnt]. Having a presentiment; with *of.*

Preserve. Wichita National Forest Game Preserve, Wichita Game Preserve, Wichita preserve.

Presidency. (office of head of government).

President. Capitalize President of the United States, the Executive, the Chief Executive, the Commander-in-Chief; the President-elect; ex-President, former President. Also capitalize references to chief executive of any other country; the President of Brazil. Capitalize with federal or international unit; BUT president of the Erie Railroad, president of George Washington University, the president.

president-elect. Pl. presidents-elect. BUT a specific person, President-elect.

president pro tempore. BUT: a specific person, President pro tem (of the Senate).

President of a college or university. ADDRESS: Robert F. Goheen, Ph.D., President of Princeton University, Princeton, N.J. or Dr. Robert F. Goheen, President of Princeton University, or (if he holds no doctor's degree) President Robert F. Goheen, Princeton University. SALUTATION: Dear Sir, My dear President Goheen, Dear President Goheen.

President of state senate. ADDRESS: The Honorable Stanley Storm, President of the State Senate of Maryland, The State Capitol. SALUTATION: Sir.

President of a theological seminary. ADDRESS: The Reverend President Jonathan A. Blue, American Theological Seminary. SALUTATION: Dear Sir, Dear President Blue.

President of the United States. ADDRESS: The President, The White House, Washington, D.C.; or The President of the United States or The President, Washington, D.C.; or President Lyndon B. Johnson, Washington, D.C.; or His Excellency, The President of the United States, Washington, D.C. SALUTATION: Sir; Dear Mr. President.

Presidential assistant. authority, order, proclamation; BUT presidential candidate, election, timber, year.

president's wife. ADDRESS: Mrs. Richard M. Nixon, The White House, Washington D.C., SALUTATION: Dear Mrs. Nixon.

presidium [preh-SIHD-ee-uhm].

Press Gallery. rotunda, stationery room, Statuary Hall, the well (House or Senate).

pressure. 1 lb. per sq. in. = 0.070302 kg. per cm.^{2}; 1 kg. per sq. cm.^{2} = 14.2235 lbs. per sq. in.

prestidigitation [prehs-tih-dij-ih-TAE-shuhn]. Sleight of hand.

prestige [prehs-TEEJ, —TEEZH]. Power to command admiration.

prestissimo. Pl. -os. In music, a very quick passage.

presto. (Mus.) Quick; prestissimo, very quick.

presume. Take for granted (with confidence). ASSUME. Take for granted (with less confidence).

Pretender, the

pretense [pree-TEHNS]. Brit. -ce. -ension, -entious.

preterit(e) [PREHT-uhr-iht]. Past. PRETERMIT. —tted, —tting. Intentionally omit or neglect; bypass without mention.

preternatural [pree-tehr-NACH-ehr-al]. Strange and inexplicable. NOT miraculous.

Pretoria [pree-toh-rih-ah]. Capital, Union of South Africa, in south-central Transvaal.

Pretorius, Andries Wilhelmus Jacobus [preh-TOO-ree-uhs, AHN-drees vihl-ehl-muhs yah-koh-buhs]. (1790–1853) South African Dutch soldier, colonizer.

prevaricate. Equivocate, quibble. NOT lie. -tor.

prevent. -able. Preferred to -ible.

preventive. Preferred to -tative. -tible.

previous. Going before, preceding in time or order. PREVIOUS TO. USE *before*. PRIOR. Refers to time only, particularly when more important because earlier. priority.

pre-war. Substitute *before the war* where practical.

Price, Mary Leontyne [LEE-ahn-tehn]. (1927–) American singer.

pricelist. price-cutting (adj.), price-fixing (adj.), price-support (adj.); price cutter, price fixer, price index.

prie-dieu [pree-DYOO]. (Lat.) "Pray God." Convertible desk or chair suitable for kneeling at prayer.

priest. ADDRESS: The Reverend or Reverend Charles B. Stone, or Reverend Father Stone, St. Andrews Church, etc. SALUTATION: Reverend Sir, Dear Reverend Father, Dear Father Stone.

prima donna [PREE-muh-DAH-nah]. Pl., -donnas.

prima facie. BUT N.Y. Times prima-facie (adj.) [PRIE-muh FAE-shee]. On first appearance.

prima facie evidence. In law, sufficient to prove the case unless contradiction is offered.

primarily [prie-MEHR-rihl-ee]. In the first place.

primary colors. In painting, red, yellow, blue; in lighting, orange-red, green, blue. Minor colors: magenta, orange, green.

primate [PRIE-maeht]. Pl. -s. In zoology, Primates [prie-MAE-teez].

Prime Minister. SEE foreign cabinets.

prime-ministerial. (adj.) prime-ministership, prime-ministry; prime minister.

primer [PRIH-muhr; Brit., PRIE-muhr]. Elementary textbook.

primeval [prie-MEE-val]. Of the first age.

primitive.

princehood. prince-priest; prince regent.

Prince Edward Island. (abbr. P.E.I.) Island in Canada. Cap., Charlottetown.

prince of the royal blood. ADDRESS: His Royal Highness Prince Albert. SALUTATION: Sir. (Good friends may say *Dear Sir*).

princess [PRIN-sihs before a name, PRIN-sehs as an independent noun].

principal. Chief, most important: *the principal city.* PRINCIPLE. A fundamental cause, truth or rule of action: *The principle of relativity.*

principal of a school. ADDRESS: Miss Helen Hill, Principal, Teaneck High School, Teaneck, N.J.; SALUTATION: Dear Madam, My dear Miss Hill, Dear Miss Hill.

prior to. Use *before*.

prise. (v.) Force.
PRIZE. (v.) Value.

Prison, Auburn. the prison.

prisonbound. prison-free (adj.), prison-made (adj.).

prisoner of war. (abbr. POW) Pl., prisoners of war. (adj.) prisoner-of-war camp.

pristine [PRIHS-teen]. Primitive; by extension, uncorrupted.

privacy [PRIE-vuh-see].

Private Res. (with number) (abbr.) private resolution.

privative. In grammar, a prefix which takes away meaning: e.g., *in*— in *in*sufficient.

privilege.

privy [prihv-ih]. privily.

Privy Council. His Majesty's. SEE Council.

prizefight. —fighter, —fighting, —holder, —taker, —taking, —winner, —worthy (all one word).

prize-winning. (adj.)

prize court. prize crew, prize ring.

Prize. Nobel Prize, Pulitzer Prize; the prize.

pron. (abbr.) pronoun.

pro-Ally. pro-vice-chancellor; pro forma, pro number, pro rata, pro tem, pro tempore.

probable. NEVER probable to: *The result is probable. The probable score will be....*

probate. In law, testing, especially in relation to wills and courts which examine wills.

probity [PROH-bih-tee]. Uprightness, not merely honesty.

problematical.

proboscis [proh-BOSS-ihs]. Pl. -scises or -scides. A long, flexible snout; e.g., an elephant's trunk.

proceed [proh-SEED]. Advance.
PROCEEDS. (only pl.) Amount realized from a sale.

process [PRAH-sehs; Brit. PROH-].

procès-verbal. Pl. procès-verbaux. Report of verbal statements; minutes.

Proclamation. Emancipation; Presidential Proclamation No. 24; Proclamation No. 24; the proclamation. BUT Presidential proclamation.

procurator [PRAHK-yoo-rae-tawr]. In law, an agent; in ancient Rome, a government fiscal agent.

prodigy [PRAHD-ih-ji]. An extraordinary person; a wonder.

produce [(n.) PRAHD-oos; (v.) proh-DOOS].

producible. Capable of being brought into existence or notice.
PRODUCTIBLE. Capable of being produced.

proem. Prelude to a speech or writing.

Prof. (abbr.) professor. Capitalize in a title.

professedly [proh-FEHS-ehd-lee].

professor in a college or university. ADDRESS: Professor Richard Peters, Department of Fine Arts, National University, Washington D.C.; or Richard Peters, Professor of Literature, National University; or Dr. Richard Peters, Department of Literature, National University. SALUTATION: Dear Sir, Dear Professor Peters, Dear Mr. Peters.

professor of dairy husbandry. the professor. Do not use the title for all college teachers. Many are instructors, hold other ranks, or have no rank at all.

professorate. Office of a professor. —oriate. Office of group of professors.

proffer [PRAHF-uhr]. Offer. —ering, —ered.

proficient in or at.

profile [PROH-fiel; Brit., -feel].

profitmaker. -making; profit-and-loss (adj.), profit-sharing (adj.).

pro forma. (Lat.) As a matter of form. In accounting, a statement as it would appear if a merger, financing, or other specified change should occur.

prognosis [prahg-NOH-sihs]. Pl. -oses [—eez]. Forecast.

prognosticate. —cable, —tor.

program. Brit. —mme [PROH-gram].

programed. -er, -ing. Some use *mm*. BUT: programmatic.

program. European recovery program, mutual defense assistance program, point 4 program, universal military training program.

progress [(n.) PRAH-grehs; (v.) proh-GREHS].

progressive. SEE conservative.

progressive average. One in which the figures from each period are added to those of the previous period.

progressive tax. One which taxes higher incomes most heavily. Also graduated tax.

prohibit from doing. NOT to do.

prohibition [proh-ih-BIHSH-uhn].

prohibitive. Preferred to prohibitory.

project [PRAHJ-ehkt]. Central Valley project, Manhattan project, McNary Dam project, Rochester atomic energy project, University of California atomic energy project.

Prokofieff, Sergei Sergeevich [prohk-KAWF-yehf]. (1891–1953) Russian composer.

prolepsis. In rhetoric, use of a figure of speech to meet an anticipated objection and weaken its force: *This Czar of parliamentary procedure may rule me out of order, but I do so move.*

prolific. Fruitful, productive, fertile.

prologue [PROH-lahg]. prologize; Brit., -guize. To deliver a prologue.

promenade [PROM-uh-nahd; PROM-uh-naed]. Walk, especially in a public place.

Prometheus [proh-MEE-thuhs]. In Greek mythology, Titan who stole fire for man and was condemned to have his liver consumed by vultures until some immortal should consent to die in his stead.

promise. -sor (legal), -ser; -ssory.

the Promised Land.

promote. Promote to the presidency, to be president. NOT . . . to president.

promptbook.

promulgate [PRAHM-uhl-gate]. -atable, -tor. *Publish* or *issue* is preferred.

pronominal adjectives. Pronouns which are also used as adjectives; *all, any, both.* Sometimes also *his, her, their, my.* Place these before other adjectives in a series.

pronounce [proh-NOUNS]. -ceable, -cedly, -cement. *Cf.* pronunciation.

PRONOUN. (abbr. pron.) A substitute for a noun. (1) Watch particularly that every pronoun has a determinable principal (antecedent), preferably nearby and preceding, to which it refers, and which agrees in number, case, person, and gender. (2) Place a pronoun as close as possible to its antecedent. NOT: *He told his friend he was feeling better.* (3) Avoid changing the person of pronouns referring to the same antecedent: *When one is young, it seems that everyone* (NOT you or he) *is young.*

There are six classes of pronoun: (1) personal: *I, we, me, us, my, ours;* (2) relative; *who, whom, which, that, whoever, whomever, whatever;* (3) interrogative; *who, whom, which, what;* (4) indefinite, *another, anyone, each, either, everyone, no one, nothing;* (5) demonstrative; *those, these;* and (6) intensive and reflexive; *myself, yourself, himself, themselves, ourselves, herself.*

A personal pronoun changes to show which person is the subject: First person: *I, we, me, us, my, mine, our, ours;* Second person: *you, your, yours;* Third person: *he, she, it, they, his, hers, its, theirs, him, her, them, their.*

The relative pronoun takes the place of a noun in the clause it introduces and connects its clause with the rest of the sentence. It must agree in number, person, and case.

The interrogative pronoun is the same in form as the relative pronoun, but asks a question.

Demonstrative pronouns may also serve as adjectives to point out or refer to a substantive which has been clearly expressed or implied: *Give these toys to the children.* But it may not otherwise be used as an adjective. An intensive pronoun intensifies a meaning: *She herself will bring the book* (no commas). A reflexive pronoun may serve as subject, direct object or its antecedent: *She gave herself a holiday.*

pronunciamento [proh-nuhn-shih-uh-MEHN-toh]. Pl., -os. Proclamation.

pronunciation [proh-nuhn-sih-AE-shuhn].

proof. Applied to liquors, the percentage of alcohol multiplied by two. 100 proof = 50% alcohol.

proofread. —reader, —reading, —room, -sheet (all one word).

proof paper. proof press, proof spirit.

propaganda. Pl. -s.

propel. -lling, -lled.

propellant. (n.); -llent (adj., fig.). Brit., -lent.

propensity [proh-PEHN-sih-tih]. Natural inclination. —to do, —for doing.

proper nouns or adjectives. In grammar, those which apply to a particular person or thing: *American, John.*

property. Pl. -ties. -tied.

prophecy [PRAF-ee-see]. (n.) Prediction.
PROPHESY [PRAF-ee-sie]. (v.) Predict.

propionate. All-weather resistant thermoplastic used for telephone hand sets, pens and pencils.

propitiate [proh-PIH-shih-aet]. Appease, conciliate. -tiable, -tor, -tion [proh-pih-shih-AE-shuhn].

propjet. -wash.

proportion. Refers to a ratio. AVOID use where *part* will do: *A large part of the class passed. Next year a larger proportion of the*

class will pass. -able, -al. Write: 2 to 7; 1: 4725; 1–3–5. *Cf.* part.

proportions. SEE dimensions.

proposal. An offering, plan, or bid. Also (colloquial) offer of marriage.
PROPOSITION. Originally a formal statement of truth to be demonstrated or discussed, as in math or logic. Now widely used as a business proposal. Also (colloquial) an immoral suggestion: *She expected a proposal but got a proposition.*

proprietary. Pertains to ownership, especially of a nonpatented medicine.
PROPRIETORY. Showing consciousness of ownership. proprietor, -tress.

pro rata [proh-RAE-tuh]. (Lat.) According to the rate; in proportion.

prorogue [proh-ROHG]. Parliamentary term meaning to discontinue meetings; e.g., at the end of a session. —ed, —guing. Adjourn for a recess; dissolve at termination.

prosaic [proh-ZAE-ihk, NOT —SAE—]. Of prose; by extension, commonplace.

proscenium [proh-SEEN-ih-uhm]. Pl. -ia. Part of stage in front of, or framing curtain.

proselyte [PRAHS-eh-liet]. A new convert. -tism, -tize.

prosody [PRAHS-oh-dih]. The science of writing verse.

prostrate [PRAHS-traet]. With face down.
PROSTATE. Muscular-glandular body organ.

protagonist. A leader; active participant, from leading character, in a play. NEVER chief protagonist.

protean [PROH-tih-an]. Versatile, changeable. From Proteus, who assumed different shapes when seized.
PROTEIN [PROH-tih-ihn, -teen]. Certain amino acids essential for living cells containing carbon, hydrogen, oxygen, nitrogen, and usually sulphur.

protégé [PROH-teh-zhae]. Pl., -s; fem., -ée, pl. -ees. One under the protection or sponsorship of another.

pro tem, pro tempore. (Lat.) Temporarily; for the time being.

protestant [PRAHT-ehs-tant, proh-TEHS-tant]. One who protests.

Protestant [PRAHT-ehs-tant, PRAHT-ihs-tant]. A Christian not of the Roman Catholic or Eastern Church; but some Anglican churches do not accept this designation. During the 17th century, only Lutherans and Anglicans.

protestation [PRAHT-ehs-TAE-shuhn].

Proteus [PROH-tyoos, PROH-tee-uhs]. Greek sea god who assumed different shapes when seized. *Cf.* protean.

protocol [PROH-tah-kahl]. Preliminary memorandum or first draft; also, rules of etiquette, especially regarding procedure and rank.

prototype. The first model. SEE archtype.

protozoa. One-celled animals. Sing., protozoon.

protrusible. Capable of being thrust out.

protrusile. So made that it can protrude.

proudhearted. proud-blooded (adj.).

Proust, Marcel [proost, mahr-SEHL]. (1871–1922) French novelist.

prove. P., proved; p.p., proved or proven.

provenance. Place of origin.

providing. Use *if* where appropriate.

province. provincial. Capitalize if referring to an administrative subdivision; Ontario Province, Province of Ontario; Maritime Provinces (Canada); the Province.

proving ground. Aberdeen, etc.; the proving ground.

proviso [pro-VIE-zoh]. Pl. -os. A clause in a law or a contract in which a condition is introduced.

provocative [proh-VAH-cuh-tihv]. Serving to incite.

provost [PRAH-vuhst; mil., PROH-voh]. An official head. Military, a military police officer.

provost marshal. Pl. -marshals.

provost marshal general. Pl. —generals.

proximo. (abbr. prox.) Of next month. Archaic commercialese: *Your order for delivery the 7th prox....*

proxy [PRAHK-sih]. Power to act for another, especially to vote as specified.

prudent. Having wisdom and judicious discrimination.

PRUDENTIAL. Considered from the prudent point of view.

prurience [PROOR-ih-ehns]. Tendency to lascivious longings.

P.S. (abbr.) post scriptum, postscript.

psalmbook [SAHM-buk].

pseudo-. [SOO-doh]. Combining form meaning false: *pseudo-Messiah, pseudomorph, pseudonym.* *Cf.* nom de plume.

pseudoformality. In rhetoric, a style utilizing wordy phrases, the passive voice, and polysyllabic terms.

p.s.f. (abbr.) pounds per square foot.

p.s.i. (abbr.) pounds per square inch.

psittacosis [siht-uh-KOH-sihs]. Disease of birds, especially parrots.

P.S.T. (abbr.) Pacific standard time.

psychic [SIE-kihk]. Psychical. *Cf.* physical.

Psyche [SIE-kee]. In mythology, a beautiful princess loved by Cupid.

PSYCHE. The mental or spiritual life spirit, in but distinct from the body.

psychiatry [sieh-KIE-uh-tree]. Medical specialty dealing with mental disorders.

PSYCHIATRIC [sie-kee-AT-trihk].

PSYCHOLOGY [sie-KAHL-oh-gee]. Science of the mind.

psycho- [SIE-koh]. Combining form meaning life, soul, mind: *psycho-organic, psychosis.*

psychopathic. Subject to mental disease or emotional disorder; overly sensitive to spiritual phenomena.

PSYCHONEUROTIC. Subject to functional disorders of the nervous system.

PSYCHOTIC. Subject to mental derangement, but not necessarily legally insane.

NEUROTIC. Subject to a nervous disease.

psychosomatic [SIE-koh-soh-MAT-ihk]. Functional interrelationship between mind and body induced by mental or emotional disturbances.

pt-. Pronounce as *t*: *Ptolemy, ptomaine.*

pt. (abbr.) part; pint.

P.t. (abbr.) Pacific time.

PTA or P-T-A. (abbr.) parent-teachers' association.

ptero-. [TEHR-oh]. Combining form meaning wing, feather: *pterosaur, pteropod.*

p.t.o. (abbr.) please turn over.

Ptolemy [TAHL-eh-mih]. Name of 14 Kings of Egypt, 367–246 B.C.

ptomaine [TOH-maen or toh-MAEN]. Alkaloid formed by putrefactive bacteria.

puberty [PYOO-buhr-tee]. Period of reaching sexual maturity.

pubic. Of the pelvic region.

Public Act 26. Public Law 9; Public 37; Public Resolution 3; public enemy No. 1.

publichearted. public-minded (adj.), public-spirited (adj.); public words.

Public Printer. the Government Printer, the Printer.

Public Res. (abbr.) public resolution.

Puccini, Giacomo [poot-CHEE-nee; angl., poo-CHEE-nee, YAH-koh-moh]. (1858–1924) Italian opera composer.

pueblo [PWEHB-loh]. A stone or adobe village of southwest United States.

puerile [PYOO-ehr-ihl; Brit., -iel]. Immature; childish.

Puerto Rico [PWEHR-tuh REE-koh]. Native and adj., Puerto Rican. Before 1932, Porto Rico [PAWR-toh REE-koh]. Commonwealth associated with U.S. Cap., San Juan.

Puerto Rico government. Governor of Puerto Rico, the Governor; Legislative Assembly of Puerto Rico, the legislative assembly; Puerto Rico Provisional Regiment, Puerto Rico regiment; Puerto Rico Resident Commissioner.

Puget Sound [PYOO-jeht or -jiht]. Arm of Pacific Ocean in West Washington.

pugilism [PYOO-jihl-ihzm]. Boxing.

puisne [PYOO-nih]. Junior in rank.

puissant [PWIH-sant pref. to Webster's first, PYOO-ihs-sant]. Potent. —ance, —antly.

Pulitzer, Joseph [PUHL-iht-suhr]. (1847–1911) Hungarian-American publisher. Pulitzer Prize.

pullback. (n. and adj.) —out (n. and adj.), —over (n. and adj.), —through (n. and adj.), —up (n. and adj.);

pull-on. (n. and adj.) pull-push (adj.); pull box.

puller-in. puller-out.

pulley. Pl. -eys.

pulmonary [PUHL-muhn-air-ee]. Of lungs. Pulmotor.

pulque [POOL-keh]. Fermented Mexican drink from maguey juice.

pulse. Pl. -s.

pulsejet. Aircraft engine which derives thrust from intermittent flow of gases.

pumice [PUHM-mihs]. Light volcanic glass used for polishing.

pummel. SEE pommel.

pumphandle. (v.) —house, —room; pump drill.

punctilio. Pl. -os. A fine point of ceremony; a trifling formality. punctilious.

punctureproof.

pundit. Wise writer or teacher, from Hindu word for scholar.

punitive [PYOO-nih-tihv].

pupa. Pl., -ae. Chrysalis stage of insect life.

pupil. One who is taught.
STUDENT. One who seeks knowledge.

puppet. Doll with movable parts for stage presentation.
MARIONETTE. Puppet manipulated by strings.

pup tent.

Purchase. Gadsden Purchase, Louisiana Purchase.

pureblood. —blooded, —bred.

puree [pyoo-RAE]. Strained pulped food.

Puritan. 16th-17th century Protestant.
PURITAN. One over-strict in religious principals, usually used in a derogatory sense. Puritanical is preferred to -ic.

purport [PUHR-pawrt]. (n.) [puhr-PORT] (v.).

pursemaking. purse-proud (adj.); purse strings.

pursue. pursuance [pehr-SYOO-uhness, per-SOO-uhness].

purulent [PYOOR-ool-ehnt]. Like pus.

purview. Scope, range: *Religion is not within the purview of the law.*

pushball. —button, —cart, —over (n. and adj.); push-pull (adj.).

pusillanimous [pyoo-sih-LAN-ih-muhs]. Cowardly. —nimity [pyoo-sih-luh-NIHM-ih-tih].

pussycat. —foot, —footing.

put. P. and p.p., put.

putback. (n. and adj.), —off (n. and adj.), —out (n. and adj.); put-on (n. and adj.), put-put (n.), put-up (n. and adj.).

putrescible. Liable to become putrid.

putsch [PUCH]. A petty rebellion.

putter. Preferred to British, potter. Dawdle; busy oneself with trifles.

Pu-yi, Henry [poo-YEE]. (1906–1969) Hsuan T'un, Puppet Chinese emperor, 1908–1912.

Pvt. (abbr.) private.

PX. (abbr.) post exchange.

pygmy. Preferred to pigmy.

pyjamas. SEE pajamas.

Pyramids of Giza [GEE-zuh]. Near Cairo.

pyrites [pie-RIET-tees or PIE-riets]. Minerals which strike fire; e.g., metallic-looking sulphides.

pyro-. [PIE-roh or PIH-roh]. Combining form meaning fire: *pyrochemical, pyromania.*

pyromania [pie-roh-MAE-nee-uh]. *Cf.* mania.

pyrotechnic [pie-roh-TEHK-nihk]. Pl. -s. Fireworks display; science of fireworks.

Pyrrhus [PIHR-uhs]. (318?–272 B.C.) King of Epirus.

Pythagoras [pih-THAG-oh-ruhs]. (Died c. 470 B.C.) Greek philosopher, mathemetician. Pythagorean [pih-thag-oh-REE-uhn].

python [PIE-thahn].

Q

Q-boat, Q-fever, Q-ship.

q. (abbr.) question; qq. (abbr.), questions.

ql. (abbr.) quintal.

Q.M. Gen. (abbr.) Quartermaster General.

Q.M. Sgt. (abbr.) quartermaster sergeant.

qt. (abbr.) quart.

qua. In the character or capacity of. Use only when comparing the same person or thing in two different settings: *Qua husband he is tender, qua financier he is hard.*

Quad Cities. Davenport (Iowa), Rock Island, Moline, and East Moline (Illinois.)

quadrant [KWAD-rant]. ¼ circle = 90°.

quadrennial [kwah-DREHN-ee-al]. Occurring every four years; or lasting four years. QUADRENNIUM. Pl. -ia. Period of four years.

quadrille [kwah-DRIHL; Brit., kah-DRIHL]. A square dance for four couples.

quadrillion. 1000 trillion. British and German, a million trillion. *Cf.* Numbers.

quagmire [KWAG-mihr]. Marsh.

Quai D'Orsay [kae DOHR-sae]. Dock in Paris on which French Ministry of Foreign Affairs is located; hence, the French Foreign Office.

quaint [KWAENT]. Strange but attractive.

qualified expert is redundant.

quality. Avoid use as an adjective meaning of high quality. NOT *quality products.*

qualm [kwahm]. Pl. -s. A sudden attack of nausea or illness; hence, sudden faint-heartedness or compunction.

quandary. [KWAN-dar-ih]. State of perplexity. Pl. quandaries. NOT quandry.

Quantico [KWAHN-tih-koh]. U.S. Marine Corps base on the Potomac River, Virginia.

quantitative. quantity. SEE Numbers.

quarantine [KWAHR-an-teen]. Condition of isolation to avoid contagion; originally 40 days.

quarrel. -ling, -led. Brit. -lling, -lled.

quart. liquid measure (abbr. liq. qt.). (1) U.S. = 0.833 Brit. qt. = 1/4 gal. = 2 liq. pt. = 8 gills = 57.75 cu. in. = 0.9463l; (2) Brit. or imperial = 1.032 U.S. dry qts. = 1.2009 U.S. liq. qts. = 2 Brit. pints = 69.35 cu. in. = 1.1365 liters.

quart. dry (abbr.) (dry qt.). Unit of capacity; (1) ⅛ peck = $\frac{1}{32}$ bu. = 2 dry pt. = 67.201 cu. in. = 1.0121. = U.S. = 0.969 Brit. or imperial qt.

quarter. (1) U.S. = 8 bushels; (2) Brit. 8 imperial bu. = 8.2564 Winchester bu.; (3) 1/4 ton; (4) 1/4 mi.

quarter-eagle. In U.S. gold coinage, $2.50.

quartermaster general. Pl. quartermaster generals. quartermaster-generalship. quartermaster sergeant.

quartet. Also -tette. A group of four.

quarto. (abbr. 4to). Pl. —s. Book size, approx. 9½ × 12½ in.

quatrain [KWAH-traen]. Four-line stanza.

quay [kee]. Paved bank or loading place beside water.

Quebec. (abbr. Que.) Province in Canada.

queen. ADDRESS: Her Gracious Majesty, the Queen, To Her Royal Highness Queen

Elizabeth, or The Queen's Most Excellent Majesty. SALUTATION: Your Royal Highness, Madam.

Quemoy [kee-MOI]. Also Kinmen, Chinmen [jun-MUN]. Island in group 5 miles off China coast; area, 50 sq. mi. Held by the Taiwan government.

querulous [KWEH-ryoo-luhs, -roo-]. Complaining, peevish.

QUESTION MARK. Warns the reader that a question is being asked or that a doubt exists. (1) The meaning rather than the form of the sentence determines whether the question mark is required. (2) If more than one question is raised, each may carry a question mark: *Will it grow? or just wither? or perhaps be destroyed by rodents?* (3) When a request is made as a formal question, a period may follow such a sentence: *Will you be good enough to sign the enclosed statement. May I request an immediate answer.*

questionnaire.

queue [kyoo]. Pigtail; waiting line. *Cf.* cue.

Quezon y Molina, Manuel Luis [KAE-sawn ee moh-LEE-nah, mah-NWEHL loo-EES]. (1878–1944) President of Phillipines, 1935–1944.

quidnunc. (Lat.) *What now.* Inquisitive busybody.

quid pro quo. (Lat.) *Something for something.*

quiescence [kwie-EHS-ehns]. State of rest. quiescent.

quiet. The state: *The hall was quiet.*

    QUIETNESS. The quality: *Her step had a special quietness.*

    QUIETUDE. The habit: *He loved the quietude of his isolated study.*

    QUIETUS [kwie-EE-tuhs]. Extinction: *The earthquake brought quietus to both the population and its problems.*

quinine [KWIE-nien, Kwih-NEEN]. Antimalarial medicine from cinchona bark.

quintet. Also —tette. A group of five.

quintillion. 1000 quadrillion (18 zeros). British and German, 1 million quadrillion (30 zeros). *Cf.* Numbers.

quintuplet [KWIHNT-tuhp-leht]. Pl., —s. A collection of five of a kind. Each of five children born at one birth.

quire. 24 or 25 folded sheets usually of writing paper = $\frac{1}{20}$th ream. *Cf.* ream.

quit. P. and p.p., quit.

quitclaim. Legal release of a right or title to property. -ed.

quite. Completely, entirely, positively: *He is quite sane.* Meaning *to a considerable degree* is colloq: *They made quite a fuss about it.*

quiver [QUIHV-uh].

qui vive [kee-VEEV]. (Fr.) *Who goes there? On the qui vive*—On the alert.

quoit [kwoit]. Pl. —s. The game *quoits* is sing.

QUOTATION MARKS. Used to enclose a direct quotation. (1) Each part of an interrupted quotation must begin and end with quotation marks: *"Never!" he said. "No," he said, "I won't go."* (2) A quotation within a quotation is indicated by single quotation marks. Where double and single quotations coincide, the single mark goes inside the double one: *Mary reported: "Mother said, 'Go to the bakery.'" Mary reported: "'Go to the bakery,' Mother said."* A quotation inside a single quotation takes a double quotation mark: *"He called loudly: 'Ship Ahoy! I see the "Battersea" off the rocks.'"* (3) Words following *said, replied, responded, entitled, the word, the term, marks, endorsed, signed,* require quotation marks: *He wrote a story entitled "Arise and Shine." After the word "peace," the group applauds. The note was signed "John Brown."* Quotation marks do not generally follow the words *called* and *so-called.* (4) In quoting more than one paragraph, a quotation mark is placed at the beginning of each paragraph but at the end of the final paragraph only. (5) Quotation marks are used for emphasis or to enclose misnomers, slang expressions, or words used out of their ordinary sense: *They called for Johnny "Red" Jones.* (6) Avoid using quotation marks for emphasis or to indicate questionable material. NOT: *The company made a "last offer."* (7) Quoted material that is indented or set in smaller type does not require quotation marks. (8) Letters reproduced with date and signature require no quotation marks. (9) The comma and the final period are always placed inside the quotation marks. Other punctuation is enclosed only if it is a part of the matter quoted: *Mary pleaded, "Please stay." She asked, "Why?" John says it's "bunk"? The captain shouted, "All aboard!" He called her "darling"! He wrote under "Announcements": "Be sure to vote today!"* (10) Capitalize the first word of a direct quotation which would be capitalized if standing alone, but not of a fragmentary quotation or an indirect quotation. *He objected "to the phraseology, not to the ideas." The maxim is well established that "a rolling stone gathers no moss."*

q.v. (abbr.) *Quod vide.* (Lat.) "Which see."; also, *qui vive* [kee-VEEV]. Who goes there?

R

R. (abbr.) Réaumur. SEE Temperature.

-r, -rr-. Words of one syllable ending in *r*, preceded by a single vowel (but not a diphthong), double the *r* when adding a suffix beginning with a vowel: *starring, charring.* Words of more than one syllable, double the *r* only when the accent falls on the last syllable: *interred, entered;* BUT *confer, infer, prefer, refer, transfer* double the *r*.

Rabat. [rah-BAHT]. City in Morocco.

Rabaul, Bismarck Archipelago [ruh-BOUL]. On East end of New Britain.

rabbet. -ing, -ed. Slot or groove.

rabbit. The animal.

rabbitskin. rabbit foot.

Rabelais, Francois [RAB-eh-lae]. (c. 1495–1553) French satirist. *Cf.* Rabelaisian.

Rabelaisian. Exuberant, with extravagant imagery; not necessarily indecent. *Cf.* Rabelais.

rabbi. Refer to Rabbi Joseph Cohen, Dr. Joseph Cohen; N.Y. Times, Rev. Dr. Joseph Cohen, Rev. Joseph Cohen. BUT among Jews, the title Rev. is applied equally to a cantor or shochet and is eschewed by rabbis. ADDRESS: Rabbi Joseph Cohen, Rev. Dr. Joseph Cohen, Dr. Joseph Cohen. SALUTATION: Dear Rabbi Cohen, Dear Dr. Cohen, Dear Sir.

Rabi, Isidor Isaac [RAE-bih]. (1898–   ) Austrian-American nuclear physicist.

rabies [RAE-bees, RAB-eez]. Virus disease of animals (dogs, squirrels) transmitted to man through a bite.

Rabin, Yitzhak (rah-BEEN YIHTZ-chawk). (1922-   ) Israeli general, diplomat, prime minister. 1974-

raccoon. Brit., one *c*.

Rachmaninoff, Sergei Wassilievitch [ruhk-MUH-nyih-nuhf, syihr-GAE-ih vuh-SYEEL-yeh-vyihch]. (1873–1943) Russian pianist, composer, conductor.

racket. (all meanings) Preferred to raquet, even for tennis.

raconteur [rah-kahn-TEUR, —tooss]. (fem.) —teuse [tooss]. Storyteller.

radar. (abbr.) radio detection and ranging. radarman, radarscope.

Radek, Karl Bernardovich [RAH-dyehk, kahrl byehr-nahr-duh-vyihch]. (1885–1939) Russian politician.

radiator [RAE-dih-ae-tawr].

Radical. Party of the extremists. Capitalize only when referring to a member of an organized party.

radio. -ed, -ing.

radio frequency. radioisotope. radio amplifier, antenna, channel, communication, control, engineer, engineering, link, range, receiver, set, spectator, transmitter, tube, wave (all separate words).

Radio Waves. Wave length of radio signals is expressed in kilocycles (KC), classified by FCC as:
VLF—Very low frequency—
   10 to 30
LF—Low frequency—
   30 to 300
MF—Medium frequency—
   300 to 3000
HF—High frequency—
   3000 to 30,000
VHF—Very high frequency—
   30,000 to 300,000
UHF—Ultra high frequency—
   300,000 to 3 million

SHF—Super high frequency—
3 million to 30 million

radio stations. Abbreviate and omit periods. *WABC.* But for broadcasting companies use periods: *N.B.C., A.B.C.*

radium therapy.

radius [RAE-dih-uhs]. Pl., radii (-ie), radiuses.

Raeder, Erich [RAE-duh, air-ihk]. (1876–1960) German admiral.

R.A.F. (abbr.) Royal Air Force.

ragout [rah-GOO]. A stew.

raillery [RAEL-ehr-ee]. Banter, especially satirical.

railroad. Brit., railway. Figuratively, *railroad a bill through* is to rush it without allowing an opportunity for the opposition to be heard.

rainbow-colored. (adj.) rainbow chaser.

Rainier III [REHN-eer]. His Serene Highness, Prince, Louis Henri Maxence, Bertrand de Grimaldi, (1923–   ). Prince of Principality of Monaco. Married Grace Kelly, 1956.

raise. A pay raise is a rise in Britain.

raise. raised, raised. A transitive verb which requires a direct object: *He raised his hat.*

RISE, ROSE, RISEN. An intransitive verb which cannot take a direct object: *She rose as he entered.*

raison d'être [REH-zohn DAET-ruh]. (Fr.) Justification for existing.

raisonné [reh-zaw-NAE]. Arranged in an order. *files raissoné.*

rajah or raja [RAH-ja]. Hindus use *raj.* Title of Indian king, prince or chief.

Rajk, Laszlo [RAH-eek, LAHS-loh]. (1909–1949) Hungarian communist, executed for Titoism.

Ramakrishna [RAH-mah-KRIHSH-nah]. (1834–86) Hindu yogi.

ramekin. Preferred to -quin. Cheese, bread crumbs, eggs, etc. baked in a mold; also, the mold.

ramie [RAM-ee]. Fiber stronger and coarser than linen, produced principally in the Orient.

ramjet. -line, -rod, -shackle.

rampant. (v.) In heraldry, rear, leap; (adj.) unrestrained.

Ramses, Rameses [RAM-eh-seez]. Name of 12 kings of Egypt, 1292 B.C.–1167 B.C.

Ranch. King Ranch, etc; the ranch.

ranchhouse. ranch hand.

rancor. Brit. -our.

range. -ing, -geable. Any description should specify top and bottom of the range.

Range. Cascade Range (mountains), the range.

rangefinder.

Ranjit Singh [RUHN-jiht SIHN-bah]. (1780–1839) Maharajah; founder of Sikh kingdom.

ransack. -ing, -ed.

Rapallo [rah-PAHL-loh]. City in Italy. Scene of treaties in 1920 and 1922.

Raphael [RAH-fah-ehl]. Raffaello Santi or Sanzio [RAHF-fah-ehl-loh SAHN-tee or SAHN-tsyoh]. (1483–1520) Italian painter.

rapier [RAE-pee-ehr].

rapine [RAPP-ihn]. Pillage, NOT necessarily sexual rape.

rapport [rap-PAWR]. Harmony.

rapprochement [ruh-prawsh-MAHN]. Return to harmonious relationship.

rapt. Intensely concentrated. Originally from raped, carried off. Enraptured.

rarebit. A delicacy NOT rabbit. BUT *Welsh rabbit* is correct.

rarefy. rarefied, rarefaction. BUT rarity. Webster accepts rarify.

rarely. *Rarely if ever,* NOT *rarely or ever.*

rase. Use raze.

raspberry [RAZ-buh-ree].

Rasputin, Grigori Efimovich [ruhs-POO-tyihn, angl., ras-PYOO-t'n, gryih-GAW-ryih yih-FYEE-muh-vyihch]. (1871–1916) Russian monk-politician.

ratable. Taxable real property.

ratbite. ratcatcher, rat-infested (adj.), rat-tailed (adj.), rat race.

rate holder. A small advertisement run in a periodical to qualify for a lower rate earned on multiple insertions.

ratemaker. rate-setting, rate-cutting (adj.), rate-fixing (adj.), rate-raising (adj.); rate base.

ratemeter. Instrument for measuring rate of radiation absorption. *Cf.* dosimeter.

ratio [RAE-shih-oh]. Pl. -os. Relation between things.

ratiocinate [rash-ih-AHS-ih-naet]. (v.) Reason.

ratiocination [RASH-ee-ahs-ih-NAE-shuhn]. A piece of thinking.

ration [RAE-shuhn; Brit. mil. RASH-uhn]. Allowance; share.

rationale [rash-uhn-AL]. A rational foundation, especially one contrived.

ratline [RAT-lihn]. Tarred ropes of ships.

rato. (abbr.) rocket assisted take-off.

rattan [rat-TAN]. Long-stemmed palm tree used for making walking sticks, wicker furniture.

raucous [RAW-kuhs]. Disagreeably harsh.

Rauschning, Hermann [ROUSH-nihng, HUHR-mahn]. (1887–) German anti-Nazi political writer.

ravage [RAV-ihj]. Violent destruction. - - geable, - - ged, - - ging.
RAVISH. To abduct or carry away; by extension, rape.
RAVISHING. (adj.) Inspiring joy or delight: *ravishing beauty*.

ravel. —led, —ling. Brit. —lled, —lling.

Ravel, Maurice Joseph [rah-VEHL, maw-REES zhoh-ZEHF]. (1875–1937) French composer.

ravine [ruh-VEEN]. Depression, larger than a gully, smaller than a valley.

raving. SEE frantic.

Rawalpindi [RAH-vahl-PIHN-dee; angl., rawl-PIHN-dih]. City in West Punjab, West Pakistan.

rawboned. rawhide; raw-edged (adj.), raw-looking (adj.).

razzle-dazzle.

RB. (abbr.) Renegotiation Board.

Rd. (abbr.) road.

R. & D. (abbr.) research and development.

RDB. (abbr.) Research and Development Board.

re-. Prefix meaning again. Use a hyphen before words beginning with *e: re-enforce* (and optionally before other vowels) *re-assess*, or where confusion in meaning might result: *re-cover* vs. *recover, re-count* vs. *recount*, or before a simple word, *re-do; re-ice, re-ink*; or to avoid mispronunciation: *re-create* (create again); *re-cross-examination*, *re-redirect*. *Cf.* Hyphenated Compounds.

re, in re. Legalese and commercialese for *in the matter of*.

-re. British ending for many words spelled -er in U.S: *theater, theatre*.

REA. N.Y. Times, R.E.A. (abbr.) Rural Electrification Administration.

read [reed]. P. and p.p., read [rehd]; reading, readable.

reading room.

ready-made. (adj.) ready room.

Reagan, Ronald [RAE-gehn]. (1911–) Governor of California (1966–).

realize. In business to convert property or paper profit into cash.

really [REE-al-lee].

Realtor [REE-al-tehr]. A member of the National Association of Real Estate Boards. Term is always capitalized.

realty [REEL-tee]. Real estate: *Money invested in realty usually brings excellent returns during periods of inflation.*

REALITY [ree-AL-ih-tee]. Something real; the quality of being real: *His dream became a reality after he inherited a fortune.* realist.

ream. 500 sheets; from 20 quires of 24 or 25 sheets. *Cf.* quire.

Rear Adm. (abbr.) rear admiral.

rear guard. rearmost, rearview (adj.); rear end.

reason is because is redundant. Use *the reason is that.*

Réaumur. (abbr. R.) Thermometric scale on which 0° is freezing and 80° is boiling point of water, invented by R. A. Réaumur

rebel. (v.) -lling, -lled.

Rebellion. Capitalize if part of name; the rebellion; Boxer Rebellion, Great Rebellion (Civil War), War of the Rebellion, Whisky Rebellion.

rebuke. —kable.

rebus [REE-buhs]. Riddle which uses pictures to represent syllables.

rebut. —tting, —tted.

rebuttal. Refutation.

recalcitrant [ree-KAL-sih-tr'nt]. Objecting to restraint; from "kicking backwards."

INTRANSIGENT. Uncompromising; from not coming to an agreement.

recapitulate. —lable, —tor.

receipt [ree-SEET].

receive.

receptible. Receivable.

reception room.

recession [reh-SEHSH-uhn]. Withdrawal; slowdown in the economic pace.

recherché [reh-shehr-SHAE]. (adj.) Choice.

recidivist [ree-SIHD-ih-vihst]. One who reverts

to antisocial behavior. —vism, —vous, —vistic.

recipe [REHS-ih-pee]. Prescription; formula, especially for cooking.

RECEIPT [ree-SEET]. Evidence of payment.

reciprocal. Shared by both sides. reciprocate. -cable.

recitative [rehs-ih-tah-TEEV]. Narrative; in music, for or like declamation.

reckon. —ing, —ed.

reclamation [rehk-luh-MAE-shuhn]. Act of reclaiming.

recluse [reh-KLOOS; REH-klyoos]. One who lives in seclusion; hermit.

recognize [REHK-ahg-niez].

re-collect. Gather together again.

RECOLLECT. Remember after searching memory.

REMEMBER. Know from previous learning.

RECALL. Bring back to memory.

recommend.

reconcile. -lable; -liation; -ilement (rare). *The minister was taken up with the reconcilement of husband and wife. The reconciliation was accomplished quickly.*

recondite [REHK-uhn-diet, ree-KAHN-diet]. Abstruse; concealed.

reconnaissance [ree-KAHN-ih-sans]. (n.) A survey: *A patrol was sent on reconnaissance to determine the number of the enemy in the area.*

reconnoiter. —tering; Brit., -tre, -tring. To examine or survey.

Reconstruction period. (usually post-Civil War).

record. All-time record, new high record, and the like are redundant.

recordbreaker. —keeper, —maker, —making (all one word).

recount. (v.) Narrate.

RE-COUNT. (v.) Count again. -ing, -ed. Avoid *recountal.*

recover, re-cover. Use hyphen to distinguish meanings.

recreation, re-creation. Use hyphen to distinguish meanings.

recrudesce. (v.) Break out again. recrudescence. (n.) Renewed morbid activity: *The recrudescense of a sore, plague, crime, malignancy.*

recti-, rect-. Combining form meaning right, straight: *rectifiable.*

rectilinear. Preferred to —neal. Formed by straight lines.

recto. Pl. —os. The right-hand page of a book: the front cover.

RECTO-. Combining form meaning rectal: *rectoscope.*

recuperate. [reh-KYOO-pehr-aet]. -rable. Recover.

recur. Preferred to reoccur.

RECURRENT. For scientific, technical use.

RECURRING. For non-scientific use.

red, reddish. *scarlet.* Yellow-red, medium brilliance.

VERMILLION. Yellow-red, medium brilliance, high saturation.

CRIMSON. Blue red, low brilliance.

PINK. Light red, high brilliance.

MAROON. Medium yellowish red, low brilliance.

FUCHSIA [FYOO-shuh]. Pink-purple-red.

MAGENTA. Purplish fuchsia.

SCOLFERINO. Blueish fuchsia.

redact. Rearrange, edit. —or, —ion.

Red army. Russian army.

Red Cross, American. SEE American.

redemptible. Redeemable is preferred.

redingote [REHD-dihng-goht]. Woman's plain long coat.

redolent. [REHD-oh-lehnt]. Odorous; hence, reminiscent of an odor, atmosphere.

redoubtable. Formidable.

redressible [ree-DREHS-ih-bl]. Able to be set right.

Reds, the. a Red (political).

reductio ad absurdum [ree-DUHK-shih-oh ad ab-SUHR-duhm]. (Lat.) *Reduction to absurdity.* In logic, disproving a proposition by extending the point or making an obvious deduction to create an obvious untruth.

redundancy. Superfluous repetition; containing unnecessary words.

PLEONASM. Superfluous wording: *Most perfect, final climax.*

TAUTOLOGY. Needless repetition of meaning in other words: *Visible to the eye.*

reef knoll. reef knot.

re-enforce. reenforce is preferred. But *reinforced concrete, troop reinforcements.*

refection. Meal.

refectory [ree-FEHK-toh-ree; Monastic, REF-]. A dining hall.

refer. —rred, —ring. reference, referable [REF-uhr-abl].

referee.

referendum. Pl. -s or da.

reflectible, reflexible. Capable of being thrown back.

reflexive pronoun. (myself, himself) *I gave myself up.* Commas isolating them are not correct. *I myself went. I hurt myself. He is as fast as myself.* -is acceptable usage (although *He is as fast as me,* -is preferred. But avoid use as subject or direct object: NOT: *My wife and myself were present.* (Use I.) *The letter was addressed to my son and myself.* (Use me.)

reform, re-form. Use hyphen to distinguish meanings.

reformation [rehf-awr-MAE-shuhn]. The Reformation, when referring to 16th-century religious revolution which divided Christendom into Catholics and Protestants.

Reformatory. Elmira; the reformatory.

Refuge. Blackwater Migratory Bird Refuge, Blackwater Bird Refuge, Blackwater refuge.

refund [ree-FUHND]. (v.) [REE-fuhnd] (n.).

refuse, re-fuse. Use hyphen to distinguish meanings.

refutable [REHF-yoo-tuh-bl]. Capable of being disproved.

regalia. (n. pl.) Royal emblems.

regard. When used to mean *consider*, requires *as*: *He considers it scandalous.* BUT: *He regards it as scandalous.* NEVER follow with an infinitive: NOT *She regards it to be an insult.* The terms *with regard to, in regard to* mean *with reference to. As regards* means *as far as it relates to.* AVOID *regarding, in regard to* for introducing a subject. As noun, use plural, *regards,* only in the formal expressions: *Give my regards to your sister.*

Regence. In French decor, period 1700–1730, identified with curvilinear feeling, elaborate carving, canework, the cabriole leg.

 REGENCY. Period in English arts and decor, 1811–1820, identified with classical motifs (Greek, Roman), including use of brass, rosettes.

regime [rae-ZHEEM]. Mode of rule. *Ancien régime,* from pre-French Revolution, now any abolished government.

Regina[ree-JIE-nah; ruh-JEE-nah]. Queen.

region. north-central region; first region, 10th region; mid-continent region; region 3; regionwide.

register. -trable, -trar.

Register of Copyrights. City Register; Register of the Treasury, the Register.

regress [REE-grehs]. (n.) [ree-GREHS] (v.).

regretful. Showing or feeling regret.

 REGRETTABLE. Causing regret: *The riot was a regrettable incident for which I am regretful.*

Regular Army. Navy; a Regular. *Cf.* Officer.

regulation. ceiling price regulation 8; regulation 56 (Navy); supplementary regulation 22; Veterans Regulation 8, (BUT veterans regulations); Regulation W.

Reign of Terror. (France, 1792).

reindeer. Singular and plural.

reinforce. Strengthen.

RE-ENFORCE. Enforce again. -ceable.

re-join, rejoin. *He re-joined* (reunited) *the links of the chain. He rejoined the party.*

rejoinder. SEE answer, plaintiff.

rejuvenate. -ting, -ted, -nable,

relater. In law, relator.

relative. Arising from any relationship; *relative facts.*

 RELATION. Person connected by blood or marriage.

 KIN. One of same stock, race, or family.

relative clause. A dependent clause introduced by a relative pronoun (who, which, that).

relative pronouns. SEE connectives, Pronouns.

relativity theory. Theory based on the premise of the equivalence of the description of the universe in terms of physical laws for various frames of reference.

relegate. Banish; remove; consign to an inferior position. -ting, -ed, -gable.

relevance [REHL-uh-vans]. Pertinence.

relict [REHL-ihkt]. Widow or a widower.

 RELIC. Something surviving from the past, especially something associated with a saint.

reliction. Extension of land due to withdrawal of a body of water: *He acquired the property by reliction.*

Religions. Bahai; Baptist; Brahman; Buddhist; Catholic, Catholicism, BUT catholic (universal); Christian; Christian Science; Evangelical United Brethren; Hebrew; Latter-day Saints, Mohammedan or Moslem; New Thought; Protestant; Roman Catholic; Seventh-Day Adventist; Seventh-Day Baptist; Zoroastrian.

Religious Terms. Capitalize all words denoting the Deity except *who, whose,* and *whom;* all names for the Bible and other sacred writings; and all names of confessions of faith and of religious bodies and their adherents, and words specifically denoting Satan. *Cf.* Bible.

Remagen [RAE-mah-gehn]. Rhine River City, West Germany; scene of Ludendorff bridge collapse after Allied troops crossing March 17, 1945.

remainder. What is left when something is taken away. Used in arithmetic and ordinary situations.

RESIDUE, RESIDUARY. Used in legal situations.

RESIDUUM. Leavings. Used in chemical situations. Pl. -dua. Residual.

BALANCE. The rest, especially in bookkeeping.

Remarque, Erich Maria [reh-MAHRK, AIR-rihk mah-REE-ah]. (1898–1970) German-American novelist.

Rembrandt van Rijn or Ryn [REHM-brant vahn RIEN]. (1606–69) Dutch painter.

remedial [reh-MEE-dee-al]. Designed to cure.

REMEDIABLE [reh-MEE-dih-uh-bl]. Curable.

remediless [REM-eh-dee-lehs].

remembrance [reh-MEHM-brehnse].

reminisce. Give oneself up to recalling past experiences. NOT remember. -iscent.

remit. —tting, —tted, —ttal, –ttance.

remissible, remission.

remodeler.

remonstrate [ree-MAHN-straet]. Say in protest; urge reasons opposed. -strance, -stration.

remove. —ving, —ved, —vable.

remunerate. —ting, —ted, —rable, —ration, —rative. NOT renumerate.

renaissance [rehn-eh-ZAHNS, -SAHNS or reh-NAE-sans]. Rebirth; revival. *A renaissance of poetry.*

The Renaissance. The period which marked transition from Middle Ages to Modern Times, characterized by great vitality in the arts, sciences, and other intellectual activities.

renascence [ree-NAES-ehns]. Rebirth. renascible.

Renault [ruh-NOH]. French automobile.

rend. (v.) rending, rent. (n.) rent. rendible.

rendezvous [RAHN-deh-voo]. (n. sing. and pl.) Meeting place; a meeting. (pl.) —vous [vooz]. (v.) To meet. —voused [vood], —vousing [-vooing].

renege [ree-NEEG, -NEHG]. Deny; renounce. In card playing, fail to follow suit. —neged, —neging.

Renoir, Pierre Auguste [reh-NWAHR, AW-gehst]. (1841–1919) French impressionist painter.

renounce. —cing, —ced, -ceable. renunciation [ree-NUHN-sih-ae-shuhn]. renunciatory [-shih-a-toh-rih; Brit., sha-trih].

Rensselaer [rehn-sih-LEER]. City in New York, near Albany.

repairman. repair shop.

reparable [REHP-uh-rabl]. (v.) Able to neutralize effects of error or injury. Repairable. Opp., irreparable.

REPAIRABLE. Able to be repaired. Opposite, unrepairable. Preferred in reference to physical things, especially those of small consequence.

repartee [reh-pahrt-TEE, NOT —TAE]. SEE answer.

repatriate [ree-PAE-tree-aet]. Return to one's own country. —iable.

repeat. (v.) Say over again.

REITERATE. (v.) say or do over again, especially for emphasis.

repel. —lling, —lled, —llent.

repercussion [ree-puh-KUHSH-uhn].

repertoire [REHP-ehr-twahr].

repertory theatre.

repetition of sounds, as of words not in parallel structure, should be avoided. NOT: *The session discussed several September dates. Long strings are wrong for John.*

repetitive. Tediously repeated, as for emphasis.

REPETITIOUS. Containing material previously noted. The words are interchangeable, but the second is more common in U.S.

replace. —ceable.

replenished. Filled again.

replete. State of being filled up. DO NOT use in negative. NOT: *The house is not replete with antiques.*

COMPLETE. Whole.

reply. SEE answer.

Report. Capitalize if part of name (with date or number); the annual report; the report; Annual Report of the Secretary of Defense for the year ended June 30, 1950; Hoover Commission Report on Paperwork, BUT Hoover Commission report, Hoover report; task force report; 1950 Report of the Chief of the Forest Service.

repoussé [reh-poo-SAE]. Art work in relief, especially metal work.

reprehensible. Culpable. —sibility, —sibleness, —sibly, —sion.

Representative. Representative at Large (U.S. Congress); Representative-elect.

Representative in Congress. ADDRESS: The Honorable Seymour Halpern, The House of Representatives, Washington, D.C., or Representative Seymour Halpern, The House of Representatives, Washington, D.C., or (if sent to his home) The Honorable Seymour Halpern, Representative in Congress (followed by postal address). SALUTATION: Dear Congressman Halpern, Dear Representative Halpern, Dear Mr. Halpern, Dear Sir, Sir.

Representative (woman). ADDRESS: As above. SALUTATION: Madam, My dear Mrs. Dwyer, Dear Madam, Dear Representative Dwyer, Dear Mrs. Dwyer.

representative at large. BUT, for a specific person with title, Representative at Large John Jones.

repress. -ssible.

reprise [ree-PRIEZ]. (n.) Obsolete for reprisal. In law, annual charge or rent. In music [ree-PREEZ], a repetition.

reproduce. -cible.

reptile [REP-tihl, -tiel]. Class of animals that includes snakes, crocodiles, salamanders, and turtles.

repudiate [ree-PYOO-dih-aet]. Renounce. -diable.

repugnant [rih-PUHG-nant]. Incongruous, incompatible, contradictory; also, distasteful. —ce or —cy.

Republic. Capitalize if part of name; capitalize standing alone if referring to a specific government: French Republic; Irish Republic; Republic of Panama; Republic of the Philippines, Philippine Republic; United Arab Republic; United States Republic; the American Republics, the Latin American Republics, South American Republics, the Republics.

Republican, a.

Republican Party. UCMS & N.Y. Times, Republican party.

requiem [REE-kwih-ehm or REHK-]. Mass for the dead.

requirement. A need: *Her qualities meet my requirements.*

REQUISITE. A thing needed to accomplish the end: *Books are requisite* (or required) *for the course.*

INDISPENSABLE. Without it, something cannot be done. *A high school diploma is a requisite for entrance into college; scholastic aptitude and a fountain pen are indispensable for staying there. Cf. necessary.*

requite. —table.

reredos [REER-dohs]. Ornamented screen.

rescind. Annul. rescission.

research [re-SUHRCH preferred to REE-suhrch]. An investigation: *research study, research worker.*

RE-SEARCH. Search again.

resentment. Against, at or of, NOT to, towards.

Reservation. (forest, military, or Indian) Capitalize if part of name: Great Sioux Reservation, Hill Military Reservation, the reservation.

Reserve. Capitalize if part of name; the Reserve *Cf.* Air Force; Army Corps; Foreign Service; Marine Corps; Merchant Marine; Naval. Active Reserve, Air Force Reserve, Army Reserve; Federal Reserve Board (SEE Federal); Civil Air Patrol Reserve, Reserve components; Enlisted Reserve; Reserve Establishment; Inactive Reserve; Naval Reserve officer; Officers' Training Corps Reserve, Ready Reserve, Retired Reserve, Standby Reserve; Volunteer Naval Reserve; Women's Reserve (SEE Women's Reserve). *Cf.* Bank.

reservedly [ree-ZUHR-vehd-lih].

Reserves, the. reservist.

reservoir [REHZ-uhr-vwahr].

Resident Commissioner. SEE Member; Puerto Rico.

residents. Those living in a place.
RESIDENCE. A home; act of living there.
RESIDENCY. An official residence, especially of a diplomat, governor.

residual [reh-ZIHD-yoo-uhl]. Remaining. —uary, residue.

res ipsa loquitur. (Lat.) *The thing speaks for itself.* In law, doctrine under which the defendant in certain cases must prove that an accident was not caused by his negligence.

resilience [reh-ZIHL-yehnss]. -cy. Elasticity. The meaning is generally the same, but elasticity cannot apply to an act of rebounding: *He showed resilience in meeting adversity.*

resin [REHZ-zihn]. Term used for liquid, chemical.
ROSIN [RAH-zihn]. Term used for the commercial product.

resist. —tible., opp., irresistible; unresisting.

resoluble, resolvable. Opposite, unresolvable, irresoluble, NOT irresolvable.

Resolution. Capitalize with number; the resolution; House Joint Resolution 3; Public Resolution 6; Resolution 42; Senate Concurrent Resolution 18; BUT Kefauver resolution.

Resolutions. The first word following *Whereas* in resolutions, contracts, and the like is not capitalized; the first word following an enacting or resolving clause is capitalized. The word *Resolved* is italicized. *Whereas the Constitution provided . . .*; and *Be it enacted, That ***** WHEREAS, we are dedicated to liberty; therefore be it Resolved, That . . .*

resonance [REHZ-uh-nehnss]. Act of resounding.

resorb [ree-SAWRB]. Absorb again. Resorption.

resource [ree-SAWRS, REE-sawrs].

respective, respectively. Each in the order given. Although in some constructions one of these may be necessary, their use should otherwise be avoided. NOT: *The corporation was dissolved and each stockholder received his respective share of the assets.*
WITH RESPECT TO. in respect of, to. AVOID.

respectworthy. Worthy of respect.

respite [REHS-piht]. (n. and v.) A delay.

responsible.

restaurant. [REHS-toh-ruhnt NOT -ant or -ahnt].
RESTAURATEUR [rehs-toh-rah-TEUR]. One who operates a restaurant (NOT -rahn-teur).

restless. Unable to stay in one place.

restroom. rest cure.

restive. Resisting control.

restrictive. (or essential) modifier. A word, phrase, or clause which identifies the person or thing modified.

résumé [rae-zyooMAE or REH-zeu-mae]. A summing up, especially a written summary of prior job experience.

resurrect [rehz-uh-REHKT]. Restore to life.

resuscitate [reh-SUHS-ih-taet]. Revive, restore. -tating, -tated, -itable (-tab'l).

retaliate. —ating, —ated, —iable.

reticent. Reserved in speech. reticence.

retina. Pl. —s or —ae.

retrace. Go back. —cing, —ced, —ceable.
RE-TRACE. Trace again.

retraction. British use retractation.

retrieve. (n.) retrieval; beyond retrieve.

retroactive [REHT-troh-ah-tihv]. Effective in a prior time.

retrogress. (v.) Move backwards, from better to worse. —gression; retrograde (adj.), —gradation.

Reuter, Paul Julius [ROI-terh]. (1816–1899) Originally Israel Beer [baer] Josaphat. German-British news agent.

Reuther, Walter Philip [ROO-thuhr]. (1907–1970) American labor leader (United Automobile Workers).

Rev. (abbr.) reverend. An honorary title given to clergyman as Hon. is given to officeholders. Must be followed by Mr., Dr., or a first name. *Cf.* reverend, clergyman.

revaluate. —ting, —ted, —ation. Preferred to re-evaluate.

reveille [REHV-ehl-ih; Brit. ree-VEHL-ih].

revel [REH-vehl]. To be noisily festive. -ling, -led, -er. Brit. *ll*.

Revelation(s). The Revelation of St. John the Divine.

reverberate. —ting, —ted, —rable, —tor.

reverend. Reverend (before a name), Rev. John Brown; the Rev. Mr. Doe; the Rev. J. P. Doe; the Rev. Dr. Doe; Rev. and Mrs. Brown; Rev. Brown, Black, and Blue; Rev. A. I. Brown, B. B. Black, and C. S. Blue. BUT NOT Rev. Doe. *Cf.* clergyman, minister, priest, abbot, bishop, monsignor, pope.

reverie. Preferred to -ry.

reverse. Turn upside down or completely about. —sing, —sed, —sible; opposite, unreversable or irreversible.

REVERT. Go back.

revertible.

revoke. —king, —ked, -vocable; -vocation, [REHV-oh-kee-shuhn].

revolt [ree-VOHLT].

Revolution, Revolutionary. Capitalize if referring to the American, French, or English Revolution. *Cf.* War.

revue [ree-VYOO]. (n.) Musical or spectacular stage presentation with little or no plot.

REVIEW. (n.) A re-examination.

Reykjavik [RAEK-yah-veek]. Seaport and capital city of Iceland.

Reynaud, Paul [rae-NOH]. (1878–1966) French statesman, premier in 1940.

RF. (abbr.) radiofrequency.

R.F.D. (abbr.) rural free delivery.

Rhee, Syngman [REE, SIHNG-mahn]. (1875–1965) President of Republic of Korea (South Korea), 1948–1960.

rhetorical question. Statement made in the form of a question which has no apparent answer: *Who can tell what time will bring?*

rhinestone [REIN-stohn]. Colorless paste or glass stone with high lustre.

rhinoceros. Singular or plural. Pl. also —oses, -otes, -i.

Rhode Island. (abbr. R.I.) Native, Rhode Islander. Cap., Providence.

Rhodesia. SEE Federation of Rhodesia and Nyasaland.

rhombus. Pl. -buses or bi. SEE shapes.

rhyme. Common sounds in line endings. Preferred to rime.

RHYTHM. Meter in words, essential in good poetry or prose. rhythmical preferred to rhythmic.

EURHYTHMY, EURYTHMY. Harmonious proportions.

riant [RIE-ant]. Literary word for laughing, gay.

ribald [RIHB-ld]. Scurrilous.

riband [RIH-band]. Archaic for ribbon.

Ribicoff, Abe (Abraham) [RIH-bih-kawf]. (1910–   ) U.S. Secretary of Health, Education and Welfare (H.E.W.) (1961–1962); former Governor of Connecticut, 1955–1961. U.S. Senator, 1963– .

riboflavin. Vitamin B_2, from eggs, green vegetables, milk, whey.

rice-throwing. rice paper, rice water.

riches. Wealth. Takes a plural verb; there is no singular.

ricochet [RIHK-oh-shae]. —eting, —eted.

rickets. Takes a singular verb.

rickety [RIHK-ih-tih]. Shaky.

rickrack.

rid. P., p.p., rid or ridden; ridding.

ride. P., rode; p.p., ridden; riding.

rider. Additional clause attached to an agreement.

riffraff [RIHF-RAFF]. Rubbish or rabble.

Riga [REE-gah]. Seaport capital of Latvia on Dvina River, U.S.S.R.

right. Correct; also, the direction.
   RITE. Ceremony.
   WRITE. Inscribe.
   WRIGHT. (suffix) A workman: *shipwright*.

right bank. When looking downstream.

right stage. From the actor's view.

rightabout. rightwing (political).

right angle. 90°.

righteous [RIE-chuhs]. Pertains to that which is right.

right-of-way. Pl. rights-of-way.

right-to-work law. Forbids requirement of membership in a union as a requisite of employment.

rigmarole. Also rigamarole. Series of foolish, confused or incoherent statements.

rigor. Brit., -our. Both, *rigorous, rigor mortis*.

Riis, Jacob August [REES, JAE-kuhb AW-guhst]. (1849–1914) Danish-American social worker-writer.

Rijswijk [RIES-vihk]; or Ryswick, [RIZ-wihk or RIEZ-]. Swiss commune near The Hague, Netherlands; scene of treaty in 1697.

rime. White frost.

Rimouski [rih-MOOS-kih]. Town on south side St. Lawrence River, Canada.

Rimski-Korsakov, Nikolai Andreyevich [RYEEM-ski KUHR-suh-kawf; angl., rihm-skih KAWR-sah-kawf, nyih-kuh-LIE uhn-dryae-yeh-vyihch]. (1844–1908) Russian composer.

ring. P. and p., rang is preferred to rung; ringing.
   RING. (encircle) ringed; ringing.

Rio de Janeiro [ree-oh deh zhuh-NAE-roh]. Seaport in Brazil.

Rio Grande [REE-oh grand or GRANN-dae or RIE-oh grand]. Mex., Rio Bravo [REE-oh VRAH-voh]. Rio means river; thus, NOT Rio Grande River.

riot. —ting, —ted.

rip cord. ripride, ripup.

riposte [rih-POHST]. Preferred to repost. Quick retort; from fencing.

Rip van Winkle. Hero in Washington Irving's story who slept for 20 years.

rise. P., rose; p.p., risen; rising.
   RISE. (n.) British for pay increase. In U.S. usually *raise*.

risible [RIHZ-ih-b'l]. Causing laughter.

risqué [rihs-KAE]. fem. —ee. Verging on the indecent; from *to risk*.

rival. —led, —ling. Brit. —lled, —lling.

rive. Tear apart. P., rived; p.p., riven or rived; riving.

Rivera, Diego [ree-VAE-rah, DYAE-goh]. (1886–1957) Mexican painter.

riverbank. —bed, —flow, —front, -man, —side, (all one word). river bottom.

rivet. —eted, —eting, —eter.

Riza Shah Pahlavi or Pahlevi [rih-ZAH SHAH PA-luh-vee]. (1877–1944) Shah of Iran, 1925–41. Son, Pahlavi.

Rjukan [RYOO-kahn]. City in Norway.

r.m.s. (abbr.) root mean square.

Roa, Roul [ROH-ah, ROU-awl]. (1909–   )
U.N. Delegate from Cuba.

Road. Capitalize if part of name: Benning
Road; the road.

roadbed.

road runner. road show.

roan [ROHN]. Brown or tan horse with gray
markings.

roast, P. and p.p., roasted; roasting. *roast beef*,
roast lamb, roasted coffee. In most cases,
—ted.

rob. robbed, robbing. Take property feloniously
from someone; in law, by force or fear of
force.
   STEAL. Take feloniously or furtively: *steal
a kiss*.

Robespierre, Maximilien Francois Marie Isidore
de [deh RAW-bes-pyair; angl., ROHBZ-
peer; mahk-see-mee-LYANN frahn-SWAH
mah-REE]. (1758–94) French revolutionist.

robot [ROH-baht]. Mechanical man. From
R.U.R. by Karl Capek.

robust [roh-BUHST]. In vigorous health.

rockaby. rock-bottom (nonliteral), rock-bound.

rock 'n 'roll.

Rockefeller [RAHK-eh-fehl-uh]. John Davison
I (1839–1937), married Laura C. Spelman.
Children: Bessie (Mrs. Charles A.) Strong,
Alta (Mrs. E. Parmalee) Prentice (1871–
1962), Edith (Mrs. Harold Fowler)
McCormick, and John Davison II.
   John D. Jr. (1874–1960), married Abby
Greene Aldrich (1901–1948). Remarried
Martha Baird Allen in 1951. Children:
Abby R. Milton, John D. 3rd, Nelson A.,
Lawrence S., Winthrop, David.

rocket age.

rococo [roh-KOH-koh]. Of baroque art, particularly when featured by ingenious curves.

rod. Unit of length = 25 links = $\frac{1}{40}$ chain =
5.5 yds. = 16.5 feet = $\frac{1}{320}$ mi. = 5.0292 m.
= 1 perch.

rodeo [ROH-dee-oh pref. to more correct roh-
DAE-oh].

roe deer.

roentgen, rontgen [RUHNT-jehn]. Of x-rays.
Unit of ray measurement. 600 is universally
lethal; 500 is lethal to half of those exposed;
300 is lethal to some.

Roentgen or Rontgen, Wilhelm Konrad
[RUHNT-gehn; angl. REHNT- or RUHNT-
geyn]. (1845–1923) Greek physicist.

Roget, Peter Mark [roh-zhae; Brit., ROZHae].
(1779–1869) British physicist-scholar (the
Thesaurus).

Rok. (abbr.) Soldier of Republic of South
Korea.

Rokossovski, Konstantin [ruh-kuh-SAWF-
skih, kuhn-stuhn-TYEEN]. (1893–1968)
Russ. marshall.

role. Actor's part. From roll of manuscript on
which actor's part was written.

rollback. roll call, roll film, rollup.

roll, wallpaper. Unit of length = 16 yds.

rolling stock. Wheeled property of a railroad.

Romains, Jules [roh-MANN]. Pseudonym of
Louis Farigoule [FAH-ree-gool] (1885–   )
French author.

ROMAN NUMBERS. May be in capitals or
small letters. (1) I; (2) II; (3) III; (4) IV or
IIII; (5) V; (6) VI; (7) VII; (8) VIII; (9) IX
or VIIII; (10) X; (11) XI; (14) XIV or XIIII;
(15) XV; (20) XX; (21) XXI; (40) XL or
XXXX; (42) XLII; (50) L; (100) C; (101)
CI; (400) CD or CCCC; (500) D; (600) DC;
(1000) M or CIƆ; (1600) MDC; (1800)
MDCCC; (1900) MCM or MDCCCC;
(1950) MCML; (2000) MM; (5000) $\overline{V}$;
(10,000) $\overline{X}$; (100,000) $\overline{C}$; 1 million, $\overline{M}$;
(1970) MCMLXX. In general, use Arabic
numerals. Use Roman numerals in small
caps or lower case (1) for preliminary pages
of a book; (2) where Roman numerals are
used in tabulations. Use Roman numerals
in capitals for (3) title of a ruler or prince:
Elizabeth II, Pope John XXIII. (4) Where
customary to distinguish other persons in
a series: *Miss America VI; Marshall Field II.*
(5) For periodical chapters, plates, graphs,
volume numbers, etc: *Vol. XXI, Map I,
Plate II, Chart III* (no periods). BUT use
Arabic numbers for text illustrations: *Fig.
3.* (6) For primary subdivisions: *Chapter*

VII; II. The Tertiary Era. (7) Common nouns used with Roman numerals are not capitalized: *book II, chapter II, part II.* (UCMS caps. Book.) BUT *Book II: Modern Types* (complete heading); *Part XI: Early Thought* (complete heading) in titles.

Romagna [roh-MAHN-yah]. Ancient Romania. Italian Province of States of the Church prior to 1860. Cap., Ravenna.

romance languages. Those derived from Rome's Latin.

Romania [roh-MAEN-yah]. Also Roumania and Rumania [roo-MAEN-yah]. SEE Rumania.

Roman Empire.

Romanov or Romanoff, Mikhail Feodorivich [ruh-MAH-ruhf, angl. ROH-mah-nof, myih-kuh-EEL fyeh-aw-duh-raw-vyihch]. (1613–45) 1st tzar of Russian dynasty.

romantic novels. Popular stories written in romance languages, generally involving strong passions and extravagant situations.

romanticism. Movement in the arts which emphasizes free expression of personality, including such diverse forms as revolution, transcendentalism, medievalism, the strange and weird. Typical 19th-century romantic writers—Byron, Coleridge, Keats, Shelley, Wadsworth.

roman type. Upright type with shaded stroke and serifs. *Cf.* italics.

Rome. Roman, Romish.

Romulo, Carlos P. [ROH-muh-loh, KAHR-lohs]. Phillipine statesman-diplomat.

rondeau, rondo. Poem of 13 (or 10) lines plus refrain with recurring word, words, or lines, and with rhymes fixed by first two lines, and with refrain after lines 8 and 13 (or 6 and 10).

RONDEL. Similar poem of 14 or 13 lines with refrain after 6th and last lines.

RONDELAY. Short simple song with a refrain.

roof garden.

rooftop. Roof is usually enough.

roomful. Pl. -s.

roominghouse.

roomkeeper. -mate; room clerk.

Roosevelt [ROH-zeh-vehlt, formerly ROOS-eh-vehlt]. Franklin Delano Roosevelt, (1882–1945). 32nd President of the United States, (1933–1945); married Anna Eleanor (1905–1962); children: Anna Eleanor (Mrs. John) Boettiger; James, Elliot, Franklin D., John A.

THEODORE (1858–1919). 26th President of the United States (1901–09); married Alice Lee, died 1884; married Edith Kermit Carow, died 1949. Children: Theodore (1887–1944), Kermit (1889–1943), Archibald Bullock (1894–   ), Quentin (1897–1918), Edith Carow (1891–   ).

root [root, not ruht].

rope. —ped, —ping; —pable, —y.

Rorschach Test [RAWR-shak]. Ink blot reaction test developed by Herman Rorschach, Swiss psychologist, to appraise personality and diagnose mental illness.

rosary [ROH-zuh-rih]. String of beads, series of prayers; garland of roses. *Cf.* Mass.

roseate [ROH-zee-aet]. Like a rose, especially in color.

Rosenwald, Julius [ROH-z'n-wawld]. (1862–1932) American merchant-philanthropist.

Rosh ha-Shanah. (N.Y. Times) Jewish spiritual New Year, in September or October. Also Rosh Hashana, Rosh Hashona.

Rosicrucians. Brethren of the Rosy Cross. Mystical moral and religious reformers who use science to interpret cryptic facets of Christianity.

rosin [RAH-zihn]. SEE resin.

roster [RAH-stehr, mil., ROH-stehr]. Roll.

Rostov [RAHS-tahv, Russ., RUH-stawf]. Also Rostov-on-Don [ahn-DAHN]. City in southeast U.S.S.R. on Don River.

rostrum [RAHS-trum]. Pl. -s except for ship's beak, -ra.

rotary. Preferred to rotatory. British for traffic circle.

Rotary Club. Local association of businessmen usually limited to one of each trade, with object of promoting service and goodwill.

ROTC. (N.Y. Times R.O.T.C.) Reserve Officers' Training Corps.

rotisserie [roh-TIHS-uh-ree]. Restaurant where meat is roasted on a spit in view; home device with same use.

rotogravure. Intaglio printing process especially suitable for large runs.

rotten. —nness.

rottenhearted.

rotund [roh-TUHND]. Round; rounded out.

roué [roo-AE]. Debauchee.

Rouen [roo-AHN]. Northern city on Seine River, France.

roughen. (v.) BUT to treat roughly or harden, use rough: *Rough up, rough a horse, rough in a sketch, rough a lens, rough it on a camping trip.*

roughing-in. (adj.).

roundabout. (n. and adj.); round robin (petition).

round trip.

rouse. Preferred for literal use: *He roused himself at 8.*

AROUSE. Preferred for abstract use: *His anger was aroused.*

rout. Set into flight: *They routed the enemy with noise alone.*

ROUTE [root, rout]. A way or course: *The shortest route is not always the easiest.*

route No. 12466. mail route 1742, railway mail route 1144, BUT cap. Route 40, State Route 9 (highways).

routine [roo-TEEN]. —tinism, —tinist.

rowboat.

roweled. —ing.

Royal Decree No. 24. Decree 24, the royal decree.

royal octavo. Book size approximately 7 × 10½ in.

royalty. Payment for use of a copyright or patent, sometimes of a mine.

r.p.m. (abbr.) revolutions per minute.

r.p.s. (abbr.) revolutions per second.

RR., R.R. (abbr.) railroad.

RRB or R.R.B. (abbr.) Railroad Retirement Board.

Rt. Rev. (abbr.) right reverend.

Ruanda [roo-AHN-dah]. Ruanda-Urundi [oo-ROON-dee]. Belgian U.N. trust territory between Congo and Tanganyika. Cap., Usumbupa. In 1962, split into Republic of Rwanda and Kingdom of Burundi.

Rubaiyat of Omar Khayyam [roo-bie-YAHT]. Arabic for quatrain. 11th-century poem translated by Edward Fitzgerald in 1859 from the Persian.

rubberband. -neck, -necker, -nose (fish), -proof-ed, -stamp (nonliteral) (n., adj., and v.), -stone (all one word); rubber-lined (adj.), rubber-stamped (adj.); rubber plant, rubber stamp.

rubdown. (n. and adj.) rub-a-dub.

Rubirosa, Porfirio [roo-bih-ROH-suh, pawr-FEE-rih-oh]. (1909–1969) Dominican Republic diplomat.

ruble. Russian currency unit = 100 kopeks.

rucksack [RUHK-sak; Brit., rook-sack]. A loose, flat pack slung over the back.

KNAPSACK. A flat case for equipment similarly carried, as by a soldier.

HAVERSACK. A canvas case for carrying provisions on a march.

Ruhr [roor]. Region in West Germany.

rule 21. rule XXI, BUT capitalize, Rule 21, when part of title: *Rule 21: Renewal of Motion.*

rule of thumb. (n.) BUT adj; *rule-of-thumb decisions.*

Ruler of the Universe. (Deity).

Rules. Of the House of Representatives; BUT rules of the House; Standing Rules of the

Senate (publication), BUT rules of the Senate; also Commission rules.

Rumania [roo-MAEN-yah]. Native, Rumanian. Cap., Bucharest (Bucuresti). Currency, leu, pl., lej; ban, pl., bani. Webster and Statesman's Yearbook prefers Romania. *Cf.* Romania.

rumba, rhumba [RUHM-buh].

rumor. Brit., -our.

rumpus room.

rumrunner. rumrunning, rumshop.

run. P., ran; p.p., run; running.

runabout. (n. and adj.), —around (n. and adj.), —away (n. and adj.), —down (n. and adj.), —out (n. and adj.), —over (n. and adj.), —through (n. and adj.), —up (n. and adj.), —way (all one word); run-in (n. and adj.), run-on (n. and adj.).

runcible [RUHN-sih-b'l]. Curved, three-prong fork. Also *runcible spoon.*

run-in. Pl., run-ins.

run of paper (ROP). In advertising, position left to the discretion of the publisher.

run-on sentence. Two or more sentences combined without connectives or sufficient punctuation. *Some people like pepper, others like salt.* IMPROVE by separating the clauses with a semicolon or inserting *but.*

ruse [RUEZ]. Trick.

russet. Reddish brown.

Russia [RUHSH-ah]. Russian, Rossiya [ruh-SYEE-yuh]. Former empire, now the *Union of Soviet Socialist Republics.* Russia often refers to *Russian Soviet Federated Socialist Republic,* largest (more than half the population) of the republics of the Soviet Union extending from Baltic to Arctic to Pacific Oceans. SEE Soviet Union.

Russian names. Where no English equivalents exist in translating, use phonetic substitutes, *zh, kh, ks, ch, sh, shch, ya. Ski* endings convert to *sky.* The feminine *a* ending is ignored.

Russian pound. $\frac{1}{40}$ pood = 0.90282 lb. avdp. (U.S.S.R.).

rustproof.

Rwanda, Republic of. Formerly Belgian mandate of Ruanda-Urundi. Independent, July 1, 1962. Native, (adj.) Rwandan (N.Y. Times) Rwanese; Cap., Kigali. Currency, franc (RF), centime.

Ry. (abbr.) railway.

rye bread. rye field.

Ryukyu Islands [rih-oo-kyoo]. Also Liukiu [lih-oo-kih-oo]; Luchu [LOO-choo]; Nansei [nahn-sae] Islands. Chain south of Japan. Occupied by U.S. since 1945.

S

S-bend. S-brake, S-iron, S-shaped, S-trap, S-wrench.

s. (abbr.) shilling.

s. and s.c. (abbr.) sized and super-calendered.

's. SEE possessives.

S. (abbr.) south; Senate bill (with number).

S.A. Sturmabteilung. German Nazi semimilitary organization. Brown Shirts. Known as storm troops, —ers. 1923-34. *Cf.* S.S.

Saar, the [zahr; Fr., sahr]. Saarland [Zahr-lant. Angl., SAHR-land]. West German territory bordering France which passed between France and Germany after each war; scene of plebiscite in 1957.

Saarbrücken [ZAHR-brihk-ehn]. Fr. Sarrebrouck [sah-reh-BROOK]. Capital of Saarland.

Sabbath. Sabbath Day. The Sabbath is observed on Saturday by Jews and Seventh-Day Adventists, on Friday by Moslems.

Sabbathbreaker. —breaking, —keeper.

Sabbatic. For religious use.

SABBATICAL. For sabbatical year, the seventh year in which Israelite fields were allowed to lie fallow. Now, a leave of absence granted every seven years (or periodically).

saber. Brit., -re.

Sabina [sah-BIE-nah]. Belgian airline.

Sabra. Native born Jewish Israeli. *Cf.* Israel.

SAC. (abbr.) Strategic Air Command.

saccharin. (n.) saccharine (adj.) [SAK-u-rihn]. Coal tar product used as a sugar substitute.

sacerdotal [sas-uh-DOH-tal]. Relating to priestly functions.

SACEUR. (abbr.) Supreme Allied Commander Europe.

sachem [SAE-chehm]. American Indian Chief; by extension, Tammany Hall official.

SACLANT. (abbr.) Supreme Allied Commander Atlantic.

sacrifice [SAK-rih-fies].

sacrilegious [sak-rih-LEE-juhs]. From sacred; stealing or desecrating sacred things.

sacrosanct. Inviolable, especially ironically.

el-Sadat, Anwar [suh-DAHT]. President of Egypt 1971–   . Commonly Sadat.

Sadducee [SAD-yoo-see]. Sect of ancient Jews who postulated freedom of will, denied resurrection, personal immortality, fate.

Sade, Comte Donatien Alphonse Francois de [deh sahd, kawnt DAW-nah-SYANN AHL-fawns FRAHN-swah]. (1740–1814) Marquis de Sade. French sadist, writer. *Cf.* sadism.

sadism [SAE-dizm]. [Though more commonly SAD-]. Delight in cruelty, from the sexual perversion which is satisfied by cruelty. *Cf.* Sade.

SAE. (abbr.) Society of Automotive Engineers, which sets product standards.

safari [suh-FAH-ree]. Expedition, especially for hunting.

saga [SAH-guh]. Epic story.

sagacious [suh-GAE-shuhs]. Keen in perception.

Sagittarius [saj-ih-TAIR-ee-uhs]. Constellation: the Archer.

Saguenay [SAG-eh-nae]. Quebec river which flows south into St. Lawrence at Tadoussac [TAHD-uh-sak].

Sahara. The word desert is inherent in the name. NEVER *Sahara Desert.*

said. Some substitute words: answered, asked, cried, continued, decried, denied, groaned, replied, shouted, whispered. NEVER: grimaced, smiled, frowned, laughed. NOT: *"I accept," he laughed.*

said, same. Commonly used for aforesaid in legal or commercial correspondence, but should otherwise be avoided.

same. SEE just as.

Saigon [sie-GAHN; Fr., sah-ee-GAWN]. Capital city of South Viet Nam.

saint. (abbr. St.; pl., SS. Brit. also S. and Sts.; Fr., Ste.). Usually abbreviate before a name: *St. Louis, St. James's Palace, St. Vitus Dance.* Omit *St.* in connection with apostles, evangelists, and Church Fathers. *Luke, Paul, Augustine.* NOT: *St. Luke etc.*

Saint Croix [saent-KROI]. River in Wisconsin, Minnesota and Maine; Island in Virgin Islands group.

Saint-Cyr-l'Ecole [sahn-SEER-lae-KAWL]. Town in northern France; site of military school, 1808–1940. The School is now at Coetquidan, Brittany.

Saint-Gaudens, Augustus [saent GAW-d'nz]. (1848–1907) Irish-American sculptor.

St. Laurent, Louis Stephen [san-law-RAHN, LOO-ih STEE-vehn]. (1882–   ) Canadian lawyer; prime minister, 1948–1957.

St. Louis [saent-LOO-ihs]. City in Missouri.

St. Maurice [sann-moh-REES]. Town in France; also river in southern Quebec.

Saint-Moritz [saent-maw-RIHTS; Fr., sann-maw-REETS; Swiss., sahm-moh-RIHITS; Ger., zanght-MOH-rits]. Resort town in Switzerland.

Saint Paul [SAENT-PAWL]. Capital of Minnesota, on Mississippi River. Twin city of Minneapolis on opposite bank.

Saint-Saens, Charles Camille [san-SAENS, kah-MEE-y]. (1835–1921) French composer.

Saipan [sie-PAN or sie-PAHN]. Japanese naval base island in Mariana group, captured by U.S., July 1944. U.S. Trust Territory.

sake [SAH-kee]. Japanese rice wine.

Sakhalin Island [SAK-ah-leen]. Russian Island formerly divided with Japan. Formerly Saghalien; Jap., Karafuto.

salable [SAEL-a-bl]. Capable of being sold. salability.

salad days. Green years of raw youth.

Saladin [SAL-ah-dihn]. (1138–1193) Sultan of Egypt and Syria.

Salamanca [sal-ah-MANG-kah; Span., sah-lah-MAHN-kah]. Former center of Arab culture in Spain.

Salazar, Antonio de Oliveira [sa-luh-ZAHR, ann-TAW-nyaw dae aw-lee VAE-ee-ruh]. (1889–1970) Portuguese dictator. Prime Minister of Portugal, 1932–1968.

salesgirl. saleswoman. AVOID saleslady.

salient [SAE-lee-ehnt]. Conspicuous, noticeable. —ce or —cy.

saline [SAE-lien]. Containing salt.

salmon [SAM-uhn].

salmon-colored. (adj.) salmon-red (adj.); salmon fishing.

Salome [sal-LOH-mee]. Niece of Herod Antipas, who received the head of John Baptist as a reward for her dancing.

"SALOME." [SAH-loh-mae]. Drama by Oscar Wilde; 1905 opera by Richard Straus.

salon. Brit., saloon. Large reception hall for exhibition of art or gathering of celebrities.

Salonica, or —ka [sal-oh-NEE-kah; sah-LAHN-ih-kah; sal-oh-NIE-kah]. Seaport in Greece; formerly Thessalonica.

saloonkeeper. saloon deck.

Salote Tupou. (1900–1965) Queen of Tonga, 1918; married Prince Uiliami Tupoulahi Tungi, 1917.

salt. For table salt.

SALTS. For chemical salts, bath salts, Epsom salts, smelling salts.

saltbox.

salubrious [sa-LOO-brih-uhs]. Conducive to good health.

Salutations. See *dear*, and each of the individual titles.

Salvador. SEE El Salvador.

salve [sahv, sav]. Healing ointment.
SALVE [salv]. (n.) Salvage. —vable.

salver [SAL-vuh]. Tray for visiting cards.

salvo [SAL-voh]. Pl. —os. A quibbling excuse, especially for saving one's own feelings or reputation; also a series of shots at intervals; a simultaneous discharge of shots or bombs.

Salzburg [ZAHLTS-buhrk; angl., SAWLZ-burg]. Resort and music center on Salzach River Austria.

SAM. (abbr.) surface-to-air missile.

Samaritan [suh-MAR-ih-t'n]. A generously helpful person.

Samarkand [SAM-uh-kand or -KAND]. Russian City in central Asia. Formerly Turkish Samarquand, ancient Maracanda.

same. DO NOT use meaning *the above mentioned*. NOT: *It is imperative that the same be delivered immediately*.

same identical. Redundant. *Same* means *identical*.

Samoa. Since 1900, U.S. territory of five islands and two coral atolls 2400 miles south of Hawaii. Cap., Pago Pago, sometimes Pango Pango.

Samos Is. [SAE-mohs]. Greek island in Aegean Sea.

Samson [SAM-s'n]. Biblical judge of great strength.

samurai [SA(M)-moor-ie]. Lesser nobility under former Japanese feudal system.

sanatorium. Pl. -s. See sanitarium.

sand, sands. Both are mass nouns. *Cf.* Collectives.

sandaled. —ing.

sandhog. Applies to tunnel diggers working under air pressure, not merely tunnel diggers.

sandy-bottomed. (adj.) sandy-red (adj.).

San Francisco, Calif. Natives object to *Frisco*.

sang-froid [SAHN-frwah]. Coolness under stress.

sanguinary [SANG-gwih-nehr-ee]. Bloody; bloodthirsty: *a sanguinary tribe of savages; a sanguinary code of justice*.
SANGUINE. Confidently hopeful; also cheerful, warm. Sometimes, sanguinary. Use is derived from an old notion that a man with a ruddy (hence, blood-filled) complexion had cheerful spirits.

Sanhedrin. Supreme council and tribunal of ancient Jews.

sanitarium. Pl. —s. Preferred to sanitorium. A place for healing.

sanitary. Hygienic.
SANATORY. Curative.

sanitation. (n.) A making sanitary; science of sanitary conditions.

sanitary district. SEE District.

San Jacinto [san juh-SIHN-toh]. River in southeast Texas.

San Joachin [san wah-KEEN]. River in southwest California.

San José [san hoh-SAE]. Capital of Costa Rica. Also city in West California southeast of San Francisco Bay.

San Juan [san WAHN]. River in Colorado, Utah. Also, seaport capital of Puerto Rico.

San Marino [san-mah-REE-noh]. Republic (and capital city) on East Italy peninsula, 38 sq. mi. Native (s. and pl.), Sanmarinese; (adj.) Sanmarinese. Currency, lira, pl. lire; centesimo, centesimi.

San Martin, Jose de [thae sahn mahr-TEEN, hoh-sae]. (1778–1850) South American soldier, statesman.

de Santa Anna, Antonio Lopez [dae sahn-tah-AH-nah]. (1795?–1876) Mexican general and president.

Santiago [sahn-tih-AH-goh]. Island in Cape Verde group; capital of Chile; and many other cities.

sapid. Flavorful. Opposite, insipid.

sapphire [SAF-ier].

SAR or S.A.R. (abbr.) Sons of the American Revolution

Sarajevo. SEE Serajevo.

Sarawak [sah-RAH-wahk]. British colony in northwest Borneo.

sarcophagus [sahr-KAHF-a-guhs]. Pl. -i or -uses. Ancient coffin.

sarsaparilla [sas-(uh)-pah-RIHL-uh; sahr -suh-puh-RIHL-uh].

Sartre, Jean-Paul [SAHRTR, zhahn pohl]. (1905–) French writer.

Saskatchewan. (abbr. Sask.) Province in Canada. Cap., Regina.

Satan [SAE-tan]. His Satanic Majesty, Father of Lies, the Devil; BUT a devil, the devils; Satanic.

satiate [SAE-shih-aet]. Fully satisfy. —tiable, —tiety, [se-TIE-ih-tih]. -ation.

Sato, Naotake [sah-toh nah-oh-tak-kee]. (1882–) Japanese diplomat.

satrap [SAE-trap; Brit., SAT-rap]. Ancient Persian provincial governor.

saturate [SAT-yuh-raet]. Impregnate completely. —rable.

Saturday [SAT-uhr-dih]. (abbr. Sat.)

Saturn. Ringed planets. Saturnian.

Saturnalia. (Sing. and pl.) Saturnalian; BUT N.Y. Times, saturnalian.

satyr [SAT'r; SAET'r]. Sylvan demigod, with tail and ears of a horse, given to lasciviousness and debauchery.

Saudi Arabia [SAH-oo-dih]. Kingdom formed in 1932 covering most of Arabian peninsula. Native, Saudi Arab(s) or Saudi; (adj.) Saudi Arabian or Saudi. Cap. and King's residence, Riyadh (ar Riyad). Diplomatic center, Jidda (Juddah). Currency, riyal (SR), piaster.

sauerbraten.

Sault Sainte Marie [soo saent mah-REE]. Waterfall in Michigan; also city opposite in Canada.

sauté [soh-TAE]. Quick fried in a little hot fat.

savable [SAEV-uh-bl]. Also saveable. saver.

Savang Vatthana [sah-VAHT-ah-nah]. (1907–). King of Laos, 1959– .

savant [sav-AHN or SAV-aNT]. Man of learning.

save-all. (n. and adj.).

save and except. A legal pleonasm.

save face.

savings. Takes a plural verb, although a mass noun. Cf. Collectives.

savings bank. NOT saving.

savior. BUT the Saviour (Christ).

Savonarola, Girolamo [sah-voh-nah-ROH-lah; angl., sav-oh-na-ROH-lah, jee-RAW-lah-moh]. (1452–1498) Italian religious reformer.

savory [SAE-vuhr-ih]. British adjective savoury

Savoyard. Native of Savoy; associated with Gilbert and Sullivan productions, from Savoy Theatre, London.

saw. (P. and p.p.) sawed, sometimes p.p. sawn; sawing.

say. P. and p.p., said. Tell, relay information: *He said he would go.*

state. Set forth formally; make a declaration: *He stated his point of view.*

say nothing. (n. and adj.) say-so (n.)

SBA or S.B.A. (abbr.) Small Business Administration.

sc., scil. (abbr.) scilicet. (Lat.) Namely. Usually italicized.

S.C. (abbr.) South Carolina.

scabland [skab-land] Bare plateau, especially in northwest U.S.

scalawag. scallawag. Preferred to scalywag in U.S. Rascal.

scallop [skahl-uhp]. —ed, —ing.

scan. Originally meant to analyze poetry, read painstakingly. Now often used for the meaning, to skim through (colloquial).

scandalmonger.

Scandinavia. Norway, Denmark, and Sweden, sometimes Iceland; NOT Finland.

Scandinavian Airlines System. (abbr. S.A.S.).

scansion. Scan a line of poetry by (A) dividing into feet, e.g. monometer, dimeter, trimeter, tetrameter, pentameter, hexameter, heptameter, octameter, nonameter; (B) indicating the meter by the rhythm of emphasis, classified as iambic (1 short or unaccented, 1 long or accented syllable); trochaic (1 long, 1 short); anapestic (2 short, 1 long); dactylic (1 long, 2 short). Most popular meter is iambic pentameter: *Draw forth thy sword, thou mighty man-at-arms.*

scant. Usually preferred to scanty.

SCAP. (abbr.) Supreme Commander for the Allied Powers (Japan.).

scapegoat. scape wheel.

Scaramouch [SKAIR-uh-mouch]. Boastful buffoon. Sabatini's book, *Scaramouche.*

scarce. May be used for scarcely.

scarcely is followed by when, NOT than: *He had scarcely washed when dinner was announced.* Avoid double negative meanings. NOT: *He could scarcely depend on no help. Without scarcely* is an impossibility.

scarf. Pl. -s or -ves.

scarface. scar-faced (adj.).

Scarlatti, Alesandro [skahr-LAHT-tee, ah-les-SAHN-droh]. (1659–1725) Italian composer.

scarlet fever.

scatterbrain. scatter rug.

scenario [sehn-NAIR-ih-oh or —NAH—, or shae-NAH-rih-oh]. Synopsis of a play. *Cf.* abbreviation.

scenic [SEEN-ihk]. Of a stage setting; picturesque; a graphic representation.

scepter. Pref. to Brit. —re. Sovereign's staff of authority.

schedule [SKED-yool; Brit., SHED-yool]. A formal list.

schedule 2, A, II. BUT Capitalize Schedule 2, when part of title: *Schedule 2: Open and Prepay Stations.*

schema [SKEE-muh]. Pl. -mata. Diagram or outline of a plan.

scherzando [SKAER-tsahnd-doh]. Pl. -os. (music) In a sportive manner.

scherzo [SKAER-tsoh]. Pl. -os. (music) Fast, humorous instrumental composition.

Schiaparelli, Elsa [skyahp-ah-REHL-ee]. French dress designer.

schism [SIHZ'm, NOT shihzm]. A division; the offense of producing one.

schizoid [SHIHZ-oid]. Tending toward or resembling schizophrenia or dementia praecox.

schizophrenia [SKIHZ-oh-free-nih-uh]. Psychoses characterized by disintegration of personality and loss of sense of reality.

School. Capitalize if part of name; capitalize any school of U.S. Army or Navy; *Hayes School,* the school, school district. *Cf.* District. Capitalize the proper names or other designations: *De Witt Clinton High School, Columbia University.* Do not write or abbreviate No. in school names: *School 5, P.S. 5, Public School 5.*

school colors. Capitalize Crimson, Violet, etc. when designating a school.

Schopenauer, Arthur [SHOH-pehn-hou-ahr, AHR-toor]. (1788–1860) German philosopher.

Schuylkill R. [SKOOL-kehl]. River in Pennsylvania.

sciatica [sie-AT-kuh]. Neuralgia or neuritis of the back.

science. Characterized by knowing facts.

ART. Generally associated with skills, doing, directions, individual workmanship: *Science of paints; art of painting.*

scilicet. (abbr. *scil* or *sc.*) (Lat.) *scire licet.* You may know, to wit.

scintilla [sihn-TIHL-uh]. Pl. —lae. The slightest trace.

scion [SIE-uhn]. Detached plant shoot, by extension descendant. For plant shoot, cion in U.S.

scissors. Although the plural form refers to one instrument, it takes a plural verb in most cases, but in some constructions a singular verb is also permissible: *Here is your scissors.* After a numeral, use *pairs of scissors* to avoid confusion. In a compound, the singular form is preferred: *scissor-handles.* The same is true of similar two-pronged instruments: *shears, tongs, calipers, clippers,* and the like.

S. Con Res. (with number) (abbr.) Senate concurrent resolution.

score. (n.) = 20: *Four score and seven years* (87 years), *scores of trains.*

scoreboard. scorecard, scoresheet.

scores. Write in numerals: *The Yankees won, 10 to 4.* Spell out numbers of runs, hits, and innings below 10, but use numerals for larger numbers.

scoria. Pl. -ial. But singular is collective. NOT scorium.

scot-free. (adj.).

Scotland. Native, Scot(s), Scotsman, Scotswoman, Scotch (collective); natives object to Scotchman. Adj., Scotch, Scottish. Scotch tweed, whiskey, terrier; Scots law. British use Scotch, Scottish, Scots, Scotchman, —woman.

Scotch plaid.

Scotch tape. Trade mark (by Minnesota Mining & Mfg. Co.).

Scottish. Scoto-Irish.

scour [SKOU-'r].

scourfish. -way.

scoutcraft. scoutmaster.

scratch pad. U.S.; British use scribbling-block.

scream. High-pitched emotional cry.
    SHRIEK. Higher pitch, more emotion.

SCREECH. Higher pitch, to the point of the comic.

scrimmage. Football play. British prefer scrummage for Rugby.

Scripture, Scriptures. Holy Scriptures (the Bible). SEE Bible. Takes singular verb.

scroll work.

scruple. Unit of apothecaries' weight = 20 grains = $\frac{1}{3}$ dram = $\frac{1}{24}$ oz. = 0.04166 oz. = 1.2959 grains.

scrupulous [SKROO-pyoo-luhs].

scull. Oar used at stern of boat for propulsion.
    SKULL. Cranial bone.

sculptress.

scurrilous [SKUHR-in-luhs]. Containing or using coarse, obscene, or indecent language.

scuttlebutt. Rumor, gossip; from ship's water casket.

scythe [sieth]. Mowing instrument with long blade, long handle.
    SICKLE. Instrument with short, curved blade, short handle.

s.d. (abbr.) (Lat.) *sine die* [SIE-nee DIE-ee]. Without date.

S. Dak. (abbr.) South Dakota.

S. Doc. (abbr.) with number, Senate document.

SE. (abbr.) southeast. Also S.E.

Seabeas. Navy construction battalion, established 1941.

seaboard. Atlantic seaboard, eastern seaboard, etc.

SEALS. Navy sea, air, and land capability (guerrilla) forces. *Cf.* Coins, Special Forces.

seamstress. Preferred to sempstress.

Sean [shawn, shuhn]. Irish for John.

seance [sae-AHNS; Brit., SAE-ahns]. Meeting to receive communications from spirits.

seasonable. Coming at the right time. *A seasonable arrival.*

SEASONAL. Connected with a season. *Seasonal employment.*

Seattle [see-AT-l]. Seaport in Washington.

SEATO. (abbr.) Southeast Asia Treaty Organization. Formed Sept. 8, 1954 by U.S., Britain, France, Australia, New Zealand, the Phillipines, Pakistan, Thailand.

Seaway. SEE geographic terms, Authority, Corporation.

sec. (abbr.) secant, second, section

SEC. (abbr.) S.E.C. N.Y. Times, Securities and Exchange Commission.

secede. secession.

sec.-ft. (abbr.) second-foot.

2d Lt. (abbr.) second lieutenant.

secondhand. (adv. and adj.); second-class (adj.), second-degree (adj.), second-guess (v.), second-rate, second in command, second sight.

Second World War. (abbr. W.W.II) SEE War.

secondary education. After elementary; i.e., high school.

secretary.

Secretary. Capitalize if head of national governmental unit: Secretary, of Defense, Secretary of State, and so on; the Secretary of State for Foreign Affairs, for the Colonies, etc. (Brit.); the Secretary of the Smithsonian Institution, the Secretary, also the Assistant Secretary, the Executive Secretary; BUT secretary of the Interstate Commerce Commission; secretary of state of Iowa; Secretaries of the Army and the Navy, BUT Secretaries of the military departments.

secretary general. Pl., secretaries general.

Secretary General of the Organization of American States (formerly Pan American Union), of the United Nations.

secretaryship. secretary-generalcy, secretary-generalship, secretary-treasurer; secretary general.

secretary-treasurer. Pl. secretaries-treasurers.

secretive [seh-CREE-tihv].

secretmonger. secret service, secret society.

section 2, A, II. BUT Section 2, when part of title: *Section 2: Test Construction Theory.* Abbreviate after the first use: *Section I . . . Sec. II.*

section crew. section gang, section hand, section man.

section of land. Unit under U.S. land laws = 1 sq. mi. = $\frac{1}{32}$ township = 640 acres.

securityholder.

seducible [see-DOOS-ih-bl].

see. P., saw; p.p., seen; seeing.

seecatch. seesaw.

seeing (that). Avoid use as a conjunction meaning *since, inasmuch as.* NOT: *Seeing that she was finished, she could not have done more work.*

seek. P. and p.p., sought.

seem. The word often produces confusion in tense. Distinguish between the time in the verb and the time in the complementary clause: *I seem to understand what he says now, what he said or what he will say. I seemed to understand yesterday, but I may have been wrong. This seems to be the case all the time. Only if they approved, as seems to be the case, would the settlement be just.*

seer [SEE-uhr]. One who sees.

seer [seer]. Prophet.

Seidlitz or Sedlitz powders [SEHD-lihtz]. Effervescing salts mixed in water as a cathartic.

Seine River [SAEN]. River in France; flows past Paris, into the English Channel.

seismic [SIEZ-mihk]. Of earthquakes.

seldom. *Seldom or never.* NOT: *Seldom or ever.*

selectman.

self-addressed. Purists note that enclosing an "addressed envelope" has the same meaning.

self-collected. self-despondent, self-evident, etc. AVOID as pleonasms. *Collected, despondent, evident* are usually better, except when great emphasis is intended.

self-liquidating premium. Premium for which the charge to the purchaser pays the cost.

sell. P. and p.p., sold.

sellers' market. One in which demand exceeds supply.

selloff. (n. and adj.). sellout (n. and adj.).

selvage. Brit. —vedge. The finished fabric edge.

SALVAGE. Rescued merchandise, or compensation for it.

semantics. The science of word meanings.

semen [SEE-m'n]. Fluid containing spermatozoa.

semester [see-MEHS-tehr]. Originally six months; now one of two periods of instruction in academic year. *Cf.* trimester.

semi-. Combining form meaning half: semi-annual, semiarid, and so on; *semi-armor-piercing* (adj.), *semi-Christian, semi-idleness,* semi-indirect, *semi-winter-hardy* (adj.).

THE SEMICOLON. Used: (1) To separate phrases or clauses containing commas: *Abraham Lincoln, President in 1861, faced the war with reluctance; Woodrow Wilson, who took office in 1913, was also a lover of peace. Never, sir; I will not go.* (2) To separate statements of contrast or statements very closely related when a sharper break than a comma is desired: *No; he received half. She said no; he said yes.* (3) To separate two distinct thoughts in a single sentence: *She loves Yogi; nothing else interests the group.*

Semite. Technically Jews and the Arab peoples, but used principally to suggest approval of or antagonism toward Jewish people (anti-Semitism). Semitism, Semitic, anti-Semitic. *Cf.* Jew.

sempstress. Use seamstress.

the Senate.

Senate. (U.S.) Capitalize titles of officers standing alone. Capitalize Chaplain, Chief Clerk, Doorkeeper, Official Reporter(s), Parliamentarian, Postmaster, President of the Senate, President pro tempore, Presiding Officer, Secretary, Sergeant at Arms.

Senate. Ohio (State), etc.; the senate.

Senator. ADDRESS: The Honorable Harrison Williams, United States Senate, Washington, D.C. or Senator Harrison Williams, The United States Senate, Washington, D.C. or (if sent to a home address) The Honorable Harrison Williams, United States Senator. SALUTATION: Sir, Dear Sir, My dear Sir, My dear Senator Williams, Dear Senator Williams.

Senator (woman). ADDRESS: As above. SALUTATION: Madam, My dear Senator Smith, Dear Madam, My dear Madam, My dear Madam Senator, Dear Mrs. Smith.

Senator (U.S. Congress). BUT lower-case if referring to a state senator, unless preceding a name.

senatorial.

send. P. and p.p., sent; sending.

sendoff. (n. and adj.), -out (n. and adj.).

Senegal [sehn-ee-GAL or SEHN]. Formerly French Soudan. Independent, August 1960. Native and adj., Senegalese. Cap., Dakar; Currency, franc (CFAF).

senile [SEE-niel]. A result of the aging process, usually characterized by mental impairment.

senior [SEEN-yuhr]. More advanced in rank or age. *Cf.* freshman.

Sennacherib [seh-NAHK-ehr-ihb]. (d., 681 B.C.). King of Assyria, 705-681 B.C.

señor [sen-YAWR]. Spanish for Mr.

señora [sen-YAWR-ah]. Spanish for Mrs.

SEÑORITA [sen-yaw-REE-tah]. Spanish for Miss.

sense in. Reason or logic in.

SENSE OF. Perception of; opinion of: *There is no sense in staying till you're thrown out. He has a sense of timing.*

sensible. Perceptible to the senses; also, having good sense.

SENSIBLE OF. Aware; responsive to an emotional stimulus.

SENSIBLENESS. Good sense

SENSIBILITY. Acuteness of feeling; often plural.

sensitive. Capable of receiving sensations.

SENSITIVE TO. Acutely responsive to a stimulus.

SENSITIVITY. Capacity to respond to stimulation.

sensuous. Appealing to the senses.

SENSUAL. Appealing to the senses, especially the grosser ones.

SENTENCE. In grammar, a group of words complete in themselves, containing subject and predicate, expressed or understood. A sentence may be a statement (declarative), a command (imperative), or a question (interrogative).

A sentence of one clause is simple; if it contains a dependent clause, it is complex; if it contains two independent clauses, it is compound.

sententious [sehn-TEHN-shuhs]. Containing too many maxims; pompous.

sentient. [SEHN-shuhnt]. Conscious, receptive of sensation.

sentinel. Anyone on watch. Sentineled, -ing.

SENTRY. Guard, especially soldier on watch.

Seoul [SOHL] or Kyongsong [kyawng-sawng] or Kei-Jo [kae-joh]. Capital city of South Korea.

separate.

sepsis [SEHP-sihs]. Pl. —ses [seez]. State of being poisoned by bacteria.

Sept. (abbr.) September.

septillion. 1000 sextillions; British and German, 1 million sextillion. *Cf.* Numbers.

septuagenarian   [sehp-chu-uh-juh-NAIR-ee-uhn].

septum. Pl. septa. Separation between two cavities; e.g., in the nose.

sepulcher [SEHP-uhl-kuhr]. Pref. to Brit. —re. Burial vault.

seq., et. seq. (abbr.) *et sequentes* (Lat.) Subsequent lines. *f.*, *ff.*, or *foll.* are more widely used.

sequela. Pl. -lae. Consequences.

SEQUENCE OF TENSES. The tense of a subordinate clause must take the tense of the principal clause: *I know he is here.* BUT not in a quotation: *I said,* "*He is here.*" And NOT in a parenthetical expression: *I thought, even as I think now, I was right.. Cf.* Subjunctive.

sequestrate [see-KWEHS-traet]. (v.) Confiscate.

ser. (abbr.) series.

seraglio [sihr-AH-lyoh]. Pl. —os or —li. Harem.

Serajevo [SAH-rah-yeh-voh]. Also Sarajevo. Capital of Bosnia and Herzegovina, Yugoslavia. Site of assassination of Archduke Ferdinand, which sparked W.W. I.

seraph [SEHR-aff]. Pl. seraphs or seraphim. Highest order of angels.

Sergeant at Arms. (U.S. Senate or House).

sergeant at arms. Pl. sergeants at arms. N.Y. Times, sergeant-at-arms.

sergeant major. Pl. sergeants major.

serif. Fine cross stroke in a typeface (T). *Sans serif,* without serif (T).

Sermon on the Mount. Christ's discourse (Mattew V. VI, VII; Luke II).

serum. Pl. -rums or -ra.

serveout. (n. and adj.).

service. -ceable.

service. Lower-case—airmail service, Army service, city delivery service, consular service, customs service, (see Bureau), diplomatic service, employment service (state), extension service (state), general delivery service, naval service, Navy service, parcel post service, postal service, postal field service, railway mail service (SEE Division), rural free delivery service, rural delivery service, free delivery service, special delivery service, star route service.

Service. Capitalize if referring to Federal unit; the service: Employment Service, Extension Service, Fish and Wildlife Service, Foreign Service (SEE Foreign Service), Forest Service, Immigration and Naturalization Service, Internal Revenue Service, Mediation and Conciliation Service, National Park Service, Officer Procurement Service, Postal Transportation Service, Secret Service (Treasure), Selective Service (SEE ALSO System); BUT selective service, in general sense; selective service classification I-A, 4-F, etc.; Soil Conservation.

serviceman. service-connected (adj.); service stripe.

serviceable.

servile [SUHR-vil, Brit. -ie].

sesame [SEHS-uh-mee]. Herb, seed, from East India.

sesqui-. Combining form meaning one and a half: *sesquialteral, sesquicentennial.*

sesquipedal [sehs-KWIP-ee-dal]. Or sesquipedalian [sehs-kwih-pee-DAE-lih-uhn]. A foot-and-a-half long. Humorously, use of long words is sesquipedalianism.

session. A sitting of a public body: *The court was in session.*
 CESSION. A giving up: *Cession of the Sudetenland became a symbol of appeasement.*
 SECESSION. A withdrawal: the *secession of the Southern states.*
 CESSATION. A stopping: *There was a cessation of fire at 11 A.M.*

set. P. and p.p., set; setting, setter. A transitive verb which requires a direct object: *I set the plate on the table.*
 SIT. P. sat, p.p. sat; sitting. An intransitive verb: *He sat on the chair.*

seta. Pl. setae. A bristle-like part.

settler. In law, settlor.

Seurat, Georges [suh-RAH, ZHAWRZH]. (1859–1891) French impressionist painter.

sever. -ered, -ering.

several. Three or more, but not many. Takes a plural verb.

severalfold.

Sevigne, Marquise de [de sae-vee-NYAE, mahr-KEEZ]. nee Marie de Rabutin-Chantal. (1629–1696) French lady of fashion, writer.

sew. p.p., sewed or sewn; sewing.

sewage. Refuse for sewers.
 SEWERAGE. Removal of sewage; a sewer system.

sextet (te). Group of six.

Sextette from Lucia [sehks-TEHT from loo-CHEE-uh].

sextodecimo. P/, —os. Book size $4\frac{1}{2} \times 6\frac{3}{4}$ in. (n.) from 16 pp. to a sheet.

Seychelles [SAE-shehl, -shelz]. British colony, island group in west Indian Ocean. Capital, Victoria. Currency, Seychelles rupee.

Sf. (abbr.) Svedberg flotation.

Sfc. (abbr.) sergeant, first class.

Sfc. (abbr.) seaman, first class.

sferics [SFEHR-ihks]. Storm detection instrument based on plotting electrical charges.

Sforza, Count Carlo [SFAWR-tsah, KAHR-loh]. (1873–1952) Italian anti-Fascist philosopher and statesman.

sforzando. (Music) Accented.

Sgt. (abbr.) Sergeant.

shade. Partial absence of light: *light and shade. Cf.* color. For window shade British use window blind.
 SHADOW. The shade of a particular object, usually with shape: *lights and shadows.*

shagbark. -tail; shag-haired (adj.).

shake. P., shook; p.p., shaken; shaking, shakable.

Shakespeare. -earian. Brit. -ere.

shaky.

shall or will, should or would. To express the idea that something will or is expected to happen: (1) Use shall or should with the first person. *I (we) shall go to school.* (2) Use will or would with the second or third person. *He (you, they) will.*
 To express determination, command, intention, promise, desire, or willingness: (1) Use will or would with the first person.

I (we) will do or die. (2) Use shall or should with the second or third person. *He, (you, they) shall do or die.*

In questions, use shall or will according to which is expected to be used in the reply: *When will I be permitted to drive?* (Answer: *You will be permitted to drive when you. . .) Shall we meet again?* (Answer: *We shall.*)

shaman [SHAH-man]. Medicine man.

shambles. A slaughterhouse; by extension, any scene of carnage, thus a scene of destruction.

shame. —mable.

Shanghai. China. Shanghai (v.), -aied; -aing.

Shangri-La. Idyllic land in James Hilton's *Lost Horizon.* In W.W. II, a secret U.S. airfield.

shape. In printing, use gothic letters to indicate shapes. *T-square, U-shaped.*

SHAPE. Words indicating shape: acerate (needle); aciniform (grape cluster); aliform (wing); alveolate (honeycomb); ampullaceous (flask, bladder); amygdaloid (almond); arciform (arch); bacillary (rod); bicorn (crescent), botyroid (bunch of grapes); bursiform (sac); campanulate (bell); capsular (capsule); cheliform (claw); claviform (club); clupeiform (herring); clypeate (shield); cochleate (snail-shell); crenate (scalloped); crescent (first-quarter moon); cordate (heart); crinoid (lily); cruciate, (cruciform cross); cucumiform (cucumber); cuneate (wedge); cystoid (bladder); dactylose (finger); deltoid (triangle); dentiform (tooth); domical (dome); ensiform (sword); feliform (cat); galeate (helmet); gliriform (rodent); helical (spiral); helicoid (snail-shell); herbaceous (leaf); ichthyomorphic (fish); infundibular (funnel); lingulate (tongue); lunate (crescent); luniform (moon); mammillary (breast); napiform (turnip); navicular (boat); nuciform (nut); nummiform (corn); olivary (olive); ovate, ovoid (egg); palmate (hand); pectinate (comb); pediform (foot); peltate (shield); petiolate (stalk, stem); piliform (hair); pisciform (fish); prolate (lemon); pyramidoid (pyramid); pyriform (pear); quadrate (roughly square); reticular, reticulate (net); rhampoid (beak); rhaboid (rod); rotate (wheel); saggittate, (arrowhead); rhombic (diamond); sagittal (arrow or arrowhead); scaphoid (boat); scutate, scutiform (shield); scyphate (cup); semilunar (half-moon); setiform (bristle); spatulate (spoon); sphenoid (wedge); spheroid (earth);

staphylo (grape); stellate (star); tabulate (table); trapeziform (trapezium); pyramid (triangle); trochal (wheel); umbilicate (navel); unciform (hook); undulant (wavy); ungulate (hoof); urceolate (urn); vermicular (worm); villiform (pile of velvet); virgate (wand); xiphoid (sword). *Cf.* -hedron, ovate, parallelephpedon, diamond, lozenge, rhombus (equilateral parallelograms without right angles): oblong; rectangle; parallelogram (four sided figure whose sides are parallel); rhomboid, (-al) equal parallelogram (with two pairs of equal sides but no two sides parallel); trapezoid (four-sided figure with two sides parallel). SEE ALSO -gon; -hedron.

SHAPE. (abbr.) Supreme Headquarters allied powers (Europe). (Webster: Supreme Headquarters Allied Powers Europe.)

shapeup. (n. and adj.). N.Y. Times, (n.) shapeup.

sharecrop. sharecropper, shareholder.

Shawn [shawn]. Irish for John. *Cf.* Sean.

shave. P., shaved; p.p., shaved or shaven; shaving.

shavehook. -tail.

Shaw, George Bernard. (1856–1950) British author, socialist. Shavian.

Shays' Rebellion. Mass., 1786–1787. For Daniel Shays, 1747–1825.

she. Nominative case. Objective and possessive, her. *She is, to her, her book.*

sheaf. Pl., -ves.

shear. P.p., -ed or shorn; shearing. Cut hair from; also, deviate.

SHEER. Transparent or pure or perpendicular or utter: *sheer stocking, gall, cliff, or folly.*

shears. *Cf.* scissors.

sheathe [sheeth]. Pl., -s [sheeths].

shed. P. and p.p., shed.

sheer. SEE shear.

sheerline. —off (n. and adj.), —up (n. and adj.).

sheik. [SHEEK, SHAEK]. Preferred to sheikh.

Shelepin, Aleksandr Nikolayevich [shehl-YEHP-ihn]. (1918–   ) Soviet politician. Formerly head of secret police.

shelf. Pl. —ves; (v.) —ve; (adj.) —ved; —fy, —vy. shelf-full.

shellack. -cked, -cking.

shepherd [SHEHP-uhrd]. Herder of sheep.

SHF. (abbr.) superhigh frequency.

shibboleth [SHIHB-oh-lehth]. Watchword, criterion, test. From the word used by Gileadites to detect Ephramites, who pronounced it [SIHB-oh-lehth].

shillelagh, shillalah [shil-AE-luh or-lee]. Irish cudgel.

Shillelagh. Raytheon surface to surface anti-tank mounted missile with infrared guidance for front line troops.

shilling. (abbr. s.) =5 pence=½ florin.

shilly-shallier. shilly-shally.

shinbone. shinplaster.

shine. (intransitive) P. and p.p., shone; shining.

shine. (transitive) P. and p.p., shined; shiny, shining.

shiner-up.

shingle. Pl. -s.; shingly.

ship. SEE boat.

ship canal no. 1. Lower-case.

ship of state. (unless personified).

shipping master. shipping office, shipping room.

SHIPS' NAMES. In. U.S. Navy, usually aircraft carriers are named for historical naval vessels or battles; battleships for states; cruisers for cities; destroyer leaders (frigates) for admirals; destroyers for naval personnel, members of Congress, or inventors; destroyer escorts and transports for naval personnel killed in action during World War II; submarines for marine creatures; ballistic-missile submarines for historical figures; ocean minesweepers for abstract qualities or birds; coastal minesweepers for birds; inshore minesweepers for seaboard features; submarine chasers and escorts for small cities; submarine tenders for those who contributed to the development of submarine technology or for mythological characters; large seaplane tenders and escort carriers for bays or sounds; small seaplane tenders for bays, inlets, and straits; ammunition ships for volcanoes or the ingredients of explosives; landing ships for countries; medium landing ships for rivers; transports for flag officers or Marine Corps officers; attack transports and cargo ships for counties; submarine rescue vessels for birds; oilers for rivers with Indian names; ocean-going tugs for Indian tribes; harbor tugs for Indian chiefs and Indian words.

shipway no. 1.

Shirer, William Lawrence [SHIE-rehr]. (1904–   ) U.S. writer, especially on Germany.

shoe. P. and p.p., shoed or shod; shoeing.

shoot. P. and p.p., shot.

shootman. —off (n. and adj.).

short circuit. (n.); short-circuit (v.).

short-lived [-lievd].

short-sighted. Lacking foresight. Also near-sighted.

NEARSIGHTED. Of the optical failing; not able to see far.

FARSIGHTED. Not able to see close objects.

MYOPIC. Nearsighted.

ASTIGMATISM. Having defect causing distortion or indistinctness of vision.

Shoshone [shoh-SHOH-nee]. Indian tribe in the Rockies.

Shostakovich, Dimitri Dimitrievich [shoss-tah-KOH-vihtch, dee-MEE-tree]. (1906–   ) Russian composer.

shot. As a collective noun for ammunition, takes a singular verb.

shotgun. -put, -putting, -star (all one word); N.Y. Times, shot-put, shot-putter, shot-putting.

should. Use with be glad, be inclined, care, like, prefer: I should like to be there. Cf. shall.

should have. NOT *should of*: *He should have stayed where he was.*

shoulder-high. (adj.) shoulder blade, shoulder strap.

shovel. —ed, —ing. Brit., —ll/lled, —lling.

show. —ed, shown; —ing.

showerproof. shower bath.

s. hp. (abbr.) shaft horsepower.

shred. P. and p.p., shredded is preferred to shred. —dding.

shredout. (n. and adj.).

shriek. SEE scream.

Shriner. a.

shrink. shrank, shrunk; shrinking (adj.); shrunken or shrunk.

shrivel. —ed, —ing. Brit., —lled, —lling.

shuffleboard.

shut. P. and p.p., shut.

shutaway. (n. and adj.), shutdown (n. and adj.), shuteye (n. and adj.), shutoff (n. and adj.), shutout (n. and adj.), shutup (adj.); shut-in (n. and adj.), shut-mouthed (adj.).

shuttlecock.

shy. shyer, —est; —ish, —ly, —ness.

Sibelius, Jean [sih-BAE-lih-uhs, zhan; angl., yahn]. (1865–1957) Finnish composer.

sibilant. In grammar, a hissing sound, as *s, z,* or *sh*. Avoid sibilants in close sequence.

sibyl. Fortune teller. -llic, sibylline.

sic. (abbr.) (Lat.) *thus.* Inserted in brackets after a quotation which may appear to be inaccurate. *Cf.* brackets.

sick. ill. Use *more* or *most* for comparison.

sick bay. -bed, -hearted, -list, -room; sick-abed (n. and adj.), sick call, sick leave.

sideward.

sidle. -led; -ling.

siege.

Siena [SYAE-nah; angl., sih-EHN-ah]. British Sienna. Province in Tuscany.

Sienkiewicz, Henryk [shehn-KYEH-veech, hehn-rihk]. (1846–1916). Polish novelist.

Sierra Leone [sih-EHR-uh lee-OHN]. In West Africa. Formerly British. Independence, April 27, 1961. Native, (adj.) Sierra Leonean. Cap., Freetown. Currency, leone, shilling.

Sierra Nevada [sih-EHR-uh neh-VAD-uh, —VAH—]. Calif. mountains. Sierra means mountain, therefore NOT Sierra Nevada Mts.

Sigismund [SIHJ-ihs-muhnt; SIHG- Ger., ZEEK-ihs-muhnt]. Holy Roman Emperor, 1410–1437.

signal. (v.) —ed, —ing; Brit. —lled, —lling. Do not confuse with single.

signalman. signal tower.

sign painter.

significant.

signor [see-NYAWAR]. signora [see-NYAWR-uh] signorina [seen-yawr-EE-nuh]. Ital. for Mr., Mrs., Miss.

Sihanouk, Norodom. SEE Norodom.

silage [SIE-lihj]. Winter fodder preserved in a silo.

silent partner. Brit., sleeping partner.

silhouette [SIHL-oo-eht].

silken. Figuratively, silk-like; otherwise, of silk cloth.

silly. sillier, silliest, sillily (adv.); silliness.

silt. -pan, -stone.

simile. A figure of speech in which similarity is expressed using *like* or *as*: *hearts that click like taxi meters.*

    METAPHOR. A comparison made by substituting a similar figurative word or phrase: *In the cathedral of my heart, a candle always burns for you.*

simon-pure. (adj.) simon pure (n.). Genuine. From Centlivre's *Bold Stroke for a Wife.*

simony [SIHM-oh-nih]. Trading in church honors.

simple-minded. (adj.) simple-rooted (adj.), simple-witted (adj.).

simpleness. Carries a deragotory sense. Use simplicity.

simulacrum [sihm-yoo-LAE-kruhm]. Pl. -cra. A sham.

simultaneous [sie-muhl-TAE-nee-uhs; Brit., sihm]. At the same time.

sin. (abbr.) sine.

sin-proof. sin-born (adj.), sin-bred (adj.)

since. Avoid the redundant use with *ago.* NOT: *It is six months ago since she arrived.*

since. SEE because.

sincerely.

sinecure [SIE-nee-kyoor, SIHN-ee-]. Position which requires little service or responsibility.

sine curve. sine wave.

sine die [SIE-nee DIE-ee or SEE-nae DEE-ae]. (Lat.) *Without setting a date. Adjourned sine die.*

sine qua non [seen kwae NAHN; Webster, SIE-nee kwae nahn]. *sine quibus non. Without which not.* Indispensable thing.

sing. P., sang; p.p., sung.

Singapore [sihng-uh-PAWR]. State of. Independence, June 3, 1959 within Commonwealth. Natives, Singaporan(s). Currency, Malayan dollar (M$), cent.

singe. singed; singeing.

Singhalese. Brit., Sinhalese. Of Ceylon. Sinhala, one of languages spoken there.

singsong.

sinh. (abbr.) hyberbolic sine.

sinister. In heraldry, on the left of the person bearing a shield. Also of lurking evil. *Cf.* dexter.

sink. P., sank or sunk; p.p., sunk; sinking. (adj.) sunken.

Sinkiang [SIHN-KYAHNG]. Province in China.

Sinn Fein [shihn-faen]. Irish nationalist party.

Sino- [SIE-noh]. Combining form meaning Chinese: *Sino-Soviet Pact.*

sinus. Sing. and pl. Pl. also -uses.

Sioux [soo; pl. soo or sooz]. American Indian tribes. Siouan.

Sioux City [sOO]. City in Iowa.

siphon [SIE-fahn].

Siqueiros, (Jose) David Alfaro [see-KAE-rohs]. (1896-1974) Mexican painter.

sir. Title placed before Christian name of a knight or baronet; also a title of respect used in addressing a man when not using his name.

Sirius [SIHR-ih-uhs]. The Dog Star.

sirocco [sih-RAHK-oh]. Pl. —os. Hot South wind from Libya.

Sister. (adherent of religious order) ADDRESS: Sister Maria Therese, Convent of the Sacred Heart. SALUTATION: Dear Sister, My dear Sister Maria Therese.

sisterhood. sister-german, sister-in-law.

sit. P. and p.p., sat.

sitdown. (n. and adj.) —fast (n. and adj.); sit-downer.

site. A place or a piece of land: *Site for a 20-story building.* NEVER: *a 20-story site.*

sitting room.

sixteenmo. (16 mo) Book size approximately $4\frac{1}{2} \times 6\frac{1}{4}$ in. 16 pages from a single sheet.

sizeup. (n. and adj.).

S.J. Res. (with number) (abbr.) Senate joint resolution.

Skaneateles [skan-ih-AT-uh-lehs]. City in New York.

skeptic. Brit., sceptic. One who questions, NOT necessarily disbelieves.

sketchbook. sketch plan.

skewbald. SEE piebald.

ski [skee, Brit. shee]. Pl. skis; (n.) ski; skied, Brit., ski'd; skiing, skier.

skiplane. ski jump, ski suit.

skidlift. (truck), —proof, —road; skid chain, skid fin.

skillful. Brit., skilful.

skim milk.

skin diver. skintight; skin-clad (adj.), skin-graft (v.); skin test.

skins. goat, sheep and calf skins. NOT calfskins.

skirt around. Redundant. *Skirt* is sufficient.

Skoda, Emil von [fahn SKOH-dah, EH-mihl]. (1839–1900) Czechoslovakian industrialist.

Skouras, Spyros [SKOO-rahs, SPIHR-ohs]. (1893–1971) Greek-American cinema producer.

skulduggery. Trickery.

skullcap.

sky blue. (n.) Adj., sky-blue.

skyscraper. A tall building. In New York City, generally one of 30 stories or more.

slack. (v.) Relax. slack-off, slacking.

slacken. (v.) Abate, slow down; become negligent.

slalom [SLAH-luhm or SLAE-]. Ski race, usually zigzag, against time.

slam-bang.

slander. In law, false and malicious defamation uttered orally.
   LIBEL. In law, false and malicious defamation, especially published or broadcast.

slantwise. slant-eyed (adj.).

slaveholder. -owner, -ownership (all one word); slave-born (adj.), slave-deserted (adj.); slave market, slave trade, slave worker.

Slavic. For ethnic references, as in nations, people.
   SLAVONIC. For cultural references, as in dances, art, literature.

slay. P., slew; p.p., slain, NOT slayed; slaying.

sleazy [SLAE-zih, SLEE-zih]. Flimsy, badly woven. sleazier, —iest.

sledgemeter. sledge-hammered (adj.); sledge hammer.

sleep. P. and p.p., slept.

sleight [sliet]. Skill, deftness: *Sleight of hand.*
   SLIGHT [sliet]. (n.) Slender, frail; (n.) treat lightly; ignore.

sleuth [slooth]. In U.S., detective.

slice. —ceable.

slide. P. and p.p., slid; p.p. sometimes slidden.

slidefilm. slide rule.

Slim Mongi [sleem, mahn-jee]. (1908–1969) Tunisian diplomat.

sling. P. and p.p., slung. NOT slang.

slingball. slingshot, slingstone.

slink. slunk. NOT slank.

slip no. 1.

slit. P. and p.p., slit.

sloop. SEE boat.

slosh, slush, sludge. This is the order of increasing viscosity.

sloth [slawth]. Laziness. slothful, —illy, —fulness.

slough [slou]. Bog: *slough of despond.*
   SLOUGH [sluhf]. Shed or cast off.

slovenly [SLUHV-ehn-lee]. Lazy and slipshod.

slow. May sometimes be used as an adverb: *Drive slow.*

sluice [slooss]. Passage or channel for water. -ceable., sluicebox, -way; sluice gate.

slumber. Especially light sleep.

slumberland.

slumberous. Preferred to -brous.

sly. —er, —est; —ly, —ness, —ish.

small. SEE little.

small-business man. Preferred to small businessman to avoid ambiguity.

smallhearted. -mouthed, -pox, -talk, -time (adj.), -town (adj.) (all one word); small-ankled (adj.), small-hipped (adj.), small-scale (adj.); small arms.

smash up. (n. and adj.).

smearcase. smear culture.

smite. P., smote; p.p., smitten.

Smithsonian Institution. SEE Institution.

smog. Smoke plus fog.

smoking room.

smolder.

Smolensk [smoh-LEHNSK]. City in U.S.S.R., on the Dnieper River.

smooth. Preferred to smoothen.

smorgasbord [SMAWR-gahs-bawrd]. Swedish buffet.

snackbar.

snake. Used rhetorically, connotes contempt, coldness, insidiousness.

    SERPENT. Used rhetorically, suggests a more venomous creature.

sniperscope [SNIE-pehr-skohp]. Periscope-like attachment on a rifle.

sniveled. -ing.

snuffbox. -maker, -making snuff-stained (adj.).

s.o. (abbr.) seller's option.

sobeit. (n. and conj.) so-and-so, so-called (adj.), so-seeming (adj.), so-so.

sobersided. sober-minded (adj.).

sobproof. sob sister, sob story, sob stuff.

sobriquet [SOH-brih-kae]. Preferred to sou-. Nickname.

so-called. An attributive adjective implying doubt: *The so-called soldiers marched up the hill.*

    SO CALLED. In predicative use: *The Happy Warrior, so called because of his . . .*

Sochi [SAW-chi]. Resort city on Black Sea, U.S.S.R.

sociable. Pleasant company.

social. Pertaining to society, friends.

socialism. An economic-political system under which the means of production and the regulation of consumption are vested in the State. socialistic.

    SOCIALIST. One who believes in socialism. A Socialist (capitalized) is a member of the Socialist Party.

Society. Capitalize if part of name; the society: American Cancer Society, Inc., Boston Medical Society.

soda jerk. soda granite, soda pop, soda water.

soddenness [SAHD-'n-ehss]. State of being boiled, stewed or soaked. Also, dissipation.

Soho [soh-HOH, SOH-hoh]. The foreign quarter of London.

soil bank.

soiree.

sojourn [SOH-juhrn pref. in U.S.]. Dwell temporarily as a stranger.

sol (sun) [sahl]. (musical) [sohl].

solace [SAH-lihs]. Comfort, alleviation of grief.

solder [SAH-duhr]. (n.) Metal used to join; (v.) join by melting.

soldierly. (Adj. and adv.) NOT soldierlily.

Soldiers' Home. Capitalize if part of name; Ohio Soldiers' Home; the soldiers' home.

solecism [SAHL-ih-sihsm]. Grammatical error; by extension, incorrect behavior.

solemn [SAHL-ehm]. solemnity [sah-LEHM-nih-tee].

Solicitor for the Department of Commerce; the Solicitor; Solicitor General.

solo. Pl. —s; for technical use, soli.

solon [SOH-lahn]. A wise man. AVOID the journalese solon for legislator, from Athenian lawgiver.

soluble, insoluble, dissolvable. For substances. SOLVABLE, SOLUBLE, INSOLUBLE, UNSOLVABLE. For problems.

Somalia [soh-MAH-leh-uh]. Formerly Italian and British Somaliland. Independence, July 1960. Natives, Somalis. Cap., Mogadishu. Currency, somali (som.)

somber. Preferred to -bre in U.S.

sombrero [suhm-BRAE-roh].

some. AVOID use for somewhat, NOT: The rain let up some.

some. Meaning approximately, should precede only round numbers. NOT: some 476 persons were present, NOR some 400-odd persons.

somehow. NOT somehows.

some of us. The possessive pronoun which follows should be our, unless the speaker is not a party: Some of us get our just desserts. BUT to a child: Some of us don't obey their parents.

someone. A person.
SOME ONE. One person, or thing.

somersault. Preferred to summerset.

something of a fool. Preferred to somewhat of a fool.

some time. (adverbial phrase) A considerable period of time: He waited for some time.

SOMETIME. (adv.) At some indefinite occasion. Sometime I will stay longer..

SOMETIME. (adj.) Former: A sometime sheriff.

SOMETIMES. An undetermined number of times: He sometimes came early. (The unusual, an adverb with a plural)

someway or somehow. Preferred to someways. Brit., somehow.

somewhere. NOT somewheres.

Somme River [suhm]. River in France; flows into English Channel. Site of battles in 1916 and 1944.

somnolent [SAHM-noh-lehnt]. Sleepy. somnolence, somnolently.

somnambulism [som-NAM-byo-lihzm]. Sleepwalking.

Somoza, Anastasio [soh-MOH-sah]. (1896–1956) President of Nicaragua, 1937–1956.

son-in-law. sons-in-law, son of man.

sonic boom. An explosion-like sound heard when a shock wave, generated by an aircraft flying at supersonic speed, reaches the ear.

sonnet. A short rhyming poem of 14 lines in iambic pentameter, composed of groups of 8 lines and 6 lines. Three varieties are represented by the works of Petrarch, Shakespeare, and Milton.

Son of Man. (Christ) Jesus' sonship, the Messiah, BUT a messiah; messiahship; messianic; messianize; christology; christological.

sonorous [soh-NOH-ruhs]. Resonant, full of sound.

Sons of the American Revolution. (organization) a Son; a Real Son.

soot [sut (as foot)].

SOP. (abbr.) standard operating procedure.

sophomore [SAHF-oh-MOUR]. Wise fool. Second-year student. Cf. freshman.

soporific [soh-pawr-RIHF-ihk]. Sleep-inducing.

soprano. Pl. -s or -ni.

Sorbonne [sawr-BUHN]. University in Paris.

sorehead. (n. and adj.) -headed, -hearted; sore-eyed (adj.), sore-footed (adj.); sore throat.

S O S. (spaces, no periods) Code signal for distress; not an abbreviation.

so that. There is no comma after *that*.

sotto voce [SOHT-oh VOH-chae]. (Ital.) In an undertone: *A comment uttered sotto voce.*

soufflé [soo-FLAE, SOO-flae]. Delicate spongy mixture of egg whites.

sough [suhf, sou]. Sighing sound, as of wind.

soupcon [SOOP-sawn]. A small amount; from *suspicion.*

Souphanouvong, Prince. (1909–   ) Leader of Pathet Lao Laotian forces.

sourcebook.

source . . . from. Redundant. NOT *The only source of water was from the Nile.*

Sousa, John Phillip [SOO-suh]. (1854–1932) American composer of marches.

Soustelle, Jacques [soos -TEHL, jahk]. (1912–   ) French-Algerian statesman, diplomat.

south. SEE east.

South. South American Republics (SEE Republic), South American States, South Atlantic, South Atlantic States, Deep South (U.S.), South Korea, Midsouth (U.S.), South Pacific, South Pole, the South (section of United States); Southland.

south, southern. Comparative: more southern; superlative: southmost, southernmost.

Southampton [south-AMP-t'n]. Seaport in England.

South Carolina. (abbr. S.C.) Native and adj., South Carolinian. Cap., Columbia.

southeast. -eastern, -going, -land, -lander, -paw, -ward, -west, -west-bound (adj.), -wester (all one word); south-born (adj.), south-central (adj.), south-sider, south-southeast; south end, south side.

southeast Asia. BUT capitalize when referring to the area as a unit. Usually Burma,

Cambodia, Indonesia, Laos, Malaya, North Borneo, North Vietnam, South Vietnam, Sarawak, and Thailand.

southerly. Southern.

Southern States. Southern United States: Alabama, Florida, Georgia, Kentucky, Mississippi, Louisiana, North Carolina, South Carolina, Tennessee, Virginia, West Virginia.

southern California. southeastern California, etc.

southerner.

southward.

Southwest, the. In U.S.: Arizona, New Mexico, Nevada, Utah, (California); sometimes also Oklahoma, Arkansas, Louisiana.

Souvanna, Phouma, H.H. Prince Tiao [soo-VAHN-uh FOO-muh]] (1901–   ) Prime Minister of Laos, 1957–1970.

sovereign [SAHV-r'n].

soviet [soh-vih-EHT]. A council. SEE ALSO U.S.S.R.

sow. P., sowed; p.p. sown.

sowback. -backed, -belly, -bug.

s.p. (abbr.) *sine prole.* Without issue.

SP. (abbr.) shore patrol.

spa [SPAH]. A mineral spring or nearby resort.

Spaak, Paul-Henri [spahk, pohl ahn-REE]. (1899–1972) Belgian statesman, diplomat.

Spaatz, Gen. Carl A. [SPAHTS]. (1891–   ) U.S. Air Force general.

spacious. With ample space.

SPECIOUS. Plausible but false.

spadeful. Pl. -s.

Spaeth, Sigmund [spaeth, SIHG-mihnd]. (1885–1966) American musicologist.

Spain. Native, Spaniard(s); (adj.) Spanish. Cap., Madrid. Currency, peseta (Pts), centimo.

span. Unit of length = 9 inches = $\frac{1}{8}$ fathom = 22.86 cm.

Span. (abbr.) Spanish, Spain.

Spanish. Spanish-born (adj.), Spanish-speaking (adj.): Spanish American.

Spanish-American War. SEE War.

Spanish Names. SEE Names.

SPAR. U.S. Coast Guard Women's Reserve. From *Semper Paratus—Always Ready.*

sparerib. spare-bodied (adj.); spare room.

speak. P., spoke; p.p., spoken; speaking.

speak-easy. (n.).

Speaker of the House of Representatives. ADDRESS: The Honorable John J. MacCormack, Speaker of the House of Representatives, Washington, D.C.; or The Honorable, The Speaker of the House of Representatives, Washington, D.C.; or The Speaker of the House of Representatives, Washington, D.C. SALUTATION: Sir: Dear Sir:, Dear Mr. Speaker:

Spear of the Nation. African black nationalist group in South Africa.

special. Distinctive.

PARTICULAR. Quality of an individual.

INDIVIDUAL. Peculiar to one of a group.

SPECIFIC. The special quality which gives a person, thing, or species its character; particular and definite: *The specific qualities of silver ore... The specific charges were.....*

Special Forces. U.S. Army guerrilla units. *Cf.* Coins, Seals.

Special Order No. 12. a special order.

specie [SPEE-shih]. Coin, not paper money.

species [SPEE-sheez or sees, SPEE-shihz]. (pl.), Biological group between genus and sub-species. Print name in *italics. Lepomis* (genus) *gibbosus* (species). *Cf.* Classification of Plants and Animals. Sing., specie.

specious [SPEE-shuhs]. Deceptively attractive; feasible but fallacious: *A specious argument.*

specter. Preferred to -re.

spectrum. Pl., —tra pref. to -s.

speech. SEE address.

speed. P. and p.p., sped

SPEED UP. P. and p.p., speeded up.

speedboat. -trap, -way, -writing (all one word); speed cop.

spell. -lled preferred to spelt; spelling.

Spencerian. Pertaining to philosopher Herbert Spencer (1820–1903).

SPENCERIAN. Pertaining to Platt Rogers Spencer (1800–1864), American penmanship stylist.

SPENSERIAN. Pertaining to the poet Edmund Spenser (1552–1599). *The Faerie Queen.*

spend. P. and p.p., spent.

spermatozoon [spuhr-muh-tuh-ZOH-uhn]. Sexual cell. Pl., —zoa.

sp. gr. (abbr.) specific gravity.

sphagnum [SFAG-n'm]. A moss used in packing.

sphere. Area of surface = $4\pi r^2$; volume = diameter $3 \times .536$.

sphinx. Pl. —es. Also —ges [-jeez]. Monster with woman's head and bust, lions body, and wings. In Egypt, image of recumbent lion with head of man. sphinxlike.

spice. —ceable.

spill. P., spilled.

spinach [spihn-ihtch].

spin-off. In finance, sale or distribution of stock of a subsidiary company to shareholders of a parent company.

Spinoza, Baruch or Benedict [spihn-OH-zuh, bah-ROOK, BAE-neh-dihkt]. (1632–77) Dutch lensmaker, philosopher.

spiraea [spie-REE-uh]. Preferred to spirea. Shrub with white or pink flowers.

Spirit of '76. (painting) But spirit of '76 (in general sense).

spiritual. Of the soul.

> SPIRITUEL. Refined, sprightly. Sometimes fem. -elle.
>
> SPIRITUOUS. Of alcoholic beverages. Note *uous*.

spit. P. and p.p., spat. spit 'n' image. Also spitting image. *The spit and image of. . . .* NOT *spittin' image.*

splendor. Preferred to Brit. —our.

splice. —ceable.

SPLIT INFINITIVES. An adverb may split an infinitive if the natural position requires this or if another position would lead to ambiguity: *It would be wise to at least call. No teacher has the right to needlessly destroy a student's ego.*

split verbs. Adverbs normally fall between auxiliary and verb, and after all auxiliaries if there are more than one: *They will not be seriously threatened.*

spoiled. Preferred to spoilt.

spoilsport. spoilsman, spoilsmonger.

Spokane [spoh-KAN]. City and River in East Washington.

spokesman.

spoliation [NOT spoil—]. Authorized plundering.

spongecake. sponge-diver; sponge-diving (adj.), sponge-shaped (adj.); sponge bath.

sponsible. Worthy of credit.

spontaneity. Preferred to -eousness.

spoonerism. Accidental transposition of sounds and letters of words: *I am gleased and prateful.* (for pleased and grateful). For Oxford's Rev. W. A. Spooner (1844–1930).

spoonful. Pl., -fuls.

sports. Use figures for scores and points. *Giants 3, Yankees 4.* Spell out numbers of runs, touchdowns, baskets, goals, strokes, hits, and so on, when less than 10, but use numerals for larger numbers. Time is written in figures: *2 : 25.* A figure less than a minute is written: *0.59.3; 2 minutes 4.3 seconds, 2 : 04.3.* Capitalize names of sports events, stadiums, bowl games: *Polo Grounds, Rose Bowl game, World Series.* Titles should precede a proper name when a position is appointive or elective: *Coach Lou Little. Cf.* scores.

spouse [SPOUS]. Husband or wife. From *espouse*, archaic, *to wed.*

spring. The season.

> SPRING. (v.) P., sprang is preferred to sprung.

springe [sprihnj]. Snare.

sprint. A short race at high speed.

> SPURT. An increase in pace.

spry. —ryer, —ryest; —ly, —ness, —ish.

Sp3c. (abbr.) specialist, third class.

spurious [SPYOOR-in-uhs]. Not from a true source; illegitimate.

spurnwater. V-shaped breakwater on a ship.

Spuyten Duyvil Creek. In N.Y. At north end of Manhattan.

spyboat. spyglass.

sq. in. or in.² (abbr.) square inch.

sq. mile (s). (abbr.) square mile(s).

squad. SEE Army Organization.

squalor, squalid [SKWAHL-lawr, —ihd]. Of filth.

Square, Lafayette. etc.; the square.

square. -rable, -rish. *NEVER more or most square,* BUT *more nearly square.*

square. Building unit = 100 sq. ft. = 9.29 m².

squinting modifier. A modifier placed so that it appears to modify both preceding and following words: *She told him this morning she was leaving. She would come back to school if required for 32 hours of work.*

S. Rept. (with number) (abbr.) Senate report.

S. Res. (with number) (abbr.) Senate resolution.

Sr. (abbr.) senior.

Sri Lanka [sree-LAHNKAH] (Prior to 1972, Ceylon). Native, adj., Sri Lankan Cap., Colombo. Curr., rupee.

SS. (abbr.) steamship, saints.

ss. (abbr.) (scilicet). In law, *namely.* SEE ALSO sc.

S.S. (abbr.) Schutzstaffel. (Blackshirts) Nazi German elite guard under Heinrich Himmler. One unit was known as the Death Head Battalion because of skull on cap.

SSA. (abbr.) Social Security Administration. Or S.S.A.

S. Sgt. (abbr.) staff sergeant.

SSM (abbr.) surface to surface missile.

SST. Supersonic transport plane. (1800 m.p.h.)

SS-10, SS-11. French anti-tank missiles.

S.S.U. (abbr.) standard Saybolt universal.

St. (abbr.) Street. Usually abbreviated in news articles and lists. Also abbreviate Ave., Blvd., Terr., BUT NOT Drive or Road. In a directory, St. is often omitted to save space, but Ave., Rd., etc. are included.

St., Ste., SS. (abbr.) Saint, Sainte, Saints.

stable. —bility, —bilize.

stadium. Pl. —dia. (meaning race courses, Greek measurement); —iums (meaning structures used for athletic events).

Stael, Mme. Anne Louise Germaine Barronne de. [deh *stahl*]. (1766–1817) Née Necker. French writer.

staff. Pl. -s; For music, sometimes for sticks, *staves.* For a group, use a singular verb.

Staff. Foreign Service. SEE Foreign Service.

stage. —geable, —gy.

stained-glass window. BUT *a panel of stained glass.*

Staked Plain.

stalactite [stuh-laq-tiet, stal-ak-tiet]. Calcium deposits hanging from the roof, resembling an icicle.

STALAGMITE [stuh-lag-miet, stal-ag-miet]. Calcium deposits formed from the floor, like an inverted icicle.

stale. stalish, staley.

Stalin [STAH-lyihn angl., STAL-in]. Original name, Joseph Vissarionovich Dzhugashvili (1879–1953). Russian dictator, 1924–1953.

Stalingrad [*stah*-lyihn-grad; *stal*-]. City on Volga River., U.S.S.R.; scene of turning point battle in W.W. II. Formerly Tsaritsyn.

stalk. Stem of a plant smaller than a bush.

TRUNK. Stem of a large tree.

Stamford, Conn.

STANFORD UNIVERSITY. Stanford, California.

stanch. See staunch.

stand. P. and p.p., stood.

standby. (n. and adj.) —down (adj and n.), —fast (n. and adj.), —off (n. and adj.), —offish –out (n. and adj.), -pat, -patter, -pattism, -pipe, -point, -post, -still (n. and adj.),–up (n. and adj.) (all one word). stand-in (n. and adj.).

standard time. SEE time.

stander-by.

staple. (1) Basic commodity; (2) wire device for holding two papers or objects together.

starboard. Right side of a ship (looking forward).

stark-mad. (adj.) stark-naked (adj.), stark-raving (adj.).

starlit. (adj.) Preferred to starlighted.

star of Bethlehem.

stars. SEE heavenly bodies.

Star-Spangled Banner. SEE flag.

start in. In is superfluous.

starter-off.

startup. (n. and adj.).

Stassen, Harold Edward [STAHS-'n]. (1907–) American lawyer, poet.

Stat. (abbr.) Statutes at Large.

-stat. Suffix meaning something stationary: *thermostat, gyrostat.*

state. When referring to the federal government, the body politic, foreign states: church and state, state of the Union message, statehood, statehouse, stateside, statewide, state's evidence, downstate, tristate, upstate, welfare state.

State government. State legislature (SEE legislature), State line, Ohio-Indiana State line; New York State; State of Israel; State of Pennsylvania; State of Veracruz; out-of-state (adjective); State prison; States rights. State-aided (adj.). State-owned (adj.); State line.

state groupings. Capitalize complete regional groups: *New England States, Middle Atlantic States.* BUT some of the mountain states.

stated that. before a fact. BUT: *He stated his demands.* NOT: *He stated he wanted more money.*

Staten Island. N.Y.C. Island containing borough and county of Richmond. Do not abbreviate.

State Representative. ADDRESS: The Honorable John J. White, The House of Representatives, The State Capitol, Jefferson City, Missouri. SALUTATION: Sir, Dear Sir, My dear Mr. White, Dear Mr. White.

States. Arab States, Balkan States, Baltic States, Communistic States, Eastern States, BUT eastern industrial States; East North Central States, East South Central States, Eastern Gulf States, Eastern North Central States, etc.; Far Western States, Gulf States, Gulf Coast States, Lake States, Latin American States, Middle States, Middle Atlantic States, Middle Western States, Midwestern States, Mountain States, New England States, North Atlantic States, Northern States, Northwestern States, etc.; Organization of American States; Pacific States, Pacific Coast States; South American States; South Atlantic States; Southern States; the six States of Australia, Thirteen Original States; West North Central States,

West South Central States, Western States, but western Gulf States; western farming states.

State's attorney. state's evidence, States rights.

State Senator. ADDRESS: The Honorable Roger Howards, The State Senate, Trenton, New Jersey; or Senator Roger Howards, The State Capitol. SALUTATION: Sir, Dear Sir, Dear Senator Howards.

statesman. -manlike, -woman.

static phrase. A phrase which denotes a condition of being rather than an action: *the beginning of,* NOT *to begin.*

Station. Capitalize if part of the name: the station; lower-case if referring to surveying or similar work: Grand Central Station, Key West Naval Station (SEE Naval), Nebraska Experimental Station; Syracuse Air Force Station, television station SWYR-RV; Union Station, Union Depot Station, the depot; WRC station, station WRC, radio station WRC, broadcasting station WRC; substation A.

station 27. Lower-case.

stationman. —master; station house, station wagon.

stationary. Fixed, not moving: *A tree is stationary.*

STATIONERY. Writing materials: *The e in envelope reminds one of the e in stationery.*

statist [stae-tist]. Advocate of statism, i.e. concentration of controls and power in the government.

statue. (sculpture).

STATURE. (height).

STATUTE. (law).

Statue of Liberty. the statue.

status [STAE-tuhs]. Position of affairs.

STATUS QUO. (Lat.) As things are.

STATUS QUO ANTE. As things were before.

statute-barred. (adj.) statute book, statute mile.

Statutes at Large. (U.S.) Revised Statutes.

staunch. Preferred to stanch. Stop the flow of.

stave [staev]. Pl., -s.

stave. (v.) P. and p.p., staved or stove.

std. c.f. (abbr.) standard cubic foot (feet).

steadfast.

steal. P., stole; p.p. stolen.

steamerload. Steamer-borne (adj.); steam line. steamship (abbr. SS., U.S.S.); United States Steamer. turbine steamship (abbr. T.SS.) His or Her Majesty's Ship (H.M.S.).

steerageway. sufficient ship speed to permit steering.

stevedore. The employer of longshoremen, who perform the labor of moving cargo.

stele [STEE-lee]. Shaft.

St. Elizabeths Hospital. (no apostrophe).

Stendhal [stann-DAHL]. Pseudonym of Marie Henri Beyle [bael]. (1783–1842) French writer.

steno-. Combining form meaning narrow, small: *stenograph, stenotic.*

stentorian [stehn-TOH-ree-uhn]. Very loud.

Stepinac, Alojzije [steh-PEE-nahtz, uh-LOIS-zih-uh]. (1898–1960) Cardinal of Yugoslavia.

steppingstone. stepping-off (adj.).

step-up. Increase gradually (U.S. only).

-ster. A suffix meaning one who does something; now often implies contempt: *gangster, punster.*

stere. (a.) Unit of volume = 1 m.^{3} = 35.314 cu. ft. = 1.308 cu. yds.

stereotype.

sterile [STEHR-ihl]. Not fertile. —ility.

sterling silver. 92.5 percent silver. Technically silver is redundant.

stern. Rear end of a vessel.

stet. Let it stand. Direction to printers to ignore correction made.

Stettin [shteh-TEEN]. Pol., Szczecin [shcheh-TSEEN]. Seaport near mouth of Oder River, Poland.

Stevens, Rise [STEEV-'nz, REE-zuh]. (1913–) American mezzo-soprano.

Stevenson, Adlai Ewing [ad-LIE]. (1900–1965) American statesman, diplomat.

stick. P. and p.p., stuck.

stick-at-it. (n. and adj.), stick-in-the-mud (n. and adj.), stick-to-itiveness (n.).

sticker-in. sticker-on, sticker-up.

Stieglitz, Alfred [STEEG-lihts]. (1864–1946) American editor, photographer.

stiff-necked. (adj.).

stifling [STEIF-lihng]. Stopping the breath.

stigma. Pl. —s; eccl., -mata. (n.). Brand; mark. (n.) Brand: stigmatize as; NOT: *He was stigmatized a liar.*

stiletto [stih-LEHT-oh]. A slender dagger. Pl. -os.

still remains. Redundant. Use *remains.*

stimulate. Excite, spur on. —lable, —tor.

stimulus [stihm-yoo-luhs]. Pl. -li. That which excites to action.

STIMULANT. Temporary exciter; e.g., alcohol.

sting. P. and p.p., stung.

stink. P., stank or stunk; p.p., stunk.

stipend [STIE-pehnd]. Compensation for service; a donation.

stirabout. A porridge of corn meal or oatmeal.

stirrup [STIHR-uhp pref. to STUHR-uhp]. Supporting ring for rider's foot.

stir-up. (n. and adj.).

stock. shares in a corporation. Brit., *shares.*

COMMON STOCK. Shares representing basic ownership. Brit., ordinary shares.

PREFERRED STOCK. Shares entitled to shares of profit (usually fixed and specified) before common stock.

CONVERTIBLE STOCK. Shares which may be converted from preferred to common stock under specified conditions.

CUMULATIVE PREFERRED STOCK. Preferred shares, of which the right to dividends accumulates if they are not paid.

stockpile.

stogie [STOH-gee]. Preferred to stogy. Cigar.

Stokowski, Leopold Antoni Stanislaw [stol-KAWF-skee]. (1887–   ) British-American conductor.

STOL. (abbr.) Short haul (distance) takeoff and landing; e.g. a helicopter.

stomacher [STUHM-ak-ehr].   Ornamental shirt-waist.

stomachache.

stone. unit of weight = 14 lbs. = 6.35 kg.

stone age. BUT UCMS and N.Y. Times, Stone Age. *Cf.* ages.

stonyhearted. stony-eyed (adj.).

stop. Stay is preferred to stop where *continue in the place* is meant: *He is staying at the Dorchester.*

storage room.

store. British prefer shop, especially for place where work is done.

story. Pl., —s or —ies. adj., —ied.

St. Peter's Church.

Stradivari, Antonio [strah-dee-VAH-ree]. (1644–1737) Italian violin maker. The violin: *Stradivarius.*

strafe [STRAEF; Brit. STRAHF].

straight. (adj. and adv.) Direct; uninterrupted.

STRAIT. Tight, narrow: *strait jacket*; *strait-laced*; *straightened circumstances.*

straightaway.   —edge,   —forward,   —way; straight-backed (adj.), straight-legged (adj.), straight-up-and-down (adj.); straight run, straight time.

stranglehold.

Strasbourg [strahz-BOOR]. City in France.

strata [STRAE-tuh]. SEE stratum.

stratagem [STRAT-a-jehm]. Ruse, deception, especially in war.

strategic [stra-TEE-jihk].

strategy. Plan or method for overall victory.

TACTIC. Method for advancing the immediate objective.

Stratford-on-Avon. English town near Birmingham, place of birth and burial of William Shakespeare.

stratosphere. Part of earth's atmosphere above troposphere, free of weather phenomena. *Cf.* atmosphere.

stratum [STRAET-'m, STRAT-'m]. Pl., -strata. (Plural is often used erroneously for singular.)

Strauss, Johann [shtrous, JOH-hahn]. Father, 1804–1849; son, 1825–1899. Austrian composers.

Straus, Richard [shtrous, REEK-ahrt; rihch-ehrd]. (1864–1949) German composer.

Strauss, Lewis Lichtenstein [STRAWS]. (1906–   ) Chairman of A.E.C., 1946–1950.

straw-hat circuit. Summer theatres.

streamlined. Designed to cut wind resistance. Extend its meaning with great restraint.

Stream, Gulf. SEE Gulf; geographic terms.

Street. Capitalize if part of name; the street: I Street (not eye); Fifteen-and-a-Half, 110th Street.

street cleaner. street-walker, street-walking; street-cleaning (adj.), street-length (adj.), street-sold (adj.).

stremma. (royal) = 0.2471 acre (Greece).

streptococcus [strehp-toh-KAHK-uhs]. A microorganism which occurs in pairs or chains.

Stresemann, Gustav [SHTRAE-ze-mahn, GUHS-tahf]. (1878–1929) German statesman.

stress. Action or pressure on bodies.
STRAIN. Change created by stress.

stretchout. (n. and adj.).

strew. P., strewed; p.p., strewn or strewed.

stria. Pl., -iae. Minute groove or channel.

stricken. P. p. of strike. Avoid adjective use for *afflicted*.

stride. P. strode; p.p., stridden.

strike. P., struck; p.p. struck or stricken: The comment was stricken from the record.

strikebreaker. —breaking, —out (n. and adj.) N.Y. Times, strike-out (n.); strike-over (n. and adj.); strike-in (n. and adj.).

string. P. and p.p., strung.

stringed. Provided with a string: *Stringed instruments*. BUT: *high strung*.

striped [STRIEPT]. Having stripes.

strive. P., strove; p.p., striven.

strongbox. —hearted, —hold, —point (n.), —room (all one word); strong-arm (adj. and v.), strong-backed (adj.), strong-minded (adj.).

Strong Opinion Words. *admirable, disgraceful, excellent, incredible, remarkable, tremendous* should not be used in neutral context. NOT: *Please bring me two remarkable steaks and two excellent books.* BUT: *He brought two excellent books from Paris.*

strychnine [STRIHK-nihn; Brit., —neen]. A poisonous alkaloid used as a stimulant.

strung. SEE stringed.

stubbornness.

stuck-up. (n. and adj.); stuck-upper, stuck-uppish (adj.).

studhorse. —mare, —work.

student. One who studies.
SCHOLAR. One who attends a school.
PUPIL. One attending secondary or elementary school.

studio. Pl. —s.

stuka [SHTOOK-ah]. German W.W. II dive bomber.

stuntman.

stupefy.

stupendous. Wonderful; astounding.

stupor [STOO-pehr]. Insensibility; lethargy.

Sturm und Drang [shtoorm-oont DRAHNG]. (Ger.) Storm and stress.

Stuttgart [SHTUHT-gahrt; angl., STUHT-gahrt]. City on Neckar River, West Germany.

sty. Pl. sties. Pig sty.
STYE. Pl., styes. Swollen gland on the eyelid.

style. Mode.
STILE. Passage.

stylebook. Manual of uniform typographic forms, spelling, capitalization, etc. for a publication.

stylus. Pl. —uses or styli. Pointed metal writing device used on stencils, tablets, etc. Also, phonograph needle.

stymie. Brit. stimy; v., stymied, —ying.

styptic [STIHP-tihk]. Astringent; stopping bleeding.

suasible [SWAES-a-bl]. Capable of being persuaded.

suave [swahv; Brit., swaev]. Urbane; smoothly, blandly pleasing.

sub-. Combining form meaning under, inferior, Usually without hyphen in U.S., with hyphen in Brit: subcommittee, submachinegun, subpolar, substandard, etc.; sub-Himalayan, etc.; sub rosa, sub specie.

subaltern [suhb-AWL-tuhrn; in logic, SUHB-]. Subordinate.

subch. (abbr.) subchapter.

subcommittee. SEE Committee. sub-subcommittee.

subdivisible.

subject of a sentence. The word or group of words which names the thing, person, place, or idea about which a statement is made in the sentence.

subject-object. subject-objectivity.

SUBJUNCTIVE MOOD. Three forms used in English are: (1) the present subjunctive, to indicate that the statement is concerned with an idea rather than with a fact; (2) the past subjunctive, to indicate that the statement is uncertain or improbable; and (3) the past perfect subjunctive, to indicate the past tense. The present subjunctive is marked by two constructions, the use of *be* directly with a subject: *They demanded that the motion be tabled.*; and the use of the third person singular without the *s* ending: *I insisted that he call me every day.* The past subjunctive is indicated by the same form as the past indicative, but expresses a present or future event: *If she studied all next week, she would still fail. If they (or she) were 90 pounds lighter, they (or she) would still be too heavy.* (*Were* is used for both sing. and pl.) The past perfect subjunctive is formed by *had*—the past participle in the indicative mood—but here implies that the facts are contrary. The words which mark this construction are *if, suppose, although, unless,* and the auxiliary verb placed before the subject: *If he had been there; had he been there....*
Several auxiliary verbs have subjunctive meanings: *may, must, shall, etc. They demand that he come at once. I wish he would stay.*
The degree of probability is expressed in the subjunctive thus: A probable event with the present subjunctive: *Though he speaks well; though he should speak well.*
A positive statement is expressed in the indicative mood: *Inasmuch as he spoke well,* (any tense may follow) *I will honor him.*
An unlikely event is expressed in the past subjunctive: *Even if he ran a three-minute mile,* (past subjunctive) *we might not honor him. If he had spoken well last week,* (past perfect subjunctive) *I might have honored him.*

sublimate. Deflect emotional drives from primitive channels to higher ones.

subliminal [SUHB LIH mihn-al]. (adj.) Below the threshold of consciousness: *Subliminal advertising reaches the consumer without his knowing it.*

submergible. Capable of being covered with water.
SUBMERSIBLE. Capable of functioning under water.

subordinate. In grammar, dependent and less important.

subordinate (or subordinating) conjunction. Used to introduce a dependent clause and join it to the main clause: *as, before, since, unless.*

subpar. (abbr.) subparagraph.

subpoena [suhb-PEE-nah]. Preferred to subpena. —naed, —naing. Legal writ requiring one to appear in court. *Subpoena duces tecum* requires the bringing of records.

subsequent to. Use *after.*

subservience. Preferred to -cy.

subsidence [suhb-SIE-dehns, pref. to Brit. SUHB-sih-dehnce]. Abatement.
SUBSISTENCE. Existence.

subsidy [SUHB-sih-dih]. Gift in financial aid. —dies.

substantiate [suhb-STAN-shih-aet]. Verify; prove. -tiable, -tiation.

substantive. In grammar, any word or group of words used as a noun.

substitute. (v.) *You replace A with B when you substitute B for A.* substitution.

subtle [SUHT'l]. —tler, —tlest; —tly. NOT subtile. Subtlety [SUHTL-tee].

Subtreasury. New York, etc.; subtreasury at New York, the subtreasury.

subtropical. subtropic(s). SEE tropical.

subvention. A subsidy.

subversive. (adj.) subversion. subvertible.

succeed.

successful achievement. Redundant.

succinct [suhk-SIHNKT]. Concise.

succor [SUHK-ehr]. Brit., —our. Aid; help.

Succoth. Jewish Feast of Tabernacles, usually in October.

succuba. (fem); pl. —ae; —bus (mas.); pl. -bi. Strumpet; demon, especially one which assumes human form to have sexual intercourse with men in their sleep.

such. Meaning *the above described,* or *those, it, them,* etc. should be avoided. NOT: *The by-laws prohibit drinking on the premises, and such drinking is in poor taste.*

such. *which, who, where, that.* AVOID. Generally incorrect. NOT: *He selected such fabrics which he felt would be suitable.* (Eliminate *such.*)

suchlike. INCORRECT.

Suchow [shoo-JOH]. City in southwest Shantung province, China.

Sudan [soo-DAN, Fr. soo-DAHN]. The Democratic Republic of the Sudan. Native, adj., Sudanese (s. and pl.). Formerly Anglo-Egyptian Sudan. Independent January 1, 1956. Cap., Khartoum. Currency, Sudanese pound (Sd £), piaster. the Sudan.

Sudan, French. Became (with Senegal) Federation of Mali (1959-1960). Since 1960, Republic of Mali.

suddenness.

Sudeten [zoo-DAE-tehn; angl., soo-]. Mountain range. West of Carpathians.

suds. There is no singular form.

sue. Sued, suing, suable.

suede [sWAED]. Tanned skin with flesh rubbed into nap to produce a rough surface.

Suez Canal [soo-EHZ]. Egyptian canal; connects Mediterranean and Red Seas.

suffer from. sufferable.

sufficient. SEE enough.

suffix. An abstract element attached at the end of a word which alters its meaning or denotes derivation, formation, or inflection; usually written without a hyphen. BUT —*elect,* —*odd,* —*wide,* are usually hyphenated. —*like* is sometimes hyphenated, and —*fold* is usually written as a separate word after words of more than one syllable: *tenfold, twenty fold, forty fold. Cf.* prefix.

suffocate. Choke, stifle, NOT necessarily fatally.

suffuse. —sable.

suggest, suggestible.

Suharto [soo-HAHR-toh]. (Only one name. *Cf.* names.) Indonesian general, premier (1968–   ).

suicide. (n.) NOT a verb.

sui juris. (Lat.) Of his own right. Entitled to act for himself.

suit [syoot]. suite [sweet]. Both mean a set of things. Custom dictates reference to a *suit* of clothes, cards, armor, sails; but to a *suite* of rooms or attendants, or furniture. (In the last sense, often pronounced [syoot]).

suitcase.

Sukarno [soekarno] Ahmed [soo-KAHR-noh]. (1901–1970) President of U.S. of Indonesia, (1950–1967). First names are almost never used in Indonesia. *Cf.* Names.

sukiyaki [soo-kee-YAH-kee]. Jap., [skee-YAH-kee]. Japanese dish.

Suleiman, The Magnificent [seu-lae-MAHN]. Also Solyman I. [suhl-ih-MAN] (1496–1566). Sultan, Ottoman empire.

sulfur. Preferred to -phur.

sullenness.

Sulu Archipelago [SOO-loo]. Philippine island group. Cap., Jolo [hoh-LOH].

sumac [SHOO-mak; SYOO-mak]. Brit., —ack.

Sumatra [soo-MAH-trah]. Equatorial island of Indonesia. Native, Sumatran.

summarily [SUHM-ma-rih-lee].

summary. SEE abbreviation.

SUMMERY. Like summer.

summer time. British for daylight-saving time.

summertime. The season.

summit meeting.

sun. Lower case unless used with names of planets or other stars.

Sunday [SUHN-dih]. (abbr. Sun.).

sundry. Several, various. *All and sundry* means each and every one.

sundries. Miscellaneous small items or articles.

sunk. SEE sink.

Sun Yat-sen [SOON-YAHT-SEHN]. (1866–1925) Father of Chinese revolution.

Suomenlinna [soo-aw-hehn-LIHN-nuh]. Swed., Sveaborg [SVAE-ah-bawr]. Island fortress on Gulf of Finland, two miles southeast of Helsinki.

Sup. Ct. (abbr.) Supreme Court Reporter.

superannuated.

supercargo. Agent of shipper on board ship.

supererogation. Doing more than duty requires.

superfluous [soo-PUHR-floo-uhs]. More than needed.

superintendent. (abbr., Supt.) Capitalize if referring to head of federal unit; Superintendent of Documents (Government Printing Office), Superintendent of the Naval (or Military) Academy.

Superintendent of schools. ADDRESS: Superintendent Harold Scribner, Teaneck Public Schools, Teaneck, N.J.; or Mr. Harold Scribner, Superintendent of Teaneck Public Schools, Teaneck, N.J. SALUTATION: Dear Sir, My dear Dr. Scribner, Dear Dr. Scribner.

Superior of Sisterhood (Roman Catholic). ADDRESS: The Reverent Mother Superior, Sisters of Notre Dame; or Sister Superior, Sisters of Notre Dame. SALUTATION: Dear Reverent Mother, My dear Reverend Mother, Dear Mother Superior, Dear Sister Superior.

superior to. NOT than.

superlative forms. Often misused where the positive or comparative form is correct. NOT: *He is in closest contact with the situation.*

supernumerary [soo-puh-NYOO-muhr-ehr-ee]. More than necessary or stated.

supersensible. Beyond what ordinary senses can detect; psychical.

supersede.

supervise.

supine [soo-PIEN]. (adj.) Lying on back, with face up.

supp. (abbr.) supplement.

suppertime.

supple [SUHP-ihl]. Flexible when bent. Adv., supplely; Brit., supply [both SUHP-lih]. suppleness.

supplement. SEE complement.

suppositious. Hypothetical, imaginary.
SUPPOSITITIOUS. Spurious, counterfeit.

suppress. —ible, —ssor.

supra [SOO-pruh]. (Lat.) Above; previously cited.

supra-. Prefix meaning above in position.

supreme. NEVER more or most supreme.

Supreme Bench. the Bench; also High Bench; High Tribunal.

Supreme Court (U.S.). the Court, High Court; titles of officers standing alone are capitalized: Associate Justice; Justice, Chief Justice, Clerk, Marshal, Reporter.

Supt. (abbr.) superintendent.

Surabaya [soo-rah-BAH-yah]. City and naval base in northeast Java.

surcease [suhr-SEES]. (n.) Cessation; end.

surcingle [SUHR-sing-gl]. Saddle belt.

sure-fire. (adj.) sure-footed (adj.), sure enough, sure thing.

surely.

surety [SHUR-tih or SHOOR-eh-tih]. One who makes himself liable for performance or payment by another.

Surg. (abbr.) surgeon.

Surgeon General. the (Army, Navy, and Public Health Service).

surgeon general. Pl. surgeons general.

Surg. Gen. (abbr.) Surgeon General.

Suribachi [suhr-ih-BAH-chih]. Volcanic island south of Iwo Jima.

Surinam [SOOY-rih-nahm]. Dutch Guiana. Native, Surinamens). Cap., Paramaribo. Currency, Surinam florin.

surly. (adv.) surlily.

surmise [suhr-MIEZ]. Guess. surmisedly [suhr-MIEZ-ehd-lih].

surprise [suhr-PRIEZ]. surprisedly [suhr-PRIEZ-ed-lee].

surreptitious [suhr-ehp-TIHSH-uhs]. surreptitiously [sur-ehp-TIH-shuhs-lee].

surrogate. Probate. Probate judge; substitute. *He is a surrogate parent for his ill sister's child.*

surround. *surround on all sides* is redundant.

survey. Capitalize if part of name of federal or state unit: Coast and Geodetic; Geological Survey; the Survey.

surveillance [suhr-VAEYL-anss]. Close supervision.

surveillant. (-ant). (n.) Overseer; (adj.) overseeing.

survivors. In a report, it is best to use the passive and the specific. *They were survived by one son and two daughters.* Other forms tend to be misleading. *They had three children* implies that the children are dead. The word children connotes young children.

susceptible [suhs-SEHP-th-bl]. Easily affected. —tibility, -tive.

Suslov, Mikhail Andreevich [soos-LAWV]. (1902–   ) Member of Presidium, U.S.S.R.

suspendable. Preferred to suspensible.

suspenders. One strap is a suspender; two pair make a set. (Brit., braces).

suspense. Mental uncertainty.

SUSPENSION. State or action of being suspended: *He awaited the decision in great suspense. The suspension of his license was a great blow.*

suspensible. Capable of being held up.

Susquehanna River. [suhs-kweh-HAHN-ah]. River in New York and Pennsylvania, flowing into Chesapeake Bay.

s.v. (abbr.) (Lat.) *sub verbo or sub voce.* Under the word or heading.

svelte. Slender.

Sverdlovsk [svehrd-LAWFSK]. City in Ural Mountains, U.S.S.R. Formerly Ekaterinburg.

SW. (abbr.) southwest.

swam. Past of swim.

swampland. swamp fever.

swan [swahn]. Aquatic bird. Cap., the constellation Cygnus.

swansdown. Webster, swan's-down. Fine, soft feathers of the swan.

swan song. A swan's fabled last outburst of song before death; hence, a last artistic work.

swap. Preferred to swop.

swarm [swawrm]. A great number of bees, etc. moving.

swarthy [SWAWR-thih]. Of dark complexion.

swastika [SWAHS-tih-kuh]. (or -ica) Symbol, Greek cross with ends bent at right angles; official emblem of the Third Reich.

swath [swahthe]. swathe [swaeth]. A row or strip cut by a scythe.

swayback. (n. and adj.); sway-backed (adj.), sway-brace (v.).

Swaziland [SWAH-see-land]. Independent since 1968. Natives, Swazi(s). Enclave in Union of South Africa. Capital, Mbabane [ehm-bow-BAWN]. Currency, Rand.

swear. P., swore; p.p., sworn.

swearword.

swearer-in.

sweat. P. and p.p., sweat is preferred to sweated in U.S.

sweatband. sweatbox; sweatshop, sweat gland, sweat pad, sweat shirt.

Sweden. Native, Swede(s); adj., Swedish. Cap., Stockholm. Currency, krona, pl. kroner (S.Kr.); ore (sing. and pl.).

Swedenborg, Emanuel [SWEE-d'n-bawrg]. (1688–1772) Swedish scientist, philosopher, founder New Jerusalem Church.

swell. P., swelled; swollen

swillbowl. —tub.

swim. P., swam; p.p., swum

swimsuit. swimwear.

swine. (sing. and pl.); swinish.
  BOAR. Wild swine, esp. male.
  SOW. Female swine.
  HOG. Adult, especially domestic swine ready for market.
  PIG. Young swine.

swing. P. and p.p., swung.

Swissair. Swiss Airline.

Switzerland [SWIHT-sur-l'nd]. Native, Swiss (sing. and pl.), Switzer. Poet., *Helvetia* (adj.) Swiss. Cap., Bern. Currency, franc (Sw. fr.), centime.

swivel. —led, —ling, Brit., —lled, —lling.

swivel chair.

swordbearer.

swordman. -woman.

sybarite [SIHB-uh-riet]. sensualist; from Sybaris. -itic [sihb-uh-RIHT-ink], -itical.

sycophant [SIHK-oh-fehnt]. Flatterer, especially for favors; false adviser.

Sydney. City in southeast Australia; capital of New South Wales.

syl-. SEE syn-.

syllable. One or several letters that form one sound.

syllabus. Pl. -buses or -bi.

syllepsis. Pl. —lepses. In rhetoric, yoking two unrelated objects with two meanings of the same verb: *He shot the picture and the man.*

sylvan. Preferred to silvan. Of the woods.

sym-. SEE syn-.

symbols.

Symington, William Stuart [SIE-mihng-tuhn]. (1901–   ) American industrialist, statesman.

symposium. Pl. symposia. SEE forum.

sympton. Pl. —s. Indication, sign.

syn-. Combining form meaning with, associated, like: *synchronize, synagogue, syntax.* syn- becomes sym- before *p, b,* and *m,* sy- before *l.*

syncope [SIHNG-koh-pee]. Dropping of a letter in a word: *ne'er for never.* There are other meanings in music and medicine.

synecdoche [sihn-NEHK-doh-kih]. Using a part to indicate the whole: *He had fifty head on his ranch.* Occasionally, the whole for a part. synecdochic, -cal.

synesis. In grammar, a departure from normal syntax to clarify meaning: *He went into the town and sold books to them.*

synod [SIHN-uhd]. Council.

synonym. Word having the same meaning as another.
  SYNONYMITY. Synonymousness.
  SYNONYMY. The study of synonyms; also, quality of being synonymous.
  SYNONYMOUS WITH. Of identical meaning. SEE ALSO homonyms.

synopsis. Pl. synopses. SEE abbreviation.

syntax. In grammar, the arrangement of word forms in a sentence to show their relationship.

synthesis. Pl. —theses. Combining of parts to form a whole.

Syosset [sie-AH-seht]. Town in Long Island, N.Y.

Syria. Native, Syrian. adj., Syriac (of the Syrian people). Currency, pound. Cap., Damascus. Native, Damascene. *Cf.* United Arab Republic.

syringe [SIHR-ihnj]. Small hand pump.

System. Capitalize if referring to federal or state unit; Alaska Communication System; the system; Federal Credit System, Federal Home Loan Bank System; Federal Reserve System; National System of Interstate and Defense Highways; National System of Interstate Highways; Interstate System of Highways; Interstate Highway System; the Interstate System; the National System; the system; BUT highway system; Federal road system; Postal Savings System; Selective Service System (SEE ALSO Service). BUT Pennsylvania Railway system; Pennsylvania system; Bell system, the system; also Federal land bank system.

systematic. Preferred to systemic except in physiology.

systematize. Preferred to systemize.

systemwide.

systole [SIHS-toh-lee]. Contraction of the heart.

Szczecin [sh-CHEH-tsihn]. Poland. Scene of 1970 riots.

Szeged [SEH-gehd]. Town in Hungary on Yugoslav border.

Szigeti, Joseph [SEE-geht-ee]. (1892–1973) Hungarian-American violinist.

Szold, Henrietta [zohld]. (1860–1945) Founder of Hadassah.

Szyk, Arthur [shihk or jeek]. (1894–1951) Miniaturist, illuminator.

Szymczak, Menc Stephen [SIHM-chah]. (1904–) American economist.

T

t. Silent after *f* or *s* when followed by *l* or *n* sounds: *chasten, fasten, listen, epistle, jostle, bustle.*

-t, -tt. Monosyllable ending in *t*, preceded by a single vowel (NOT a diphthong, or a double vowel) double the *t* before a suffix beginning with a vowel. Polysyllables follow the same rule if the accent is on the last syllable.

-t or -ed. bereaved, bereft; burned, burnt; dreamed, dreamt; kneeled, knelt; leaned, leant; leaped, leapt; learned, learnt; spilled, spilt; spoiled, spoilt; tossed, tost. Both forms are in use, but written usage tends towards *-ed*, pronunciation towards *-t* (burnt). *Bereaved* has a more emotional connotation than *bereft*.

T., Tps. (abbrs.) township, townships.

T-beam. T-iron, T-shape, T-square, T-boat, T-man, T-scale.

tableau. Pl. -eaux.

table d'hote [TAH-bl-DOHT]. Restaurant meal at a set price. Opposite, à la carte.

table tennis. Ping-Pong is a trade name.

table 2, II, A. Lower-case; but Table 2, when part of title: *Table 2: Degrees of Land Deterioration.*

table a motion. In U.S., suspend discussion of the motion till a later date; Brit., place on the agenda.

taboo [ta-BOO]. P. and p.p., -ooed.

taboret or tabouret [TAB-oh-reht]. Stool; in music, a small drum.

tabulate. -lable.

tacit [TASS-iht]. Implied but not expressed: *tacit consent.*

Tacitus, Cornelius [TAS-ih-tuhs]. (c. 55—117) Roman historian.

tack. Change direction by manipulating sail (nautical); by extension, direction.

TACT. Ability to deal with others.

tactician [tak-TIHSH-'n]. A skillful maneuverer.

tactics. SEE strategy.

tactile. Capable of being felt or feeling.

TACTUAL. Of touch.

Tadoussac, Que., Can. SEE Saguenay.

taffeta. Smooth, shiny weave of silk or rayon.

taffy. Brit., toffee.

Tag [TAHK]. (Ger.) Day.

Tahiti [tuh-HEE-tee]. Fr., Taiti, [tah-ee-tee]. French South Pacific island in Windward Island group. Formerly Otaheite [OH-tuh-HEE-tee].

Tahoe, Lake [TAH-hoh]. Resort on California-Nevada border.

Taipeh [tie-PAE]. Capital of Formosa. Formerly Taihoku.

Taipong [tie-PIHNG]. Town in Malaya.

Taiwan [TIE-wahn]. Formosa. SEE China.

Taj Mahal [TAHJ-muh-HAHL]. *The distinguished one of the palace.* (Title of the wife of Shah Jahan); mausoleum built for her (1631–1645) at Agra, India.

take. p., took; p.p., taken; taking.

takedown. (n. and adj.), —off (n. and adj.) (N.Y. Times and Web., take off); —out (n. and adj.), —over (n. and adj.), —up (n. and adj.); take-all (n.), take-home (adj.), take-in (n. and adj.).

take-home pay. Wages or salary after taxes and other deductions.

take it easy.

talent. Ancient weight and money unit = 60 minos = 300 or 360 shekels = £57.85 = approx. current values, $40,000 (in gold); $1900 (in silver).

Taliaferro County [TAHL-ih-vehr]. County in Georgia.

talisman. Engraved figure charm. Pl. —s. —manic, —manical.

talkfest.

talking-to. (n.); talking film.

Talmud [TAHL-muhd]. (Heb.). Commentary on the Bible. Talmudist, by extension, an argumentative person.

tan. (abbr.) tangent.

Tanganyika [tan-gan-YEE-kuh]. U.N. Trust Territory in Africa administered by Great Britain. Formerly German East Africa. Independent, December 28, 1961. Native Tanganyikan. Cap., Dar es Salaam. Currency, EACB shilling = $\frac{1}{20}$ Brit. Combined in April, 1964 with Zanzibar and Pemba to form Tanzania.

tangelo. Pl. —os. Hybrid tangerine-grapefruit.

tangible [TAN-jih-bl]. Capable of being touched, realized or appraised: *tangible assets.*

Tangier [tan-JEE'R]. City in Morocco, at west end of Gibraltar Strait.

tanh. (abbr.) hyperbolic tangent.

Tannhauser [TAHN-hoi-zehr]. Legendary hero in Wagner's opera.

Tanzania, United Republic of. Established 1964 by combining Tanganyika, Zanzibar and Pemba. Cap., Dar es Salaam. [SAHR-ehs-LAHM]. Currency, East Africa shilling.

Taos [touss]. Town in New Mexico.

tap. British for faucet.

tapir [TAE-puhr]. Large nocturnal relative of the horse.

Tarascon [tah-rahs-KOHN]. Town in southeast France.

Tarawa Island [tah-RAH-wah]. Island in Gilbert and Ellice group, British protectorate. Group was scene of U.S. Marine landing November 21–24, 1943.

tarragon [TAR-uh-gahn]. A spice.

Tasman Sea [TAZ-m'n]. Pacific Ocean southeast of Australia.

tassel. -led, -ling. Brit., -lled, -lling.

Tassigny, Jean de Lattre de [tah-seen-YEE, jahn duh LAH-truh duh]. (1890–1952) French general.

tasty. (Collog.) savory.

tattler. Teller of secrets, especially inadvertently.

TATTLETAIL. Teller of secrets, especially intentionally, to make trouble.

tattoo. To mark skin by pricking with coloring. —ed, —ing.

taupe [TOHP]. Tannish yellow.

tautology [taw-TAHL-uh-jih]. A repetition in other words without point.

taxi. Pl. -s. taxied, -iing, or -ying.

taximeter [TAKS-ihm-mee-tr]. Gauge for measuring taxi fare.

TB. (abbr.) tuberculosis.

tbs. (abbr.) tablespoonful.

Tchaikovsky, Petr Ilich [chie-KAWF-skih, PYAW-tuhr ihl-YEHCH]. (1840–1893) Russian composer.

T.D. (abbr.) Treasury Decisions.

TDN (abbr.) total digestible nutrients.

teach. P. and p.p., taught.

teammate. -play, -wise, -work.

tear [taer]. P., tore; p.p., torn; tearing.

tear bomb. —drop, —sheet, —stain; tear-dimmed (adj.), tear-off (n. and adj.), tear-out (n. and adj.), tear-stained (adj.); tear gas.

teasable.

technic [TEHK-nihk]. Used for more technological meanings.

TECHNIQUE [tehk-NEEK]. Used for ordinary arts and sciences.

tedious [TEE-dee-uhs, TEED-yuhs, TEE-juhs]. Tiresome.

Te deum [tee-DAE-uhm]. (Lat.) Thee, God.

TE DEUM [tee DEE-uhm]. Ancient Latin hymn.

tedium [TEE-dee-uhm]. Boredom.

teenage. (adj.) teenager. N.Y. Times and Webster, teen-age, teen-ager. DO NOT USE teen-aged as adj.

tee shirt.

teetotaler [tee-TOH-t'l-uhr]. Brit., ll. One who abstains entirely from intoxicating drinks.

Tegucigalpa [teh-GOO-see-GAL-pah]. Capital of Honduras.

Teheran [teh-huh-RAHN]. Also Tehran. Capital of Iran.

Tehuantepec [tae-WAHN-tah-pek]. Town in Mexico.

Tel Aviv [tehl-ah-VEEV]. Seaport in Israel, northwest of Jerusalem.

telegraphy [teh-LEHG-ruh-fih].

Telemachus [tih-LEHM-uh-kuhs]. Son of Odysseus.

telemetering. Collection and transmission of data by instruments.

televise. (v.) Transmit or receive; photograph for telecasting.

TELECAST. (v.) Broadcast by television.

television station. SEE station.

Tell, Guillaume [TEHL gee-YAWRM; angl., William Tell]. Legendary Swiss archer immortalized by Johann Christopher Friedrich von Schiller's play.

telltale.

temerity. Boldness: *He had the temerity to ask for an increase although all prices were down.*

TIMIDITY. Shyness: *His timidity prevented his asking for a fair price.*

temptress. SEE feminine designation.

tempus fugit [TEHM-puhs FYOO-jiht]. (Lat.) *Time flies.*

tendentious. Preferred to -cious. Having a tendency with a purpose, usually to change something: *His analyses showed a tendentious leaning toward the right.*

tender. (n.) Offer or the thing offered: *legal tender.*

tenfold. –penny (nail), –pins; ten-strike.

tenebrous [TEHN-uh-bruhs, TEHN-nehb-rih-uhs]. Gloomy.

tenement house.

tenet [TEHN-eht, -iht]. Principle held to be true.

Tennessee [tehn-eh-SEE]. (abbr. Tenn.) Native and adj., Tennessean. Webster's accepts Tennesseean.

Tennyson, Alfred Lord [TEHN-ihs-sehn]. (1809–1902) First Baron: English poet laureate, 1850–1892.

tenor. Course or direction; nature. In law, a transcript. In music, highest male voice except falsetto.

TENURE [TEHN-yoor]. Period in office or tenancy.

tenpenny nail. About three inches long. *Cf.* penny.

tenpins. The American game, said to have been established when ninepins was outlawed. British, usually ninepins (which SEE). Knocking down all ten pins with one throw is a strike (Brit., ten-strike); with two throws, a spare.

TENSE. In grammar, tense is the property that describes the time of an action or state of being. English has three simple tenses—present, *talk;* past, *talked;* and future, *will talk*—and three compound or perfect tenses which show that an action has been perfected or completed—present perfect, *have or has talked;* past perfect, *had talked;* and future perfect, *shall or will have talked.* In addition, there are progressive forms of each tense which indicate that the action is continuing. The progressive forms are made up of the present participle , *talking,* and a form of the auxiliary verb, to be: present progressive, *I am talking;* past progressive, *I was talking;* future progressive, *I shall be talking;* present perfect progressive, *I have been talking;* past perfect progressive, *I had been talking;* future perfect progressive, *I shall have been talking.* Tense is indicated both by changes in the verb and by auxiliary verbs. Verb forms that indicate tense are called the principal parts: infinitive or present, *talk;* past, *talked;* past participle, *talked.* The past participle is always used with an auxiliary verb. When actions occur at the same time, the same tense may be used, but if a series of actions is interrupted by an action that occurred earlier or will occur later, the tense must be changed to show this change in time.

The past tense is usually formed by adding (-ed) to the present tense form. *Cf.* Irregular Verbs. The habitual past of most verbs is formed by the auxiliary *used to: She used to read every book she could find.* The emphatic past is formed with the auxiliary *did: She did read it.*

Simple past tense is also used of complete action: *He spoke to me. He came here.* Past perfect progressive is also used to show habitual past action: *I had been teaching for many years.*

In the subjunctive mood, the simple past tense, used as the past subjunctive, refers to either present or future: *If he spoke well today or tomorrow, he could win.* BUT the past subjunctive of *to be* requires *were* as both singular and plural form: *If I were you. . . .* Use of *was* or *were,* followed by a *to* infinitive refers to either the present or the future: *If she were to say no. . . .* BUT when followed by any other form, this construction refers only to the present: *If they were near, we could see them.* To show that something is not a fact, *were* and *had* may be used without *if. Had you been ten feet tall, and were I as strong as Hercules, we could not have been defeated by them.* A verb in the past tense may be used with *if* to refer to the past in the simple indicative mood: *If he went, he will tell me about it.*

Tense in a subordinate clause is past if the principle clause is past; but it may be in any tense, according to the sense to be expressed, if the principle clause is in the present or future tense. This rule does not apply to verbs expressing habitual action. In clauses of result or purpose, introduced by such conjunctions as *in the order that, so that,* (a) if the verb in the principal clause is

in the past or past perfect tense, use one of the past auxiliaries (*might, could, would*) in the subordinate clause: *He walked (or had walked) to the store, so that he could have rolls for breakfast.*

tensible [TEHN-suh-bl]. Capable of being extended. —bleness, tensibly, tensibility.

tensile strength. Resistance to longitudinal stress.

tenterhooks. Nail-hooks used to fasten cloth to a drying tenter. NOT *tenderhooks.*

tenure. SEE tenor.

tepee [TEE-pee]. Preferred to teepee. Conical tent used by some American Indians.

tepid [TEHP-ihd]. Lukewarm. —ity, —ly, —ness.

Ter-. Preceding a name, SEE Le-.

Ter. (abbr.) terrace.

teraphim [TEHR-uh-fihm]. Images of primitive Jewish household gods.

terazzo [tehr-AHT-soh]. Also terrazzo. Polished flooring of marble chips set in cement.

tercentenary. 300th anniversary.

terminal. U.S., starting or ending point for buses and trains. Brit., terminals (pl. only) are charges for use of a station.

TERMINATE [TUHR-mih-nate]. End; have its end, —nable, —ter.

TERMINUS. Pl. termini. U.S., end of line. British, also for terminal station.

terneplate [TUHRN-plaet]. Lead-tin plated sheet iron or steel.

terpsichore [tuhrp-SIH-kawr-ih]. The Muse of dance and choral song; (Cap.), thus dance. terpsichorean [tuhrp-sih-kuh-REE-uhn].

terr. (abbr.) Terrace. Usually abbreviated in the news report or informal address.

terra-cotta. (adj.); terra cotta (n.), terra firma.

Terre Haute [TEHR-uh-hoht]. City in Indiana.

terrible [TEHR-ih-bl]. Afflicting severely; exciting terror.

terrified. SEE afraid.

territorial. Capitalize if referring to a political subdivision.

Territory. Capitalize if part of name; Northwest Territory (1799), the territory; Trust Territory of the Pacific Islands, Pacific Islands Trust Territory, BUT trust territory; the territory; territory of Guam, the territory.

terror-stricken. SEE afraid.

tertiary [TUHR-shih-ehr-ih; Brit., TUHR-shuh-rih]. Of the third order.

tertiary era. The Cenozoic period. *Cf.* Time.

tertium quid [TUHR-shih-uhm, kwihd]. (Lat.) A third something. Another alternative where there appeared to be only two exhaustive and mutually exclusive categories.

tessera [TEHS-ehr-uh]. Pl. -rae [-ree]. Square, faced marble or glass used in mosaic.

Test. Otis Mental Ability Group Test, etc.; the group test; the test.

testator [tehs-TAE-tehr]. Man who leaves a will. fem., testatrix [-trihks]; pl. -trices [trie-seez].

testimony. Write: Q: Did she arrive?—A: Yes.

tête-à-tête [TAET-uh-TAET]. Fr. *Head to head*. Private or confidential conversation.

tetralogy. Four connected literary works.

Texarkana [tehk-sahr-KAN-uh]. Border city between Texas and Arkansas.

Texas. (abbr. Tex.) adj. Texan. Cap., Austin.

textile [TEHKS-tihl]. Woven fabrics.

T.F. (abbr.) Till forbid. Advertising order to run copy until further notice.

T.H. (abbr.) Territory of Hawaii. Now a state, and not abbreviated.

Thailand [TAE-land]. Native, Thai(s), adj., Thai [TIE]. Cap., Bangkok Krung Thep [kruhng kahk]. Formerly Siam. Currency, baht (B), satong.

thalamus [THAL-uh-muhs]. Part of forebrain. Pl. -mi.

Thalia [THAE-lee-uh]. Muse of pastoral poetry, comedy.

Thames River [tehms]. River flowing past London into North Sea.

than. (coordinating conjunction) Use only with *other, rather, else* and the comparative form of an adjective or adverb: *They arrived sooner than we expected.* BUT: *Scarcely had they arrived when we started.*

than, as. If the word following is the subject of a clause, even if part of the clause is understood, that word must be in the nominative case. But if the word following is not the subject of a clause, it must be in the objective case: *I have more money than she (has). I know him better than (I know) her.*

thanking you in advance. AVOID. The assumption that a favor will be granted is considered insolent by many, and the phrase has become a meaningless cliché.

thanksgiver. —giving.

Thanksgiving Day.

Thant, U [THAHNT, OO]. (1909–) Acting U.N. Secretary-General (1961–1962), Secretary-General (1962–1971). Thant means *clean;* U is a national term of respect similar to *Mr. Cf.* Names.

thank you. But formally: *I thank you;* other formalities: *thanks; many, a thousand, best thanks, thanks a million; much thanks* is archaic. *Thanks so much, a ton, shipload.*

that. (adj., adv.) To such an extent. AVOID: *that section which is involved* and other uses where *the* or *very* will do as well. NOT: *He was that rich. After examining the arm, the surgeon removed that part infected.* USE *the part infected* or *the part which was infected.*

that-which. *That* is pref. as a defining relative in all cases; which or who is used as defining or non-defining relative. Although *who* is used for individual persons, *that* may be used for a group, class, or type of persons: *Any groups that were on active duty may be relieved.* A non-defining clause is preceded by a comma: *This house, which I built with my own hands, is one of the most beautiful in town.*

that for who. Most authorities hold *that* is acceptable, especially where no specific person is mentioned. *The first governor that ordered police protection.*

that. Possessive form is *whose: That store is the one whose advertisements are outstanding.*

that. (relative pronoun) *This is the world that man has made.* NOT with a question: *I question that had he been well, he would have done better on the examination.* Use *whether.*

that. Introducing parallel clauses. When *that* or *which* introduces a series of parallel clauses, the conjunction should be repeated for each clause: *They recalled that seven persons were present and that six wore wigs.*

that. (conj. omitted) *I knew* (that) *he was here.* Omission of *that* is good idiomatic English, esp. with such verbs as *believe, presume, suppose, think, assert, aver, calculate, conceive, learn, maintain, reckon, state, suggest.* BUT *that* is seldom omitted after *acknowledge.*

that ... that. AVOID: *All of us know that he would live up to the promises that his mother had made for him in good faith.* USE *that ... which,* or omit second *that.*

The. Capitalize only when it is a part of the name: *The Hague,* BUT *the Hague Conference; The Times* (of London), *The Adjutant General* (when so in copy), The Dallas, BUT *the Dallas Dam, the Dallas region;* The Weirs, BUT the Weirs streets; the National Archives; the Archives; the Times; the Mermaid; the Federal Express.

theater. Brit., —re [THEE-uh-tuhr].

theatergoer. -going. The profession prefers theatre.

the —— and the ——. *The first and the second classes have 30 pupils* (meaning each). *The first and second classes have 60 pupils* (meaning together). *The blue and red flags* (many flags of two colors); *The blue and the red flags* (flags of a single color). Usually repeat *the* with each adjective except after *some.* With two nouns, elimination of the second *the* indicates a single, combined quality: *The strength and courage of the people is of historic importance. The strength and the courage of the people are of historic importance.*

the——. In question. AVOID. Use *this* or *that: This hat is mine,* NOT *The hat in question is mine.*

their. Posessive form of *they, them.* Make certain the antecedent is clear. Do not confuse with *his* or *its. They spoke their thoughts. Each to his own choice. Everyone* (everybody) *has his faults.*

theirs. *This prize of theirs. The book is theirs. Theirs is the winner.* NOT *their's.*

theirselves. NOT literate. Use *themselves.*

theism. Belief in a deity. SEE atheism.

thence [thehnss]. SEE hence.

thenceforth. -forward, -ward.

thenceforth. From there on. NOT *from thenceforth.*

then-existing.

theoretical. Preferred to theoretic.

there. Use as anticipatory expletive. Except after verb *to be,* omit *there* as part of a verb in an inverted position: *It was evident that whatever* (there) *remained belonged to him.*

thereabout(s). —above, —after, —among, —around, —at, —away, —before, —between, —by, —for, —fore, —from, —in, —inafter, —inbefore, —into, —of, —on, —over, —through, —to, —tofore, —under, —until, —unto, —upon, —with (all one word).

thereat, therein, thereof. AVOID except in legal forms.

thereby. AVOID use before an unattached present participle. NOT *The horse ran last, thereby losing our bet.*

therefor [thair-FAWR]. (adverb or adjective phrase) A legalism for *for that: He was paid therefor.*

    THEREFORE [THAIR-fawr]. (adverbial conjunction) For that reason. Commas before *therefore* accent the preceding word. Avoid *therefore* after *and, it,* and other weak words.

thesaurus. Pl. -ri. Treasury, especially of words.

these. *This kind, these kinds.*

thesis [THEE-sihs]. A proposition; postulate. Pl. -es [eez].

THI. Temperature-humidity index. Weather Bureau ratio designed to measure discomfort (originally Discomfort Index). At THI 75, 50% of the population is uncomfortable.

thiamine. B-1 vitamin, preventative for beriberi and some types of neuritis.

thine [THEIN]. Archaic possessive of *thou*. now only for poetical use. Use only before a vowel or an *h* except when it follows its antecedent: *mine and thine; thine ox*. NOT *thine house*.

things—. *Things American*, etc. is an affectation and should be avoided except for titles or other special uses.

think that. *I think* (that) *he is bright*. Omit *that* after think.

think to do. AVOID.

thinness.

third-hand. (adv. and adj.); third-class (adj.), third-degree (adj.), third-rate (adj.), third-rater; third house.

Thirteen American Colonies. etc. SEE Colonies.

Thirteen Original States.

thirties. SEE Numbers.

thirty-twomo. (abbr. 32mo.) Book size, approx. $3\frac{1}{8} \times 3\frac{1}{2}$ in., made of 32 papes from one sheet.

this. *This two months is* ... Acceptable grammatically if the period is a unit.

thorax [THOH-raks]. Pl., thoraxes or —ces. Part of body between neck and abdomen, containing esophagus, heart, lungs.

Thoreau, Henry David [THAW-roh]. (1817–1862) American writer, philosopher.

Thorvaldsen or Thorwaldsen, Bertel [TUHR-vah-s'n, buhr-tehl]. (1768–1844) Danish sculptor.

those. *Those persons who are selected. The persons selected. Those selected.* NOT: *Those persons selected.*

though, although. (conj.) Although is more formal.

as though. *She wooed as though she had to win.*

thrall. Bondage; one in bondage. thralldom; Brit., thraldom.

thrash. For animals, people.
  THRESH. For grain.

thrasonical. In grammar, bold, bragging. *I came, I saw, I conquered.*

three, 3, III. thirteen, thirty. SEE four.

threefold. —folded, —penny (nail), —score, —some; three-bagger, three-cornered (adj.), three-dimensional (adj.), three-in-hand, three-ply (adj.), three-spot, three-square.

threepence [thrihp'ns].

three quarters. (n.) *A yard and three quarters.*
  THREE-QUARTER. (adj.) *He had a three-quarter coat.*

threnody [THREHN-oh-dih]. Dirge. Pl. —dies (—dic).

threshingtime.

threshold [THREHSH-ohld]. Part of a structure under the door; by ext., entering point.

thriftbox.

thrive. P., thrived or throve; p.p., thrived is pref. to thriven.

throughout the whole of is redundant.

throw. P., threw; p.p., thrown; throwing.

thru. Avoid this spelling.

thrust-power. thrust-pound.

Thruway, New York. the thruway.

Thule [THYOO-lee]. City in northwest Greenland, site of U.S. Air Force base.

thurible [TH (Y) UHR-uh-bl]. Frankincense.

Thurs. (abbr.) Thursday [THUHRZ-dih].

thus. AVOID use before a present participle. NOT: *thus making himself important.*

thusly. Do not use.

thwart [THWAWRT]. Placed across something else.

thwartman. -ship.

thy, thine. Archaic. Use only in special situations (poetry, prayers, etc.). *Cf.* thine.

thyme [tiem]. Seasoning related to mint.

thyroid [THIE-roid]. Gland near larynx which influences growth.

Thyssen, Fritz [TIE-sehn, frihts]. (1873-1951) German industrialist. Father, August (1842-1926).

Tibet [tih-BEHT]. Native, Tibetan. Cap., Lhasa [LAH-sah]. Occupied by People's Republic of China (Communist China).

tickler file. Record based on the calendar, esp. for reminders.

tidal wave.

tidbit. British use titbit.

tiddlywinks [TIHD-lih-WIHNGKS]. Game with objective of snapping small disks into cup.

tie-in sale. tie-in. Pl. tie-ins. Sale in which the buyer must take additional merchandise or services to be able to buy what he wants.

Tientsin [tihn-TSIHN; Chin., tih-en-JIN]. City in northeast China on Pei River and Grand Canal.

Tierra del Fuego Island [TYEHR-uh del FWAE-goh]. Chile-Argentina archipelago at southern tip of South America.

Tiflis [TIHF-lihs; TIF-flees]. City in Georgia, U.S.S.R.; birthplace of Stalin.

Tiglath-pileser III [TIHG-lath pih-LEE-zuhr]. (d. 727 B.C.) King of Assyria, 745-27.

tilde [TIHL-dueh, —dih]. Diacritical mark over Span. *ñ* which adds a palatal sound: canon [KAN-yohn]. *Cf.* diacritical marks.

till, until. Until is more formal. NOT *til.* AVOID *'til.*

timber [TIHM-buhr]. Wood.

TIMBRE [TAM-br]. Resonance.

Timbuktu [tihm-BUHK-too]. Also Timbuctoo. City in Mali, near Nigeria. Great city of 15th and 16th centuries.

time. *The years 1957-1961. The club meets Monday-Friday at 9 o'clock.* But the short dash may be substituted by *through* or *to. From May to September 1960.* NOT: *From May-September 1960. Cf.* days, weeks, months, years, decades, centuries, Ages, Numerals.

CAPITALIZATION. Atlantic time, Atlantic Standard time, central time, central standard time, mountain time, mountain standard time, Pacific time, Pacific standard time, universal time.

COMPUTATION. Noon in New York City (Eastern Standard Time) is 11 A.M. in Chicago (Central Standard Time); 10 A.M. in Denver (Mountain Standard Time); 9 A.M. in San Francisco (Pacific Standard Time); 7 A.M. in Nome and Honolulu (daylight saving time is 1 hour later). Similarly, 5 P.M. in Greenwich, London, Paris; 6 P.M. in Berlin; 7 P.M. in Moscow, Bucharest, Istanbul; 2 A.M. the following day in Tokyo.

FORM. SEE ALSO Dates, Years. *12 m.* (noon); *12 p.m.* (midnight); *3: 40 p.m.: 7 o'clock; 7 p.m.* BUT NOT *7 o'clock p.m.; half past 7; 4^h 30^m or 4.5^h in scientific work; 0025, 2359 in astronomy. 6 hours 8 minutes 4 seconds: four centuries. three decades.*

timeborn. —bound, —card, —clerk, —clock, —keep (v.), —keeper, —killer, —killing, —lag, —lock, —out (n. and adj.), —piece, —pleaser, —proof, —saver, —saving, —server, —serving, —sheet, —span, —table, —taker, —taking, —waster, —wasting, —work, —worker, —worn (all one word); time-consuming (adj.), time-honored (adj.), time-stamp (v.).

timid. Applied to people, animals. *Cf.* afraid, temerity.

TIMOROUS. Also, applied to ideas, actions, animals: *A timorous program.*

Timon [TIE-m'n].

Timor Island. [tee-MAWR]. Island in Indonesia. Portuguese since 1563.

tin. British for can.

tinderbox. tinder-dry (adj.).

tinge. -geable, tinged, -ging.

Tinian [tee-nee-AHN; angl., tihn-ih-AN]. Island in south Mariana group.

tinsel. -seled, -ing.

tintblock. (printing).

Tipperary [tihp-uhr-AIR-ih]. County in south Ireland.

tiptoe. tiptoed, tiptoeing.

tirade [TIE-raed or tih-RAED]. Long speech, especially an intemperate one.

Tirana [tih-RAH-nah]. Capital of Albania.

tire. (n.) Brit., tyre.

tiro [TIE-roh]. tyro is pref. Beginner.

Tirol, Tyrol [tih-ROHL or TIHR]. Ital., Tirolo, [tee-RAW-loh]. Mountain region (Alps) in Austria, Bavaria, Italy.

tissue [TIH-shoo, pref. to -shyoo].

titan [TIE-t'n]. From Titan, mythological primeval giant.

titanium. *titanosaurus, titanous. Cf.* Ti.

titbit. Brit; U.S., tidbit.

Titian [TIHSH-an]. Tíziano Vecellio (1477–1576). Italian painter.

title. In law, proof of ownership.

titleholder. —winner; title-holding (adj.), title-winning (adj.); title page.

title 2, II, A, etc. Lower-case; BUT Title 2, when part of title: *Title 2: General Provisions.*

titled. Use entitled. BUT *a well-titled novel, a titled family.*

TITLES. Capitalize principal words in titles of acts, addresses, articles, books, captions, chapter and part headings, documents, editorials, essays, headings, headlines, motion pictures and plays (including TV and radio programs), papers, pamphlets, short poems, reports (not annual reports), songs, subheadings, subjects, laws, treaties, and themes. Capitalize both parts of compound words: *Record of First-Class Mer-*

chants Club. In printing, titles are set in italics for books, essays, plays, motion pictures, symphonies, operas, pamphlets, published documents, newspapers, magazines, and collections of paper, BUT NOT in long lists of these. N.Y. Times places these titles in quotation marks.

Also capitalize titles of heads of state, governmental units, members of the diplomatic corps, princes and rulers, BUT NOT officers of the armed forces, professors, corporate officers, or nonofficial titles.

Hyphenate a double title, but not a civil or military title denoting a single office: *ambassador at large; sergeant at arms;* BUT *secretary-treasurer.*

Abbreviate a civil, military, or naval title and honorable, reverend, monsignor, mister, mistress, messieurs when followed by a Christian name or initial; *Lt. A.B. White, Insp. Gen. Black.*

Italicize the titles of legal cases (except the verb), BUT NOT title of legal reports: *John Doe* v. *Richard Roe. Cf.* Capitalization.

The capitalization of the titles of books, etc., written in a foreign language conforms to national practice in that language.

title search. Examination of records to determine liens, encumbrances, or defects in ownership.

Tito. Josip Broz-Tito. (1890–   ) President of Yugoslavia (1953–   ).

titration. Process of determining strength of a solution in terms of smallest amount (titer) required to effect reaction.

titular [TIHT-yoo-lahr]. Of a title; in name only.

Titus [TIE-tuhs].

Tivoli [TEE-voi-lee]. Commune east-north-east of Rome, Italy.

TIVOLI [TIH-voh-lee]. Park in Copenhagen.

t.l.o. (abbr.) total loss only.

t.m. (abbr.) true mean.

T-man. Treasury investigator.

tmeses [TMEE-sihs, MEE-sihs]. In grammar. separation of parts of a compound word by insertion of another word: *so parenthetically called.*

TNT. (abbr.) trinitrotoluol, or trinitrotoluene.

today. tomorrow, tonight; to-and-fro, to-do (n.); to wit.

-to. lean-to, etc.

tobacco. Pl. -s.

tobacco-growing. (adj.); tobacco shop.

Tobago [toh-BAE-goh]. Island in West Indies Federation, adjacent to Trinidad. Cap., Scarborough.

Tobruk [toh-BRUHK]. City in Libya.

Tocqueville, de, Alexis Charles Henri Maurice Clerel [duh-TAWK-vehl, ah-LEHK-see]. (1805–1859) French writer, statesman.

tocsin [TAHK-sihn]. Alarm.

Togliatti, Palmero [toh-lih-YAHT-tee, pahl-MIH-roh]. (1893–1946) Italian Communist politician.

Togo [TOH-goh]. Native, Togolese. Formerly French, independent since April 1960. Situated on Atlantic Ocean. Cap., Lomé [loh-MAE]. Currency, CFA franc.

Togo, Marquis Heihachiro [TOH-goh, hae-hay-chee-roh]. (1847–1934) Japanese admiral.

Togo, Shigenori [TOH-goh, shee-geh-noh-ree]. (1882–1950) Japanese diplomat.

toilet [TOI-leht]. U.S., *bathroom;* Brit., *W.C.* or *water closet.*

toilette. Lady's bath, hair dressing, use of cosmetics and dressing.

Tojo, Hedeki [TOH-joh, hee-deh-kee]. (1885–1948) Japanese general, statesman.

Tokyo [TOH-kyoh]. Capital city of Japan.

Toledano, Ralph De [ton-lae-DAH-noh]. (1916–   ) Editor, writer, political analyst.

tolerance. Allowable deviation from the standard specification in a manufacture.

tolerant. of or towards.

toll. *For Whom the Bell Tolls.* NOT *bells toll.*

tollhouse. —keeper, —master, —payer, —paying, —taker (all one word); toll bridge, toll line, toll road.

tomato [toh-MAE-toh; Brit. AH-]. Pl. -oes.

Tomb. Grant's Tomb, the tomb; Tomb of the Unknown Soldier, Unknown Soldier's Tomb, Tomb of the Unknowns, the tomb. *Cf.* Unknown Soldier.

tombstone. tomb-strewn (adj.).

ton. (Not abbreviated.) Pl. -s. Unit of weight: (1) U.S. = 2000 lbs. avoirdupois = 907.2 kilograms; (2) Brit., gross or long ton = 2240 lbs. = 1016 kilograms; (3) displacement ton, unit for ship size measurement = 35 cu. ft. = volume of 1 long ton of water; (4) measurement ton, unit for ship charges = 40 cu. ft. = vol. use of 1 long ton of average cargo; (5) metric ton = 1000 kilograms = 2,204.6 lbs. avoirdupois; (6) registered ton, a unit of ship measurement = 100 cu. ft. of internal space. The adj. is always sing.: *three-ton load.*

tongs. *Cf.* scissors.

tongue tied. (N.Y. Times, tongue-tied) tongue-lash (v.), tongueshaped (adj.), tongue-twisting (adj.); tongue lashing, tongue twister.

tonneau [TUHN-OH]. Body of an automobile. Pl. -s or —x.

tonsil. Pl., —s. tonsillitis, inflammation of the tonsils; tonsillectomy, removal of the tonsils.

tonsorial. Of a barber or barbering.

too. When too qualifies a following adj. or adv. it means *more than is desirable: too big.* BUT never use with a comparative or superlative form.
  When used to mean *in excess,* use only as an intensive: *He was only too happy to join us.* BUT avoid use without *only.* NOT: *It was too wonderful.*

too much. Use *too much* meaning *very* to modify a verb, if required: *Too much concerned with,* NOT *too concerned with.* Watch, especially, use with negative adverbs. *Cf. very.*

top. topmost.

topology. In mathematics, geometric algebra used for measuring surfaces.

topsy-turvy.

Topsy. The quotation is: "I 'spect I grow'd." Avoid the cliché: "Just grow'd like Topsy."

Torah [TOH-rah]. The Pentateuch.

torah or -ra [TOH-rah]. A law; divine interpretation. Pl. —roth.

torchbearer. —bearing, —light, —lighted, —like, —lit, —man (all one word); torch song.

torment. —ntor, —ntress.

tornado [tawr-NAE-doh]. Pl. —oes. tornadic [tawr-NAD-ihk].

Toronto [tuh-RAHN-toh]. City in Canada.

torpedo. Pl. -oes.

torpor. Suspended animation; sluggishness.

torque [tawrk]. Rotational force.

Torquemada, Tomas de [dthae-taw-kae-MAH-dthah, toh-MAHS]. (1420–1498) Spanish inquisitor.

torquemeter.

tort. In law, a private, actionable injury; e.g., vehicular negligence, libel.

tortilla [TAWR-TEE-yuh]. Thin, unleavened flat cakes.

tortoise [TAWR-tuhs]. A turtle; by extension, a slow-moving person.

tortuous. Twisting or winding: *The road followed a tortuous course.*

    TORTUROUS. From torture: *The barbarians employed torturous rituals to obtain favors from their gods.*

    TORTIOUS. Involving a tort.

Toscanini, Arturo [TOHS-kah-nee-nee angl., TAHS-kah-nee-nih]. (1867–1957) Italian conductor.

toss. P. and p.p., tossed; poet., tost.

tosspot. -up (n. and adj.).

total. —ize; —ity; —ed; —ing; —ly; Brit., —llize, —llity, etc. AVOID *a total of* except as a device to avoid beginning a sentence with a number.

total effect of all is redundant

totalitarian [toh-tal-ih-TAIR-ee-uhn]. Centralized government which permits no opposition.

totally destroyed. Meaning *demolished*, is redundant.

Totowa [TOH-toh-wah]. Town in New Jersey.

touché. Hit, especially at a sensitive spot.

Toulon [too-LAHN; Fr., too-LAWN]. Seaport, naval base in southeast France.

Toulouse-Lautrec, Henri Marie Raymond de [too-LOOZ loh-TREHK]. (1864–1900) French painter of Paris life.

toupee [too-PAE; Brit.,-peht]. Pl. -s. A small wig.

tour de force. (Fr.) Feat of strength, skill, or ingenuity.

Touré, Sekou [too-RAE, sae-KOO]. (1922–) President of Guinea, 1958–

tourmaline [TUR-muh-lihn]. Semi-precious stone, usually black, sometimes blue, red, brown or colorless. Brittle, pyro-electric borosilicate with a vitreous lustre.

tourney [TOOR-nih].

tourniquet [TOOR-nih-kae, TUR-nih-keht].

Tours [TOOR]. City in France.

tousle [TOU-z'l]. -led, -sling.

toward. [(adj.) TOH-ahrd; (prep.) tohrd]. For prep. use British prefer *towards.*

towboat. towline, towrope; tow-haired (adj.), tow car.

toweled. -ing.

Tower, Eiffel. the tower.

townbound. —folk, —gate, —goer, —house, —ship, —site, —wear (all one word); town-bred (adj.), town-dotted (adj.), town-weary (adj.); town clerk, town crier, town hall, town meeting.

townsboy. —fellow, —man, —people.

Township. Union; Township of Union.

toxemia.

trace. —ceable.

trachea [TRAE-kee-uh]. Windpipe. Pl. —eae [—ee].

tradebound. trade-mark, trade-in (n. and adj.), trade-laden (adj.), trade-made (adj.); trade name, trade school, trade union, trade wind.

tradesfolk. -man, -people, -woman; trades union, trades unionism.

trade union. Pl. trade unions.

trade wind. A drying wind, easterly toward the equator.

trading stamp. Premium in stamp form, given to stimulate trade, usually redeemable for merchandise.

traduce. Slander; defame. -cible.

traffic. -icked, -icking, -icker.

trafficway. traffic-mile.

tragedian [tra-JEE-dih-uhn]. Fem., -ienne [-dih-EHN]. Writer or actor of tragedy.

tragedy. The adjective *tragic* is preferred to *tragical*. Applies to art, drama; by extension, to life. Misfortune is more appropriate for a person, disaster or calamity in a real-life situation.

   TRAGICO-, TRAGI-. Combining form meaning tragedy: *tragicomical, tragical, tragicomedy, tragicomic.*

trailblazer. —blazing, —breaker, —maker, —making, —side, —sight (all one word); trail-marked (adj.), trail-weary (adj.).

training camp. training ship.

traipse or trapse [TRAEPS]. Trudge.

trait [treat; Brit., trae]. Characteristic; peculiarity.

traitor. traitress; —torous.

Trajan [TRAE-jan]. (53?–117) Roman emperor, 98–117.

tramcar. —line, —load, —man, —rail, —way, —wayman, —yard (all one word); tramborne (adj.).

trammeled. -ing.

tranquil. -ize, -izer; Brit. -llize, -llizer. -quilly, -quillity or -quility.

Trans-Canada Air Lines. Canadian airline.

transcendental. Visionary, beyond experience; of Emerson's religious philosophy.

transfer. -ferred, -ferring, -ferrer, -ferable, ference; -feree (who receives). In law, -feror, (who conveys).

transfuse [trans-FYOOZ]. Pour, transfer. -sible. *transfuse blood.*

transgress [trans-GREHS]. Go beyond limits, especially of the law. -essor.

transients. Those passing through.

transitive verbs. Require a direct object: *Put the chair in the place.* Cf. Verbs.

translate. Reproduce meaning.

   CONSTRUE. Show grammatical structure, especially for something that requires translation.

   CONSTRUCT. Older form of construe.

   TRANSLITERATE. Reproduce sounds in a different alphabet.

translucent. -cence, -cency, -cently. Cf. transparent.

transmit. To send from one person or place to another. Destination should be indicated NOT merely implied: *He sent the letter. He transmitted the letter to Dr. B.* -mitted, -mitting, -mittance, -mitter, -missible, -mittible.

transom. Cross piece over the door. In U.S., by ext., the window above.

transonic. Of the speed exceeding 1087 ft. per second, the speed of sound. Cf. Mach.

transparency. Preferred to -ce.

transparent. Transmitting light so that what lies beyond is visible, as glass.

   DIAPHANOUS. So fine-textured that it is transparent or translucent, as chiffon, membranes, vapor.

PELLUCID [peh-LOO-sihd]. Transparent, clear, easy to understand. As water, good writing. *Cf.* turbid.

TRANSLUCENT. Diffusing light so objects cannot be seen clearly. As tortoise shell, frosted glass.

transpire. (v.) leak out; occur; emerge, from secrecy; exhale; perspire: *It transpired that he had left his money to charity.* ALSO happen.

transposition. Preferred to transposal. Change in order. transpose.

transship. Preferred to tranship. Brit., tranship.

Transvaal [trans-VAHL]. Province in northeast Union of South Africa. Cap., Pretoria.

trapezium. Irregular four-sided figure. Pl. -ia or -s.

travail [TRAV-ael]. Toil, esp. with great effort.

travel [TRAV-ehl]. -led, -ler, -ing. Brit., -lled, -ller, -lling.

travelogue. or -log.

travesty. Ludicrous distortion.

trawl boat. —net.

trayful. Pl. -fuls.

tray maker. tray cloth.

treacle [TREE-kl]. Molasses; an old remedy against poison.

tred. P., trod; p.p., trodden. trod; pres. p., treading, NOT trodding.

treadboard. —mill, —wheel.

Treasurer. Assistant, of the United States; the Assistant Treasurer. BUT assistant treasurer of New York, etc.

Treasury, of the United States. General Treasury, National Treasury, Public Treasury, Register of the Treasury; Treasury notes, treasuries.

Treaty. Capitalize if part of name; the treaty: Jay Treaty, North Atlantic Treaty, North Atlantic Defense Treaty, Treaty of Versailles. BUT treaty of 1919.

treaty bound.

treble [TREHBL]. triple. (music) highpitched.

trecento. (Ital.) 1300. In art, 1300–1399; quattrocento, 1400–1499; cinquecento, 1500–1599.

trek. -kked, -kking.

trellis. —ed; trellis-work; trellis-covered (adj.).

tremendous. SEE Strong Opinion Words.

tremolo. Pl. -os.

tremor [TREH-mer].

trepan [tree-PAN]. —nned, —nning. Entrap; in surgery, saw for skull perforation.

triad [TRIE-ad]. Group of three clearly related; trinity. *Cf.* groups.

trial [TRIE-'L].
TRAIL [TRAEL].

tribesman. —people.

tribunal [trie-BYOO-nal]. Court.

Tribunal. Capitalize standing alone only in minutes and official reports of a specific arbitration; also High Tribunal, the Tribunal (Supreme Court).

tricentenary. Use tercentenary.

triceps. Pl. —cepses. SEE biceps.

trick proof. -work.

Tricolore. The French flag; angl., Tricolor, -our [TRIE-kuhl-ehr, trih-kuhl-ehr].

Trieste [tree-EHS-tae; angl., tree-EHST]. Native, Triestini. Adriatic seaport between Italy and Yugoslavia.

trillion. 1000 billion in U.S. and France; 1 million billion in Britain and Germany. *Cf.* numbers.

trilogy. Three associated literary or musical works by the same author.

Trinidad and Tobago, W.I. Capital, Port of Spain. Natives, Trinidadian(s) or Tobagan(s). Currency, TT dollar, cent.

Trinity.

trio. Pl. -os.

triolet. An 8-line poem in which the first line is repeated as the 4th and 7th, the second line as the 8th, and the other lines rhyme with first and second.

tripartite [trie-PAHR-tiet, TRIHP-uhr-tiet]. Divided into three parts. tripartible.

triple. British prefer treble.

Triple A. (any three A Group). *American Automobile Association.*

tripod [TRIE-pahd]. Stand, etc., with three legs.

Tripolitania [trihp-oh-lih-TAEN-yah]. Region of northwest Libya on Mediterranean Sea. Native, Tripolitanian. Cap., Tripoli [TRIHP-oh-lih].

Trippe, Juan [trihp, wahn]. (1899–   ) American airline executive.

triptych [TRIHP-tihk]. Three-part folded writing tablet or picture.

trireme [TRIE-reem]. Galley with three banks of oars. *Cf.* boats.

triton [TRIE-t'n]. Nucleus of tritium.

TRITON. In mythology, Greek sea god with fishlike lower body.

triumphal. Pertains to or used in celebration of victory.

TRIUMPHANT. Victorious, exultant.

triumvir. One of three men in public office (Roman). Pl. -s, sometimes-ri. triumvirate, triumviral.

trivia [TRIHV-ih-uh]. Plural form only. Trifles.

-trix. Agent suffix from Latin, feminine equivalent of -tor: *administratrix, testatrix, prosecutrix.* Pl. -trices [-seez].

Trizonia. trizonal, trizone. Area in West Germany occupied and controlled by three powers, U.S., Britain and France.

troche [TROH-kee]. Medicinal lozenge.

TROCHEE [TROH-kee]. Poetic foot with one long, one short beat. *Cf.* scansion.

Trondheim [TRAWN-haem]. Seaport in Norway. Formerly *Trondhjem* [TRAWN-yehm].

troop. A company, especially military. troops. Soldiers.

TROUPE. A company of actors.

trope [TROHP]. Figure of speech, especially a word used in an unusual sense: *Two incipient chandeliers hanging from her ears.*

tropical. neotropic, neotropical, subtropic(s), subtropical; the Tropics (of Cancer and Capricorn).

Tropic of Cancer. Area from the Equator to 23°27′ N. lat.

Tropic of Capricorn. Area from the Equator to 23°27′ S. lat.

tropopause. Surface separating troposphere from stratosphere, approx. 55,000 ft. above sea level at equator, 25,000 ft. at poles.

troposphere. SEE atmosphere.

Trotsky, Leon [TRAWTS-kih. angl., TRAHT-skih]. Originally Leib or Lev Davydovich Bronstein. (1877–1940). Russian Communist War Minister, theoretician.

troubadour [TROO-buh-dawr]. Lyric singer of the 11th–13th centuries.

troublemaker. –making, –proof, –shooting, –some (all one word); troublefree (adj.). trouble-shooter.

trounce. [TROUNSS]. Thrash. —cing, —ced; —ceable.

trousseau [troo-SOH, TRR-soh]. Pl. —eaux —eaus. Bride's personal outfit.

trout. Singular and plural.

troweled. —ing.

troy weight. System of measurement used for precious stones and metals based on 5760 grains = 1 lb. = 12 ou. = 240 pennyweights.

trucebreaker. truce-seeking (adj.).

truculent [TRUHK-yoo-lehnt]. Displaying fierceness, cruelty. —ly, —lence, —lency.

true facts is a tautology

Trujillo Molina, Rafael Leonidas [troo-HEE-yoh moh-LEE-nah, rah-fah-EHL lae-oh-NEE-dthahs]. (1891–1967) Dominican Republic dictator, general. Son: Rafael, Jr. (1930–1969). Nickname: *Ramfis.*

truly.

truncheon [TRUHN-ch'n]. Short stick, especially a policeman's.

trundle [TRUHN-dl or TRUHN'l]. Low-wheeled cart or its noise.

trundlehead. trundle bed.

trunkful. Pl. -fulls.

trust.

    BENEFICIAL TRUST. One in which the trustee is a beneficiary.

    CONSTRUCTIVE TRUST. One without a formal writing, implied in a situation and declared a trust by a court.

    INTER VIVOS TRUST [IHN-tehr vie vohs]. "Between living persons." Living trust; a gift from one person to another.

    LIVING TRUST. Voluntary trust created without consideration, usually for a person's support.

trust territory. SEE Territory.

trysail [TRIE-sl]. A fore-and-aft-sail bent to a gaff.

tryst [trihst; Brit., triest].

T(s)chaikovsky, Peter (Pëtr) Ilyich [chie-KAEF-skih, PEAT-ehr IL-yihch]. (1840–1893) Russian composer.

tsetse [TSEH-tsih]. The fly that carries sleeping sickness.

T. Sgt. (abbr.) technical sergeant.

Tshombe, Moise-Kapenda [CHAHM-bae, MOI-suh]. (1919–1969) Premier of Katanga, Congo, 1960–1961.

tsp. (abbr.) teaspoonful(s).

T-square. BUT tee shirt.

T2g. (abbr.) technician, second grade.

tube. British use *valves* for radio tubes.

tubercle [TOO-buhr-k'l]. Nodule; morbid skin growth, especially in tuberculosis.

tuberculine [too-BUHR-kyoo-lih liquid used to test for and treat v .

tuberculosis [tyoo-buhr-kyoo-LOH-sihs]. A lung disease.

tuberose [TYOO-buhr-ohs]. Bulb of amaryllis family with spiked white flowers.

tubful. Pl., -s.

Tucson [too-SAHN or TOO-sahn]. City in Arizona.

Tuesday [TOOZ-dih]. (abbr., Tues.)

tugboat. —boatman; tug of war.

Tuileries [TWEE-luhr-eez]. Place in Paris near the Louvre.

Tula [TOO-lah]. City in Russia on tributary of Oka River. Town in Mexico, site of Toltec ruins.

tularemia. A disease, especially of rodents

tulipgrower. tulip-growing (adj.).

tulle [tool]. A fine net for veils, etc.

tumefy. Swell, become swelled. —fied, —fying. tumidity.

tumultuous. (NOT tumultus) Full of noise: *tumultuous commotion, applause, seas, joy.*

    TUMULTUARY. Less common form which emphasizes the unorganized: *Tumultuary mob, thoughts*

tumulus. Pl. -li. Artificial mound, especially over an ancient grave.

tuna. A species of the fish *tunny.* Also a prickly pear: *tunafish, tuna oil.*

tun. Large wine cask; unit of capacity measure = 252 wine gallons = 953.9 1. = 2 pipes. = 8 bbls.

Tunisia [tyoo-NIHZH-ih-ah]. Country in North Africa. Native, Tunisians(s); (adj.) Tunisian. Capital, Tunis [tyoo-nihs]. French, Tunisie [teu-nee-zee]. Currency, millime(s) dinar(s).

tunnel. -led, -ling; tunneler. Brit., -lled, -lling. -ller.

Tunnel, Lincoln. the tunnel. BUT lower-case irrigation tunnel, railroad tunnel etc.; tunnel no. 1.

Tunney, Gene James Joseph [TUHN-ıh]. (1897–). American boxer, businessman. World heavyweight champion, 1926–1928.

Tuolumne R. [too-AHL-uh-mee]. River in California.

Tuomioja, Sakari Severi. "*thou also.*" (Lat.) [TWOO-mee-oh-yah, SAHK-uh-ree]. (1911–1964). Premier of Finland, 1953–1954. Mediator at Cyprus, 1954.

tu quoque. In rhetoric, answering an argument by attacking the one presenting it.

turbid. Confused, muddy. —idness is preferred to —ity, except poetically.

turbine [TUHRB-bin, pref. to -bien]. Rotary engine driven by fluid, especially water, or by heated air, as in a jet engine.

turbot [TEHR-buht, TOOR-boh]. Luxury food fish from France; ordinary food fish from Greenland.

tureen [tuh-REEN, commonly too-REEN; Brit., tyoo]. Vessel from which soup is served.

turf. Pl. -s.

Turgenev, Ivan Sergeevich [toor-GEHN-yehf, ee-VAHN syihr-gae-yeh-vyihch]. (1818–1883) Russian novelist.

turgid. Swollen; vainly ostentatious.

turbid [THUHR-bihd]. Clouded, muddy.

Turk. Turkoman.

Turkestan or -istan [tuhr-keh-STAN]. Central Asian region in U.S.S.R., China, Afghanistan.

Turkey. Native, Turk(s); (adj.) Turkish. Cap., Ankara. Currency, lira (Tl), kuruş.

turner-off.

turnover tax. Sales tax, especially in U.S.S.R.

turnpike. Pennsylvania, etc.; the turnpike.

turquoise [TUHRK-kwoiz]. Blue-green, from semi-precious stone of this color.

AQUAMARINE. Green-blue.

turret. A little tower. -eted.

Tuskegee [tuhs-KEE-gih]. College in Alabama.

Tutankhamen or -mon [toot-ahngk-AH-mehn or -mahn]. (c. 1358 B.C.) King of Egypt.

Tuva [TOO-vah]. Autonomous region in U.S.S.R. near Mongolia. Formerly Tannu Tuva [TAN-oo TOO-vah].

TV. (abbr.) television. NOT T.V.

TVA. N.Y. Times, T.V.A. (abbr.) Tennesee Valley Authority.

Twad. (abbr.) Twaddell.

twelfth.

twenties. SEE numbers.

twentyfold. —leaf, —penny (nail); twenty-first, twenty-one.

twice-born. (adj.) twice-reviewed (adj.), twice-told (adj.).

twilighted. Preferred to twilit.

twinborn. twin-engined (adj.), twin-jet (adj.), twin-motor (adj.), twin-screw (adj.), twin boat, twin ship.

Twin Cities. Minneapolis and St. Paul, Minnesota.

twins. A pair of twins is four people. The expression is redundant if the meaning is two people.

two. Pl. twos.

twofold. two-penny (nail), twoscore, twosome; two-a-day (adj.) two-along (bookbinding) (n.), two-decker, —faced (adj.), two-handed (adj.), two-piece (adj.), two-ply (adj.,) two-seater, two-spot, two-step (dance), two-striper, two-suiter, two-thirder, two-up (n. and adj.), two-way (adj.), two-wheeler.

2, 4-D. A weed killer.

tying.

tyke. Preferred to tike. A dog.

tympanist. Drum player.

tympanum [tihmp-uh-nuhm]. Pl. -s. Ear drum.

Tyne River [tien]. River in England; flows into North Sea.

type. *O-type blood.* BUT NOT *intellectual type person.* BETTER: *intellectual type of person.*

type case. —cast, —caster, —casting, —cutter, —cutting, —face, –holder, –script, –set, —setter, –setting, –write (v.), –writing, —written (all one word); type-high (adj.); type founder, type foundry, type metal, type page.

type size. Based on 72 points = 1 inch, type faces are manufactured in 5, 5½, 6, 7, 8, 9, 10, 11, 12, 14, 16, 18, 24, 30, 36, 42, 48, 60, and 72 points. 1 pica = 12 points = 2 nonparils.

typhoon. Tropical cyclone in China Sea area.

typify. Embody essential characteristics of -fied, -fying.

tyranny [TIHR-a-nih]. Despotism. tyrannical.

Tyre [tier]. Town in southwest Lebanon; ancient capital of Phoenicia.

tyro [TIE-roh]. Beginner. Pl. -s.

Tyrol [tih-ROHl]. SEE Tirol.

Tyrrhenian Sea [tie-REE-nih-an]. Part of Mediterranean Sea, southwest of Italy, north of Sicily, east of Corsica and Sardinia.

Tzar. Czar is preferred in U.S. Fem., Tzarina.

tzigane, -ny [tsee-GAHN]. Hungarian Gyspy.

U

U-boat. U-cut, U-magnet, U-rail, U-shaped, U-tube.

U.A.W. (abbr.) United Auto Workers.

Uaxactun [wah-sahk-TOON]. Town in Guatamala.

Ubangi [yoo-BANG(g)-ee; OO-BAHNG(g)-ee]. French, Oubangui [yoo-bahn-GEE]. River and people in central Africa, near border of French Equatorial Africa and former Belgian Congo.

ubiety [yoo-BIE-eh-tih]. Being in position.

ubiquitous [yoo-BIHK-wih-tuhs]. Being everywhere.

uc or u.c. (abbr.) uppercase, capital letters. *Cf.* lc, lowercase.

Ucayali River [oo-kah-YAH-lih]. River in Peru; flows into Marañón River.

UCMS. (abbr.) University of Chicago Manual of Style.

Udall, Stewart Lee [yoo-DAHL]. (1920–   ) U.S. Secretary of Interior, 1961-1968.

Ufa River [OO-fah]. River in U.S.S.R.

Uganda [yoo-GAN-duh]. British Protectorate west of Kenya. Independent, 1962. Cap., Entebbe. Currency, Uganda shilling.

Ugarteche, Manuel Prado y. SEE Prado.

UHF. (abbr.) ultrahigh frequency.

uhlan [YOO-1'n]. Type of lancer.

Ujpest [OO-yuh-pehsht]. City in Hungary.

ukase [yoo-KAES]. An official decree.

Ukraine [yoo-KRAEN]. Native, Ukrainian(s); (adj.) Ukrainian. Russ. Ukraina [oo-KRAH-ih-nae] Republic in east central Europe on Black Sea, noted for soil fertility. Part of U.S.S.R.

ukulele [YOO-kuh-LAE-lee]. Small guitar, originally from Portugal.

Ulbricht, Walter [OOL-brihkt]. (1893-1973) East German chief of state; First Secretary of Communist Party. (1950–1973)

ulna. Inner of forearm bones. Pl., -nae.

ultima [UHL-tih-muh]. Last syllable of a word.
    ULTIMO [UHL-tih-moh]. (abbr. ult.) In the preceding month. Old-fashioned business form. *Yours of the 17th ult.* is archaic.

ultimatum [uhl-tih-MAE-tehm]. Final offer or condition. Pl. -s or -ta.

ultra-. Combining prefix meaning beyond, excessively. Usually in one word except preceding a vowel. *Ultra-ambitious, ultra-exclusive, ultra-high-speed* (adj.), *ultramodern, ultrareligious.*

ultra-high frequency. (abbr., UHF). Radio or television range 30 to 300 megacycles.

ultra vires. (Lat.) Beyond the power: *An ultra vires act is not binding.*

ululate [YOOL-yoo-laet]. Howl like a dog. —lated, —lating, —lation, uluant.

umber. Brown.

umbilicus [um-BIHL-ih-kuhs]. Navel. Pl. -ci.

umbrage. Shadow, or that which casts it; by extension, resentment.

umlaut [OOM-lout]. Mark of two dots over a vowel to indicate pronunciation change caused by another vowel in the same syllable, especially in German. ä, ö, or ü: röentgen. *Cf.* diacritical marks.

UMTS. (abbr.) Universal Military Training Service (or System).

un-. Combining prefix meaning *not; un-American,* etc., *uncalled-for* (adj.), *unheard-of* (adj.), *un-ionized* (adj.), *unself-conscious, unsent-for* (adj.), *unthought-of* (adj.), *unthought-on* (adj.); *un-uniformity; unaided, unbearable,* etc. Cf. *in-*.

U.N. [YOO-ehn]. (abbr.) United Nations. (Webster, also UN.)

unable. Not able; not usually incapable.

INCAPABLE. Lacking capacity. *She was not able to be here because she had guests; he is incapable of finding this place.*

unadmissible. NOT correct. Use inadmissible.

Unalaska [oo-nuh-LAS-kuh]. Island in the Aleutians.

Unamuno y Ugo, Miguel de [dae oo-nah-MOO-noh ee HOO-goh, mee-gee]. (1864–1936) Spanish philosopher.

unanimous [yoo-NAN-ih-muhs]. With the consent of all. Never *more* or *most* unanimous.

unappeasable. Implacable.

unapt. Not likely to; unsuitable.

INEPT. Preferred to *unapt* for backward, without aptitude.

unartistic. Not interested in art.

INARTISTIC. Not a work of art; not artistic.

unattached adjective and participles. Avoid in complete sentences. NOT: *Walking down the street, two tall buildings could be seen.*

unauspicious. Inauspicious is preferred.

una voce [YOO-nuh VOH-see]. *With one voice:* unanimously.

unaware. (adj.) Ignorant, not knowing: *They were unaware of his presence.*

UNAWARES. (adj.) Without preparation, suddenly: *The troops move forward unaware of their objective: they came upon the enemy unawares.*

unbeknown. Unknown.

unbeknownst [uhn-bee-NOHNST]. Avoid.

unbiased [uhn-BIE-uhst]. Preferred to unbiassed. Unprejudiced.

unceasing. Incessant, continuous. —ly.

uncomparable. Cannot be compared: *Pens and mice are uncomparable.*

INCOMPARABLE [ihn-KAHMP-rabl]. Unequalled: *An incomparable accomplishment.*

unconscionable [uhn-KAHN-shuhn-uh-b'l]. Unreasonable; unscrupulous.

uncontrollable. Preferred to in-.

uncorruptible.

unctuous. [UHNG-choo-uhs]. Oily; hence, ingratiating; gushing.

undependable.

under. SEE *below*.

underage [UHN-deh-ehj]. Deficit.

UNDERAGE [uhn-dehr-AEJ]. Not old enough.

underground. Brit. for subway. U.S. for anti-establishment.

under secretary. Pl. under secretaries.

Under Secretary. Capitalize if referring to officer of federal government; the Under Secretary of Agriculture, of State, of the Treasury.

Under Secretary of State. ADDRESS: The Under Secretary of State, Washington, D.C.; or The Honorable David K. Bruce, Under Secretary of State. SALUTATION: Sir, Dear Sir, Dear Mr. Bruce.

under the counter. Surreptitious.

underwrite. Agree to accept the risk, as in insurance and security flotations.

undigested. Preferred to in-.

undisciplined. Preferred to in-.

undiscriminating. Preferred to in-. Not discriminating, especially among races.

INDISCRIMINATE. Showing no sense of discrimination; e.g., between the wise and the unwise.

undisposed. SEE indisposed.

undissolvable.

undistinguishable. *In-* is preferred BUT undistinguished.

undue. Avoid a double negative: NOT: *There was no need for undue fear.*

uneconomic. Bad business sense, especially of a community or goverment.

UNECONOMICAL. Bad budget sense. Bringing ice to Alaska is uneconomic; buying ice cubes for home use when your refrigerator can make them is uneconomical.

unequaled. Brit., -lled.

unescapable. Preferred to in-.

UNESCO. (abbr.) United Nations Educational, Scientific, and Cultural Organization. Sometimes Unesco.

unessential. Preferred to in-. *Cf.* essential.

unexhaustible.

unexpressible.

unfrequented [uhn-free-KWEHNT-ehd]. Not in-.

unquent [UHNG-gwehnt, NOT uhn—]. Salve; ointment.

unhuman. Not a human being.

INHUMAN. Not having the traits of civilized human beings.

uni-. Combining form meaning one: *united, univalent, uniform, universal.*

UNICEF. (abbr.) United Nations Children's Fund. (International and Emergency have been dropped from the name, but not from the acronym.) Sometimes *Unicef.*

Uniform Code of Military Justice. SEE Code.

unimproved property. Property in the natural state; i.e., with no construction, sewers, sidewalks, and similar development.

unintelligible.

Union. Capitalize if part of proper name; capitalize standing alone if synonym for United States or if referring to international unit: European Payments Union, the Union; International Typographical Union, the

Typographical Union, the union; Pan American Union (SEE Organization of American States); Union Station, union passenger station, union freight station; Teamsters Union, the Teamsters, the union; also the Auto Workers Union; Universal Postal Union, the Postal Union, the union; Western Union (SEE alliances); Woman's Christian Temperance Union. BUT: a painters union, printers union.

un-ionized. Not ionized.

Union of South African States. Ghana, Guinea, Mali Republic.

Union of South Africa. Since 1961, Republic of South Aftrica. Native, Afrikaner; of original Dutch or Huguenot immigrant stock, by ext. of white stock. (Afrikander is a breed of cattle.) Language, Afrikaans. adj., South African. Cap., Pretoria, seat of administration; Cape Town, seat of legislature. Currency, rand.

Union of Soviet Socialist Republics. (abbr., U.S.S.R.) Native, Soviets (pl. only); adj., Soviet. Cap. Moscow (Moskva). Currency, ruble, kopek. NOT to be confused with Russia (RSFSR), Ruskaya Socialisticheskaya Federationaya Sovietskaya Republika (Great Russian Republic), largest of the republics, with more than half the total population. Soviet is capitalized if part of name; capitalized standing alone if referring to central governmental unit: Soviet Government, BUT Communist government; Moscow Soviet, National Soviet, Soviet of Labor and Defense. BUT a soviet (meaning council); sovietic; sovietism; sovietize.

Union Jack. SEE flags.

unionman. union-made (adj.); union card union shop.

unique. Only one of its kind. NOT *rather, more* or *most, very, somewhat,* or *comparatively unique.* BUT *almost, really, certainly, perhaps,* or *in many ways* are correct. Some grammarians assess the meaning of unique as "unparalleled" and accept *more* and *quite unique* in this sense.

Unit. Capitalize if referring to federal or state branch: Alcohol Tax Unit, Income Tax Unit, the Unit; BUT Pasco unit.

United Arab Republic. (abbr. U.A.R.). Native, Egyptian(s) (Egyptian region), Syrian(s) (Syrian region) until 1961. adj., United Arab

Republic. Cap., Cairo (Al Quahira). Currency, pound, piaster.

United Kingdom. (abbr. U.K.) Great Britain, made up of England, Scotland and Wales, and Northern Ireland. Capital, London. Currency, £1 = 100 pence. *Cf.* Great Britain, Britain.

United Nations. United Nations Charter, the charter; United Nations Children's Fund (UNICEF), the Fund; United Nations Conference on International Organization, the Conference; United Nations Economic and Social Council, the Council; United Nations Educational, Scientific, and Cultural Organization (UNESCO) (SEE Organization); United Nations Food and Agriculture Organization (FAO), the Organization; United Nations General Assembly, the Assembly; United Nations International Court of Justice, the Court; United Nations International Labor Organization (SEE Organization); United Nations Assembly, the Assembly; United Nations Permanent Court of Arbitration (SEE Court); United Nations Secretariat, the; Secretary General of the United Nations; United Nations Security Council, the Council; Special United Nations Fund for Economic Development (SUNFED); United Nations Trusteeship Council, the Council; World Health Organization (WHO), the Organization.

United States. (abbr. U.S.) Takes singular verb.

United States. the Republic; the Nation; the Union; the Government; Federal, Federal Government; republic (when not referring specifically to one such entity); republican (in general sense).

United States of America. (abbr., U.S.A.) Native, American(s); adj., American (preferred), United States.

unit fraction. unit price.

unit modifier. An adjective which modifies a following noun. Compounds are usually hyphenated: *five-day week*, *ten-year-old wine*, *7-hour day*. BUT: *.30 caliber bore*. In this text, especially in matter relating to hyphenation, the abbreviation *adj.* refers to unit modifier only.

units of measure. (number) When a number is used with a plural noun as a unit of measurement (fractions, money, time, etc.) use a singular verb except when the term is viewed as made of individual parts: *Here is $20.*

unity, dramatic. Consists of unities of time (a single day), place, and action. Only the last is considered essential in modern drama.

Universal Postal Union.

University. Capitalize if part of name: Stanford University, the university. *Cf.* college.

Unknown Quantities. Are represented by lower case letters. $(a + b)/c$ and are usually italicized. BUT NOT abbreviations or representations of persons' names: *A sold B two items*.

unknown. NOT unknownst.

Unknown Soldier. Unknown Soldier of World War II, World War II Unknown Soldier, Unknown Soldier of Korea, Korea Unknown Soldier; the Unknowns (SEE ALSO Tomb).

unlearned. Pref. to -nt.

unlisted security. One not traded on a registered securities exchange.

unmaterial. Not consisting of matter. *Immaterial* is pref. for all meanings.

unmoral. SEE amoral.

unnavigable.

unparalleled.

unpractical. NOT in-.

unquiet.

unredeemed.

unresponsible. Not responsible.

IRRESPONSIBLE. Not able or not willing to assume required responsibility.

unsanitary. Of a place that neither requires nor has sanitation.

INSANITARY. Without sanitation, implying a dangerous condition; unhealthful.

unsolvable. Not capable of being solved.

unstable [uhn-STAE-bl]. Not constant.

unsusceptible.

until. Up to or before the time or point. AVOID *until such time as.*

untoward [uhn-TOH-uhrd]. Perverse; awkward; inconvenient.

U Nu [oo noo]. (1907–   ). Burmese statesman, premier. *Cf.* Names.

unwieldy [uhn-WEEL-dih]. Unmanageable. unwieldiness.

up-along. (adv.) upbeat, up-bow, up-coast, upcountry (adv. and adj.), upend (v.) upgrade, up-gradient, upkeep, uplift, up-river, upstairs, upstate, upstream, up-street, upswing, uptake, uptown, up-trend, upturn; up-anchor (adj. and v.), up-and-coming (adj.), up-over (adj.), up-to-date (adj.); up and up, up oars.

upon, on. *On* is preferred when position would create two unaccented syllables; *upon* is preferred at the end of a sentence.

Upper. Capitalize if part of name: Upper Colorado River Basin, Upper Egypt, Upper Peninsula (of Michigan); BUT upper House of Congress.

upper case. (n.) In printing, capital letters. Upper cased. (adj., v.) upper-case.

upper classman. upper crust (n. and adj.); uppermost; upper class, upper deck, upper grade, upper hand.

Upper Volta [VAHL-tuh]. Independent since Aug., 1960. Situated north of Ghana, formerly in French West Africa. Cap., Ouagadougou [WAH-gul-DOO-goo]. adj., Voltaic. Natives, Upper Voltan(s). Currency, CFAF franc.

Uppsala or Upsala [UHP-sah-luh]. City and university in Sweden.

UPSALA COLLEGE [uhp-SAH-luh]. College in East Orange, N.J.

upward. (s) SEE backward.

upwards of. Meaning *more than.* AVOID.

Ural Mountains [YOO-r'l]. Mountains in U.S.S.R.

uraniun 235. BUT U^{235}; Sr^{90}; $92U^{234}$.

Uranus [YOOR-uh-nahs]. The planet. URANOUS. Containing uranium.

urban. Characteristic of or pertaining to a city.

URBANE. Suave. *Her urbane manner and sophisticated clothes impressed the naive visitor.*

uremia. Pref. to uraemia [uh-REE-mih-uh]. Toxic condition caused by insufficient urine secretion.

ureter [yoo-REE-tuhr]. Duct from kidney to bladder.

urethane. Polyurethane foam plastic.

urethra. Canal which carries urine from the bladder.

urinalysis [yoo-ruh-NAL-ih-sihs]. Analysis of urine, especially for sugar or bacterial content.

Uruguay [OO-ruh-gwie, —gwae]. Native, Uruguayan(s); adj. Uruguayan. Cap., Montevideo. Currency, peso (Ur. $) centesimo.

us. (objective); we (nominative); *They know as much as we* (know); or *more than we; We Americans can join . . . Let us join.* BUT formal grammatical rules may be breached in this respect in conversation.

U.S. (abbr.) U.S. Supreme Court Reports.

USA. (abbr.) U.S. Army.

U.S.A. (abbr.) United States of America.

USAF. (abbr.) U.S. Air Force.

usage. Customary practice.

USAREUR. (abbr.) U.S. Army, Europe.

U.S.C. (abbr.) United States Code.

U.S.C.A. (abbr.) United States Code Annotated.

USCG. (abbr.) U.S. Coast Guard.

U.S. Congress.

U.S.C. Supp. (abbr.) United States Code Supplement.

use. An act of employing something.

USES or U.S.E.S. (abbr.) U.S. Employment Service.

USIA or U.S.I.A. (abbr.) U.S. Information Agency.

USMC or U.S.M.C. (abbr.) U.S. Marine Corps.

USN or U.S.N. (abbr.) U.S. Navy.

USNR or U.S.N.R. (abbr.) U.S. Naval Reserve.

U.S.-owned property.

U.S.P. (abbr.) United States Pharmacopoeia.

U.S.S. (abbr.) U.S. Senate; U.S. ship.
ussc. (abbr.) United States Strike Command. Unified TAC-SAC FORCE.

U.S.S.R. (abbr.) Union of Soviet Socialist Republics.

Ustinov, Peter Alexander [oo-STEEN-AWf]. (1921–   ) British writer, dramatist, actor.

usually. Place immediately before or after verb: *She is usually in bed by nine.*

usufruct. Legal right to use of another's property without ownership.

usurp [yoo-ZUHRP]. Seize without right. —ed, —ing.

usury [YOO-zhoo-ree]. Charge of interest rate higher than that allowed by law. usurious [yoo-ZHOOR-ih-uhs].

u.t. (abbr.) universal time.

Utah [YOO-taw]. (No abbr.) (Web. "unofficial," *Ut.*) Native, Utahan. Cap., Salt Lake City.

U Thant [oo-THAHNT]. (1901–   ) Burmese diplomat; Sec.-Gen., U.N. 1962–1972. *Cf.* NAMES.

Utica [YOO-tih-kuh]. City in New York State.

utilization. Use *use.*

utmost. Preferred to uttermost.

Utopia [yoo-TOH-pih-uh]. utopian.

Uusikaupunki [oo-sih-KOU-poong-kie]. Town in Finland.

uxorious [uhks-OH-rih-uhs]. Excessive fondness for or submissiveness to a wife. uxorial, uxoricide.

Uzbek [OOZ-behk]. Republic in U.S.S.R.

V

V-boat. V-connection, V-curve, V-engine, V-man, V-neck, V-shaped, V-type.

v. (abbr.) Pref. to vs. versus, against.

v. (abbr.) volt; verb.

VA. (abbr.) Veterans Administration.

Va. (abbr.) Virginia.

Vaasa [VAH-sah]. Town in Finland.

vacation. SEE holidays.

vaccine [VAK-seen]. Substance for preventive innoculation. vaccinate, -nable, nator.

vacillate [VASLih-laet]. Waver.

vacuous [VAK-yoo-uhs]. —cuity, —cuousness. Empty.

vacuum [VAK-yoo-m]. Pl. -s or vacua.

vagary [vah-GAIR-ih]. Pl. -ies. Eccentric action.

vain. Empty of value. vainly.
  IN VAIN. Without result.

vainglorious [vaen-GLOH-rih-uhs]. Boastful.

vainglory. Excessive pride, shown in boasting.

vainness. Devoid of value; *The vainness of the revolution.*
  VANITY. That which is useless; having excessive pride in one's appearance or attainments: *The woman's vanity.*

valance [VAL-ans]. Drapery hanging.
  VALENCE. [VAEL-ens]. (n.) In chemistry, combining power.

DeValera, Eamon [dehv-uh-LAE-rah, AFM-muhn]. (1881-1975) Irish president (1959-1973), revolutionist. Prime minister 1937-1948, 1951-1954, 1957-1959.

Valerian, Publicius Licinius Valerianus. [vah-LEER-ih-an]. Roman emperor (253-260).

valet [VAL-iht, VAL-ae]. Man servant. -eted, -eting.

Valhalla [val-HAL-uh]. In Norse myth., Hall of Odin, for dead heroes.

Valkyrie [val-KIH-rih, val-KIE-rih]. Pl., Valkyries. In Norse myth., maidens of Odin who select those to be slain in battle and guide the worthy to Valhalla. *Die Walkure* is the 1876 opera by Wagner. Valkyrian.

Valley. Shenandoah, the valley; BUT the valleys of Maryland and Virginia.

valor. Brit., -our. valorous.

Valparaiso [vahl-pah-RAH-ee-soh; angl., val-pah-RIE-zoh or -rae-]. Chief seaport of Chile.

valse [VAHLS]. A waltz, especially a concert waltz.

value. Monetary worth of anything; market price. *Of what value is that; What value has that?* valuable.

vandriver. vanguard, vanload.

Van Gogh, Vincent. SEE Gogh.

vapid [VAP-ihd]. Lifeless, dull. -ness pref. to -ity, except regarding comments. Pl. -ities.

vapor. Brit., —our. —orish, —orless, —ory. vaporific, -ize, -ization, -izer, -osity.

Vargas, Getulio Dornelles [VAHR-gahs, zhe-TOO-lyoh thoor-NEH-leez]. (1883-1954) President of Brazil, 1930-1945, 1951-1954.

variability [var-ih-uh-BIHL-ih-tih]. Or variableness. Being subject to change.
  VARIANT [VAIR-ih-ant]. Concretely different from the norm.

VARIATION. A slight change; music, repetition of a theme, with modifications.

VARIETY. The smallest classification in biology or geology: *A variety of Mollienesia caucana.*

varicolored.

variegate [VAIR-ee-eh-gaet]. Diversify.

variorum [vaer-ee-OR-uhm]. Classical text with notes.

various. Avoid use as *several* or *some.*

vase [vaeze-vahz].

Vaterland [FAH-ter-lahnt]. (Ger.) Fatherland.

vaudeville [VOHD-vihl].

vault. A room in which safe deposit boxes and valuables are kept; NOT a safe.

Vauxhall [VAHKS-hawl]. French automobile.

VD. (abbr.) venereal disease.

Veda [VAE-duh; VEE-duh]. Sacred book of Hindus.

V-E Day. V-J Day. SEE holidays.

vehicle [VEE-ihk'L; Webster, also VEE-hih-K'l].

vehicular [vee-HIHK-yoo-lahr]. Of a vehicle.

Velasco Ibarra, Jose [veh-LAHS-koh ee-BAH-rah, hoh-SAE]. (1896–   ) President of Ecuador (1944–1947).

Velazquez or Velasquez, Diego Rodriquez de Sylva y [vae-LATH-kaeth or -LAHS, DYAE-goh raw-DTHREE-gaeth dthae SEEL-vah ee]. (1599–1660) Spanish painter.

veld [VEHLT]. Preferred to -dt. African grassland with some shrubs or trees.

volition. Implies exercise of free choice. *Most people in these countries do not go to the polls of their own volition.*

vellum. Pl. -s; adj., -y. Prepared skin of a lamb, kid or calf used for bookbinding; a velvety paper made to imitate it.

velodrom [VEEL-oh-drohm]. Cycle track.

venal [VEE-nal]. Capable of being bought or bribed.

VENIAL [VEE-nih-al]. Capable of being forgiven; excusable.

vend. —ible.

vendee. (buyer); vendor (seller). —or is pref. to —er, esp. when contrasted with buyer. *Caveat vendor. "Let the seller beware."* Cf. emptor.

Venetia [veh-NEE-shih-ah]. Also Venezia [veh-NEHTS-yah]. Ancient Roman tripartite division of Italy (Three Venetias); continued until 1942.

vengeance. Retribution, punishment. SEE revenge.

REVENGE. Retaliation; returning evil for evil.

venial [VEE-nih-al]. SEE venal.

venire [vih-NIE-ree]. venire fascias [veh-NIE-ree FAE-shih-as]. In law, jury-duty notice.

VENEER. Thin sheet of overlay, especially of fine wood.

venireman. Member of a jury panel.

ventilate. -lable, -lator.

ventral. Abdominal; in man, front.

venue [VEHN-yoo]. Place of a trial.

Venus. Pl. -es; poss. -us's.

veracious. Habitually truthful.

veranda. Preferred to -ah. Porch.

VERB. In grammar, a word or group of words which expresses being or action to or by the subject. The verb, its modifiers and complements constitute the predicate of a sentence. Every sentence must have a verb. Verb form may vary in person (1st, 2nd, 3rd), number (sing. and pl.), tense (past, present, etc.), voice (active, passive), mood (indicative, subjunctive, imperative), and, a relatively new concept, aspect (intention of tense revealed by context). Cf. number, person, tense, mood, voice, aspect.

A transitive verb has a direct receiver of the action (an object): *He put the chair there.* An intransitive verb does not have an object: *That man lies. The chair stands where he put it.* An intransitive verb cannot take a passive form. A copulative or linking verb joins two ideas without the action of one or the other: *He was a big man. She seems bright.*

Verbal. In grammar, of verbs, gerunds, participles, and infinitives, not necessarily preceded by *to.* Verbals may serve as subject, complement, or modifier, but cannot act as verbs. Verbals express time only in relation to the time of the main verb in the sentence; they may show that an action occurred at the same time or at an earlier time.

verbal. Of words. A verbal promise is an oral one.

ORAL. Of or with the mouth.

AURAL. Of hearing.

verbal noun. In grammar, the gerund or participle: *Going is better than coming.*

verbatim [ver-BAE-t'm]. In the same words.

verboten [fehr-BOH-t'n]. (Ger.) Forbidden.

verbum sap. (Lat.) *A word is enough to the wise.*

Verdi, Giuseppe [VAIR-dee, joo-ZEHP-pae]. (1813–1901) Italian composer.

verdigris [VUHR-dih-grees]. Greenish, poisonous pigment created by the effect of acetic acid on copper.

Vergil or Virgil Publius Vergilius Maro [VUHR-jihl]. (70–19 B.C.) Roman poet.

verily [VEHR-ih-lee]. Truly. Archaic except in *I verily believe.*

Vermeer, Jan [ver MAER, jahn]. Jan van der Meer von Delft (1632–1675). Dutch painter.

vermin [VUHR-mihn]. Singular, plural and collective. Disgusting insects or animals.

Vermont. (abbr. Vt.) Native, Vermonter. Cap., Montpelier.

vermouth [vehr-MOOTH; Brit., VUHR-]. Flavored white wine.

vernacular. SEE language.

Verne, Jules [vehrn]. (1828–1905) French writer. *Around the World in 80 Days, Twenty Thousand Leagues Under the Sea*, etc.

Veronese, Paolo [vae-roh-nae-sae, PAH-oh -loh]. Paolo Cagliari (1528–1588). Italian painter.

Verrazano da or —zz—, Andrea [dah vair-a-TSAH-noh or —raht-TSAH-noh]. Florentine navigator (1480–1527).

Verrazano Bridge, N.Y.C.

Versailles [ver-SAELZ; ver-SIE]. City near Paris, site of Louis XIV palace, beginnings of French revolution, and treaty of 1918.

versatile [vuhr-suh-tihl, Brit. -iel]. Able to turn easily from one thing to another.

verse. Metrical composition in general. Takes a singular verb.

STANZA. Pl. stanzas. A group of metrical lines in succession.

vertebra [VUHR-teh-bruh]. A segment of the spinal column. Pl. —brae (in biology); otherwise —s.

vertex. Pl. -es or -ices.

vertigo. [VEHR-tih-goh]. Pl. -os. Dizziness.

Verwoerd, D. Hendryk Frensch [feh-FOORT]. (1901–1966) Nationalist prime minister of Union of South Africa, 1958–1966.

very, very much. Unlike other adverbs, which can modify verbs, adverbs, and adjectives, *very* can modify only adjectives and adverbs. The difficulty in applying this rule arises in the case of participles: When a participle is used as an adjective, *very* can properly modify it; when a participle is part of the verb, *very much* must be used: *She is very pretty* (modifying an adjective). *He is very comfortably situated,* (modifying an adverb). *The very drunk man in the corner is the president of the company* (modifying a participle used as an adjective). BUT: *He is very much distressed* (modifying a participle that is part of the verb), NOT: *He is very distressed.* A fairly reliable rule of thumb is: Wherever *much* can be used, *very* by itself cannot be; wherever *much* cannot be used, *very* alone is correct.

vesper. Pl. vespers. Late afternoon or evening services. Usually used in plural form with plural verb.

Vespucci, Amerigo [vehs-POO-cheh; Ital., vas-POOT-cheh]. Americus Vespucius [uh-

MEHR-ih-kuhs vehs-PYOO-shuhs]. (1451–1512) Italian explorer; eponym of America

vessel. Any boat or ship. *Cf.* boat.

veteran. World War.

Veterans Administration. SEE administration.

veto. Pl. -oes.

VHF. (abbr.) very high frequency.

V.I. (abbr.) Virgin Islands.

via [VIE-uh]. By way of. *Via media*, the middle way.

viable [VIE-uh-bl]. Capable of living. -bility.

viand [VIE-and]. Pl. -s. Food; usually in plural.

Viborg [VEE-bahrk]. City in Denmark.

VIBORG [VEE-bahr-yuh]. City in Finland (Fin., Viipuri [VEE-puh-ree]).

vicarious [vie-KAIR-ee-uhs]. Done for another, delegated; substitutional.

Vice Adm. (abbr.) vice admiral.

vice-chairman. Pl. vice-chairmen.

vice consul. British, etc.

vice. —regal, —royal, —royalty (all one word). Otherwise usually hyphenated.

Vicenze [vee-CHEHN-tsah]. Community in northeast Italy; Ancient Vincentia.

vice president. For capitalization SEE president. vice president (Webster, vice-president); pl., vice presidents, BUT vice-presidency.

Vice President of the United States. ADDRESS: The Honorable Spiro Agnew, Vice President of the United States, Washington D.C.; or The Honorable, The Vice President of the United States; or The Vice President, Washington, D.C. SALUTATION: Sir; Dear Sir; My dear Mr. Vice President; Dear Mr. Vice President.

vice-regent. Deputy regent.

VICEREGENT. One selected by a ruler to act for him.

vicereine [VIES-raen]. Viceroy's wife.

vice versa [VIE-suh VUHR-suh]. The relations reversed; conversely.

Vichy [VIHSH-ih, VEE-shih]. Seat of French government, July 1940—Nov. 1942.

VICHY [VIH-shih]. Mineral water from Vichy, or similar water.

vichyssoise [vih-shee-SWAHZ, VEE—, —shih —]. Leek soup.

vicissitude [vih-SIHS-ih-t-ood; or -tood].

Victor Emmanuel, King [vihk-TOHR eh-man-YOO-ehl]. I of Sardinia (1759–1824); II of Sardinia and Italy (1820–1878); III of Italy (1869–1947).

victoria. A type of carriage.

Victory bond. Victory ship. BUT lowercase victory garden, victory speaker. *Cf.* bond.

vicuña [VIE-kyoo-nuh]. Andean ruminant related to the llama.

victual [VIH-tl]. -er. (v.) -ed, -ing. Food especially prepared for human beings.

Vidal, Gore [vee-DAHL, gawr]. (1925–   ). American writer, politician.

vide [VIE-deh]. (Lat.). Used in referring to another document, text, or passage for illustration or proof: *The King was adamant; vide the 1651 statute.*

video. (adj.) The image portion of television. *Cf.* audio, the sound portion.

Viet Cong. N.Y. Times, Vietcong, Communists in South Vietnam.

Vientiane [vyahn-TYAHN]. Capital city of Laos.

Viet-Nam or Vietnam or Viet Nam [vee-eht-NAHM; -NAM: VEET-]. Formerly part of Indochina, divided into North and South. North (Communist) Democratic Republic of Vietnam (abbr. DRVN). Capital, Hanoi. Currency, dong, sau. South, Republic of Vietnam. Capital, Saigon. Native, adj., Vietnamese. Currency, piaster (VN$), cent.

Vietnamese names. SEE Names.

viewfinder. viewpoint.

vigilante [VIH-jih-LAN-tee]. One of a volunteer group organized for protection, especially against crime.

vignette [vihn-YEHT]. Small decorative illustration. In printing, a picture which shades gradually into the background.

viking [VIE-kihng]. Plunderers of Europe. Pirate Northman, 8th-10th century.

vilify [VIHL-ih-fie]. Debase; defame.

Villa, Francisco (Pancho) [VEE-yah, PAHN-choh]. (1877–1923) Mexican bandit, revolutionist.

villain [VIHL-ihn].

Villon, Francois [vee-YAWNN, frahn-SWAH]. Francois de Montcarbier (1431–1462?) French poet.

vinaigrette [vinn-ae-GREHT]. Ornamented container with perforated top for vinegar or smelling salts. Also a small two-wheeled vehicle.

Vinci, Leonardo, da [dah-VEEN-chih, lae-oh-NAHR-doh]. (1452–1519) Florentine genius in arts and engineering.

vincible [VIHN-sih-bl]. Capable of being conquered.

vindicate. Justify; defend successfully: *He vindicated his honor.*

VINDICTIVE. Vengeful: *Let us encourage a merciful attitude rather than a vindictive one.*

vineyard [VIHN-yehrd].

viola [vie-OH-luh]. [vee-OH-luh] (the instrument); [VIE-uh-luh] (the flower).

violate. —lable, —tor.

violoncello [vee-oh-lahn-CHEHL-oh; vie-]. Bass instrument. Usually called *cello* [CHEHL-oh].

VIP. (abbr.) very important person.

virago [vih-RAE-goh]. Amazon; a quarrelsome woman.

Virginia. (abbr. Va.) Native, Virginian. Cap., Richmond.

Virginia creeper.

Virgin Islands. (abbr. V.I.) U.S. territory in West Indies. There are three chief islands: St. Thomas, St. Croix [saent-KROI], and St. John. Cap., Charlotte Amalie [SHAHR-laht uh-MAHL-yuh].

virile [VIH-rihl; pref. to VIE-].

virtu [vehr-TOO]. Love of objects d'art; also, objects d'art collectively: *A piece of virtu.*

VIRTUE. Moral excellence.

virtually. In essence or effect, although not in face. *Virtually* does not mean *very nearly* or *almost: Hitler was virtually the ruler of France, although Petain was nominally the chief of state.*

virtuoso. [vehr-choo-OH-soh]. Pl. -s or -si. Scholar. -osity.

virulent [VIH-ryoo-lent]. Deadly, malignant. virulence.

virus. [VIE-ruhs]. Microscopic infective agent. Pl., -es.

visa [VEE-zuh]. (v.) -ed, -ing. Brit., vise [VEE-zae].

visage [VIHZ-ahz]. The face.

vis-a-vis [vee-zah-VEE]. Face to face.

viscera [VIS-lhr-uh]. Internal body organs. Singular is viscus.

viscid, viscous [VIHS-ihd, VIHS-kuhs]. Sticky.

viscount [VIE-kount]. Noble with rank between earl and baron, usual courtesy title for earl's eldest son. *Cf.* Nobility.

vise. British use *vice.*

visé. French form of *visa.*

visibility. Ability to see; used for light and weather conditions.

VISIBLE.

VISIBLENESS. Ability to be seen.

vision. Sight; foresight; supernatural sight.

visit. AVOID *visitation.* -or.

visor [VIE-zuar pref. to VIHZ-zuhr]. Front piece of a helmet.

Vistula River [VIES-tyoo-lah]. Polish river.

Visla [VEES-luh]. Russ. VISLA [vyees-lah]; Ger. *Weichsel* [VIEK-sehl]. River flowing past Warsaw into Gulf of Danzig on the Baltic.

VISTA. Volunteers in Service to America.

Vitebsk [VEE-tyehpsk]. City on the Dvina River, in White Russia.

vitiate [VIHSH-ih-aet]. Corrupt; invalidate. vitiable.

vitrify. Change to glass by heat. —fiable or vitrescible, vitrification.

vitriol [VIHT-ree-uhl]. A caustic acid; by ext., virulent, caustic speech. virulence. —ize, —ization.

vituperate [vie-TYOO-puhr-aet]. Censure severely; berate.

vivace [vee-VAH-chae]. In music, in a lively manner.

vivacious [vih-VAE-shuhs, vie-]. Lively, spirited.

viva voce [VIE-vuh- VOH-sih]. (Lat.) Orally: *A vote viva voce.*

viz. (abbr.) videlicet [vih-DEHL-ih-seht]. Namely. Always precede with a comma or semicolon.

vizier [vih-ZEER, VIHZ-yEHR, VIHZ-ih-ehr]. State official in Islamic countries, especially Turkish empire. -ial, -irial.

V-J Day. Aug. 14 or Sept. 2, 1945. Days of Japan's surrender and formal ceremony aboard U.S.S. Missouri.

Vladivostok [vlah-dih-vahs-TAWK]. City in U.S.S.R.

VLF. (abbr.) very low frequency. *Cf.* Radio Frequency.

Vocabulary. High school students have an average vocabulary of 5000 to 8000 words in speech; college graduates use approximately 15,000 to 25,000 words in speech, write with fewer, but should understand 50,000 words before they graduate. In less wordy years, Shakespeare used only 24,000 words, Milton 14,000. Woodrow Wilson is credited with a 60,000 word vocabulary.

vocative case. In Latin, the case for direct address.

Vo Giap, Nguyen [nwihn ZAHP]. (1910–   ) North Vietnamese general, victor at Dienbienphu.

Voice. In a verb, property indicating whether subject is agent or receiver of an action; i.e., active, *I hit him*; passive, *I was hit.*

Voice of America. the Voice.

voilà! [vwah-LAH]. (Fr.) There! Behold!

voilà tout [TOO]. That's all.

vol. (abbr.) volume.

volatile [VAHL-uh-tihl; Brit., -tiel]. Readily vaporized; lighthearted; fickle.

vol-au-vent [vahl-loh-VAHNN]. (Fr.) Meat pie made with rich puff paste.

volcano [vahl-KAE-noh]. Pl., -oes. May be active, dormant, or extinct. volcanic.

Volga River [VAHL-guh]. River in U.S.S.R.

Volkslied [FOHKS-leet]. (Ger.) Folksong.

volley. Pl., -s.

volleyball. volley fire.

Volpe, John Anthony [VAHL-pae]. (1909–   ) Governor of Mass., 1961–1962.

Voltaire [vahl-TAER]. Pen name of Francois Marie Arouet [ah-RWEH]. (1694–1778) French writer, philosopher.

volume 2, A, II. Lower-case; BUT Volume 2, when part of title: *Volume 2: Five Rivers in America's Future.*

voluminous [vah-LOO-mih-nuhs]. Of many books; by extension, of great length.

Volunteer Naval Reserve. SEE Reserve.

V-1. German W.W. II gyroscopically guided explosive plane.

V-2. German W.W. II liquid-fueled rocket used in Battle of Britain.

Voroshilov, Klimentiy Efremovich [vuh-ruh-SHIH-luhf, KLYEE-mynt-yih FRAE-muh-vyihch]. (1881–1969) Russian marshall, politician.

Vorster, Balthazar Johannes [FAWRS-tehr]. Prime minister, Republic South Africa (1968–   ).

vortex [VAWR-tehks]. Pl. -es or -tices. Whirlpool.

Vosges Mountains [vohzh]. Mountains in France, west of Rhine River.

votable or voteable. Capable of voting or being submitted to a vote.

vote-getter. vote-casting (adj.), vote-getting (adj.).

vouch. Pledge one's word: *He was prepared to vouch for my honesty.*

vouchsafe [vouch-SAEF]. Condescend to grant.

vox populi [vahks PAHP-yoo-lie]. (Lat.) Voice of the people.

Vrsac [VUHR-shahts]. Town in Yugoslavia.

Vt. (abbr.) Vermont.

VTOL. (abbr.) Vertical takeoff and landing; *e.g.* helicopter.

vying [VIE-ihng]. vie, vied; adj., —ly.

W

W-engine. W-shaped, W-type.

W. west.

w. watt.

WAAF. (abbr.) Woman's Auxiliary Air Force (Brit.) changed to WRAF, Woman's Royal Air Force.

Wabash River [WAW-bash]. Flows north through Indiana and Illinois to Ohio River.

WAC. (abbr.) Woman's Army Corps; a WAC.

W.A.C.B. (abbr.) West African Currency Board.

wacky. Slang for eccentric. NOT whacky.

w.a.e. (abbr.) when actually employed.

WAF. (abbr.) Women in the Air Force; a Waf.

waft [waft].

wage. Pl. —s; *wages* is sometimes accepted as singular;compensation for servant and workmen, especially when hired by hour, day or week.

SALARY. Compensation for executives, sometimes white collar workers on a continuous payroll.

Wagner, Wilhelm Richard [VAHG-nehr, VIL-helm RIK-ahrt]. (1813–1883) German composer.

wagon. Brit., waggon.

wagon-lit [va-gawn-LEE]. Fr., sleeping car.

Waichow [IE-choh]. City in China.

Waikiki Beach [WIE-kih-kee]. Resort in Honolulu, Hawaii.

wainscot [WAEN-skuht]. Wood molding or lining usually placed three or four feet from floor. wainscoting, —ed.

waistcoat [WAEST-koht is pref. to WES-kuht]. Vest.

wait. *He waits to hear from you.* NOT: *He awaits.*

AWAIT. Must have an object: *He awaits your arrival.*

waive. Abandon, overlook, forgo.

WAVE. The physical motion.

waiver. (n.) relinquishing of a right: *A waiver of immunity would leave him open to prosecution.*

WAVER (n.) Hesitate; also, totter: *He will not waver in his efforts to clear your name.*

wake. P., woke, sometimes waked; p.p., waked. wakened, woke, or woken.

Wales. Native, Welshman (men), Welsh (collective, pl.); adj., Welsh. *Cf.* Celts, Cymric, Gallic.

walkie-talkie.

Walkyrie. SEE Valkyrie.

Wall. (abbr.) Wallace (U.S. Supreme Court Reports).

Walla Walla [WAH-lah WAH-lah]. City in Washington.

wall-less.

Walloon [wah-LOO'N]. Celtic people of South Belgium. (adj.) Walloon.

wallop. —ed, —ing, —er.

wallpaper. Brit., wall-paper.

Walpurgis Night [vahl-PUHR-gihs]. Eve of May Day, Witches Sabbath. Ger., Walpurgisnacht [—nahkt].

walrus [WAWL-ruhs].

Walter, Bruno [VAHL-tehr, BROO-noh] (1878–1962). German-American musician.

waltz. *Valse* is sometimes used for programs.

wan [WAHN]. Pallid, sickly in color; faint: *wan hope.*

wanderlust [Brit., Ger., VAHN-dehr-luhst, angl., WAHN-dehr-luhst]. Impulse to wander.

wanton [WAHN-tuhn]. Unrestrained, unchaste. -ness.

War of Independence. British for the American Revolutionary War.

War Between the States. Preferred in the South for U.S. Civil War.

War. Capitalize if part of name: War Between the States, Civil War; First World War, World War I (W.W. I), World War, Great War; Second World War (World War II); French and Indian War (1754–63); Mexican War; War of the Nations; War of the Rebellion, BUT the rebellion; War of the Revolution, the Revolution; War of 1812, but war of 1914; Philippine Insurrection; Revolutionary War; Seven Years War; Spanish-American War; the two World Wars; post-World War.

war. cold war, hot war, European war, French and Indian wars, Indian war, Korean war; third world war, world war III; war with Mexico, war with Spain.

war bond. SEE bond.

War College. National. SEE College.

-ward [-wehrd, -wehrds; formerly -ehrd, -ehrds]. (adj.), -wards (adj.) Suffix meaning direction to or motion towards.

ward 1, 2, 3. lower-case; first ward, 11th ward, and so on.

Wards Island. N.Y.C.

warmed-over. (adj.).

War Mothers. SEE American.

warp [wawrp]. (n.) Threads which make the length in a loom. *Cf.* woof.

warrant. -y (agreement), -or (maker), -eε (receiver). *Cf.* guaranty.

Warsaw Pact Nations. U.S.S.R., Bulgaria, Rumania, Hungary, Czechoslovakia, Poland, East Germany in military alliance.

was. 1st and 3rd person sing., past of the verb *be.* NOT *we was, they was.* Use *were.* Plural past of the verb *be,* also used in the singular with *you: You were here yesterday. Were* is sometimes used in the past subjunctive of *be,* after *if, suppose,* and *wish,* and in hypothetical statements: *I wish I were home now. If I were home now.* . . BUT *was* may also be used in these constructions. *Were* is pref. in *If I were you.* . . and is required if the verb precedes the subject. *Were I to go to school.* . . In a statement about the past expressing uncertainty, use *was: If Tom was late, I will find out about it.*

Washington. (abbr. Wash.) Native, Washingtonian. Cap., Olympia.

Washington's Birthday.

Washington's Farewell Address.

wassail [WAHS-'l, WAHS-ael]. (n.) A toast; a sweet, spiced alcoholic drink; (v.) drink a wassail.

wastage. Sometimes preferred to *waste* where no blame is indicated.

waste. wastable.

wastrel [WAES-trehl]. Spendthrift, profligate.

waterway. inland waterway, intercoastal waterway, etc: BUT Intracoastal Waterway.

Watteau, Jean Antoine [vah-TOH, angl., wah-TOH, ahn-TWANN]. (1684–1721) French painter.

Waugh, Evelyn Arthur St. John [WAW, EEV-ehl-ihn sant-jahn; Brit. sihn-juhn]. (1903–1966). English writer.

Waukegan [waw-KEE-gan]. City in Illinois.

wave. wavable, wavy.

WAVES. (U.S. Navy) Women Accepted for Volunteer Emergency Service; a Wave.

wax. (adj.) Made of wax: *Wax candles.*

WAXEN. Appearance of wax: waxen faces, images.

waybill. Official list of goods in a rail or motor shipment.

-ways, -wise. Both of these suffixes are correct and have the same meaning. Usage has established one suffix with some words, the other with others: *sideways, clockwise.* In forming spur-of-the-moment combinations, —wise is generally preferred. SEE -wise.

W.C. (abbr.) water closet, Brit. bathroom.

W.C.T.U. (abbr.) Women's Christian Temperance Union.

weal [WEEL]. Obsolete, wealth; used only in *public weal, commonweal.*

wear. P., wore; p.p., worn.

weather-beaten. —blown, —board, —boarding, -glass, -going, -maker, -making, -man, -most, -proof, -proofed, -proofing, -strip, -tight, -worn (all one word); weather-hardened (adj.), weather-marked (adj.), weather-stain (v.), weather-stripped (adj.); weather-wise; weather-bound; weather eye, weather gauge, weatherman.

weave. P., wove or weaved; p.p., woven or weaved. BUT *He weaved his way through the land mines.*

web. Fabric on a loom.

WEB PRESS. Rotary printing press which prints on a roll of paper. A *perfecting web press* imprints both sides of the sheet at the same time.

wed. P. and p.p., wed; Brit., wedded.

wedge. wedgeable.

Wednesday [WEHNZ-dih]. (abbr., Wed.)

weedkiller. —killing; weed-choked (adj.), weed-hidden (adj.).

Week. Fire Prevention; and the like.

weeviled. —ing.

weft [WEHFT]. Woof; cross threads in a loom.

weigh [wae]. Hoist: weigh anchor; anchors aweigh. BUT: *The ship is under way.*

weird [WEERD]. Of witchcraft; unearthly. —ly, —ness.

Weirton [WEER-t'n]. City in West Virginia.

Weizmann, Chaim [VIETS-mahn, HIE-im]. (1874–1952) First president of Israel, 1948–52.

welder.

welfare state.

as well as. And not only. NOT *besides*: *The U.S. as well as Britain is in need of increasing exports.*

Wellesley [WEHLZ-lih]. Town and college in Massachusetts.

well-nigh. (adj.) Nearly. Used with adjectives of time: *The house is well-nigh 200 years old.*

well plus participle. Hyphenate when an attributive adj. *His well-heralded approach.* BUT DO NOT hyphenate predicate adj.: *His approach was well heralded. Well-trained schoolteachers are necessary for all schools, and his teachers were well trained.*

welsh [WEHLSH]. Preferred to welch [WEHLCH]. (Slang) Avoid payment of a debt.

WELSH. preferred to Welch. Pertains to Wales or its inhabitants.

welterweight.

weltgeist. —politik, —schmerz. Spirit of the age.

were [wuhr; Brit., waer].

werewolf. Preferred to werwolf.

Weser River [VAE-zehr]. River in West Germany; flows into North Sea.

West Coast. (Africa) BUT west coast (U.S.); West End, etc. (section of city); West Europe (political entity); Far West, Far Western States; West Germany (political entity); Middle West (U.S.), Midwest; West South Central States, etc.; the West (section of U.S.; also world political entity).

west. western, more western, westernmost.

westbound. westmost, westward; west-central (adj.), west-faced (adj.), west-northwest, west-sider; west end, west side.

Western civilization. Western countries; Western Europe (an) (political entity); Western Germany (political entity); Western Hemisphere, the hemisphere; Western North Central States; Western Powers; Western States; Western Union (SEE alliances); Western United States; Western World. BUT for western; western farming states (U.S.).

West Indies Federation. Established January 3, 1958. Antigua, Barbados, Dominica, Grenada, Jamaica, Montserrat, St. Lucia, St. Vincent, and St. Kitts-Nevis. Dissolved 1962 by withdrawal of Jamaica and Trinidad and Tobago.

Westminster [WES(T)-mihn-stuhr]. City and borough in London, England.

West Virginia. (abbr. W.Va.) Native, West Virginian. Cap., Charleston.

westward. (adj.). —s (adv.).

wetback. Illegal immigrant from Mexico (presumably across the Rio Grande). wetback, wetwash; wet-cheeked (adj.), wet-nurse (v.).

Weygand, Gen. Maxime [vae-GAHNN, MAK-seam]. (1867–1965) French general.

wf or w.f. (abbr.) wrong font.

wharf [hwawrf]. Pl. —ves; Brit., —s.

wharfage. Fee for use of dock.

wharfinger [WHAWR-fihn-juhr]. Wharf manager.

Wharton, Edith Newbold née Jones [HWAWR-t'n]. (1862–1937) American novelist.

what [hwaht].
  WHATEVER. whatnot (n.), whatsoever; what-is-it (n.), what-you-may-call-it (n.).
  WHATEVER. All that: *They have whatever they need; no matter what: Whatever you say, don't tell.*
  WHAT EVER. Avoid as the emphatic of what. NOT: *What ever did he say?*
  WHATSOEVER. Formal for whatever.
  WHEN [hwen].

WHILE [hwiel].

Wheat Belt. SEE Belt.

when. AVOID using *when* to introduce a definition unless time is involved. NOT: *Success is when you make money.*

whence [hwehns]. From where: *Let them return whence they came.*
  WHITHER. To what place.
  WHENCESOEVER. From what place [or cause] soever.

when ever. Colloquial use for emphasis of when: *When ever will they get here?*
  WHENEVER. (conjunction) At whatever time: *They visit us whenever their ship is in port.*
  WHENSOEVER. (adverb and conjunction) Use whenever.

whereabouts. -after, -as, -at, -by, -for, -fore, -from, -in, -insoever, -into, -of, -on, -over, -soever, -through, -to -under, -upon, -with, -withal (all one word).

where. AVOID use to introduce a definition except where place is involved. NOT: *A book where the hero dies is called a tragedy.*

wherever. At or to whatever place: *He goes wherever help is needed.* Avoid colloquial use as an emphatic of where, expressing a strong question or puzzlement.

whether or not. *Or not* is essential. *Tell him whether or not you have sent the package.*

whether, as to. Avoid. NOT: *The question as to whether he would come was posed.*

which [hwich]. (1) Place in a position reasonably close to its antecedents. (2) *Which* can introduce a defining clause (in which case no punctuation is used), but is better used in nondefining clauses (in which case commas enclose the clause). (3) *One of the greatest books which have* (NOT *has*) *ever been written.* (The greatest books determines the number of which, the subject here.) *Cf. that . . . which.*

whichever. which ever.

whiffletree.

while. (conjunction) Brit., often whilst. During the time that; whereas. AVOID use with unattached participles. NOT: *Tears streamed* *down his face while reading the story* (while he was reading the story). AVOID use to introduce a definition not involving time, or as a substitute for *though, although, whereas, and,* or *but.* NOT: *While he does not recall the agreement, he will pay the bill.* Use *although.*

whimsey. Preferred to Brit., -sy.

whip, the. Of a political party in Congress, legislator appointed to enforce party discipline in attendance and voting.

whippoorwill.

whir. British whirr. Buzzing or whizzing sound: *Motion picture cameras may whir but TV cameras are silent.*

whirlabout. (n. and adj.).

whirlybird. A helicopter.

whisk broom. whisk tail.

whisky. Preferred to whiskey. Brit. Scotch whisky, Irish whiskey. Pl. —ies.

Whisky Rebellion. SEE Rebellion.

Whistler, James Abbott McNeill [HWIHS-luhr, —mak-NEEL]. (1834–1903) American painter, etcher.

whistle stop.

white elephant. An expensive, useless possession.

White House. Blue Room, East Room, Red Room, State Dining Room. White House Police (SEE Police).

whiten. -ed. -ing.

white paper. British, and the like.

White Plains [hwiet PLAENZ]. City in New York.

white space. Area of an advertisement not covered by ink.

Whitsunday. Whit Sunday, Whitsuntide. 7th Sun. after Easter. The Feast of Pentecost. NOT Whitsun Day.

whiz. —zzed, —zzing.

who. *Who* is nominative; *whom* objective. But who is often acceptable at the beginning of a sentence where whom is grammatically correct. *Who are you seeking?* BUT generally, use *whom* after *to, for, from, with,* and *than. He is a man who* is redundant (except for rhetorical emphasis).

who (agreement). The verb must agree in person and number with the antecedent of who: *To him who has everything. . . For me who have* (NOT *has*) *nothing.*

who (interrogative pronoun). *Who* and *what* are used in reference to an unlimited group, *who* for persons and *what* for inanimate things, animals, and in reference to persons' status, interests, and so on. *Who is he? What did you get? What are his interests?*

who (relative pronoun). Avoid use for inanimate objects unless personification has been established previously. NOT: *Canada, who sold wheat to China.*
  Who is preferred if the antecedent is a person or personal pronoun. *Which* refers to inanimate things but may in some instances refer to persons in an impersonal way, as in official reports: *He spoke of the child which was killed in the flood. That* is used to refer to an unidentifiable person and is ordinarily used to refer to either a person or a thing. *Cf.* that, which. *Who* and *whom* are preferred for introducing nondefining clauses; *that* for defining clauses: *The man, whom I think you know, was here. He knew John, who was a bright boy. We expected John, whom he liked. The boy that was here yesterday was John. Cf.* whom.

who. Meaning *whoever,* is somewhat archaic. NOT: *He who comes on Monday,* BUT: *Whoever comes on Monday.*

WHO. N.Y. Times, W.H.O. (abbr.), World Health Organization.

whoever. whoso, whosoever.

wholehearted. (Brit., whole-hearted).

wholly. [HOH-lee]. Fully.

whom. (relative proun). *Whom* is required after *than: Lincoln, than whom no man earned more respect, was a humble man,* although theoretically *who* is the correct form. *Who* is required as the subject when it is placed before a verb; *whom* may be used in a normally nominative position after the verb: *You heard whom?*

Whom may also be used as the subject of a verb, and is preferred by most grammarians, when a parenthetical clause intervenes. The classic example is Shakespeare's: *Arthur, whom they say is killed tonight...* Use *whom* as the object of a preposition: *The girl to whom you gave the book...* BUT the object of a verb requires *that* wherever possible, and *whom* only where necessary, e.g., after an identified person: *The teacher that he knew best; Miss Jones, whom you knew. Who* is also acceptable in this construction.

whomsoever.

whooping cough [HWOOP-ihng-cawf; preferred to HOOP-ihng].

whose. Possessive of who, but *whose* may apply to things as well as people: *The company whose stock we bought.*

WHO's. Who is. May refer to animate or inanimate objects. *Cf.* who.

w.-hr. (abbr.) watt-hour.

w.i. (abbr.) when issued.

Wichita [WIHCH-ih-taw]. City in Kansas.

wicketkeeper. -keeping.

—wide. SEE Suffix.

wide. SEE broad.

wide awake. (n.); wide-awake (adj.).

widow. In printing, a word or short line carried over to the top of the next page, creating an unsightly margin. *Cf.* Names, Filing, divorcee.

widow. Address by former title: Mrs. John Brown, NOT Mrs. Anne Smith, unless a preference is expressed.

widthway. widthwise.

Wiesbaden [VEES-bah-d'n]. City in Germany.

wild cat. Untamed cat.

WILDCAT, WILD-CAT. Wild animal native of U.S.; lynx.

Willemstad [VIHL-'m-stht]. Capitol of Curacao [KYOOR-uh-sou] Dutch West Indies.

Wilhelmina [vihl-hehl-MEE-nah]. (1880–1962). Queen of the Netherlands (1890–1948).

Wilkes-Barre [WIHLKS-bar-ih; -bar-ee]. City in Pennsylvania.

will. (v.) Intend to have come to pass: *She willed her father's death.* wills, willed, willable, willing.

Willamette River. Ore. [wih-LAM-eht].

willful. Preferred to wilful.

Williamsburg, Va.

willinghearted.

will-o'-the-wisp. Pl. -wisps.

willy nilly. Without choice. (Webster, willy-nilly).

wilt-resistant. (adj.) wilt disease.

wilton carpet.

win. P. and p.p., won.

wind [wiend]. Twist. P. and p.p., wound [wound].
WIND [wihnd; poetically, wiend]. Movement of air.

windsail [WIHND-sael].

Windsor, Duke of [WIHN-zehr]. Edward VIII (1894–1972). Reigned and abdicated 1936.

winebibber. Brit., wine-bibber.

Winnebago Lake [wihn-eh-BAE-goh]. Lake in Wisconsin.

Winnipesaukee Lake [wihn-ih-peh-SAW-kee]. Lake in New Hampshire.

Winterthur [VIHN-tehr-TOOR]. Town in Switzerland. Also Dupont museum of Americana near Wilmington, Delaware.

Wisconsin. (abbr. Wis.) Native, Wisconsinite. Nickname, *Badger State.* Cap., Madison.

—wise. no-wise or nowise. BUT *in any wise, in no wise; clockwise, dollarwise, lengthwise.*

wishbone.

Wisla River [VEES-lah]. River in Poland.

wistaria [wihs-TAER-ih-uh]. Preferred to wisteria [wihs-TEER-ih-uh].

withdraw. withhold.

withe [wihth]. A flexible twig. Also (v.) *to bind with a withe.* -ed, -ing.

without. Meaning *not with.* Use meaning *outside* is archaic. AVOID use for *unless*, NOT: *No representative of the people should vote for this measure without he first sees for himself the deplorable conditions involved.*

with reference to. with regard to. *About* is preferred.

witness. Avoid use meaning *see*, except in legal sense.

wizened [WIHZ-'nd].

WMAL, WRC. radio stations.

WO. (abbr.) warrant officer.

WO. (jg.) (abbr.) warrant officer (junior grade).

w.o.c. (abbr.) without compensation.

Wodehouse, Pelham Grenville [WOHD-hous]. (1881–   ) Eng. writer.

woebegone.

wolf. Pl., wolves; (v.) wolf, wolfed, -fing.

woman [WUH-men].
WOMEN [WIHM-men].

woman aviator. Plural, women aviators.

womanly. SEE female, lady.

woman marine. SEE Marine Corps.

woman student. Plural, women students.

woman writer. Plural, women writers.

Women in the Air Force. (abbr. WAF) a Waf, Wafs (individuals).

Women's Army Corps. SEE Corps.

Women's Reserve of the Coast Guard Reserve. Women's Reserve; the Reserve. SPAR is a popular name, made up of the initial letters of the motto *semper paratus* (*always ready*); a Spar.

Women's Reserve of the Naval Reserve. Women's Reserve; the Reserve; WAVES (Women Accepted for Volunteer Emergency Service); a Wave.

wont [wuhnt, wohnt]. (adj.) Accustomed to. (n.) custom; habit.
WON'T [WOHNT]. Will not.

wood. Capitalize if part of name: Belleau Wood, House in the woods (palace).

Woodbridge, N.J. In Middlesex County.

wooden. (adj.) Preferred to wood. —enness.

Wood-Ridge, N.J. In Bergen County.

Woods Hole, Mass.

woodsman.

woof. Also weft. Cross threads on a loom.

woofer. Loudspeaker for low acoustic frequencies, used to reproduce low-pitch sound.

wool. woolen (adj. pref. to wool); wooly: Brit.. -llen, -lly.

Worcestershire County [WUHS-tuhr-shihr]. County in England.
WORCESTER, MASS [WUHS-tuhr]. City in Massachusetts.

work. P. and p.p., worked, wrought.

World. New World, Old World.

World Series.

World War. (W.W., W.W. I, W.W. II). SEE War. World War II veteran.

Worms [Ger., vohrms; angl., wehrmz]. City in Germany.

worndown. (adj.) worn-out (adj.).

worrywart. One who worries unduly.

worsen. (v.) Become or make worse.

worship. —ed, —ing. Brit., —pped, —pping.

worsted [WUHS-tid is pref. to wihrst-ed]. Hard-twisted long-stapled wool yarn and cloth made from it.

worthwhile. (n and adj.), —ness; worth while (adv.).

Wouk, Herman [wohk]. (1915–   ) American writer.

would, should. SEE shall.

wove paper.

wrack. (destruction) and ruin.

wrap around. (n. and adj.); wrap-up (n. and adj.).

wrath [rath]. (n.) Anger. *The king's wrath.* -ful. *A wrathful king.*

WROTH [RAWTH]. (adj.) Angry: *The king was wroth.*

wreathmaker. making, -work; wreath-crowned (adj.).

wreckfish. -master; wreck-free (adj.); wreck buoy.

wring. P. and p.p., wrung.

writ. A mandatory court order to perform a specific act.

write. P., write; p.p., written. *I wrote her yesterday.* Brit., *I wrote to her yesterday. I wrote her a letter.*

writeback. (n. and adj.), write-off (n. and adj.), write-up (n. and adj.); write-in (n. and adj.).

write down In accounting, reduce the value of an asse   books of account. *writedown,* The reduction.

write off. In accounting, remove the value of an asset from the books of account. *writeoff,* The amount removed.

write up. In accounting, increase the value of an asset on the book of account. *Writeup, the amount increased.*

writing desk. writing room.

wrong. (adj.) *His work was done wrong.* Wrongly. (adv.) *His wrongly done work.*

wrongdoer. wrongdoing, wronghearted; wrongended (adj.), wrong-minded (adj.), wrongthinking (adj).

wrong font. (abbr. wf or w.f.) Error in typesetting caused by a character from another type face or style.

wrought. SEE work.

wrought-up. (adj.)

wrought iron. Handcrafted malleable iron.

wry. wrier, wriest; Brit., wryer, wryest; wryly, wryish.

Wurttemberg [VEUR-tehm-buhrk;   angl., WERT-tehm-buhrg]. City in Germany.

W. Va. (abbr.) West Virginia.

W.W. I, II. (abbr.) World War I, II.

Wyoming. [wie-OH-mihng]. (abbr. Wyo.) Native Wyomingite. Cap., Cheyenne.

X

—x. French words ending in —*eau* or —*eu* usually take —*x* for a plural form: *beau, beaux* (or *beaus*). Exception: *adieus, plateaus*.

X. U.S. Air Force symbol for *experimental* in numbering aircraft: *X-15*.

x-body. x-disease, x-shaped, x-virus.

Xanthippe. angl., Iantippe [zan-TIHP-ee]. Socrates' peevish wife, 5th cent. B.C.

Xavier, Saint Francis [ZAE-vih-ehr or ZAV-ih-ehr]. Francisco Xavier (1506–52). Apostle of the Indies. Spanish Jesuit, missionary.

xenophobia [zehn-oh-FOH-bee-uh]. Fear or hatred of foreigners.

Xenophon [ZEHN-uh-f'n]. Greek historian-soldier, c. 434–355 B.C.

Xerxes I [ZUHRK-seez]. (519?–465 B.C.). King of Persia.

Xieng Khouang [see-EHN kwahng]. Pathet Lao headquarters in Laos.

—xion. Common in Britain; in U.S., -*ction* is pref.

Xmas. Christmas is preferred. (X = Christ.) N.Y. Times, "never use."

Xochimilco [soh-cheh-MEEL-koh]. Town in Mexico.

X-ray. (n.) (Webster X ray) Electromagnetic wave with radiation wavelength of 0.1 to 2.0 angstroms. X-ray (v.); X-ray (adj.): *X-ray photograph*.

xylem [ZIE-l'm]. Woody plant tissue.

xylophone [ZIE-loh-fohn]. Percussion instrument.

xyster [ZIHSS-tehr]. Surgical bone scraper.

Y

Y-. U.S. Air Force symbol for *prototype* in numbering aircraft: *YTM-61*.

Y-chromosome. Y-joint, Y-level, Y-potential, Y-shaped, Y-track, Y-tube.

y endings. When adding a suffix to a word ending in *y*: (1) if *y* is preceded by a consonant, usually change *y* to *i*: *beauty, beautiful, beautify*. (2) BUT when the suffix begins with *i*, retain the *y*: *satisfy, satisfying*. (3) When *y* is preceded by a vowel, retain the *y*: *enjoy, enjoying, enjoyable*.

yacht [YAHT].

yachtsman. yachtsmanship.

Yahweh [YAH-weh]. Also Jahveh. Jehovah.

Yakima [YAHK-ih-muh]. City in Washington.

Yakutsk [yeh-KOOTSK]. Republic in East Central Russia, Asia.

Yalta [YAWL-tah]. Town on Crimean coast, U.S.S.R., scene of W.W. II conference, 1945.

Yalu River [YAH-loo]. Divides Manchuria from North Korea.

Yamamoto, Isoroku [yah-mah-MOH-toh, ee-soh-ROH-koo]. (1884–1943) Japanese admiral.

Yangtze River [YANG(T)-see]. Yangtze Kiang [kih-ANG]. Principal river in China.

Yankee. New Englander. By extension, in the U.S. South, a northerner; abroad, an American.

Yankee-Doodle. Yankeedom, -ism, -land.

Yap Island [yap or yahp]. Also *Uap* [wohp]. U.S. Trust territory southeast of P.I.

yard. Unit of length = 3 ft. = 36 in. = 0.9144 meter

yardarm. yardmaster, yardstick; yard-long (adj.), yard-wide (adj.).

Yarmouth [YAHR-muhth]. Seaport in England; seaport in Nova Scotia.

y-clept [ee-KLEHPT]. Called, named (archaic).

yd. (abbr.) yard.

yea [YAE]. Yes.

year. Period of 365 days (366 in a leap year). A calendar year begins January 1; a fiscal year may begin at any time selected.

Year. International Geophysical; the Geophysical Year, the Year.

Years. Style for indicating a period of two or more years: *1907–17: 1898–1902: 1900–1902:* BUT *1900, 1902* (individually). *From 1901 through 1906*, NOT: *between 1901–1906; use between 1921 and 1923. 1937 to 1945 inclusive; the year nineteen hundred and sixty three; 193* B.C.; A.D. *1888.* (A.D. and B.C. are usually printed in small caps.) *Cf.* Age, Time.

Yeats, William Butler [YAETS]. (1865–1939) Irish poet.

Yemen Republic or Yemen Arab Republic. 1972 unification of Yemen and South Yemen (People's Democratic Republic of Yemen). Cap., Sana.

yeoman [YOH-m'n]. A freeborn man, subordinate to an esquire.

yes man. yes-no.

yesterday. yesteryear.

Yiddish. Language made of Hebrew, German and Slavic languages, used by middle-European Jews. *Cf.* Hebrew.

yoga [YOH-guh]. In Hinduism, mental concentration on an object to obtain identification in consciousness

YOGI [YOH-gee]. One who practices yoga.

yogurt.

yoke. A pair of draft animals; wood frame by which they are connected.

Yokohama [YOH-kuh-HAH-mah]. City in Japan.

yolk [yohk]. Yellow of an egg.

Yom Kippur [yohm-KIHP-uhr]. Jewish Day of Atonement. In Sept. or Oct.

Yosemite National Park [yoh-SEHM-ih-tee]. In California.

Yoshihito [yoh-shee-HEE-toh]. (1879–1926) Emperor of Japan, 1921–1926.

you-all. AVOID. Southern U.S. colloquialism used to emphasize inclusiveness. Takes a plural verb.

Youlou, Fulbert [yoo-loo]. (1917–1972) President, Premier, Republic of Congo (formerly French), 1958–1963.

younker [YUHNG-ker]. Young gentleman.

your. (poss.); you're (you are).

your. *Your and our and my* (his, her) *books.* NOT *yours and ours and my books.* BETTER: *Your books and ours and mine*: BUT: *her and his books.*

Your Excellency. Your Honor, Your Majesty.

youth [yooth]. A young person, especially male Pl., youths [yooths].

youthlike.

Ypres [EE-pr]. Town in Belgium.

Ypsilanti, Alexander and Demetrius [uhp-sih-LAN-tih]. or Hypselantes [ee-psee-LAHN-des]. (1792–1828 and 1793–1832) Greek revolutionists.

Ypsilanti [IHP-sih-LAN-tih]. Town in Michigan.

yr. (abbr.) year.

Yuan Shih-k'at [yeu-AHN shihr-KIE]. (1850–1916). Chinese statesman.

Yucatan [yoo-kuh-TAN]. State and peninsula in Central America and Mexico.

Yucca Flat [YUHK-ah]. Town in Nevada.

Yugoslavia. Serbian and British, Jugoslavia [yoo-goh-SLAH-vih-ah]. Formerly (1918–1929) Kingdom of the Serbs, Croats, and Slovenes. Native, Yugoslav(s); adj. Yugoslav. Cap., Belgrade [BEHL-grad]. Currency, dinar (Din), para.

Yukon [YOO-kahn]. River and territory in Alaska and Canada.

yuletide, yule log.

Z

Z-bar. Z-chromosome.

zabaglione [zah-BEHL-yoh-nee]. Dessert of eggs, wine, creamed fruit.

Zagreb [zah-grehb]; Hungarian, **Zagrab** [ZAH-grahb]. City in Yugoslavia.

Zaharoff, Sir Basil [suh-KAH-ruf; angl., Zah-HAH-rahff]. (1850–1936) Russian-British banker, munitions merchant.

Zaire. Formerly Belgian Congo, Republic of Congo 1960-1971. (Cf.) Proclaimed Oct. 27, 1971. Capital, Kinshasa (formerly Leopold-wille). Native, Zairian(s). Currency, zaire, makuta.

Zambesi Riber [zam-BEE-zih]. River in northern Rhodesia; flows into Mozambique Channel.

Zambia. Formerly Northern Rhodesia. Independent since 1964. Natives, Zambian(s). Cap. Lusaka. Currency, kwacha (K), ngwee(n).

zany [ZAE-nee]. Mildly insane. zanier, —iest.

Zarathustra. —trian. Zoroaster [ZAWR-oh-ASS-tehr]. founder of ancient Persian religion.

zealot [ZEHL-uht]. A zealous person; in Hebrew history, a fanatical anti-Roman.

zebrafish. zebralike.

zed. Brit. for *z*.

zenith [ZEE-nith; Brit., ZEHN-]. Heavenly point directly overhead; by extension, summit.

Zenoviev, Grigori Evseevid [ehn-NAWV-yehr, gryih-GAW-ryih yihf-SYAE-yeh-vyihch]. (1883–1936) Originally, Hirsch Apfelbaum. Russian Communist.

zephyr [ZEHF-eh]. A gentle wind.

zero. Pl. -os.

zero hour. Starting time for an action.

zeugma [ZYOOG-muh]. Pl. —ata or —as. Figure of speech in which one word is used to modify or affect two words, taking a different meaning in each case: *The Senator picked up his hat and his courage. He sometimes took counsel, sometimes tea.*

Zeus [zooss, YOOS]. Chief Greek god.

Zhdanov, Andrei Aleksandrovich [ZHDAH-nuhf, un-DRYAE-ih uh-lyihks-AHN-druh-vyihch]. (1896–1948) Russian general, politician.

Zhivago, Dr. [zhee-VAH-goh]. 1958 Nobel Prize-winning novel by Boris Pasternak.

Zhukov, Konstantinovich Grigory, Marshall of the Soviet Union [ZHOO-kuf, grih-GAWR-geh kuhn-stuhn-TYEE-nuh-vyihch]. (1895–) Russian marshal.

zigzag. -gged, -gging.

zillion. An undefinably large number.

zingaro [TSEENG-gah-roh]. Fem., —ara. Pl. —ari. A gypsy.

zither.

zloty [ZLAH-tih]. Polish monetary unit.

zodiacal [zoh-DIE-ih-kal].

Zog ı. ₍zohg]. Ahmed Bey Zogu (1895–1961) King of the Albanians, 1928–1946.

Zola, Émile [ZOH-luh, ae-MUHL]. (1840–1902) French novelist.

Zone. Capitalize if part of name; the zone: BUT Bizonia, bizonal; British Zone (in Germany); Canal Zone (Panama), Canal

Zone Government; Eastern Zone, Western Zone, (Germany); Frigid Zone; New York Foreign Trade Zone; Foreign Trade Zone No. 1, BUT the foreign trade zone; Zone of Interior (see Command); Temperate Zone, Torrid Zone, BUT the zone; Trizonia, trizonal. BUT Arctic Zone, eastern standard time zone, polar zone, tropical zone.

zoning. Municipal control of types and use of structures which may be constructed in specified areas.

Zoological Park. (National); the zoo; the park.

Zorin, Valaerian Alexandrovitch [ZAW-rihn]. (1902–   ) U.S.S.R. diplomat.

Zouave [zoo-AHV]. French infantry body.

zweibach [TSVEE-bahk; angl., TSWEE-or SWIE-]. A toasted biscuit.

Zweig, Arnold [tsviek, AHR-nawlt]. (1887–1968) German writer.

Zweig, Stefan [tsviek, stehf-AHN]. (1881–1942) Austrian-British writer.

Zwingliun, Huldreich or Ulrich [ZWIHNG-glee-uhn]. (1484–1531) Swiss Reformation leader.

zygote [ZIE-goht]. Cell formed by two gametes, matured sex cells.

zyme [ziem]. Ferment.

Zzyzx [Zie-zihks]. Health resort in California named *to have the last word.*

PROOFREADER'S MARKS

∧	Make correction indicated in margin.	⌐⌐	Raise to proper position.
Stet	Retain crossed-out word or letter; let it stand.	⌐⌐	Lower to proper position.
		////	Hair space letters.
.... Stet	Retain words under which dots appear; write "Stet" in margin.	w.f.	Wrong font; change to proper font.
		Qu?	Is this right?
X	Appears battered; examine.	l.c.	Put in lower case (small letters).
≡	Straighten lines.	s.c.	Put in small capitals.
∨∨∨	Unevenly spaced; correct spacing.	Caps	Put in capitals.
//	Line up; i.e., make lines even with other matter.	C+s.c.	Put in caps and small caps.
		rom.	Change to Roman.
run in	Make no break in the reading; no ¶	ital.	Change to Italic.
no ¶	No paragraph; sometimes written "run in."	≡	Under letter or word means caps.
		=	Under letter or word, small caps.
out see copy	Here is an omission; see copy.	—	Under letter or word means Italic.
¶	Make a paragraph here.	∼∼	Under letter or word, bold face.
tr	Transpose words or letters as indicated.	,/	Insert comma.
		;/	Insert semicolon.
ℐ	Take out matter indicated; dele.	:/	Insert colon.
ℐ	Take out character indicated and close up.	⊙	Insert period.
		/?/	Insert interrogation mark.
ℓ̸	Line drawn through a cap means lower case.	(!)	Insert exclamation mark.
		/=/	Insert hyphen.
ℰ	Upside down; reverse.	✓	Insert apostrophe.
⌒	Close up; no space.	✓✓	Insert quotation marks.
#	Insert a space here.	ℰ	Insert superior letter or figure.
⊥	Push down this space.	∏	Insert inferior letter or figure.
□	Indent line one em.	[/]	Insert brackets.
⌐	Move this to the left.	(/)	Insert parenthesis.
⌐	Move this to the right.	1/m	One-em dash.
		2/m	Two-em parallel dash.

HOW TO CORRECT PROOF

s.c. It does not appear that the earliest printers had any method of e/

✓ ✓ ✓ correcting errors, before the form, was on the press/ The learned The ⊙ ℒ

ℒ learned correctors of the first two centuries of printing were not

;/ proof/readers in our sense/ they were rather what we should term ℒ 9

not/ office editors. Their labors were chiefly to see that the proof corre, /·/

sponded to the copy, but that the printed page was correct in its

Cap/:/ /atinity / that the words were there, and that the sense was right. stet

ℒ They cared but little about orthography, bad letters or purely printers, ;/tr

errors, and when the text seemed to them wrong they consulted fresh

authorities or altered it on their own responsibility. Good proofs in ,/

not # the modern sense, were impossible until professional readers were ×

ᵛ⁄m employed/men who had first a printer's education, and then spent tr

i/ many years in the correction of proof. · The orthography of English,

which for the past century has undergone little change, was very

w.f. = fluctuating until after the publication of Johnson's Dictionary, and

capitals, which have been used with considerable regularity for the ℒ ld

Spell past 80 years, were previously used on the miss or hit plan. The tr

9 approach to regularity, so far as we have may be attributed to the it/

growth of a class of professional proof readers, and it is to them that

we owe the correctness of modern printing. ∧More errors have been ℛ rl

found in the Bible than in any other one work. For many generations

it was frequently the case that Bibles were brought out stealthily, — lead

from fear of governmental interference. ∧They were frequently printed out, see copy

[[from imperfect texts, and were often modified to meet the views of

h/ those who publised them.The story is related that a certain woman ⌂

ℒ . in Germany, who was the wife of a printer, and had become disgusted l.c./who

ℒ/f/ with the continual assertions of the superiority of man over woman rom.

which she had heard, hurried into the composing room while her

husband was at supper and altered a sentence in the ◡bible, which he uf. ◡

ℰ⁄ ℐℐ was printing, so that it read Narr instead of Herr, thus making the ℰ⁄ ℐℐ

verse read "And he shall be thy fool" instead of "∧nd he shall be thy ℓ

Cap ℐℐ lord." The word, not, was omitted by Barker, the ◣ing's printer in ≋

England in 1632, in printing the seventh commandment. He was fined ⊙

41 £3,000 on this account.

342